Sixteenth-Century English Poetry

The Harper English Literature Series

Under the editorship of
KARL J. HOLZKNECHT

Sixteenth-Century
ENGLISH POETRY

Edited by

NORMAN E. McCLURE
Ursinus College

NEW YORK
Harper & Brothers Publishers

SIXTEENTH-CENTURY ENGLISH POETRY

C-D

Library of Congress catalog card number: 54-6707

CONTENTS

FOREWORD

THE PURPOSE of The Harper English Literature Series is to present, in a pair of volumes for each century from the sixteenth through the nineteenth, the most significant poetry and prose of the time. The texts reproduced are taken not from modern reprints, but directly from the original manuscript or the best early edition; there has been a minimum of editorial alteration or emendation, and the source of the text is clearly indicated. Major writers of each century are adequately represented, but proportionate space is also allotted to lesser authors. Although it has not been possible to ignore the "anthology canon" of selections that every anthology is expected to include, room has nevertheless been found for much fresh material, including some prose fiction and narrative verse. The presentation of mere snippets has been avoided as far as possible; either the selections chosen are complete, or they are substantial units in themselves, representative of both the individual authors and the age which produced them. But when it has been necessary to detach a selection from a longer work, the context is usually briefly synopsized for the convenience of the reader.

In the interest of flexibility a chronological arrangement by authors has been adopted. Compressed biographical and critical headnotes—printed with the selections—emphasize the significance of each author's work to his age. The final paragraphs of these headnotes contain concise bibliographies, including important editions, monographs, and articles. The notes, placed at the foot of each page where they will be most useful, are mainly glossarial or else present information necessary to an understanding of what the author wrote; textual notes are rare and record only variants or emendations which affect the meaning. An effort has been made to unify each volume by an introductory essay confined to an interpretation of the literature and thought of the time, and estimating the contribution of the particular century to the history of English literature as a whole. Thus again attention is focused on the main picture, and the backgrounds are relegated to a properly subordinate place.

Karl J. Holzknecht

New York University

PREFACE

THE PURPOSE of this book is to include in one volume the best and most representative nondramatic verse of the sixteenth century. Much that is familiar is included—the best work of the great Tudor poets. With the best, however, the "most representative" deserves a place if one is to follow the development of English poetry through the century. Much of the verse included is accessible only in scarce or expensive editions.

No verse written before 1500 is included. It is, however, very difficult to draw a line at the end of the century. Shakespeare, Raleigh, Daniel, and Campion are included. So, too, are songs from songbooks and plays up to 1615, and a few epigrams written between 1600 and 1615. Drayton's sonnets and the songs from Jonson's plays are included; their other poetry and the poetry of Chapman and Donne will appear in a later volume.

The text of the poems reproduces as closely as possible the form in which each poet wished his work to stand. To this general rule one exception is made in that the 1594 text of Samuel Daniel is used in preference to his revisions of that text.

The abbreviations common in sixteenth-century books and manuscripts, such as ye, yt, &, and the tilde for nasals, are expanded. Obvious errors (the transposition or omission of letters, faulty lineation, etc.) are corrected without comment. All important changes in the text are indicated in the footnotes.

The original spelling and punctuation are important to every serious student. It is true that sixteenth-century spelling and punctuation sometimes represent the printer's carelessness or caprice rather than the poet's intention. But even when it is the printer's rather than the poet's, the spelling of that period is a more reliable guide to sixteenth-century pronunciation than modern spelling can be. Although sixteenth-century punctuation is often chaotic in printed books and even more in manuscript, it is not always so; sometimes it is clear that the poet—or the printer—has used pointing to direct the reader's attention to the rhythm of the line or to the structure of the stanza. The punctuation of Dunbar, Hawes, and Skelton is the present editor's because in the early editions of these poets the punctuation is so scanty as to be meaningless or misleading. So, too, is the punctuation in Wyatt's manuscripts and in several other manuscripts and broadsides.

A one-volume collection of sixteenth-century nondramatic verse can at best serve only as an introduction to the poetry of this period. It is hoped that many who use this book will continue their reading and study in the original texts and standard editions.

I gratefully acknowledge my debt to many scholars, of whom only a few are named in this book, and to the officials and staffs of the libraries mentioned in the footnotes. My greatest debt is to my guide and friend of many years ago, the late Felix E. Schelling. For generous and helpful advice I owe a special debt of gratitude to Dr. A. C. Baugh, University of Pennsylvania, to Dr. Karl J. Holzknecht, New York University, and to Dr. C. D. Yost, Jr., Ursinus College.

N. E. McClure

Ursinus College

Sixteenth-Century English Poetry

Introduction

THE LONG tradition of medieval poetry ends about 1500. For the dearth of good poetry during the fifteenth century the wars in France and the Wars of the Roses were in part responsible. The medieval tradition continues in the miracle play, in the morality play, and in the lyric, both religious and secular, especially in the carol and the English and Scottish ballad. But no longer are the medieval themes enriched by ideas from France and Italy, and no fifteenth-century poetry equals Chaucer's in variety and artistry. Although medieval thought and feeling survive in much sixteenth-century poetry, the main tradition ends with Henryson and Dunbar, Hawes and Skelton.

Although the reign of Henry VII (1485–1509) brought peace, prosperity, a strong central government, and a settled court life, the poetry of these years was largely retrospective; the rebirth of English poetry was to come a generation later. Caxton and his early successors printed Chaucer and Gower and Lydgate, and the poets of the period imitated them. But during the fifteenth century many of the traditional poetic forms had grown obsolete, and the language itself had changed; many inflectional endings which had helped to make Chaucer's verse graceful and fluid were no longer given syllabic value. The poets no longer understood his versification, his pronunciation of syllabic *-e*, *-es*, and *-ed*, his rules of elision, and his accentuation of words of French origin. The inaccurate text of his poetry in Caxton's editions and in sixteenth-century editions made it difficult—or almost impossible—to read his lines as he intended them to be read, and his fluid pentameters became clumsy tetrameters, the "riding rhyme" that Gascoigne and Puttenham considered suitable for "a merie tale." Sixteenth-century readers—and later readers—of Chaucer heard in his graceful verse what Dryden in 1700 described as "the rough sweetness of a Scotch tune." Deaf to the music of his verse, poets valued Chaucer as a moralist; and Hawes gave higher rank to Lydgate, lamenting the fact that after his death poets lacked his seriousness:

They fayne no fables pleasaunt and covert,
But spende theyr time in vaynful vanyte,
Makynge balades of fervent amyte.
As gestes and tryfles wythout frutefulnes;
Thus al in vayne they spende their besynes.

Hawes will imitate his master Lydgate and will write "fables pleasaunt and covert," moral allegories; but most of the poets of the court of Henry VII and of his successor will choose "balades of fervent amyte."

The reign of Henry VIII (1509–1547) marks the beginning of a new period in the history of English poetry. Though Henry was neither a scholar nor a patron of learning or poetry, he became the center of a cultivated court, and at least by example gave encouragement to those courtiers who shared his own interest in poetry and music. The accomplished young king, who at this time in no way resembled the coarse and brutal tyrant of later years, played the lute, the organ, and the harpsichord, and wrote verses and set them to music. His songs telling of his pleasure in "pastime with good company" are to the modern reader less surprising than his songs of constancy in love. The surviving songs of the courtiers and musicians in the early years of his reign are various in subject; they include love songs, hunting songs, gnomic verses, lullabies, patriotic songs, devotional poems. Their form is in the tradition of the minstrel; they make use of repeated rhyme, internal rhyme, repetition of phrase, refrain, and they usually employ the irregular rhythms of the old native verse or follow the ballad pattern. Nothing that survives from the early years of the reign gives promise of the important developments soon to come.

The later years of the reign of Henry VIII saw the new birth of English poetry. It was in France and Italy that Chaucer had found his models, and now English poets—chief among them Wyatt and Surrey—turned again to Italy, still as in Chaucer's day the home of Renaissance culture. The greatest debt of Wyatt and Surrey and their fellows was to Petrarch and to his Italian and French followers. Petrarch, like Dante, celebrated in his sonnets an idealized love, and both his matter and his disciplined verse appealed strongly to his English imitators. Using his verse and that of other Italians as models, Wyatt and Surrey learned how the old patterns of Chaucer, adjusted to the new pronunciation, could be recovered from the disorder into which they had fallen during the fifteenth century. Though the verse of Wyatt's translations and imitations of Petrarch retains much of the old irregularity, Surrey achieved a smoothness which in time became one of the characteristics of English verse. Wyatt introduced into England the sonnet, *ottava rima,* and *terza rima;* Surrey originated both the English form of the sonnet and blank verse. But they not only gave English poetry new patterns; they also gave it new life and vigor. They were indeed, as George Puttenham wrote in 1589, "the first reformers of our English meetre and stile" and "the two chief lanternes of light to all others who haue since employed their pennes vpon English Poesie."

Wyatt and Surrey are interesting for yet another reason. The reign of Henry VIII produced in England the cultivated gentleman of the Renaissance described in Baldassare Castiglione's *Il Cortegiano.* As G. M. Trevelyan has observed, "The mediaeval distinction between the learned clerk and the barbarous fighting baron was coming to an end, blending in the ideal of the all-accomplished 'gentleman.'" Wyatt and Surrey are early representatives of this new type, the courtier-soldier-scholar, who throughout the century did much to shape the course of English poetry and of English history. It is well to remember that a great deal of the best sixteenth-century poetry was written by men who lived full and active lives as soldiers, statesmen, and public servants of various ranks, and whose love of action was balanced by a love of learning and of poetry. Sir Philip Sidney remains the ideal representative of this important type.

From the death of Surrey in 1547 to the publication of Spenser's *Shepheardes Calender* in 1579 English poetry made little progress. Although after the Reformation England did not suffer from "wars of religion" such as devastated France, economic distress was acute, and during the reigns of Edward VI (1547–1553) and Mary (1553–1558) England was too sorely distracted by political confusion and religious controversy to give much encouragement to poets. But the relatively quiet twenty years after Elizabeth's accession were almost equally barren of good poetry. The best work of Wyatt and Surrey remained unequaled before Spenser if we except Sackville's *Induction* and the scattered poems of a few others. It was a time of preparation rather than of achievement.

It is hard to explain the dearth of good poetry in the 1560's and 1570's. The Elizabethans themselves do not agree. George Puttenham, in a section of *The Arte of English Poesie* that dates probably from the late 1560's, writes:

Peraduenture in this iron and malitious age of ours, Princes are lesse delighted in it, being ouer earnestly bent and affected to the affaires of Empire and ambition, whereby they are as it were inforced to indeuour them selues to armes and practises of hostilitie, or to entend to the right pollicing of their states, and haue not one houre to bestow vpon any other ciuill or delectable Art of naturall or morall doctrine: nor scarce any leisure to thincke one good thought in perfect and godly contemplation, whereby their troubled mindes might be moderated and brought to tranquillitie. . . . Of such among the nobilitie or gentrie as be very well seene in many laudable sciences, and especially in making or Poesie, it is so come to passe that they haue no courage to write and if they haue, yet are they loath to be a knowen of their skill. So as I know very many notable Gentlemen in the Court that haue written commendably, and suppressed it agayne, or els suffred it to be publisht without their owne names to it: as if it were a discredit for a Gentleman, to seeme learned, and to shew him selfe amorous of any good Art.

And Sir Philip Sidney in the early 1580's attributes the dearth to lack of spirit and to ignorance of the art of poetry. "Heertofore Poets haue in England . . . florished; and, which is to be noted, euen in those times when the trumpet of *Mars* did sound loudest." But the peaceful years, with their "ouer-faint quietnes," have bred spiritless men; and poetry is now written by

base men with seruile wits . . . who think it inough if they can be rewarded by the Printer . . . while, in the mean tyme, they

Queis meliore luto finxit praecordia Titan,

are better content to suppresse the out-flowing of their wit, then by publishing them to bee accounted Knights of the same order, But I . . . doe finde the very true cause of our wanting estimation is want of desert; taking vpon vs to be Poets in despight of *Pallas*. . . . They that delight in Poesie it selfe should seeke to knowe what they doe, and how they doe.

Perhaps, as Sir Edmund Chambers suggests, the simplest explanation is that no new genius happened to be born.

A taste for medieval poetry persisted from the 1550's through the 1570's. Chaucer, Gower, and Langland were read, the work of early sixteenth-century poets who wrote in the medieval tradition—Hawes, Skelton, Heywood—was reprinted, and the thoroughly medieval *Mirror for Magistrates* was the most popular narrative poetry of the period. The themes of love and honor that attracted Wyatt and Surrey were no longer in favor, and in their place we find doleful reflections about the brevity and vanity of life and the need for preparing for death. The melancholy tone of *The Paradise of Dainty Devices* (1576) is fairly representative of the period: friendship is fleeting, love is folly, life is short, death is certain. Even the brisk and cheerful Thomas Tusser includes in his advice to farmers his translation of the famous verses on the vanity of life attributed to St. Bernard of Clairvaux, another translation of which is included in *The Paradise*. During the period from 1547 to 1579 a host of translators labored to acquaint English readers with the masterpieces of ancient and modern literature, and although their work made new matter and new models available, it had little effect on the original poetry written during these years.

Throughout these years Turberville, Googe, Howell, Gascoigne, and lesser men whose poems are preserved in the miscellanies were attempting to standardize the forms of English verse with which Wyatt, Surrey, and their contemporaries had experimented. Their principal concern appears to have been to bring order and discipline to the line. Skelton had reverted to purely accentual verse; Wyatt's lines, especially in the sonnets, were confusingly irregular. The mid-century poets chose Surrey as their model. In imitating him they attained a wooden "correctness"; most of the verse of the period has a heavy iambic beat, the syllables march with monotonous regularity, and the caesuras are fixed and strongly marked.

In the parts of *The Arte of English Poesie* that he wrote in the late 1560's George Puttenham reveals many mid-century preferences. He likes best lines of from eight to twelve syllables; the fourteener "kepeth the eare too long from his delight." He dislikes long stanzas and favors clear, strong, masculine rhyme and "entertangled" rhyme to bind the lines of a stanza together. He implies that the line was read rapidly, with the stressed syllables, the caesuras, and the rhyming syllables strongly marked: "The Poetes chiefe Musicke lying in his rime or concorde, to heare the Simphonie, he maketh all the hast he can to be at an end of his verse." It is almost certain that in this manner mid-century readers read tumbling verse and Chaucer's misunderstood pentameters—and probably much other verse. Puttenham, and doubtless many of the earlier and contemporary poets, failed to hear within the English line the "stirres," the ripple, the modulation of the classical line. Gascoigne, like Puttenham, laments the lack of modulation within the line and the almost invariable use of iambic verse: "Commonly now a dayes in English rimes . . . we vse none other order but a foote of two sillables, wherof the first is depressed or made short, and the second is eleuate or made long; and that sound or scanning continueth throughout the verse. . . . And surely I can lament that wee are fallen into suche a playne and simple manner of wryting, that there is none other foote vsed but one. . . . But since it is so, let vs take the forde as we finde it."

Both Puttenham and Gascoigne allow the poets little freedom in the placing of the caesura. "In euery long verse," Puttenham writes, "the *Cesure* ought to be kept precisely, if it were but to serve as a law to correct the licentiousnesse of rymers"; and he explains: "In a verse of twelve sillables the *Cesure* ought to fall right vpon the sixt sillable: in a verse of eleuen vpon the sixt also leauing fiue to follow. In a verse of ten vpon the fourth, leauing sixe to follow. In a verse of nine vpon the fourth, leauing fiue to follow. In a verse of seuen, either vpon the fourth or none at all, the meeter very ill brooking any pause. In a verse of sixe sillables and vnder is needeful no *Cesure* at all, because the breath asketh no reliefe: yet if ye giue any *Comma*, it is to make distinction of sense more then for any thing else." In his *Certain Notes of Instruction Concerning the Making of Verse or Ryme in English* (1575), Gascoigne, though allowing the writer some choice in the placing of the caesura, records his own preferences, which are in general the same as Puttenham's:

> There are . . . certayne pauses or restes in a verse, whiche may be called *Ceasures*, whereof I woulde be lothe to stande long, since it is at discretion of the wryter, . . . but yet thus much I will aduenture to wryte, that in mine opinion in a verse of eight sillables the pause will stand best in the middest; in a verse of tenne it will best be placed at the ende of the first foure sillables; in a verse of twelue, in the midst; in verses of twelue in the firste and fouretene in the seconde wee place the pause commonly in the midst of the first, and at the ende of the first eight sillables in the second. In Rithme royall it is at the wryters discretion, and forceth not where the pause be vntill the ende of the line.

So important was the fixed caesura that in much of the verse, especially in Alexandrines and fourteeners, punctuation was used to mark it. Punctuation that appears to be purely metrical is found frequently, but not consistently, in many of the poems in *A Mirror for Magistrates*, in Googe, Turberville, and Gascoigne, in *The Paradise of Dainty Devices*, *A Gorgeous Gallery of Gallant Inventions*, and elsewhere.

From the formless and jumbled line of Skelton, Heywood, and many of their contemporaries, the mid-century poets developed a line marked by iambic iteration, heavy and fixed caesuras, and strong rhyme. It remained for Sidney and Spenser to add variety to the basic pattern of the line.

The verse forms most widely used from 1547 to 1579 were the rhyme royal, the Alexandrine, the fourteener, and the combination of the Alexandrine and fourteener to which Gascoigne gave the name "poulter's measure." Rhyme royal (iambic pentameter, ababbcc), originated by Chaucer, was used by Lydgate, Hoccleve, Dunbar, Hawes, Barclay, Gascoigne, and many of the writers in *A Mirror for Magistrates*, and Shakespeare was to use it in *Lucrece* and Davies in *Orchestra*. Puttenham calls it "the chiefe of our ancient proportions vsed by any rimer writing any thing of historical or graue poeme," and Gascoigne writes: "Surely it is a royall kinde of verse, serving best for graue discourses." Of all the poets of the period

Sackville alone writes rhyme royal with distinction; the grave and stately beauty of the verse in his *Induction* is unspoiled by the heavy iambic beat and the fixed caesuras that mar the rhyme royal of his contemporaries.

During these years the Alexandrine was written sometimes as a variant of the decasyllabic line but more frequently in combination with the fourteener. Sidney was later to experiment with it, for example, in *Astrophel and Stella*, Sonnet 1 and Song 4; and early in the next century Drayton was to use it, rhymed in couplets, for the many thousand lines of his *Poly-Olbion*. The fourteener, rhymed in couplets, is deeply rooted in English tradition; divided into two lines of eight syllables and six syllables, it is the "common meter" of the ballads and of the psalms of Sternhold and Hopkins. Much early Elizabethan translation is in the fourteener couplet, the most important being Thomas Phaer's translation of the *Aeneid* (1558) and Arthur Golding's translation of Ovid's *Metamorphoses* (1565); Chapman used it for his translation of the *Iliad* (1598). More widely used than either the Alexandrine or the fourteener is the combination of the two in poulter's measure, "the commonest sort of verse which we vse now adayes," wrote Gascoigne in 1575; "although it be now adayes vsed in all Theames, yet in my iudgement it would serue best for Psalmes and Himpnes." But the poets in this period use it for all purposes, and many of them wrote it with a fatal facility. Surrey's use of it and Sternhold's use of the fourteener couplet probably did much to establish the vogue of these measures. The monotonous iambic beat and the fixed caesuras often reduce the rhythm to a painful jog trot.

Early Elizabethan poets gave careful attention to ornament, to verbal dexterity, to "copious varying," to the elaborate patterning of verse. Ornament should be used, writes Puttenham, "to such purpose as it may delight and lure as well the mynde as the eare of the hearers with a certaine noueltie and strange maner of conueyance, disguising it no litle from the ordinary and accustomed." The Third Book of his *Arte of English Poesie* is devoted to the explanation and illustration of more than a hundred rhetorical figures. Since every educated Elizabethan had studied these figures in school, the poet made copious use of them, and the reader or hearer found pleasure in recognizing them. The Elizabethans considered elaborate decoration as essential to their poetry as to their architecture, gardens, painting, music, dress. Puttenham's statement is illuminating:

> Great Madames of honour . . . perchance do then thinke themselues more amiable in euery mans eye, when they be in their richest attire, suppose of silkes or tyssewes and costly embroderies, then when they go in

cloth or in any other plaine and simple apparell. Euen so cannot our vulgar Poesie shew it selfe either gallant or gorgious, if any lymme be left naked and bare and not clad in his kindly clothes and coulours, such as may conuey them somwhat out of sight, that is from the common course of ordinary speach and capacitie of the vulgar iudgement, and yet being artificially handled must needes yeld it much more bewtie and commendation. This ornament we speake of is given to it by figures and figurative speaches, which be the flowers as it were and coulours that a Poet setteth vpon his language by arte, as the embroderer doth his stone and perle, or passements of gold vpon the stuffe of a Princely garment.

The imitation of Petrarch's "conceited" style, the use of the many varieties of balance and antithesis and repetition, the piling up of analogies, the elaborate patterning—these are characteristic of early Elizabethan poetry; and although the fashion declines in the 1580's and 1590's it survives in some of the verse of Sidney, Spenser, Shakespeare, and lesser men. The style of *Richard III*, for instance, is early Elizabethan; Henry VI's speech on the miseries of kingship (*3 Henry VI*, II, v, 1–54) and Sonnet 66 ("Tyr'd with all these for restfull death I cry") provide good examples of anaphora; and a list of illustrations of the use of other figures could be extended to great length. But Shakespeare and his contemporaries were freeing themselves from "figures pedanticall." In *Love's Labour's Lost* there is pleasant burlesque of

> Taffata phrases, silken tearmes precise,
> Three-pil'd Hyperboles, spruce affectation,
> Figures pedanticall,

and in *Hamlet*, when the old Polonius exhibits his skill in the use of the figures, the Queen in her impatient protest speaks with the voice of the new age, "More matter, with lesse Art."

Throughout the sixteenth century the vocabulary of English increased rapidly, and the question of proper diction in prose and poetry gave rise to sharply conflicting views, especially after 1550. One group of writers and critics favored the free borrowing of words from other languages both ancient and modern; but purists, moved in part by patriotic pride, believed that the language should grow from within, that English writers should form new words from old roots or should revive archaic or obsolete words. Sir John Cheke in his translation of the Gospel of St. Matthew into "Saxon" English carefully avoids Latin and Greek derivatives and uses native words whenever possible: *hundreder* instead of *centurion*, *foresayer* instead of *prophet*, *crossed* instead of *crucified*, *gainrising* instead of *resurrection*. In a letter prefaced to Sir Thomas Hoby's translation of *The Courtier* (1561) Cheke wrote:

> I am of this opinion that our own tung shold be written cleane and pure, vnmixt and vnmangeled with borowing of other tunges. . . . For then doth our tung naturallie and praisablie vtter her meaning, when she bourоweth no counterfeitness of other tunges to attire her self withall, but vseth plainlie her own, . . . and if she want at ani tijm (as being vnperfight she must) yet let her borow with suche bashfulnes, that it mai appeer that, if either the mould of our own tung could serue us to fascion a woord of our own, or if the old denisoned wordes could content and ease this neede, we wold not boldly venture of vnknowen wordes.

Similar views were expressed by such humanists as Sir Thomas Chaloner in his translation of Erasmus's *Praise of Folly* (1549), by Thomas Wilson in his famous *Arte of Rhetorique* (1553), and by Roger Ascham in *The Scholemaster* (1570). Gascoigne in 1575 advises the poet to avoid the polysyllables of classical borrowings because "the more monasyllables that you vse the truer Englishman you shall seeme, and the lesse you shall smell of the Inkehorne." Saxon purism is in part responsible for the drab and awkward diction of much mid-century verse. But in spite of the purists the use of inkhorn terms continued, and opposition gradually decreased.

The early Elizabethan poets were interested also in the propriety of archaisms and of overseas language, especially Italian words. Throughout the century the diction of English poetry differed from the diction of prose. Most of the poets were influenced—directly or indirectly—by Chaucer's diction. The language of the poets in *Tottel's Miscellany* as a whole is more archaic, more aureate, more "poetic" than the language of contemporary prose, and their example—and the continuing influence of Chaucer—colored the diction of English poetry during the next quarter-century. For a discussion of diction in mid-century poetry a passage in Puttenham's chapter "Of Language" (III, iv) is the *locus classicus:*

> This part in our maker or Poet must be heedyly looked vnto, that it be naturall, pure, and the most vsuall of all his countrey: and for the same purpose rather that which is spoken in the kings Court, or in the good townes and Cities within the land, then in the marches and frontiers, or in port townes, where straungers haunt for traffike sake, or yet in Vniuersities where Schollers vse much peeuish affectation of words out of the primatiue languages, or finally, in any vplandish village or corner of a Realme, where is no resort but of poore rusticall or vnciuill people: neither shall he follow the speach of a craftes man or carter, or other of the inferiour sort, though he be inhabitant or bred in the best towne and Citie in this Realme, for

such persons doe abuse good speaches by strange accents or ill shapen soundes, and false ortographie. But he shall follow generally the better brought vp sort, . . . men ciuill and graciously behauoured and bred. Our maker therfore at these dayes shall not follow *Piers plowman* nor *Gower* nor *Lydgate* nor yet *Chaucer*, for their language is now out of vse with vs: neither shall he take the termes of Northern-men, such as they vse in dayly talke, whether they be noble men or gentlemen, or of their best clarkes all is a matter: nor in effect any speach vsed beyond the riuer of Trent, though no man can deny but theirs is the purer English Saxon at this day, yet it is not so Courtly nor so currant as our Southerne English is, no more is the far Westerne mans speach: ye shall therfore take the vsuall speach of the Court, and that of London and the shires lying about London within lx. myles, and not much aboue. I say not this but that in euery shyre of England there be gentlemen and others that speake but specially write as good Southerne as we of Middlesex or Surrey do, but not the common people of euery shire, to whom the gentlemen, and also their learned clarkes do for the most part condescend, but herein we are already ruled by th'English Dictionaries and other bookes written by learned men, and therefore it needeth none other direction in that behalfe. Albeit peraduenture some small admonition be not impertinent, for we finde in our English writers many wordes and speaches amendable, and ye shall see in some many inkhorne termes so ill affected brought in by men of learning as preachers and schoolemasters: and many straunge termes of other languages by Secretaries and Merchaunts and trauailours, and many darke wordes and not vsuall nor well sounding, though they be dayly spoken in Court. Wherefore great heed must be taken by our maker in this point that his choise be good.

Sidney objects to "so farre fette words" that "may seeme Monsters, but must seeme straungers to any poore English man," and he objects also to Spenser's "framing of his stile to an old rustick language" in *The Shepheardes Calender*. Spenser's use of archaisms is of course defended by his friend "E.K.," who points out that "auncient solemne wordes are a great ornament" in Livy and Sallust, that Cicero believed "ofttimes an auncient worde maketh the style seeme graue, and as it were reuerend," and that Spenser "hath laboured to restore, as to theyr rightfull heritage, such good and naturall English words as have ben long time out of vse and almost cleane disherited"; and he complains that some writers have borrowed so freely from French, Italian, and Latin that "now they have made our English tongue a gallimaufray or hodgepodge of al other speches."

The controversy about diction continued to the end of the century, with many poets, like Shakespeare, borrowing freely, and others carefully avoiding both archaisms and borrowings. Samuel Daniel in *A Defence of Ryme* (c. 1602) laments "our affectation, wherein we alwayes bewray our selues to be both vnkinde, and vnnaturall to our owne natiue language, in disguising or forging strange or vnvsuall wordes, as if it were to make our verse seeme an other kind of speach out of the course of our vsuall practise, displacing our wordes, or inuesting new, onely vpon a singularitie: when our owne accustomed phrase, set in the due place, would expresse vs more familiarly and to better delight, than all this idle affectation of antiquitie, or noueltie can euer doe."

The Elizabethan interest in diction enriched and disciplined the language. "As the Book of Common Prayer and the Bible had already demonstrated," writes Professor Douglas Bush, "the special power and beauty of English were to spring from its combinations of Anglo-Saxon brevity, weight, and strength with the sonority, speed, and connotative richness of classical polysyllables." The care that the mid-century poets and critics gave to language —the choice of words, the shape and design of sentences, the use of ornament—prepared the ground for Sidney and Spenser and their contemporaries.

Although the poets of the third quarter of the century wrote much verse that is dull, flat, and labored, and indeed little that is memorable, their achievement is important; they restored rhythm to English poetry and by their studious attention to diction they revealed to their successors the growing richness of the language. It remained for Sidney and Spenser and their contemporaries to add to the line a varied and subtle music, to give to stanza forms a new fluidity and grace, and to bring to their use of language a fresh beauty and strength.

The difference between the poetry of the third quarter of the century and that of the fourth is striking. Puttenham complains that he knows "very many notable Gentlemen in the Court that haue written commendably, and suppressed it agayne." Doubtless much good poetry perished. If more of the poetry of Dyer, Raleigh, Oxford, Greville, and other courtiers had survived, the changes wrought by Sidney and Spenser would perhaps seem less abrupt and surprising. Sidney's and Spenser's experiments in metrics, in stanza forms, and in diction achieve a new freedom and variety in both language and prosody. Their innovations mark the beginning of the great age of Elizabethan poetry. Sidney's experiments in his translations of some of the Psalms and in the poems included in the *Arcadia* and Spenser's experiments in *The Shepheardes Calender* did much to free English poetry from the stiffness and awkwardness, the rigid patterns and rhetorical schemes, of the 1560's and 1570's. The ease and "naturalness" of the verse of Sidney and Spenser are perhaps their great contributions to the art of English poetry.

The closing years of the century are years of eager experiment and innovation. The poetry of the 1590's is marked not only by new techniques—new experiments in diction, in the use of ornament, in the ordering of syllables, in verse patterns—but by the modification of established conventions, by new emphases, and in general by continuous change. A few of these changes deserve mention here. The emphasis in Arthur Golding's translation of Ovid's *Metamorphoses* (1565, 1567) is very different not only from that of Ovid but from that of the Ovidian poetry of Lodge and Marlowe and Shakespeare, and Drayton's Ovidian poetry in turn differs from that of the early 1590's. The sonnet in the early 1590's is very different from the sonnet a few years later. The "complaint," long popular in the successive editions of *A Mirror for Magistrates*, is given a changed emphasis by Churchyard, Daniel, and their imitators. Philosophical poems of a new kind are written by Daniel, Davies, Greville, and Chapman. Closely related to these are the grave and beautiful verse epistles of Daniel and the later epistles of Drayton, Jonson, and others. Daniel and Drayton write historical poetry of a new kind. In the closing years of the century satire in the manner of Juvenal and Persius is for the first time attempted in English. The greatest nondramatic poetry of the century is to be found in a new kind of heroic poem, *The Faerie Queene*. The more important of these developments are discussed in the individual introductions.

One important convention that developed in English poetry in the second half of the century, and especially after 1580, is classical and Italianate pastoralism. The pastoral convention represents life in the rural peace of a golden age of simplicity and virtue. It is unnecessary to trace here the development of the convention from Theocritus through Virgil, Longus, and their imitators in Latin, Italian, and French. The strongest influence on the pastoral in early Elizabethan England was that of Baptista Spagnuoli Mantuanus (1448–1516), the "good old Mantuan" of *Love's Labour's Lost*, whose stiffly didactic Latin eclogues were studied by English schoolboys. Alexander Barclay's imitations of the eclogues of Virgil and Mantuan were printed about 1515 and 1521, but it does not appear that Elizabethan poets knew them. Barnabe Googe included eight eclogues in his *Eglogs, Epytaphes, and Sonettes* (1563), and in 1567 George Turberville's translation of Mantuan appeared. When in the early 1570's Michael Drayton, then "scarse ten yeares of age," asked his "milde Tutor" to make him a poet, that wise man first read him "honest Mantuan, Then Virgils Eglogues." But it was probably Sidney's *Arcadia* and Spenser's *The Shepheardes Calender* that made pastoralism the most pervasive literary influence in the 1580's and 1590's. Pastoralism is to be found in much of the drama, in the prose romance, and in poems so diverse in form and purpose as the amatory sonnets of Lodge and Spenser's *Colin Clouts Come Home Againe*, *Epithalamion*, *Prothalamion*, and *The Faerie Queene*, especially in the sixth book. There is pastoralism in Shakespeare's plays, not only in many of the songs but in *A Midsummer Night's Dream*, *As You Like It*, the fourth act of *A Winter's Tale*, and the speeches of several of his kings who, burdened with the cares of authority, long for the simple pastoral life.

The chief glory of Elizabethan pastoral is the pastoral lyric in the drama, in the prose romance, in the songbooks, and in such miscellanies as *The Phoenix Nest* and *England's Helicon*. These are songs that tell of delight in natural and spiritual beauty, of spring and youth, of honest loves and quiet lives. "A certain Dorique delicacy," which Sir Henry Wotton found in Milton's *Comus*, marks the pastoral lyric in general, although there is homely realism too, as in Shakespeare's "When icicles hang by the wall."

The deep melancholy that lay beneath the gaiety and brilliance of Elizabethan life and found expression in so much of Elizabethan literature doubtless accounts in part for the strong and enduring appeal of the pastoral. Closely related to the pastoral are, of course, the Horatian praise of the life of the country gentleman, as in Wyatt's first epistle, and the long tradition of dispraise of life at court; and complementing the idealization of the retired life and the mean estate is praise of the life of heroic endeavor. In the pastoral episode in Book VI of *The Faerie Queene* Spenser discusses these complementary ideals. Sir Calidore visits the shepherds and longs for the "lowly quiet life" free from "warres, and wreckes, and wicked enmitie," and "fearlesse of foes, or fortunes wrackfull yre," but the wise old shepherd Melibee, who has been a courtier, reproves him (ix, 30); Providence knows what is best for men, and the mind is its own place:

It is the mynd, that maketh good or ill,
  That maketh wretch or happie, rich or poore:
  For some, that hath abundance at his will,
  Hath not enough, but wants in greatest store;
  And other, that hath litle, askes no more,
  But in that litle is both rich and wise.
  For wisdome is most riches; fooles therefore
  They are, which fortunes doe by vowes deuize,
Sith each vnto himselfe his life may fortunize.

Melibee's answer is orthodox Elizabethan doctrine.

In the sixteenth century the purpose of serious poetry was avowedly didactic—in Sidney's words, "to teach and delight." This belief, which had come down from Greece and Rome, was strengthened by Christianity, and it informs much of medieval literature, especially the drama and such compilations as Lydgate's *Fall of Princes.* To the humanists in Tudor England the Greek and Latin classics were a treasury of wisdom second only to the Bible. Sir Thomas Elyot in *The Governour* writes of Homer as a teacher "from whom as from a fountaine proceded all eloquence and lernyng" and of Virgil as "most lyke to Homere." Even Plautus and Terence, Ovid and Martial, have good counsel mixed with less serious matter. Thomas Wilson in *The Arte of Rhetorique* (1553) maintains that every tale of the poets contains something that pertains to the knowledge of truth or to the amendment of manners. The view of scholars like Wilson is based in part on the medieval tradition which found allegory in narratives as diverse as those in the Bible and in Ovid. The allegorical method appealed strongly to the sixteenth-century reader, with his belief in the interrelation of all things in heaven and earth. This inherited tradition is exemplified in Arthur Golding's translation of Ovid's *Metamorphoses;* in the epistle to his completed translation (1567) he explains the moral lesson of each of the fifteen books. Another example is the allegorizing of *Orlando Furioso.* Italian critics turned Ariosto's romantic epic into an edifying allegory; and when Sir John Harington published his English translation (1591), he added to almost every one of the forty-six books notes explaining the "moral" and the "allegory," and to his translation he added "A Briefe and Summarie Allegorie" of some seven thousand words. Whatever Harington's real purpose may have been, he admits that many readers will be interested only in the story or in the sweetness of the verse. He explains that one reason for writing allegorical narrative is "to be able with one kinde of meate and one dish (as I may so call it) to feed diuers tastes. For the weaker capacities will feed themselues with the pleasantnesse of the historie and sweetnes of the verse, some that haue stronger stomackes will as it were take a further tast of the Morall sence, a third sort more high conceited then they, will digest the Allegorie." To Sidney the poet's use of allegory makes him the best of teachers:

The Philosopher teacheth, but he teacheth obscurely, so as the learned onely can vnderstande him, that is to say, he teacheth them that are already taught; but the Poet is the foode for the tenderest stomacks, the Poet is indeed the right Popular Philosopher. . . . He beginneth not with obscure definitions, which must blur the margent with interpretations, and load the memory with doubtfulnesse; but he commeth to you with words set in delightfull proportion, either accompanied with, or prepared for, the well inchaunting skill of Musicke; and with a tale forsooth he commeth vnto you, with a tale which holdeth children from play, and old men from the chimney corner. And, pretending no more, doth intende the winning of the mind from wickednesse to vertue: euen as the childe is often brought to take most wholsom things by hiding them in such other as haue a pleasant tast: . . . So is it in men (most of which are childish in the best things, till they bee cradled in their graues).

And he believes that poetry is a surer guide to virtue and patriotism than history is, for the historian "beeing captiued to the trueth of a foolish world" is "tyed, not to what shoulde bee but to what is," whereas poetry "euer setteth vertue so out in her best cullours, making Fortune her wel-wayting hand-mayd, that one must needs be enamored of her."

The Elizabethan critics use the words "heroic," "epic," and "historical" almost interchangeably, but they agree that such poetry is the highest kind of poetry. Puttenham writes: "The Poesie historicall is of all other next the diuine most honorable and worthy, as well for the common benefit as for the speciall comfort euery man receiueth by it." And Sidney writes that "the Heroicall" is "the best and most accomplished kinde of Poetry. For as the image of each action styrreth and instructeth the mind, so the loftie image of such Worthies most inflameth the mind with desire to be worthy, and informes with counsel how to be worthy." To Chapman the poetry of Homer is "full of gouernment and direction to all estates: . . . Soldiers shall neuer spende their idle howres more profitablie then with his studious and industrious perusall. . . . Counsellors haue neuer better oracles then his lines: fathers have no morales so profitable for their children as his counsailes. . . . Husbands, wiues, louers, friends, and allies hauing in him mirrors for all their duties." Spenser in *The Faerie Queene* and Chapman in his translation of Homer offered the reader examples of virtue and true gentility. Milton believed that Spenser was a better teacher than Scotus or Aquinas.

To the humanist in Tudor England the aim of all learning was preparation for the active Christian life. For the serious poet the function of poetry was not only to direct the mind to truth but to move the will to right action. The end of learning and of serious poetry was to make good men who would be also good citizens and responsible leaders. Many Elizabethan poets—Sidney, Dyer, Greville, Raleigh, Spenser, to name only a few—were men of action, and their poetry reflects the interests and outlook of the educated community. To them the good life was a life of honorable achievement or of heroic action. Although the Elizabethans longed at times for the quiet life of the pastoral, they did not often praise a fugitive and cloistered virtue. Belphoebe states the accepted view in *The Faerie Queene* (II, iii, 40–41):

Who so in pompe of proud estate (quoth she)
Does swim, and bathes himselfe in courtly blis,
Does waste his dayes in darke obscuritee,
And in obliuion euer buried is:
Where ease abounds, yt's eath to doe amis;
But who his limbs with labours, and his mind
Behaues with cares, cannot so easie mis.
Abroad in armes, at home in studious kind
Who seekes with painfull toile, shall honor soonest find.

In woods, in waues, in warres she wonts to dwell
And will be found with perill and with paine;
Ne can the man, that moulds in idle cell,
Vnto her happie mansion attaine:
Before her gate high God did Sweat ordaine,
And wakefull watches euer to abide:
But easie is the way, and passage plaine
To pleasures pallace; it may soone be spide,
And day and night her dores to all stand open wide.

Man's first duty is to serve God and his vicegerent, Queen Elizabeth. This obligation, implicit in all serious literature of the period, is emphasized by many of the writers from *A Mirror for Magistrates* to *The Faerie Queene*. In most of the literature that deals with the fall of princes—and this includes not only a great many plays and such poems as William Warner's *Albion's England*, Daniel's *Civil Wars*, and Drayton's *The Barons' Wars*, but also such prose as Sir Thomas North's *Dial of Princes* and his translation of Plutarch's *Lives*—the emphasis is political as well as moral and religious; the sins of the mighty at last overthrow them, vaulting ambition leads to disaster, order and "degree" must be maintained, civil war is the most horrible of all catastrophes. Truth and right action—in private and in public life—are the great ends of poetry. Daniel speaks for the serious poets of his age in the lines:

What good is like to this,
To do worthy the writing, and to write
Worthy the reading, and the worlds delight?

To the educated people of Elizabethan England poetry was a noble and necessary part of life. They passed it from hand to hand in the author's manuscript or copied it into commonplace books or permitted it to perish, for most gentlemen were unwilling to have their verse appear in print. They assembled to hear it read. They sang their lovely lyrics at home to the music of the virginals or the lute. Poets were secretaries or tutors in the houses of many of the noble and gentle families. There can be no doubt that the Elizabethans devoted much time to the serious reading of poetry. In *Mother Hubberds Tale* (760–770) Spenser has given us a picture—not wholly fanciful, we may suppose—of the courtier after his busy day:

His minde vnto the Muses he withdrawes;
Sweete Ladie Muses, Ladies of delight,
Delights of life, and ornaments of light:
With whom he close confers with wise discourse,
Of Natures workes, of heauens continuall course,
Of forreine lands, of people different,
Of kingdomes change, of diuers gouernment,
Of dreadfull battailes of renowmed Knights;
With which he kindleth his ambitious sprights
To like desire and praise of noble fame,
The onely vpshot whereto he doth ayme.

To write good poetry in English was to men like Sidney and Spenser and Daniel much more than a polite accomplishment for a gentleman. It was an act of patriotism; and they—and many like them—labored to bring England to a place of honor among the nations in poetry as in war and exploration and commerce. Samuel Daniel in *Musophilus* (951–962) speaks with the patriotism of a true Elizabethan when he tells of his pride in England and in the greatness of his native tongue:

Or should we carelesse come behind the rest
  In powre of wordes, that go before in worth,
  When as our accents equall to the best
  Is able greater wonders to bring forth:
  When all that euer hotter spirits exprest
  Comes bettered by the patience of the North?
And who in time knowes whither we may vent
  The treasure of our tongue, to what strange shores
  This gaine of our best glorie shal be sent,
  T'inrich vnknowing nations with our stores?
  What worlds in th'yet vnformed Occident
  May come refin'd with th'accents that are ours?

Queen Elizabeth, who as sovereign for so many years had brought England peace and strength and honor, became to her people the symbol of all that they loved and revered in sovereignty and womanhood. From the poets came a growing chorus of praise. Some of it, of course, was flattery; some of it was certainly extravagant; but there can be no doubt that much of it was sincere—and deserved—and more than a little of it is memorable poetry. *The Faerie Queene*, the greatest idealization of Elizabeth, is also the greatest poem of the century.

Various and striking as the praise of Elizabeth and her England had been while she lived, the most impressive praise was written after her death. In his *Life of the Renowned Sir Philip Sidney* written about 1612, Greville describes himself as one "who hath euer since been dying to all those glories of Life which he formerly enjoyed under the blessed, and blessing presence of this unmatchable Queen and woman." In 1620 John Chamberlain, the letter writer, like many another man who had reached middle age in Queen Elizabeth's reign, is saddened by the evils that have overtaken England under King James, and alludes to November 17, the anniversary of Elizabeth's accession, as "the happiest day that ever England had to my remembraunce." Ten years after her death came the most beautiful tribute of all—and from the greatest of her poets. Shakespeare, in perhaps his last play, *Henry VIII*, chooses the theme of mutability. The great ones—Buckingham, Katherine, Wolsey—fall, but with the birth of the Princess Elizabeth there comes the hope of a golden age. As Archbishop Cranmer holds the infant Elizabeth in his arms, he speaks of the great age to come (V, v, 18–39):

This Royall Infant, Heauen still moue about her;
Though in her Cradle; yet now promises
Vpon this Land a thousand thousand Blessings,
Which Time shall bring to ripenesse: She shall be,
(But few now liuing can behold that goodnesse)
A Patterne to all Princes liuing with her,
And all that shall succeed: *Saba* was neuer
More couetous of Wisdome, and faire Vertue
Then this pure Soule shall be. All Princely Graces
That mould vp such a mighty Piece as this is,
With all the Vertues that attend the good,
Shall still be doubled on her. Truth shall nurse her,
Holy and Heauenly thoughts still Counsell her.
She shall be lou'd and fear'd. Her owne shall blesse her;
Her Foes shake like a Field of beaten Corne,
And hang their heads with sorrow.
Good growes with her.
In her dayes, Euery Man shall eate in safety,
Vnder his owne Vine what he plants; and sing
The merry Songs of Peace to all his Neighbours.
God shall be truely knowne, and those about her,
From her shall read the perfect way of Honour,
And by those claime their greatnesse; not by Blood.

These lines are an eloquent summary of what Queen Elizabeth meant to her people and of Shakespeare's view of a world and a way of life that had ended with her.

William Dunbar

[c. 1460–c. 1520]

AT THE close of the fifteenth century the best English poetry was being written by Scottish Chaucerians who followed the tradition established in Scotland by King James I in *The Kingis Quair* (the king's book). written about 1423. The best of these poets—Robert Henryson (c. 1430–1506), Gavin Douglas (c. 1475–1522), and William Dunbar (c. 1460–c. 1520)—wrote a great variety of admirable verse. The poetry of Douglas, especially his translation of the *Aeneid* in homely rhymed couplets, gives him an honorable place in the history of English literature. Of the three, Henryson, especially in his *Testament of Cresseid*, is closest to Chaucer in spirit, but his work belongs to the fifteenth century. Dunbar, writing a generation later than Henryson, is the best poet of his time, and the last true poet among the followers of Chaucer.

Little is known of Dunbar's life. It is probable that he was of good family and well educated. A William Dunbar—probably but not certainly the poet—became Master of Arts at St. Andrews in 1479. Many accounts of Dunbar state without proof that he became a novice in the order of Franciscans. It is certain that for several years he served King James IV, though the nature of his service is not known. In 1500 King James granted him a pension, and records of the payment of the pension continue until 1513.

Nearly one hundred of Dunbar's poems survive. Though he was primarily a court poet, he wrote poems of many kinds, from the "flyting" and satire to religious lyric. *The Thistle and the Rose* is a beautiful allegory, written after the manner of Chaucer's *Parliament of Fowls* and celebrating the marriage of King James IV and the Princess Margaret Tudor. *The Merle and the Nightingale* is a graceful *débat*. *The Dance of the Seven Deadly Sins* is a satirical, witty, macabre picture of hell. Many of his short poems deal with common medieval themes: the uncertainty and brevity of life, the *ubi sunt?* motif, the fear of hell, the hope of heaven.

In meter and in verse patterns Dunbar shows great versatility and skill. He employs the old alliterative verse in *The Two Married Women and the Widow*. He uses many of Chaucer's verse patterns, especially the ten-syllable couplet and the rhyme royal, which King James had written with exceptional grace in *The Kingis Quair*, and which Dunbar uses in *The Thistle and the Rose.* In *The Golden Targe* he uses the difficult stanza of Chaucer's *Womanly Noblesse* and *Anelida and Arcite* (aabaabbab), and he uses some French verse forms—for example, the *kyrielle*, a stanza of two rhyming couplets with a refrain, used in his *Lament for the Makaris.*

In his satirical and humorous verse Dunbar makes effective use of the coarse and pungent vernacular. For the more lofty themes of his allegories and his devotional poems he developed an aureate style ornamented with Latin derivatives from Chaucer and Lydgate or coined directly from Latin.

The Golden Targe, written about 1503, is a courtly allegory; the poet, defended by the shield of reason, is at last wounded by the arrows of beauty. Dunbar, like Chaucer and many of his followers, adopted the conventions of the great French poem, *The Romance of the Rose:* the dream, the beautiful garden, the May morning, the river, the singing birds, the gods and goddesses, the personified abstractions—the last convention familiar to Dunbar's hearers and readers not only through poetry but through stage plays and pictorial art. His aureate style, "dulce and redolent," gives the poem a peculiar brightness and splendor. His *Lament for the Makaris*, thoroughly medieval in tone and written in Middle Scots adorned with aureate terms, is a good example of his serious verse. The closing stanzas of *The Golden Targe* show that Dunbar understood Chaucer's success in doing for the English language what Dante had done earlier for Italian —Chaucer established English as a literary language and enriched it with much that was best in medieval poetry. Dunbar tried to do the same for Middle Scots.

For manuscripts and early editions of Dunbar see *CBEL*, i, 258. Facsimiles of the earliest editions are included in *The Chepman and Myllar Prints. Nine tracts from the first Scottish press, Edinburgh* 1508, *followed by the two other tracts in the same volume in the National Library of Scotland. A facsimile with a bibliographical note by William Beattie*, Edinburgh Bibliographical Society, 1950. The first collected edition of Dunbar is *The Poems of William Dunbar*, ed. D. Laing, 2 vols., 1834. Later editions are *The Poems of William Dunbar*, ed. John Small, Scottish Text Society, 3 vols., 1884–1893; and *The Poems of William Dunbar*, ed. H. B. Baildon, 1907. The most convenient modern edition is *The Poems of William Dunbar*, ed. W. M. Mackenzie, 1932. The best biography is J. W. Baxter, *William Dunbar*, 1952. The most useful studies are the following: J. Schipper, *William Dunbar, sein Leben und seine Gedichte*, Berlin, 1884; R. A. Taylor, *Dunbar*, 1932; W. M. Mackenzie, Introduction to *The Poems of William Dunbar*, 1932; P. H. Nichols, "William Dunbar as a Scottish Lydgatian," *PMLA*, xlvi (1931), 214–224.

THE GOLDYN TARGE[1]

Ryght[2] as the stern[3] of day begouth[4] to schyne,
Quhen[5] gone to bed war[6] Vesper and Lucyne,[7]
I raise[8] and by a rosere[9] did me rest.
Up sprang the goldyn candill matutyne,[10]
With clere depurit[11] bemes cristallyne,
Glading the mery foulis in thair nest.
Or[12] Phebus was in purpur[13] cape reuest,[14]
Up raise the lark, the hevyns menstrale fyne
In May, in till[15] a morow[16] myrthfullest.

Full angellike thir[17] birdis sang thair houris[18]
Within thair courtyns grene, in to[19] thair bouris
Apparalit quhite and red wyth blomes suete.
Anamalit[20] was the felde wyth all colouris;
The perly droppis schake in silvir schouris
Quhill[21] all in balme did branch and leuis flete.[22]
To part fra Phebus did Aurora grete;[23]
Hir cristall teris I saw hyng[24] on the flouris,
Quhilk[25] he for lufe[26] all drank vp wyth his hete.

For mirth of May, wyth skippis and wyth happis,
The birdis sang vpon the tender croppis,[27]
With curiouse note, as Venus chapell clerkis.
The rosis yong, new spreding of thair knopis,[28]
War powderit brycht with hevinly beriall[29] droppis,
Throu bemes rede birnyng as ruby sperkis.
The skyes rang for schoutyng of the larkis;
The purpur hevyn, ourscailit[30] in silvir sloppis,[31]
Ourgilt[32] the treis, branchis, lef, and barkis.

Doune throu the ryce[33] a ryuir[34] ran wyth stremys
So lustily[35] agayn thai lykand lemys,[36]
That all the lake[37] as lamp did leme of licht,

---

1 *The goldyn targe,* [1508 ?], STC 7349, National Library of Scotland. "Targe" means "round shield."
2 just.
3 star.
4 began.
5 when.
6 were.
7 The moon.
8 rose.
9 rose garden.
10 morning.
11 purified.
12 before.
13 purple.
14 clothed.
15 into.
16 morning.
17 these.
18 The canonical hours, the offices or services prescribed for stated times of the day; here the birds sing "matins."
19 in.
20 enameled.
21 until.
22 float.
23 weep.
24 hang.
25 which.
26 love.
27 young growths.
28 buds.
29 beryl.
30 scaled over.
31 mantles, clouds.
32 gilded over.
33 branches, brushwood.
34 river.
35 pleasantly.
36 those pleasing gleams.
37 water.

Quhilk schadowit all about wyth twynkling glemis,
That bewis[38] bathit war in secund[39] bemys
Throu the reflex of Phebus visage brycht.
On every syde the hegies[40] raise on hicht,
The bank was grene, the bruke[41] was full of bremys,[42]
The stanneris[43] clere as stern in frosty nycht.

The cristall air, the sapher firmament,
The ruby skyes of the orient,
Kest[44] beriall bemes on emeraut bewis grene.
The rosy garth[45] depaynt[46] and redolent
With purpur, azure, gold, and goulis[47] gent[48]
Arayed was, by dame Flora the quene,
So nobily that ioy was for to sene.
The roch[49] agayn the rivir resplendent
As low[50] enlumynit all the leues schene.[51]

Quhat throu the mery foulys armony,
And throu the ryueris soune[52] rycht ran me by,
On Florais mantill I slepit as I lay;
Quhare sone in to my dremes fantasy
I saw approch, agayn the orient sky,
A saill als quhite as blossum vpon spray,
Wyth merse[53] of gold, brycht as the stern[54] of day,
Quhilk tendit to the land full lustily,
As falcoune swift desyrouse of hir pray.

And hard on burd vnto[55] the blomyt medis,
Amang the grene rispis[56] and the redis,
Arrivit sche, quhar fro anone thare landis
Ane hundreth ladyes, lusty in to wedis,[57]
Als fresch as flouris that in May vp spredis,
In kirtillis grene, withoutyn kell[58] or bandis.
Thair brycht hairis hang gletering on the strandis
In tressis clere, wyppit[59] wyth goldyn thredis;
With pappis quhite and mydlis small as wandis.

Discrive[60] I wald, bot quho coud wele endyte[61]
How all the feldis wyth thai[62] lilies quhite
Depaynt war brycht, quhilk to the hevyn did glete.[63]
Noucht thou, Omer, als fair as thou coud wryte,
For all thine ornate stilis so perfyte,

---

38 boughs.
39 reflected.
40 hedges.
41 brook.
42 breams.
43 pebbles.
44 cast.
45 garden.
46 painted.
47 gules, red.
48 soft, beautiful.
49 rock.
50 flame.
51 bright, beautiful.
52 sound.
53 Round top of mast.
54 star.
55 close alongside.
56 sedges.
57 gay as to clothing.
58 coif, headdress.
59 tied.
60 describe.
61 write.
62 those.
63 shine.

Nor yit thou, Tullius,[64] quhois[65] lippis suete
Off rethorike did in to termes flete[66]—
Your aureate tongis both bene all to lyte[67]
For to compile that paradise complete.

Thare saw I Nature and Venus, quene and quene,
The fresch Aurora, and lady Flora schene,[68]
Juno, Appollo, and Proserpyna,
Dyane the goddesse chaste of woddis[69] grene,
My lady Cleo, that help of makaris[70] bene,
Thetes, Pallas, and prudent Minerua,
Fair feynit[71] Fortune, and lemand[72] Lucina;
Thir[73] mychti quenis in crounis mycht be sene,
Wyth bemys blith, bricht as Lucifera.

Thare saw I May, of myrthfull monethis quene,
Betuix Aprile and June, her sistir schene,
Within the gardyng walking vp and doune,
Quham of[74] the foulis gladdith al bedene;[75]
Scho[76] was full tender in hir yeris grene.
Thare saw I Nature present hir a goune,
Rich to behald and nobil of renoune,
Off eviry hew vnder the hevin that bene,
Depaynt and broud[77] be gude proporcioun.

Full lustily thir ladyes all in fere[78]
Enterit within this park of most plesere,
Quhare that I lay our helit[79] wyth leuis ronk.[80]
The mery foulis, blisfullest of chere,
Salust[81] Nature, me thoucht,[82] on thair manere,
And eviry blome on branch and eke on bonk
Opnyt and spred thair balmy leuis donk,
Full low enclynyng to thair Quene so clere,
Quham of thair nobill norising[83] thay thonk.

Syne[84] to dame Flora on the samyn[85] wyse
Thay saluse, and thay thank a thousand syse;[86]
And to dame Venus lufis[87] mychti quene
Thay sang ballettis in lufe, as was the gyse,[88]
With amourouse notis lusty to devise,[89]
As thay that had lufe in thair hertis grene.
Thair hony throtis, opnyt fro the splene,[90]

---

64 Cicero.
65 whose.
66 abound in figures of rhetoric.
67 small.
68 beautiful.
69 woods.
70 poets.
71 feigned, disguised.
72 gleaming.
73 these.
74 of whom.
75 together.
76 she.
77 embroidered in.
78 together.
79 covered over.
80 luxuriant.
81 saluted.
82 it seemed to me.
83 nourishing.
84 after.
85 same.
86 times.
87 love's.
88 fashion.
89 pleasant to contrive.
90 heart.

With werblis suete did perse the hevinly skyes,
Quhill[91] loud resownyt the firmament serene.

Ane othir court thare saw I consequent,[92]
Cupide the king, wyth bow in hand ybent,
And dredefull arowis grundyn[93] scharp and square.
Thare saw I Mars, the god armypotent,
Of rethorike that fand[97] the flouris faire.
Aufull and sterne, strong and corpolent.
Thare saw I crabbit[94] Saturn ald and haire;[95]
His luke[96] was lyke for to perturb the aire.
Thare was Mercurius, wise and eloquent,

Thare was the god of gardingis, Priapus;
Thare was the god of wildernes, Phanus;[98]
And Janus, god of entree delytable;
Thare was the god of fludis, Neptunus;
Thare was the god of wyndis, Eolus,
With variand luke, rycht lyke a lord vnstable;
Thare was Bacus, the gladder of the table;
Thare was Pluto, the elrich[99] incubus,
In cloke of grene—his court vsit no sable.

And euiry one of thir,[1] in grene arayit,
On harp or lute full merily thai playit,
And sang ballettis with michty notis clere;
Ladyes to dance full sobirly assayit;[2]
Endlang the lusty ryuir so thai mayit,[3]
Thair observance rycht hevynly was to here.
Than crap[4] I throu the leuis and drew nere,
Quhare that I was rycht sudaynly affrayt,
All throu a luke quhilk I have boucht[5] full dere.

And schortly for to speke, be[6] lufis quene
I was aspyit; scho bad hir archearis kene
Go me arrest, and thay no time delayit.
Than[7] ladyes fair lete fall thair mantillis grene;
With bowis[8] big in tressit hairis schene,
All sudaynly thay had a felde arayit;[9]
And yit rycht gretly was I noucht affrayit,
The party was so plesand for to sene;
A wonder lusty bikkir[10] me assayit.

And first of all, with bow in hand ybent,
Come dame Beautee, rycht as scho wald me schent;[11]

[91] until.
[92] afterwards.
[93] ground.
[94] sullen.
[95] hoar.
[96] look.
[97] found, devised.
[98] Faunus.
[99] elfish, fairy.
[1] these.
[2] ventured.
[3] along the pleasant river so they celebrated May.
[4] crept.
[5] bought.
[6] by.
[7] then.
[8] *bowis*] *lowis* STC 7349.
[9] prepared for battle.
[10] pleasant attack.
[11] just as though she wished to injure me.

Syne[12] folowit all hir dameselis yfere,[13]
With mony diuerse aufull instrument,
Unto the pres;[14] Fair Having wyth hir went,
Fyne Portrature, Plesance, and Lusty Chere.[15]
Than come Resoun, with schelde of gold so clere,
In plate and maille, as Mars armypotent,
Defendit me, that nobil cheuallere.

Syne tender Youth come wyth hir virgyns ying,[16]
Grene Innocence, and schamefull Abaising,[17]
And quaking Drede, wyth humble Obedience.
The Goldyn Targe harmyt thay no thing;[18]
Curage in thame was noucht begonne to spring;
Full sore thay dred to done a violence.
Suete Womanhede I saw cum in presence;
Of artilye[19] a warld[20] sche did in bring,
Seruit wyth ladyes full of reuerence.

Sche led wyth hir Nurture and Lawlynes,[21]
Contenence, Pacience, Gude Fame, and Stedfastnes,
Discrecioun, Gentrise,[22] and Considerance,
Leuefell[23] Company, and Honest Besynes,
Benigne Luke,[24] Mylde Chere, and Sobirnes.
All thir bure ganyeis[25] to do me greuance
But Resoun bure the Targe wyth sik constance,
Thair scharp assayes mycht do no dures[26]
To me for all thair aufull ordynance.

Unto the pres persewit Hie Degree;
Hir folowit ay Estate, and Dignitee,
Comparisoun, Honour, and Noble Array,
Will, Wantonnes, Renoun, and Libertee,
Richesse, Fredome,[27] and eke Nobilitee.
Wit[28] ye thay did thair baner hye display;
A cloud of arowis as hayle schour lousit[29] thay,
And schot quhill[30] wastit was thair artilye,
Syne went abak reboytit[31] of thair pray.

Quhen Venus had persauit[32] this rebute,[33]
Dissymilance[34] scho bad go mak persute,
At all powere[35] to perse the Goldyn Targe;
And scho, that was of doubilnes[36] the rute,[37]

---

[12] after.
[13] together.
[14] throng.
[15] pleasant countenance.
[16] young.
[17] modest humility.
[18] not at all.
[19] artillery.
[20] world.
[21] lowliness.
[22] gentleness.
[23] lawful, becoming.
[24] look.
[25] these bore arrows.
[26] injuries.
[27] generosity.
[28] know.
[29] loosed.
[30] until.
[31] repulsed.
[32] perceived.
[33] repulse.
[34] dissembling.
[35] with all her might.
[36] duplicity.
[37] root.

Askit hir choise of archeris in refute.
Venus the best bad hir go wale[38] at large;
Scho tuke Presence, plicht ankers[39] of the barge,
And Fair Callyng, that wele a flayn[40] coud schute,
And Cherising for to complete hir charge.

Dame Hamelynes[41] scho tuke in company,
That hardy was and hende[42] in archery,
And broucht dame Beautee to the felde agayn.
With all the choise of Venus cheualry
Thay come and bikkerit vnabaisitly.[43]
The schour of arowis rappit[44] on as rayn.
Perilouse Presence, that mony syre[45] has slayne,
The bataill broucht on bordour[46] hard vs by.
The salt[47] was all the sarar,[48] suth to sayn.[49]

Thik was the schote of grundyn[50] dartis kene,
Bot Resoun with the Scheld of Gold so schene
Warly[51] defendit quho so euir assayit.[52]
The aufull stoure[53] he manly did sustene,
Quhill Presence kest a pulder in his ene,[54]
And than as drunkyn man he all forvayit.[55]
Quhen he was blynd, the fule wyth hym thay playit,
And banyst[56] hym amang the bewis grene;
That sory sicht me sudaynly affrayit.

Than was I woundit to the deth wele nere,
And yoldyn[57] as a wofull prisonnere
To lady Beautee in a moment space.
Me thoucht scho semyt lustiar of chere[58]
Efter that Resoun tynt[59] had his eyne clere,
Than of before, and lufliare of face.
Quhy was thou blyndit, Resoun, quhi, allace,
And gert[60] ane hell my paradise appere,
And mercy seme,[61] quhare that I fand[62] no grace?

Dissymulance was besy me to sile,[63]
And Fair Calling did oft apon me smyle,
And Cherising me fed wyth wordis fair;
New Acquyntance enbracit me a quhile
And favouryt me, quhill men mycht go a myle,
Syne tuk hir leve—I saw hir nevir mare.

38 choose.
39 principal anchors.
40 arrow.
41 familiarity.
42 skillful.
43 attacked boldly.
44 struck.
45 men.
46 border.
47 assault.
48 sorer.
49 to tell the truth.
50 ground.
51 warily or (perhaps) in a warlike manner.
52 *assayit*] *assayes* STC 7349.
53 conflict.
54 cast a powder in his eye.
55 went astray.
56 banished.
57 yielded.
58 pleasanter of face.
59 lost.
60 made.
61 seem (to be).
62 found.
63 mislead.

Than saw I Dangere[64] toward me repair;
I coud eschew hir presence be[65] no wyle;
On syde scho lukit wyth ane fremyt fare,[66]

And at the last departing coud hir dresse,[67]
And me delyuerit vnto Hevynesse
For to remayne, and scho in cure[68] me tuke.[69]
Be this[70] the Lord of Wyndis, wyth wodenes,[71]
God Eolus, his bugill blew, I gesse,
That with the blast the leuis all to-schuke,[72]
And sudaynly in the space of a luke
All was hyne[73] went; thare was bot wildernes;
Thare was no more bot birdis, bank, and bruke.

In twynkling of ane eye to schip thai went,
And swyth[74] vp saile vnto the top thai stent,[75]
And with swift course atour[76] the flude thai frak.[77]
Thai fyrit gunnis wyth powder violent,
Till that the reke[78] raise to the firmament
The rochis all resownyt wyth the rak;[79]
For rede[80] it semyt that the raynbow brak.
Wyth spirit affrayde apon my fete I sprent[81]
Amang the clewis,[82] so carefull[83] was the crak.

And as I did awake of my sueving,[84]
The ioyfull birds merily did syng
For myrth of Phebus tendir bemes schene.
Suete war the vapouris, soft the morowing,[85]
Halesum[86] the vale, depaynt wyth flouris ying;
The air attemperit, sobir, and amene;[87]
In quhite and rede was all the felde besene,[88]
Throu Naturis nobil fresch anamalyng,
In mirthfull May, of euiry moneth Quene.

O reverend Chaucere, rose of rethoris[89] all,
As in oure tong ane[90] flour imperiall,
That raise in Britane euir, quho redis rycht,
Thou beris of makaris the tryumph riall.[91]
Thy frech anamalit termes celicall[92]
This mater coud illumynit haue full brycht.
Was thou noucht of oure Inglisch all the lycht,

---

64 coyness, disdain.
65 by.
66 in a strange or unfriendly manner.
67 (?) made ready to depart.
68 care.
69 *tuke.*] *take* STC 7349.
70 by this time.
71 madness.
72 *to-schuke;*] *to-schake* STC 7349.
73 hence.
74 quickly.
75 stretched.
76 over.
77 sped.
78 smoke.
79 crack, shock.
80 noise, roar.
81 sprang.
82 cliffs.
83 awful.
84 dreaming.
85 morning.
86 wholesome.
87 pleasant.
88 arrayed.
89 writers.
90 *ane*] *and* STC 7349.
91 royal.
92 heavenly.

Surmounting euiry tong terrestriall,
Alls fer[93] as Mayes morow dois mydnycht?

O morall Gower, and Ludgate laureate,
Your sugurit lippis and tongis aureate
Bene to oure eris cause of grete delyte.
Your angel mouthis most mellifluate[94]
Oure rude langage has clere illumynate,
And faire ourgilt[95] oure speche that imperfyte
Stude or[96] your goldyn pennis schupe[97] to wryte.[98]
This Ile before was bare and desolate
Off rethorike or lusty[99] fresch endyte.[1]

Thou lytill quair,[2] be euir obedient,
Humble, subiect, and symple of entent,
Before the face of euiry connyng wicht.[3]
I knaw quhat thou of rethorike has[4] spent;
Off all hir lusty rosis redolent
Is none in to thy gerland[5] sett on hicht;
Eschame[6] thar of and draw the out of sicht.
Rude is thy wede,[7] disteynit,[8] bare, and rent.
Wele aucht[9] thou be aferit[10] of the licht.

[LAMENT FOR THE MAKARIS][11]

I, that in heill[12] wes[13] and gladnes,
Am trublit now with gret seiknes[14]
And feblit[15] with infermite;
Timor mortis conturbat me.[16]

Our plesance[17] heir[18] is all vane glory;
This fals warld is bot transitory;
The flesche is brukle;[19] the fend is sle;[20]
Timor mortis conturbat me.

The stait of man dois change and[21] vary,
Now sound, now seik, now blith, now sary,[22]
Now dansand[23] mery, now like to dee;[24]
Timor mortis conturbat me.

No stait in erd[25] heir standis sickir;[26]
As with the wynd wavis the wickir,[27]
Wavis this warldis vainte;
Timor mortis conturbat me.

One to the ded[28] gois all estatis,

---

[93] as far.
[94] mellifluous.
[95] gilded over.
[96] before.
[97] shaped, undertook.
[98] *wryte;*] *write* STC 7349.
[99] pleasant.
[1] writing.
[2] book.
[3] learned person.
[4] *has*] *may* STC 7349.
[5] in thy garland.
[6] be ashamed.
[7] clothing.
[8] stained.
[9] ought.
[10] afraid.
[11] from *The tua mariit wemen and the wedo,* [1508?]; STC 7350, National Library of Scotland. Although the poem has no title in the oldest extant edition, editors usually give it the title *Lament for the Makaris,* that is, "for the makers, the poets."
[12] health.
[13] was.
[14] sickness.
[15] enfeebled.
[16] This sentence occurs in the *Responsorium* to the seventh lesson in the Office for the Dead, and it is used as a refrain by Lydgate and by other poets of Lydgate's time.
[17] pleasure.
[18] here.
[19] brittle.
[20] fiend is sly.
[21] *and*] *et* STC 7350.
[22] sorry.
[23] dancing.
[24] die.
[25] earth.
[26] secure.
[27] willow.
[28] death.

Princis, prelotis, and potestatis,[29]
Baith[30] riche and pur[31] of al degre;
Timor mortis conturbat me.

He takis the knythis in to[32] feild,
Anarmyt[33] vnder helme and scheild;
Victour he is at all melle;[34]
Timor mortis conturbat me.

That strang[35] vnmercifull tyrand
Takis, one the moderis[36] breist sowkand,[37]
The bab full of benignite;
Timor mortis conturbat me.

He takis the campion[38] in the stour,[39]
The capitane closit in the tour,
The lady in bour full of bewte;
Timor mortis conturbat me.

He sparis no lord for his piscence,[40]
Na[41] clerk[42] for his intelligence;
His awful strak[43] may no man fle;
Timor mortis conturbat me.

Art-magicianis[44] and astrologgis,
Rethoris,[45] logicianis, and theologgis,
Thame helpis no conclusionis sle;[46]
Timor mortis conturbat me.

In medicyne the most practicianis,[47]
Lechis,[48] surrigianis, and phisicianis,
Thame self fra ded[49] may not supple;[50]
Timor mortis conturbat me.

I se that makaris[51] amang the laif[52]
Playis heir ther pageant, syne[53] gois to graif;[54]
Sparit is nought ther faculte;[55]
Timor mortis conturbat me.

He has done petuously devour[56]
The noble Chaucer, of makaris flour,
The Monk of Bery,[57] and Gower,[58] all thre;
Timor mortis conturbat me.

The gud Syr Hew of Eglintoun,[59]
And[60] eik[61] Heryot and[62] Wyntoun,[63]
He has tane out of this cuntre;
Timor mortis conturbat me.

That scorpion fell has done infek[64]
Maister Iohne Clerk and[65] Iames Afflek
Fra balat-making and[65] trigidie;
Timor mortis conturbat me.

Holland[66] and[67] Barbour[68] he has berevit;[69]
Allace[70] that[71] he nought[72] with us levit[73]
Schir Mungo Lokert of the Le;
Timor mortis conturbat me.

Clerk of Tranent eik he has tane,
That maid[74] the Anteris[75] of Gawane;

[29] potentates.
[30] both.
[31] poor.
[32] in.
[33] armed.
[34] fight.
[35] strong.
[36] mother's.
[37] sucking.
[38] champion.
[39] battle.
[40] puissance, power.
[41] no.
[42] learned man.
[43] stroke.
[44] magicians.
[45] eloquent writers.
[46] clever.
[47] most skillful.
[48] doctors.
[49] from death.
[50] help, deliver.
[51] poets.
[52] rest.
[53] then, afterwards.
[54] grave.
[55] profession.
[56] he has piteously devoured.
[57] John Lydgate (c. 1370–c. 1449), of Bury St. Edmunds.
[58] John Gower (c. 1330–1408).
[59] Little or nothing is known about some of the poets that Dunbar mentions.
[60] *and*] *et* STC 7350.
[61] also.
[62] *and*] *et* STC 7350.
[63] Andrew of Wyntown, author of the *Orygynale cronykil*, c. 1420.
[64] has infected.
[65] *and*] *et* STC 7350.
[66] Sir Richard Holland, author of *The buke of the howlet*, c. 1480.
[67] *and*] *et* STC 7350.
[68] John Barbour, author of *The Bruce*, 1376.
[69] taken away.
[70] alas.
[71] *that*] *taht* STC 7350.
[72] not.
[73] left.
[74] wrote.
[75] adventures.

Schir Gilbert Hay[76] endit has he;
Timor mortis conturbat me.

He has Blind Hary and Sandy Traill
Slaine with his schour of mortall haill,
Quhilk[77] Patrik Iohnestoun myght nought fle;
Timor mortis conturbat me.

He has reft Merseir his endite,[78]
That did in luf[79] so lifly[80] write,
So schort, so quyk, of sentence hie;[81]
Timor mortis conturbat me.

He has tane Roull of Aberdene,
And gentill Roull of Corstorphin;
Two bettir fallowis did no man se;
Timor mortis conturbat me.

In Dumfermelyne he has done rovne[82]
With Maister Robert Henrisoun;[83]
Schir Iohne the Ros[84] enbrast has he;
Timor mortis conturbat me.

And he has now tane last of aw[85]
Gud gentill Stobo and[86] Quintyne Schaw,
Of quham all wichtis has pete;[87]
Timor mortis conturbat me.

Gud Maister Walter Kennedy
In poynt of dede lyis veraly,[88]
Gret reuth[89] it wer that so suld be;
Timor mortis conturbat me.

Sen[90] he has all my brether[91] tane,
He will naught lat me lif alane;[92]
Of forse I man his nyxt pray be;[93]
Timor mortis conturbat me.

Sen for the deid[94] remeid[95] is none,
Best is that we for dede dispone,[96]
Eftir our deid that lif may me;
Timor mortis conturbat me.

Quod Dunbar quhen he wes sek.

[76] Sir Gilbert Hay (fl. 1456), translator.
[77] which.
[78] he has deprived Merseir of his writing.
[79] love.
[80] spiritedly.
[81] noble of sentiment.
[82] has whispered.
[83] Robert Henryson (c. 1430–1506), well-known poet, was schoolmaster at Dunfermline.
[84] Sir John the Ross, John Reid alias Stobo, Quentin Shaw, and Walter Kennedy were contemporaries of Dunbar and are mentioned elsewhere in his poems.
[85] all.
[86] *and*] *et* STC 7350.
[87] of whom all creatures have pity.
[88] lies truly at point of death.
[89] pity.
[90] since.
[91] brothers.
[92] he will not let me live alone.
[93] perforce I must his next prey be.
[94] death.
[95] remedy.
[96] dispose ourselves for death.

Stephen Hawes

[c. 1474–c. 1523]

STEPHEN HAWES was a Suffolk man, educated at Oxford, and a groom of the chamber to Henry VII, to whom in 1503–1504 he dedicated *The Example of Virtue* and in 1505–1506 *The Pastime of Pleasure*. Hawes's reputation rests upon these two poems.

The Example of Virtue is an allegory of some three hundred stanzas of rhyme royal. The hero, Youth, conducted by Discretion and instructed by Nature, Hardiness (courage), Fortune, and Wisdom, resists Sensuality and Pride, and, wearing the armor of St. Paul, conquers the three-headed dragon (the world, the flesh, and the devil), changes his name to Virtue, and marries Cleanness.

The same theme—the life of the Christian knight—is developed more elaborately in *The Pastime of Pleasure*. Into his long, cloudy allegory this scholarly moralist introduces most of the conventional machinery and characters of medieval allegory: the dream, the painted wall, the Tower of Doctrine, the Temple of Mars, the Temple of Venus, the digressions, the descriptions, the debates, the gods and goddesses, the Nine Worthies, the Seven Liberal Arts, the Seven Deadly Sins, the host of personified abstractions, the giants and dragons, the fantastic adventures. There is no originality; he is content to follow his predecessors, especially his master Lydgate.

The Pastime is a medieval "pilgrim's progress." The hero, Graund Amoure, passes through the fair meadow of Youth and must choose between the two highways: the way of Contemplation (life in a religious order) or the way of Active Life. He chooses the latter, and Fame tells him of La Bel Pucell (who symbolizes the good life), attainable only with great difficulty. He visits the Tower of Doctrine, where the Seven Liberal Arts instruct him. He passes through many trials and dangers and finally reaches the palace of La Bel Pucell, where he is welcomed by Peace, Mercy, Justice, Reason, Grace, and Memory, and is married to La Bel Pucell by *Lex Ecclesiae* (Law of the Church). After happy years with her, Old Age visits him, Policy and Avarice tempt him, he becomes eager for riches, Death warns him, Contrition and Conscience come to him before he dies. He speaks from the grave; the Seven Deadly Sins, Fame, and

Time make their pronouncements; and the poem ends with the solemn exhortation of Dame Eternity, who is "of heuen quene and of hell empres."

The Pastime belongs in the tradition of Deguilleville's famous fourteenth-century poem, *Le Pèlerinage de la Vie Humaine*, translated by Lydgate (1426–1430). When Hawes wrote, the moral allegory was already antiquated, and *The Pastime* is the last important English poem of its kind until *The Faerie Queene*.

The rhythm of Hawes's verse is puzzling to the modern reader. The gradual disappearance of many inflectional endings and the shift in accent, especially in words borrowed from the French—changes which had embarrassed poets during the fifteenth century—were troublesome to Hawes. Like his contemporaries, he failed to understand the verse technique of Chaucer, and he relied upon his own sense of metrical movement. In *The Pastime* he employs two kinds of verse: the rhymed pentameter couplet, which he used in the more than four hundred lines of the Godfrey Gobelyve episode, and the conventional rhyme royal. His lines, normally pentameter, have from eight to twelve syllables and from four to six stresses.

The best modern edition is *The Pastime of Pleasure*, ed. W. E. Mead, Early English Text Society, vol. 173, 1928. The best accounts of Hawes are given in the Introduction in Mead's edition; J. M. Berdan, *Early Tudor Poetry*, 1920; and C. S. Lewis, *The Allegory of Love*, 1936.

HERE BEGYNNETH THE PASSE TYME OF PLEASURE[1]

Ryght myghty prynce and redoubted souerayne,[2]
Saylynge forthe well in the shyppe of grace
Ouer the wawes of this lyfe vncertayne
Ryght towarde heuen to haue dwellynge place,
Grace doth you guyde in euery doubtfull cace;
Your gouernaunce dothe euermore eschewe
The synne of slouthe,[3] enemy to vertewe.

Grace stereth well; the grace of God is grete
Whiche you hathe brought to your ryall se,
And in your ryght it hath you surely sette
Aboue vs all to haue the souerayntе;
Whose worthy power and regall dygnyte
All our rancour and our debate gan[4] ceace
And hath vs[5] brought bothe welthe, reste, and peace.

Frome whome dyscendeth by the ryghtfull lyne
Noble prynce Henry[6] to succede the crowne,
That in his youthe dothe so clerely shyne

[1] From *The passe tyme of pleasure*, 1517, STC 12949, Morgan Library.

[2] Henry VII, to whom Hawes was a groom of the chamber.

[3] Sloth, one of the Seven Deadly Sins.

[4] *gan* STC 12950]; *and* STC 12949.

[5] *And hath vs* STC 12950]; *Hath to vs* STC 12949.

[6] Henry VIII.

In euery vertu, castynge the vyce adowne.
He shall of fame attayne the hye renowne;
No doubt but grace shall hym well enclose,
Whiche by trewe ryght sprange of the reed rose.[7]

Your noble grace and excellent hyenes
For to accepte I beseche ryght humbly
This lytell boke opprest with rudenes,
Without rethorycke or colour crafty.
Nothynge[8] I am experte in poetry
As the monke or Bury,[9] floure of eloquence,
Whiche was in tyme of grete excellence

Of your predecessour the v. kynge henry;
Vnto whose grace he dyde present
Ryght famous bokes of parfyte[10] memory,
Of his faynynge with termes eloquent,
Whose fatall fyccyons are yet permanent,
Grounded on reason; with clowdy fygures
He cloked the trouthe of all his scryptures.[11]

The lyght of trouthe I lacke connynge to cloke;
To drawe a curtayne I dare not to presume,
Nor hyde my mater with a mysty smoke,
My rudenes connynge dothe so sore consume.
Yet as I maye I shall blowe out a fume
To hyde my mynde vnderneth a fable,
By couert[12] colour[13] well and probable,

Beschynge your grace to pardon myne ignoraunce,
Whiche this fayned fable to eschewe ydlenesse
Haue so compyled, now without doubtaunce,
For to present to your hye worthynesse;
To folowe the trace and all the parfytenesse
Of my mayster Lydgate with due exercyse,
Suche fayned tales I do fynde and deuyse.

For vnder a colour a truthe maye aryse,
As was the guyse in olde antyquyte
Of the poetes olde a tale to surmyse
To cloke the trouthe of theyr infyrmyte,
Or yet on Ioye to haue moralyte,
I me excuse yf by neclygence
That I do offende for lacke of scyence.

. . . .

The good dame mercy with dame charyte[14]
My body buryed full ryght humbly

[7] The red rose of Lancaster.

[8] not at all.

[9] John Lydgate, of Bury St. Edmunds, whom Hawes admired and imitated.

[10] perfect.

[11] in his writings he shrouded his meaning in allegory.

[12] *couert* STC 12950]; *conuert* STC 12949.

[13] rhetorical embellishment or fiction or allegory.

[14] Here 765 stanzas are omitted. Graunde Amour speaks from his grave, and each of the Seven Deadly Sins addresses him. The Seven Deadly Sins appear often in medieval literature. Hawes was probably familiar with the accounts in Chaucer's "Parson's Tale," Gower's *Mirour de l'Omme* and *Confessio Amantis,* and Lydgate's *Courte of Sapyence.*

In a fayre temple of olde antyquyte,
Where was for me a dyryge[15] deuoutely,
And with many a masse full ryght solempnely,
And ouer my graue to be in memory
Remembraunce made this lytell epytaphy:

O erthe, on erthe it is a wonders cace[16]
That thou arte blynde and wyll not the knowe;
Though vpon erthe thou hast thy dwellynge place,
Yet erthe at laste must nedes the ouerthrowe.
Thou thynkest the to be none[17] erthe, I trowe;
For yf thou dydest thou woldest than apply
To forsake pleasure and to lerne to dy.

Pryde

O erthe, of erthe why arte thou so proude?
Now what thou arte call to remembraunce.
Open thyn eres vnto my songe aloude.
Is not thy beaute, strength, and puyssaunce,
Though it be[18] cladde with clothes of pleasaunce,
Very erthe and also wormes fode,
Whan, erthe, to erthe shall to tourne the blode?[19]

Wrathe

And, erthe, with erthe why arte thou so wrothe?
Remembre the that it vayleth[20] ryght nought,
For thou mayst thynke of a perfyte trothe[21]
Yf with the erthe thou hast a quarell sought.
Amyddes the erthe there is a place ywrought,
Whan erthe to erthe is torned proprely,
The for thy synne to punysshe wonderly.

Enuy

And, erthe, for erthe why hast thou enuy,
And the, erthe, vpon erthe to be more prosperous
Than thou thy selfe fretynge[22] the inwardly?
It is a synne ryght foule and vycyous,
And vnto god also full odyous.
Thou thynkest, I trowe, there is no punysshemente
Ordeyned for synne by egall[23] Iugemente.

Slouthe

Towarde heuen to folowe on the way
Thou arte full slowe and thynkest nothynge[24]
That thy nature dooth full sore dekay,
And dethe ryght fast is to the comynge.
God graunte the mercy, but no tyme enlongynge;[25]

15 dirge.
16 wondrous condition.
17 *the to be none* STC 12948]; *the do be none* STC 12949.
18 *Though it be* STC 12948]; *Though be* STC 12949.
19 when the blood shall completely turn to earth.
20 avails.
21 perfect truth.
22 cutting, consuming.
23 just.
24 not at all.
25 prolonging of time.

Whan thou hast tyme, take tyme and space;
Whan tyme is past, lost is the tyme of grace.

Couetyse[26]

And whan erthe to erthe is nexte[27] to reuerte,
And nature lowe in the laste aege,
Of[28] erthely treasure erthe doth set his herte,
Insacyatly vpon couetyse to rage.
He thynketh not his lyfe shall aswage;[29]
His good is his god with his grete ryches;
He thynketh not for to leue it, doutles.

Glotony

The pomped[30] carkes[31] with fode delycyous
Erthe often fedeth with corrupte glotony,
And nothynge[32] with werkes vertuous.
The soule doth fede ryght well ententyfly;[33]
But without mesure full inordynatly
The body lyueth and wyll not remembre
How erthe to erthe must his strength surrendre.

Lechery

The vyle carkes set vpon a fyre
Dooth often haunte the synne of lechery,
Fulfyllynge the foule carnall desyre.
Thus erthe with erthe is corrupte meruaylously,
And erthe on erthe wyll nothynge puryfye,[34]
Tyll erthe to erthe be nere subuerted,[35]
For erthe with erthe is so peruerted.

O mortall folke, you may beholde and se
How I lye here, somtyme a mygthy knyght.
The ende of Ioye and all prosperyte
Is dethe at last through his course and myght.
After the day there cometh the derke nyght,
For though the day be neuer so longe,
At last the belles ryngeth to euensonge.

And my selfe called la graunde amoure,
Sekynge aduenture in the worldly glory,
For to attayne the ryches and honoure,
Dyde thynke full lytell that I sholde here ly,
Tyll dethe dyde mate[36] me full ryght pryuely.
Lo, what I am and where to you must;[37]
Lyke as I am so shall you be all dust.

Than in your mynde inwardely dyspyse
The bryttle worlde so full of doublenes,

---

26 Covetousness.
27 about.
28 on.
29 decrease.
30 pampered.
31 carcass. All early editions read *clerkes*. As Mead points out, line 547 reads *The pomped carkes with fode delycyous*, which is probably the true reading of the present line (line 5460).
32 not at all.
33 intently.
34 *puryfye* STC 12948]; *purfye* STC 12949.
35 overthrown.
36 *mate* STC 12948]; *marke* STC 12949: confound.
37 must go.

With the vyle flesshe, and ryght soone aryse
Out of your slepe of mortall heuynes.
Subdue the deuyll with grace and mekenes
That after your lyfe, frayle and transytory,
You may than lyue in Ioye perdurably.[38]

. . . .

"Withouten tyme is no erthely thynge,[39]
Nature, fortune, or yet dame sapyence,
Hardynes, clergy,[40] or yet lernynge,
Past, future, or yet in presence.
Wherfore I am of more hye preemynence,
As cause of fame, honoure, and clergy;
They can nothynge without hym magnyfy.

"Do not I, tyme, cause nature to augment?
Do not I, tyme, cause nature to decay?
Do not I, tyme, cause man to be present?
Do not I, tyme, take his lyfe away?
Do not I, tyme, cause dethe take his say?[41]
Do not I, tyme, passe his youth and age?
Do not I, tyme, euery thynge aswage?[42]

"In tyme Troye the cyte was edefyed;[43]
By tyme also was the dystruccyon.
Nothynge without tyme can be fortefyed;
No erthely Ioye nor trybulacyon
Without tyme is for to suffre passyon;[44]
The tyme of erthe was our dystruccyon,
And the tyme of erthe was our redempcyon.

"Adam of erthe, sone of vyrgynyte,
And Eue by god of adam create,
These two the worlde dampned[45] in certaynte,
By dysobedyence so foule and vycyate,[46]
And all other than frome them generate,
Tyll peace and mercy made ryght to enclyne
Out the lyon to entre the vyrgyne.[47]

"Lyke as the worlde was dystroyed totally
By the vyrgyns sone, so it semed well
A vyrgyns sone to redeme it pyteously,
Whose hye godheed in the chosen vessell
Forty wekes naturally dyde dwell,
Nature takynge as the hye god of kynde;[48]
In the vyrgyn he dyde suche nature fynde.

---

[38] eternally.

[39] Here 26 stanzas are omitted. Time is speaking.

[40] learning.

[41] assay; i.e., taste his food.

[42] diminish.

[43] built.

[44] can be felt without time.

[45] damned.

[46] wicked.

[47] Leo and Virgo are the fifth and sixth signs of the zodiac. Hawes probably suggests here the transition from Judaism to Christianity.

[48] So STC 12948. STC 12949 here prints three words from the preceding line. The meaning is probably "taking human nature as the high God of nature."

"Thus without nature, nature wonderly
In a vyrgyn pure openly hath wrought;
To the god of nature nothynge truely
Impossyble is, for he made of nought
Nature fyrst, whiche naturynge hath tought
Naturately ryght naturate to make;[49]
Why may not he than the pure nature take

"By his godhede of the vyrgyn Mary?
His electe moder and arke of testament,
Of holy chyrche the blessyd lumynary;
After the byrthe of her sone excellent
Vyrgyn she was yet alway permanent,
Dysnullynge[50] the sectes of false ydolatry,
And castynge downe the fatall heresy.

"Thus whan I, tyme, in euery nacyon
Raygned[51] in rest and also in peace,
And Octauyan in his domynacyon
Thorough the worlde and the peopled preace[52]
Lettres had sent, his honoure to encreace,
Of all the nombre for to be certayne
For to obey hym as theyr souerayne,

"In whose tyme god toke his natyuyte,
For to redeme vs with his precyous blode
Frome the deuylles bonde of grete iniquyte;
His herte was perst, hangynge on the rood;
Was not this tyme vnto man ryght good?
Shall not I, tyme, euermore abyde
Tyll that in libra[53] at the dredefull tyde[54]

"Of the day of dome, than in the balaunce,[55]
Almyghty god shall be Iust and egall
To euery persone withouten doubtaunce?
Eche as they dyde deserue in generall,
Some to haue Ioye, some payne eternall.
Than I am past; I may no lenger[56] be,
And after me is dame eternyte."

And thus as tyme made his conclusyon,
Eternyte in a fayre whyte vesture
To the temple came with hole[57] affeccyon,
And on her hede a dyademe ryght pure,
With thre crownes of precyous treasure.
"Eterne,"[58] she sayde, "I am, nowe doubtles
Of heuen quene and of hell empres.

[49] The meaning of this and the preceding line is perhaps "nature, which has taught the creative power to make, by nature, created things."
[50] destroying.
[51] *Raygned* STC 12950]; *Reygne* STC 12949.
[52] press, throng.
[53] Libra, the scales, the seventh sign of the zodiac.
[54] time.
[55] scales of justice.
[56] longer.
[57] whole.
[58] *Eterne* STC 12948]; *Eternitie* STC 12949.

"Fyrst god made heuen his propre habytacle;
Though that his power be in euery place,
In eterne heuen is his tabernacle;
Tyme is there in no maner of cace;
Tyme renneth[59] alwaye his ende to enbrace.
Now I my selfe shall haue none endynge,
And my maker had no begynnynge.

"In heuen and hell I am contynually,
Withouten ende to be inextynguyssyble,
As euermore to reygne full ryally.[60]
Of euery thynge I am inuyncyble;
Man of my power shall be intellygyble
Whan the soule shall ryse agaynst the body
To haue Iugemente to lyue eternally,

"In heuen or hell, as he dothe deserue.
Who that loueth god aboue euery thynge
All his commaundementes he wyll then obserue,
And spende his tyme in vertuous lyuynge;
Ydlenes wyll euermore be[61] eschewynge;
Eternall Ioye he shall then attayne
After his laboure and his besy[62] payne.

"O mortall folke, reuolue in your mynde
That worldly Ioye and frayle prosperyte;
What is it lyke but a blaste of wynde,
For you therof can haue no certaynte,
It is now so full of mutabylyte.
Set not your mynde vpon worldly welthe,
But euermore regarde your soules helthe.

"Whan erthe in erth hath tane[63] his corrupte taste,
Than to repente it is for you to late.
When you haue tyme, spende it nothynge[64] in waste;
Tyme past with vertue must entre the gate
Of Ioye and blysse, with myn hye estate,
Withoute tyme for to be euerlastynge,
Whiche god graunte vs at our last endynge."

Now blyssed lady of the helthe eternall,
The quene of comforte and of heuenly glorye,
Pray to thy swete sone, whiche is infynall,[65]
To gyue me grace to wynne the vyctory
Of the deuyll, the worlde, and of my body,
And that I may my selfe well apply,
Thy sone and the to laude and magnyfy.

---

59 runs.
60 royally.
61 *euermore be* STC 12950]; *euermore* STC 12949: He will evermore avoid idleness.
62 busy.
63 taken.
64 not at all.
65 infinite.

THE EXCUSACYON OF THE AUCTORE

Vnto all poetes I do me excuse
Yf that I offende for lacke of scyence.[66]
This lytell boke yet do ye not refuse
Though it be deuoyde of famous eloquence.
Adde or detray[67] by your hye sapyence,
And pardon me of my hye enterpryse,
Whiche of late this fable dyde fayne and deuyse.

Go, lytell boke, I pray god the saue
Frome myssemetrynge by wronge Impressyon;
And who that euer lyst the for to haue
That he perceyue well thyn entencyon
For to be grounded withoute presumpcyon,
As for to eschewe the synne of ydlenes
To make suche bokes I apply my besynes,

Besechynge God for to gyue me grace
Bokes to compyle of morall vertue,
Of my mayster Lydgate to folowe the trace,[68]
His noble fame for to laude and renue,[69]
Whiche in his lyfe the slouthe dyde eschewe,
Makynge grete bokes to be in memory,
On whose soule I pray God haue mercy.[70]

---

[66] knowledge, skill.
[67] subtract.
[68] track, path.
[69] *renue* STC 12950]; *reneue* STC 12948; *remeue* STC 12949.
[70] Many medieval poems end in this manner.

John Skelton

[c. 1460–1529]

IN HIS own day John Skelton was honored as a scholar and poet. By 1493 he had received from Oxford and Cambridge, and perhaps from Louvain, the academic title of poet laureate. For a time he was tutor to the future Henry VIII. In 1498 he entered holy orders, and from about 1502 to 1512 he was rector of Diss in Norfolk. Then he returned to court, where he became Orator Regius and a member of the king's household.

Skelton wrote a vast amount of verse—religious, elegiac, complimentary, patriotic, satiric. He wrote charming lyrics. Many of the poems that he names in *The Garland of Laurel* are lost.

One of his more famous poems is *The Tunning of Elinor Rumming*, a coarse and realistic picture of low life that concludes with a warning to avoid what the poem describes. Of his morality plays only one, *Magnificence*, is extant. The most pleasant and playful of his poems is *Philip Sparrow*, in which he reveals the sweet and simple innocence of a well-bred schoolgirl who laments the death of her pet sparrow. This poem and the lyrics that he addresses to young ladies in *The Garland of Laurel* have the fresh beauty of many of the lyrics written later in the century.

Skelton's most striking poems are a series of satires. *The Bowge of Court* (i.e., "the food of court"), written about 1498, is an allegorical satire on life at court, which he describes as a place of selfishness and deceit and hatred. The form is medieval, but the theme and the tone are Renaissance. *Speak, Parrot* (1521) attacks the new learning, the new extravagance in manners and dress, the new politics, especially the power of Cardinal Wolsey. *Colin Clout* (1522) denounces the corruption of the higher clergy, especially Wolsey. *Why Come Ye Not To Court?* (1522) is another and more savage attack on Wolsey.

The Garland of Laurel (1523) and later poems attempt to conciliate Wolsey. *The Garland* is notable for its conventional medieval machinery, the beauty of its rhyme royal, the fresh and graceful lyrics in Skeltonic verse, the poet's self-praise, the catalogue of his poems, and the complimentary conclusion addressed to Wolsey.

Though at times Skelton uses rhyme royal and other conventional verse forms, he writes often in a succession of short lines, heavily alliterated and irregular in rhythm, usually containing two or three accented syllables and a varying number of unaccented syllables, and rhyming in groups of two, three, four, or more, but never cross-rhymed. This distinctive verse, usually termed "Skeltonic," he probably developed from the classical prose figure "like ending," from the native alliterative verse, and from the rhythm of ordinary speech. Whatever its origin, Skeltonic verse has never become a conventional verse pattern, although its rhythm resembles the "sprung rhythm" of Gerard Manley Hopkins, and the form in general has perhaps influenced Edith Sitwell, Robert Graves, W. H. Auden, and other modern poets. Skelton uses the form effectively for various purposes—for torrents of invective as well as for graceful lyrics. His diction is at times aureate, at times simple, fresh, and vivid.

Skelton is the most vigorous and original poet of his day. He belongs to a changing age, partly medieval, partly Renaissance. His themes and his tone are at times medieval; at times he uses medieval machinery and verse forms. Though his work shows little or nothing of the foreign influences that were very soon to shape the development of English poetry, much of his work has that lightness and exuberance and vigor which mark one aspect of the Tudor Renaissance. To his contemporaries he was an innovator; to Wyatt and Surrey and the other poets of the second quarter of the sixteenth century he was already old-fashioned.

Skelton was widely read during the sixteenth century. The publication of his collected poems in 1568 and of *Merie Tales newly imprinted and made by Master Skelton* in 1567 is evidence of his fame a generation after his death. As Professor William Nelson has pointed out, the Skelton of the *Merie Tales* is a witty rhetorician rather than a mountebank. But to George Puttenham (*The Arte of English Poesie*, 1589) he seemed "but a rude rayling rimer, and all his doings ridiculous," and it is not surprising that the readers of the great Elizabethan poets shared this view. It is impossible to estimate the extent of his indirect influence upon the development of English poetry.

For manuscripts and early editions see *CBEL*, i, 408–410. The standard edition of Skelton is *The Poetical Works of John Skelton*, ed. Alexander Dyce, 2 vols., 1843. A useful edition in modernized spelling is *The Complete Poems of John Skelton*, ed. Philip Henderson, 1931; revised, 1948. The standard accounts of Skelton follow: biography and criticism in Dyce; J. M. Berdan, *Early Tudor Poetry*, 1920; W. H. Auden, "John Skelton," *The Great Tudors*, ed. K. Garvin, 1935, a stimulating essay; L. J. Lloyd, *John Skelton, a Sketch of His Life and Writings*, 1938; William Nelson, *John Skelton, Laureate*, 1939, an excellent account; I. A. Gordon, *John Skelton, Poet Laureate*, 1943; H. L. R. Edwards, *Skelton, the Life and Times of an Early Tudor Poet*, 1949, the best biography.

A PRAYER TO THE FATHER OF HEAUEN[1]

O radiant luminary of light interminable,
  Celestiall father, potenciall God of might,
Of heauen and earth O lord incomperable,
  Of al perfections the essenciall most perfighte,[2]
  O maker of mankind, that formed day and night,
Whose power imperial comprehendeth euery place,
  Mine hart, my mind, my thought, my hole delite
Is, after this lyfe, to se thy glorious face.

Whose magnificence is incomprehensible,
  Al argumentes of reason which far doth excede,
Whose deite doutles is indiuisible,
  From whom al goodnes and vertue doth procede,
  Of thy support al creatures haue nede.
Assist me, good Lord, and graunt me of thy grace
  To liue to thy pleasure in word, thought, and dede,
And, after this lyfe, to see thy glorious face.

SKELTON LAUREAT, VPPON A DEED MANS HED THAT WAS SENT TO HYM FROM AN HONORABLE IENTIL WOMAN FOR A TOKEN, DEUYSYD THIS GOSTLY MEDITACION IN ENGLISH, COUENABLE IN SENTENCE,[3] COMENDABLE, LAMENTABLE, LACRIMABLE, PROFITABLE FOR THE SOULE

Youre vgly tokyn
My mynd hath brokyn
From worldly lust.
For I haue dyscust[4]
We are but dust,
And dy we must.
  It is generall
To be mortall.
I haue well espyde
No man may hym hyde
From deth holow eyed,
With sinnews wyderyd,
With bonys shyderyd,[5]
With hys worme etyn maw,
And his gastly Iaw
Gaspyng asyde,
Nakyd of hyde
Neyther flesh nor fell.[6]
  Then by my councell
Loke that ye spel[7]
Well thys gospell.
For wher so we dwell
Deth wil vs qwell[8]
And with vs mell.[9]
  For all our pamperde paunchis
Ther may no fraunchys,[10]
Nor worldly blys,
Redeme vs from this.
Oure days be datyd
To be chek matyd
With drauttys[11] of deth
Stoppyng oure breth,
Oure eyen synkyng,
Oure bodys stynkyng,
Oure gummys grynnyng,
Oure soulys brynnyng.[12]

[1] All of Skelton's verse presented here is from *Pithy, pleasaunt and profitable workes of Maister Skelton,* 1568, STC 22608, New York Public Library, Berg Collection. The passage from *Philip Sparrow* includes lines 261–322; the passage from *Colin Clout* includes lines 1–91, 287–345, 594–624.

[2] perfect.

[3] suitable in meaning.

[4] decided.

[5] splintered.

[6] skin.

[7] understand.

[8] kill.

[9] meddle.

[10] franchise, privilege.

[11] A draught is a move at chess.

[12] burning.

To whom then shall we sew
For to haue reskew
But to swete Iesu
On vs then for to rew.
O goodly child
Of Mary mylde,
Then be oure shylde,
That we be not exyld
To the dyne dale[13]
Of botemles bale,
Nor to the lake
Of fendys[14] blake.
But graunt vs grace
To se thy face
And to purchase
Thyne heuenly place
And thy palace,
Full of solace,
Aboue the sky
That is so hy,
Eternally
To beholde and se
The Trynyte.
Amen.
Mirres vous y.[15]

From PHILIP SPARROW

That vengeaunce I aske and cry,
By way of exclamacion,
On al the whole nacion
Of Cattes wilde and tame:
God send them sorow and shame!
That Cat specially
That slew so cruelly
My litle prety sparow
That I brought vp at Carow.
O cat of churlyshe kynde,
The feend was in thy minde
Whan thou my byrd vntwynde.[16]
I wolde thou haddest ben blynd!
The leopardes sauage,
The lyons in their rage,
Might catche the in their pawes
And gnaw the in theyr iawes!
These serpentes of Libany[17]
Might sting the venemously!
The dragons with their tunges
Might poison thy liuer and lunges!
The manticors[18] in the mountaynes
Mighte feed them on thy braines!
Melanchates, that hound
That plucked Acteon to the grounde,
Gave him his mortal wound,
Chaunged to a deere;
The story doth appere,
Was chaunged to an harte:
So thou, foule cat that thou arte,
The selfe same hounde
Might the confound,
That his own Lord bote,[19]
Mighte bite asunder thy throte!
Of Inde the gredy gripes[20]
Might teare out all thy tripes!
Of Arcady the beares
Might plucke awaye thine eares!
The wilde wolfe Licaon[21]
Bite asondre thy backe bone!
Of Ethna the brenning[22] hyl,
That day and night brenneth styll,
Set in thy tayle a blase
That al the world may gase
And wonder vpon thee,
From Occion the greate sea
Unto the Iles of Orchadye,[23]
From Tilbery fery
To the playne of Salisberye!
So trayterously my byrd to kyll
That neuer ought the euil will!
Was neuer bird in cage
More gentil of corage[24]
In doing his homage
Unto his soueraine.
Alas, I say agayne,
Death[25] hath departed[26] vs twayne!
The false cat hath the slaine.
Fare well, Philip, adewe!
Our Lorde thy soule rescewe!
Farewell without restore,
Farewell for euer more!

---

[13] dark valley.
[14] friends.
[15] see yourself therein.
[16] destroyed.
[17] Libya.
[18] fabled monsters.
[19] bit.
[20] griffins.
[21] Lycaon, king of Arcadia, was turned into a wolf by Zeus.
[22] burning.
[23] the Orkneys.
[24] heart.
[25] *Death*] *Deate* STC 22608.
[26] separated.

From COLIN CLOUT[27]

Quis consurget[28] *mecum aduersus malignantes? Aut quis stabit mecum aduersus operantes iniquitatem? Nemo, domine!*[29]

What can it auaile
To dryue forth a snayle
Or to make a sayle
Of an herynges tayle?
To ryme or to raile,[30]
To write or to indyte,
Eyther for delite
Or els for despite?
Or bookes to compile
Of diuers maner style,
Vyce to reuile
And sinne to exyle?
To teache or to preche
As reason wyll reach?
Saye this and saye that,
His head is so fat,
He wotteth neuer what
Nor wherof he speaketh;
He cryeth and he creketh,[31]
He pryeth and he peketh,
He chydes and he chatters,
He prates and he patters,
He clytters[32] and he clatters,
He medles and he smatters,
He gloses[33] and he flatters;
Or if he speake plaine,
Than he lacketh brayne,
He is but a foole;
Let him go to scoole—
A three foted stoole,
That he may downe syt,
For he lacketh wit.
And if that he hit
The nayle on the head
It standeth in no stede.
The Deuyll, they say, is dead,
The Deuill is dead.
 It may wel so be,
Or els they wold see
Otherwise, and flee
From worldly vanitie,
And foule couetousnes,
And other wretchednes,
Fickell falsenesse,
Uaryablenesse,
With vnstablenesse.
 And if ye stand in dout
Who brought this ryme about,
My name is Colyn Clout.
I purpose to shake out
All my conning bagge
Lyke a clarkely hagge;
For though my rime be ragged,
Tattered and iagged,
Rudely rayne beaten,
Rusty and moothe eaten,
If ye take[34] well therewyth
It hath in it some pith.
For, as farre as I can see,
It is wrong with eche degree:
For the temporalty
Accuseth the spiritualty;
The spirituall agayn
Doth grudge and complain
Vpon temporall men;
Thus eche of other blother[35]
The tone against the tother;
Alas, they make me shoder.
For in hoder moder[36]
The churche is put in faulte;[37]
The prelates ben so haut,
They say, and loke so hye
As though they wold flye
Aboue the sterry sky.
 Lay men say in dede
How they take no hede
Their sely[38] shepe to fede,
But plucke away and pul

---

[27] The name is here used to represent the speaker as a man of the people. Spenser used it in his pastoral verse when he spoke of himself.

[28] *consurget*] *consurgat* STC 22608.

[29] Who will rise up with me against the wicked? Or who will stand with me against the evil-doers? No one, O Lord.—Psalm xciv, 16.

[30] In STC 22608 *raile* is the last word in this line, and *tayle* is the last word in the line above.

[31] boasts.

[32] chatters.

[33] flatters.

[34] *take* STC 22601]; *talke* STC 22608.

[35] gabble.

[36] in secret, or in confusion.

[37] misfortune.

[38] simple, harmless.

The fleces of their wull;
Vnnethes[39] they leue a locke
Of wull amonge their flocke;
And as for theyr connyng,[40]
A glumming[41] and a mummyng,
And to make therof a iape.[42]
They gaspe and they gape
Al to haue promocion;
There is their whole deuocion,
With money, if it will hap,
To catch the forked cap;[43]
Forsoth they are to lewd[44]
To say so, all beshrewd.[45]

. . . .

Thus I, Colin Clout,
As I go about,
And wandryng as I walke,
I heare the people talke.
Men say, for syluer and Golde
Miters are bought and sold;
There shall no clergy appose[46]
A myter nor a crose[47]
But a full purse;
A straw for goddes curse!
What are they the worse?
For a simoniake[48]
Is but a hermoniake;[49]
And no more ye make
Of Symony, men say,
But a childes play.
Ouer this, the forsayd laye[50]
Report how the Pope maye
A holy anker[51] call
Out of the stony wall
And hym a bysshopp make,
If he on him dare take
To kepe so hard a rule
To ryde vpon a Mule
Wyth golde all betrapped,
In purple and paule[52] belapped;
Some hatted and some capped,
Rychely bewrapped,
God wot to theyr great paynes,
In Rotchettes[53] of fine raynes,[54]
Whyte as morowes[55] mylke;
Their tabertes[56] of fine silke,
Their stirops of mixt golde begarred;[57]
There may no cost be spared;
Their Moyles[58] Golde doth eate,
Theyr neyghbours dye for meat.
What care they though Gill sweat,
Or Iacke of the Noke?[59]
The pore people they yoke
With Sommons and Citacions
And excommunications,
Aboute churches and market.
The byshop on his carpet
At home full soft doth syt.
This is a feareful fyt,[60]
To heare the people iangle,
How warely they wrangle.
Alas, why do ye not handle
And them all mangle?
Full falsly on you they lye,
And shamefully you ascry,[61]
And say as vntruly
As the butter fly,
A man might say in mocke,
Ware the Wethercocke
Of thee steple of Poules;[62]
And thus they hurt their soules
In sclaunderyng you, for truth
Alas, it is great ruthe!

. . . .

Ye are so puffed wyth pryde
That no man may abide
Your high and lordly lokes;
Ye cast vp then your bokes

[39] scarcely.
[40] learning.
[41] looking gloomy.
[42] joke.
[43] The miter, symbol of the bishop's office. STC 22608 reads *cath* for *catch*.
[44] base.
[45] altogether accursed.
[46] approach.
[47] *crose* STC 22601]; *Crosse* STC 22608. *Crose* is *crozier*, symbol of the bishop's office.
[48] One who practices simony.
[49] Perhaps, one who seeks to preserve harmony.
[50] the aforesaid laity.
[51] anchorite, hermit.
[52] pall.
[53] A rochet is a vestment resembling a surplice.
[54] Linen manufactured at Rennes.
[55] morning's.
[56] tabards; short, sleeveless coats.
[57] *begarred* STC 22601]; *begarded* STC 22608: trimmed.
[58] mules.
[59] Conventional names for rustics.
[60] experience.
[61] denounce.
[62] St. Paul's, the cathedral in London.

And vertue is forgotten;
For then ye wyl be wroken[63]
Of euery light quarel,
And cal a Lord a iauel,[64]
A knight a knaue to make;
Ye boste, ye face, ye crake,[65]
And vpon you take
To rule king and kayser;
And if you maye haue layser
Ye bryng all to nought,
And that is all your thought.
For the Lordes temporall,
Their rule is very small,
Almost nothing at al.
Men say how ye appal
The noble bloud royal.
In ernest and in game,
Ye are the lesse to blame,
For Lordes of noble bloude,
If they wel vnderstood[66]
How conning[67] might them auaunce,[68]
They would pype you another daunce.
But noble men borne,
To learne they haue scorne,
But hunt and blow an horne,
Leape ouer lakes and dikes,
Set nothing by[69] politikes.
Therfore ye kepe them bace,
And mocke them to their face.
This is a petious case!
To you that ouer the wheele[70]
Lordes must couch[71] and knele,
And breake theyr hose at the knee,
As daily men may see
And to remembraunce call.
Fortune so turneth the ball
And ruleth so ouer all,
That honour hath a great fall.

[63] avenged.
[64] knave.
[65] boast.
[66] *vnderstood*] *vnderstand* STC 22608.
[67] learning.
[68] advance.
[69] consider of no importance.
[70] at the top of fortune's wheel.
[71] bow.
[72] merry.

From THE GARLAND OF LAUREL

To Maistres Margaret Hussey

Mirry[72] Margaret,
As midsomer flowre,
Gentyll as faucoun
Or hauck of the towre;[73]
With solace and gladnes,
Moch mirth and no madnes,
All good and no badnes,
So ioyously,
So maydenly,
So womanly,
Her demenynge;
In euery thynge
Far, far passynge
That I can endite
Or suffice to write
Of mirry Margarete,
As mydsomer flowre,
Gentill as faucoun
Or hauke of the towre.
As pacient and as styll
And as ful of good wil,
As fayre Isiphill,[74]
Coliander,[75]
Swete pomaunder,[76]
Good[77] Cassander;[78]
Stedfast[79] of thought,
Wel made, wel wroght;
Far may be sought
Erst[80] that ye can fynde
So curteise, so kynde,
As mirry Margarete,
This midsomer flowre,
Gentyll as faucoun
Or hauke of the towre.

[73] a hawk trained to fly high.
[74] Hypsipyle, in classical legend a beautiful woman of Lemnos. She appears also in medieval romances.
[75] coriander, an aromatic herb.
[76] pomander, a ball or bag of perfume.
[77] *Good*] *Oood* STC 22608.
[78] Cassandra, daughter of Priam, king of Troy.
[79] *Stedfast*] *Stefast* STC 22608.
[80] before.

John Heywood

[c. 1497–c. 1580]

JOHN HEYWOOD was a musician and writer of interludes at the court of Henry VIII, Edward VI, and Queen Mary. His wife was the daughter of John Rastell, the printer, and the niece of Sir Thomas More, and his grandson was John Donne. Because of his adherence to the old faith, Heywood left England in 1564 and never returned. At least one of his poems is included in *Tottel's Miscellany*. He is best known for his interludes and epigrams. A collection of his epigrams appeared in 1556, and other collections followed. Six hundred epigrams are included in his *Works* (1562, 1566, 1576, 1587, 1598).

In his epigrams he uses the old "tumbling verse" which was already old-fashioned. He is bluff, hearty, vigorous, homely. More than half of the epigrams are based on proverbs, to each of which he adds comment, humorous or didactic. Many of the epigrams are humorous anecdotes, often no more than bits of repartee, in the manner of the contemporary jestbooks. His satirical epigrams are blunt and rough, without subtlety. Unlike the later epigrammatists, he owes little to Martial.

Heywood's epigrams were reprinted by the Spenser Society, 1867, and edited by J. S. Farmer, 1906. The best accounts of Heywood are R. W. Bolwell, *The Life and Works of John Heywood*, 1922; R. de la Bere, *John Heywood, Entertainer*, 1937; and L. I. Guiney, *Recusant Poets*, 1939. For bibliography see *CBEL*, i, 518–519; and Samuel A. Tannenbaum, *John Heywood, a Concise Bibliography*, 1946.

A PRAISE OF HIS LADYE[1]

Geue place you Ladies and be gone,
Boast not your selues at all:
For here at hand approcheth one:
Whose face will staine[2] you all.

[1] From *Songes and sonettes written by the right honorable Lorde Henry Haward late Earle of Surrey, and other*, July 31, 1557, STC 13861, Huntington Library. It is probable that in 1534 Heywood wrote this poem in praise of the Princess Mary, who was then eighteen. (H. E. Rollins, *Tottel's Miscellany*, ii, 274–276; L. I. Guiney, *Recusant Poets*, pp. 115–118.)

[2] surpass.

The vertue of her liuely lokes,
Excels the precious stone:
I wish to haue none other bokes
To read or loke vpon.

In eche of her two cristall eyes,
Smileth a naked boye:[3]
It would you all in hart suffice
To see that lampe of ioye.

I thinke nature hath lost the moulde,
Where she her shape did take:
Or els I doubt if nature could,
So faire a creature make.

She may be well comparde
Vnto the Phenix kinde:
Whose like was neuer sene nor heard,
That any man can finde.

In life she is Diana chast,
In trouth Penelopey:
In word and eke in dede stedfast,
What wil you more we sey.

If all the world were sought so farre,
Who could finde such a wight:[4]
Her beuty twinkleth like a starre,
Within the frosty night.

Her rosiall colour comes and goes,
With such a comely grace:
More redier[5] to then doth the rose,
Within her liuely face.

At Bacchus feast none shall her mete,
Ne at no wanton play:
Nor gasyng in an open strete,
Nor gaddyng as a stray.[6]

The modest mirth that she dothe vse,
Is mixt with shamefastnesse:[7]
All vice she dothe wholy refuse,
And hateth ydlenesse.

O lord it is a world to see,
How vertue can repaire:
And decke in her such honestie,
Whom nature made so faire.

[3] Cupid.
[4] creature.
[5] more readily. The edition of 1559 (STC 13863) reads *more ruddier.*
[6] vagabond.
[7] modesty.

Truely she dothe as farre excede,
Our women now adayes:
As doth the Ielifloure,[8] a wede,
And more a thousand waies.

How might I do to get a graffe:
Of this vnspotted tree.
For all the rest are plaine but chaffe,
Which seme good corne to be.

This gift alone I shall her geue,
When death doth what he can:
Her honest fame shall euer liue,
Within the mouth of man.

EPIGRAMS[9]

A FOOLES TOUNGE

Vpon a fooles prouocation
A wise man will not talke:
But euery light instigacion
May make a fooles toung walke.

WEDDING AND HANGING

Weddyng and hangyng, are desteny I see.
Weddyng or hangyng, which is best, sir (quoth shee?)
Forsooth good wife, hangyng I thinke best (quoth hee)
So helpe me god, good husbande, so thinketh mee.
Oh how like lambes, man and wyfe here agree.

OF BYRDES AND BYRDERS

Better one byrde in hande, then ten in the wood.
Better for byrders, but for byrdes not so good.

BIYNG A PYG

I will neuer bye the pyg in the poke:
Thers many a foule pyg in a feyre cloke.

OF LOUING A DOG

Loue me, loue my dog: by loue to agree,
I loue thy dog, as well as I loue thee.

OF NOTHYNG AND ALTHING

Where nothing is, a little thyng doth ease.
Where al thyng is, nothyng can fully please.

---

[8] gillyflower, clove pink.
[9] From *John Heywoodes woorkes*, 1562, STC 13285, New York Public Library, Berg Collection.

HOW GOD WILL NOT DO FOR VS

Euery man for him self, and God for vs all:
God will not seale that writing, write it who shall.

OF A SHEEPES IYE

He cast a sheepes eye at her: a straunge eye spred,
To se a sheepes eye, looke out of a calues hed.

OF A CATTES LOOKE

A cat may looke on a kyng, and what of that.
When a cat so looketh: a cat is but a cat.

OF COMMON MEDLERS

He that medleth with all thyng, may shooe the goslyng:
If all such medlers were set to goose shoyng:
No goose neede go barfote betwene this and Greese,
For so: we should haue as many goose shooers as geese.

OF ENOUGH AND A FEAST

As good ynough as a feast: ye God saue it.
Inough were euen as good, if we might haue it.

OF HEYWOOD

Art thou Heywood with the mad mery wit?
Ye forsooth maister, that same is euen hit.
Art thou Heywood that applieth mirth more then thrift?
Ye sir, I take mery mirth a golden gift.
Art thou Heywood that hath made many mad plaies?
Ye many plaies, fewe good woorkes in all my daies.
Art thou Heywood that hath made men mery long?
Ye: and will, if I be made mery among.
Art thou Heywood that woulde be made mery now?
Ye sir: helpe me to it now I beseche yow.

Sir Thomas Wyatt

[c. 1503–1542]

IN THE latter end of the same kings [Henry VIII's] raigne sprong vp a new company of courtly makers, of whom Sir *Thomas Wyat* th'elder and *Henry* Earle of Surrey were the two chieftaines, who hauing trauailed into Italie, and there tasted the sweete and stately measures and stile of the Italian Poesie as nouices newly crept out of the schooles of *Dante Arioste* and *Petrarch,* they greatly pollished our rude and homely maner of vulgar Poesie, from that it had bene before, and for that cause may iustly be sayd the first reformers of our English meetre and stile." So wrote George Puttenham in *The Arte of English Poesie* late in the reign of Queen Elizabeth.

It is impossible to name many of the poets who wrote at the court of Henry VIII. Skill in music, in dancing, and in the writing of verse was expected of every gentleman. It is certain that, like King Henry himself, many of his courtiers wrote verse, but very little of it survives either in manuscript or in print. Many persons interested in poetry kept notebooks or commonplace books in which they wrote verse—their own or others'—that they wished to preserve. Several such books were probably used by Richard Tottel, the publisher of the largest and most important collection of these poems, which appeared with the title *Songs and Sonnets* (usually known as *Tottel's Miscellany*) on June 5, 1557, and again, with omissions and additions, on July 31. This miscellany achieved immediate and continuing popularity; a third edition appeared in 1559, and at least five other editions followed during the next thirty years.

The first two editions of this famous book contain three hundred and ten poems: ninety-six by Wyatt, forty by Surrey, forty by Grimald, and the rest assigned by Tottel or his editor to "uncertain authors," of whom only a few can be identified.

Most of the poems in *Tottel's Miscellany* are lyrics; others are epigrams, epitaphs, elegies, satires, epistles, pastorals, short narratives. Some are translations or imitations of Greek or Latin, and others of later Latin, French, and Italian.

Sir Thomas Wyatt was born at Allington Castle in Kent, and educated at St. John's College, Cambridge. He spent the rest of his life, except for a few brief intervals, in the service of Henry VIII. In 1524 he was appointed clerk of the king's jewels. During the next few years he went on diplomatic missions to France and Italy. He was appointed to the Privy Council in 1533 and was knighted in 1536. In May of the same year he was imprisoned in the Tower, but a month later he was released, and for a time he remained in his father's custody at Allington Castle. The suspicion–probably unwarranted–that he had been a lover of Anne Boleyn attached to his name then and later. In 1537 he was appointed ambassador to Spain, and he remained abroad on various missions during most of the next two years. In January, 1541, he was imprisoned on charges of treason, and two months later was pardoned. In October, 1542, while on a diplomatic mission, he died.

It is probable that during his lifetime his poems were known only to those who had manuscript copies. His *Seven Penitential Psalms* appeared in 1549. Ninety-six of his poems were included in *Tottel's Miscellany* (1557). Most of these and many others are preserved in early manuscripts, the three most important being Wyatt's own manuscript (Egerton 2711), which contains several poems in Wyatt's autograph and others with his autograph revisions, and which was later owned by John Harington and his son Sir John, the epigrammatist and translator of *Orlando Furioso;* the manuscript preserved at Arundel Castle, which contains poems collected by the Haringtons; and the "Devonshire manuscript" (Addit. MS. 17492), which, according to Miss Foxwell, was owned by the poet Surrey, Mary Queen of Scots, the Earl of Shrewsbury, and others, before it was acquired by the Duke of Devonshire and finally by the British Museum.

The rhythm of much of Wyatt's verse in the manuscripts is irregular. Whether this irregularity was intentional or the result of his failure to understand Chaucer's pronunciation or of awkward experiment or of literal translation or of hasty writing that he intended to revise (all these causes have been suggested), the unknown editor or the transcriber of the manuscripts used by the printer of *Tottel's Miscellany* removed much of the roughness and irregularity. In the surviving manuscripts the *e* of the genitive and plural forms is sometimes retained, and a Romance accent is given to many words of French and Latin origin. In *Tottel's Miscellany* not only are these archaisms in part eliminated, but iambic feet are substituted for trochees and anapests.

Wyatt's poetry contains both native and foreign elements. Although in many of his lyrical "balettes" he expresses the love longings of Petrarch, his verse forms in these poems are in the English medieval tradition, and the rhythms are borrowed from medieval carols and from songs for the lute. He uses also the English rhyme royal and poulter's measure. His other verse forms are of foreign origin. From the French he borrowed the rondeau. He was the first English poet to write *terza rima* and the sonnet. Most of his sonnets are translations, adaptations, or imitations of Petrarch (1304–1374). He usually follows Petrarch's rhyme pattern in the octave, but his sestet ordinarily ends with a couplet. He gives the Petrarchan conventions a Tudor coloring. In Wyatt's sonnets we see little of the constant lover and the lady worthy of all devotion; he seldom praises the lady's beauty; he does not idealize her; Dame Fortune turns the wheel; joy is fleeting; women are cruel and false; he, too, can be cruel; perhaps others can learn from his experience. From Serafino (1466–1500) he borrowed the *strambotto,* a poem complete in one stanza of *ottava rima.* Most of Wyatt's epigrams are written in this form. His verse epistles, or satires as they are sometimes called, are the first English poems in *terza rima,* which he wrote without keeping the tercets closed; that is, he wrote not in the manner of Dante but in the manner of the cinquecento and especially in the manner of Alamanni, whose satires appeared in 1532–1533, and whom he followed in his first epistle. The epistles, with their plain and easy style, their intimate tone, their praise of country life, their sly humor, their homeliness, reveal an aspect of Wyatt's personality that is not elsewhere disclosed. *The Penitential Psalms* he adapted from the prose paraphrase of Aretino, using *terza rima* and adding prologues in *ottava rima.*

Wyatt, like Surrey and Sidney, approaches the ideal of the sixteenth-century courtier-scholar-statesman. In one of his letters he urges his son to acquire "wisdome, gentlenes, sobrenes, disire to do good, frendlines to get the loue of manye, and trougth aboue all the rest." And he adds, "A great part to haue al thes things is to desire to haue them" and "of these things the chiefest and infallible grond is the dread and Reuerens of God, wherapon shall ensue the eschewing of the contraries of thes sayd vertues,—that is to say, Ignorans, unkindnes, Raschnes, desire of harme, unquiet enmytie, hatred, manye and crafty falshed, the verie Rote of al shame and dishonestye." His poems, even when they are translations, reveal his energy, directness, humor, and the seriousness that is displayed also in his choosing to translate *The Penitential Psalms* and Plutarch's *Quiet of Mind.* In general, these are the qualities that Surrey stresses in his poems about Wyatt.

Wyatt's poetry is a landmark in English literature. He recaptured the grace and rhythm of the older lyric. With the exception of the heroic couplet and blank verse he used most of the verse forms that were to be used during the century. In Surrey's words, he "taught what might be said in ryme." His diction is relatively free from archaisms and from aureate terms. He exerted a strong influence upon the Earl of Surrey, who in turn set fashions that poets followed through most of the century. In 1589 Puttenham called Wyatt and Surrey "the two chief lanternes of light to all others who haue since employed their pennes vpon English Poesie."

The first important edition of Wyatt is that of G. F. Nott, *The Works of Henry Howard Earl of Surrey and of Sir Thomas Wyatt the Elder,* 2 vols., 1815–1816. It is based on a collation of the manuscripts; spelling and punctuation are modernized. A. K. Foxwell, *The Poems of Sir Thomas Wiat,* 2 vols., 1913, though faulty in some respects (see H. E. Rollins, *Tottel's Miscellany,* ii, 62), remained for many years the best edition. The most useful edition is Kenneth Muir, *The Collected Poems of Sir Thomas Wyatt,* 1949. A definitive edition of

Wyatt is needed. For Wyatt's prose see his letters to his son in Muir and his translation of Plutarch's *Quyete of Mynde*, 1527, ed. C. R. Baskervill, 1931. For discussion of Wyatt see A. K. Foxwell, *A Study of Sir Thomas Wyatt's Poetry*, 1911; J. M. Berdan, *Early Tudor Poetry*, 1920; H. E. Rollins, *Tottel's Miscellany*, 2 vols., 1928–1929; E. M. W. Tillyard, *The Poetry of Sir Thomas Wyatt, a Selection and a Study*, 1929; E. K. Chambers, *Sir Thomas Wyatt and Some Collected Studies*, 1933; Ruth Hughey, "The Harington Manuscript at Arundel Castle and Related Documents," *The Library*, Fourth Series, xv (1934–1935), 388–444; Hallett Smith, "The Art of Sir Thomas Wyatt," *The Huntington Library Quarterly*, ix (1946), 323–355.

From EGERTON MS. 2711, BRITISH MUSEUM

The longe love that in my thought doeth harbar,[1]
And in myn hert doeth kepe his residence,
Into my face preseth with bolde pretence[2]
And therin campeth, spreding his baner.
She that me lerneth too love and suffre
And willes that my trust and lustes negligence
Be rayned by reason, shame,[3] and reverence,
With his hardines[4] taketh displeasur.
Wherewithall vnto the hertes forrest he fleith,
Leving his entreprise with payn and cry,
And ther him hideth and not appereth.
What may I doo when my maister fereth[5]
But in the feld[6] with him too lyve and dye?
For goode is the liff ending faithfully.

Farewell, Love, and all thy lawes for ever;
Thy bayted hookes shall tangill me no more.
Senec and Plato call me from thy lore
To perfaict welth my wit for to endever.
In blynde error when I did perseuer,
Thy sherpe repulce that pricketh ay so sore
Hath taught me to sett in tryfels no store,
And scape fourth, syns libertie is lever.[7]
Therefore, farewell; goo trouble yonger hertes,
And in me clayme no more authoritie.
With idill youth goo vse thy propertie,
And theron spend thy many brittill dertes.
For hetherto though I have lost all my tyme,
Me lusteth[8] no lenger[9] rotten boughes to clyme.

---

[1] This sonnet is a translation of Petrarch, *Sonetto in vita*, 91. So also is Surrey's *Complaint of a louer rebuked*.
[2] claim to authority.
[3] modesty.
[4] boldness.
[5] fears.
[6] field.
[7] since liberty is preferable.
[8] it pleases me.
[9] longer.

Helpe me to seke, for I lost it there,
And if that ye have founde it, ye that be here,
And seke to convaye it secretely,
Handell it soft and trete it tenderly,
Or els it will plain[10] and then appere.[11]
But prithee[12] restore it mannerly,
Syns that I do aske it thus honestly,
For to lese[13] it, it sitteth me to neere.[14]
Helpe me to seke.

Alas, and is there no remedy?
But have I thus lost it wilfully?
I wis it was a thing all to dere
To be bestowed, and wist not where.
It was myn hert. I pray you hertely
Helpe me to seke.

My galy charged with forgetfulnes[15]
Thorrough sharpe sees in wynter nyghtes doeth pas
Twene Rock and Rock; and eke myn ennemy,[16] alas,
That is my lorde,[16] sterith[17] with cruelnes;
And every owre, a thought in redines,
As tho that deth were light in suche a case.[18]
An endles wynd doeth tere the sayll apase,
Of forced sightes[19] and trusty ferefulnes.
A rayn of teris, a clowde of derk disdain,
Hath done the wered[20] cordes great hinderaunce,
Wrethed[21] with errour and eke with ignoraunce.
The starres be hid that led me to this pain.
Drowned is reason, that should me consort,[22]
And I remain dispering of the port.

Like to these vnmesurable montayns,[23]
Is my painfull lyff, the burden of Ire,
For of great height be they, and high is my desire,
And I of teres, and they be full of fontayns.
Vnder craggy rockes they have full barren playns,
Herd thoughtes in me my wofull mynde doeth tyre;
Small fruyt and many leves their toppes do atyre,
Small effect with great trust in me remayns.

---

10 complain.
11 "appair" (deteriorate) or perhaps "appear" (make its presence known).
12 In the manuscript this word is illegible.
13 lose.
14 it concerns me deeply.
15 A translation of Petrarch, *Sonetto in vita*, 137. This line means "my galley is so freighted with love as to forget all else."
16 Cupid.
17 steers.
18 every oar is a thought ready to remind me that death is easy in such a situation.
19 sighs.
20 wearied.
21 wreathed.
22 accompany. Tottel reads *comfort*.
23 From Sannazaro, *Rime*, Part iii, *sonetto* 3.

The boyseus[24] wyndes oft their high bowghes do blast,
Hote sighes from me continuelly be shed;
Cattell in them, and in me love is fed;
Immovable ame I, and they are full stedfast.
  Of restles[25] birdes they have the tune and note,
  And I alwayes plaintes that passe thorough my throte.

They fle from me, that sometyme did me seke,
With naked fote stalking[26] in my chambre.
I have sene theim gentill, tame, and meke,
That nowe are wyld and do not remembre
That sometyme they put theimself in daunger[27]
To take bred at my hand; and nowe they raunge,
Besely seking with a continuell chaunge.

Thancked be fortune it hath ben othrewise,
Twenty tymes better; but ons in speciall,
In thyn arraye, after a pleasaunt gyse,
When her lose gowne from her shoulders did fall,
And she me caught in her armes long and small,
Therewithall swetely did me kysse,
And softely saide, dere hert, howe like you this?

It was no dreme; I lay brode waking.
But all is torned, thorough my gentilnes,
Into a straunge fasshion of forsaking;
And I have leve to goo, of her goodenes,
And she also to vse new fangilnes.[28]
But syns that I so kyndely ame serued,
I would fain knowe what she hath deserued.

Patience, though I have not
  The thing that I require,
I must of force, God wot,
  Forbere my moost desire;
For no ways can I fynde
To saile against the wynde.

Patience, do what they will
  To worke me woo or spite,
I shall content me still
  To thyncke boeth daye and nyte;
To thyncke and hold my peace,
Syns there is no redresse.

Patience withouten blame,
  For I offended nought;
I knowe they knowe the same,
  Though they have chaunged their thought.
Was ever thought so moved
To hate that it haith loved?

Patience of all my harme,
  For fortune is my foo;
Patience must be the charme
  To hele me of my woo.
Patience withoute offence
Is a painfull patience.

24 boisterous.
25 *Of restles*] *Of that restles* MS.
26 walking gently.
27 in my power. Cf. Chaucer, *Canterbury Tales*, Prologue, 663–664.
28 fickleness.

My lute, awake, perfourme the last
Labour that thou and I shall wast,
  And end that I have now begon;
For when this song is sung and past,
  My lute, be still, for I have done.

As to be herd where ere is none,
As lede to grave in marbill stone,
  My song may perse her hert as sone.[29]
Should we then sigh, or syng, or mone?
  No, no, my lute, for I have done.

The Rokkes do not so cruelly
Repulse the waves continuelly,
  As she my suyte and affection,
So that I ame past remedy;
  Whereby my lute and I have done.

Prowd of the spoyll that thou hast gott
Of simple hertes thorough loves shot;
  By whome, vnkynd, thou hast theim wone,
Thinck not he haith his bow forgot,
  All tho my lute and I have done.

Vengeaunce shall fall on thy disdain,
That makest but game on ernest pain.
  Thinck not alone vnder the sonne
Vnquyt[30] to cause thy lovers plain,[31]
  All tho my lute and I have done.

Perchaunce the[32] lye wethered[33] and old
The wynter nightes[34] that are so cold,
  Playnyng in vain vnto the mone.
Thy wisshes then dare not be told.
  Care then who lyst, for I have done.

And then may chaunce the to repent
The tyme that thou hast lost and spent
  To cause thy lovers sigh and swoune.
Then shalt thou knowe beaultie but lent,
  And wisshe and want as I have done.

Now cesse, my lute; this is the last
Labour that thou and I shall wast,
  And ended is that we begon.
Now is this song boeth sung and past;
  My lute be still, for I have done.

Tagus,[35] fare well, that westward with thy stremes
  Torns vp the grayns off gold alredy tryd;
With spurr and sayle for I go seke the Tems,[36]
  Gaynward[37] the sonne that shewth her welthi pryd,
And to the town which Brutus sowght by drems,[38]
  Like bendyd mone,[39] doth lend[40] her lusty syd.
My Kyng, my Contry, alone for whome I lyve,
Of myghty love the winges for this me gyve.

From ADDIT. MS. 17492, BRITISH MUSEUM

And wylt thow leve me thus?
Say nay, say nay, for shame,
To save the from the Blame
Of all my greffe and grame.[41]
And wylt thow leve me thus?
  Say nay, Say nay.

And wylt thow leve me thus,
That hathe lovyd the so long
In welthe and woo among?[42]
And ys thy hart so strong
As for to leve me thus?
  Say nay, Say nay.

---

29 my song will pierce her heart as soon as sound can be heard where there is no ear, as soon as lead can engrave marble.
30 unrequited.
31 complain.
32 thee.
33 withered.
34 *nightes* Tottel]; *nyght* Egerton 2711.
35 The principal river of Spain. This epigram refers to Wyatt's return to England in 1539 after two years in Spain.
36 Tottel reads *For I with spurre and saile go seke the temmes.*
37 flowing against.
38 According to Geoffrey of Monmouth, Brutus, a great-grandson of Aeneas, was directed by Diana in a dream to sail to the white cliffs of Albion and build another Troy, which became London.
39 crescent moon.
40 Tottel reads *that leanes.*
41 sorrow, scorn.
42 all the while.

And wylt thow leve me thus,
That hathe gevyn the my hart,
Never for to Depart
Nother[43] for payn nor smart?
And wylt thow leve me thus?
Say nay, Say nay.

And wylt thow leve me thus,
And have no more Pyttye
Of hym that lovythe the?
Helas,[44] thy cruellte!
And wylt thow leve me thus?
Say nay, Say nay.

Forget not yet the tryde entent[45]
Of suche a truthe as I haue ment,
My gret travayle so gladly spent,
Forget not yet.

Forget not yet when fyrst began
The wery lyffe ye know, syns whan
The sute, the seruys none tell can,
Forgett not yett.

Forget not yet the gret assays,[46]
The cruell wrong, the skornfull ways,
The paynfull pacyence in denays,[47]
Forgett not yet.

Forget not yet, forget not thys,
How long ago hathe ben and ys
The mynd that neuer ment amys,
Forget not yet.

Forget not, then, thyn owne aprovyd,
The whyche so long hathe the so lovyd,
Whose stedfast faythe yet neuer movyd,
Forget not thys.

Blame not my lute, for he must sownde
Of thes or that as liketh me;
For lake of wytt the lutte is bownde
To gyve suche tunes as plesithe me.
Tho my songes be sume what strange,
And spekes suche wordes as toche thy change,
Blame not my lutte.

My lutte, alas, doth not ofende,
Tho that perforus[48] he must agre
To sownde suche teunes as I entende
To sing to them that hereth me.
Then tho my songes be some what plain,
And tochethe some that vse to fayn,
Blame not my lutte.

My lute and strynges may not deny,
But as I strike they must obay.
Brake not them than soo wrongfully,
But wryeke[49] thy selff some wyser way;
And tho the songes whiche I endight
Do[50] qwytt[51] thy chainge with rightfull spight,
Blame not my lute.

Spyght askyth spight and changing change,
And falsyd faith must nides[52] be knowne;
The faute so grett, the case so strange,
Of right it must abrode be blown.
Then sins that by thyn own desartt
My soinges[53] do tell how trew thou artt,
Blame not my lute.

Blame but the selffe that hast mysdewn[54]
And well desaruide to haue blame;
Change thou thy way so evyll bygown,[55]
And then my lute shall sownde that same;
But if tyll then my fyngeres play
By thy desartt their wontyd way,
Blame not my lutte.

Farwell, vnknowne, for tho thow brake
My strynges in spight with grett desdayn,
Yet haue I fownde owtt for thy sake
Stringes for to strynge my lute agayne.

---

[43] neither.
[44] alas.
[45] endeavor.
[46] tribulations.
[47] refusals, frustrations.
[48] perforce.
[49] wreak.
[50] *Do*] *To* MS.
[51] requite.
[52] needs.
[53] songs.
[54] misdone.
[55] begun.

And yf perchance this folys[56] Ryme[57]
Do make the blushe at any tyme,
Blame nott my lutte.

Sins you will nedes that I shall sing,
Take yt in worth,[58] siche as I have,
Plentye of plaint, mone, and morning,
Yn depe dispaire and dedlye[59] payne,
Boteles for boote, crying to crave,
To crave yn vayne.

Suche hammers worke within my hed
That sounde nought els vnto my eris
But faste at borde and wake abed;
Suche tune the tempre to my song
To waile my wrong, that I wante teris
To waile my wrong.

Dethe and dispaire afore my face
My dayes dekaes, my grefe doth gro;[60]
The cause thereof is in this place,
Whom crueltye dothe still constraine
For to reioise, tho yt be wo
To here me plaine.

A brokin lute, vntunid stringes,
With such a song maye well bere parte,
That nether pleasith him that singes
Nor theim that here, but her alone
That with her herte wold straine my herte
To here yt grone.

Yf it greve you to here this same
That you do fele but in my voyse,
Considre then what plesaunt game
I do sustaine in everye parte
To cause me sing or to reioyse
Within my herte.

What shulde I saye,
Sins faithe is dede,
And truthe awaye
From you ys fled?
Shulde I be led
With doblenesse?
Naye, naye, mistresse!

I promiside you,
And you promisid me,
To be as true
As I wolde bee.
But sins I se
Your doble herte,
Farewell, my perte![61]

Though for to take
Yt ys not my minde,
But to forsake
. . . . .[62]
And as I finde
So will I truste.
Farewell, vniuste!

Can ye saye naye
But you saide
That I allwaye
Shulde be obeide,
And thus betraide
Or that I wiste?[63]
Fare well, vnkiste!

Dyvers dothe vse, as I have hard and kno,
When that to chaunge ther ladies do beginne,
To morne and waile and neuer for to lynne,[64]
Hoping therbye to pease[65] ther painefull woo.
And some ther be that, when it chanseth soo
That women change, and hate where love hath bene,
Thei call them fals and think with wordes to wynne

56 foolish.
57 *Ryme*] *Rymyme* MS.
58 in good part.
59 *dedlye*] *delye* MS.
60 *Dethe* and *dispaire* are subjects of the verbs *dekaes* and *doth gro*, which are here transitive.

61 part.
62 The line is missing in the manuscript.
63 before I knew.
64 stop.
65 appease.

The hartes of them wich otherwhere dothe gro.
But as for me, though that by chaunse indede
Change hath outworne the favor that I had,
I will not wayle, lament, nor yet be sad,
Nor call her fals that falsley ded me fede;[66]
But let it passe and think it is of kinde[67]
That often chaunge doth plese a womans minde.

The wofull dayes so full of paine,
The werye night all spent in vayne,
The labor lost for so small gayne,
To wryt them all yt will not bee.
But ha, ha, ha, full well is me,
For I am now at libretye.

Everye thing that faire doth sho,
When prof is made yt provithe not soo,
But tournith mirthe to bittre woo,
Wiche in this case full well I see.
But ha, ha, ha, full well is me,
For I am now at libretye.

To grete desire was my guide,
And wanton will went bye my syde;
Hope rulid still, and made me byde
Of loves craft th' extremitye.
But ha, ha, ha, full well is me,
For I am now at libretye.

With faynid wordes wich ware but winde
To long delayes I was assind;
Her wylye lokes my wyttes ded blinde;
Thus as she wolde I ded agree.
But ha, ha, ha, full well is me,
For I am now at libretye.

Was never birde tanglid yn lyme[69]
That brake awaye yn bettre tyme
Than I, that rotten bowes ded clyme,
And had no hurte, but scaped fre.
Now ha, ha, ha, full well is me,
For I am nowe at libretye.

Hate whome ye list, for I kare not;
Love whom ye list and spare not;
Do what ye list and drede not;
Think what ye liste, I fere not;
For, as for me, I am not
But even as one that reckes not
Whyther ye hate or hate not;
For yn your love I dote not;
Wherefor I praye you forget not,
But love whom ye liste, for I care not.

Tanglid I was yn loves snare,[68]
Opprest with payne, tormente with care,
Of grefe right sure, of Joye full bare,
Clene in dispaire bye crueltye.
But ha, ha, ha, full well is me,
For I am now at libretye.

From ADDIT. MS. 36529, BRITISH MUSEUM

Luckes,[70] my faire falcon, and your fellowes all,
How well plesaunt yt were, your libertie!
Ye not forsake me that faire might ye befall.
But they that somtyme lykt my companye
Like lyse awaye from ded bodies thei crall;
Loe, what a profe in light adversytie!
But ye, my birdes, I swear by all your belles,
Ye be my fryndes, and so be but few elles.

---

66 feed (with false hopes).
67 nature.
68 An imitation of Serafino's first *barzalleto*.
69 A sticky substance spread on boughs to catch birds.
70 Lux, the name of a falcon.

A face that shuld content me wonders[71] well
Shuld not be faire but louelie to behold,
With gladsome cheare all grief for to expell,
With sober lookes, so wold I that it should
Speake without wordes such woordes as non can tell;
The tresse also should be of crysped gold.
With witt and these perchance[72] I might be tyde,
And knyt agayne the knott that should not slide.

HE RULETH NOT THOUGH HE RAIGNE OUER REALMES THAT IS SUBIECT TO HIS OWNE LUSTES[73]

If thou wilt mighty be, flee from the rage
Of cruel wyll and see thou kepe thee free
From the foule yoke of sensuall bondage,
For though thyne empyre stretche to Indian sea,
And for thy feare trembleth the fardest Thylee,[74]
If thy desire haue ouer thee the power,
Subiect then art thou and no gouernour.

If to be noble and high thy minde be meued,[75]
Consider well thy grounde and thy beginning:
For he that hath eche starre in heauen fixed,
And geues the Moone her hornes and her eclipsing:
Alike hath made the noble in his working,
So that wretched no way may thou bee,
Except foule lust and vice do conquer thee.

All were it so thou had a flood of gold,
Vnto thy thirst yet should it not suffice.
And though with Indian stones a thousande folde,
More precious then can thy selfe deuise,
Ycharged were thy backe: thy couitise
And busy biting yet should neuer let,
Thy wretchid life, ne do thy death profet.[76]

WIATE BEING IN PRISON, TO BRIAN[77]

Syghes are my foode: my drink are my teares.
Clinking of fetters would such musick craue.
Stink, and close ayre away my life it weares.
Poore innocence is all the hope I haue.

[71] wondrous.

[72] *these perchance* Tottel]; *thus might chaunce* MS.

[73] From *Songes and sonettes* STC 13861, Huntington Library. This poem is based on Boethius' *De consolatio philosophiae,* Book iii, meters 5, 6, 3.

[74] Ultima Thule.

[75] moved.

[76] Even though you had great wealth, it would not satisfy you. Your covetousness and avarice would never stop, and your wretched life would not profit you after death. Wyatt seems to follow Chaucer's translation: "Nevere ne schal his bytynge busynesse forleeten hym whil he lyveth, ne the lyghte richesses ne schal nat beren hym companye whan he is deed."

[77] STC 13861. Probably written during Wyatt's imprisonment early in 1541. It is addressed to his friend, Sir Francis Bryan.

Rain, winde, or wether iudge I by mine eares.
Malice assaultes, that righteousnesse should haue.
Sure am I, Brian, this wound shall heale again:
But yet alas, the skarre shall still remayn.

OF DISSEMBLING WORDES[78]

Throughout the world if it wer sought,
Faire wordes inough a man shall finde:
They be good chepe[79] they cost right nought.
Their substance is but onely winde:
But well to say and so to mene,
That swete acord is seldom sene.

OF THE MEANE AND SURE ESTATE[80]

Stond who so list vpon the slipper[81] wheele,
Of hye astate and let me here reioyce.
And vse my life in quietnesse eche dele,[82]
Vnknowen in court that hath the wanton toyes,
In hidden place my time shal slowly passe
And when my yeres be past withouten noyce
Let me dye olde after the common trace[83]
For gripes[84] of death doth he to hardly passe
That knowen is to all: but to him selfe alas,
He dyeth vnknowen, dased with dreadfull face.

OF THE COURTIERS LIFE WRITTEN TO IHON POINS[85]

Myne owne Ihon Poyns: sins ye delite to know
The causes why that homeward I me draw,
And fle the prease[86] of courtes, where so they go:
Rather then to liue thrall vnder the awe,
Of lordly lokes, wrapped within my cloke,
To will and lust learning to set a law:
It is not that because I scorne or mocke
The power of them: whom fortune here hath lent
Charge ouer vs, of ryght to strike the stroke.
But true it is that I haue alwayes ment
Lesse to esteme them, then the common sort
Of outward thinges: that iudge in their entent,
Without regarde, what inward doth resort.[87]
I graunt, sometime of glory that the fire
Doth touch my hart. Me list not to report

---

[78] STC 13861.
[79] bargain.
[80] STC 13861. Translated from Seneca, *Thyestes*, ii, 391–403.
[81] slippery, variable (wheel of fortune).
[82] part.
[83] manner.
[84] torments.
[85] From Egerton MS. 2711. The first 51 lines, missing in the manuscript, and the title are printed from STC 13861. Of John Poynz little is known. Holbein painted his portrait. The poem is based on Luigi Alamanni's tenth satire, published in 1532. Wyatt doubtless wrote this poem when he was at his father's house in Kent after his release from prison in 1536.
[86] throng.
[87] He values rank and outward appearances less than do the "common sort."

Blame by honour,[88] and honour to desire.
But how may I this honour now attaine?
That can not dye the colour blacke a lier.
My Poyns, I can not frame my tune to fayn:
To cloke the truth, for prayse without desert,
Of them that list all vice for to retaine.
I can not honour them, that set their part
With Venus, and Bacchus, all their life long:
Nor holde my peace of them, although I smart.
I can not crouch nor knele to such a wrong:
To worship them like God on earth alone:
That are as wolues these sely[89] lambes among.
I can not with my wordes complaine and mone,
And suffer nought: nor smart without complaynt:
Nor turne the word that from my mouth is gone,
I can not speak and loke like as a saint:
Vse wiles for wit, and make disceyt a pleasure:
Call craft counsaile, for lucre still to paint.
I can not wrest the law to fill the coffer:
With innocent bloud to fede my selfe fatte:
And do most hurt: where that most helpe I offer.
I am not he, that can alow the state
Of hye Ceasar, and damne Cato to dye:
That with his death did scape out of the gate,
From Ceasars handes, if Liuye doth not lye:
And would not liue, where libertie was lost,
So did his hart the common wealth apply.[90]
I am not he, such eloquence to bost:
To make the crow in singyng, as the swanne:
Nor call the lyon of coward beastes the most.
That can not take a mouse, as the cat can.
And he that dieth for honger of the golde,[91]
Call him Alexander, and say that Pan
Passeth Appollo in musike manifold:
Praise syr Topas for a noble tale,
And scorne the story that the knight tolde:[92]
Praise him for counceill that is droncke of ale,
Grynne when he laugheth that bereth all the swaye,
Frowne when he frowneth and grone when he is[93] pale,
On othres lust[94] to hang boeth nyght and daye,—
None of these poyntes would ever frame[95] in me;
My wit is nought; I cannot lerne the waye;
And much the lesse of thinges that greater be
That asken helpe of colours[96] of devise
To joyne the mene with eche extremitie.
With the neryst vertue to cloke alwaye the vise,
And as to pourpose, like wise it shall fall[97]
To presse the vertue that it may not rise;
As dronkenes, good fellowshippe to call;

[88] about honor.
[89] innocent.
[90] work for.
[91] Midas.
[92] The foolish tale of Sir Tophas and the noble tale of the knight in Chaucer's *Canterbury Tales.*
[93] *he is* STC 13861]; *he* MS.
[94] wishes.
[95] succeed.
[96] falsehood.
[97] in conversation as it may suit the occasion.

The frendly Foo with his dowble face
Say he is gentill and courtois therewithall;
And say that favell[98] hath a goodly grace
In eloquence; and crueltie to name
Zele of justice, and chaunge in tyme and place;[99]
And he that sufferth offence withoute blame,
Call him pitefull, and him true and playn
That raileth rekles to every mans shame,
Say he is rude that cannot lye and fayn,
The letcher a lover, and tirannye
To be the right of a prynces reigne.
I cannot, I; no, no, it will not be.
This is the cause that I could never yet
Hang on their slevis that way, as thou maist se,
A chippe of chaunce more then a pownde of witt.
This maketh me at home to hounte and to hawke,
And in fowle weder at my booke to sitt,
In frost and snowe then with my bow to stawke.
No man doeth marke where so I ride or goo.
In lusty lees[1] at libertie I walke,
And of these newes[2] I fele nor wele nor woo,
Sauf[3] that a clogg doeth hang yet at my hele.[4]
No force[5] for that, for it is ordered so
That I may lepe boeth hedge and dike full well.
I ame not now in Fraunce to judge the wyne,
With saffry[6] sauce the delicates to fele;
Nor yet in Spaigne where oon must him inclyne,
Rather then to be, owtewerdly to seme;
I meddill not with wittes that be so fyne;
Nor Flaunders chiere letteth not my sight to deme[7]
Of black and white, nor taketh my wit awaye
With bestlynes; they beestes do so esteme.
Nor I ame not where Christe is geven in pray[8]
For mony, poison, and traison, at Rome—
A commune practise, vsed nyght and daie.
But here I ame in Kent and Christendome
Emong the muses, where I rede and ryme;
Where if thou list, my Poynz, for to come,
Thou shalt be judge how I do spend my tyme.

OF THE MEANE AND SURE ESTATE WRITEN TO IOHN POINS[9]

My mothers maydes, when they did sowe and spynne,
They sang sometyme a song of the feld mowse,
That forbicause her lyvelood[10] was but thynne
Would nedes goo seke her townysshe systers howse.

98 flattery, duplicity.
99 Cruelty is just in some times and places.
1 delightful meadows.
2 matter.
3 save.
4 Wyatt was paroled in his father's custody.
5 Probably news that Poynz had sent him.
6 Savory.
7 the strong drink of Flanders does not hinder my sight from judging.
8 as a prey.
9 The title is from STC 13861, the text from Egerton 2711. The story is perhaps from Horace, *Satires*, ii, 6, although, as Rollins points out, the tone and many of the phrases are Chaucerian.
10 livelihood.

She thought her self endured to much pain;
The stormy blastes her cave so sore did sowse,
That when the forowse[11] swymmed with the rain,
She must lye cold and whete, in sorry plight;
And wours then that, bare meet there did remain
To comfort her when she her howse had dight[12]—
Sometyme a barly corne, sometyme a bene,
For which she laboured hard boeth daye and nyght
In harvest tyme whilest she myght goo and glyne.[13]
And when her[14] stoore was stroyed with the flodd
Then, wellawaye, for she vndone was clene.[15]
Then was she fayne to take in stede of fode
Slepe, if she myght, her hounger to begile.
"My syster," quoth she, "hath a lyving good,
And hens from me she dwelleth not a myle.
In cold and storme she lieth warme and dry
In bed of downe; the dyrt doeth not defile
Her tender fote; she laboureth not as I.
Richely she fedeth and at the richemans cost,
And for her meet she nydes not crave nor cry.
By se, by land, of the delicates the moost
Her Cater[16] sekes and spareth for no perell.
She fedeth on boyled, bacon[17] meet, and roost,
And hath therof neither charge nor travaill.
And when she list, the licor of the grape
Doeth glad her hert till that her belly swell."
And at this jorney she maketh but a jape;[18]
So fourth she goeth, trusting of all this welth
With her syster her part so for to shape
That, if she myght kepe her self in helth,
To lyve a Lady while her liff doeth last.
And to the dore now is she come by stelth,
And with her foote anon she scrapeth full fast.
Thothre[19] for fere durst not well scarse appere,
Of every noyse so was the wretche agast.
At last she asked softly who was there.
And in her langage as well as she cowd
"Pepe," quoth the othre, "syster, I ame here."
"Peace," quoth the townysshe mowse, "why spekest thou so lowde?"
And by the hand she toke her fayer and well.
"Welcom," quoth she, "my sister, by the Roode."
She fested her that joy it was to tell
The faere[20] they had; they drancke the wyne so clere;
And as to purpose[21] now and then it fell
She chered her with, "How, syster, what chiere?"
Amyddes this joye befell a sorry chaunce,
That, well awaye, the straunger bought full dere
The fare she had, for as she loked[22] ascaunce

---

11 furrows.
12 put in order.
13 glean.
14 *when her* STC 13861]; *wher* MS.
15 entirely.
16 caterer.
17 baked.
18 makes light of.
19 the other.
20 fare.
21 *purpose* STC 13861]; *poupose* MS.: conversation.
22 *lookt* STC 13861]; *loke* MS.

Vnder a stole[23] she spied two stemyng[24] Ise
In a rownde hed with sherp erys; in Fraunce
Was never mowse so ferd, for the vnwise[25]
Had not Isene[26] suche a beest before;
Yet had nature taught her after her gyse
To knowe her Foo and dred him evermore.
The towney mowse fled; she knowe whether[27] to goo.
Thothre had not shift but, wonders[28] sore
Ferd of her liff, at home she wyshed her tho;
And to the dore, alas, as she did skipp—
Thevyn[29] it would, lo, and eke her chaunce was so—
At the threshold her sely[30] fote did tripp,
And ere she myght recover it again,
The traytor Catt had caught her by the hipp,
And made her there against her will remain,
That had forgotten her poure suretie[31] and rest,
For semyng welth wherin she thought to rayne.
Alas, my Poynz, how men do seke the best
And fynde the wourst, by error as they stray!
And no marvaill, when sight is so opprest,
And blynde the gyde; anon owte of the way
Goeth gyde and all in seking quyete liff.
O wretched myndes, there is no gold that may
Graunt that ye seke, no warr, no peace, no stryff.
No, no, all tho thy hed were howpt[32] with gold,
Sergeaunt with mace, hawbert, sword, nor knyff,
Cannot repulse the care that folowe should.
Eche kynd of lyff hath with hym his disease.[33]
Lyve in delight evyn as thy lust[34] would,
And thou shalt fynde, when lust doeth moost the please,
It irketh straite and by it self doth fade.
A small thing it is that may thy mynde apese.
Non of ye all there is that is so madde
To seke grapes vpon brambles or breers;[35]
Nor none I trow that hath his wit so badd
To set his hay for Conys[36] over Ryvers;
Ne ye set[37] not a dragg net for an hare.
And yet the thing that moost is your desire
Ye do mysseke with more travaill and care.
Make playn thyn hert, that it be not knotted[38]
With hope or dred; and se thy will be bare
From all affectes whome vice hath ever spotted.[39]
Thy self content with that is the assigned,
And vse it well that is to the allotted.
Then seke no more owte of thy self to fynde

[23] stool.
[24] steaming, flaming.
[25] *for the vnwise* STC 13861]; *for tho* MS.
[26] seen.
[27] whither.
[28] wondrous.
[29] the heaven.
[30] unfortunate.
[31] the security that she derived from her poverty.
[32] hooped, crowned.
[33] discomfort.
[34] pleasure, in a general sense.
[35] briars.
[36] hunting net for conies.
[37] *set* STC 13861]; *se* MS.
[38] entangled.
[39] free from all affections or passions that vice has defiled.

The thing that thou haist sought so long before,
For thou shalt fele it sitting in thy mynde;
Madde, if ye list to continue your sore.[40]
Let present passe, and gape on[41] tyme to come,
And diepe your self in travaill more and more.[42]
Hens fourth, my Poyngz, this shalbe all and some;[43]
These wretched fooles shall have nought els of me.
But to the great God and to his high dome[44]
None othre pain pray I for theim to be,
But when the rage doeth led them from the right,
That lowking backwards, vertue they may se
Evyn as she is, so goodly fayre and bright.
And whilst they claspe their lustes in armes a crosse,
Graunt theim, goode Lorde, as thou maist of thy myght,
To frete inwards for losing suche a losse.

40 do not look for happiness outside yourself; you are mad if you do.
41 long for.
42 (?) enter more deeply into work and study.
43 everything.
44 doom, judgment.

Henry Howard, Earl of Surrey

[c. 1517–1547]

HENRY HOWARD, eldest son of Thomas Howard, third Duke of Norfolk, was educated at Windsor and at the French court as the companion of Henry VIII's natural son, the Duke of Richmond, who married Surrey's sister. His ancestry and his family connections made him the greatest noble of the age. His fortunes rose and declined with the fortunes of the Howard family; when his cousin, Catherine Howard, was queen (1540–1542) he held important posts, but in 1546 his enemies arrested him on a charge of treason, and he was executed in January, 1547. Courtier, scholar, soldier, envoy abroad, he was described by a contemporary as "the most folish prowde boye that ys in England." Proud, high-spirited, adventurous, he was also the most accomplished and brilliant aristocrat of his day.

Only two of his poems survive in manuscripts older than *Tottel's Miscellany.* In these and in Tottel's text Surrey's rhythm is smoother than Wyatt's. The word accent and the diction are less archaic. Writing only a few years later than Wyatt, Surrey seems much more modern. Although he uses a variety of metrical patterns, his innovations are in the sonnet and in blank verse. Most of the fifteen or sixteen sonnets attributed to him have the English or "Shakespearian" rhyme scheme, three quatrains followed by a couplet. Although he was not the first to use this pattern, his success with it helped to make it the usual Elizabethan form. The first blank verse in English appears in his translation of the fourth book of the *Aeneid,* which was printed about 1554. In 1557 Richard Tottel published another text of this book, together with Surrey's translation of the second book. Not for thirty years were English poets to write blank verse as good as Surrey's.

For a third contribution by Surrey later poets have less reason to be thankful. Surrey wrote eighteen of his poems (about a thousand lines) in iambic couplets, the first line of twelve syllables, the second of fourteen. George Gascoigne gave this couplet the name (poulter's measure) by which it is still known. In his *Certain Notes of Instruction,* 1575, he wrote: "The commonest sort of verse which we vse now adayes (*viz.* the long verse of twelue and fourtene sillables) I know not certainly howe to name it, vnlesse I should say that it doth consist of Poulters measure, which giueth xii. for one dozen and xiiii. for another." Although earlier poets, including Wyatt, had used this measure, it was probably Surrey's example, especially in his paraphrases of Ecclesiastes and the Psalms, that gave this lumbering meter—and the almost equally clumsy "fourteener" couplet—the unfortunate vogue that both forms enjoyed for several decades, and indeed much longer in devotional verse. When each line of poulter's measure is printed as two lines, we have the stanza known in the hymnbooks as "short meter"; when the "fourteener" couplet is so printed, we have the hymnbook "common meter."

Surrey's verse in general is more melodious, more graceful, more pictorial and discursive, less vigorous, less sententious than Wyatt's. His amatory verse lacks Wyatt's intensely personal note. Like Wyatt, he sought to do what Petrarch had done—make the vernacular suitable for polite and courtly poetry. During the sixteenth century his reputation as a poet was greater than Wyatt's; it was he, rather than Wyatt, who was imitated by the poets of the next half-century. In his verse they found, as they did not find in Wyatt's, a skillful adjustment of the conflicting claims of word accent, rhetorical accent, and metrical accent. Verse technique had passed beyond the experimental stage. The language of Skelton and Wyatt had already become archaic; Surrey's English was to remain current for several decades. To the poets of those decades Surrey seemed to be the first modern poet.

The best early edition is G. F. Nott, *The Works of Henry Howard Earl of Surrey and of Sir Thomas Wyatt the Elder*, 2 vols., 1815–1816. The best modern editions are F. M. Padelford, *The Poems of Henry Howard, Earl of Surrey*, 1920, revised, 1928; and H. E. Rollins, *Tottel's Miscellany*, 2 vols., 1928–1929. An excellent account of Surrey is given in J. M. Berdan, *Early Tudor Poetry*, 1920. The standard biography is Edwin Casady, *Henry Howard, Earl of Surrey*, 1938. For bibliography see *CBEL*, i, 412–413.

DESCRIPTION OF SPRING, WHERIN ECHE THING RENEWES, SAUE ONELY THE LOUER[1]

The soote[2] season, that bud and blome forth brings,
With grene hath clad the hill, and eke[3] the vale:
The nightingale, with fethers new she sings:
The turtle[4] to her make[5] hath tolde her tale:
The adder all her slough away she slings:
The hart hath hong his old hed on the pale:[6]
The buck in brake his winter coate he flings:
The fishes flete[7] with new repayred scale:

[1] From *Songes and sonettes, written by the right honorable Lorde Henry Haward late Earle of Surrey, and other.* 31 July, 1557, STC 13861, Huntington Library. This poem is adapted from Petrarch, *Sonetto in morte*, 42.

[2] *soote* STC 13860]; *foote* STC 13861: sweet.

[3] also.

[4] turtledove.

[5] mate.

[6] has shed his antlers on the palings (fence of the enclosure).

[7] float.

The adder all her slough away she slings:
The swift swallow pursueth the flies smalle:
The busy bee her hony now she minges:[8]
Winter is worne that was the flowers bale:
And thus I see among these pleasant things,
Eche care decayes, and yet my sorow springs.

COMPLAINT OF A LOUER, THAT DEFIED LOUE, AND WAS BY LOUE AFTER THE MORE TORMENTED

When sommer toke in hand the winter to assail,
With force of might, and vertue gret, his stormy blasts to quail,
And when he clothed faire the earth about with grene,
And euery tree new garmented, that pleasure was to sene:
Mine hart gane new reuiue, and changed blood did stur,
Me to withdrawe my winter woes, that kept within the dore.
Abrode, quod[9] my desire: assay to set thy fote,
Where thou shalt finde the sauour swete: for sprong is euery rote.
And to thy health, if thou were sick in any case,
Nothing more good, than in the spring the aire to fele a space.
There shalt thou heare and se all kindes of birdes ywrought,[10]
Well tune their voice with warble smal, as nature hath them tought.
Thus pricked me my lust[11] the sluggish house to leaue:
And for my health I thought it best such counsail to receaue.
So on a morow furth, vnwist[12] of any wight,[13]
I went to proue how well it would my heauy burden light.
And when I felt the aire so pleasant round about,
Lord, to my self how glad I was that I had gotten out.
There might I se how Ver[14] had euery blossom hent:[15]
And eke the new betrothed birdes ycoupled[16] how they went.
And in their songes me thought they thanked nature much,
That by her licence all that yere to loue their happe was such,
Right as they could deuise to chose them feres[17] throughout:
With much reioycing to their Lord thus flew they al about.
Which when I gan resolue, and in my head conceaue,
What pleasant life, what heapes of ioy these litle birdes receaue,
And saw in what estate I wery man was brought,
By want of what they had at will, and I reiect at nought:
Lord how I gan in wrath vnwisely me demeane.[18]
I cursed loue[19] and him defied: I thought to turne the streame,
But when I well beheld he had me vnder awe,
I asked mercy for my fault, that so transgrest his lawe.
Thou blinded God (quod I) forgeue me this offence,
Unwittingly I went about, to malice thy pretence.[20]
Wherwith he gave a beck, and thus me thought he swore,
Thy sorowe ought suffice to purge thy fault, if it were more.
The vertue of which sound mine hart did so reuiue,

---

8 mixes.
9 quoth.
10 created.
11 wish.
12 unknown.
13 person.
14 spring.
15 seized.
16 mated.
17 mates.
18 behave.
19 Cupid.
20 to seek to injure Cupid's claim to authority.

That I, me thought, was made as whole as any man aliue,
But here I may perceiue mine errour all and some,[21]
For that I thought that so it was: yet was it still vndone.
And all that was no more but mine expressed minde,
That faine would haue some good reliefe, of Cupide well assinde.
I turned home forthwith, and might perceue it well,
That he agreued was right sore with me for my rebell.[22]
My harmes haue euer since, encreased more and more,
And I remaine without his help, vndone for euermore,
A mirror let me be vnto ye louers all:
Strive not with loue, for if ye do, it will ye thus befall.

COMPLAINT OF A LOUER REBUKED[23]

Loue, that liueth, and raigneth in my thought,
That built his seat within my captiue brest,
Clad in the armes, wherin with me he fought,
Oft in my face he doth his banner rest.
She, that me taught to loue, and suffer payne,
My doutfull hope, and eke my hot desire,
With shamefast[24] cloke to shadow and restraine,
Her smiling grace conuerteth straight to yre.
And coward loue then to the hart apace
Taketh his flight, wheras he lurkes and plaines[25]
His purpose lost, and dare not shew his face.
For my lordes gilt thus faultlesse bide I paines,
Yet from my lorde shall not my foote remoue.
Swete is his death, that takes his end by loue.

DESCRIPTION AND PRAISE OF HIS LOUE GERALDINE[26]

From Tuskane[27] came my Ladies worthy race:
Faire Florence was sometime her auncient seate:
The Western yle, whose pleasaunt shore dothe face
Wilde Cambers[28] clifs, furst gaue her liuely heate:
Fostred she was with milke of Irishe brest:
Her sire, an Earle: her dame, of princes blood.[29]
From tender yeres, in Britain did she rest,
With a kinges childe,[30] who tasteth ghostly[31] food.
Honsdon[32] did first present her to mine iyen:
Bright is her hewe, and Geraldine she hight.[33]

---

21 entirely.

22 rebellion.

23 Translated from Petrarch, *Sonetto in vita,* 91.

24 modest.

25 complains.

26 This sonnet gave rise to the legend of Surrey's love for "the fair Geraldine" and to the belief that he addressed his love poetry to her. The chief sixteenth-century sources for the legend are Thomas Nashe's *The Unfortunate Traveller,* 1594, and Michael Drayton's *Heroical Epistles,* 1598. The sonnet was addressed to Elizabeth Fitzgerald, daughter of the ninth Earl of Kildare. In 1537, the probable date of the sonnet, Elizabeth was about nine years old. See H. E. Rollins, *Tottel's Miscellany,* ii, 70–75.

27 The Fitzgeralds were believed to be descended from the Giraldi of Florence.

28 of Cambria, of Wales.

29 Her mother was granddaughter of Edward IV's queen.

30 She was attached to the household of Princess Mary.

31 spiritual. STC 13860 reads *where she tasteth costly food.*

32 Hunsdon.

33 is named.

Hampton[34] me taught to wishe her first for mine:
And Windsor,[35] alas, dothe chase me from her sight.
Her beauty of kinde[36] her vertues from aboue.
Happy is he, that can obtaine her loue.

THE FRAILTIE AND HURTFULNES OF BEAUTIE[37]

Brittle beautie, that nature made so fraile,
Wherof the gift is small, and short the season,
Flowring to day, to morowe apt to faile,
Tickell[38] treasure abhorred of reason,
Daungerous to dele with, vaine, of none auaile,
Costly in keping, past not worthe two peason,[39]
Slipper[40] in sliding as is an eles taile,
Harde to attaine, once gotten not geason,[41]
Iewel of ieopardie that perill dothe assaile,
False and vntrue, enticed oft to treason,
Enmy to youth: that moste may I bewaile.
Ah bitter swete infecting as the poyson:
Thou farest as frute that with the frost is taken,
To day redy ripe, to morowe all to shaken.[42]

VOW TO LOUE FAITHFULLIE HOWSOEUER HE BE REWARDED[43]

Set me wheras the Sunne do parche the grene,
Or where his beames do not dissolue the yse:
In temperate heate where he is felt and sene:
In presence prest[44] of people madde or wise.
Set me in hye, or yet in lowe degree:
In longest night, or in the shortest day:
In clearest skie, or where clowdes thickest be:
In lusty youth, or when my heares are gray.
Set me in heauen, in earth, or els in hell,
In hill, or dale, or in the foming flood:
Thrall, or at large, aliue where so I dwell:
Sicke, or in health: in euyll fame, or good,
Hers will I be, and onely with this thought
Content my selfe, although my chaunce be nought.

A COMPLAINT BY NIGHT OF THE LOUER NOT BELOUED[45]

Alas so all things nowe do hold their peace.
Heauen and earth disturbed in nothing:
The beasts, the ayre, the birdes their song do cease:

---

34 Hampton Court.
35 Surrey was a prisoner in Windsor in July, 1537.
36 nature.
37 Usually attributed to Surrey; probably by Lord Vaux.
38 insecure.
39 peas.
40 slippery, variable.
41 rare.
42 completely shaken down.
43 Translated from Petrarch, *Sonetto in vita,* 95.
44 crowded.
45 Adapted from Petrarch, *Sonetto in vita,* 113.

The nightes chare[46] the starres aboute doth bring:
Calme is the Sea, the waues worke lesse and lesse:
So am not I, whom loue alas doth wring,
Bringing before my face the great encrease
Of my desires, whereat I wepe and sing,
In ioy and wo, as in a doutfull ease.
For my swete thoughtes sometime do pleasure bring:
But by and by the cause of my disease[47]
Geues me a pang, that inwardly doth sting,
When that I thinke what griefe it is againe,
To liue and lacke the thing should[48] ridde my paine.

PRISONED IN WINDSOR, HE RECOUNTETH HIS PLEASURE THERE PASSED[49]

So cruell prison how could betide, alas,
As proude Windsor? where I in lust[50] and ioy,
With a kinges sonne, my childishe yeres did passe,
In greater feastes than Priams sonnes of Troy:
Where eche swete place returns a taste full sower,
The large grene courtes, where we were wont to houe,[51]
With eyes cast vp into the maydens tower.
And easie sighes, such as folke drawe in loue:
The stately seates,[52] the ladies bright of hewe:[53]
The daunces shorte, longe tales of great delight:
With wordes and lokes, that tygers coulde but rewe,[54]
Where eche of vs did pleade the others right:
The palme play,[55] where, dispoyled[56] for the game,
With dazed eies oft we by gleames of loue,
Haue mist the ball, and got sight of our dame,
To baite[57] her eyes, which kept the leads[58] aboue:
The grauell grounde, with sleues tyed on the helme:
On foming horse, with swordes and frendly hartes:
With cheare,[59] as though one should another whelme:[60]
Where we haue fought, and chased oft with dartes,
With siluer droppes the meade yet spred for ruth,
In actiue games of nimblenes, and strength,
Where we did straine, trained with swarmes of youth.
Our tender limmes, that yet shot vp in length:
The secret groues, which oft we made resound
Of pleasaunt plaint, and of our ladies praise,
Recording ofte what grace eche one had found,
What hope of spede, what dread of long delaies:
The wilde forest, the clothed holtes with grene:

[46] chariot.
[47] lack of ease.
[48] thing that should.
[49] In July, 1537, Surrey was imprisoned in Windsor for striking a courtier. In the poem he recalls his boyhood there with Henry Fitzroy, Duke of Richmond, who was the husband of Surrey's sister, Mary Howard, and who died in 1536, aged seventeen.
[50] pleasure.
[51] linger.
[52] Addit. MS. 36529 reads *sales:* halls.
[53] *hewe:* STC 13860]; *hewe* STC 13861.
[54] pity.
[55] Old form of tennis, resembling modern handball.
[56] disrobed.
[57] attract.
[58] Lead-covered windowsills or roof.
[59] countenance.
[60] overwhelm.

With rains auailed,[61] and swift ybreathed horse,
With crie of houndes, and mery blastes betwene,
Where we did chase the fearfull hart of force,[62]
The wide vales eke, that harborde vs ech night,
Wherwith (alas) reuiueth in my brest
The swete accord: such slepes as yet delight:
The pleasant dreames, the quiet bed of rest:
The secrete thoughtes imparted with such trust:
The wanton[63] talke, the diuers change of play:
The frenship sworne, eche promise kept so iust:[64]
Wherwith we past the winter nightes away.
And, with this thought, the bloud forsakes the face,
The teares beraine my chekes of deadly hewe:
The whiche as soone as sobbing sighes (alas)
Vpsupped haue, thus I my plaint renew:
O place of blisse, renuer of my woes,
Geue me accompt, where is my noble fere:[65]
Whom in thy walles thou doest eche night enclose,
To other leefe,[66] but vnto me most dere.
Eccho (alas) that doth my sorow rewe,
Returns therto a hollow sounde of plaint.
Thus I alone, where all my freedome grewe,
In prison pyne, with bondage and restraint,
And with remembrance of the greater griefe
To banish the lesse, I finde my chief reliefe.

THE LOUER COMFORTETH HIMSELFE WITH THE WORTHINESSE OF HIS LOUE

When raging loue with extreme payne
Most cruelly distrains[67] my hart:
When that my teares, as floudes of rayne,
Beare witnes of my wofull smart:
When sighes haue wasted so my breath,
That I lye at the point of death.

I call to minde the nauie great,
That the Grekes brought to Troye town:
And how the boysteous[68] windes did beate
Their ships, and rent their sayles adown,
Till Agamemnons daughters blood[69]
Appeasde the goddes, that them withstood.

And how that in those ten yeres warre,
Full many a bloodie dede was done,
And many a lord, that came full farre,
There caught his bane (alas) to soone:

61 lowered.
62 in the open with hounds.
63 playful.
64 exactly.
65 companion.
66 dear.
67 oppresses, subdues.
68 boisterous.
69 Iphigenia, who according to Aeschylus was sacrificed by Agamemnon to appease the goddess Diana.

And many a good knight ouerron,
Before the Grekes had Helene won.

Then thinck I thus: sithe[70] such repaire,[71]
So longe time warre of valiant men,
Was all to winne a ladye faire:
Shall I not learne to suffer then,
And thinck my life well spent to be,
Seruing a worthier wight[72] than she?

Therfore I neuer will repent,
But paines contented still endure.
For like as when, rough winter spent,
The pleasant spring straight draweth in vre:[73]
So after raging stormes of care
Ioyful at length may be my fare.[74]

COMPLAINT OF THE ABSENCE OF HER LOUER BEING VPON THE SEA[75]

O happy dames, that may embrace
The frute of your delight,
Help to bewaile the wofull case,
And eke the heauy plight
Of me, that wonted to reioyce
The fortune of my pleasant choyce:
Good Ladies, help to fill my moorning voyce.

In ship, freight with remembrance
Of thoughts, and pleasures past,
He sailes that hath in gouernance
My life, while it will last:
With scalding sighes, for lack of gale,
Furdering his hope, that is his sail
Toward me, the swete port of his auail.[76]

Alas, how oft in dreames I see
Those eyes, that were my food,
Which somtime so delited me,
That yet they do me good.
Wherwith I wake with his returne,
Whose absent flame did make me burne.
But when I find the lacke, Lord how I mourne?

When other louers in armes acrosse,
Reioyce their chiefe delight:
Drowned in teares to mourne my losse,
I stand the bitter night,
In my window, where I may see,

[70] since.
[71] concourse of men.
[72] person.
[73] use, practice.
[74] The initial letters of the five stanzas spell "Wiatt."
[75] Adapted from Serafino's fifth epistle.
[76] disembarking.

Before the windes how the clowdes flee.
Lo, what a Mariner loue hath made me.

And in grene waues when the salt flood
Doth rise by rage of winde:
A thousand fansies in that mood
Assaile my restlesse mind.
Alas, now drencheth[77] my swete fo,
That with the spoyle of my hart did go,
And left me but (alas) why did he so?

And when the seas waxe calme againe,
To chase fro me annoye.
My doutful hope doth cause me plaine:
So dread cuts of my ioye.
Thus is my wealth mingled with wo,
And of ech thought a dout doth growe,
Now he comes, will he come? alas, no no.

THE MEANES TO ATTAIN HAPPY LIFE[78]

Martial, the thinges that do attain
The happy life, be these, I finde.
The richesse left, not got with pain:
The frutefull ground: the quiet minde:
The egall[79] frend, no grudge, no strife:
No charge of rule, nor gouernance:
Without disease the healthful life:
The houshold of continuance:[80]
The meane diet, no delicate fare:
Trew wisdom ioyned with simplenesse:
The night discharged of all care,
Where wine the wit may not oppresse:
The faithful wife, without debate:
Such slepes, as may begile[81] the night:
Contented with thine owne estate,
Ne wish for death, ne feare his might.

[OF THE DEATH OF SIR THOMAS WYATT]

W. resteth here, that quick[82] could neuer rest:
Whose heauenly giftes encreased by disdain,[83]
And vertue sank the deper in his brest.
Such profit he by enuy could obtain.
A head, where wisdom misteries did frame:
Whose hammers bet still in that liuely brain,
As on a stithe:[84] where that some work of fame
Was dayly wrought, to turne to Britaines gaine.
A visage, stern, and mylde: where both did grow,

[77] drowns.
[78] Translated from Martial, x, 47.
[79] equal.
[80] stability, permanence.
[81] make pass.
[82] living.
[83] gifts increased by his disdain of them.
[84] anvil.

Vice to contemne, in vertue to reioyce:
Amid great stormes, whom grace assured so,
To liue vpright, and smile at fortunes choyce.
A hand, that taught, what might be sayd in rime:
That reft Chaucer the glory of his wit:
A mark, the which (vnparfited,[85] for time)
Some may approch, but neuer none shal hit.
A toung, that serued in forein realmes his king:
Whose courteous talke to vertue did enflame[86]
Eche noble hart: a worthy guide to bring
Our English youth, by trauail, vnto fame.
An eye, whose iudgement none affect[87] could blinde,
Frendes to allure, and foes to reconcile:
Whose persing[88] loke did represent a minde
With vertue fraught, reposed, void of gile.
A hart, where dreade was neuer so imprest,
To hide the thought, that might the trouth auance:[89]
In neither fortune loft,[90] nor yet represt,
To swel in wealth, or yeld vnto mischance.
A valiaunt corps,[91] where force, and beawty met:
Happy, alas, to happy, but for foes:
Liued, and ran the race, that nature set:
Of manhodes shape, where she the mold did lose.
But to the heauens that simple soule is fled:
Which left with such, as couet Christ to know,
Witnesse of faith, that neuer shall be ded:
Sent for our helth, but not receiued so.
Thus, for our gilte, this iewel haue we lost:
The earth his bones, the heauens possesse his gost.

HOW NO AGE IS CONTENT WITH HIS OWN ESTATE, AND HOW THE AGE OF CHILDREN IS THE HAPPIEST, IF THEY HAD SKILL TO VNDERSTAND IT

Layd in my quiet bed, in study as I were,
I saw within my troubled head, a heape of thoughtes appere:
And euery thought did shew so liuely in myne eyes,
That now I sighed, and then I smilde, as cause of thought dyd rise.
I saw the litle boy in thought, how oft that he
Did wish of God, to scape the rod, a tall yongman to be.
The yongman eke that feles, his bones with paines opprest
How he would be a rich olde man, to lyue, and lye at rest.
The rych old man that sees his end draw on so sore,
How he would be a boy again, to liue so much the more.
Wherat full oft I smilde, to se, how all these three,
From boy to man, from man to boy, would chop[92] and change degree.
And musing thus I think, the case is very strange,
That man from welth, to liue in wo, doth euer seke to change.
Thus thoughtfull as I lay, I saw my witherd skyn,

[85] unfinished.
[86] *enflame*] *enflame.* STC 13861.
[87] passion.
[88] piercing.
[89] advance.
[90] raised aloft.
[91] body.
[92] trade, barter.

How it doth show my dented chewes,[93] the flesh was worne so thyn:
And eke my tothelesse chaps,[94] the gates of my rightway,
That opes and shuts, as I do speake, doe thus vnto me say:
Thy white and horish heares, the messengers of age,
That shew, like lines of true belife, that this life doth asswage,
Byds thee lay hand, and fele them hanging on thy chin:
The whiche do write two ages past, the third now comming in.
Hang vp therfore the bit of thy yong wanton time:
And thou that therin beaten art, the happiest life define.
Wherat I sighed, and sayd, farewell, my wonted ioy:
Trusse vp thy pack, and trudge from me to euery litle boy:
And tell them thus from me, their tyme most happy is:
If, to their time, they reason had to know the trueth of this.

EXHORTACION TO LEARNE BY OTHERS TROUBLE

My Ratclif,[95] when thy retchlesse youth offendes:
Receue thy scourge by others chastisement.
For such calling, when it workes none amendes:
Then plages are sent without aduertisement.[96]
Yet Salomon said,[97] the wronged shall recure:[98]
But Wiat said true,[99] the skarre doth aye endure.

THE SECOND BOKE OF VIRGILES AENAEIS[1]

They whisted[2] all, with fixed face attent,
When prince Aeneas from the royal seat
Thus gan to speak. O Quene, it is thy wil,
I shold renew a woe cannot be told:
How that the Grekes did spoile, and ouerthrow
The Phrygian wealth, and wailful realm of Troy,
Those ruthfull things that I my self beheld,
And wherof no small part fel to my share.
Which to expresse, who could refraine from teres?
What Myrmidon? or yet what Dolopes?[3]
What stern Ulysses waged[4] soldiar?
And loe moist night now from the welkin falles,
And sterres declining counsel vs to rest.
But sins so great is thy delight to here
Of our mishaps, and Troyes last decay:
Though to record the same my minde abhorres,
And plaint eschues: yet thus wil I begyn.
The Grekes chieftains all irked with the war,
Wherin they wasted had so many yeres,
And oft repulst by fatal destinie,
A huge hors made, hye raised like a hill,

[93] jaws.
[94] jaws.
[95] Perhaps addressed to Thomas Radcliffe, third Earl of Sussex, who in 1544, when he was about eighteen years old, was with Surrey as a soldier in France.
[96] warning.
[97] Perhaps Proverbs xii, 13, or xxiv, 16.
[98] be cured.
[99] See Wyatt's *Syghes are my foode: my drink are my teares*, line 8.
[1] From *Certain bokes of Virgiles Aeneis*, 1557, STC 24798, Princeton.
[2] grew silent.
[3] Thessalian.
[4] mercenary.

By the diuine science of Minerua:
Of clouen fir compacted were his ribbs:
For their return a fained sacrifice:
The fame wherof so wandred it at point.[5]
In the dark bulk they closde bodies of men
Chosen by lot, and did enstuff by stealth
The hollow womb with armed soldiars.
  There stands in sight an isle hight Tenedon,[6]
Rich, and of fame, while Priams kingdom stood:
Now but a bay, and rode vnsure for ship.
Hether them secretly the Grekes withdrew,
Shrouding themselues vnder the desert shore.
And, wening we they had ben fled and gone,
And with that winde had fet[7] the land of Grece,
Troye discharged her long continued dole:
The gates cast vp, we issued out to play,
The Grekish camp desirous to behold,
The places void and the forsaken costes.
Here Pyrrhus band, there ferce Achilles pight:[8]
Here rode their shippes, there did their battells ioyne.
Astonnied, some the scathefull gift beheld:
Behight[9] by vow vnto the chast Minerue,
All wondring at the hugenesse of the horse.
  And fyrst of all Timoetes gan aduise,
Wythin the walles to leade and drawe the same,
And place it eke amidde the palace court:
Whether of guile, or Troyes fate it would.
Capys, wyth some of iudgement more discrete,
Wild it to drown, or vnderset with flame
The suspect present of the Grekes deceit,
Or bore and gage the hallowe caues uncouth.
So diuerse ranne the giddy peoples minde.
  Loe formest of a rout[10] that followd him,
Kindled Laocoon hasted from the towre,
Crieng far of: O wreched citezens,
What so great kind of frensie freteth you?
Deme ye the Grekes our enemies to be gone?
Or any Grekish giftes can you suppose
Deuoid of guile? Is so Ulysses known?
Either the Grekes ar in this timber hid:
Or this an engin is to anoy our walles,
To view our toures, and ouerwhelme our towne.
Here lurkes some craft. Good Troyans, geue no trust
Unto this horse, for what so euer it be,
I dred the Grekes, yea when they offer gyftes.
And with that word, with all his force a dart
He launced then into that croked wombe:
Which tremling stack,[11] and shoke within the side.
Wherwith the caues gan hollowly resound.
And, but for faites and for our blind forcast,
The Grekes deuise and guile had he discried:
Troy yet had stand, and Priams toures so hie.

---

[5] the rumor so spread about conveniently.
[6] Tenedos.
[7] fetched, reached by sailing.
[8] pitched (their tents).
[9] pledged.
[10] throng.
[11] stuck.

Minor "Courtly Makers"

[1500–1560]

THOMAS VAUX, Lord Vaux of Harrowden (1510–1556), holds a place among the "courtly makers" second only to Wyatt and Surrey. Vaux succeeded to the barony in 1523, accompanied Cardinal Wolsey to France in 1527, and in 1532 was in the train of Henry VIII when he went to Calais. He became a member of the House of Lords in 1531.

Puttenham (1589) names Vaux as one of the best poets of his day and commends him for "the facillitie of his meetre, and the aptnesse of his descriptions." Sir Egerton Brydges (1810) finds in Vaux's poems "an awful sense of religion" and the expression of a heart "sick of the bustle of a turbulent, inconstant, and treacherous world."

None of Vaux's verse was printed during his lifetime. At least two of his poems are in *Tottel's Miscellany*, 1557, and at least twelve in *The Paradise of Dainty Devices*, 1576. His poems were reprinted by A. B. Grosart in *Miscellanies of the Fuller Worthies' Library*, vol. iv, 1884. The best accounts of Vaux are in *The Paradise of Dainty Devices*, ed. H. E. Rollins, 1927, and in *Tottel's Miscellany*, ed. H. E. Rollins, 2 vols., 1928–1929.

Nicholas Grimald (c. 1519–c. 1562), scholar, translator, poet, is remembered chiefly for his forty poems in the first edition of *Tottel's Miscellany*. All but ten of these were, for reasons unknown, omitted from later editions. Some scholars have supposed that he edited the miscellany, but this view is no longer held. Grimald was of both universities and for a time lectured on rhetoric at Oxford. He became chaplain to Nicholas Ridley, Bishop of London, and was later imprisoned. It is probable that he obtained his release by recanting, and it is possible that by acting as a spy he helped to bring to their deaths the Protestant martyrs Ridley, Latimer, Cranmer, and others.

Much of Grimald's writing has perished. Among his extant work are two plays in Latin and a translation of Cicero's *De Officiis*. Many of his poems in *Tottel's Miscellany* are translations from Latin. Two of these are in blank verse which may be as early as Surrey's. Though he crowds his poems with learned allusions and at times uses "poulter's measure," his verse generally is more disciplined and terse than that of most of his contemporaries. His poetry as a whole is the work of the careful scholar rather than of the courtier for whom the writing of verse was a polite accomplishment.

There are good discussions of Grimald in J. M. Berdan, *Early Tudor Poetry*, 1920; H. E. Rollins, *Tottel's Miscellany*, 2 vols., 1928–1929; L. I. Guiney, *Recusant Poets*, 1939. The fullest account is in L. R. Merrill, *The Life and Poems of Nicholas Grimald*, 1925. For comment on Merrill's views see C. R. Baskervill in *Modern Philology*, xxiii (1926), 377–378, and G. C. Moore Smith in *The Modern Language Review*, xxi (1926), 81–83.

POEMS BY VAUX

THE AGED LOUER RENOUNCETH LOUE[1]

I lothe that I did loue,
In youth that I thought swete:
As time requires for my behoue,[2]
Me thinkes they are not mete.

My lustes they do me leaue,
My fansies all be fled:
And tract[3] of time begins to weaue,
Gray heares vpon my hed.

For age with steling steps,
Hath clawed me with his clutch:[4]
And lusty life[5] away she leapes,
As there had bene none such.

My muse dothe not delight
Me as she did before:
My hand and pen are not in plight,[6]
As they haue bene of yore.

For reason me denies,
This youthly idle rime:
And day by day to me she cries,
Leaue of these toyes in time.

The wrinkles in my brow,
The furrowes in my face:
Say limping age will hedge him now,
Where youth must geue him place.

The harbinger of death,
To me I see him ride:
The cough, the cold, the gasping breath,
Doth bid me to prouide.

A pikeax and a spade,
And eke a shrowding shete,
A house of claye for to be made,
For such a gest most mete.

Me thinkes I heare the clarke,
That knoles the carefull knell:
And bids me leaue my wofull warke,
Ere nature me compell.

My kepers knit the knot,[7]
That youth did laugh to scorne:
Of me that clene shalbe forgot,
As I had not bene borne.

Thus must I youth giue vp,
Whose badge I long did weare:
To them I yelde the wanton cup
That better may it beare.

Loe here the bared scull,
By whose balde signe I know:
That stouping age away shall pull,
Which youthfull yeres did sow.

For beauty with her band
These croked cares hath wrought:
And shipped me into the land,
From whence I first was brought.

And ye that bide behinde,
Haue ye none other trust:
As ye of claye were cast by kinde,[8]
So shall ye waste to dust.

---

[1] From *Songes and sonettes,* 31 July 1557, STC 13861, Huntington Library. The first grave-digger in *Hamlet* (V, i, 69 ff.) sings three stanzas of this song. Goethe included two stanzas in *Faust,* II, v, 6. In 1563–1564 it was registered for publication as a ballad.

[2] behoof, advantage.

[3] passage.

[4] *clutch*] *cowche* STC 13860; *crowch* STC 13861. Early manuscripts read *crutche.* Shakespeare reads *clutch.*

[5] Some early manuscripts read *youth.*

[6] condition.

[7] The meaning is obscure.

[8] nature.

NO PLEASURE WITHOUT SOME PAINE[9]

How can the tree but wast, and wither awaie,
That hath not sometyme comfort of the Sonne:
How can that flower but fade, and sone decaie,
That alwaies is with darke clouds ouer ronne.
Is this a life, naie death you maie it call,
That feeles eche paine, and knoweth no ioye at all.

What foodles beast can liue long in good plight,
Or is it life, where sences there be none:
Or what auaileth eyes without their light:
Or else a tonge, to hym that is alone.
Is this a life? naie death you maie it call,
That feeles eche paine, and knowes no ioye at all.

Whereto serue eares, if that there be no sounde,
Or suche a head, where no deuise[10] doeth growe:
But all of plaints, since sorrowe is the grounde,[11]
Whereby the harte doeth pine in deadly woe.
Is this a life, naie death you maie it call,
That feeles eche paine, and knows no ioye at all.[12]

OF THE MEANE ESTATE[13]

The higher that the Ceder tree, vnder the heauens doe growe,
The more in danger is the top, when sturdie winds gan[14] blowe,
Who iudges then in princely throne, to be deuoide of hate,
Doeth not yet knowe, what heapes of ill, lies hid in suche estate.
Suche dangers greate, suche gripes[15] of minde, suche toile doe thei sustaine,
That oftentimes, of God thei wishe, to be vnkyngde againe.

For as the huge and mightie rocks, withstande the ragyng seas,
So kyngdoms in subiection be, whereas dame Fortune please:
Of brittle ioye, of smilyng cheare, of honie mixt with gall,
Allotted is to euery Prince, in fredome to be thrall.
What watches longe, what stepps vnsure, what grefes and cares of minde:
What bitter broiles, what endles toiles, to kyngdoms be assingde.

The subiect then maie well compare with prince for plesant daies,
Whose silent might[16] bryngs quiet rest, whose might[17] no storme bewraies:[18]
How muche be we, then bounde to God, who suche prouision maks
To laye our cares vpon the Prince thus doeth he for our saks.
To hym therefore, let vs lift vp our harts, and praie a maine:
That euery Prince that he hath plast, maie long in quiet raigne.[19]

---

[9] From *The paradyse of daynty devises,* 1576, STC 7516, Morgan Library.
[10] thought.
[11] only of laments since all his thought arises from sorrow.
[12] Signed *"L. Vaux."*

[13] From *The paradyse of daynty devises,* 1576.
[14] Perhaps a misprint for *gin* or *can.*
[15] grief.
[16] Probably a misprint for *night.*
[17] Probably a misprint for *rest.*
[18] reveals.
[19] Signed *"L. V."*

OF A CONTENTED MYNDE[20]

When all is doen and saied, in the ende thus shall you finde,
He[21] moste of all doeth bathe in blisse, that hath a quiet minde:
And clere from worldly cares, to deame can be content,
The swetest tyme, in all his life, in thinkyng to be spent.

The bodie subiect is, to fickle Fortunes power,
And to a million of mishapps, is casuall[22] euery hower:
And death in tyme doeth chaunge it to a clodde of claye,
When as the mynde whiche is deuine, runnes neuer to decaie.

Companion none is like, vnto the mynde alone,
For many haue been harmde by speache, through thinking fewe or none:
Fewe oftentymes restraineth words, but maks not thoughts to cease,
And he speaks best that hath the skill,[23] when for to holde his peace.

Our wealth leaues vs at death, our kinsmen at the graue,
But vertues of the mynde, vnto the heauens with vs we haue:
Wherefore for vertues sake, I can be well content,
The swetest tyme of all my life, to deme in thinkyng spent.[24]

BETHINCKING HYM SELF OF HIS ENDE, WRITETH THUS[25]

When I behold the baier,[26] my last and postyng[27] Horse,
That bare shall to the graue, my vile and carren corse.[28]
Then saie I seely[29] wretche, why doest thou put thy trust,
In thyngs eithe[30] made of clay, that soone will turne to dust.

Doest thou not see the yong, the hardy and the fayre,
That now are past and gone, as though thei neuer were,
Doest thou not see thy selfe, draw howerly to thy last,
As shaftes which that is shotte, at byrdes that flieth fast.

Doest thou not see how death, through smiteth with his launce,
Some by warre, some by plague, and some by worldlie chaunce,
What thyng is there on earth, for pleasure that was made,
But goeth more swifte awaie, then doth the Sommer shade.

Loe heare the Sommer flower, that sprong this other day,
But Wynter weareth as fast, and bloweth cleane[31] away,
Euen so shalt thou consume, from youth to lothsome age,
For death he doth not spare, the prince more then the page.

Thy house shalbe of clay a clotte vnder thy head,
Vntill the latter day the graue shall be thy bed.
Vntill the blowing tromp doth say to all and some,[32]
Rise vp out of your graue, for now the Iudge is come.[33]

---

[20] From *The paradyse of daynty devises,* 1576.
[21] *He*] *The* STC 7516.
[22] subject to change or accident.
[23] knowledge.
[24] Signed "*L. Vaux.*"
[25] From *The paradyse of daintie devises,* 1580, STC 7518, Folger Library.
[26] bier.
[27] *postyng* STC 7517]; *hosting* STC 7518.
[28] carrion corpse.
[29] helpless.
[30] easily.
[31] entirely.
[32] everyone.
[33] Signed "*L. Vaux.*"

POEMS BY GRIMALD

DESCRIPTION OF VERTUE[34]

What one art thou, thus in torn weed yclad?
Vertue, in price[35] whom auncient sages had.
Why, poorely rayd?[36] For fading goodes past care.
Why doublefaced? I marke ech fortunes fare.
This bridle, what? Mindes rages to restrain.
Tooles why beare you? I loue to take great pain.
Why, winges? I teache aboue the starres to flye.
Why tread[37] you death? I onely cannot dye.

MANS LIFE AFTER POSSIDONIUS, OR CRATES[38]

What path list you to tread? what trade will you assay?
The courts of plea, by braul, and bate,[39] driue gentle peace away.
In house, for wife, and childe, there is but cark and care:
With trauail, and with toyl ynough, in feelds we vse to fare.
Vpon the seas lieth dreed: the riche, in foraine land,
Doo fear the losse: and there, the poore, like misers poorely stand.
Strife, with a wife, without, your thrift full hard to see:
Yong brats, a trouble: none at all, a maym[40] it seems to bee:
Youth, fond:[41] age hath no hert, and pincheth all to nye.
Choose then the leefer[42] of these twoo, no life, or soon to dye.

METRODORUS MINDE TO THE CONTRARIE[43]

What race of life roone you? what trade will you assay?
In courts, is glory got, and wit encreased daye by daye.
At home, wee take our ease, and beak[44] our selues in rest:
The feeldes our nature doo refresh with pleasures of the best.
On seas, is gayn to get: the straunger, hee shall bee
Estemed: hauing much: if not, none knoweth his lack, but hee.
A wife will trim thy house: no wife? then art thou free.
Brood is a louely thing: without, thy life is loose[45] to thee.
Yong bloods be strong: old sires in double honour dwell.
Do way[46] that choyse, no life, or soon to dye: for all is well.

OF FRENDSHIP[47]

Of all the heauenly giftes, that mortall men commend,
What trusty treasure in the world can counteruail[48] a frend?
Our helth is soon decayd: goodes, casuall,[49] light, and vain:
Broke haue we sene the force of powre, and honour suffer stain.

---

[34] From *Songes and sonettes,* July 31, 1557, STC 13861, Huntington Library. The source is Beza's epigram *Descriptio virtutis* (*Poemata,* 1548, p. 68).
[35] in high regard.
[36] arrayed.
[37] crush under foot.
[38] From *Songes and sonettes,* July 31, 1557. This and the following poem are based on epigrams in the Greek anthology; Grimald probably used the Latin translations of Erasmus or George Buchanan. See Bacon's version in his poem beginning "The world's a bubble."
[39] debate, strife.
[40] calamity.
[41] foolish.
[42] more desirable.
[43] From *Songes and sonettes,* July 31, 1557.
[44] warm, bask.
[45] easy(?)
[46] do away with.
[47] From *Songes and sonettes,* July 31, 1557.
[48] equal.
[49] uncertain.

In bodies lust, man doth resemble but base brute:
True vertue gets, and keeps a frend, good guide of our pursute:
Whose harty zeale with ours accords, in euery case:
No terme of time, no space of place, no storme can it deface.
When fickle fortune failes, this knot endureth still:
Thy kin out of their kinde[50] may swarue, when frends owe the good will.
What sweeter solace shall befall, than one to finde,
Vpon whose brest thou mayst repose the secretes of thy minde?
Hee wayleth at thy wo, his teares with thine be shed:
With thee doth he all ioyes enioy: so leef[51] a life is led.
Behold thy frend, and of thy self the patern see:
One soull, a wonder shall it seem, in bodies twain to bee.
In absence, present, rich in want, in sickenesse sound,
Yea after death aliue, mayst thou by thy sure frend be found.
Eche house, eche towne, eche realm by stedfast loue doth stand:
Where fowl debate breeds bitter bale, in eche deuided land.
O frendship, flowr of flowrs: O liuely sprite of life,
O sacred bond of blisfull peace, the stalworth staunch of strife:
Scipio with Lelius[52] didst thou conioyn in care,
At home, in warrs, for weal and wo, with egall[53] faith to fare.
Gesippus eke with Tite,[54] Damon with Pythias,
And with Menetus sonne Achill, by thee combined was.[55]
Euryalus, and Nisus gaue Virgil[56] cause to sing:
Of Pylades doo many rimes, and of Orestes ring.
Down Theseus went to hell, Pirith, his frend to finde:
O that the wiues, in these our dayes, were to their mates so kinde.
Cicero,[57] the frendly man, to Atticus, his frend,
Of frendship wrote: such couples lo doth lot[58] but seldome lend.
Recount thy race, now ronne: how few shalt thou there see,
Of whome to say: This same is he, that neuer fayled mee.
So rare a iewell then must nedes be holden dere:
And as thou wilt esteem thy self, so take thy chosen fere.[59]
The tirant, in dispaire, no lacke of gold bewayls.
But, Out I am vndoon (saith hee) for all my frendship fails.
Wherfore sins nothing is more kindely[60] for our kinde:
Next wisdome thus that teacheth vs, loue we the frendful minde.

ANONYMOUS POEMS FROM TOTTEL'S MISCELLANY

THEY OF THE MEANE ESTATE ARE HAPPIEST[61]

If right be rackt,[62] and ouerronne:
And power take part with open wrong:
If feare by[63] force do yelde to soone,
The lack is like to last to long.

If God for goodes shalbe vnplaced:
If right for riches lose his shape:
If world for wisdome be embraced:
The gesse is great, much hurt may hap.

Among good thinges, I proue and finde,

[50] natural obligations.
[51] agreeable.
[52] Scipio Africanus the younger and Gaius Laelius, lifelong friends, are the interlocutors in Cicero's *De Senectute*. In Cicero's *De Amicitia* Laelius eulogizes Scipio.
[53] equal.
[54] The friendship of Gisippus and Titus Quintus Fulvius is celebrated in Boccaccio's *Decameron*, x, 8.
[55] The friendship of Achilles and Patroclus, the son of Menoetius, is celebrated in the *Iliad*.
[56] *Aeneid*, ix, 176 ff.
[57] Cicero's letter to Atticus.
[58] fortune.
[59] companion.
[60] pleasing.
[61] From *Songes and sonettes*, July 31, 1557, STC 13861, Huntington Library.
[62] wracked, overthrown.
[63] *by* STC 13860]; *my* STC 13861.

The quiet life doth most abound:
And sure to the contented minde
There is no riches may be found.

For riches hates to be content:
Rule is enmy to quietnesse.
Power is most part impacient:
And seldom likes to liue in pease.

I heard a herdman once compare:
That quiet nightes he had mo slept:
And had mo mery dayes to spare:
Then he, which ought[64] the beastes, he kept.

I would not haue it thought hereby
The Dolphin swimme I meane to teache:
Nor yet to learne the Fawcon fly:
I rowe not so farre past my reache.

But as my part aboue the rest,
Is well to wish and well to will:
So till my breath shall fail my brest,
I will not ceasse to wish you still.

VPON CONSIDERATION OF THE STATE OF THIS LIFE HE WISHETH DEATH[65]

The lenger[66] life, the more offence:
The more offence the greater paine:
The greater paine, the lesse defence:
The lesse defence, the lesser gaine.
The losse of gaine long yll doth trye:
Wherfore come death, and let me dye.

The shorter life, lesse count I fynde:
The lesse account, the soner made:
The count soone made, the merier mind:
The merier minde doth thought euade,
Short life in truth this thing doth trie.[67]
Wherefore come death, and let me dye.

Come gentle death, the ebbe of care,
The ebbe of care,[68] the flood of lyfe,
The flood of lyfe, the ioifull fare,
The ioyfull fare, the end of strife,
The ende of strife, that thing wishe I:
Wherefore come death, and let me dye.

OF A NEW MARIED STUDENT[69]

A student at his boke so plast:
That welth he might haue wonne,
From boke to wife did flete in hast,
From wealth to wo to runne.
Now, who hath plaied a feater cast,
Since iugling first begonne?
In knitting of him self so fast,
Him selfe he hath vndonne.

THE PORE ESTATE TO BE HOLDEN FOR BEST[70]

Experience now doth shew what God vs taught before,
Desired pompe is vaine, and seldome doth it last:
Who climbes to raigne with kinges, may rue his fate full sore.
Alas the woful ende that comes with care full fast,
Reiect him doth renowne,[71] his pompe full low is caste.
Deceiued is the birde by swetenesse of the call
Expell that pleasant taste, wherein is bitter gall.

Such as with oten cakes in poore estate abides,
Of care haue they no cure,[72] the crab[73] with mirth they rost,
More ease fele they then those, that from their height down slides.[74]
Excesse doth brede their wo, they saile in Scillas cost,[75]
Remainyng in the stormes till shyp and al be lost.
Serue God therfore thou pore, for lo, thou liues in rest,
Eschue the golden hall, thy thatched house is best.

---

64 owned.

65 From *Songes and sonettes,* July 31, 1557. The rhetorical echo device employed in this poem Puttenham calls "the marching figure" or "the climbing figure." (*The Arte of English Poesie,* 1591, ed. Willcock and Walker, p. 208.)

66 longer.

67 prove.

68 *care,* STC 13860]; *care* STC 13861.

69 From *Songes and sonettes,* July 31, 1557.

70 *Ibid.* The initial letter of each line and the last letter of the last line spell the name "Edwarde Somerset." The poem was probably written after the execution in 1552 of Edward Seymour, Duke of Somerset, the Protector.

71 *renowne,*] *renowne* STC 13861.

72 care, heed.

73 crabapple.

74 *slides.*] *slides* STC 13861.

75 coast.

TOTUS MUNDUS IN MALIGNO POSITUS[76]

Complaine we may: much is amisse:
Hope is nye gone to haue redresse:
These daies ben ill, nothing sure is:
Kinde hart is wrapt in heauinesse.

The sterne is broke: the saile is rent:
The ship is geuen to winde and waue:
All helpe is gone: the rocke present.
That will be lost, what man can saue?

Thinges hard, therefore are now refused.
Labour in youth is thought but vaine:
Duty by (will not)[77] is excused.
Remoue the stop the way is plaine.

Learning is lewd,[78] and held a foole:
Wisdome is shent,[79] counted to raile:
Reason is banisht out of schoole:
The blinde is bold, and wordes preuaile.

Power, without care, slepeth at ease:
Will, without law, runth where he list:
Might without mercy can not please.
A wise man saith not, had I wist.[80]

When power lackes care and forceth not:
When care is feable and may not:
When might is slouthfull and will not:
Wedes may grow where good herbes cannot.

Take wrong away, law nedeth not:
For law to wrong is bridle and paine.
Take feare away, law booteth[81] not.
To striue gainst streame, it is but vaine.

Wyly is witty: brainsicke is wise:
Trouth is folly: and might is right:
Wordes are reason: and reason is lies:
The bad is good: darknesse is light.

Wrong to redresse, wisdome dare not.
Hardy is happy, and ruleth most.
Wilfull is witlesse, and careth not,
Which end go first, till all be lost.

Few right do loue, and wrong refuse.
Pleasure is sought in euery state.
Liking is lust: there is no chuse.
The low geue to the hye checke mate.

Order is broke in thinges of weight.
Measure and meane who doth not flee?
Two thinges preuaile: money, and sleight.[82]
To seme is better then to be.

The bowle is round, and doth downe slide,
Eche one thrusteth: none doth vphold.
A fall failes not, where blinde is guide.
The stay is gone: who can him hold?

Folly and falshed prayeth apace.
Trouth vnder bushell is faine to crepe.
Flattry is treble, pride singes the bace.
The meane the best part scant doth pepe.[83]

This firy plage the world infectes.
To vertue and trouth it geues no rest:
Mens harts are burnde with sundry sectes,
And to eche man his way is best.

With floods and stormes thus be we tost,
Awake good Lord, to thee we crye.
Our ship is almost sonk and lost.
Thy mercy help our miserye.

Mans strength is weake: mans wit is dull:
Mans reason is blinde. These thinges tamend,[84]
Thy hand (O Lord) of might is full,
Awake betime, and helpe vs send.

In thee we trust, and in no wight:[85]
Saue vs as chickens vnder the hen.[86]
Our crokednesse thou canst make right,
Glory to thee for aye. Amen.

---

[76] From *Songes and sonettes,* July 31, 1557. The title is from I John v, 19 (Vulgate). The poem is possibly by Sir John Cheke.

[77] The parentheses are used where we would now use quotation marks.

[78] ignorant.

[79] rebuked.

[80] A proverb common in the sixteenth century.

[81] helps.

[82] trickery.

[83] make a sound.

[84] to amend.

[85] creature.

[86] Cf. Matthew xxiii, 37.

OF THE VANITIE OF MANS LYFE[87]

Vaine is the fleting welth,
Whereon the world stayes:
Sithe[88] stalking time by priuy stelth,
Encrocheth on our dayes.

And elde[89] which creepeth fast,
To taynte vs with her wounde:
Will turne eche blysse vnto a blast,
Which lasteth but a stounde.[90]

Of youth the lusty floure,
Which whylome[91] stoode in price:[92]
Shall vanish quite within an houre,
As fire consumes the ice.

Where is become that wight,[93]
For whose sake Troy towne:
Withstode the grekes till ten yeres fight,
Had rasde their walles adowne.

Did not the wormes consume,
Her caryon to the dust?
Did dreadfull death forbeare his fume[94]
For beauty, pride, or lust?

[87] From *Songes and sonettes,* July 31, 1557.
[88] since.
[89] old age.
[90] short time.
[91] formerly.
[92] in esteem.
[93] person.
[94] smoke, anger.

Thomas Sternhold

[?–1549]

DURING the sixteenth century a great many persons wrote metrical versions of some or all of the Psalms—among them Wyatt seven in *terza rima,* Surrey three in poulter's measure and one in unrhymed hexameters, Sir Philip Sidney and his sister, Mary, Countess of Pembroke, all the Psalms in a wide variety of metrical patterns.

Thomas Sternhold, a Hampshire gentleman and groom of the robes to Henry VIII and Edward VI, translated into English verse some forty of the Psalms. Nineteen of these were published about 1547 with a dedication to Edward VI. After Sternhold's death, John Hopkins published Sternhold's version of thirty-seven Psalms with seven of his own in 1549. In later editions the number was increased, and in 1562 appeared *The Whole Booke of Psalmes . . . with apt notes to synge them withal,* translated by Sternhold, Hopkins, Thomas Norton, and others. It was many times reprinted and became the best-known metrical version.

It was Sternhold who determined the verse form and the style of the entire collection. The verse form that he chose is the "fourteener" couplet, which, whether it is printed in two lines or four, is the most common form of the popular ballad. Because his translations were to be memorized and sung, Sternhold simplified the form as much as possible by avoiding variation in the number of syllables and by giving nearly always only one syllable to a note of music. The verse is iambic, with a strong caesura after the fourth stress and usually a strong one after the second stress. The great popularity of these metrical psalms may be in part responsible for the vogue of the "fourteener" couplet and for the prolixity of much early Elizabethan verse in that measure; it may be in part responsible also for the preference after 1550 for iambic verse that is regular in stress, strictly measured, with caesuras strongly marked. Sternhold's plain, bare, "mere English" style contrasts sharply with the ornate, stylized manner, with its figures of rhetoric and its "inkhorn" terms, that marks much English verse after 1550.

The best account of Sternhold and Hopkins is Hallett Smith, "English Metrical Psalms in the Sixteenth Century and Their Literary Significance," *The Hunting-*

ton Library Quarterly, ix (1945–1946), 249–271. For a most unfavorable estimate of their work, see Thomas Warton, *The History of English Poetry*, 1824, iii, 449–464. The standard book of reference is John Julian, *Dictionary of Hymnology*, 1892; revised, 1907.

PSALM 1[1]

BEATUS VIR

How happy be the righteous men
this Psalme declareth playne.
And howe the wayes of wieked men,
be damnable and vayne.

The man is blest that hath not goen
by wycked rede[2] astraye,
Ne sate in chayer of pestilence,
Nor walkt in sinners waye.

But in the lawe of God the lorde
doeth set his whole delight,
And in that lawe doeth exercise
hymself bothe daye and nyght.

And as the tree that planted is
fast by the ryuer syde
Euen so shal he bring furth his fruite,
in his due tyme and tyde.

His leaf shal neuer fall away,
but florysh styl and stande,
Eche thyng shal prosper wonderous wel
that he doth take in hande.

So shall not the vngodly do.
they shall be nothyng so,
But as the dust which from the earth,
the wyndes dryue to and fro.

Therfore shal not the wieked men
in iudgement stande vpright,
Ne yet in counsell of the iust,
but shal be voyde of myght.

For why[3] the way of godly men
vnto the lorde is knowen,
And eke the waye of wieked men
shall quyte be ouerthrowen.

PSALM 3

DOMINE QUID MULTIPLICATI SUNT

The passion here is figured,
and how Christ rose againe.
So is the churche and faythful men,
theyr trouble and theyr payne.

O lorde how many do increase,
and trouble me ful sore,
How many say vnto my soule,
God wyl him saue no more?

But thou O lorde art my defence
Whan I am harde bestead,
My worship and myne honor bothe
and thou holdest vp my head.

And with my voyce vpon the lorde
I do both cal and crye,
And he out of his holy hyl,
doth heare me by and by.

I layde me doune, and quietly
I slept, and rose againe,
For why, I knowe assuredly,
the lorde wyl me sustayne.

Ten thousand men have compast[4] me
yet am I not afrayde,
For thou art styl my lorde my God,
my sauiour and myne ayde.

Thou smitest all thine enemies,
euen on the harde cheke bone.
And thou hast broken all the teeth
of eche vngodly one.

Saluacion onely doeth belong
to the O Lorde aboue,
Bestowe therfore vpon thy folke,
thy blessyng and thy loue.

[1] From Thomas Sternhold, *Certayne psalmes chosen out of the psalter of David, and drawen into English metre,* c. 1550, STC Huntington Library. This issue (or edition) is different from STC 2419. It contains nineteen psalms.

[2] advice.

[3] because.

[4] encircled.

PSALM 4

CUM INUOCAREM

God heard the praier of the churche,
mennes vanities are shent.[5]
With sacrifice of righteousnes,
the lorde is best content.

O God that art my right wisnes
lorde heare me when I cal,
Thou hast set me at libertie,
whan I was bonde and thral.

O mortal men how long wyl ye,
the glory of God dispise.
Why wander ye in vanitie,
and folowe after lyes.

Knowyng that good and godly men
the lorde doeth take and chuse,
And when to him I make my plaint
he doth me not refuse.

Synne not, but stand in awe therfore,
examine well thine heart
And in thy chambre quietly,
thou shalt thy selfe conuert.

Offre to God the sacrifice,
of righteousnes I say,
And loke that in the liuyng lorde,
thou put thy trust alway.

The greater sorte craue worldely goodes
and riches do embrace,
But lord graunt vs thi countenaunce
thy fauour and thy grace.

Wherwith thou shalt make all our heartes
more ioyful and more glad,
Than they that of thy corne and wyne
ful great increase haue had.

In peace therfore lye doune wyll I
takyng my rest and slepe,
For thou art he that onely doest,
al men in safetie kepe.

PSALM 128

BEATI OMNES

God blesseth with his benefites,
the man and eke the wyfe,
That in his wayes do rightly walke
and feare him all their life.

Blessed art thou that fearest god
and walkest in his way,
For of thy laboure thou shalt eate,
happy art thou I say.

Lyke fruiteful vynes on the house sides
so doth thy wyfe spryng out,
Thy children stand like Oliue buddes
thy table round about.

Thus art thou blessed that fearest God
and he shal let thee see
The promise of Ierusalem,
and his felicitie.

Thou shalt thy childrens children see
to thy great ioyes encrease,
Full quietly in Israel,
to passe their tyme in peace.

---

[5] reproved.

A Mirror for Magistrates

THE MOST popular and influential collection of narrative verse written during the sixteenth century, *A Mirror for Magistrates* appeared in 1559. Planned several years earlier, the first edition contained nineteen "tragedies"; later editions gradually increased the number to about one hundred.

The *Mirror* was planned as a continuation of John Lydgate's *The Fall of Princes,* which was written in 1431–1438 and first printed in 1494, and which was read and reprinted until the *Mirror* appeared. Lydgate's book was itself an expansion and elaboration of Boccaccio's *De Casibus Virorum Illustrium,* written about 1360.

The *Mirror* is a series of poems in each of which a great man, addressing the editor, speaks from the grave to tell the story of his rise and fall. The poems are linked together by passages in prose in which the editor and his collaborators discuss the tragedy just rehearsed. William Baldwin, printer, philosopher, poet, and later clergyman, was the first editor. He was known as the translator of *The Canticles or Ballads of Solomon,* 1549, and as the author of *A Treatise of Moral Philosophy, containing the Sayings of the Wise,* which appeared in 1547 and was reprinted many times during the next fifty years. For the first edition of the *Mirror* Baldwin wrote the address "To the nobilitye and all other in office," "William Baldwin to the Reader," and probably *Jack Cade* and most of the nineteen tragedies and the prose links. He chose as his collaborators men of learning and position, responsible men of affairs. Their avowed purpose was to compile a collection of *exempla* for the guidance of magistrates and people alike.

"To the nobilitye and all other in office" Baldwin writes: "Ye be all Gods, as many as have in your charge any ministracion of Iustice. What a fowle shame wer it for any now to take vpon them the name and office of God, and in their doinges to shew themselves divyls? God can not of Iustice, but plage such shameles presumption and hipocrisy, and that with shamefull death, diseases, or infamy. Howe he hath plaged euill rulers from time to time, in other nacions, you may see gathered in Boccas booke intituled the fall of Princes, translated into Englishe by Lydgate. How he hath delt with sum of our countreymen your auncestors, for sundrye vices not yet left, this booke named *A Myrrour for Magistrates,* can shew: which therfore I humbly offre vnto your honors, beseching you to accept it fauorably. For here as in a loking glas, you shall see (if any vice be in you) howe the like hath bene punished in other heretofore, whereby admonished, I trust it will be a good occasion to move you to the soner amendment. This is the chiefest ende, whye it is set furth, which God graunt it may attayne. . . . And although you shall finde in it, that sum haue for their vertue been enuied and murdered, yet cease not you to be vertuous, but do your offices to the vttermost: punish sinne boldly, both in your selues and other, so shall God (whose lieutenauntes you are) eyther so mayntayne you, that no malice shall preuayle, or if it do, it shall be for your good, and to your eternall glory both here and in heaven." In his address to the reader Baldwin explains that he plans to tell the stories "chiefly of suche as Fortune had dalyed with here in this ylande: whiche might be as a myrrour for al men as well noble as others, to shewe the slyppery deceytes of the waueryng lady, and the due rewarde of all kinde of vices."

The *Mirror* is both medieval and Renaissance in its emphasis. Many of the narratives are colored by the spirit of earlier tales *de contemptu mundi.* Capricious Fortune turns her wheel and casts down the mighty, both the wicked and the innocent. Humility and otherworldliness are the best defense against her blows. Although these ideas appear throughout the *Mirror*, of at least equal importance is the moralist's emphasis upon sin and punishment.

The Elizabethans believed that history was a mirror in which the present might see and learn the patterns of conduct that had brought happiness or unhappiness in the past. They believed, further, that the poet could provide such a mirror with more profit and delight to the reader than could the historian.

Ths *Mirror* is in part the product of the growing interest in kingship and government which found expression in Guevara's *The Dial of Princes*, Machiavelli's *The Prince*, Castiglione's *The Courtier*, and Elyot's *The Governour*. The decision to include in the *Mirror* only stories of English history reflects the increasing nationalism, the ardent patriotism, the desire to strengthen the Tudor monarchy.

The political doctrine of the *Mirror* is the orthodox Tudor doctrine emphasized in Calvin's *Institutes*, in the addresses of Tudor rulers to their people, and in certain homilies appointed to be read in churches. The subject owes obedience to the king and to all magistrates as God's deputies, and rebellion is therefore a sin against God; but the *Mirror* emphasizes the responsibility of kings to the King of Kings, and condemns injustice and selfish ambition in all magistrates.

The verse form used in most of the narratives in the *Mirror* is rhyme royal, which Chaucer used beautifully in *Troilus and Criseyde*, and which Lydgate employed laboriously throughout *The Fall of Princes*. The grace and dignity of Sackville's rhyme royal are equaled by no other contributor to the *Mirror*.

Despite the undistinguished quality of the verse in most of the narratives and the monotony of the immense gallery of gloomy portraits, the *Mirror* was read throughout the century. It exerted a powerful influence on the development of the Elizabethan interest in historical poetry and on the emphasis in much of that poetry—for example, the epics of Daniel and Drayton warning against the evils of civil war. It became the inspiration of much of the dramatic and nondramatic poetry of the next half-century.

Baldwin explains that he was willing to undertake the task of editing the *Mirror* only with "the helpe of suche, as in wyt were apte, in learning allowed, and in iudgemente and estymacion able to wield and furnysh so weighty an enterpryse."

Among the contributors to the various editions of the *Mirror* Thomas Sackville (1536–1608) is the most distinguished both as a man and as a poet. He was the cousin of Queen Elizabeth through his grandmother, Margaret Boleyn, and heir to the vast fortune of his father, Sir Richard Sackville. At the age of twenty-one he was elected to Parliament. In or before 1561 he collaborated with Thomas Norton in writing *Gorboduc*, the first English tragedy in blank verse, and by 1563 he had completed his two contributions to the *Mirror*. After that date he devoted his life to public service and, so far as is known, wrote no more poetry. Queen Elizabeth knighted him, created him Lord Buckhurst, and gave him her palace of Knole in Kent. He held various ambassadorships, and in 1599 became Lord High Treasurer of England. In 1604 King James created him Earl of Dorset. Throughout his long life he remained the faithful and upright counselor of Queen Elizabeth and King James.

Sackville's poetry, written thirty years before Spenser's and Shakespeare's, is noteworthy for its graceful verse, for the freshness of its imagery, for the stateliness and grandeur of its style, and for its emphasis upon the tragedy and nobility of human life. In Sackville, more clearly than in Wyatt and Surrey, are heard the new music and cadence that mark the great poetry written later in the century. The *Induction* is rightly regarded as the best English poem between Chaucer and Spenser.

Thomas Churchyard (c. 1520–1604), born in Shrewsbury, served as a page in the household of Henry Howard, Earl of Surrey, and later spent some years as a soldier in Scotland, Ireland, France, and the Low Countries. For a half-century he wrote verse of many kinds. Some of his poems, he affirmed, were included in *Tottel's Miscellany*. *Shore's Wife*, in the second edition of the *Mirror*, 1563, is his most famous poem, but probably of greater interest is his story of Cardinal Wolsey, which was included in the 1587 edition. Though his verse here and elsewhere is often flat and monotonous, in the years before the great Elizabethan poets he did his share to restore form and order to English poetry.

The standard edition is *The Mirror for Magistrates*, ed. Lily B. Campbell, 1938, and *Parts Added to the Mirror for Magistrates by John Higgins and Thomas Blenerhasset*, ed. Lily B. Campbell, 1946. Sackville's poems in the *Mirror* are edited from his manuscript, with a valuable Introduction, in *The Complaint of Henry Duke of Buckingham*, ed. Marguerite Hearsey, 1936. For the background and influence of the *Mirror*, see the following: Louis B. Wright, *Middle-Class Culture in Elizabethan England*, 1935; Lily B. Campbell, *Tudor Conceptions of History and Tragedy in "A Mirror for Magistrates,"* 1936; Willard Farnham, *The Medieval Heritage of Elizabethan Tragedy*, 1936; Homer Nearing, Jr., *English Historical Poetry*, 1599–1641 (University of Pennsylvania dissertation), 1945, chapters 1–4; Lily B. Campbell, *Shakespeare's "Histories": Mirrors of Elizabethan Policy*, 1947, chapters 1–10; Louis R. Zocca, *Elizabethan Narrative Poetry*, 1950, chapters 1–7; Lewis F. Ball, "The Background of the Minor English Renaissance Epic," *ELH*, i (1934), 63–89. The best account of Churchyard is that by Henry W. Adnitt, *Transactions of the Shropshire Archaeological and Natural History Society*, iii (1880), 1–68. For Churchyard's probable contributions to *Tottel's Miscellany*, see Rollins's edition, ii, 83–84.

HOW IACKE CADE TRAITEROUSLY REBELLING AGAYNST HIS KYNG, WAS FOR HIS TREASONS AND CRUELL DOINGES WURTHELY PUNYSHED[1]

Shal I cal it Fortune or my froward folly
That lifted me, and layed me downe below?
Or was it courage that me made so Ioly,[2]
Which of the starres and bodyes grement[3] grow?
What euer it were this one poynt sure I know,
Which shal be mete for euery man to marke:
Our lust[4] and wils our evils chefely warke.[5]

It may be wel that planetes doe enclyne,[6]
And our complexions[7] move our myndes to yll,
But such is Reason, that they brynge to fine[8]
No worke, vnayded of our lust and wyl:
For heauen and earth are subiect both to skyl.[9]
The skyl of God ruleth al, it is so strong,
Man may by skyl gyde thinges that to him long.

Though lust be sturdy[10] and wyl inclined to nought,[11]
This forst by mixture, that by heavens course,
Yet through the skyl God hath in Reason wrought
And geuen man, no lust nor wyl so course
But may be stayed or swaged[12] of the sourse,
So that it shal in nothing force the mynde
To worke our wo, or leaue the proper kynde.[13]

---

[1] From *A myrroure for magistrates*, 1559, STC 1247, Huntington Library; probably by William Baldwin.
[2] jolly, arrogant.
[3] agreement.
[4] desire.
[5] work.
[6] submit, accede to.
[7] temperaments.
[8] end.
[9] knowledge, reason.
[10] stubborn.
[11] wickedness.
[12] assuaged.
[13] nature.

But though this skil be geven every man
To rule the wyl, and kepe the minde aloft,
For lacke of grace[14] ful fewe vse it can,
These worldly pleasures tickle[15] vs so oft:
Skyl is not weake, but wyl strong, flesh is soft
And yeldes it selfe to pleasure that it loueth,
And hales the mynde to that it most reproueth.

Now if this happe[16] wherby we yelde our mynde
To lust and wyll, be fortune, as we name her,
Than is she iustly called false and blynde,
And no reproche can be to much to blame her:
Yet is the shame our owne when so we shame her,
For sure this hap if it be rightly knowen,
Cummeth of our selves, and so the blame our owne.

For who so lyveth in the skole of skyll
And medleth not with any worldes affaires,
Forsaketh pompes and honors that do spyl[17]
The myndes recourse to Graces quiet stayers,
His state no Fortune by no meane appayers:[18]
For Fortune is the folly and plage of those
Which to the worlde their wretched willes dispose.

Among which Fooles (Marke Baldwyn)[19] I am one
That would not stay my selfe in mine estate.[20]
I thought to rule, but to obey to none,
And therfore fel I with my Kyng at bate.[21]
And to the ende I might him better mate,[22]
Iohn Mortimer I caused my selfe be called,
Whose Kingly blood the Henries nye had thralled.[23]

This shift I vsed the people to perswade
To leave their Prince, on my side more to sticke,
Wheras in deede my fathers name was Kade
Whose noble stocke was never wurth a sticke.
But touching wit I was both rype and quicke,
Had strength of lims, large stature, cumly face,
Which made men wene[24] my lynage were not base.

And seing stoutnes stucke by men in Kent
Whose Valiaunt hartes refuse none enterprise,
With false perswasions straite to them I went,
And sayd they suffred to great iniuryes:
By meane wherof I caused them to rise,
And battayle wyse to cum to blacke heth[25] playne
And thence their grefes vnto the Kyng complayne.

---

14 God's favor.
15 entice.
16 chance.
17 destroy.
18 impairs.
19 William Baldwin, editor of *A Mirror for Magistrates*.
20 position in society. In the Catechism in *The Book of Common Prayer*, 1549, part of the Christian's duty to his neighbor is to do his duty "in that state of life unto which it shall please God" to call him.
21 strife.
22 rival, vie with.
23 conquered.
24 suppose.
25 Blackheath near London.

Who being deafe (as men say) on that eare,
For we desired releace of subsidies,
Refused roughly our requestes to heare
And came against vs as his enemies.
But we to trap hym, sought out subtiltyes,
Remoued our campe, and backe to Senocke[26] went,
After whom the Staffordes[27] with their power wer sent.

Se here how Fortune setting vs a flote
Brought to our nettes a porcion of our pray.
For why the Staffordes with their army hote
Assayled vs at Senocke, where we laye:
From whence alive they parted not away,
Which whan the Kynges retinew vnderstode
They all affirmed my quarel to be good.[28]

Which caused the king, and quene whom al did hate,
To raise their campe, and sodaynely depart:
And that they might the peoples grudge abate,
To imprison sum ful sore against their hart.
Lord Sayes was one, whom I made after smart.
For after the Staffordes and their oast[29] was slaine,
To Blackheath fyelde I marched backe againe.

And where the king would nothing heare before,
Nowe was he glad to send to know my minde:
And I therby enflamed much the more,
Refused his grauntes, so folly made me blind.
For this he flewe and left lord Skales[30] behind,
Mo helpe the towne, and strengthen London tower,
Towardes which I marched forward with my power.

And found there all thinges after my desier,
I entred London, did there what I list,
The Treasurer, lord Sayes, I did conspier
To have condemned: wherof whan I mist,
(For he by lawe my malice did resist)
By force I tooke him in Guyld hall fro the heape,
And headed him before the crosse in cheape.[31]

His sonne in law, Iames Cromer shrive[32] of Kent,
I caught at Myle ende, where as than he laye:
Beheaded him, and on a poale I sent
His head to London, where his fathers laye.
With these two heades I made a prety play,
For pight[33] on poales I bare them through the strete,
And for my sport made ech kisse other swete.

---

[26] Sevenoaks.
[27] Sir Humphrey Stafford.
[28] *good.*] *good* STC 1247.
[29] host.
[30] Lord Scales, the governor of the Tower of London.
[31] Cheapside, a London street.
[32] sheriff.
[33] fixed.

Than brake I prisons, let furth whom I woulde,
And vsed the citie as it had ben[34] mine:
Tooke fram the marchanntes, money, ware, and golde:
From sum by force, from other sum by fine.
This at the length did cause them to repine,
So that lord Skales consenting with the mayre,
Forbad vs to their citie to repayre.

For al this while mine hoast in Southwarke lay,
Who whan they knewe our passage was denyed,
Came boldly to the bridge and made a fraye,
For in we would, the townes men vs defied:
But whan with strokes we had the matter tryed,
We wan the bridge and set much part on fire,
This doen, to Southwarke backe we did retier.

The morowe after came the Chauncellour
With generall pardon for my men halfe gone,
Which heard and read, the rest within an houre
Shranke all awaye, eche man to shift for one.
And whan I sawe they left me post alone,[35]
I did disguise me like a knight of the post,[36]
And into Sussex roade away in poste.[37]

And there I lurked, till that cursed coyne
That restles begle[38] sought and found me out.
For strayt the king by promise did enioyne
A thousand marke, to whosoever mought
Apprend my corse:[39] which made men seke about.
Among the which one Alexander Iden,
Found out the hole wherin the fox was hidden.

But ere he tooke me, I put him to his trumpes,[40]
For yeeld I would not while my handes would holde
But hope of money made him stur his stumpes,[41]
And to assault me valiauntly and bolde.
Two howres and more our cumbate was not colde,
Til at the last he lent me such a stroke,
That downe I fell, and never after spoke.

Than was my carkas caried like a hog,
To Southwarke borow where it lay a night,
The next day drawen to Newgate like a dog,
All men reioycing at the rufull sight:
Than were on poales my parboylde quarters pight,
And set aloft for vermine to deuower,
Meete graue for rebels that resist the power.

Full litell knowe we wretches what we do.
Whan we presume our princes to resist,[42]

---

[34] *ben* STC 1248]; *be* STC 1247.
[35] entirely alone.
[36] The usual meaning is "perjuror"; here probably "courier."
[37] haste.
[38] beagle.
[39] apprehend my body.
[40] put him to the last expedient.
[41] walk briskly, work zealously.
[42] *resist,*] *resist.* STC 1247.

We war with God, against his glory to,
That placeth in his office whom he list,
Therfore was never traytour yet but mist
The marke he shot, and came to shamefull ende
Nor never shall til God be forst to bend.

God hath ordayned the power, all princes be
His Lieutenauntes, or debities[43] in realmes,
Against their foes still therfore fighteth he,
And as his enmies drives them to extremes,
Their wise deuises prove but doltish dreames.
No subject ought for any kind of cause,
To force the lord, but yeeld him to the lawes.

And therefore Baldwin warne men folow reason
Subdue theyr wylles, and be not Fortunes slaues,
A troublous ende doth ever folowe treason,
There is no trust in rebelles, raskall knaues,
In Fortune lesse, whiche wurketh as the waves:
From whose assautes who lyst to stande at large,[44]
Must folowe skyll, and flye all worldly charge.[45]

MAYSTER SACKUILLES INDUCTION[46]

The wrathfull winter prochinge[47] on a pace,
With blustring blastes had al ybared[48] the treen,
And olde Saturnus with his frosty face
With chilling colde had pearst the tender green:
The mantels rent, wherein enwrapped been
The gladsom groves that nowe laye ouerthrowen,
The tapets[49] torne, and euery tree downe blowen.

The soyle that earst[50] so seemely was to seen
Was all despoyled of her beauties hewe:
And soot[51] freshe flowers (wherwith the sommers queen
Had clad the earth) now Boreas blastes downe blewe.
And small fowles flocking, in theyr song did rewe

---

[43] deputies.

[44] free.

[45] In the prose link that follows this narrative Baldwin writes: "By saint mary (quoth one) yf Iacke wer as well learned, as you haue made his oracion, what so ever he was by byrth, I warraunt hym a gentylman by his learnyng. How notably and Philosopher like hath he discryved Fortune and the causes of worldly cumbraunce? howe vpryghtly also and howe lyke a deuine hath he determined the states both of officers and Rebelles. For in dede officers be gods deputies, and it is gods office which they beare, and it is he whiche ordeyneth thereto suche as himselfe lysteth, good whan he fauoreth the people, and evyll whan he wyll punysth theim. And therefore whosoever rebelleth agaynst any ruler either good or bad, rebelleth against *God,* and shalbe sure of a wretched ende: For God can not but maintein his deputie. Yet this I note by the waye concernyng rebelles and rebellions. Although the deuyll rayse theim, yet God alwayes vseth them to his glory, as a parte of his Iustice. For whan Kynges and chiefe rulers, suffer theyr vnder officers to mysuse their subiectes, and wil not heare nor remedye theyr peoples wronges whan they complayne, than suffreth *God* the Rebell to rage, and to execute that parte of his Iustice, which the parcyall prince woulde not." The prose link then states that Lord Saye was a "very corrupt officer" and the Bishop of Salisbury "a proude and coueitous prelate," and that both deserved God's punishment with Cade as the agent.

[46] From *A myrroure for magistrates,* 1563, STC 1248, Huntington Library.

[47] approaching.

[48] made bare.

[49] tapestries (here, foliage).

[50] formerly.

[51] sweet.

The winters wrath, wherwith eche thing defaste[52]
In woful wise bewayld the sommer past.

Hawthorne had lost his motley lyverye,
The naked twigges were shivering all for colde:
And dropping downe the teares abundantly,
Eche thing (me thought) with weping eye me tolde
The cruell season, bidding me withholde
My selfe within, for I was gotten out
Into the feldes where as I walkte about.

When loe the night with mistie mantels spred
Gan darke the daye, and dim the azure skyes,
And Venus[53] in her message Hermes sped
To bluddy Mars, to wyl him not to ryse,
While she her selfe approcht in speedy wise:
And Virgo hiding her disdaineful brest
With Thetis nowe had layd her downe to rest.

Whiles Scorpio dreading Sagittarius dart,
Whose bowe prest[54] bent in sight, the string had slypt,
Downe slyd into the Ocean flud aparte,
The Beare that in the Iryshe seas had dipt
His griesly feete, with spede from thence he whypt:
For Thetis hasting from the Virgines bed,
Pursued the Bear, that ear[55] she came was fled.

And Phaeton[56] nowe neare reaching to his race
With glistering beames, gold streamynge where they bent,
Was prest to enter in his resting place.
Erythius[57] that in the cart fyrste went
Had euen nowe attaynde his iourneyes stent.[58]
And fast declining hid away his head,
While Titan couched him in his purple bed.

And pale Cinthea with her borowed light
Beginning to supply her brothers place,
Was past the Noonesteede syxe degrees in sight
When sparklyng starres amyd the heauens face
With twinkling light shoen on the earth apace,
That whyle they brought about the nightes chare,[59]
The darke had dimmed the daye ear I was ware.

And sorowing I to see the sommer flowers,
The liuely greene, the lusty[60] leas forlorne,
The sturdy trees so shattered with the showers,
The fieldes so fade that floorisht so beforne,
It taught me wel all earthly thinges be borne
To dye the death, for nought long time may last.
The sommers beauty yeeldes to winters blast.

---

52 defaced.

53 These introductory stanzas follow the medieval convention by describing the season and the astronomical setting.

54 ready.

55 ere.

56 The sun.

57 Erythraeus, one of the four horses that draw the chariot of the sun.

58 end.

59 chariot, car.

60 pleasant.

Then looking vpward to the heauens leames[61]
With nightes starres thicke powdred euery where,
Which erst so glistened with the golden streames
That chearefull Phebus spred downe from his sphere,
Beholding darke oppressing day so neare:
The sodayne sight reduced[62] to my minde,
The sundry chaunges that in earth we fynde.

That musing on this worldly wealth in thought,
Which comes and goes more faster than we see
The flyckering flame that with the fyer is wrought,
My busie minde presented vnto me
Such fall of pieres as in this realme had be:
That ofte I wisht some would their woes descryue.[63]
To warne the rest whom fortune left aliue.

And strayt forth stalking with redoubled pace
For that I sawe the night drewe on so fast,
In blacke all clad there fell before my face
A piteous wight,[64] whom woe had al forwaste,[65]
Furth from her iyen the cristall teares outbrast,[66]
And syghing sore her handes she wrong and folde,
Tare al her heare that ruth was to beholde.

Her body small forwithered and forespent,[67]
As is the stalke that sommers drought opprest,
Her wealked[68] face with woful teares besprent,[69]
Her colour pale, and (as it seemd her best)
In woe and playnt reposed was her rest.
And as the stone that droppes of water weares,
So dented were her cheekes with fall of teares.

Her iyes swollen with flowing streames aflote,
Wherewith her lookes throwen vp full piteouslye,
Her forceles handes together ofte she smote,
With dolefull shrikes, that eckoed in the skye:
Whose playnt such sighes dyd strayt accompany,
That in my doome[70] was neuer man did see
A wight but halfe so woe begon as she.

I stoode agast beholding all her plight,
Tweene dread and dolour so distreynd[71] in hart
That while my heares vpstarted with the sight,
The teares out streamde for sorowe of her smart:
But when I sawe no ende that could aparte[72]
The deadly dewle,[73] which she so sore dyd make,
With dolefull voice then thus to her I spake.

---

[61] lights.
[62] brought back.
[63] describe.
[64] creature.
[65] wasted utterly.
[66] burst.
[67] exhausted.
[68] withered.
[69] sprinkled.
[70] judgment.
[71] distressed, torn asunder.
[72] separate.
[73] lamentation.

Vnwrap thy woes what euer wight thou be
And stint[74] betime to spill[75] thy selfe wyth playnt,
Tell what thou art, and whence, for well I see
Thou canst not dure[76] wyth sorowe thus attaynt.
She looked vp, and prostrate as she laye
With piteous sound loe thus she gan to saye.

Alas, I wretche whom thus thou seest distreyned
With wasting woes that neuer shall aslake,[77]
Sorrowe I am, in endeles tormentes payned,
Among the furies in the infernall lake:
Where Pluto god of Hel so griesly blacke
Doth holde his throne, and *Letheus* deadly taste
Doth rieue[78] remembraunce of eche thyng forepast.

Whence come I am, the drery destinie
And luckeles lot for to bemone of those,
Whom Fortune in this maze of miserie
Of wretched chaunce most wofull myrrours chose
That when thou seest how lightly they did lose
Theyr pompe, theyr power, and that they thought most sure,
Thou mayest soone deeme no earthly ioye may dure.

Whose rufull voyce no sooner had out brayed[79]
Those wofull wordes, wherewith she sorrowed so,
But out alas she shryght[80] and never stayed,[81]
Fell downe, and all to dasht[82] her selfe for woe.
The colde pale dread my lyms gan overgo,
And I so sorrowed at her sorowes eft,[83]
That what with griefe and feare my wittes were reft.

I strecht my selfe, and strayt my hart reuiues,
That dread and dolour erst did so appale,[84]
Lyke him that with the feruent feuer stryves
When sickenes seekes his castell health to skale:
With gathered spirites so forst I feare to auale.[85]
And rearing her with anguishe all fordone,[86]
My spirits returnd, and then I thus begonne.

O Sorrowe, alas, sith Sorrowe is thy name,
And that to thee this drere doth well pertayne,
In vayne it were to seeke to ceas the same:
But as a man hym selfe with sorrowe slayne,
So I alas do comfort thee in payne,
That here in sorrowe art forsonke so depe
That at thy sight I can but sigh and wepe.

---

[74] stop.
[75] destroy.
[76] endure.
[77] diminish.
[78] rob.
[79] called out.
[80] shrieked.
[81] stopped.
[82] dashed in pieces.
[83] again.
[84] grow pale.
[85] yield, subside.
[86] overcome.

I had no sooner spoken of a sike[87]
But that the storme so rumbled in her brest,
As Eolus could neuer roare the like,
And showers downe rayned from her iyen so fast,
That all bedreynt[88] the place, till at the last
Well eased they the dolour of her minde,
As rage of rayne doth swage[89] the stormy wynde.

For furth she paced in her fearfull tale:
Cum, cum, (quod she) and see what I shall shewe,
Cum heare the playning, and the bytter bale
Of worthy men, by Fortune ouerthrowe.
Cum thou and see them rewing al in rowe.
They were but shades that erst in minde thou rolde.
Cum, cum with me, thine iyes shall them beholde.

What could these wordes but make me more agast?
To heare her tell whereon I musde while eare?[90]
So was I mazed therewyth, tyll at the last,
Musing vpon her wurdes, and what they were,
All sodaynly well lessoned was my feare:
For to my minde returned howe she telde
Both what she was, and where her wun[91] she helde.

Whereby I knewe that she a Goddesse was,
And therewithall resorted to my minde
My thought, that late presented me the glas
Of brittle state, of cares that here we finde,
Of thousand woes to silly[92] men assynde:
And howe she nowe byd me come and beholde,
To see with iye that erst in thought I rolde.

Flat downe I fell, and with al reuerence
Adored her, perceyuing nowe that she
A Goddesse sent by godly prouidence,
In earthly shape thus showed her selfe to me,
To wayle and rue this worldes vncertayntye:
And while I honourd thus her godheds might,
With playning voyce these wurdes to me she shryght.

I shal the guyde first to the griesly lake,
And thence vnto the blisfull place of rest.
Where thou shalt see and heare the playnt they make,
That whilom here bare swinge[93] among the best.
This shalt thou see, but great is the vnrest
That thou must byde before thou canst attayne
Vnto the dreadfull place where these remayne.

And with these wurdes as I vpraysed stood,
And gan to folowe her that strayght furth paced,

87 *sike*] *stike* STC 1248: sigh.
88 drenched.
89 assuage.
90 formerly.
91 abode.
92 helpless, miserable.
93 sway.

Eare I was ware, into a desert wood
We nowe were cum: where hand in hand imbraced,
She led the way, and through the thicke so traced,
As but I had bene guyded by her might,
It was no waye for any mortall wight.

But loe, while thus amid the desert darke,
We passed on with steppes and pace vnmete:
A rumbling roar confusde with howle and barke
Of Dogs, shoke all the ground vnder our feete,
And stroke the din within our eares so deepe,
As halfe distraught vnto the ground I fell,
Besought retourne, and not to visite hell.

But she forthwith vplifting me apace
Remoued my dread, and with a stedfast minde,
Bad me come on, for here was now the place,
The place where we our trauayle ende should finde.
Wherewith I arose, and to the place assynde
Astoynde[94] I stalke, when strayt we approched nere
The dredfull place, that you wil dread to here.[95]

An hydeous hole al vaste, withouten shape,
Of endles depth, orewhelmde with ragged stone,
Wyth ougly mouth, and grisly Iawes doth gape,
And to our sight confounds it selfe in one.
Here entred we, and yeding[96] forth, anone
An horrible lothly lake we might discerne
As blacke as pitche, that cleped[97] is Auerne.

A deadly gulfe where nought but rubbishe growes,
With fowle blacke swelth[98] in thickned lumpes that lyes,
Which vp in the ayer such stinking vapors throwes
That ouer there, may flye no fowle but dyes,
Choakt with the pestilent sauours that aryse.
Hither we cum, whence forth we still dyd pace,
In dreadful feare amid the dreadfull place.

And first within the portche and iawes of Hell
Sate diepe Remorse of conscience, al besprent
With teares: and to her selfe oft would she tell
Her wretchedness, and cursing neuer stent[99]
To sob and sigh: but euer thus lament,
With thoughtful care, as she that all in vayne
Would weare and waste continually in payne.

Her iyes vnstedfast rolling here and there,
Whurld on eche place, as place that vengeauns[1] brought,
So was her minde continually in feare,
Tossed and tormented with the tedious thought

---

[94] astonished, stunned.
[95] Sackville's description of hell is based on Virgil, *Aeneid,* vi, 237 ff.
[96] going.
[97] called.
[98] foul water.
[99] ceased.
[1] *vengeauns*] *vegeauns* STC 1248.

Of those detested crymes which she had wrought:
With dreadful cheare[2] and lookes throwen to the skye,
Wyshyng for death, and yet she could not dye.

Next sawe we Dread al tremblyng how he shooke,
With foote vncertayne profered here and there:
Benumde of speache, and with a gastly looke
Searcht euery place al pale and dead for feare,
His cap borne vp with staring of his heare,[3]
Stoynde[4] and amazde at his owne shade for dreed,
And fearing greater daungers than was nede.

And next within the entry of this lake
Sate fell Reuenge gnashing her teeth for yre,
Deuising meanes howe she may vengeaunce take,
Neuer in rest tyll she haue her desire:
But frets within so farforth with the fyer
Of wreaking[5] flames, that nowe determines she,
To dye by death, or vengde by death to be.

When fell Reuenge with bloudy foule pretence[6]
Had showed her selfe as next in order set,
With trembling limmes we softly parted thence,
Tyll in our iyes another sight we met:
When fro my hart a sigh forthwith I fet[7]
Rewing alas vpon the wofull plight
Of Miserie, that next appered in sight.

His face was leane, and sumdeale pyned away,
And eke his handes consumed to the bone,
But what his body was I can not say,
For on his carkas, rayment had he none
Saue cloutes and patches pieced one by one.
With staffe in hand, and skrip[8] on shoulders cast,
His chiefe defence agaynst the winters blast.

His foode for most, was wylde fruytes of the tree,
Vnles sumtime sum crummes fell to his share:
Which in his wallet, long God wote kept he.
As on the which full dayntlye would he fare.
His drinke the running streame: his cup the bare
Of his palme closed, his bed the hard colde grounde.
To this poore life was Miserie ybound.

Whose wretched state when we had well behelde
With tender ruth on him and on his feres,
In thoughtful cares, furth then our pace we helde.
And by and by, an other shape apperes
Of Greedy care, stil brushing vp the breres,[9]

---

2 countenance.
3 his hair standing on end.
4 astonished.
5 avenging.
6 purpose, intention.
7 fetched.
8 pouch, bag.
9 briars.

His knuckles knobd, his fleshe deepe dented in,
With tawed[10] handes, and hard ytanned skyn.

The morrowe graye no sooner hath begunne
To spreade his light euen peping in our iyes,
When he is vp and to his worke yrunne,
But let the nightes blacke mistye mantels rise,
And with fowle darke neuer so much disguyse
The fayre bright day, yet ceasseth he no whyle,
But hath his candels to prolong his toyle.

By him lay Heauy slepe the cosin of death
Flat on the ground, and stil as any stone,
A very corps, save yelding forth a breath.
Small kepe tooke he whom Fortune frowned on.
Or whom she lifted vp into the trone[11]
Of high renowne, but as a liuing death,
So dead alyve, of lyef he drewe the breath.

The bodyes rest, the quyete of the hart,
The travayles ease, the still nightes feer[12] was he.
And of our life in earth the better parte,
Reuer[13] of sight, and yet in whom we see
Thinges oft that tide,[14] and ofte that neuer bee.
Without respect esteming equally.
Kyng Cresus pompe, and Irus[15] pouertie.

And next in order sad Olde age we found
His beard al hoare, his iyes hollow and blynde,
With drouping chere still poring on the ground,
As on the place where nature him assinde
To rest, when that the sisters had vntwynde
His vitall threde, and ended with theyr knyfe
The fleting course of fast declining life.

There heard we him with broken and hollow playnt
Rewe with him selfe his ende approching fast,
And all for nought his wretched minde torment.
With swete remembraunce of his pleasures past,
And freshe delites of lusty youth forwaste.
Recounting which, how would he sob and shrike?
And to be yong againe of Ioue beseke.[16]

But and[17] the cruell fates so fixed be
That time forepast can not retourne agayne,
This one request of Ioue yet prayed he:
That in such withered plight, and wretched paine,
As elde[18] (accompanied with his lothsom trayne)[19]
Had brought on him, all were it woe and griefe.
He myght a while yet linger forth his lief,

[10] hardened.
[11] throne.
[12] companion.
[13] robber.
[14] betide, happen.
[15] Irus, the beggar in Homer's *Odyssey*.
[16] beseech.
[17] = an, if.
[18] old age.
[19] *trayne*] *trayne*. STC 1248.

And not so soone descend into the pit:
Where death, when he the mortall corps hath slayne,
With retcheles[20] hande in grave doth couer it,
Thereafter neuer to enioye agayne
The gladsome light, but in the ground ylayne,
In depth of darkenes waste and weare to nought,
As he had neuer into the world been brought.

But who had seene him sobbing, howe he stoode
Vnto him selfe and howe he would bemone
His youth forepast, as though it wrought hym good
To talke of youth, al wer his youth foregone,
He would haue mused, and meruayld much whereon
This wretched age should life desyre so fayne,
And knowes ful wel life doth but length his payne.

Crookebackt he was, toothshaken, and blere iyed,
Went on three feete, and sometime crept on fower,
With olde lame bones, that ratled by his syde,
His skalpe all pilde,[21] and he with elde forlore:
His withered fist stil knocking at deathes dore,
Fumbling and driueling as he drawes his breth,
For briefe the shape and messenger of death.

And fast by him pale Maladie was plaste,
Sore sicke in bed, her colour al forgone,
Bereft of stomake, sauor, and of taste,
Ne could she brooke no meat but brothes alone.
Her breath corrupt, her kepers euery one
Abhorring her, her sickenes past recure,[22]
Detesting phisicke, and all phisickes cure.

But oh the doleful sight that then we see,
We turnde our looke and on the other side
A griesly shape of Famine mought[23] we see,
With greedy lookes, and gaping mouth that cryed,
And roard for meat as she should there haue dyed,
Her body thin and bare as any bone,
Wherto was left nought but the case alone.

And that alas was knawen on euery where,
All full of holes, that I ne mought refrayne
From teares, to se how she her armes could teare
And with her teeth gnashe on the bones in vayne:
When all for nought she fayne would so sustayne
Her starven corps, that rather seemde a shade,
Then any substaunce of a creature made.

Great was her force whom stonewall could not stay,
Her tearyng nayles snatching at all she sawe:

---

[20] reckless, careless.
[21] bald.
[22] remedy.
[23] might.

With gaping Iawes that by no meanes ymay
Be satisfyed from hunger of her mawe,
But eates her selfe as she that hath no lawe:
Gnawyng alas her carkas all in vayne,
Where you may count eche sinow, bone, and vayne.

On her while we thus firmely fixt our iyes,
That bled for ruth of such a drery sight,
Loe sodaynelye she shryght in so huge wyse,
As made hell gates to shyver with the myght.
Wherewith a darte we sawe howe it did lyght[24]
Ryght on her brest, and therewithal pale death
Enthryllyng[25] it to reve her of her breath.

And by and by a dum dead corps we sawe,
Heauy and colde, the shape of death aryght,
That dauntes all earthly creatures to his lawe:
Agaynst whose force in vayne it is to fyght:
Ne piers, ne princes, nor no mortall wyght,
No townes, ne realmes, cities ne strongest tower,
But al perforce must yeeld vnto his power.

His Dart anon out of the corps he tooke,
And in his hand (a dreadfull sight to see)
With great tryumphe eftsones the same he shooke,
That most of all my feares affrayed[26] me:
His bodie dight with nought but bones perdye
The naked shape of man there sawe I playne,
All save the fleshe, the synowe, and the vayne.

Lastly stoode Warre in glitteryng armes yclad.
With visage grym, sterne lookes, and blackely hewed
In his right hand a naked sworde he had,
That to the hiltes was al with blud embrewed:
And in his left (that kinges and kingdomes rewed)
Famine and fyer he held, and therewythall
He razed townes, and threwe downe towers and all.

Cities he sakt, and realmes that whilom flowred,
In honor, glory, and rule above the best,
He overwhelmde, and all theyr fame deuowred,
Consumed, destroyed, wasted, and neuer ceast,
Tyll he theyr wealth, theyr name, and all opprest.
His face forhewed with woundes, and by his side,
There hunge his targe with gashes depe and wyde.

In mids of which, depaynted there we founde
Deadly debate, al ful of snaky heare,
That with a blouddy fillet was ybound,
Outbrething nought but discord euery where.
And round about were portrayd here and there
The hugie hostes, Darius and his power,
His kynges, prynces, his pieres, and all his flower.

---

[24] *light*] *light.* STC 1248.

[25] piercing.

[26] frightened.

Whom great Macedo[27] vanquisht there in sight,
With diepe slaughter, dispoylyng all his pryde,
Pearst through his realmes, and daunted all his might.
Duke Hanniball beheld I there beside,
In Cannas field, victor howe he did ride,
And woful Romaynes that in vayne withstoode
And Consull Paulus[28] covered all in blood.

Yet sawe I more the fight at Trasimene,[29]
And Trebery fyeld,[30] and eke when Hanniball
And worthy Scipio last in armes were seene
Before Carthago gate, to trye for all
The worldes empyre, to whom it should befal.
There sawe I Pompeye, and Cesar clad in armes,
Theyr hostes alyed and al theyr civil harmes.

With conquerours hands forbathde in their owne blood,
And Cesar weping ouer Pompeyes head.
Yet sawe I Scilla and Marius where they stoode,
Theyr great crueltie, and the diepe bludshed
Of frendes: Cyrus I sawe and his host dead,
And howe the Queene with great despyte hath flonge
His head in bloud of them she overcome.

Xerxes the Percian kyng yet sawe I there
With his huge host that dranke the riuers drye,
Dismounted hilles, and made the vales vprere,
His hoste and all yet sawe I slayne perdye.
Thebes I sawe all razde howe it dyd lye
In heapes of stones, and Tyrus put to spoyle,
With walles and towers flat euened with the soyle.

But Troy alas (me thought) aboue them all,
It made myne iyes in very teares consume:
When I beheld the wofull werd befall,
That by the wrathfull wyl of Gods was come:
And Ioves vnmooved sentence and foredoome
On Priam kyng, and on his towne so bent.
I could not lyn,[31] but I must there lament.

And that the more sith destinie was so sterne
As force perforce,[32] there might no force auayle,
But she must fall: and by her fall we learne,
That cities, towres, wealth, world, and al shall quayle.[33]
No manhoode, might, nor nothing mought preuayle,
Al were there prest[34] ful many a prynce and piere
And many a knight that solde his death full deere.

---

27 Alexander the Great, of Macedon.
28 Lucius Paulus, killed in the battle of Cannae.
29 *Trasimene,*] *Trasimene*. STC 1248.
30 Trebia, a river in Italy, where Hannibal defeated the Romans.
31 cease.
32 *perforce,*] *perfore,* STC 1248.
33 decline.
34 ready.

Not wurthy Hector wurthyest of them all,
Her hope, her ioye, his force is nowe for nought.
O Troy, Troy, there is no boote but bale,[35]
The hugie horse within thy walles is brought:
Thy turrets fall, thy knightes that whilom fought
In armes amyd the fyeld, are slayne in bed,
Thy Gods defylde, and all thy honour dead.

The flames vpspring, and cruelly they crepe
From wall to roofe, til all to cindres waste,
Some fyer the houses where the wretches slepe,
Sum rushe in here, sum run in there as fast.
In euery where or sworde or fyer they taste.
The walles are torne, the towers whurld to the ground,
There is no mischiefe but may there be found.

Cassandra yet there sawe I howe they haled
From Pallas house, with spercled[36] tresse vndone,
Her wristes fast bound, and with Greeks rout[37] empaled:[38]
And Priam eke in vayne howe he did runne
To armes, whom Pyrrhus with despite hath done
To cruel death, and bathed him in the bayne[39]
Of his sonnes blud before the altare slayne.

But howe can I descryve[40] the doleful sight,
That in the shylde so liuelike fayer did shyne?
Sith in this world I thinke was neuer wyght
Could haue set furth the halfe, not halfe so fyne.
I can no more but tell howe there is seene
Fayer Ilium fal in burning red gledes[41] downe,
And from the soyle great Troy Neptunus towne.

Herefrom when scarce I could mine iyes withdrawe
That fylde with teares as doeth the spryngyng well,
We passed on so far furth tyl we sawe
Rude Acheron, a lothsome lake to tell
That boyles and bubs[42] vp swelth[43] as blacke as hell,[44]
Where grisly Charon at theyr fixed tide
Stil ferreies ghostes vnto the farder side.[45]

The aged God no sooner sorowe spyed,
But hasting strayt vnto the banke apace
With hollow call vnto the rout he cryed,
To swarve apart, and geue the Goddesse place.
Strayt it was done, when to the shoar we pace,
Where hand in hand as we then linked fast,
Within the boate we are together plaste.

---

[35] there is no remedy but affliction.
[36] sparkled, flowing.
[37] troop.
[38] hemmed in.
[39] bath.
[40] describe.
[41] glowing ashes.
[42] bubbles.
[43] filth.
[44] *hell,*] *hell.* STC 1248.
[45] *side.*] *side,* STC 1248.

And furth we launch ful fraughted to the brinke,
Whan with the vnwonted weyght, the rustye keele
Began to cracke as if the same should sinke.
We hoyse vp mast and sayle, that in a whyle[46]
We fet[47] the shore, where scarcely we had while
For to arryve, but that we heard anone
A thre sound barke confounded al in one.

We had not long furth past, but that we sawe,
Blacke Cerberus the hydeous hound of hell,
With bristles reard, and with a thre mouthed Iawe,
Foredinning the ayer[48] with his horrible yel.
Out of the diepe darke cave where he did dwell,
The Goddesse strayt he knewe, and by and by
He peaste[49] and couched, while that we passed by.

Thence cum we to the horrour and the hel,
The large great kyngdomes, and the dreadful raygne
Of Pluto in his trone where he dyd dwell,
The wyde waste places, and the hugye playne:
The waylinges, shrykes, and sundry sortes of payne,
The syghes, the sobbes, the diepe and deadly groane,
Earth, ayer, and all resounding playnt and moane.

Here pewled the babes, and here the maydes vnwed
With folded handes theyr sory chaunce bewayled,
Here wept the gyltles slayne, and louers dead,
That slewe them selues when nothyng els auayled;
A thousand sortes of sorrowes here that wayled
With sighes and teares, sobs, shrykes, and all yfere,[50]
That (oh alas) it was a hel to heare.

We stayed vs strayt, and wyth a rufull feare,
Beheld this heauy sight, while from mine eyes,
The vapored teares downstilled here and there,
And Sorowe eke in far more woful wyse[51]
Tooke on with playnt, vp heauing to the skyes
Her wretched handes, that with her crye the rout
Gan all in heapes to swarme vs round about.

Loe here (quoth Sorowe) Prynces of renowne,
That whilom[52] sat on top of Fortunes wheele
Nowe layed ful lowe, like wretches whurled downe,
Euen with one frowne, that stayed but with a smyle,
And nowe behold the thing that thou erewhile,
Saw only in thought, and what thou now shalt heare
Recompt[53] the same to Kesar, King, and Pier.

Then first came Henry duke of Buckingham,
His cloke of blacke al pilde[54] and quite forworne,

[46] *whyle*] *whyle*. STC 1248.
[47] reached.
[48] making a great noise in the air.
[49] became still.
[50] together.
[51] *wyse*] *wyse*. STC 1248.
[52] formerly, at times.
[53] recount.
[54] torn, threadbare.

Wringing his handes, and Fortune ofte doth blame,
Which of a duke[55] hath made him nowe her skorne.
With gastly lookes as one in maner lorne,
Oft spred his armes, stretcht handes he ioynes as fast,
With ruful chere,[56] and vapored eyes vpcast.

His cloke he rent, his manly breast he beat,
His heare al torne about the place it laye,
My hart so molte[57] to see his griefe so great,
As felingly me thought it dropt awaye:
His iyes they whurled about withouten staye,
With stormy syghes the place dyd so complayne,
As if his hart at eche had burst in twayne.

Thryse he began to tell his doleful tale,
And thrise the sighes did swalowe vp his voyce,
At eche of which he shryked so wythal
As though the heauens rived with the noyse:
Tyll at the last recovering his voyce,
Supping[58] the teares that all his brest beraynde
On cruel Fortune weping thus he playnde.

HOW THOMAS WOLSEY DID ARISE VNTO GREAT AUTHORITY AND GOUERNMENT, HIS MANER OF LIFE, POMPE, AND DIGNITY, AND HOW HEE FELL DOWNE INTO GREAT DISGRACE, AND WAS ARESTED OF HIGH TREASON[59]

Shall I looke on, when states[60] step on the stage,
And play theyr parts, before the peoples face?
Some men liue now, scarce four score years of age,
Who in time past, did know the Cardnalls grace.
A gamesom worlde, when Byshops run at bace,[61]
Yea, get a fall, in striuing for the gole,
And body loase, and hazarde seely[62] sole.

Ambitious minde, a world of wealth would haue,
So scrats[63] and scrapes, for scorfe,[64] and scoruy drosse:
And till the flesh, and bones, be layde in graue,
Wit neuer rests, to grope for mucke and mosse.
Fye on prowde pompe, and gilted bridels bosse:[65]
O glorious golde, the gaping after thee,
So blindes mens eyes, they can no daunger see.

Now note my byrth, and marke how I began,
Beholde from whence, rose all this pryde of mine.
My father but, a playne poore honest man,

55 Buckingham.
56 countenance.
57 melted.
58 consuming.
59 *The mirror for magistrates,* 1587, STC 13445, Huntington Library; by Churchyard.
60 persons of high rank.
61 A boys' game.
62 blessed.
63 struggles to get money.
64 scurf, worthless things.
65 Raised ornaments on bridle.

And I his son, of wit and iudgement fine,
Brought vp at schoole, and prou'd a good diuine:
For which great gifts, degree of schoole I had,
And Batchler was, and I a litle lad.

So, tasting some, of Fortunes sweete consayts,[66]
I clapt the hoode, on shoulder, braue as Son,[67]
And hopt at length, to bite at better bayts,
And fill my mouth, ere banket halfe were don.
Thus holding on, the course I thought to ron:
By many a feast, my belly grue so big,
That *Wolsey* streight,[68] became a wanton[69] twig.[70]

Lo what it is, to feede on daynty meate,
And pamper vp, the gorge,[71] with suger plate:[72]
Nay, see how lads, in hope of higher seate
Rise early vp, and study learning late.
But hee thriues best, that hath a blessed fate,
And hee speeds[73] worst, that worlde will nere aduance,
Nor neuer knowes, what meanes good lucke nor chaunce.

My chaunce was great, for from a poore mans son,
I rose aloft, and chopt[74] and chaungde degree:
In *Oxford* first, my famous name begon,
Where many a day, the scholers honourd mee.
Then thought I how, I might a courtier bee:
So came to Court, and fethred there my wing,
With *Henry* th'eight, who was a worthy King.

Hee did with words, assay[75] mee once or twice,
To see what wit, and ready sprite[76] I had:
And when hee saw, I was both graue and wice,
For some good cause, the King was wondrous glad.
Than downe I lookt, with sober countnaunce sad,[77]
But heart was vp, as high as hope could go,
That suttell fox, might win some fauour so.

Wee worke with wiles, the mindes of men like wax,
The fawning whelp, gets many a peece of bred:
Wee follow Kings, with many coning knacks,[78]
By searching out, how are theyr humours fed.
Hee haunts no Court, that hath a doltish hed:
For as in golde, the pretious stone is set,
So finest wits, in Court the credit get.

I quickly learnde, to kneele and kysse the hand,
To waite at heele, and turne like top about,
To stretch out necke, and lyke an Image stand,

---

66 conceits, inventions.
67 as finely arrayed as the sun.
68 straightway.
69 luxury-loving.
70 slender shoot (used figuratively).
71 stomach.
72 A confection of sugar flavored with orange.
73 fares, succeeds.
74 bartered (but in this alliterative phrase the meaning has grown indistinct).
75 test.
76 spirit.
77 serious, grave.
78 cunning tricks.

To taunt, to skoffe, and face the matter out,
To preace[79] in place, among the greatest rout:[80]
Yet like a priest, my selfe did well behaue,
In fayre long gowne, and goodly garments graue.

Where *Wolsey* went, the world like Bees would swarme,
To heare my speach, and note my nature well.
I coulde with tongue, vse such a kinde of charme,
That voyce full cleare, should sounde like siluer bell.
When head deuisde, a long discours to tell,
With stories straunge, my speach should spised bee,
To make the worlde, to muse the more on mee.

Each tale was sweete, each worde a sentence[81] wayde,
Each eare I pleasde, each eye gaue mee the vewe,
Each Iudgment markt, and paysed[82] what I sayde,
Each minde I fed, with matter rare and newe,
Each day and howre, my grace and credit grewe:
So that the King, in hearing of this newes,
Deuysed howe, hee might my seruice vse.

Hee made mee then, his Chaplayne, to say masse
Before his grace, yea twise or thrise a weeke:
Now had I time, to trym[83] my selfe by glasse,[84]
Now founde I meane, some liuing for to seeke,
Now I became, both humble, mylde, and meeke,
Now I applyde, my wyts and sences throwe,[85]
To reape some corne, if God would speede[86] the plowe.

Whom most I sawe, in fauour with the King,
I followde fast, to get some hap thereby:
But I obserude, a nother fyner thing,
That was, to keepe, mee styll in Princes eye.
As vnder wyng, the hawke in winde doth lye,
So for a pray, I prowlled here and there,
And tryed frendes, and Fortune euery where.

The King at length, sent mee beyonde the seas,
Embastour[87] then, with message good and greate:
And in that time, I did the King so pleas,
By short dispatch, and wrought so fine a feate,
That did aduaunce my selfe to higher seate,
The deanrie then, of *Lincolne* hee me gaue:
And bownty shewde, before I gan to craue.

His Amner[88] to, hee made mee all in haste,
And threefolde gyftes, hee threwe vpon mee still:
His counslour straight, listewise was *Wolsey* plaste,
Thus in shorte time, I had the world at will:

---

79 push forward.
80 crowd, throng.
81 meaning.
82 weighed.
83 attire.
84 mirror.
85 thoroughly.
86 aid.
87 ambassador.
88 almoner.

Which passed far, mans reason, wit, and skill.
O hap, thou haste, great secrets in thy might,
Which long lye hyd, from wily worldlyngs sight.

As shures of raine, fall quickly on the grasse,
That fading flowres, are soone refresht thereby:
Or as with Sun, the morning dewe doth passe,
And quiet calme, makes cleare a troubled skye:
So Princes powre, at twinkling of an eye
Sets vp a lofte, a favret on the wheele,
When giddy braynes, about the streetes doe reele.

They are but blinde, that wake where Fortune sleepes,
They worke in vayne, that striue with streame and tyde:
In double garde, they dwell, that destnye keepes,
In simple sorte,[89] they liue that lacke a gyde:
They misse the marke, that shoote theyr arrowes wide,
They hit the pricke,[90] that make theyr flight to glaunce
So nere the white, that shafte may light on chaunce.

Such was my lucke, I shot no shafte in vayne,
My bow stoode bent, and brased[91] all the yeere:
I wayted harde, but neuer lost my payne:
Such wealth came in, to beare the charges cleere.
And in the end, I was the greatest peere
Among them all, for I so rulde the land,
By Kings consent, that all was in my hand.

Within on yeare, three Bishoprickes I had,
And in small space, a Cardnall I was made:
With long red robes, rich *Wolsey* then was clad,
I walkte in Sun, when others sate in shade:
I went abroade, with such a trayne and trade,[92]
With crosses borne, before mee where I past,
That man was thought, to bee some God at last.

With sonnes of Earles, and Lordes I serued was,
An hundreth chaynes,[93] at leaste were in my trayne:
I dayly dranke, in gold, but not in glas,
My bread was made, of fynest flowre and grayne:
My daynty mouth, did common meates disdayne,
I fed like Prince, on fowles most deare and straunge,
And bankets made, of fine conceites for chaunge.

My hall was full, of Knightes, and Squires of name,
And gentlemen, two hundreth tolde by powle:[94]
Tale yeomen to, did howrely serue the same,
Whose names each weeke, I saw within checke rowle.
All went to church, when seruis bell did knowle,

---

[89] manner.
[90] Spot in the center of a target.
[91] braced, tightened.
[92] body of retainers, coming and going.
[93] Gold chains were worn by gentlemen; the wealthy sometimes provided them for their retainers.
[94] counted exactly (literally, "by poll," head).

All dinde and supte, and slepte at Cardnalls charge,
And all would wayte, when *Wolsey* tooke his barge.

My householde stuffe, my wealth and siluer plate,
Mighte well suffice, a Monarke at this day:
I neuer fed, but vnder cloth of state,
Nor walkt abroade, till Vshars clearde the way.
In house I had, musitions for to play,
In open streete, my trompets lowde did sownde,
Which pearst the skies, and seemde to shake the grownde.

My men most braue,[95] martcht two and two in ranke,[96]
Who helde in length, much more then half a mile:
Not one of these, but gaue his maister thanke,
For some good turne, or pleasure got some while.
I did not feede, my seruantes with a smile,
Or glosing[97] wordes, that neuer bring forth frute,
But gaue them golde, or else preferde theyr sute.

In surety so, whiles God was pleasde, I stoode,
I knewe I must, leaue all my wealth behinde:
I sawe they lou'd, mee not for byrth or bloode,
But serude a space, to try my noble minde.
The more men gieue, the more in deede they finde
Of loue, and troth, and seruice, euery way:
The more they spare, the more doth loue decay.

I ioyde to see, my seruantes thriue so well,
And go so gay, with little that they gote:
For as I did, in honour still excell,
So would I oft, the wante of seruantes note:
Which made my men, on maister so to dote,
That when I sayde, let such a thing bee donne,
They would in deede, through fyre and water ronne.

I had in house, so many ofsars still,
Which were obayde, and honourde for their place,
That carelesse I, might sleepe or walke at will,
Saue that sometyme, I wayde a poore mans case,
And salude such sores, whose griefe might breede disgrace.
Thus men did wayte, and wicked world did gaze,
On mee and them, that brought vs all in maze.

For worlde was whist,[98] and durst not speake a woorde
Of that they sawe, my credite curbde them so:
I waded far, and passed ore the foorde,
And mynded not, for to returne I troe.[99]
The worlde was wise, yet scarce it selfe did knoe,
When wonder made, of men that rose by hap:
For Fortune rare, falls not in each mans lap.

---

95 finely arrayed.
96 order.
97 flattering.
98 silenced.
99 trow, believe; here, "assure you."

I climde the clouds, by knowledge and good wit,
My men sought chaunce, by seruice or good lucke:
The worlde walkte lowe, when I aboue did sit,
Or downe did come, to trample on this mucke:
And I did swim, as dainty as a ducke,
When water serues, to keepe the body braue,
And to enioy, the gyftes that Fortune gaue.

And though my pompe, surpast all Prelates nowe,
And like a Prince, I liu'd and pleasure tooke:
That was not sure, so great a blur[1] in browe,
If on my workes, indiffrent[2] eyes doe looke.
I thought great scorne, such liuings heare to brooke,[3]
Except I built, some howses for the poore,
And order tooke, to gieue great almes at doore.

A Colledge fayre,[4] in *Oxford* I did make,
A sumptuous house, a stately worke in deede.
I gaue great lands, to that, for learning sake,
To bring vp youth, and succour scholers neede.
That charge of myne, full many a mouth did feede,
When I in Courte, was seeking some good turne,
To mend my torch, or make my candell burne.

More houses gay, I builte, then thowsands do
That haue enough, yet will no goodnes shoe:
And where I built, I did mayntayne it to,
With such great cost, as few bestowes I troe.
Of buildings large, I could reherse a roe,
That by mischaunce, this day haue lost my name,
Whereof I do, deserue the only fame.

And as for sutes, about the King was none
So apte as I, to speake and purchase grace.
Though long before, some say *Shores* wife[5] was one,
That oft kneelde downe, before the Princes face
For poore mens sutes, and holpe theire woefull case,[6]
Yet shee had not, such credite as I gate,
Although a King, would heare the parret prate.

My wordes were graue, and bore an equall poyes,
In ballaunce iust,[7] for many a weighty cause:
Shee pleasde a Prince, with pretty merry toyes,
And had no sight, in state, nor course of lawes.
I coulde perswade, and make a Prince to pawes,
And take a breath, before hee drew the sworde,
And spy the time, to rule him with a worde.

I will not say, but fancy may do much,
Yet worlde will graunt, that wisdom may do more:

[1] stain.
[2] impartial.
[3] enjoy.
[4] Christ Church.
[5] Jane Shore, mistress of Edward IV. The preceding poem in this edition of the *Mirror* is Churchyard's *Shore's Wife*.
[6] condition.
[7] exact.

To wanton gyrls, affection is not such,
That Princes wise, will bee abusde[8] therefore:
One sute of mine, was surely worth a score
Of hers indeede, for shee her time must watch,
And at all howres, I durst go draw the latch.

My voyce but heard, the dore was open streyght,
Shee might not come, till shee were calde or brought;
I rulde the King, by custom, arte, and sleight,[9]
And knew full well, the secrets of his thought.
Without my minde, all that was done was nought,
In wars or peace, my counsayle swayed all,
For still the King, would for the Cardnall call.

I kept a court, my selfe, as great as his,
(I not compare, vnto my maister heere)
But looke my Lords, what liuely worlde was this,
That one poore man, became so great a peere?
Yet though this tale, be very straunge to heere,
Wit wins a worlde: and who hath hap and wit,
With triumph longe, in Princely throne may sit.

What man like mee, bare rule in any age,
I shone like Sun, more cleare then morning star:
Was neuer parte, so playde in open stage
As mine, nor fame, of man flewe halfe so far.
I sate on bench, when thowsands at the bar
Did pleade for right: for I in publique weale
Lorde Chaunclour was, and had the great broad seale.[10]

Now haue I tolde, how I did rise aloft,
And sate with pride, and pomp, in golden hall,
And set my feete, on costly carpets soft,
And playde at goale, with goodly golden ball:
But after, Lord, I must rehearse my fall.
O trembling heart, thou canst not now for teares
Present that tale, vnto the hearers eares.

Best weepe it out, and sodayne silence keepe,
Till priuy pangs, make pinched heart complayne:
Or cast thy selfe, into some slumbring sleepe,
Till wakened wits, remembraunce bring agayne.
When heauy tears, do hollow cheekes distayne,[11]
The world will thinke, thy sprits[12] are growne so weake,
The feeble tongue, hath sure no powre to speake.

A tale by signes, with sighes and sobs set out,
Moues peoples mindes, to pity plaged men:
With howling voyce, do rather cry and showt,
And so by arte, shew forth thy sorrow then.
For if thou speake, some man will note with pen

8 deceived.
9 cunning.
10 *seale.*] *seale,* STC 13445.
11 discolor.
12 spirits.

What *Wolsey* sayde, and what thrue *Wolsey* downe,
And vnder foote, flings *Wolseys* great renowne.

What force of that, my fall must needs be herd,
Before I fell, I had a time to rise:
As fatall chaunce, and Fortune mee preferd,
So mischiefe came, and did my state despise.
Yf I might pleade, my case among the wise,
I could excuse, right much of mine offence:
But leaue a while, such matter in suspence.

The Pope, or pride, or peeuish parts of mine,
Made King to frowne, and take the seale from mee:
Now seru'd no words, nor pleasaunt speeches fine,
Now *Wolsey,* lo, must needs disgraced bee.
Yet had I leaue (as dolefull prisner free)
To keepe a house (Got wot) with heauy cheere,
Where that I founde, no wine, ne bread, nor beere.

My time was come, I coulde no longer liue,
What should I make, my sorrow further knowne?
Vpon some cause, that King that all did giue
Tooke all agayne, and so possest his owne.
My goods, my plate, and all was ouerthrowne,
And looke what I, had gathred many a day,
Withine one howre, was cleanly[13] swept away.

But harken now, how that my Fortune fell,
To *Yorke* I must, where I the Bishop was:
Where I by right, in grace a while did dwell,
And was in stawle,[14] with honour great to pas.[15]
The Priors then, and Abbots gan to smell,
Howe Cardnall must, bee honourd as hee ought,
And for that day, was great prouision brought.

At *Cawood* then, where I great buildings made,
And did through cause, exspect[16] my stawling day,[17]
The King deuisde, a secrete vnder shade,
Howe Cardnall shoulde, bee reste[18] and brought away.
One *Wealsh* a Knight, came downe in good aray,
And seasned[19] sure, because from Courte hee cam,
On *Wolsey* wolfe, that spoyled many a lam.

Then was I led, toward Courte, like dog in string,
And brought as biefe, that Butcherrowe must see:
But still I hoapt, to come before the King,
And that repayre, was not denyde to mee.
But hee that kept, the Towre, my guide must bee.
Ah there I saw, what King thereby did meane,
And so I searcht, yf conscience now were cleane.

---

13 completely.
14 stall.
15 go beyond all bounds.
16 await.
17 George Cavendish, one of Wolsey's gentleman ushers, writes of this in detail in *The Life and Death of Thomas Wolsey.*
18 arrested.
19 seized.

Some spots I founde, of pryde and popishe partes,
That might accuse, a better man then I:
Now *Oxford* came, to minde, with all theire artes,
And *Cambridge* to, but all not worth a flye:
For schoolemen can, no fowle defects supplye.
My sauce was sowre, though meate before was sweete,
Nowe *Wolsey* lackte, both conning, wit, and spreete.

A deepe conceyte,[20] of that, possest my heade,
So fell I sicke, consumde[21] as some did thinke.
So tooke in haste, my chamber and my bed,
On which deuise,[22] perhaps the worlde might winke.[23]
But in the heart, sharpe sorrow so did sinke,
That gladnes sweete, (forsooke my senses all)
In those extremes, did yeelde vnto my fall.

O let mee curse, the popish Cardnall hat,
Those myters big, beset with pearle and stones,
And all the rest, of trash I know not what,
The saints in shrine, theyr flesh and rotten bones,
The maske of Monkes, deuised for the nones,[24]
And all the flocke, of Freers, what ere they are,
That brought mee vp, and left mee there so bare.

O cursed priestes, that prate for profits sake,
And follow floud, and tyde, where ere it floes:
O marchaunts fine, that do aduauntage take
Of euery grayne, how euer market goes.
O fie on wolues, that march in masking cloes,
For to deuoure, the lambs, when shepperd sleepes,
And woe to you, that promise neuer keepes.

You sayd I should, be reskude if I neede,
And you would curse, with candell, booke, and bell:
But when yee should, now serue my turne indeede,
Yee haue no house, I know not where yee dwell.
O Freers and Monkes, your harbour is in hell,
For in this world, yee haue no rightfull place,
Nor dare not once, in heauen shew your face.

Your fault not halfe, so great as was my pryde,
For which offence, fell *Lucifer* from skyes:
Although I would, that wilfull folly hyde,
The thing lyes playne, before the peoples eyes,
On which hye heart, a hatefull name doth ryes.
It hath beene sayde, of olde, and dayly will,
Pryde goes before, and shame coms after still.

Pryde is a thing, that God and man abores,
A swelling tode, that poysons euery place,

---

20 idea, plan.
21 wasted with disease.
22 plan.
23 close its eyes.
24 occasion.

A stinking wounde, that breedeth many sores,
A priuy plague, found out in stately face,
A paynted byrd, that keepes a pecocks pace,
A lothsome lowt, that lookes like tinkers dog,
A hellish hownd, a swinish hatefull hog

That grunts and groanes, at euery thing it sees,
And holds vp snowt, like pig that coms from draffe.[25]
Why should I make, of pride all these degrees,
That first tooke roote, from filthy drosse and chaffe,
And makes men stay,[26] vpon a broken staffe?
No weakenes more, than thinke to stand vpright,
When stumbling blocke, makes men to fall downe right.

Hee needes must fall, that looks not where hee goes,
And on the starrs, walkes staring goezling[27] like:
On sodayne oft, a blostring tempest bloes,
Than downe great trees, are tumbled in the dike.[28]
Who knowes the time, and howre when God will strike?
Then looke about, and marke what steps yee take,
Before you pace, the pilgrimage yee make.

Run not on head,[29] as all the worlde were youres,
Nor thrust them backe, that cannot bide a shocke:
Who striues for place, his owne decay procures:
Who always brawles, is sure to catch a knocke:
Who beards a King, his head is neere the blocke:
But who doth stand, in feare, and worldly dreede,
Ere mischiefe coms, had neede to take good heede.

I hauing hap,[30] did make account of none,
But such as fed, my humour good or bad.
To fawning doggs, sometimes I gaue a bone,
And flong some scrapps, to such as nothing had:
But in my hands, still kept the golden gad,[31]
That seru'd my turne, and laught the rest to skorne,
As for himselfe, was Cardnall *Wolsey* borne.

No, no, good men, wee liue not for our selues,
Though each one catch, as mutch as hee may get:
Wee ought to looke, to those that diggs and delues,
That alwayes dwell, and liue in endles det.
Yf in such sort, wee would our compas set,
Wee should haue loue, where now but hate wee finde,
And hedstrong will, with cruell hollow minde.

I thought nothing, of duty, loue, or feare,
I snatcht vp all, and alwayes sought to clime:
I punisht all, and would with no man beare,
I sought for all, and so could take the time.[32]

25 refuse, dregs.
26 rely.
27 gosling, young goose, foolish person.
28 ditch.
29 straight forward.
30 good fortune.
31 goad.
32 use the present moment.

I plide the Prince, whiles Fortune was in prime,[33]
I fild the bags, and gold in hoorde I heapt,
Thought not on those, that thresht the corne I reapt.

So all I lost, and all I gat was nought,
And all by pride, and pompe lay in the dust:
I aske you all, what man aliue had thought,
That in this world, had beene so litle trust?
Why, all thinges heare, with time decline they must.
Than all is vaine, so all not worth a flye,
Yf all shall thinke, that all are borne to dye.

Yf all bee bace, and of so small a count,
Why doe wee all, in folly so abound?
Why doe the meane, and mighty seeke to mount,
Beyonde all hope, where is no surety found,
And where the wheele, is alwayes turning round?
The case is plaine, if all bee vnderstood,
Wee are so vaine, wee knowe not what is good.

Yet some will say, when they haue heapes of golde,
With flocks of friends, and seruaunts at theyr call,
They liue like Gods, in pleasure treble folde,
And haue no cause, to finde no fault at all.
O blinde conceite, these gloryes are but small,
And as for friends, they change their mindes so mych,
They stay not long, with neither poore nor rich.

With hope of friends, our selues wee do deceaue,
With feare of foes, we threatned are in sleepe:
But friends speake fayre, yet men alone they leaue
To sinke or swim, to mourne, to laugh, or weepe.
Yet whan foe smiles, the snake begins to creepe,
As world falles out, these dayes in compasse iust,
Wee knowe not howe, the friend or foe to trust.

Both can betray, the truest man aliue,
Both are to doubt, in matters of greate weight,
Both will somtime, for goodes and honour striue,
Both seemeth playne, yet both can shewe great sleight,[34]
Both stoups full lowe, yet both can looke on height,
And best of both, not worth a cracked crowne:
Yet least of both, may loase a walled towne.

Talke not of frends, the name thereof is nought,
Then trust no foes, if frendes theire credit loes:
If foes and frendes, of on[35] bare earth were wrought,
Blame nere of both, though both one nature shoes.
Grace passeth kinde,[36] where grace and vertue floes,
But where grace wantes,[37] make foes and frends alike,
The on drawes sworde, the other sure will strike.

[33] favorable.
[34] deceit.
[35] one.
[36] God's favor surpasses nature.
[37] is lacking.

I prou'd that true, by tryall twenty times,
When *Wolsey* stoode, on top of Fortunes wheele:
But such as to, the height of ladder climes,
Knowe not what led, lies hanging on their heele,
Tell me my mates, that heauy Fortune feele,
Yf rising vp, breede not a gyddy brayne,
And faling downe, bee not a greuous payne.

I tolde you how, from *Cawood* I was led,
And so fell sicke, when I arested was:
What needeth nowe, more wordes heere in bee sed?
I knewe full well, I must to pryson passe,
And sawe my state, as brittell as a glasse:
So gaue vp ghost, and bad the worlde farewell,
Where in, God wot, I could no longer dwell.

Thus vnto dust, and ashes I returnde,
When blase of life, and vitall breath went out,
Like glowing cole, that is to sinders burnde:
All fleshe and bloud, so ende, you neede not dout.
But when the bruite,[38] of this was blowne aboute,
The worlde was glad, the Cardnall was in graue,
This is of worlde, lo all the hope wee haue.

Full many a yeare, the world lookt for my fall,
And whan I fell, I made as great a cracke,
As doth an oake, or mighty tottring wall,
That whirling winde, doth bring to ruin and wracke.
Now babling world, wil talke behinde my backe
A thousand things, to my reproache and shame:
So will it to, of others do the same.

But what of that? the best is wee are gone,
And worst of all, when wee our tales haue tolde,
Our open plagues, will warning bee to none,
Men are by hap, and courage made so bolde:
They thinke all is, theyr owne, they haue in holde.
Well, let them say, and thinke what thing they please,
This weltring[39] world, both flowes and ebs like seas.

[38] rumor.

[39] rolling.

Barnabe Googe

[c. 1540–1594]

THE FIRST twenty years of Queen Elizabeth's reign produced no great poetry. During these two decades hundreds of poets translated into English verse the best that had been written in other languages, and hundreds wrote original verse which was for the most part imitative of Surrey. The verse translations are inferior to the prose translations of the period; and the original verse, imitative or cautiously experimental, marks little advance beyond the verse of *Tottel's Miscellany*.

Although the poets of this period learned their art from *Tottel's Miscellany*, they are in general more serious, more solemnly didactic, than the Tottel poets. In many thousands of lines of melancholy, moralizing verse they repeat the commonplaces about the sorrows of love, the instability of fortune, the brevity of life. Their metrical patterns and rhetorical devices are those of the Tottel poets. Despite the awkwardness and stiffness of much of their verse, with its lumbering or jigging rhythms, its alliterative singsong, some of these poets show here and there a surer sense of rhythm, more flexibility, greater skill in the use of simple, colloquial speech, and in general a growing appreciation of the richness and vigor of Elizabethan English.

Poets fairly representative of the period are Googe, Turberville, Howell, Gascoigne, and the many others—known and unknown—whose verse is included in the miscellanies *The Paradise of Dainty Devices* and *A Gorgeous Gallery of Gallant Inventions*.

Barnabe Googe studied at both universities, and after travel in France and Spain he was taken into the service of his kinsman Lord Burghley. From 1574 to 1585 he was a government official in Ireland. His translation of the now forgotten *Zodiacus Vitae* of Marcellus Palingenius was reprinted several times. In 1563 appeared a volume of original poems, *Eclogues, Epitaphs, and Sonnets*. The eight eclogues, which make up about one-half of the book, are among the earliest examples of pastoral poetry in English. The fifth and sixth eclogues are derived from the prose of Montemayor's *Diana Enamorada*, a book that later influenced many English writers of pastoral verse and prose. The eclogues, as well as the longest poem in the volume, *Cupido Conquered*, are written in lumbering fourteeners. The book contains also a group of poems in a variety of measures—epistles to friends, epitaphs upon famous men, short love poems. In most of his shorter poems as well as in his eclogues, Googe is an earnest moralist. The diction and the metrical patterns are representative of the 1560's.

A convenient modern edition is *Eglogs, Epytaphes, and Sonettes*, ed. Edward Arber, 1871. For discussion see Arber's Introduction; T. P. Harrison, "Googe's *Eglogs* and Montemayor's *Diana*," *University of Texas Studies in English*, v (1925), 68–78; H. H. Hudson, "Sonnets by Barnabe Googe," *PMLA*, xlviii (1933), 293–294; Clay Hunt, "The Elizabethan Background of Neo-Classic Polite Verse," *ELH*, viii (1941), 273–304.

AN EPYTAPHE OF THE DEATH OF NICOLAS GRIMAOLD[1]

Beholde this fletyng world how al things fade,[2]
Howe euery thyng doth passe and weare awaye,
Eche state of lyfe, by comon course and trade,
Abydes no tyme, but hath a passyng daye.
For looke as lyfe, that pleasaunt Dame hath brought,
The pleasaunt yeares, and dayes of lustynes,
So Death our Foe, consumeth all to nought,
Enuyeng these, with Darte doth vs oppresse,
And that whiche is, the greatest gryfe of all,
The gredye Grype,[3] doth no estate respect,
But wher he comes, he makes them down to fall,
Ne stayes he at, the hie sharpe wytted sect.[4]
For yf that wytt, or worthy Eloquens,
Or learnyng deape, could moue hym to forbeare,
O *Grimaold* then, thou hadste not yet gon hence
But heare hadest sene, full many an aged yeare.
Ne had the Muses loste so fyne a Floure,
Nor had *Minerua* wept to leaue the so,
If wysdome myght haue fled the fatall howre,
Thou hadste not yet ben suffred for to go,
A thousande doltysh Geese we myght haue sparde,
A thousande wytles heads, death might haue found
And taken them, for whom no man had carde,
And layde them lowe, in deepe obliuious grounde,
But Fortune fauours Fooles as old men saye
And lets them lyue, and take the wyse awaye.

TO M. HENRYE COBHAM OF THE MOST BLESSED STATE OF LYFE

The happyest lyfe that here we haue,
My *Cobham* yf I shall defyne,
The goodlyest state, twyxte byrth and graue,
Most gracious dayes and swetest tyme,

[1] From *Eglogs, epytaphes, and sonettes,* 1563, STC 12048, Huntington Library.
[2] *fade,*] *fade* STC 12048.
[3] vulture.
[4] class, group.

The fayrest face, of fadynge Lyfe,
Race ryghtlyest ronne, in ruthfull wayes,
The safest meanes to shun all stryfe:
The surest Staffe, in fyckle Dayes:
I take not I as some do take,
To gape and gawne,[5] for Honoures hye,
But Court and *Cayser*[6] to forsake,
And lyue at home, full quyetlye,
I well do mynde, what he once sayde,
Who bad, Courte not in any case,
For Vertue is, in Courtes decayed,
And Vyce with States,[7] hath chyefest place,
Not Courte but Countreye I do iudge,
Is it wheare lyes, the happyest lyfe,
In Countreye growes, no gratynge grudge,
In Countreye standes not sturdye[8] stryfe,
In Countreye, *Bacchus* hath no place,
In Countreye *Venus* hath defecte,[9]
In Countreye *Thraso*[10] hath no grace,[11]
In Countreye fewe of Gnatoes[12] Secte.
But these same foure and many moe,
In Courte, thou shalt be sure to fynde,
For they haue vowed, not thence to goe,
Bycause in Courte, dwels ydle mynde.
In Countreye mayste thou safelye rest,
And flye all these, yf that thou lyste,
The Countrey therfore, iudge I best,
Where godly lyfe, doth vyce resyste,
Where vertuous exercyse with ioye,
Doth spende the yeares that are to run,
Where Vyces fewe, maye the annoye,
This lyfe is best whan all is done.

Ons musynge as I sat, and Candle burnynge bye,
When all were husht I myght discern a symple selye[13] Flye.
That flewe before myne eyes, with free reioysynge Hart,
And here and there, with wings did play as voyde of payne and smart,
Somtyme by me she sat, when she had playde her fyll,
And euer when she rested had aboute she flyttered styll.
When I perceyud her well, reioysyng in her place,
O happy Flye quoth I, and eake, O worme in happy case.
Whiche two of vs is best? I that haue reason? no:
But thou that reason art without and therwith voyde of woe.
I lyue and so doste thou, but I lyue all in payne,

5 stare.
6 Caesar.
7 persons of high rank.
8 stubborn, rebellious.
9 wane or eclipse (of the heavenly bodies).
10 A boastful soldier in Terence, *The Eunuch*.
11 favor.
12 Gnatho, the parasite, a character in Terence, *The Eunuch*.
13 innocent, harmless.

And Subiect am to her alas, that makes my Gryefe her gayne.
Thou lyuest, but feelst no gryefe, no Loue doth the torment,
A happye thynge for me it were, If God were so content.
That thou with Pen, wert placed here and I sat in thy place,
Then I shuld Ioye as thou dost nowe and thou shuldst wayle thy case.

OCULI AUGENT DOLOREM
OUT OF SYGHT, OUT OF MYND

The oftener sene, the more I lust,
The more I lust, the more I smart,
The more I smart, the more I trust,
The more I trust, the heauyer hart,
The heuy hart, breedes myne vnrest,
Thy absence therfore, lyke I best.

The rarer sene, the lesse in mynde,
The lesse in mynde, the lesser payne,
The lesser payne, lesse gryefe I fynd,
The lesser gryefe, the greater gayne,
The greater gayne, the meryer I,
Therefore I wysh thy syght to flye.

The further of, the more I ioye.
The more I ioye, the happyer lyfe,
The happyer lyfe, lesse hurts annoye,
The lesser hurts, pleasure most ryfe,
Suche pleasures ryfe, shall I obtayne
When Distaunce doth depart[14] vs twaine.

THE VNCERTAYNTIE OF LYFE

No vayner thing ther can be found amyd this vale of stryfe,
As Auncient men reporte haue made then truste vncertayne lyfe.
This trew we dayly fynde, by proofes of many yeares,
And many tymes the trothe is tryed, by losse of frendly fears,
Hope who so lyst in lyfe hath but vncertayne stay,[15]
As tayle of Ele that harder held, doth sooner slyde away.
When least we thynk therof, most neare approcheth it,[16]
And sodaynly posses the place, wher lyfe before did sytt:
How many haue byn seen, in Helth to go to rest,
And yet eare mornyng tyde haue ben, with Cruell Death opprest,
How many in their meales, haue Ioyfully ben sett,
That sodaynly in all their Feaste, hath yealded Earth theyr dett.
Syth thus the lyfe is nought, that in this world we trust,
And that for all the pompe and Pryde, the Bodie tournes to dust:
Hope for the lyfe aboue, whiche far surmounteth all.
With vertuous mind await the time, when God, for vs doth call.

---

[14] separate.
[15] *stay,*] *stay.* STC 12048.
[16] *it,*] *it.* STC 12048.

GOYNG TOWARDES SPAYNE

Farewell thou fertyll soyle, that *Brutus*[17] fyrst out founde,
When he poore soule, was driuen clean from out his Countrey ground,[18]
That Northward layst thy lusty sides amyd the ragyng Seas,[19]
Whose welthy Land doth foster vpp, thy people all in ease,
While others scrape and carke[20] abroad, theyr symple foode to gett,
And selye Soules take all for good, that commeth to the Net.
Which they with painfull paynes do pynch,[21] in barrain burning Realmes:
While we haue all with out restreint among thy welthy streames.
O blest of God thou Pleasaunt Ile, where welth her self doth dwell:
Wherin my tender yeares I past, I byd thee now farewell.
For Fancy dryues me forth abrode, and byds me take delyght,
In leuyng thee and raungyng far, to se some straunger syght,[22]
And sayth I was not framed[23] heare, to lyue at home with eas:
But passynge foorth for knowledge sake to cut the fomyng seas.

COMMYNG HOME WARDE OUT OF SPAYNE

O ragyng Seas, and myghty Neptunes rayne,
In monstrous Hylles, that throwest thy selfe so hye,
That wyth thy fludes, doest beate the shores of Spayne:
And breake the Clyues, that dare thy force enuie.[24]
Cease now thy rage, and laye thyne Ire a syde,
And thou that hast, the goueruaunce of all,
O myghty God, graunt Wether Wynd and Tyde,
Tyll in my Countreye Coast, our Anker fall.

[17] The grandson of Aeneas and the legendary founder of England.

[18] *ground,*] *ground.* STC 12048.

[19] *Seas,*] *Seas.* STC 12048.

[20] labor painfully.

[21] *pynch,*] *pych,* STC 12048.

[22] *syght,*] *syght.* STC 12048.

[23] made, molded.

[24] oppose.

George Turberville

[c. 1540–c. 1595]

GEORGE TURBERVILLE was educated at Winchester and Oxford, but left without taking a degree. He went to London and lived for a time in one of the Inns of Court. In 1567 three of his books were published: his translations of Ovid's *Heroides* and of Mantuan's *Eclogues* and his *Epitaphs, Epigrams, Songs, and Sonnets,* the last a collection of original poems with a few translations. In 1568, as secretary, he accompanied Queen Elizabeth's ambassador to Russia, where he wrote verse letters and other poems. About 1575 he acquired property in Dorset and lived in retirement. In 1587 appeared his *Tragical Tales,* verse translations from the Italian with a few "epitaphs and sonnets."

Six of the epistles translated from Ovid are in blank verse, but most of his poetry is in poulter's measure and fourteeners. After Sidney and Spenser began to write, Turberville's verse soon seemed old-fashioned, but some of the younger poets remembered him with respect and gratitude. After Turberville's death Sir John Harington wrote:

> When rimes were yet but rude, thy pen endeuored
> To pollish Barbarisme with purer stile:
> When times were grown most old, thy heart perseuered
> Sincere and iust, vnstaind with gifts or guile.

The most useful modern editions are the following: Ovid's *Heroides,* ed. F. S. Boas, 1928; Mantuan's *Eclogues,* ed. Douglas Bush, 1937; *Epitaphs, Epigrams, Songs and Sonnets,* ed. J. P. Collier, 1869; *Tragical Tales,* ed. J. P. Collier, 1867. For biography and criticism see H. E. Rollins, "New Facts About George Turberville," *Modern Philology,* xv (1918), 129; J. E. Hankins, *The Life and Works of George Turberville,* 1940.

VERSE IN PRAYSE OF LORDE HENRYE HOWARDE EARLE OF SURREY[1]

What should I speake in prayse of *Surreys* skill
Unlesse I had a thousand tongues at will?
No one is able to depaint at full,

[1] From *Epitaphes, epigrams, songs and sonets,* 1567, STC 24326, Huntington Library.

The flowing fountaine of his sacred Skull.
Whose Pen approoude what wit he had in mue[2]
Where such a skill in making Sonets grue.
Eche worde in place with such a sleight[3] is coucht,
Eche thing whereof he treates so firmely toucht,
As *Pallas* seemde within his Noble breast
To haue soiournde, and beene a daylie guest.
Our mother tongue by him hath got such light,
As ruder speach thereby is banisht quight:
Reproue him not for fansies that he wrought,
For Fame thereby and nothing else he sought.
What though his verse with pleasant toyes are fright?[4]
Yet was his honours life a Lampe of light.
A Mirrour he the simple sort to traine,
That euer beate his brayne for Britans gaine.
By him the Nobles had their vertues blazde,[5]
When spitefull death their honors liues had razde.
Eche that in life had well deserued aught,
By *Surreys* meanes an endles fame hath caught.
To quite his boone and aye well meaning minde,
Whereby he did his Sequell seeme to binde:[6]
Though want of skill to silence me procures,
I write of him whose fame for aye endures,
A worthie Wight,[7] a Noble for his race,[8]
A learned Lorde that had an Earles place.

THE LOUER TO HIS LADIE THAT GASED MUCH VP TO THE SKIES[9]

My Girle, thou gazest much
  vpon the golden Skies:
Would I were Heauen, I would behold
  thie then with all mine eies.

THAT HE FINDETH OTHERS AS FAIRE, BUT NOT SO FAITHFULL AS HIS FREND[10]

I sundry see for beuties glosse
  that with my mistresse may compare:
But few I finde for true good wil
  that to their frends so frendly are.
Looke what she saies I may assure
  my selfe thereof, she wil not faine:
What others speake is hard to trust
  they measure all their words by gaine.
Her lookes declare her louing minde,
  her countnance and her heart agree:
When others laugh they looke as smooth,
  but loue not halfe so wel as she:

---

[2] in mew, in keeping (a term from falconry).
[3] art, skill.
[4] freighted.
[5] made known.
[6] to repay his goodness, an obligation that he seems to have required of us who follow him.
[7] man.
[8] because of his ancestry.
[9] From the Greek anthology, where it is attributed to Plato.
[10] From *Tragical tales,* 1587, STC 24330, Huntington Library.

The greefe is hers when I am grypte,[11]
my fingers ache is her disease:[12]
With me though others mourne to sight,
yet are their hearts at quiet ease.
So that I marke in Cupids court,
are many faire and fresh to see:
Each where is sowen dame beuties seede
but faire and faithfull few there bee.

TO HIS FREND PROMISING THAT THOUGH HER BEAUTIE FADE, YET HIS LOUE SHALL LAST[13]

I wotte full well that bewtie cannot laste,
No rose that springs, but lightly[14] doth decay,
And feature like a lillie leafe doth waste,
Or as the Cowslip in the midst of May:
I know that tract[15] of time doth conquer all,
And beuties buddes like fading floures do fall.

That famous Dame fayre *Helen,* lost her hewe
When withred age with wrinckles chaungd her cheeks,
Her louely lookes did loathsomnesse ensewe,
That was the *A per se*[16] of all the Greekes:
And sundrie moe that were as fayre as shee
Yet *Helen* was as freshe as fresh might bee.

No force[17] for that, I price your beautie light,
If so I finde you stedfast in good will:
Though fewe there are that doe in age delight,
I was your friend, and so doe purpose still,
No change of lookes shall breede my change of loue
Nor beauties want, my first goodwill remoue.

[11] griped, distressed.
[12] discomfort.
[13] From *Tragical tales*, 1587.
[14] quickly.
[15] duration.
[16] first, best.
[17] matter.

Thomas Howell

[fl. 1568–1581]

THOMAS HOWELL was a minor poet whose verse is more interesting than that of most of his contemporaries. Of his life almost nothing is known except that his birthplace was probably Dunster in Somerset, that he probably spent some time at Oxford, and that for many years he was a gentleman-retainer in the related families of the Earls of Shrewsbury and of Pembroke. He is the author of three small volumes of short poems: *The Arbor of Amity*, 1568; *Pleasant Songs and Pretty Pamphlets*, 1568; *Howell, His Devices*, 1581.

Although he writes the inevitable fourteener, he uses also rhyme royal, the six-line stanza of *Venus and Adonis*, and various other measures; and some of his verse has the grace and flexibility that were to mark the lyric poetry of the eighties and nineties.

The modern editions of Howell are *The Poems of Thomas Howell*, ed. A. B. Grosart, 1879; and *Howell, His Devices*, ed. Sir Walter Raleigh, 1906.

TO THE READER[1]

Where none but Nature is the guyde, *Minerva* hath no parte,
Then you her Nurcelings beare with him, that knows no aide of arte.
I wake my wyts to please my selfe, nought reaking[2] praise or blame,
I force my pen to purge my brayne, though matter small I frame.
In which attempt, if lack of skill, haue led my Muse awry,
Let my well meaning minde the misse, in eche respect supply.
If patterns wrought by Arte, of curious workman here thou seeke,
Thy trauayle then thou shalt but lose, to looke and neuer leeke.
But if good will may thee suffise, peruse, and take thy pleasure,
In Natures schoole my little skill: I learned all by leasure.
Here nothing placed is, that may the vertuous sorte offende,
Though enuious Carpers barke and snarle, at things they scarce can mende.
Whose chiefest grace is wise to seeme, by blotting others deedes,
Whose paynted flowers in proofe full oft, fall out but stincking weedes.
The chaste desyre with honest ryme, mislykes[3] no whitt in minde,
But venomde Spyders poyson take, where Bee doth honey finde.

[1] From *H. his deuises, for his owne exercise, and his friends pleasure*, 1581, STC 13875, Bodleian Library.

[2] recking, heeding.

[3] displeases.

With greater ease a fault is founde, then well to welde[4] the reste:
It differs much to tell the tale, and words misplaste to wreste.
By patterns here displayed to thee, thou mayst perhaps preuente
The poysoning bayts of bitter sweete, whose blisse brings sharp euente.
Disloyall loue and filthie lust, thou here art taught to flee:
With other Sawes to sundry endes, though hewed rough they bee.
That lyfe is lyke a Bubble blowne, or smoke that soone doth passe,
That all our pleasures are but paynes, our glorie brittle glasse.
That Fortunes fruites are variable, no holde[5] in Princely mace:
That womens myndes are mutable, that death drawes on apace.
That worldly pompe is vanity, that youth vnwares decayes:
That high estate is slipperie, that onely vertue stayes,
Here learne thou mayst: with diuers notes, gaynst fraude and flattery,
That may suffise to warne the wise, to voyde such battery.
And eke thou here mayst viewe and see, howe Bewtie cruell haste[6]
Doth make, to shun the gallant face, where she but late was plaste.
That she is Natures prieuledge, and so is sayd to bee
Because she seldom giues that gyfte, but where she cause doth see.
That beawtie is a dumbe disceite, not hauing worde or arte:
And yet with silente crafte she can, perswade the hardest harte.
She conqueres where she coms by kinde:[7] for Creatures faire procure,
By naked lookes, such yeelding harts, as they wishe to allure.
Whose vayne delyghts if thou desier, thy thryfte goes to the grounde.
(And yet by honest loue we see, the greatest wealth is founde.)
Apollos troope my faults will passe, and waye my want herein,
Whose friendly fauor if I gaine, I prise not *Pan* a pin.
The trauell myne, the pleasure thine, if ought thou here doe leeke,
Thy good reporte, for paynes ymployed is sole rewarde I seeke.

A WINTERS MORNING MUSE[8]

As by occasion late, towards *Brutus* Citie[9] olde,
With quiet pace alone I rode, in winter sharp and colde.
In my delating[10] brains, a thousand thoughts were fed,
And battailewise a warre they made, in my perplexed hed.
I thought on tymely change, and musde on yerely waste,
How winter aye deuours the welth, that pleasant sommer plast.
I sawe the naked Fields vnclothde on euery side,
The beaten bushes stand al bare, that late were deckt with pride.
Whose fainting sap was fled, and falne from top to roote,
Eche tree had newe cast of his Cote, and laid him at his foote.
The smale and syllie[11] Byrds, sat houering in the hedge,
And water Fowles by Wynter forst, forsooke the Fenny sedge.
Thus Nature altering quite, her earthly childrens cheere,
Doth shewe what brittle stay of state, and feeble holde is heere.
Who as in slender things, she shewes her yerely might,
So doth she like attempt her force, in all degrees aright.
For as I musing rode, I plainely might perceaue,

---

[4] wield, govern.
[5] defense, protection.
[6] *haste*] *haste:* STC 13875.
[7] nature.
[8] From *H. his deuises*, . . . 1581.
[9] London.
[10] dilating.
[11] weak.

That like both change and chance there was, mans state that did bereaue.[12]
I sawe the mounting minde, that clymbde to reach the Skyes,
Aduanced vp by Fortunes wheele, on tickle[13] stay that lyes,
Fall soone to flat[14] decay, and headlong downe doth reele,
As fickle Fortune list to whyrle, her rounde vnstable wheele.
Was neuer Prince of power, so safe in his degree,
But deemde sometime the meaner sort, to syt more sure than hee.
Then to my selfe I sayde, if Fortune stande vnsure,
And highest type of worldly hap, vncertaine doe endure,[15]
Why thirst we so to raigne? why hunger we for heape?[16]
Why presse we forth for worldly pompe, with brech of quiet sleape?
Which lyke a Mothe eates out, the gaine of godly lyfe,
With all that stretch their vaine desyre, to wrest thys worlde in stryfe.
Whose fruite of toyling paine, by sweate and sorrow sought,
Is lost in twinckling of an eye, our name consumde to nought.
Yea though by worldly wyles, we thousande driftes[17] deuise,
A God there is that laughes to scorne, the wisedome of the wise.
When thus along my waye, I diuersly had musde,
I found whome Fortune high did heaue,[18] on sodaine she refusde.
Then he by Vertue stayde, me thought the rest did passe,
So farre as doth the purest Golde, the vile and basest brasse.
Euen he I deemed blest, that wearing Vertues Crowne,
Doth liue content, not caring ought, how Fortune smile or frowne.

MANS LYFE LIKENED TO A STAGE PLAY[19]

Sithe[20] earth is Stage, whereon we play our partes,
And deedes are deemde according to desartes,
Be warie how thou walkst vpon the same,
In playing thy parte, thy course vprightly frame.

Remember when thy tale is tolde, straight way
Another steps on stage his part to playe,
To whome thou must resigne thy former state,
As one that hath already playde his mate.[21]

All welth, pompe, powre, high hap and princely Mace,
Must yeelden be to such as shall take place,
As things but lente, to play our parts withall,
Our meede no more, then our desarts doe fall.

Not he that playeth the stateliest parte most praise,
Nor he that weares the ryches robe alwaies,
But he whose Vertues shall exceede the reast,
How so his seate be with the great or least.

Take heede therfore, and kepe eche Cue so right,
That Heauen for hyre vnto thy lotte may light.

---

12 impair.
13 insecure.
14 absolute.
15 *endure,*] *endure.* STC 13875.
16 wealth.
17 schemes.
18 lift.
19 From *H. his deuises,* . . . 1581.
20 since.
21 been checkmated, defeated.

With greedie minde so wrest not worldly gayne,
That soule doe spill,[22] for slyding pleasures vayne.

Suffised be with that sufficient is,
And seeke the things that bring eternall blisse,
So shalt thou here not onely purchase prayse,
But after eke enioy most happie dayes.

REWARDE DOTH NOT ALWAYES AUNSWERE DESERTE[23]

Sith my desyre is prest[24] to please,
Though not with glosing[25] showe:
And eke my deeds if proofe were made,
Should tell what fayth I owe,[26]
Whereto shall I impute my hap,
To Fate or wante of skill:
When nought I finde but tickle[27] trust,
Where most I meane good will.

OF THE GOLDEN WORLDE[28]

The golden worlde is past sayth some,
But nowe say I that worlde is come:
Now all things may for Golde be had,
For gayne of Golde, both good and bad.
Now honour hie for Golde is bought,
That earst[29] of greater price was thought.
For Golde the Foole alofte doth rise,
And ofte is plaste aboue the wise.
For Golde the subtile shewe their skill,
For Golde the wicked winne their will.
For Golde who shunnes to wrest a wrong,
And make it seeme as right and strong?
Who spares to pleade as pleaseth thee,
If bring thou doe a golden fee?
The Fatherlesse is quyte forgot,
Where golden giftes doe fall to lot.
For Golde the Wyddow is opprest,
And rightfull heyres are dispossest.
Poore *Irus*[30] cause at dore doth stande,
If *Croesus* come with Golde in hande.
What mischiefe may almost be thought,
That now for Golde not daylie wrought?
A heape of ylles for Golde are clokte,
Yea vice for Golde hath vertue chokte.
For gayne of Golde the Flatterer smyles,
And on thee fawnes with sundry wyles.
I will not here through golden traps,
Say Louers light in Ladies laps.
But briefe to bee, what can you craue,
That now for Golde you may not haue?
Then truth to tell, and not to fayne,
Right now the golden worlde doth raygne.

22 destroy.
23 From *H. his deuises*, . . . 1581.
24 eager.
25 flattering.
26 *owe*,] *owe*. STC 13875: own.
27 insecure.
28 From *H. his deuises*, . . . 1581.
29 formerly.
30 A beggar in Homer's *Odyssey*.

George Gascoigne

[c. 1539–1577]

GEORGE GASCOIGNE was perhaps the best-known English writer of his day and, after Sackville, the most important man of letters between Surrey and Spenser. The son of Sir John Gascoigne of Cardington, Bedfordshire, he spent several years as a student at Trinity College, Cambridge, and at Gray's Inn, to which he was admitted in 1555. From 1557 to 1559 he was a member of Parliament. In 1561 he became the stepfather of the poet Nicholas Breton.

Improvident and quarrelsome, he was in turn a disappointed courtier, an unhappy country gentleman, an unfortunate soldier, and finally a writer perhaps too facile and versatile. Gabriel Harvey, in the marginalia that he wrote in his copy of *The Posies,* attributes Gascoigne's misfortunes to his vanity, levity, and "want of resolution and constancy."

With his friend Francis Kinwelmarsh he wrote in blank verse the tragedy *Jocasta,* a free translation of Lodovico Dolce's Senecan tragedy *Giocasta* which itself is an adaptation of *The Phoenissae* of Euripides. He wrote the prose comedy *Supposes,* a translation of Ariosto's *I Suppositi.* Both plays were performed at Gray's Inn in 1566. He wrote also the school play *The Glass of Government,* printed in 1575. There is no record of when or where this play was presented. He wrote a masque for the double wedding of Viscount Montague's son and daughter in 1572, and he assisted in the preparation of entertainment for Queen Elizabeth at Woodstock and Kenilworth in 1575.

In 1573, while Gascoigne was in Holland, a miscellany was printed with the title *A Hundreth Sundry Flowers,* which contained "divers discourses and verses, invented uppon sundrie occasions, by sundrie gentlemen." It is probable, however, that Gascoigne planned the publication and wrote everything in it. In 1575 the book was reissued, with some alterations and additions, as *The Posies of George Gascoigne Esquire.* In 1576 appeared *The Steel Glass,* a satire in blank verse.

Gascoigne is remarkable for the range and variety of his writing. *The Supposes* is the first prose comedy in English. *Jocasta* is the first example of Greek tragedy on the English stage. *The Adventures of Master F. J.* may be considered the first English novel. *Dan Bartholomew* is the first attempt in English to tell a love story in a series of poems. *Certain Notes of Instruction* is the first treatise on English prosody. *The Steel Glass* is the first original nondramatic blank verse in English.

Most of Gascoigne's poetry is written in rhyme royal, poulter's measure, and blank verse. He prefers iambic measures, the fixed medial caesura, the end-stopped line, natural word order, native and homely words. Despite his vigor, eloquence, and skill, his verse generally exhibits the defects of that of his contemporaries. He is the last—and perhaps the most interesting—of the early Elizabethans.

After the publication of Spenser's *Shepheardes Calender* in 1579, Gascoigne's verse soon became representative of an age that had ended. In the "glosse" to the November eclogue of *The Shepheardes Calender* E. K. calls him "a wittie gentleman, and the very chefe of our late rymers," and Nashe in his preface to Robert Greene's *Menaphon*, 1589, mentions him as the one "who first beate the path to that perfection which our best Poets haue aspired too since his departure."

The standard modern editions are *The Works of George Gascoigne*, ed. J. W. Cunliffe, 2 vol., 1907–1910, and *George Gascoigne's A Hundreth Sundrie Flowres*, ed. C. T. Prouty (University of Missouri Studies, xvii, no. 2), 1942. An early account of Gascoigne is F. E. Schelling, *The Life and Writings of George Gascoigne* (Publications of the University of Pennsylvania), 1893. The most complete account is C. T. Prouty, *George Gascoigne, Elizabethan Courtier, Soldier, and Poet*, 1942. For bibliography see *CBEL*, i, 414–415; S. A. Tannenbaum, *George Gascoigne, A Concise Bibliography*, 1942.

THE ARRAIGNMENT OF A LOUER[1]

At Beautyes barre as I dyd stande,
When false suspect accused mee,
George (quod[2] the Iudge) holde vp thy hande.
Thou art arraignde of Flatterye:
Tell therefore howe thou wylt bee tryde?
Whose iudgment here wylt thou abyde.

My Lorde (quod I) this Lady here,
Whome I esteeme aboue the rest,
Doth knowe my guilte if any were:
Wherefore hir doome[3] shall please me best,
Let hir bee Iudge and Iurour boathe,
To trye mee guiltlesse by myne oathe.

Quod Beautie, no, it fitteth not,
A Prince hir selfe to iudge the cause:

[1] The following five poems are from *The posies of George Gascoigne esquire. Corrected, perfected, and augmented by the authour*, 1575, STC 11636, Morgan Library.

[2] quoth.

[3] judgment.

Wyll is our Iustice well you wot,
Appointed to discusse our Lawes:
If you wyll guiltlesse seeme to goe,
God and your countrey quitte you so.

Then crafte the cryer cal'd a quest,[4]
Of whome was falshoode formost feere,[5]
A packe of pickethankes[6] were the rest,
Which came false witnesse for to beare,
The Iurye suche, the Iudge vniust,
Sentence was sayde I should be trust.

Ielous the Iayler bound mee fast,
To heare the verdite of the byll,
George (quod the Judge) nowe thou art cast,[7]
Thou must goe hence to heauie hill,
And there be hangde all but the head,
God rest thy soule when thou art dead.

Downe fell I then vpon my knee,
All flatte before Dame Beauties face,
And cryed, good Ladye pardon mee,
Which here appeale vnto your grace,
You knowe if I haue beene vntrue,
It was in too much praysing you.

And though this Iudge doe make suche haste,
To shead with shame my guiltlesse blood:
Yet let your pittie first bee plaste,
To saue the man that meant you good,
So shall you shewe your selfe a Queene,
And I maye bee your seruaunt seene.

(Quod Beautie) well: bicause I guesse,
What thou dost meane hencefoorth to bee,
Although thy faultes deserue no lesse,
Than Iustice here hath iudged thee,
Wylt thou be bounde to stynt[8] all strife,
And be true prisoner all thy lyfe?

Yea Madame (quod I) that I shall,
Loe fayth and trueth my suerties:
Why then (quod shee) come when I call,
I aske no better warrantise.
Thus am I Beauties bounden thrall,
At hir commaunde when shee doth call.

[4] inquest.
[5] companion.
[6] flatterers.
[7] convicted.

A STRAUNGE PASSION OF A LOUER

Amid my Bale[9] I bath in blisse,
I swim in heauen, I sinke in hell:
I find amends for euery misse,
And yet my moane no tongue can tell.
I liue and loue, what wold you more:
As neuer louer liu'd before.

I laugh sometimes with little lust,
So iest I oft and feele no ioye:
Myne ease is builded all on trust:
And yit mistrust breedes myne anoye.
I liue and lacke, I lacke and haue:
I haue and misse the thing I craue.

These things seeme strange, yet are they trew,
Beleeue me sweete my state is such,
One pleasure which I wold eschew,
Both slakes my grief and breedes my grutch.[10]
So doth one paine which I would shoon,
Renew my ioyes where grief begoon.

Then like the larke that past the night.
In heavy sleepe with cares opprest:
Yit when shee spies the pleasaunt light,
She sends sweete notes from out hir brest.
So sing I now because I thinke
How ioyes approch, when sorrowes shrinke.

And as fayre *Philomene* againe,
Can watch and singe when other sleepe:
And taketh pleasure in hir payne,
To wray the woo that makes hir weepe.
So sing I now for to bewray[11]
The lothsome life I lead alway.

The which to thee (deare wenche) I write,
That know'st my mirth, but not my moane:
I praye God graunt thee deepe delight,
To liue in ioyes when I am gone.
I cannot liue, it wyll not bee:
I dye to thinke to part from thee.
Ferenda Natura.[12]

[8] stop.
[9] torment.
[10] grudge.
[11] reveal.
[12] *Feranda* STC 11635]; *Ferendo* STC 11636.

THE LULLABIE OF A LOUER

Sing lullaby, as women doe,
Wherewith they bring their babes to rest,
And lullaby can I sing to,
As womanly as can the best.
With lullaby they still the childe,
And if I be not much beguild,
Full many wanton babes haue I,
Which must be stild with lullabie.

First lullaby my youthfull yeares,
It is nowe time to go to bed,
For croocked age and hoary heares,
Have wone the hauen with in my head:
With Lullaby then youth be still,
With Lullaby content thy will,
Since courage quayles, and commes behind,
Go sleepe, and so beguile thy minde.

Next Lullaby my gazing eyes,
Which wonted were to glaunce apace.
For every Glasse maye now suffise,
To shewe the furrowes in my face:
With Lullabye then winke[13] awhile,
With Lullabye your lookes beguile:
Lette no fayre face, nor beautie brighte,
Entice you efte[14] with vayne delighte.

And Lullaby my wanton will,
Lette reasons rule, nowe reigne thy thought,
Since all to late I finde by skyll,[15]
Howe deare I haue thy fansies bought:
With Lullaby nowe tak thyne ease,
With Lullaby thy doubtes appease:
For trust to this, if thou be styll,
My body shall obey thy will.

Eke Lullaby my louing boye,
My little Robyn take thy rest,
Since age is colde, and nothing coye,
Keepe close thy coyne, for so is best:
With Lullaby be thou content,
With Lullaby thy lustes relente,
Lette others pay which hath mo pence,
Thou art to pore for such expence.

Thus Lullabye my youth, myne eyes,
My will, my ware, and all that was,
I can no mo delayes deuise,
But welcome payne, let pleasure passe:
With Lullaby now take your leaue,
With Lullaby your dreames deceiue,
And when you rise with waking eye,
Remember then this Lullabye.

GASCOIGNES GOOD MORROW

You that haue spent the silent night,
In sleepe and quiet rest,
And ioye to see the cheerefull lyght
That ryseth in the East:
Now cleare your voyce, now chere your hart,
Come helpe me nowe to sing:
Eche willing wight come beare a part,
To prayse the heauenly King.

And you whome care in prison keepes,
Or sickenes doth suppresse,
Or secret sorowe breakes your sleepes,
Or dolours doe distresse:
Yet beare a parte in dolfull wise,
Yea thinke it good accorde,
And exceptable sacrifice,
Eche sprite to prayse the lorde.

The dreadfull night with darkesomnesse,
Had ouer spread the light,
And sluggish sleepe with drowsynesse,
Had ouer prest our might:
A glasse wherin you may beholde,
Eche storme that stopes our breath,
Our bed the graue, our clothes lyke molde,
And sleepe like dreadfull death.

Yet as this deadly night did laste,
But for a little space,
And heauenly daye nowe night is past,
Doth shewe his pleasaunt face:
So must we hope to see Gods face,
At last in heauen on hie,
When we haue chang'd this mortall place,
For Immortalitie.

---

[13] close your eyes.
[14] again.
[15] knowledge.

And of such happes and heauenly ioyes,
As then we hope to holde,
All earthly sightes and worldly[16] toyes,
Are tokens to beholde.
The daye is like the daye of doome,
The sunne, the Sonne of man,
The skyes the heauens, the earth the tombe
Wherein we rest till than.

The Rainbowe bending in the skye,
Bedeckte with sundrye hewes,
Is like the seate of God on hye,
And seemes to tell these newes:
That as thereby he promised,
To drowne the world no more,
So by the bloud which Christ hath shead,
He will our helth restore.

The mistie cloudes that fall somtime,
And ouercast the skyes,
Are like to troubles of our time,
Which do but dymme our eyes:
But as suche dewes are dryed vp quite,
When *Phoebus* shewes his face,
So are such fansies put to flighte,
Where God doth guide by grace.

The caryon Crowe, that lothsome beast,
Which cryes agaynst the rayne,
Both for hir hewe and for the rest,
The Deuill resembleth playne:
And as with gonnes we kill the Crowe,
For spoyling our releefe,
The Deuill so must we ouerthrowe,
With gonshote of beleefe.

The little byrdes which sing so swete,
Are like the angelles voyce,
Which render God his prayses meete,
And teache vs to reioyce:
And as they more esteeme that myrth,
Than dread the nights anoy,
So muste we deeme our days on earth,
But hell to heauenly ioye.

Vnto which Ioyes for to attayne
God graunt vs all his grace,
And sende vs after worldly payne,
In heauen to haue a place.
Where wee maye still enioy that light,
Which neuer shall decaye:
Lorde for thy mercy lend vs might,
To see that ioyfull daye.

GASCOYGNES GOOD NIGHT

When thou hast spent the lingring day in pleasure and delight,
Or after toyle and wearie waye, dost seeke to rest at nighte:
Vnto thy paynes or pleasures past, adde this one labour yet,
Ere sleepe close vp thyne eye to fast, do not thy God forget,
But searche within thy secret thoughts, what deeds did thee befal:
And if thou find amisse in ought, to God for mercy call.
Yea though thou find nothing amisse, which thou canst cal to mind,
Yet euer more remember this, there is the more behind:
And thinke how well so euer it be, that thou hast spent the daye,
It came of God, and not of thee, so to direct thy waye.
Thus if thou trie thy dayly deedes, and pleasure in this payne,
Thy life shall clense thy corne from weeds, and thine shal be the gaine:
But if thy sinfull sluggishe eye, will venter for to winke,
Before thy wading will may trye, how far thy soule maye sinke,
Beware and wake, for else thy bed, which soft and smoth is made,
May heape more harm vpon thy head, than blowes of enmies blade.
Thus if this paine procure thine ease, in bed as thou doest lye,
Perhaps it shall not God displease, to sing thus soberly:
I see that sleepe is lent me here, to ease my wearye bones,
As death at laste shall eke appeere, to ease my greeuous grones.
My dayly sportes, my panch full fed, have causde my drousie eye,
As carelesse life in quiet led, might cause my soule to dye:
The stretching armes, the yauning breath, which I to bedward vse,
Are patternes of the pangs of death, when life will me refuse:

[16] *worldly*] *wordly* STC 11636.

And of my bed eche sundrye part in shaddowes doth resemble,
The sundry shapes of deth, whose dart shal make my flesh to tremble.
My bed it selfe is like the graue, my sheetes the winding sheete,
My clothes the mould which I must haue, to couer me most meete:
The hungry fleas which friske so freshe, to wormes I can compare,
Which greedily shall gnaw my fleshe, and leaue the bones ful bare:
The waking Cock that early crowes to weare the night awaye,
Puts in my minde the trumpe that blowes before the latter day.
And as I ryse vp lustily, when sluggish sleepe is past,
So hope I to rise ioyfully, to Iudgement at the last.
Thus wyll I wake, thus wyll I sleepe, thus wyl I hope to ryse,
Thus wyll I neither waile nor weepe, but sing in godly wyse.
My bones shall in this bed remaine, my soule in God shall trust,
By whome I hope to ryse againe from death and earthly dust.

From THE STEEL GLASS[17]

For whyles[18] I mark this weak and wretched world,[19]
Wherin I see, howe euery kind of man
Can flatter still, and yet deceiues himselfe.
I seeme to muse, from whence such errour springs,
Such grosse conceits,[20] such mistes of darke mistake,
Such *Surcuydry,*[21] such weening ouer well,
And yet in dede, such dealings too too badde.
And as I stretch my weary wittes, to weighe
The cause therof, and whence it should proceede,
My battred braynes, (which now he shrewdly brusde,
With cannon shot, of much misgouernment)
Can spye no cause, but onely one conceite,
Which makes me thinke, the world goeth stil awry.

I see and sigh, (bycause it makes me sadde)
That peuishe pryde, doth al the world possesse,
And euery wight, will have a looking glasse
To see himselfe, yet so he seeth him not:
Yea, shal I say? a glasse of common glasse,
Which glistreth bright, and shewes a seemely shew,
Is not enough, the days are past and gon,
That Berral[22] glasse, with foyles of louely brown,
Might serue to shew, a seemely fauord face.
That age is deade, and vanisht long ago,
Which thought that steele, both trusty was and true,
And needed not, a foyle of contraries,
But shewde al things, euen as they were in deede.
In steade whereof, our curious yeares can finde
The christal glas, which glimseth braue and bright,
And shewes the thing, much better than it is,

[17] From *The steele glas,* 1576, STC 11645, Morgan Library. The passages printed here are about one-sixth of the poem.
[18] at times.
[19] Marginal note: *Here the substance of the theame beginneth.*
[20] ideas.
[21] pride.
[22] beryl.

Beguylde with foyles, of sundry subtil sights,
So that they seeme, and couet not to be.

This is the cause (beleue me now my Lorde)[23]
That Realmes do rewe,[24] from high prosperity,
That kings decline, from princely gouernment,
That Lords do lacke, their auncestors good wil,
That knights consume, their patrimonie still,
That gentlemen, do make the merchant rise,
That plowmen begge, and craftesmen cannot thriue,
That clergie quayles,[25] and hath smal reuerence,
That laymen liue, by mouing mischiefe stil,
That courtiers thriue, at latter Lammas day,[26]
That officers, can scarce enrich their heyres,
That Souldiours sterue, or prech at Tiborne crosse,[27]
That lawyers buye, and purchase deadly hate,
That merchants clyme, and fal againe as fast,
That roysters brag, aboue their betters rome,
That sicophants, are counted iolly guests,
That *Lais*[28] leades a Ladies life alofte,
And *Lucrece*[29] lurkes, with sobre bashful grace.

This is the cause (or else my Muze mistakes)
That things are thought, which neuer yet were wrought,
And castels buylt, aboue in lofty skies,
Which neuer yet, had good foundation.
And that the same may seme no feined dreame,
But words of worth, and worthy to be wayed,
I haue presumde, my Lord for to present
With this poore glasse, which is of trustie Steele,
And came to me, by wil and testament
Of one that was, a Glassemaker in deede.

Lucylius,[30] this worthy man was namde,
Who at his death, bequeathed the christal glasse,
To such as loue, to seme but not to be,
And vnto those, that loue to see themselues,
How foule or fayre, soeuer that they are,
He gan bequeath, a glasse of trustie Steele,
Wherin they may be bolde alwayes to looke,
Bycause it shewes, all things in their degree.
And since myselfe (now pride of youth is past)
Do loue to be, and let al seeming passe,
Since I desire, to see my selfe in deed,
Not what I would, but what I am or should,
Therfore I like this trustie glasse of Steele.

. . . .

[23] Gascoigne dedicated this poem to Lord Gray of Wilton.
[24] decline, fall.
[25] declines.
[26] at a time that will never come.
[27] beg or be executed at Tyburn, the usual place of public execution in London.
[28] Type name for a light woman.
[29] Type name for a faithful wife.
[30] Marginal note: *A famous old satyrical Poete.*

But now (aye me) the glasing[31] christal glasse[32]
Doth make vs thinke, that realmes and townes are rych
Where fauor sways, the sentence of the law,
Where al is fishe, that cometh to the net,
Where mighty power, doth ouer rule the right,
Where iniuries, do foster secret grudge,
Where bloudy sword, maks euery booty prize,
Where banquetting, is compted comly cost,
Where officers grow rich by princes pens,
Where purchase commes, by covyn[33] and deceit,
And no man dreads, but he that cannot shift,
Nor none serue God, but only tongtide men.
Againe I see, within my glasse of Steele,
But foure estates, to serue eche country Soyle,
The King, the Knight, the Pesant, and the Priest.
The King should care for al the subiectes still,
The Knight should fight, for to defende the same,
The Peasant he, should labor for their ease,
And Priests shuld pray, for them and for themselues.

But out alas, such mists do bleare our eyes,
And christal glosse, doth glister so therwith,
That Kings conceiue, their care is wonderous great[34]
When as they beat, their busie restles braynes,
To maintaine pompe, and high triumphant sights,
To fede their fil, of daintie delicates,
To glad their harts, with sight of pleasant sports,
To fil their eares, with sound of instruments,
To breake with bit, the hot coragious horse,
To deck their haules, with sumpteous cloth of gold,
To cloth themselues, with silkes of straunge deuise,
To search the rocks, for pearles and pretious stones,
To delue the ground, for mines of glistering gold:
And neuer care, to maynteine peace and rest,
To yeld reliefe, where needy lacke appears,
To stop one eare, vntil the poore man speake,
To seme to sleepe, when Iustice still doth wake,
To gard their lands, from sodaine sword and fier,
To feare the cries of giltles suckling babes,
Whose ghosts may cal, for vengeance on their bloud,
And stirre the wrath, of mightie thundring Ioue.

I speake not this, by any english king,
Nor by our Queene, whose high forsight prouids,
That dyre debate,[35] is fledde to foraine Realmes,
Whiles we inioy the golden fleece of peace.
But there to turne my tale, from whence it came,
In olden dayes, good kings and worthy dukes,
(Who sawe themselves, in glasse of trusty Steele)
Contented were, with pompes of little pryce,
And set their thoughtes, on regal governement.

. . . .

[31] making to shine like glass, deceiving.
[32] Marginal note: *Common woe.*
[33] deceit.
[34] Marginal note: *Kings.*
[35] dissension.

Oh Christal Glasse, thou settest things to shew,
Which are (God knoweth) of little worth in dede.
Al eyes behold, with eagre deepe desire,
The Faulcon flye, the grehounde runne his course,
The bayted Bul, and Beare at stately stake,
These Enterluds, these newe Italian sportes,
And every gawde, that glads the minde of man:
But fewe regard, their needy neighbours lacke,
And fewe beholde, by contemplation,
The ioyes of heaven, ne yet the paines of hel.
Fewe loke to lawe, but al men gaze on lust.

A swete consent, of Musicks sacred sound,
Doth rayse our mindes, (as rapt) al vp on high,
But sweeter soundes, of concorde, peace, and loue,
Are out of tune, and iarre in every stoppe.

To tosse and turne, the sturdie trampling stede,
To bridle him, and make him meete to serue,
Deserues (no doubt) great commendation.
But such as haue, their stables ful yfraught,
With pampred Iades, ought therwithal to wey,
What great excesse, vpon them may be spent,
How many pore, (which nede nor brake nor bit)
Might therwithal, in godly wise be fedde,[36]
And kings ought not, so many horse to haue.

The sumpteous house, declares the princes state,
But vaine excesse, bewrayes[37] a princes faults.

Our bumbast[38] hose, our treble double ruffes,
Our sutes of Silke, our comely garded[39] capes,
Our knit silke stockes, and spanish lether shoes,
(Yea velvet serues, ofttimes to trample in)
Our plumes, our spangs,[40] and al our queint aray,
Are pricking spurres, prouoking filthy pride,
And snares (vnseen) which leade a man to hel.

. . . .

O Knights, O Squires, O Gentle blouds yborne,
You were not borne, al onely for your selues:
Your countrie claymes, some part of al your paines.
There should you liue, and therin should you toyle,
To hold vp right, and banish cruel wrong,
To helpe the pore, to bridle backe the riche,
To punish vice, and vertue to aduance,
To see God serude, and *Belzebub* supprest.
You should not trust, lieftenaunts in your rome,
And let them sway, the scepter of your charge,
Whiles you (meane while) know scarcely what is don,
Nor yet can yeld, accompt if you were callde.

---

[36] Marginal note: *Deut. 18.*
[37] reveals.
[38] padded.
[39] ornamented.
[40] spangles.

The stately lord, which woonted was to kepe
A court at home, is now come vp to courte,
And leaues the country for a common prey,
To pilling,[41] polling,[42] brybing, and deceit:
(Al which his presence might have pacified,
Or else haue made offenders smel the smoke.)
And now the youth which might have serued him,
In comely wise, with countrey clothes yclad,
And yet therby bin able to preferre
Vnto the prince, and there to seke aduance:
Is faine to sell, his landes for courtly cloutes,[43]
Or else sits still, and liueth like a loute,
(Yet of these two, the last fault is the lesse:)
And so those imps[44] which might in time haue sprong
Alofte (good lord) and servde to shielde the state,
Are either nipt, with such vntimely frosts,
Or else growe crookt, bycause they be not proynd.

. . . .

Behold him (priests) and though he stink of sweat[45]
Disdaine him not: for shal I tel you what?
Such clime to heaven, before the shauen crownes.[46]
But how? forsooth, with true humilytie.
Not that they hoord, their grain when it is cheape,
Nor that they kill, the calfe to haue the milke,
Nor that they set, debate betwene their lords,
By earing vp the balks,[47] that part their bounds:
Nor for because, they can both crowche and creep
(The guilefulst men, that euer God yet made)
When as they meane, most mischiefe and deceite,
Nor that they can, crie out on landelordes lowde,
And say they racke, their rents an ace to high,[48]
When they themselues, do sel their landlords lambe
For greater price, then ewe was wont be worth.
I see you *Peerce,*[49] my glasse was lately scowrde.
But for they feed, with frutes of their gret paines,
Both King and Knight, and priests in cloyster pent:
Therefore I say, that sooner some of them
Shal scale the walles which leade vs vp to heauen,
Than cornfed beasts, whose bellie is their God,
Although they preach, of more perfection.

. . . .

But here me thinks, my priests begin to frowne,
And say, that thus they shal be ouerchargde,
To pray for al, which seme to do amisse:
And one I heare, more saucie than the rest,
Which asketh me, when shal our prayers end?

---

41 robbing.
42 plundering by excessive rent-raising.
43 clothes.
44 children.
45 Marginal note: *The plowman.*
46 tonsured monks.
47 by plowing the strips of sod that mark boundaries.
48 raise their rents a trifle too high.
49 Type name for the plowman since the fourteenth-century poem *Piers Plowman.*

I tel thee (priest) when shoomakers make shoes,
That are wel sowed, with neuer a stitch amisse,
And vse no crafte,[50] in vttring[51] of the same:
When Taylours steale, no stuffe from gentlemen,
When Tanners are, with Corriers[52] wel agreede,
And both so dresse their hydes, that we go dry:
When Cutlers leaue, to sel olde rustie blades,
And hide no crackes, with soder nor deceit:
When tinkers make, no more holes than they founde,
When thatchers thinke, their wages worth their worke,
When colliers put, no dust into their sacks,
When maltemen make, vs drinke no firmentie,[53]
When Dauie Diker[54] diggs, and dallies not,
When smithes shoo horses, as they would be shod,
When millers, toll[55] not with a golden thumbe,
When bakers make, not barme[56] beare price of wheat,
When brewers put, no bagage[57] in their beere,
When butchers blowe, not ouer al their fleshe,
When horsecorsers, beguile no friends with Iades,
When weauers weight, is found in huswiues web.
(But why dwel I, so long among these lowts?)

When mercers make, more bones to swere and lye,[58]
When vintners mix, no water with their wine,
When printers passe, none errours in their bookes,
When hatters vse, to bye none olde cast robes,
When goldsmithes get, no gains by sodred crownes,
When vpholsters, sel fethers without dust,
When pewterers, infect no Tin with leade,
When drapers draw, no gaines by giuing day,[59]
When perchmentiers,[60] put in no ferret Silke,[61]
When Surgeons heale, al wounds without delay.
(Tush these are toys, but yet my glas sheweth al.)

When purueyours, prouide not for themselues,
When Takers,[62] take no brybes, nor vse no brags,
When customers,[63] conceale no covine[64] vsde,
When Searchers see, al corners in a shippe,
(And spie no pens[65] by any sight they see)
When shriues[66] do serue, al processe as they ought,
When baylifes strain,[67] none other thing but strays,
When auditours, their counters cannot change,
When proude surueyours, take no parting pens,
When Siluer sticks not on the Tellers fingers,

[50] deceit.
[51] selling.
[52] curriers, those who dress and color leather after it is tanned.
[53] frumenty, a drink made of grain boiled in milk.
[54] Type name for a diker or ditch-digger.
[55] rob.
[56] yeast.
[57] refuse, poor ingredients.
[58] are less ready to swear and lie. There is here a punning reference to the bones (spindles) of the mercer.
[59] giving credit.
[60] makers of parchment.
[61] floss silk.
[62] Officers who took or exacted supplies for the sovereign.
[63] custom-house officers.
[64] deceit.
[65] pence.
[66] sheriffs.
[67] distrain, take up as stray animals.

And when receiuers, pay as they receiue,
When al these folke, haue quite forgotten fraude.

(Againe (my priests) a little by your leaue)
When Sicophants, can finde no place in courte,
But are espied, for *Ecchoes,* as they are,
When roysters ruffle not aboue their rule,
Nor colour crafte, by swearing precious coles:[68]
When Fencers fees, are like to apes rewards,
A peece of breade, and therwithal a bobbe,[69]
When *Lays*[70] liues, not like a ladies peare,
Nor vseth art, in dying of hir heare.
When al these things, are ordred as they ought,
And see themselues, within my glasse of steele,
Euen then (my priests) may you make holyday,
And pray no more but ordinarie prayers.

And yet therin, I pray you (my good priests)
Pray stil for me, and for my Glasse of steele
That it (nor I) do any minde offend,
Bycause we shew, all colours[71] in their kinde.
And pray for me, that (since my hap is such
To see men so) I may perceiue myselfe.
O worthy words, to ende my worthlesse verse,
Pray for me Priests, I pray you pray for me.

---

[68] an obsolete oath.
[69] *bobbe,*] *bobbe* STC 11636: a blow or a taunt.
[70] Lais. See note 28.
[71] appearances.

Early Miscellanies

THE MOST popular miscellany printed during the reign of Elizabeth, *The Paradise of Dainty Devices,* was first published in 1576 and by 1600 had reached at least eight editions. It was published by the printer Henry Disle from a collection of poetry made by a distinguished lyricist and playwright, Richard Edwards. If Disle's statement that the poems in the first edition were "collected togeather" by Edwards "for his priuate vse" is true, none of the poems in the 1576 edition can be later in date than 1566, the year of Edwards's death. The first edition contained ninety-nine poems; in later editions poems were added and omitted; the several editions included, at one time or another, one hundred twenty-five poems by about thirty poets.

The contributors to the earliest editions (1576, 1578, 1580) included many of the best poets of the time, among them Edwards, Lord Vaux, the Earl of Oxford, Jasper Heywood, Kinwelmarsh, Churchyard, as well as others of whom little or nothing is known.

Richard Edwards (c. 1524–1566), who compiled the original collection and is represented by thirteen poems, was born in Somersetshire, became B.A. at Oxford in 1544, and in 1561 was appointed Master of the Children of the Chapel Royal.

In the several editions of the *Paradise* eight poems are attributed to Jasper Heywood (1535–1598). He was the son of John Heywood, the famous writer of epigrams and interludes, and as a boy was a page to the Princess Elizabeth. After several years at Oxford he became a fellow of All Souls' College in 1558, but soon thereafter he left Oxford, went to Rome, and in 1562 was admitted to the Society of Jesus. In 1581 he returned to England as the head of a Jesuit mission; in 1583 he was imprisoned, in 1585 he was deported, and in 1598 he died in Naples. He is best known for his translations of Seneca's *Troas,* 1559, *Thyestes,* 1560, and *Hercules Furens,* 1561.

Francis Kinwelmarsh (1538–c. 1600) was born in London, was admitted to Gray's Inn in 1557, and collaborated with Gascoigne in writing *Jocasta.* In 1572 he was elected to Parliament. He died before 1600.

Of Bew nothing is known, and of John Thorn nothing except that two poems are ascribed to him in the *Paradise* and three ballads in a contemporary manuscript.

The *Paradise* is remarkable for the serious tone of most of its lyrics. Proverbial wisdom and earnest didacticism, common in the verse of the sixties and seventies, are especially conspicuous here. The taste of the age accounts for the peculiarities of the style: the many trite phrases and rhetorical devices, the many literary allusions, the excessive use of alliteration. The stanza found most frequently is the pentameter stanza rhyming ababcc, used later by Spenser, by Howell, and by Shakespeare in *Venus and Adonis.*

In 1578 appeared the only known edition of *A Gorgeous Gallery of Gallant Inventions.* The title page states that the poems were "first framed and fashioned in sundrie formes, by diuers worthy workemen of late dayes: and now, ioyned together and builded up: By T. P." Of "T. P." (Thomas Proctor) little is known; several of the poems are signed with his name or with his initials, and he may have written or revised others that are not signed. The themes and the style are conventional, and the diction seems more archaic than that of the *Paradise.* The book as a whole reflects the taste of the period.

The standard edition of *The Paradise of Dainty Devices* is that edited by H. E. Rollins, 1927. For discussion see Rollins's Introduction; W. Y. Durand, "Notes on Richard Edwards," *Journal of Germanic Philology*, iv (1902), 348–369, and "Some Errors Concerning Richard Edwards," *Modern Language Notes,* xxiii (1908), 129–131. For an account of Jasper Heywood see L. I. Guiney, *Recusant Poets*, 1939. The standard edition of *A Gorgeous Gallery of Gallant Inventions* is that edited by H. E. Rollins, 1926.

From THE PARADISE OF DAINTY DEVICES[1]

M. EDWARDES. M A Y.

When May is in his prime, then may eche hart reioyce,
When May bedeckes eche branch with green, eche bird straines forth his voice;
The liuely sappe creepes vp, into the bloming thorne,
The flowres which cold in prison kept, now laughes the frost to scorne.
All natures Impes[2] triumphes whyles ioyfull May dooth last,
When May is gone, of all the yeere the pleasant time is past.

May makes the cherefull hue, May breeds and bringes newe blood,[3]
May marcheth throughout euery limme, May makes the mery mood.[3]
May pricketh tender hartes, their warbling notes to tune:
Ful strange it is, yet some wee see, doo make their May in June,
Thus thinges are straungely wrought, whyles ioyfull May doth last,[3]
Take May in time, when May is gone, the pleasant time is past.

All ye that liue on earth, and haue your May at will,
Reioyce in May as I doo now, and vse your May with skill.
Vse May while that you may, for May hath but his time:

[1]From *The paradyse of daynty deuises,* 1576, STC 7516, Morgan Library.
[2] children.
[3] In STC 7516 the punctuation is crowded off.

When all the fruite is gone, it is to late the tree to clime,
Your liking and your lust[4] is freshe whyles May dooth last,
When May is gone, of all the yeere the pleasaunt time is past.

FOR WHITSUNDAY

Come holy ghost eternall God, and ease the wofull greefe:
That thorough the heapes of heauy sinne, can no where find releefe.
Doo thou O God redresse
The great distresse
Of sinfull heauinesse.

Come comfort the aflicted thoughtes, of my consumed hart:
O ryd the pearcing pricking paynes, of my tormenting smart.
O holy Ghost graunt me
That I by thee
From sinne may purged be.

Thou art my God, to thee alone,
I wyll commend my cause:
Not glittering golde nor precious stone,
Shall make me leaue thy lawes.
O teache me then the way
Whereby I may
Make thee my onely stay.

My lippes, my tongue, my hart and al,
Shall spreade thy mightie name:
My voyce shall neuer cease to sound,
The prayses of the same.
Yea euery liuing thing
Shall sweetely syng
To thee (O heauenly king.)[5]

WHO MINDES TO BRING HIS SHIPPE TO HAPPY SHORE, MUST CARE TO KNOWE THE LAWES OF WYSDOMES LORE.

My freend, yf thou wylt credite me in ought,[6]
To whom the trueth by tryall well appeares:
Nought woorth is wit, till it be dearely bought,
There is no wysedome but in hoarie heares.
Yet yf I may of wysedome ought[7] define,
As well as others haue of happinesse:
Then to my woordes my freende, thy eare encline,
The thinges that make thee wyse, are these I gesse.[8]

Feare God, and knowe thy selfe in eche degree,
Be freend to all, familier but to fewe:
Too light of credite, see thou neuer be,
For tryall oft in trust, dooth treason shewe.
To others faultes cast not to much thy eyes,[9]
Accuse no man of gilt, amend thy owne:

[4] wish.
[5] Signed *"M. Kindlemarsh."*
[6] aught.
[7] *ought*] *oft* STC 7516.
[8] think.
[9] *eyes,*] *eye,* STC 7516.

Of medling much, dooth mischiefe oft aryse,
And oft debate,[10] by tickle[11] tongue is sowne.

What thing thou wylt haue hid, to none declare,
In woorde or deede, beware of had I wist:
So spend thy good, that some thou euer spare,
For freendes like Haukes, doo soare from emptie fist.
Cut out thy coate, according to thy cloth,
Suspected persons see thou alwayes flee:
Beleeue not him that once hath broke his troth,
Nor yet of gift, without desart be free.

Time quickly slips beware how thou it spend,
Of wanton youth, repentes a painefull age:
Beginne nothing without an eye to thend,
Nor bowe thyne eare from counsell of the sage.
If thou to farre let out thy fancie slip,
And witlesse wyll from reasons rule outstart:
Thy folly, shall at length be made thy whippe,
And sore, the stripes of shame, shal cause thee smart.

To doo too much for olde men is but lost,
Of freendship had to women comes like gaine:
Bestowe not thou on children to much cost,
For what thou dooest for these, is all in vayne.
The olde man or he can requite, he dyes,
Vnconstant is the womans waueryng minde:
Full soone the boy thy freendship wyl despise,
And him for loue thou shalt vngratefull finde.

The aged man is like the barren ground,
The woman like the Reede that wagges with winde:
There may no trust in tender yeeres be found,
And of the three, the boy is most vnkinde.
If thou haue found a faithfull freend in deede,
Beware thou lose not loue of such a one:
He shall sometime stand thee in better steede,
Then treasure great of golde or precious stone.[12]

MANS FLITTING LIFE, FYNDES SUREST STAY, WHERE SACRED VERTUE BEARETH SWAY.

The sturdy Rocke, for all his strength,
By raaging Seas, is rent in twayne:
The Marble stone, is pearst at length,
With little droppes, of drislyng rayne.
The Oxe dooth yeelde vnto the yoke,
The Steele obeyeth the hammer stroke.

The stately Stagge, that seemes so stout,
By yalpyng Houndes, at bay is set:
The swiftest Bird, that flees about,

[10] strife.
[11] uncertain.
[12] Signed "*Iasper Hewood.*"

Is caught at length in Fowlers net.
The greatest Fishe in deepest Brooke,
Is soone deceiued with subtil hooke.

Yea[13] man him selfe, vnto whose wyll,
All thinges are bounden to obay:
For all his witte, and woorthy skill,
Dooth fade at length, and fall away.
There is nothing, but time dooth wast,
The Heauens, the Earth, consume at last.

But *Vertue* sittes, triumphing still,
Vpon the Trone, of glorious *Fame:*
Though spitefull Death, mans body kill,
Yet hurtes he not, his vertuous name.
By Life or death, what so be tides,
The state of *Vertue,* neuer slides.[14]

AMANTIUM IRAE AMORIS REDINTIGRATIA EST[15]

In goyng to my naked bedde,[16] as one that would haue slept,
I heard a wife syng to her child, that long before had wept:
She sighed sore and sang full sweet,[17] to bryng the babe to rest,
That would not cease[18] but cried still, in suckyng at her brest.
She was full wearie of her watche,[19] and greued with her child,
She rocked it and rated[20] it, vntill on her it smilde:
Then did she saie now haue I founde, the prouerbe true to proue,
The fallyng out of faithfull frends, is the renuyng of loue.[21]

Then tooke I paper, penne and ynke, this prouerbe for to write,
In regester for to remaine, of suche a worthie wight:[22]
As she proceded thus, in song vnto her little bratte,[23]
Muche matter vttered she of waight, in place whereas she satte.
And proued plaine, there was no beast, nor creature bearyng life,
Could well be knowne to liue in loue, without discorde and strife:
Then kissed she her little babe, and sware by God aboue,
The fallyng out of faithfull frends, is the renuyng of loue.

She saied that neither kyng ne prince, ne lorde could liue aright,
Vntill their puissance thei did proue, their manhode and their might.
When manhode shalbe matched so, that feare can take no place,
Then wearie works makes warriours, eche other to embrace,[24]
And leaue their forse that failed them, whiche did consume the rout,[25]
That might before haue liued their tyme,[26] and nature out:

---

13 *Yea*] *Ye* STC 7516.
14 Signed "*M.T.*" i.e., Master John Thorn.
15 The title is from Terence's *Andria,* III, iii, 23 (Rollins, p. 214).
16 naked to my bed.
17 *sweet,* (ed. of 1578) STC 7517]; *sore,* STC 7616.
18 *cease* STC 7517]; *rest* STC 7516.
19 wakefulness.
20 berated.
21 In later editions: *renewing is of love.*
22 person.
23 child.
24 *embrace,*] *embrace.* STC 7516.
25 throng.
26 H. E. Rollins points out that the edition of 1600 supplies the reading *time, and days,* which the meter requires. Norman Ault (*Elizabethan Lyrics,* 1949, pp. 47, 520) substitutes the reading of a version in Br. Mus. Addit. Ms. 26737: *That might by force with love have lived the term of nature out.*

Then did she syng as one that thought, no man could her reproue,
The fallyng out of faithfull frendes, is the renuyng of loue.

She saied she sawe no fishe ne foule, nor beast within her haunt,
That mett a straunger in their kinde, but could geue it a taunt:
Since fleshe might not indure, but reste must wrathe succede,
And forse the fight to fall to plaie, in pasture where thei feede.
So noble nature can well ende, the works she hath begone,
And bridle well that will not cease, her tragedy in some:
Thus in her songe she oft reherst, as did her well behoue,
The fallyng out of faithfull frends, is the renuyng of loue.

I meruaile muche pardy quoth she, for to beholde the route,
To see man, woman, boy and beast, to tosse the worlde about:
Some knele, some crouch, some beck, some check, and some can smothly smile,
And some embrace others in armes, and there thinke many a wile.
Some stand aloufe at cap and knee, some humble and some stout,
Yet are thei neuer frends indeede, vntill thei once fall out:
Thus ended she her song, and saied before she did remoue,
The fallyng out of faithful frends, is the renuyng of loue.[27]

Why should I lenger[28] long to liue,
In this desease of fantasie,
Sins fortune doeth not cease to giue,
Things to my mynde most contrarie.
And at my ioyes doeth lowre and froune,
Till she hath tourned them vpsidoune.[29]

A Frende I had to me moste dere,
And of long tyme faithfull and iuste:
There was no one, my harte so nere,
Nor one in whom I had more truste.
Whom now of late without cause why,
Fortune hath made my enemie.

The grasse me thinks should growe in skie
The starres, vnto the yearth cleaue faste:
The water streame should passe awrie,
The winds should leue their strengt of blast.
The Sonne and Moone by one assent,
Should bothe forsake the firmament.

The fishe in ayer should flie with finne,
The foules in floud should bryng forth fry,[30]
All thyngs me thinks should erst[31] beginne,
To take their course vnnaturally.
Afore my frende should alter so,
Without a cause to bee my foe.

27 Signed "*M. Edwardes,*" i.e., Master Richard Edwards.

28 longer.

29 upside down.

30 *fry,*] *fry* STC 7516: young fish.

31 first.

But suche is Fortunes hate I saie,
Suche is her will on me to wreake:
Suche spite she hath at me alwaie,
And ceasseth not my harte to breake.
With suche dispite of crueltie,
Wherefore then longer liue should I.[32]

When sage *Vlisses* sailed by,
The perillous seas, where *Cirens* syng:
Hym self vnto the mast did tye,
Lest their alluryng tunes might bryng,
His mynde on maze and make hym staie,
And he with his become their praie.

Vlisses O thou valiant wight,
It semed dame *Circes* loued thee well:
What tyme she told, to thee aright,[33]
The seas wherein the *Sirens* dwell.
By meane where,[34] against thy saile,
Their subtill songes, could not preuaile.

Were thou amongs vs here againe,
And heard our *Sirens* melodie:
Not *Circes* skill nor yet thy braine,
Could kepe thee from their trecherie.
Suche *Sirens* haue we now adaies,
That tempt vs by a thousande waies.

Thei syng thei daunce, thei sport, thei plaie,[35]
Thei humbly fall vpon their knees:
Thei sigh, thei sobb, thei prate, thei praie,
With suche dissemblyng shifts as these,
Thei calculate, thei chaunt, thei charme,
To conquere vs that meane no harme.

Good ladies all letts ioyne in one,
And banishe cleane[36] this *Siren* kinde:
What nede we yelde, to heare their mone,
Since their deceipt we daiely finde.
Let not your harts to them apply,
Defie them all for so will I.

And if where *Circes* now doeth dwell,
You wish your[37] witt aduise, to learne:[38]
Loe I am he[39] that best can tell,

32 Signed "*E.S.*" The author is unknown.
33 *aright*,] *aright*. STC 7516.
34 means whereby.
35 *plaie*,] *plaie* STC 7516.
36 entirely.
37 *wish your*] *wisht you* STC 7516.
38 if you wish your wit to get information where Circes now dwell.
39 *he*] *she* STC 7516.

Their *Sirens* songes and them discerne.
For why[40] experience yeldeth skill,
To me that scapt that *Sirens* ill.[41]

LOOKE OR[42] YOU LEAPE

If thou in suertie safe wilt sitt,
If thou delight at rest to dwell:
Spende no more words then shall seme fitt,
Let tonge in silence talke expell.
In all thyngs that thou seest men bent,
Se all, saie nought, holde thee content.

In worldly works degrees are three,
Makers, doers, and lookers on:
The lookers on haue libertie,
Bothe the others to iudge vpon.
Wherefore in all, as men are bent,
Se all, saie nought, holde thee content.

The makers oft are in fault founde,
The doers doubt of praise or shame:
The lookers on finde surest grounde,
Thei haue the fruite, yet free from blame.
This doeth persuade in all here ment,
Se all, saie nought, holde thee content.

The prouerbe is not South and West,[43]
Whiche hath be saied, long tyme agoe:
Of little medlyng cometh rest,
The busie man neuer wanteth woe.
The best waie is in all worlds sent,
Se all, saie nought, holde thee content.[44]

From A GORGEOUS GALLERY OF GALLANT INVENTIONS[45]

A PROPER SONET, HOW TIME CONSUMETH ALL EARTHLY THINGES

Ay mee, ay mee, I sighe to see, the Sythe a fielde,
Downe goeth the Grasse, soone wrought to withered Hay:
Ay mee alas, ay mee alas, that beauty needes must yeeld,
And Princes passe, as Grasse doth fade away.

Ay mee, ay mee, that life cannot haue lasting leaue,
Nor Golde, take holde, of euerlasting ioy:
Ay mee alas, ay mee alas, that time hath talents to receyue,
And yet no time, can make a suer stay.

Ay mee, ay mee, that wit can not haue wished choyce,
Nor wish can win, that will desires to see:

[40] because.
[41] Signed "*M. Bew.*" The author is unknown.
[42] ere, before.
[43] Perhaps this line means that the proverb (two lines below) is universally applicable.
[44] Signed "*Iasper Haywood.*"
[45] From *A gorgious gallery of gallant inuentions*, 1578, STC 20402, Bodleian Library. The author of this poem is unknown.

Ay mee alas, ay mee alas, that mirth can promis no reioyce,
Nor study tell, what afterward shalbee.

Ay mee, ay mee, that no sure staffe, is giuen to age,
Nor age can giue, sure wit, that youth will take:
Ay mee alas, ay mee alas, that no counsell wise and sage,
Will shun the show,[46] that all doth marre and make.

Ay mee, ay mee, come time, sheare on, and shake thy Hay,
It is no boote,[47] to baulke thy bitter blowes:
Ay mee alas, ay mee alas, come time, take euery thing away,
For all is thine, bee it good or bad that growes.

RESPICE FINEM

Lo here the state of euery mortall wight,[48]
See here, the fine,[49] of all their gallant ioyes:
Beholde their pompe, their beauty and delight,
Wherof they vaunt, as safe from all annoyes:
To earth the stout, the prowd, the ritch shall yeeld,
The weake, the meeke, the poore, shall shrowded lye
In dampish mould, the stout with Speare and Sheeld
Cannot defend, himselfe when hee shal dye.
The prowdest wight, for all his lyuely showes,
Shall leaue his pompe, cut of by dreadfull death:
The ritch, whose Hutch,[50] with golden Ruddocks[51] flowes,
At length shall rest, vncoynd in dampish earth:
By Natures law, wee all are borne to dye,
But where or when, the best vncertayne bee:
No time prefixt, no goods our life shall buye,
Of dreadfull death, no freends shall set vs free.
Wee subiect bee, a thousand wayes to death,
Small sicknesse moues the valiaunts[52] hart to feare:
A litle push bereaues your breathing breath,
Of braue[53] delights, wherto you subiect are:
Your world is vayne, no trust in earth you finde,
Your valyaunst prime, is but a brytle glasse:
Your pleasures vade, your thoughts a puffe of winde,
Your auncient yeres, are but a withered grasse.[54]

---

[46] deceptive appearance.
[47] there is no remedy.
[48] creature.
[49] end.
[50] chest, coffer.
[51] gold coins.
[52] most valiant.
[53] fair.
[54] Signed "*T.P.*" i.e., Thomas Proctor.

Thomas Tusser

[c. 1523–1580]

THE POETRY of the translators and scholars—Googe, Turberville, Howell, Gascoigne, and the like—reached a rather limited public. The verse of Tusser, like the psalms of Sternhold and Hopkins and the narratives of the ballad writers, was addressed to the people.

Thomas Tusser attended Eton and Cambridge, was for ten years in the service of Lord Paget, probably as a musician, and later was for many years a farmer. His *A Hundred Good Points of Husbandry* was published by Tottel in 1557, 1570, 1571. In 1573 it appeared, greatly expanded, as *Five Hundred Points of Good Husbandry*, and was reprinted many times before 1600.

Tusser's book is a collection of maxims on farming, thrift, religion, and the conduct of life in general. It has a peculiar charm. His shrewd and kindly humor, his quaint and homely phrases, his rustic music, his unaffected love of country things—these make his book unique in his age. His verse shows remarkable metrical ingenuity and a wider variety of metrical experiment than that of his contemporaries. He is especially skillful in his use of trisyllabic measures, which are uncommon in his century, and which may in his verse be reminiscent of the rhythm of country dances. His favorite measure is the anapestic tetrameter couplet. The simplicity and terseness of his style, together with his easy rhythms, doubtless helped to fix his precepts in the memory of the sixteenth-century reader. Though much of his book is prosaic, it was very popular in its day, and has since become a minor classic.

The standard edition is *Five Hundred Points of Good Husbandrie*, ed. W. Paine and S. J. Herrtage, English Dialect Society, 1878. An edition of part of Tusser's verse, with interesting notes, is *Tusser Redivivus*, 1744. Attractive recent editions are *Five Hundred Points of Good Husbandry, with an Introduction by Sir Walter Scott and a Benediction by Rudyard Kipling incorporated in a Foreword by E. V. Lucas*, 1931, and *Thomas Tusser . . . His Good Points of Husbandry*, ed. D. Hartley, 1931.

A PREFACE TO THE BUIER OF THIS BOOKE[1]

What lookest thou herein to haue?
Fine verses thy fansie to please?
Of many my betters that craue,
Looke nothing but rudenes in thease.

What other thing lookest thou then?
Graue sentences[2] many to finde?
Such, Poets haue twentie and ten,[3]
Yea thousands contenting the minde.

What looke ye, I praie you shew what?
Termes painted with Rhetorike fine?
Good husbandrie seeketh not that,
Nor ist any meaning of mine.

What lookest thou, speake at the last?
Good lessons for thee and thy wife?
Then keepe them in memorie fast,
To helpe as a comfort to life.

What looke ye for more in my booke?
Points needfull and meete to be knowne?
Then dailie be suer to looke,
To saue to be suer thine owne.

AS TRUE AS THY FAITH, THIS RIDDLE THUS SAITH:[4]

I seeme but a drudge, yet I passe any King
To such as can vse me, great wealth I do bring.
Since Adam first liued, I neuer did die,
When Noe was shipman, there also was I.
The earth to susteine me, the sea for my fish:
Be readie to pleasure me, as I would wish.
What hath any life, but I helpe to preserue,
What wight[5] without me, but is ready to sterue.
In woodland, in Champion,[6] Citie or towne,
If long I be absent, what falleth not downe?
If long I be present, what goodnes can want?[7]
Though things at my comming, were neuer so scant.
So many as looue me, and vse me aright,
With treasure and pleasure, I richly acquite.[8]
Great kings I doe succour, else wrong it would go,
The King of al kings hath appointed it so.

THE LADDER TO THRIFT

To take thy calling thankfully,
and shun the path to beggery.

2 To grudge in youth no drudgery,
to come by knowledge perfectly.

3 To count no trauell slauerie,
that brings in penie sauerlie.[9]

4 To folow profit earnestlie:
but meddle not with pilferie,

5 To get by honest practisie,[10]
and keepe thy gettings couertlie.

6 To lash not out too lashinglie,[11]
for feare of pinching penurie.

7 To get good plot to occupie,
and store and vse it husbandlie.

8 To shew to landlord curtesie,
and keepe thy couenants orderlie.

9 To hold that thine is lawfullie,
for stoutnes[12] or for flatterie.

10 To wed good wife for companie,
and liue in wedlock honestlie.

11 To furnish house with housholdry,
and make prouision skilfully.

[1] All of Tusser's verse printed here is from *Fiue hundreth points of good husbandrie,* 1580, STC 24380, Folger Library.
[2] sententious sayings.
[3] a large number.
[4] In margin: *The praise of husbandrie* (the answer to the riddle).
[5] creature.
[6] champaign, open country.
[7] be lacking.
[8] requite, repay.
[9] frugally.
[10] conduct.
[11] spend too freely.
[12] in spite of blustering or arrogance.

12 To ioine to wife good familie,[13]
and none to keepe for brauerie.[14]

13 To suffer none liue idlelie,
for feare of idle knauerie.

14 To courage wife in huswiferie,
and vse well dooers gentilie.

15 To keepe no more but needfullie,
and count excesse unsauerie.

16 To raise betimes the lubberlie,
both snorting[15] Hob and Margerie.

17 To walke thy pastures vsuallie,
to spie ill neighbours subtiltie.

18 To hate reuengement hastilie,
for loosing loue and amitie.

19 To loue thy neighbor neighborly,
and shew him no discurtesy.

20 To answere stranger ciuilie,
but shew him not thy secrecie.

21 To vse no friend deceitfully,
to offer no man villeny.

22 To learne how foe to pacifie,
but trust him not too trustilie.

23 To keepe thy touch[16] substanciallie,
and in thy word vse constancie.

24 To make thy bandes[17] advisedly,
and com not bound through suerty.[18]

25 To meddle not with vsurie,
nor lend, thy monie foolishlie.

26 To hate to liue in infamie,
through craft, and liuing shiftingly.

27 To shun, all kinde of treachery,
for treason, endeth horribly.

28 To learne, to eschew ill company,
and such as liue dishonestly.

29 To banish house of blasphemie,
least crosses, crosse vnluckelie.

30 To stop mischance, through policy[19]
for chancing too vnhappily.

31 To beare thy crosses paciently,
for worldly things are slippery.

32 To laie[20] to keepe from miserie,
age comming on, so creepinglie.

33 To praie to God continuallie,
for aide against thine enimie.

34 To spend thy Sabboth holilie,
and helpe the needie pouertie.

35 To liue in conscience quietly,
and keepe thy selfe from malady.

36 To ease thy sicknes speedilie,
er helth be past recouerie,

37 To seeke to God for remedie,
for witches proue vnluckilie.

These be the steps vnfainedlie:
to climbe to thrift, by husbandrie.

These steps both reach, and teach thee shall:
To come by thrift, to shift withall.

A DESCRIPTION OF THE PROPERTIES OF WINDES ALL THE TIMES OF THE YEERE

North winds send haile, South winds bring raine,
East winds we bewail, West winds blow amaine:
North east is too cold, South east not too warme,
North west is too bold, South west doth no harme.

The north is a noyer,[21] to grasse of all suites,[22]
The east a destroyer, to herbe, and all fruites:

13 household, servants.
14 keep no servants for show.
15 snoring.
16 keep faith.
17 bonds, agreements.
18 being security or surety.
19 stratagem.
20 lay by, save; or apply oneself to.
21 One who annoys or injures.
22 kinds.

The south, with his showers, refresheth the corne,
The west, to all flowers, may not be forborne.

The West, as a father, all goodnes doth bring,
The East, a forbearer no manner of thing:[23]
The South as vnkind, draweth sicknesse too neere,
The North, as a friend, maketh all againe cleere.

With temperate winde, we be blessed of God,[24]
With tempest, we finde, we are beat with his rod:
All power, we knowe, to remaine in his hand,
How euer winde blowe, by sea, or by land.

Though windes doe rage, as windes were wood,[25]
And cause spring tydes, to raise great flood,
And loftie ships leaue anker in mud,
Bereafing many, of life, and of blud:

Yet true it is, as cow chawes cud,
And trees at spring, doe yeeld forth bud,
Except winde stands as neuer it stood:
It is an ill winde turnes none to good.

A DIGRESSION TO HOSPITALITIE

Leaue husbandrie sleeping, a while ye must doo:
to learne of housekeeping, a lesson or twoo.
What euer is sent thee, by trauell[26] and paine:
a time there is lent thee, to rendrit[27] againe.
Although ye defend it, vnspent for to bee:
another shall spend it, no thanke vnto thee.
How euer we clime, to accomplish[28] the mind:
we haue but a time, thereof profit to find.

A DESCRIPTION OF TIME, AND THE YEARE

Of God to thy dooings, a time there is sent,
which endeth with time, that in dooing is spent.
For time is it selfe but a time for a time:
forgotten ful soone, as the tune of a chime.

In Spring time we reare, we doo sowe, and we plant,
in Sommer get vittels, least after we want.
In Haruest, we carie in corne, and the fruit:
in Winter to spend, as we neede of ech suit.[29]

The yeere I compare, as I find for a truth,
the Spring vnto childhood, the Sommer to youth.
The Haruest to manhood, the Winter to age:
all quickly forgot, as a play on a stage.

---

23 The meaning is obscure. The east wind is kind to nothing, or the east wind is (unlike the west wind) the parent of nothing.

24 Marginal note: *God is the gouernor of windes and weather.*

25 mad, crazy.

26 work.

27 render it, return it.

28 equip.

29 kind.

Time past is forgotten, er men be aware,
time present is thought on, with woonderfull care.
Time coming is feared, and therefore we saue:
yet oft er it come, we be gone to the graue.

A DESCRIPTION OF LIFE AND RICHES

Who liuing, but daily discerne it he may,
how life as a shadow, doth vanish away;
And nothing to count on, so suer to trust:
as suer of death, and to turne into dust.

The lands and the riches, that here we possesse,
be none of our owne, if a God we professe.
But lent vs of him, as his talent of gold:[30]
which being demanded, who can it withhold?

God maketh no writing, that iustly[31] doth say,
how long we shall haue it, a yeere or a day.
But leaue it we must (how soeuer we leeue:)
when Atrop[32] shall pluck vs, from hence by the sleeue.

To death we must stoupe, be we high, be we lowe,
but how, and how sodenly, few be that knowe.
What carie we then, but a sheete to the graue:
to couer this carkas, of all that we haue?

CHRISTMAS HUSBANDLIE FARE

Good husband and huswife, now cheefly be glad,
things handsom to haue, as they ought to be had.
They both doo provide, against[33] Christmas doo come:
to welcome good neighbour, good cheere to haue some.

Good bread and good drinke, a good fier in the hall,
brawne,[34] pudding and souse,[35] and good mustard withall.

Beefe, mutton and porke, shred pies[36] of the best,
pig, veale, goose and capon, and turkey well drest.
Cheese, apples and nuts, ioly Carols to heare:
as then in the countrie, is counted good cheare.

What cost to good husband is any of this?
good houshold provision, onely it is.
Of other the like, I doo leave out a menie:[37]
that costeth the husbandman neuer a penie.

POSIES FOR THINE OWNE BED CHAMBER

What wisdom more, what better life, than pleseth God to send?
what worldly goods, what longer vse, than pleseth God to lend?

30 Matthew xxv, 14–30.
31 exactly.
32 Marginal note: *Atrop, or death.*
33 before, in expectation of the time when.
34 Originally, the flesh of the wild boar; later, flesh of any kind.
35 Pigs' feet pickled.
36 mince pies.
37 many.

2 What better fare, than well content, agreeing with thy wealth?
what better gest, than trustie friend, in sicknes and in health?

3 What better bed, than conscience good, to passe the night with sleepe?
what better worke, than daily care, fro sinne thy selfe to keepe?

4 What better thought, than think on God, and daily him to serue?
what better gift, than to the poore, that ready be to sterue?

5 What greater praise of God and man, than mercie for to shew?
who merciles, shall mercie finde, that mercie shewes to few?

6 What worse despaire, than loth to die, for feare to go to hell?
what greater faith, than trust in God, through Christ in heauen to dwell?

THE DESCRIPTION OF AN ENUIOUS AND NAUGHTIE NEIGHBOUR

An enuious neighbour, is easie to finde,
His cumbersome fetches,[38] are seldome behinde.
His hatred procureth,[39] from naughtie to wurse,
His friendship like Judas that carried the purse.
His head is a storehouse, with quarrels full fraught,
His braine is vnquiet, till all come to naught.
His memorie pregnant, old euils to recite,
His mind euer fixed, each euill to requite.
His mouth full of venim, his lips out of frame,[40]
His tongue a false witnes, his friend to defame.
His eies be promooters,[41] some trespas to spie,
His eares be as spials, alarum to crie.
His hands be as tyrants, reuenging ech thing,
His feete at thine elbow, as serpent to sting.
His breast full of rancor, like Canker to freat,[42]
His hart like a Lion, his neighbour to eat.
His gate like a sheepebiter, fleering[43] aside,
His looke like a coxcombe, vp puffed with pride.
His face made of brasse, like a vice[44] in a game,
His iesture like Dauus,[45] whom Terence doth name.
His brag as Thersites,[46] with elbowes abrode,
His cheekes in his furie, shall swell like a tode.
His colour like ashes, his cap in his eies,
His nose in the aire, his snout in the skies.
His promise to trust to, as slipprie as ice,
His credit much like, to the chance of the dice.
His knowledge, or skill, is in prating too much,
His companie shunned, and so be all such.
His friendship is counterfait, seldome to trust,
His dooings vnluckie and euer vniust,
His fetch is to flatter, to get what he can,
His purpose once gotten, a pin for thee than.

38 tricks.
39 brings about.
40 order.
41 informers.
42 worm to eat away.
43 grinning, sneering, like a sneaking person.
44 buffoon.
45 Davus is the name that Terence gave to the cunning, plotting servant.
46 Thersites is the scurrilous Greek in Homer.

A SONET VPON THE AUTHORS FIRST SEUEN YEERES SERUICE

Seuen times hath Janus, tane new yeere by hand,
Seuen times hath blustring March, blowne forth his powre:
To driue out Aprils buds, by sea and land,
For minion Maie, to decke most trim[47] with flowre.
Seuen times hath temperate Uer,[48] like pageant plaide,
And pleasant Aestas,[49] eke hir flowers told:[50]
Seuen times Autumnes heate hath been delaide,[51]
With Hyems[52] boistrous blaste, and bitter cold.
Seuen times the thirteene Moones haue changed hew,
Seuen times the Sunne, his course hath gone about:
Seuen times ech bird, hir nest hath built anew,
Since first time you to serue, I choosed out.
Still yours am I, though thus the time hath past:
And trust to be, as long as life shall last.

THE PREFACE TO THE BOOKE OF HUSWIFERIE

Take weapon away, of what force is a man?
Take huswif from husband, and what is he than?

As louers desireth, together to dwell,
So husbandrie loueth, good huswiferie well.

Though husbandrie seemeth, to bring in the gaines,
Yet huswiferie labours, seems equall in paines.

Some respit to husbands, the weather may send,
But huswiues affaires, haue neuer an end.

EIGHT OF S. BARNARDS VERSES, BOTH IN LATINE AND ENGLISH, WITH ONE NOTE[53] TO THEM BOTH

Cur mundus militat, sub vana gloria,
Cuius prosperitas, est transitoria?
Tam cito labitur, eius potentia,
Quam vasa figuli, quae sunt fragilia?

1 Why so triumphes the world, in pompe and glorie vaine,
Whose state so happie thought, so fickle doth remaine?
Whose brauerie[54] slipprie stands, and doth so soone decaie:
As doth the potters pan, compact of brittle claie?

47 neat, fine.
48 Ver, spring.
49 summer.
50 counted.
51 tempered, moderated.
52 winter.
53 music, meter. An anonymous translation of this poem is included in *The Paradise of Dainty Devices,* 1576. The Latin poem, attributed to St. Bernard of Clairvaux (c. 1090–1153), was popular throughout the Middle English and Tudor periods.
54 splendor.

2 Plus crede literis, scriptis in glacie,
Quam mundi fragilis, vanae fallaciae,
Fallax in praemiis, virtutis specie,
Quae nunquam habuit, tempus fiduciae.

2 More credite see thou giue, to letters wrote in ise,
Than vnto vaine deceits, of brittle worlds deuise.
In gifts to vertue due, beguiling many one:
Yet those same neuer haue, long time to hope vpon.

3 Magis credendum est, viris fallacibus,
Quam mundi miseris prosperitatibus,
Falsis insaniis et voluptatibus,
Falsis quoque studiis et vanitatibus.

3 To false dissembling men, more trust is to be had,
Than to the prosperous state, of wretched world so bad.
What with voluptuousnes, and other maddish toies:
False studies won with paine, false vanities and ioies.

4 Dic vbi *Salomon,* olim tam nobilis?
Vel vbi *Samson* est, dux inuincibilis?
Vel dulcis *Ionathas,* multum amabilis?
Vel pulcher *Absolon,* vultu mirabilis?

4 Tell where is *Salomon,* that once so noble was?
Or where now Samson is, in strength whome none could pas?
Or woorthie *Ionathas,* that prince so louely bold?
Or faier *Absolon,* so goodlie to behold?

5 Quo *Caesar* abiit, celsus imperio?
Vel *Diues* splendidus, totus in prandio?
Dic vbi *Tullius,* clarus eloquio?
Vel *Aristoteles,* summus ingenio?

5 Shew whither is *Caesar* gone, which conquered far and neere?
Or that rich famous *Carle,*[55] so given to bellie cheere:
Shew where is *Tullie*[56] now, for eloquence so fit?
Or *Aristoteles,* of such a pregnant wit?

6 O esca vermium! o massa pulueris!
O ros! o vanitas! cur sic extolleris?
Ignoras penitus vtrum cras vixeris,
Fac bonum omnibus, quam diu poteris.

6 O thou fit bait for wormes! O thou great heape of dust!
O dewe! O vanitie! Why so extolst thy lust?[57]
Thou therefore ignorant, what time thou hast to liue:
Doe good to erie[58] man, while here thou hast to giue.

7 Quam breue festum est, haec mundi gloria?
Vt umbra hominis, sic eius gaudia.

55 churl; namely, Dives.
56 Cicero.
57 desire in general.
58 every.

Quae semper subtrahit, aeternia praemia,
Et ducunt hominem, ad dura deuia.

7 How short a feast (to count,) is this same worlds renowne?
Such as mens shadowes be, such ioies it bringes to towne.
Which alway plucketh vs, from Gods eternall blis:
And leadeth man to hell, a iust reward of his.

8 Haec mundi gloria, quae magni penditur,
Sacris in literis, flos foeni dicitur.
Vt leue folium, quod vento rapitur,
Sic vita hominum, hac vita tollitur.

8 The brauerie of this world, esteemed here so much,
In Scripture likened is, to flowre of grasse and such.
Like as the leafe so light, through winde abrode is blowne:
So light[59] is this our life, full soone is ouerthrowne.

[59] *light*] *life* STC 24380.

Broadside Ballads

THE SURVIVING broadside ballads are representative of the verse enjoyed by the least literate readers in sixteenth-century England. The traditional ballads of medieval times, composed by unknown authors and handed down orally, are not broadside ballads and are not included here, though some of them were printed during the sixteenth century.

The broadside ballad was printed in black letter on a single sheet of paper, often with a woodcut and an ornamental border, and with the name of the tune to which the ballad was to be sung. Sometimes the buyers pasted the broadsides on the walls of inns and houses. Squire Cokes in Ben Jonson's *Bartholomew Fair* asks his sister, "Do you remember the ballads over the nursery chimney o' my pasting up?"

Relatively few of the many hundreds of sixteenth-century ballads survive, some in the original broadside form, some in reprints or collections, and some in manuscripts. The most interesting sixteenth-century collection is Clement Robinson's *A Handful of Pleasant Delights*, printed probably in 1566 and again in 1576 and 1584.

These broadsides reveal the tastes, the interests, the habits of ordinary men and women, the stories they liked, the allusions they understood. The diction of most of the ballads is simple enough to be intelligible to those who could barely read. The shepherdess Mopsa in *The Winter's Tale* could read them.

The broadsides were sold by ballad singers in the streets, on village greens, at markets and fairs, wherever people congregated. The ballad men are mentioned often by contemporary writers. In *Kind Heart's Dream*, 1592, Henry Chettle describes them: "A company of idle youths, loathing honest labour and dispising lawfull trades, betake themselues to a vagrant and vicious life, in euery corner of Cities and market Townes of the Realme, singing and selling of ballads and pamplets full of ribaudrie, and all scurrilous vanity, to the prophanation of God's name, and withdrawing people from christian exercises, especially at faires, markets, and such publike meetings." Ben Jonson in *Bartholomew Fair* introduces the ballad singer Nightingale who sings to the prospective buyers while his confederate picks their pockets. Shakespeare in *The Winter's Tale* brings Autolycus, engaging rogue and ballad singer, to the sheep shearing, where the country people buy his broadsides telling of marvels, and Mopsa exclaims, "I love a ballad in print . . . for then we are sure they are true." In 1600 Sir William Cornwallis wrote: "I haue not been ashamed to aduenture mine eares with a ballad-singer, and they haue come home loaden to my liking, doubly satisfied with profit and with recreation. The profit, to see earthlings satisfied with such course stuffe, to heare vice rebuked, and to see the power of Vertue that pierceth the head of such a base Historian and vile Auditorie. The recreation to see how thoroughly the standers by are affected; what strange gestures come from them; what strayned stuffe from their Poet; what shift they make to stand to heare; what extremitie he is driuen to for Rime; how they aduenture their purses, hee his wits."

The broadsides provided entertainment, information, and instruction of many kinds. The narrative ballads told stories from the Bible, from the mythology and history of Greece and Rome, from English legend and history. Many ballads told of current events, the Armada, battles abroad, floods, earthquakes, destructive fires, sensational happenings of all kinds, the latest murders, the latest public executions. Some ballads were based on popular plays such as *Titus Andronicus* and *Romeo and Juliet*. Some protested against high prices, monopolies, enclosures. Some inveighed against new fashions in dress. A great many were love songs or tales of love; and if these seemed objectionable or too trivial, there were always ballad writers to "moralize" them. Soon after the publication of the ballad *Fain wold I haue a pretie thing to giue vnto my Ladie* there appeared the moralizations *Fayne wolde I have a godly Thynge to shewe vnto my ladye* and *Fayne wolde I haue a vertuous wyfe adourned with all modeste bothe mylde and meke of quyett lyf esteemynge chef hyr chastetye*. The publication of the famous *Lady Greensleeves* was followed by *Greene Sleves moralised to the Scripture Declaringe the manifold benefites and blessings of God bestowed on sinfull manne* and *A Reprehension against Greene Sleves*. Many broadsides attacked specific sins, or exhorted the reader to repentance, or offered him practical advice about the conduct of life, or outlined his whole duty to God and to his neighbor as in the following: *An Hundred Godly Lessons, That a Mother on her Death-Bed gaue to her Children, whereby they may learn how to guide themselues towards God and Man, to the benefit of the Commonwealth, joy of their Parents, and good to themselues*. Hundreds of ballads were religious, stories from the Bible, instruction, devotional songs. Some of these were colored by the religious prejudices of the writers and readers; for example, the ballad beginning *Ierusalem my happy home, when shall I come to thee* survives in several versions, some Catholic in emphasis, some Protestant, some Puritan.

Most of the ballads are anonymous, but a few of the professional ballad writers are known. William Elderton (fl. 1559–1584) was the most famous of his day. Thomas Deloney (c. 1543–c. 1599), silk weaver of Norwich and London and well known as a ballad writer in the nineties, was even better known as the author of the prose romances *Jack of Newbury*, *Thomas of Reading*, and *The Gentle Craft*.

The most useful collections are the following: *Broadside Black-Letter Ballads*, ed. J. P. Collier, 1868; *Ballads from Manuscripts*, ed. F. J. Furnivall and W. R. Morfill, 2 vols., 1868–1873; *The Roxburghe Ballads*, ed. William Chappell and J. W. Ebsworth, 10 vols., 1871–1899; *The Shirburn Ballads, 1585–1616*, ed. Andrew Clark, 1907; *The Works of Thomas Deloney*, ed. F. O. Mann, 1912; *Old English Ballads*, 1553–1625, ed. H. E. Rollins, 1920; *A Handful of Pleasant Delights*, ed. H. E. Rollins, 1924; *The Pepys Ballads*, ed. H. E. Rollins, 8 vols., 1929–1932. The best accounts of the broadside ballad are the following: Sir Charles Firth, "The Ballad History of the Reigns of Henry VII and Henry VIII," *Transactions of the Royal Historical Society*, Third Series, ii (1908), 21–50; "The Ballad History of the Reigns of the Later Tudors," *ibid.*, iii (1909), 51–124; "The Ballad History of the Reign of James I," *ibid.*, v (1911), 21–61; "Ballads and Broadsides," *Shakespeare's England*, 1916, ii, 511–538, reprinted in *Essays Historical and Literary*, 1928, pp. 1–33; H. E. Rollins, "The Black-Letter Broadside Ballad," *PMLA*, xxxiv (1919), 258–339; M. A. Shaaber, *Some Forerunners of the Newspaper in England*, 1476–1622, 1929; L. B. Wright, *Middle-Class Culture in Elizabethan England*, 1935, chapter 11 *et passim.* An invaluable guide is H. E. Rollins, *An Analytical Index to the Ballad-Entries (1557–1709) in the Registers of the Company of Stationers of London*, 1924, which lists the titles, subjects, and first lines of more than three thousand ballads, and adds notes on many of them. For the ballad writers see H. E. Rollins, "William Elderton: Elizabethan Actor and Ballad Writer," *Studies in Philology*, xvii (1920), 199–245; Introduction, *The Works of Thomas Deloney*, ed. F. O. Mann, 1912. For the music of the ballads see William Chappell, *Popular Music of the Olden Time*, ed. H. E. Wooldridge, 2 vols., 1893; C. M. Simpson, "Tudor Popular Music: Its Social Significance," *The Huntington Library Quarterly*, v (1941–1942), 176–179.

BECAUSE HE [JOHN CARELESS] MAKETH MENTION IN THE FORMER LETTER AND OTHER HERETOFORE, OF THE MOST GODLYE AND CHRISTIAN CONFLICTES WHICH HE HAD SUBTEYNED, WE THOUGHT GOOD TO ADIOYNE HERETO THIS SWETE AND HEAUENLY EXERCISE FOLLOWYNG, WHEREBY IT MAY APPEARE WHAT FRUITE THESE CONFLICTES WROUGHTE IN HYS MOST GODLY AND CHRISTIAN CONSCIENCE[1]

Some men for sodayne ioye do wepe,
  And some in sorow syng:[2]
When that they lie in daunger depe,
  To put away mournyng.

[1] From Miles Coverdale, *Certain most godly, fruitful, and comfortable letters of such true Saintes and holy Martyrs of God, as in the late bloodye persecution here within this Realme gaue their lyues for the defence of Christes holy gospel: written in the tyme of theyr affliction and cruell imprysonment*, 1564, STC 5886, Union Theological Seminary, McAlpin Collection. The date and author of this ballad are unknown.

[2] The first two lines are quoted in Shakespeare's *King Lear*, I, iv, 191.

Betwene them both will I beginne,
  Being in ioy and payne:
In sighing to lament my sinne,
  But yet reioyce agayne.

My sinfull life doth still increase,
  My sorow is the more:
From wyckednes I cannot cease,
  Wo is my hart therfore.

Sometimes when I thinke to do wel,
  And serue God night and day:
My wycked nature doth rebell,
  And leadeth me astray.

As bonde and captiue vnto sinne
  Which greueth me full sore:
This miserye do I liue in
  Wo is my harte therfore.

In dede sometyme I do repent
  And pardon doe obtaine:
But yet (alas) incontinent,
  I fall to sinne agayne.

My corrupte nature is so yll,
  Offending more and more:
That I displease my Lord god still,
  Wo is my harte therfore.

Wo is my harte, wo is my mynd,
  Woe is my soule and sprite:
That to my God I am vnkynde,
  In whome I shoulde delite.

Hys loue alwayes I should regard,
  Which towarde me was so pure:
But I wyth synne do him rewarde,
  O most vnkynd creature.

The beast, the byrde, the fishe, the foule,
  Their maker doe obey:
But I that am a liuing soule,
  Am farre much worse then they.

For they accordyng to their kinde,[3]
  To serue him do not cease:
But I wyth sinfull hert and mynde,
  Do daily him displease.

Thus do I sore complayne of synne,
  And with kyng Dauyd wepe:
For I do feele my harte within,
  The wrath of God full deepe.

To heauen myne eyes I dare not lift,
  Agaynst it I haue trespaste:
And in the earth I fynde no shifte,
  Nor succour that can last.

What shall I do? shall I dispaire,
  And from my Sauiour slide?
Nay god forbid, there is no feare,
  Syth Christ for me hath dyed.

God became man, and for vs men,
  He dyed and rose againe:
His mercy great we may see then,
  For euer doth remayne.

Therefore my sinne I will confesse,
  To God, and mourning make:
Who wil forgeue the same doutlesse,
  For hys sonne Christes sake.

Yf sinne in me god should respecte,
  Then do I know full well,
His iustice would me sone reiecte,
  To the deepe pit of hel.

Hys glorious eies cannot abide
  The foule and filthy smoke:
Wherwith I am on euerye syde,
  Couered as with a cloke.

But he in Christ doth me behold,
  In whom he doth delite,
And myne offences manyfold,
  Through him releaseth quite.

Reputyng me amongest the iust,
  Forgeuyng al my sinne:
Therfore my faith, my hope, my truste,
  Shall euer be in hym.

O Lord encrease true faith in me,
  Thy good spirite to me geue:
That I may grow in loue toward thee,
  And euer seeke to liue,

In true obedience of thy will
  And thankefulnes of hart,
And with thy grace so guide me stil,
  That I neuer departe

[3] nature.

From thy true word and testament,
All the dayes of my life:
Nor from thy churche most innocent,
Thine owne true spouse and wife.

But from that filthy whore of Rome,
Lord kepe me euermore:
As gratiously thou hast yet done,
Thankes be to thee therfore.

And sith thou haste of thy goodnes,
Forgeuen me all my sinne
Strength me, thy truth for to confesse,
And boldly die therin.

That as I haue confessed thee,
Before the wicked sort:
Thou maiest in thy good time know me
To my ioy and comfort.

My soule returne vnto thy reste,
Thou art wel satisfied:
The Lord hath graunted thy request,
And nothyng thee denied.

Prayse be God the father of myght,
Praise be to thee O Christ:
Praise be to thee O holy sprite,
Three in one God most hyest.

A PROPER SONG, INTITULED: FAIN WOLD I HAUE A PRETIE THING TO GIUE VNTO MY LADIE. TO THE TUNE OF LUSTIE GALLANT[4]

Fain would I have a pretie thing,
to giue vnto my Ladie:
I name no thing, nor I meane no thing,
But as pretie a thing as may bee.

Twentie iorneyes would I make,
and twentie waies would hie me,
To make aduenture for her sake,
to set some matter by me:
But I would faine haue a pretie thing, &c,
I name nothing, nor I mean nothing, &c.

Some do long for pretie knackes,
and some for straunge deuices:
God send me that my Ladie lackes,
I care not what the price is, thus faine, &c.

Some goe here, and some go there,
wheare gases[5] be not geason:[6]
And I goe gaping euery where,
But still come out of season. Yet faine, &c.

I walke the towne, and tread the streete,
in euery corner seeking:
The pretie thinge I cannot meete,
thats for my Ladies liking. Faine, &c.

The Mercers pull me going by,
the Silkie wiues say, what lacke ye?
The thing you haue not, then say I.
ye foolish fooles, go packe ye. But faine, &c.

It is not all the Silke in Cheape,[7]
nor all the golden treasure:
Nor twentie Bushels on a heape,
can do my Ladie pleasure. But faine, &c.

The Grauers of the golden showes,
with Iuelles do beset me.
The Shemsters[8] in the shoppes that sowes,
They do nothing but let[9] me: But faine, &c.

But were it in the wit of man,
by any meanes to make it,
I could for Money buy it than,
and say, faire Lady, take it. Thus, fain, &c.

O Lady, what a lucke is this:
that my good willing misseth:
To finde what pretie thing it is,
that my good Lady wisheth.

---

[4] From *A handefull of pleasant delites, containing sundrie new Sonets and delectable histories . . . by Clement Robinson, and diuers others,* 1584, STC 21105, Harvard photostat. This ballad was in print by 1566. The tune, "Lusty Gallant," is in Chappell, i, 234.

[5] gazes, staring.

[6] rare.

[7] Cheapside, the street of fine shops in Elizabethan London.

[8] seamstresses.

[9] hinder.

Thus fain wold I haue had this preti thing
to giue vnto my Ladie:
I said no harme, nor I ment no harme,
but as pretie a thing as may be.

A NEW COURTLY SONET, OF THE LADY GREEN SLEEUES. TO THE NEW TUNE OF GREENSLEEUES[10]

Greensleeues was all my ioy,
Greensleeues was my delight:
Greensleeues was my hart of gold,
And who but Ladie Greensleeues.

Alas my loue, ye do me wrong,
to cast me off discourteously:
And I haue loued you so long,
Delighting in your companie.
Greensleeues was all my ioy,
Greensleeues was my delight:
Greensleeues was my heart of gold,
And who but Ladie Greensleeues.

I haue been readie at your hand,
to grant what euer you would craue.
I haue both waged[11] life and land,
your loue and good will for to haue.
Greensleeues was all my ioy, &c.

I bought thee kerchers to thy head,
that were wrought fine and gallantly:
I kept thee both at boord and bed,
Which cost my purse wel fauouredly,[12]
Greensleeues was al my ioie, &c.

I bought thee peticotes of the best,
the cloth so fine as fine might be:
I gaue thee iewels for thy chest,
and all this cost I spent on thee.
Greensleeues was all my ioie, &c.

Thy smock of silk, both faire and white,
with gold embrodered gorgeously:
Thy peticote of Sendall[13] right:
and thus I bought thee gladly.
Greensleeues was all my ioie, &c.

Thy girdle of gold so red,
with pearles bedecked sumptuously:
The like no other lasses had,
and yet thou wouldst not loue me,
Greensleeues was all my ioy, &c.

Thy purse and eke thy gay guilt kniues,
thy pincase gallant to the eie:
No better wore the Burgesse wiues,
and yet thou wouldst not loue me.
Greensleeues was all my ioy, &c.

Thy crimson stockings all of silk,
with golde all wrought aboue the knee,
Thy pumps as white as was the milk,
and yet thou wouldst not loue me.
Greensleeues was all my ioy, &c.

Thy gown was of the grossie[14] green,
thy sleeues of Satten hanging by:
Which made thee be our haruest Queen,
and yet thou wouldst not loue me.
Greensleeues was all my ioy, &c.

Thy garters fringed with the golde,
And siluer aglets[15] hanging by,
Which made thee blithe for to beholde,
And yet thou wouldst not loue me.
Greensleeues was all my ioy, &c.

My gayest gelding I thee gaue,
To ride where euer liked thee,
No Ladie euer was so braue,[16]
And yet thou wouldst not loue me.
Greensleeues was all my ioy, &c.

My men were clothed all in green,
And they did euer wait on thee:
Al this was gallant to be seen,
and yet thou wouldst not loue me.
Greensleeues was all my ioy, &c.

They set thee vp, they took thee downe,
they serued thee with humilitie,
Thy foote might not once touch the ground,
and yet thou wouldst not loue me.
Greensleeues was all my ioy, &c.

[10] From *A handefull of pleasant delites*, 1584. This ballad was almost certainly in print by 1580. In *The Merry Wives of Windsor* Shakespeare twice refers to this ballad (II, i, 64; V, v, 22). The tune is in Chappell, i, 239.

[11] wagered, ventured.

[12] handsomely.

[13] Thin silken material.

[14] luxuriant, vigorous; or perhaps a misprint for *grassie*.

[15] Metallic tags or ornaments.

[16] handsomely arrayed.

For euerie morning when thou rose,
  I sent thee dainties orderly:
To cheare thy stomack from all woes,
  and yet thou wouldst not loue me.
    Greensleeuevs was all my ioy, &c.

Thou couldst desire no earthly thing.
  But stil thou hadst it readily:
Thy musicke still to play and sing,
  And yet thou wouldst not loue me.
    Greensleeues was all my ioy, &c.

And who did pay for all this geare,
  that thou didst spend when pleased thee?
Euen I that am reiected here,
  and thou disdainst to loue me.
    Greensleeues was all my ioy, &c.

Wel, I wil pray to God on hie,
  that thou my constancie maist see:
And that yet once before I die,
  thou wilt vouchsafe to loue me.
    Greensleeues was all my ioy, &c.

Greensleeues now farewel adue,
  God I pray to prosper thee:
For I am stil thy louer true,
  come once againe and loue me.
    Greensleeues was all my ioy, &c.

THE LAMENTATION OF BECKLES[17]

With sobbing sighes and trickling teares,
  my state I doe lament,
Perceuing how Gods heauie wrath
  against my sinnes is bent;
Let all men viewe my woefull fall,
  and rue my woefull case,
And learne hereby in speedy sort
  repentaunce to embrace.

For late in Suffoclke was I seen
  to be a stately towne,
Replenished with riches store,
  and had in great renowne;
Yea, planted on a pleasant soyle,
  so faire as heart could wish,
And had my markets, once a weeke,
  well storde with flesh and fish.

A faire fresh Riuer running by,
  to profite me withall,
Who with a cristall cleered streame
  about my bankes did fall;
My fayres in somer welthely
  for to increase my store;
My medowes greene and commons great,
  what could I wish for more?

But now beholde my great decay,
  which on a sodaine came;
My sumptuous buildings burned be
  by force of fires flame;
A careless wretch, most rude in life,
  his chymney set on fire,
The instrument, I must confesse,
  of Gods most heauie ire.

The flame whereof increasing stil
  the blustering windes did blowe,
And into diuers buildings by
  disperst it to and fro;
So, kindling in most grieuous sort,
  it waxed huge and hie;
The riuer then was frozen, so
  no water they could come by.

Great was the crye that then was made
  among both great and small;
The wemen wept and wrong their handes,
  whose goods consumed all;
No helpe was founde to slacke the fyre,
  theyr paines was spent in vaine;
To beare theyr goods into the fieldes
  for safegarde they were fayne.

And yet, amid this great distresse,
  a number set theyr minde,
To filtch, and steale, and beare away
  so much as they could finde;
Theyr neighbors wealth, which wasted lay
  about the streetes that time,
They secretly conuayde away,
  o most accursed crime!

---

[17] *A proper newe sonet declaring the lamentation of Beckles (a market towne in Suffolke) which was in the great winde vpon S. Andrewes eue last past most pittifully burned with fire, to the losse by estimation of twentie thousande pound and vpwarde, and to the number of foure score dwelling houses. 1586. To Wilsons tune.*, STC 6564, University Library, Cambridge. Entered in the Stationers' Registers on December 13, 1586. The fire occurred November 29. The original lacks punctuation except for a period at the end of each stanza.

Thus, from the morning nyne a clocke
till four a clocke at night,
Fourescore houses in Beckles towne
was burnd to ashes quite;
And that which most laments my heart,
the house of God, I say,
The church and temple by this fyre
is cleane consumde away.

The market-place and houses fayre,
that stood about the same,
Hath felt the force and violence
of this most fearefull flame;
So that there is no christian man
but in his heart would grieue,
To see the smart I did sustaine
vpon saint Andrewes eue.

Wherefore, good Christian people, now
take warning by my fall;
Liue not in strife and enuious hate
to breed each other thrall;
Seeke not your neighbors lasting spoyle
by greedy sute in Lawe;
Liue not in discord and debate,
which doth destruction draw.

And flatter not your selues in sinne;
holde not Gods worde in scorne;
Repine not at his Ministers,
nor be not false forsworne;
For where such vices doth remaine
Gods grace will neuer be;
And in your health and happie state
haue yet some minde on me.

Whose songes is changd to sorrowes sore,
my ioyes to wayling woe,
My mirth to mourning sighes and grones,
the which from griefe doth growe;
My wealth to want and scarsetie,
my pleasure into payne,
All for the sinne and wickednesse
which did in me remaine.

If then you wish prosperitie,
be louing meeke and kinde,
Lay rage and rancour cleane aside,
set malice from your minde;
And liue in loue and charitie,
all hatefull pride detest,
And so you shall with happie dayes
for euermore be blest.

And thus I ende my wofull song,
beseeching God I may
Remaine a mirrour to all such
that doe in pleasure stay;
And that amongest their greatest mirth
and chiefest ioye of all,
They yet may haue a heart to thinke
of Beckles sodaine fall.[18]

QUEEN ELIZABETH AT TILBURY[19]

Within the yeare of Christ our Lord
a thousand and fiue hundreth full:
And eightie eight by iust record
the which no man may disanull.
And in the thirtieth yeare remaining,
of good Queene Elizabeths raigning,
A mightie power there was prepared
by Philip, then the king of Spaine:
Against the maiden Queene of England,
which in peace before did raigne.

Her Ryall ships to sea she sent,
to garde the coast on euerie side:
And seeing how her foes were bent,
her realme full well she did prouide.
With many thousands so prepared:
as like was neuer erst declared.
Of horsemen and of footemen plentie,
whose good harts full well is seene:
In the safegarde of their countrie,
and the seruice of our Queene.

In Essex faire that fertill soile,
vpon the hill of Tilsbury:
To giue our Spanish foes the foile,
in gallant campe they now do lye.
Where good orders is ordained,
and true iustice eke maintained,
For the punishment of persons,
that are leude or badly bent.
To see a sight so straunge in England,
t'was our gracious Queenes intent.

And on the eight of August she,
from faire Saint Iames tooke her way:

---

18 Signed *T.D.*, (i.e., Thomas Deloney).

19 *The Queenes visiting of the campe at Tilsburie with her entertainment there. To the tune of Wilsons Wilde,* 1588, STC 6565, British Museum. This ballad was entered in the Stationers' Registers on August 10, the day following the events described.

With many Lords of high degree,
in princely robes and rich aray.
And to bardge vpon the water,
being King Henryes royall daughter,
She did goe with trumpets sounding,
and with dubbing drums apace:
Along the Thames that famous riuer,
for to view the campe a space.

When she as farre as Grauesend came,
right ouer against that prettie towne:
Her royall grace with all her traine,
was landed there with great renowne.
The Lords and Captaines of her forces,
mounted on their gallant horses.
Readie stood to entertaine her,
like martiall men of courage bold:
Welcome to the campe dread soueraigne,
thus they said both yong and old.

The Bulworkes strong that stood thereby,
well garded with sufficient men:
Their flags were spred couragiously,
their cannons were discharged then.
Ech Gunner did declare his cunning,
for ioy conceiued of her coming.
All the way her Grace was riding,
on each side stood armed men:
With Muskets, Pikes, and good Caleeuers,[20]
for her Graces safegarde then.

The Lord generall of the field,
had there his bloudie auncient[21] borne:
The Lord marshals coulors eke,
were carried there all rent and torne.
The which with bullets was so burned,
when in Flaunders he soiourned.
Thus in warlike wise they martched
euen as soft as foote could fall:
Because her Grace was fully minded,
perfectly to view them all.

Her faithfull souldiers great and small,
as each one stood within his place:
Vpon their knees began to fall,
desiring God to saue her Grace.
For ioy whereof her eyes was filled,
that the water downe distilled.
Lord blesse you all my friendes, she said,
but doe not kneele so much to me:
Then sent she warning to the rest,
they should not let such reuerence be.

Then casting vp her Princely eyes,
vnto the hill with perfect sight:
The ground all couered she espyes,
with feet of armed souldiers bright.
Whereat her royall hart so leaped,
on her feet vpright she stepped.
Tossing vp her plume of feathers,
to them all as they did stand:
Chearefully her body bending,
wauing of her royall hand.

Thus through the campe she passed quite,
in manner as I haue declared:
At maister Riches for that night,
her graces lodging was preparde.
The morrow after her abiding,
on a princely paulfrey riding.
To the camp she cam to dinner,
with her Lordes and Ladies all:
The Lord generall went to meete her,
with his Guarde of yeomen tall.

The Sargeant trumpet with his mace,
And nyne with trumpets after him:
Bare headed went before her grace,
in coats of scarlet colour trim.
The king of Heralds tall and comely,
was the next in order duely.
With the famous Armes of England,
wrought with rich imbroidered gold:
On finest veluet blew and crimson,
that for siluer can be sold.

With Maces of cleane beaten gold,
the Queenes two Sargeants then did ride,[22]
Most comely men for to behold,
in veluet coates and chaines beside.
The Lord generall then came riding,
and Lord marshall hard beside him.
Richly were they both atired,
in princelie garments of great price:
Bearing still their hats and fethers
in their handes in comely wise.[23]

Then came the Queene on pranceing steede
atired like an Angell bright:
And eight braue footemen at her feete,

[20] light muskets.
[21] ensign.
[22] *ride,*] *ride* STC 6565.
[23] *wise.*] *wise* STC 6565.

whose Ierkins were most rich in sight.
Her Ladies likewise of great honor,
most sumpteously did waite vpon her.
With pearles and diamonds braue adorned,
and in costly cales[24] of gold:
Her Guarde in scarlet then rid after,
with bowes and arrowes stoute and bold.

The valiant Captaines of the field,
meane space them selues in order set:
And each of them with speare and sheelde,
to ioyne in battaile[25] did not let.[26]
With such a warlike skill extended,
as the same was much commended.
Such a battaile pitcht in England,
many a day hath not beene seene:
Thus they stood in order waiting,
for the presence of our Queene.

At length her grace most royally
receiued was and brought againe:
Where she might see most loyally
this noble hoast and warlike traine.
How they cam martching all together,
like a wood in winters weather.
With the strokes of drummers sounding,
and with trampling horses than:
The earth and aire did sound like thunder,
to the eares of euerie man.

The warlike Armie then stood still,
and drummers left their dubbing sound:
Because it was our Princes will,
to ride about the Armie round.
Her Ladies she did leaue behind her,
and her Guarde which still did minde her.
The Lord generall and Lord marshall,
did conduct her to each place:
The pikes, the colours, and the lances,
at her approch fell downe apace.

And then bespake our Noble Queene,
my louing friends and countriemen:
I hope this day the worst is seene,
that in our wars ye shall sustaine.
But if our enimies doe assaile you,
neuer let your stomackes faile you.
For in the midst of all your troupe,
we our selues will be in place:
To be your ioy, your guide and comfort,
euen before our enimies face.

This done the souldiers all at once,
a mightie shout or crye did giue:
Which forced from the Assure skyes,
an Ecco loud from thence to driue.
Which fild her grace with ioy and pleasure,
and riding then from them by leasure,[27]
With trumpets sound most loyally,
along the Court of guarde she went:
Who did conduct her Maiestie,
vnto the Lord chiefe generals tent.

Where she was feasted royally,
with dainties of most costly price:
And when that night aproched nye,
Her Maiestie with sage aduice,[28]
In gracious manner then returned,
from the Campe where she soiourned.
And when that she was safely set,
within her Barge, and past away:
Her farewell then the trumpets sounded,
and the cannons fast did play.[29]

A SONG OF THE BANISHMENT OF TWO DUKES, HEREFORD AND NORFOLKE[30]

Two Noble Dukes of great renowne,
that long had liu'd in fame,
Through hatefull enuie were cast downe,
and brought to sudden shame.
The Duke of *Hereford* was the one,
a prudent Prince and wise:
Gainst whom such malice there was showne,
which soone in sight did rise.

The Duke of *Norfolk* most vntrue,
declared to the King:

[24] cauls. A caul is the plain part at the back of a woman's cap.
[25] line of troops in battle array.
[26] forbear.
[27] *leasure,*] *leasure.* STC 6565.
[28] *aduice,*] *aduice.* STC 6565.
[29] Signed *T.D.*, (i.e., Thomas Deloney).
[30] From Thomas Deloney, *The garland of good will,* 1631, STC 6554, Bodleian Library. The earliest edition was probably 1593.

The Duke of *Hereford* greatly grew
in hatred of each thing,
Which by his grace was acted still,
against both high and low:
And how he had a trayterous will,
his state to ouerthrow.

The Duke of *Hereford* then in hast,
was sent for to the King:
And by his Lords in order plac't,
examined of each thing.
Which being guiltlesse of this crime,
which was against him laid:
The Duke of Norfolk at that time,
these words vnto him said.

How canst thou with a shamelesse face,
deny a truth so stout:
And here before his Royall Grace,
so falsly face it out:
Did not these treasons from thee passe,
when we together were,
How that the King vnworthy was,
the Royall Crown to beare:

Wherefore, my gracious lord (quoth he)
and you his noble Peeres:
To whom I wish long life to be,
with many happy yeares.
I doe pronounce before you all,
the Duke of *Hereford* here,
A traitor to our noble King,
as time shall shew it cleare.

The Duke of *Hereford* hearing that
in mind was grieued much:
And did returne this answer flat,
which did Duke *Norfolke* touch.
The terme of traitor trothlesse Duke,
in scorne and deepe disdaine:
With flat defiance to thy face
I do returne againe.

And therefore if it please your Grace,
to grant me leaue (quoth he)
To combate with my knowne foe,
that here accuseth me;
I doe not doubt but plainly proue:
that like a periur'd Knight,
He hath most falsly sought my shame,
against all truth and right.

[31] stop.

The King did grant this iust request,
and did therewith agree:
At Couentry in August next,
this combate fought should be.
The Dukes on backed steeds full stout,
in coats of steel most bright:
With spears in rests did enter lists,
this combate fierce to fight.

The King then cast his warder downe,
commanding them to stay:
And with his Lords he counsell tooke,
to stint[31] that mortall fray.
At length vnto these noble Dukes,
the King of Heralds came,
And vnto them with lofty speech,
this sentence did proclaime.

Sir *Henry Bullingbrooke* this day,
the Duke of *Hereford* here,
And *Thomas Moubray, Norfolkes* Duke,
so valiant did appeare:
And hauing in honourable sort,[32]
repaired to this place:
Our noble King, for speciall cause,
hath altred thus the case.

First *Henry* Duke of *Hereford,*
ere fifteene dayes be past:
Shall part this Realme on paine of death,
while ten yeares space doth last.
And *Thomas* Duke of *Norfolke,* thou,
that hast begun this strife,
And therefore no good proofe canst bring,
I say for terme of life.

By iudgement of our Soueraigne Lord,
which now in place doth stand:
For euermore I banish thee,
out of thy natiue Land:
Charging thee on paine of death,
when fifteene dayes are past:
Thou neuer tread on English ground,
so long as life doth last.

Thus they were sworne before the King
ere they did further passe:
The one should neuer come in place,
where as the other was.

[32] manner.

Then both the Dukes with heauy hearts,
were parted presently:[33]
Their vncooth[34] streams of froward chance,
in forraigne Lands to try.

The Duke of *Norfolke* comming then,
where hee should shipping take:
The bitter tears fell downe his cheeks,
and thus his mone did make.
Now let me sob and sigh my fill,
ere I from hence depart:
That inward pangs with speed may burst
my sore afflicted heart.

Ah cursed man whose loathed life
is held so much in scorne:
Whose company is cleane[35] despis'd,
and left as one forlorn.
Now take thy leaue and last adue,
of this thy countrey deare.
Which neuer more thou must behold
nor yet approach it neare.

How happy should I count my self,
if death my heart had torne:
That I might haue my bones entomb'd
where I was bred and borne.
Or that by Neptunes wrathfull rage,
I might be prest[36] to dye;
Whilst that sweet *Englands* pleasant banks,
did stand before mine eye.

How sweet a sent hath English ground,
within my senses now:
How faire vnto my outward sight,
seemes euery branch and bow.
The fields and flowers, the trees and stones,
seeme such vnto my mind:
That in all other Countries sure,
the like I shall not find.

Oh that the Sun with shining face,
would stay his Steeds by strength:
That this same day might stretched be
to twenty yeares of length.
And that the true performed tides,
their hasty course would stay:
That *Eolus*[37] would neuer yeeld,
to beare me hence away.
That by the Fountaine of mine eye,
the fields might watred be:
That I might graue my grieuous plaints,
vpon each springing tree.
But time I see with Eagles wings,
too swift doth flye away:
And dusky clouds begin to dim
the brightnes of the day.

The fatall houre draweth on,
the winds and tides agree:
And now sweet England ouer soone,
I must depart from thee.
The mariners haue hoisted sailes,
and call to catch me in:
And now in wofull heart I feele,
my torments to begin.

Wherefore farwell for euermore,
sweet England vnto thee:
And farwell all my freinds which I
againe shall neuer see.
And England here I kisse thy ground
vpon my bended knee:
Whereby to shew to all the world,
how deare I loued thee.

This being said, away he went,
as fortune did him guide:
And at the length with griefe of hart,
in Venice there he died.
The Duke in dolefull sort,
did leade his life in France:
And at the last the mighty Lord,
did him full high aduance.

The Lords of *England* afterward,
did send for him againe:
While that King *Richard* at the wars,
in Ireland did remaine.
Who through the vile and great abuse,
which through his deeds did spring,
Deposed was, and then the Duke
was truly crowned King.

THE WIDDOWES SOLACE, TO THE TUNE OF ROBINSONS ALMAINE[38]

Mourne no more faire widdow,
teares are all in vaine:

[33] at once.
[34] unknown.
[35] completely.
[36] ready, eager.
[37] Aeolus, ruler of the winds.
[38] From Thomas Deloney, *The garland of good will,* 1631.

Tis neither griefe nor sorrow,
can call the dead againe.
Man's well enough compared
vnto the Summers flower:
Which now is faire and pleasant,
yet withered in an houre.
And mourne no more in vaine,
as one whose faith is small:
Be patient in affliction,
and giue god thanks for all.

All men are borne to dye,
the Scripture telleth plaine,
Of earth we are created,
to earth we must againe.
Twas neither *Cressus* treasure,
nor *Alexanders* fame,
Nor *Solomon* by wisdome,
that could deaths fury tame.
No Physicke might preserue them
when nature did decay:
What man can hold for euer,
the thing that will away.
Then mourn no more, &c.

Though you haue lost your husband,
your comfort in distresse:
Consider God regardeth
the widdowes heauinesse.
And hath straightly charged,
such as his children be,
The fatherlesse and widdow,
to shield from iniury.
Then mourn no more, &c.

If he were true and faithfull,
and louing vnto thee:
Doubt not but ther's in England,
enough as good as he.
But if that such affection,
within his heart was none:
Then giue God praise and glory,
that he is dead and gone.
And mourne no more, &c.

Receiue such sutors friendly,
as do resort to thee:
Respect[39] not the outward person,
but the inward grauity:
And with aduised iudgment,
chuse him aboue the rest:
Whom thou by proofe hast tried,
in heart to loue thee best.
Then mourne no more, &c.

Then shalt thou leade a life,
exempt from all annoy:
And whensoeuer it chanceth,
I pray God giue thee ioy.
And thus I make an end,
with true humilitie,
In hope my simple solace,
shall well accepted be.
Then mourne no more in vaine, &c.

THE WEAUERS SONG[40]

When *Hercules* did vse to spin,
and *Pallas* wrought vpon the Loome,
Our trade to flourish did begin,
while Conscience went not selling Broome.[41]
Then loue and friendship did agree,
To keepe the band of amitie.

When Princes sonnes kept sheep in field,
and Queenes made cakes of wheaten flower,
Then men to lucre did not yeeld,
which brought good cheare in euery bower.
Then loue and friendship did agree,
To hold the bands of amitie.

But when that Giants huge and hie,
did fight with speares like Weauers beames,[42]
Then they in Iron beds did lie,[43]
and brought poore men to hard extreames.
Yet loue and friendship did agree,
To hold the bands of amitie.

Then *Dauid* tooke his sling and stone,
not fearing great *Golias* strength:
He pearc't his braines and broke the bone,

[39] consider.

[40] From Thomas Deloney, *The pleasant historie of Iohn Winchcomb, in his younger yeares called Iack of Newbery*, 1619, STC 6569, Huntington Library; written about 1597.

[41] Selling broom was considered a mean occupation.

[42] I Samuel xvii, 7 (Geneva Bible, 1560): "And the shafte of his speare was like a weauers beame."

[43] Deuteronomy iii, 11 (Geneva Bible): "For onelie Og King of Bashan remained of the remnant of the gyants, whose bed was a bed of yron."

though he were fifty foote of length.
For loue and friendship &c.

But while the Greekes besieged *Troy,*
Penelope apace did spin,
And Weauers wrought with mickle ioy,
though little gaines were comming in.
For loue and friendship, &c.

Had *Helen* then sate carding wooll
(whose beautious face did breed such strife)
She had not beene sir *Paris* trull,
nor caused so many lose their life.
Yet we by loue did still agree, &c.

Or had King *Priams* wanton sonne,
beene making quils[44] with sweet content,
He had not then his friends vndone,
when he to *Greece* a gadding went,
For loue and friendship did agree, &c.

The Cedar tree indures more stormes,
than little shrubs, that sprout not hie:
The Weauers liue more voyd of harmes,
than Princes of great dignitie.
While loue and friendship doth agree, &c.

The Shepheard sitting in the field,
doth tune his pipe with hearts delight:
When Princes watch with speare and shield,
the poore man soundly sleepes all night.
While loue and friendship doth agree, &c.

Yet this by proofe is daily tride,
for Gods good gifts wee are ingrate:
And no man through the World so wide,
liues well contented with his state.
No loue and friendship wee can see,
To hold the bands of amitie.

Ierusalem my happy home,[45]
when shall I come to thee:
When shall my sorrows haue an end,
thy ioyes when shall I see?

O happy Citty of the Saintes!
o sweet and pleasant soyle!
In thee no sorrow may be found,
no griefe, no care, no toyle.

There is no dampe nor foggy mist,
no clowde nor darksome night:
There, euery Saint shines like the Sunne,
there, God himselfe giues light.

In thee no sicknes may be found,
no hurt, no ache, no sore:
In thee there is no dread of death,
There's life for euermore.

There is no raine, no sleete, no snow,
no filth may there be found:
There is no sorrow, nor no care,
all ioy doth there abound.

Ierusalem, *my happy home,*
When shall I come to thee:
When shall my sorrowes haue an end,
Thy ioyes when shall I see.

Thy walles are all of precious stones,
thy streetes paued with golde:
Thy gates are eke of precious pearle,
most glorious to beholde.

Thy Pinacles and Carbuncles,
With Diamondes doe shine:[46]
Thy houses couered are with golde,
most perfect, pure and fine.

Thy gardens and thy pleasant walkes,
continually are greene:
There growes the sweet and fairest flowers
that euer erst was seene.

There, Sinamon, there, Ciuet sweet,
there, Balme springs from the ground:
No tongue can tell, no heart conceiue,
the ioyes that there abound.

Thy happy Saints (Ierusalem)
doe bathe in endlesse blisse:

[44] Reeds or other hollow stems on which yarn is wound.

[45] From *The Song of Mary the Mother of Christ,* 1601, STC 17547, New York Public Library, Berg Collection.

[46] British Museum, Addit. Ms. 15225, f. 36v reads *Thy turrettes, and thy Pinacles/with Carbuncles Doe shine.*

None but those blessed soules, can tell
how great thy glory is.

Throughout thy streetes with siluer streames,
the flood of life doth flowe;
Vpon whose bankes, on euery side,
the wood of life doth growe.

Those trees doe euermore beare fruite,
and euermore doe spring:
There, euermore the Saints doe sit,
and euermore doe sing.

There *Dauid* stands with Harpe in hand,
as Master of the Quire:
Ten thousand times that man were blest,
that might his musique heare.

Our Lady sings *Magnificat,*
with tune surpassing sweet:
And all the Virgins beare their parts,
sitting about her feete.

Te deum doth Saint Ambrose sing,
Saint *Augustine* the like:
Old *Simeon*[47] and good *Zacharie,*[48]
haue not their songs to seeke.

There *Magdalen* hath lost her moane,
and she likewise doth sing
With happy Saints, whose harmony
in euery streete doth ring.

There all doe liue in such delight,
such pleasure and such play:
That thousand thousand yeares agoe,
doth seeme but yesterday.

Ierusalem my happy home,
when shall I come to thee:
When shall my sorrowes haue an end,
thy ioyes when shall I see?

---

47 *Nunc dimittis,* Luke ii, 29–32.

48 *Benedictus,* Luke i, 68–79.

Sir Philip Sidney

[1554–1586]

SIR PHILIP SIDNEY, famous in his own day as scholar, poet, courtier, diplomat, and soldier, exhibited in life and literature the qualities of the ideal Renaissance gentleman. The son of Sir Henry Sidney and the nephew of the famous Earl of Leicester, he was born at Penshurst in Kent. In 1563 he entered Shrewsbury School; here he met Fulke Greville, who became his lifelong friend. He was at Oxford for four years but he took no degree. From 1572 to 1575 he traveled in France, Germany, Hungary, Italy, and the Netherlands. In 1577 he went abroad again, this time as ambassador to the emperor and the elector palatine. At about this time he became associated with a group of young men —Greville, Edward Dyer, and others—who were interested in writing poetry and especially in experiments with classical prosody in English. In 1579 one Stephan Gosson published *The School of Abuse*, attacking plays and poetry, and dedicated it to Sidney; Sidney's *Defence of Poesy* (written, c. 1583; printed, 1595) replies to Gosson's attack. In 1580, when for a short time he lost Queen Elizabeth's favor, he retired to Wilton, the home of his sister Mary, Countess of Pembroke, and wrote for her entertainment at least part of his pastoral romance *Arcadia*. He was knighted in 1583, and in 1585 he was sent to Holland as governor of Flushing. In 1586 he died from a wound that he received in combat at Zutphen.

Nothing that Sidney wrote was published during his lifetime. *The Countess of Pembroke's Arcadia* was published in 1590 in Sidney's incomplete revision of his first draft, and again in 1593 with additions from the unrevised first draft. His sonnet sequence, *Astrophel and Stella*, was published in unauthorized form in 1591; a second edition appeared in the same year, and a third with some revisions in 1592; the authorized edition appeared in 1598, together with all his principal works, prepared for the printer by the Countess of Pembroke.

Between the time of Wyatt and Surrey and the time of Sidney and Spenser English poetry made little progress. The rhythm of English verse grew stiff and monotonous; heavily stressed, regular iambic verse, with fixed caesuras, was used almost exclusively; the sing-song of poulter's measure and the heavy fourteener were the favorite patterns; and there was excessive alliteration. In his *Defence of Poesy* Sidney finds little that is praiseworthy in recent English poetry. He admires Chaucer's *Troilus*, Surrey, the *Mirror for Magistrates*, and Spenser's *Shepheardes Calender*, though he "dare not alowe" the "framing of his stile to an old rustick language." He continues: "Besides these, doe I not remember to haue seene but fewe (to speake boldely) printed, that haue poeticall sinnewes in them: for proofe whereof, let but most of the verses bee put in Prose, and then aske the meaning; and it will be found that one verse did but beget another, without ordering at the first what should be at the last; which becomes a confused masse of words, with a tingling sound of ryme, barely accompanied with reason." Elsewhere in the *Defence* he objects to the diction of the poets, to their "painted affectation," their "far fette words" that "must seeme straungers to any poore English man." In *Astrophel and Stella* (in Sonnet 15 and elsewhere) Sidney mentions other faults of contemporary poets: the use of too many classical allusions and of too much alliteration, subservience to Petrarch, a lack of genuine emotion. These faults he sought to avoid.

Before writing *Astrophel and Stella* Sidney experimented with a variety of verse forms and rhetorical devices. In his metrical translation of the first forty-three Psalms he used the simplest diction and a wide variety of stanzaic patterns. The *Arcadia*, though written in prose, contains some eighty songs and eclogues, many of them experiments in classical meters and Italian verse forms. It was probably from his experiments with classical prosody that he learned to free the line from the shackles of the too regular iambic rhythm. His experiments with various Italian verse forms gave him practice in elaborate rhyme patterns and trained his ear to a more varied stanzaic music. Many of the poems in *Arcadia* are mere exercises, but there are a few remarkable achievements, among them the slow, haunting music of the double sestina "Ye Gote-heard Gods, that loue the grassie mountaines" and the monosyllabic simplicity and perfect movement of the sonnet "My true loue hath my hart, and I haue his."

From his laborious experiments he learned to achieve variety within the line and throughout the poem as a whole. He learned also that control of movement, that logical ordering of the thought, that directness, that fresh and simple language, which mark the best sonnets and songs in *Astrophel and Stella*. This sonnet sequence, which revived an interest in Petrarchan amatory verse, was influential in establishing the vogue of the sonnet cycle in the 1590's. It is generally believed that the one hundred eight sonnets and eleven songs in *Astrophel and Stella* (the star-lover and the star) tell of Sidney's love for the first Earl of Essex's daughter, Penelope Devereux. In 1581 she was married to Robert, Lord Rich, and in 1584 Sidney married Frances, daughter of Sir Francis Walsingham. It is probable that Sidney wrote about one third of the sonnets before Penelope's marriage. Whatever the autobiographical element in the sequence, Stella was a symbol that prompted Sidney to write a few of the best sonnets in our language.

The simplicity, force, depth, and music of his poetry made him a major influence in his day—an influence that would doubtless have been greater if his verse had been printed in the 1580's.

The standard edition is *The Complete Works of Sir Philip Sidney*, ed. A. Feuillerat, 4 vols., 1912–1926. For a discussion of the poetry see H. H. Hudson, "Penelope Devereux as Sidney's Stella," *Huntington Library Bulletin*, vii (1935), 89–129; J. M. Purcell, "Sidney's *Astrophel and Stella* and Greville's *Caelica*," *PMLA*, l (1935), 413–422; Theodore Spencer, "The Poetry of Sir Philip Sidney," *English Literary History*, xii (1945), 251–278. The best biographies are Fulke Greville, *Life of Sir Philip Sidney*, 1652, ed. Nowell Smith, 1907; M. W. Wallace, *The Life of Sir Philip Sidney*, 1915; Mona Wilson, *Sir Philip Sidney*, 1931; A. H. Bill, *Astrophel*, 1937. For bibliography see S. A. Tannenbaum, *Sir Philip Sidney, a Concise Bibliography*, 1941.

From ASTROPHEL AND STELLA[1]

1

Louing in truth, and faine in verse my loue to show,[2]
That she (deare she) might take some pleasure of my paine:
Pleasure might cause her reade, reading might make her know,
Knowledge might pitie winne, and pitie grace obtaine,
I sought fit words to paint the blackest face of woe,
Studying inuentions[3] fine, her wits to entertaine:
Oft turning others leaues, to see if thence would flow
Some fresh and fruitfull showers vpon my sunne-burn'd braine
But words came halting forth, wanting Inuentions stay,[4]
Inuention Natures child, fled step-dame Studies blowes,
And others feete still seem'd but strangers in my way.
Thus great with child to speake, and helplesse in my throwes,
Biting my trewand pen, beating my selfe for spite,
Foole, said my Muse to me, looke in thy heart and write.

2

Not at the first sight, nor with a dribbed[5] shot
Loue gaue the wound, which while I breathe will bleed:
But knowne worth did in mine[6] of time proceed,
Till by degrees it had full conquest got.
I saw and liked, I liked but loued not,
I loued, but straight did not what *Loue* decreed:
At length to *Loues* decrees, I forc'd, agreed,
Yet with repining at so partiall[7] lot.
Now euen that footstep of lost libertie

[1] From *The Countesse of Pembrokes Arcadia*, 1598, STC 22541, Huntington Library.
[2] This and a few other sonnets in the sequence are in hexameter.
[3] rhetorical devices.
[4] lacking the help of imagination.
[5] inaccurate.
[6] tunnel dug under a fortification.
[7] unjust.

Is gone, and now like slaue-borne *Muscouite,*
I call it praise to suffer Tyrannie;
And now employ the remnant of my wit,
To make my[8] selfe beleeue, that all is well,
While with a feeling skill I paint my hell.

3

Let daintie wits crie on the Sisters nine,[9]
That brauely[10] maskt, their fancies may be told:
Or *Pindares* Apes,[11] flaunt they in phrases fine,
Enam'ling with pied flowers[12] their thoughts of gold:
Or else let them in statelier glorie shine,
Ennobling new found Tropes with problemes old:
Or with strange similies enrich each line,
Of herbes or beastes, which *Inde* or *Afrike* hold.[13]
For me in sooth, no Muse but one I know:
Phrases and Problemes from my reach do grow,
And strange things cost too deare for my poore sprites.[14]
How then? euen thus: in *Stellas* face I reed,
What Loue and Beautie be, then all my deed
But Copying is, what in her Nature writes.

5

It is most true, that eyes are form'd to serue
The inward light: and that the heauenly part
Ought to be king, from whose rules who do swerue,
Rebels to Nature striue for their owne smart.[15]
It is most true, what we call *Cupids* dart,
An image is, which for our selues we carue;
And, fooles, adore in temple of our hart,
Till that good God make Church and Churchman starue.
True, that true Beautie Vertue is indeed,
Whereof this Beautie can be but a shade,
Which elements with mortall mixture breed:
True, that on earth we are but pilgrims made,
And should in soule vp to our countrey moue:
True, and yet true that I must *Stella* loue.

7

When Nature made her chiefe worke, *Stellas* eyes,
In colour blacke, why wrapt she beames so bright?
Would she in beamie blacke, like painter wise,
Frame daintiest lustre, mixt of shades and light?
Or did she else that sober hue deuise,
In obiect best to knit and strength our sight,

---

8 *my* STC 22538]; *me* STC 22541.
9 The Muses.
10 splendidly.
11 Imitators of Pindar, Greek lyric poet, 522–448 B.C.
12 adorning with varicolored flowers (of rhetoric).
13 These lines refer to the peculiarities of euphuistic prose.
14 spirits.
15 pain.

Least if no vaile these braue gleames did disguise,
They sun-like should more dazle then delight?
Or would she her miraculous power show,
That whereas blacke seemes Beauties contrary,
She euen in blacke doth make all beauties flow?
Both so and thus, she minding[16] *Loue* should be
Placed euer there, gaue him this mourning weed,[17]
To honor all their deaths, who for her bleed.

10

Reason, in faith thou art well seru'd, that still
Wouldst brabling[18] be with sence and loue in me:
I rather wisht thee clime the Muses hill,
Or reach the fruite of Natures choisest tree,
Or seeke heau'ns course, or heau'ns inside to see:
Why shouldst thou toyle our thornie soile to till?
Leaue sense, and those which senses obiects be:
Deale thou with powers of thoughts, leaue loue to will.
But thou wouldst needs fight both with loue and sence,
With sword of wit, giuing wounds of dispraise,
Till downe-right blowes did foyle thy cunning fence:[19]
For soone as they strake thee with *Stellas* rayes,
Reason thou kneel'dst, and offeredst straight to proue
By reason good, good reason her to loue.

11

In truth, O loue,[20] with what a boyish kind[21]
Thou doest proceed in thy most serious wayes:
That when the heau'n to thee his best displayes,
Yet of that best thou leau'st the best behind.
For like a child that some faire booke doth find,
With guilded leaues or colourd Velume playes,
Or at the most on some fine picture stayes,
But neuer heeds the fruit of writers mind:
So when thou saw'st in Natures cabinet
Stella, thou straight lookst babies in her eyes,[22]
In her cheekes pit[23] thou didst thy pitfould[24] set:
And in her breast bopeepe or couching[25] lyes,
Playing and shining in each outward part:
But, foole, seekst not to get into her hart.

15

You that do search for euerie purling spring,
Which from the ribs of old *Parnassus* flowes,
And euerie floure not sweet perhaps, which growes

---

16 intending.
17 clothing.
18 quarreling.
19 defense.
20 Cupid.
21 fashion.
22 see tiny reflections of yourself.
23 dimple.
24 pitfall, snare.
25 hiding.

Neare thereabouts, into your Poesie wring.[26]
You that do Dictionaries methode bring
Into your rimes, running in ratling rowes:
You that poore *Petrarchs* long deceased woes,
With new-borne sighes and denisend[27] wit do sing.
You take wrong waies:[28] those far-fet[29] helpes be such,
As do bewray[30] a want of inward tuch:[31]
And sure at length stolne goods do come to light.
But if (both for your loue and skill) your name
You seeke to nurse at fullest breasts of Fame,
Stella behold, and then begin to endite.[32]

21

Your words my friend (right healthfull caustiks)[33] blame
My young mind marde, whom *Loue* doth windlas[34] so,[35]
That mine owne writings like bad seruants show
My wits, quicke in vaine thoughts, in vertue lame:
That *Plato* I read for nought, but if he tame
Such coltish yeeres, that to my birth I owe
Nobler desires, least else that friendly foe,
Great expectation, weare a traine of shame.
For since mad March great promise made of me,
If now the May of my yeares much decline,
What can be hoped my haruest time will be?
Sure you say well, your wisdomes golden mine,
Dig deepe with learnings spade, now tell me this,
Hath this world ought so faire as *Stella* is?

24

Rich[36] fooles there be, whose base and filthy hart
Lies hatching[37] still the goods wherein they flow:
And damning their owne selues to *Tantals* smart,[38]
Wealth breeding want, more blist,[39] more wretched grow.
Yet to those fooles heau'n such wit doth impart,
As what their hands do hold, their heads do know,
And knowing *Loue,* and louing lay apart,
As sacred things, far from all daungers show.
But that rich foole who by blind Fortunes lot,
The richest gemme of Loue and life enioyes,
And can with foule abuse such beauties blot;
Let him depriued of sweet but vnfelt ioyes,
(Exil'd for ay from those high treasures, which
He knowes not) grow in only follie rich.

26 force violently.

27 denizened, admitted to the rights of citizenship.

28 *waies:*] *wayes,* STC 22538; *waies* STC 22541.

29 far-fetched.

30 reveal.

31 emotion.

32 write.

33 Remedies that burn.

34 ensnare, deceive or bewilder by leading through winding or roundabout paths.

35 In lines 2–11 of this sonnet Sidney quotes his friend; in lines 12–14 he replies.

36 This is one of several sonnets that contain puns on the name of Penelope's husband, Lord Rich.

37 obstructing, damming up.

38 The "smart" of Tantalus was to suffer from hunger and thirst with food and water just beyond his reach.

39 blest. STC 22538 reads *rich.*

27

Because I oft in darke abstracted guise,
Seeme most alone in greatest companie:
With dearth of words, or answers quite awrie,
To them that would make speech of speech arise.
They deeme, and of their doome the rumour flies,
That poison foule of bubling pride doth lie:
So in my swelling breast that only I
Fawne on my selfe, and others do despise:
Yet pride I thinke doth not my soule possesse,
Which lookes too oft in his vnflattring glasse:
But one worse fault *Ambition* I confesse,
That makes me oft my best friends ouerpasse,
Vnseene, vnheard, while thought to highest place
Bends all his powers, euen vnto *Stellas* grace.

28

You that with allegories curious frame,
Of others children changelings vse to make,[40]
With me those paines for Gods sake do not take:[41]
I list not dig so deepe for brasen fame.
When I say, *Stella,* I do meane the same
Princesse of Beautie, for whose only sake,
The raines[42] of *Loue* I loue, though neuer slake,[43]
And ioy therein, though Nations count it shame.
I beg no subiect to vse eloquence,
Nor in hid wayes do guide Philosophie:
Looke at my hands for no such quintessence;[44]
But know that I in pure simplicitie,
Breathe out the flames which burne within my heart,
Loue onely reading vnto me this art.

31

With how sad steps, O Moone, thou climb'st the skies,
How silently, and with how wanne a face,
What may it be, that euen in heau'nly place
That busie archer[45] his sharpe arrowes tries?
Sure if that long with *Loue* acquainted eyes
Can iudge of *Loue,* thou feel'st a Louers case;
I reade it in thy lookes, thy languisht grace
To me that feele the like, thy state descries.[46]
Then eu'n of fellowship, O Moone, tell me
Is constant *Loue* deem'd there but want of wit?
Are Beauties there as proud as here they be?
Do they aboue loue to be lou'd, and yet
Those Louers scorne whom that *Loue* doth possesse?
Do they call *Vertue* there vngratefulnesse?[47]

---

[40] you who interpret all poetry as though it were allegory.

[41] *take:*] *take,* STC 22538; *take* STC 22541.

[42] reins.

[43] slack.

[44] mystery, the fifth essence sought by the philosophers.

[45] Cupid.

[46] reveals.

[47] Do they call ungratefulness a virtue there?

35

What may words say, or what may words not say,
  Where truth it selfe must speake like flatterie?
  Within what bounds can one his liking stay,[48]
  Where Nature doth with infinite agree?
What *Nestors* counsell can my flames alay,
  Since Reason selfe doth blow the cole in me?
  And ah what hope, that hope should once see day,
  Where *Cupid* is sworne page to Chastity?
Honour is honour'd, that thou doest possesse
  Him as thy slaue, and now long needy Fame
  Doth euen grow rich, naming my *Stellas* name.
Wit learnes in thee perfection to expresse,
  Not thou by praise, but praise in thee is raisde:
  It is a praise to praise, when thou art praisde.

39

Come sleepe, O sleepe, the certaine knot of peace,
  The baiting place[49] of wit, the balme of woe,
  The poore mans wealth, the prisoners release,
  Th'indifferent[50] Iudge betweene the high and low;
With shield of proofe[51] shield me from out the prease[52]
  Of those fierce darts, dispaire at me doth throw:
  O make in me those ciuill warres to cease;
  I will good tribute pay if thou do so.
Take thou of me smooth pillowes, sweetest bed,
  A chamber deafe to noise, and blind to light:
  A rosie[53] garland, and a wearie hed:
And if these things, as being thine by right,
  Moue not thy heauy grace, thou shalt in me
  Liuelier then else-where *Stellas* image see.

41

Hauing this day[54] my horse, my hand, my launce
  Guided so well, that I obtain'd the prize,
  Both by the iudgement of the English eyes,
  And of some sent from that sweet enemie *Fraunce.*
Horsemen my skill in horsmanship aduance:[55]
  Towne-folkes my strength, a daintier iudge applies
  His praise to sleight,[56] which from good vse[57] doth rise:
  Some luckie wits impute it but to chaunce:
Others, because of both sides I do take
  My bloud from them, who did excell in this,
  Thinke Nature me a man of armes did make.
How farre they shot awrie? the true cause is,

---

48 restrain.
49 Place for rest on a journey.
50 impartial.
51 proven strength.
52 press, throng.
53 This adjective implies comfort and hope and perhaps also silence.
54 A tournament in 1581.
55 praise.
56 skill.
57 practice.

Stella lookt on, and from her heau'nly[58] face
Sent forth the beames, which made so faire my race.

45

Stella oft sees the verie face of wo
Painted in my beclowded stormie face:
But cannot skill to pitie my disgrace,
Not though thereof the cause her selfe she know:
Yet hearing late a fable, which did show
Of Louers neuer knowne, a grieuous case,
Pitie thereof gate in her breast such place,
That from that sea deriu'd teares spring did flow.
Alas, if Fancy drawne by imag'd things,
Though false, yet with free scope more grace doth breed
Then seruants wracke,[59] where new doubts honor brings;
Then thinke my deare, that you in me do reed
Of Louers ruine some sad Tragedie:
I am not I, pitie the tale of me.

54

Because I breathe not loue to euerie one,
Nor do not vse set colours for to weare,
Nor nourish speciall lockes of vowed haire,
Nor giue each speech a full point[60] of a grone.
The courtly Nymphs, acquainted with the mone
Of them, who in their lips *Loues* standerd beare;
What he? say they of me, now I dare sweare,
He cannot loue: no, no, let him alone.
And thinke so still, so *Stella* know my mind,
Professe in deed I do not *Cupids* art;
But you faire maides, at length this true shall find,
That his right badge is but worne in the hart:
Dumbe Swannes, not chatring Pies,[61] do Louers proue,
They loue indeed, who quake to say they loue.

FIRST SONG[62]

Doubt you to whom my Muse these notes entendeth,
Which now my breast orecharg'd to Musicke lendeth:
To you, to you, all song of praise is due,
Only in you my song begins and endeth.

Who hath the eyes which marrie state with pleasure,[63]
Who keepes the key of Natures chiefest treasure:
To you, to you, all song of praise is due,
Only for you the heau'n forgate all measure.[64]

Who hath the lips, where wit in fairenesse raigneth,
Who womankind at once both deckes and stayneth:[65]

[58] *heau'nly*] *heauenly* STC 22538; *hau'nly* STC 22541.
[59] than the wrack (wreck, ruin) of your servant.
[60] period.
[61] magpies.
[62] This song follows Sonnet 63 in STC 22541.
[63] combine dignity with vivacity.
[64] i.e., when heaven made you.
[65] i.e., eclipses.

To you, to you, all song of praise is due,
Onely by you *Cupid* his crowne maintaineth.

Who hath the feet, whose step of sweetnesse planteth,
Who else for whom *Fame* worthy trumpets wanteth:
To you, to you, all song of praise is due,
Onely to you her Scepter *Venus* granteth.

Who hath the breast, whose milke doth passions[66] nourish,
Whose grace is such, that when it chides doth cherish,
To you, to you, all song of praise is due,
Onelie through you the tree of life doth flourish.

Who hath the hand which without stroke subdueth,
Who long dead beautie with increase reneweth:[67]
To you, to you, all song of praise is due,
Onely at you all enuie hopelesse rueth.[68]

Who hath the haire which loosest fastest tieth,
Who makes a man liue then glad when he dieth:
To you, to you, all song of praise is due:
Only of you the flatterer neuer lieth.

Who hath the voyce, which soule from sences sunders,
Whose force but yours the bolts of beautie thunders:
To you, to you, all song of praise is due:
Only with you not miracles are wonders.[69]

Doubt you to whom my Muse these notes intendeth,
Which now my breast orecharg'd to Musicke lendeth:
To you, to you, all song of praise is due:
Only in you my song begins and endeth.

64

No more, my deare, no more these counsels trie,
O giue my passions leaue to run their race:
Let Fortune lay on me her worst disgrace,
Let folke orecharg'd with braine against me crie.
Let clouds bedimme my face, breake in mine yee,
Let me no steps but of lost labour trace:[70]
Let all the earth with scorne recount my case,
But do not will me from my *Loue* to flie.
I do not enuie *Aristotles* wit,
Nor do aspire to *Caesars* bleeding fame;
Nor ought do care, though some aboue me sit:
Nor hope, nor with another course to frame,
But that which once may win thy cruell hart
Thou art my Wit, and thou my Vertue art.

---

[66] *passions* STC 22541]; *patience* STC 22538.
[67] revives and increases in herself charm of beauties long since dead.
[68] grieves.
[69] miracles are not wonders.
[70] follow.

69

O ioy, too high for my low stile to show:
  O blisse, fit for a nobler state then me:
  Enuie, put out thine eyes, least thou do see
  What Oceans of delight in me do flow.
My friend, that oft saw through all maskes my wo,
  Come, come, and let me powre my selfe on thee;
  Gone is the winter of my miserie,
  My spring appeares, O see what here doth grow.
For *Stella* hath with words where faith doth shine,
  Of her high heart giu'n me the monarchie:
  I, I, O I may say, that she is mine.
And though she giue but thus conditionly
  This realme of blisse, while vertuous course I take,
  No kings be crown'd, but they some couenants make.[71]

71

Who will in fairest booke of Nature know,
  How Vertue may best lodg'd in beautie be,
  Let him but learne of *Loue* to reade in thee
  Stella, those faire lines, which true goodnesse show.
There shall he find all vices ouerthrow,
  Not by rude force, but sweetest soueraigntie
  Of reason, from whose light those night-birds flie;
  That inward sunne in thine eyes shineth so.
And not content to be Perfections heire
  Thy selfe, doest striue all minds that way to moue:
  Who marke in thee what is in thee most faire.
So while thy beautie drawes the heart to loue,
  As fast thy Vertue bends that loue to good:
  But ah, Desire still cries, giue me some food.

74

I neuer dranke of *Aganippe* well,[72]
  Nor euer did in shade of *Tempe*[73] sit:
  And Muses scorne with vulgar braines to dwell,
  Poore Layman I, for sacred rites vnfit.
Some do I heare of Poets furie tell,
  But (God wot) wot not what they meane by it:
  And this I sweare by blackest brooke of hell,
  I am no pick-purse of anothers wit.
How falles it then, that with so smooth an ease
  My thoughts I speake, and what I speake doth flow
  In verse, and that my verse best wits doth please?
Guesse we the cause, what is it thus? fie no:
  Or so? much lesse: how then? sure thus it is:
  My lips are sweet, inspired with *Stellas* kisse.

---

[71] *make.* STC 22539]; *make,* STC 22541.
[72] A well or fountain on Mount Helicon, sacred to the Muses.
[73] A valley near Mount Olympus, sacred to Apollo.

FOURTH SONG[74]

Onely ioy, now here you are,
Fit to heare and ease my care:
Let my whispering voyce obtaine,
Sweete reward for sharpest paine:
Take me to thee, and thee to me.
No, no, no, no, my Deare, let be.

Night hath closd all in her cloke,
Twinckling starres Loue-thoughts prouoke:
Danger hence good care doth keepe,
Iealousie it selfe doth sleepe:
Take me to thee, and thee to me.
No, no, no, no, my Deare, let be.

Better place no wit can find,
Cupids yoke to loose or bind:
These sweet flowers on fine bed too,
Vs in their best language woo:
Take me to thee, and thee to me.
No, no, no, no, my Deare, let be.

This small light the Moone bestowes,
Serues thy beames but to disclose,
So to raise my hap more hie;
Feare not else, none can vs spie:
Take me to thee, and thee to me.
No, no, no, no, my Deare, let be.

That you heard was but a Mouse,
Dumbe sleepe holdeth all the house:
Yet a sleepe, me thinkes they say,
Yong folkes, take time while you may:
Take me to thee, and thee to me.
No, no, no, no, my Deare, let be.

Niggard Time threats, if we misse
This large offer of our blisse:
Long stay ere he graunt the same:
Sweet then, while each thing doth frame:[75]
Take me to thee, and thee to me.
No, no, no, no, my Deare, let be.

Your faire mother is abed,
Candles out, and curtaines spread:
She thinkes you do letters write:
Write, but let me first endite:[76]
Take me to thee, and thee to me.
No, no, no, no, my Deare, let be.

Sweet alas, why striue you thus?

---

[74] This song follows Sonnet 85 in STC 22541.

[75] is convenient.

[76] dictate.

Concord better fitteth vs:
Leaue to *Mars* the force of hands,
Your power in your beautie stands:
Take thee to me, and me to thee.
No, no, no, no, my Deare, let be.

Wo to me, and do you sweare
Me to hate, but I forbeare,
Cursed be my destines all,
That brought me so high to fall:
Soone with my death I will please thee.
No, no, no, no, my Deare, let be.

90

Stella thinke not that I by verse seeke fame,
Who seeke, who hope, who loue, who liue but thee;
Thine eyes my pride, thy lips mine history:
If thou praise not, all other praise is shame.
Nor so ambitious am I, as to frame
A nest for my yong praise in Lawrell tree:
In truth I sweare, I wish not there should be
Graued[77] in mine Epitaph a Poets name:
Ne[78] if I would, I could iust title make,
That any laud to me thereof should grow,
Without[79] my plumes from others wings I take,
For nothing from my wit or will doth flow,
Since all my words thy beauty doth endite,[80]
And loue doth hold my hand, and makes me write.

ELEUENTH SONG[81]

Who is it that this darke night,
Vnderneath my window playneth?
It is one who from thy sight,[82]
Being (ah) exild, disdayneth
Euery other vulgar light.

Why alas, and are you he?
Be not yet those fancies changed?
Deere when you find change in me,
Though from me you be estranged,
Let my chaunge to ruine be.

Well in absence this will dy,
Leaue to see, and leaue to wonder:
Absence sure will helpe, if I
Can learne, how my selfe to sunder
From what in my hart doth ly.

---

[77] engraved.
[78] nor.
[79] unless.
[80] inspire me to write.

[81] This song follows Sonnet 104 in STC 22541.
[82] Lines 3–5 in each stanza are the reply to lines 1–2.

But time will these thoughts remoue:
Time doth worke what no man knoweth,
Time doth as the subiect proue,
With time still the affection groweth
In the faithfull Turtle doue.

What if you new beauties see,
Will not they stir new affection?
I will thinke they pictures be,
(Imagelike of Saints perfection)
Poorely counterfeting thee.

But your reasons purest light,
Bids you leaue such minds to nourish?
Deere, do reason no such spite,
Neuer doth thy beauty florish
More, then in my reasons sight.

But the wrongs loue beares, will make
Loue at length leaue vndertaking,
No the more fooles it do shake,
In a ground of so firme making,
Deeper still they driue the stake.

Peace, I thinke that some giue eare:
Come no more, least I get anger.
Blisse, I will my blisse forbeare,
Fearing (sweete) you to endanger,
But my soule shall harbour there.[83]

Well, be gone, be gone I say,
Lest that *Argus*[84] eyes perceiue you,
O vniust fortunes sway,
Which can make me thus to leaue you,
And from lowts to run away.

From ARCADIA[85]

My sheepe are thoughts, which I both guide and serue:
Their pasture is faire hilles of fruitlesse loue:
  On barren sweetes they feed, and feeding sterue:
  I waile their lott, but will not other proue.[86]

My sheepehooke is wanne hope, which all vpholds:
My weedes,[87] Desire, cut out in endlesse folds.
  What wooll my sheepe shall beare, whiles thus they liue,
  In you it is, you must the iudgement giue.

[83] *there.*] *thee.* STC 22541.
[84] In Greek legend, Argus was a giant with a hundred eyes.

[85] From *The Countesse of Pembrokes Arcadia*, 1598, STC 22541, Huntington Library.
[86] test.
[87] clothing.

Strephon

Ye Gote-heard Gods, that loue the grassie mountaines,[88]
Ye Nymphs that haunt the springs in pleasant vallies,
Ye Satyrs ioy'd with free and quiet forrests,
Vouchsafe your silent eares to plaining musike,
Which to my woes giue still an earlie morning,
And drawes the dolor on till wearie euening.

Klaius

O *Mercurie,* foregoer to the euening,
O heauenly huntresse of the sauage mountaines,
O louely starre, entitled of the morning,
While that my voice doth fill these wofull vallies,
Vouchsafe your silent eares to plaining musike,
Which oft hath Echo tyr'd in secret forrests.

Strephon

I that was once free burgesse of the forrests,
Where shade from Sunne, and sports I sought at euening,
I that was once esteem'd for pleasant musike,
Am banisht now among the monstrous mountaines
Of huge despaire, and foule afflictions vallies,
Am growne a shrich-owle to my selfe each morning.

Klaius

I that was once delighted euerie morning,
Hunting the wild inhabiters of forrests:
I that was once the musike of these vallies,
So darkened am, that all my day is euening,
Hart broken so, that molehilles seeme high mountaines,
And fill the vales with cries in steed of musike.

Strephon

Long since alas, my deadlie swannish musike,
Hath made it selfe a crier of the morning,
And hath with wailing strength clim'd highest mountaines:
Long since my thoughts more desert be then forrests:
Long since I see my ioyes come to their euening,
And state throwne downe to ouertroden vallies.

Klaius

Long since the happie dwellers of these vallies,
Haue pray'd me leaue my straunge exclaming musike,
Which troubles their dayes worke, and ioyes of euening:
Long since I hate the night, more hate the morning:
Long since my thoughts chase me like beasts in forrests,
And make me wish my selfe laid vnder mountaines.

Strephon

Me seemes I see the high and statelie mountaines,

---

[88] Sidney calls this verse form a "double sestine." The sestina, developed in France and Italy, is rare in English. The common form of the sestina has six stanzas of six lines each, with a tercet at the end. There is usually no rhyme, and only six end words are used, the order of these words changing in each stanza.

Transforme themselues to low deiected vallies:
Me seemes I heare in these ill chaunged forrests,
The Nightingales do learne of Owles their musike:
Me seemes I feele the comfort of the morning,
Turn'd to the mortall serene of an euening.

Klaius

Me seemes I see a filthy cloudy euening,
As soone as Sunne begins to clime the mountaines:
Me seemes I feele a noysome sent, the morning
When I doo smell the flowers of these vallies:
Me seemes I heare, when I doo heare sweete musicke,
The dreadfull cries of murdred men in forrests.

Strephon

I wish to fire the trees of all those forrests,
I giue the Sunne a last farewell each euening,
I curse the fidling finders out of musicke:
With enuie I doo hate the loftie mountaines;
And with dispite despise the humble vallies;
I doo detest night, euening, day, and morning.

Klaius

Curse to my selfe my praier is, the morning;
My fire is more then can be made with forrests;
My state more base, then are the basest vallies
I wish no euenings more to see, each euening;
Shamed I hate my selfe in sight of mountaines,
And stoppe mine eares, lest I grow mad with musicke.

Strephon

For she whose parts maintainde a perfect musicke,
Whose beautie shin'de more then the blushing morning,
Who much did passe in state[89] the stately mountaines,
In streightnesse past the Cedars of the forrests,
Hath cast me wretch into eternall euening,
By taking her two Sunnes from these darke vallies.

Klaius

For she, to whome compar'd, the Alps are vallies,
She, whose least word brings from the sphears their musick,
At whose approch the Sunne rose in the euening,
Who where she went bare in her forhead morning,
Is gone, is gone, from these our spoyled forrests,
Turning to desarts our best pastur'de mountaines.

Strephon

These mountaines witnesse shall, so shal these vallies,
These forrests eke, made wretched by our musicke,

Klaius

Our morning hymne is this, and song at euening.

---

[89] surpass in grandeur.

O sweet woods the delight of solitarinesse![90]
O how much I do like your solitarinesse!
Where mans mind hath a freed consideration
Of goodnesse to receiue louely direction.
Where senses do beholde th'order of heau'nly hoste,
And wise thoughts do behold what the creator is:
Contemplation here holdeth his only seate:
Bounded with no limits, borne with a wing of hope
Clymes euen vnto the starres, Nature is vnder it.
Nought disturbs thy quiet, all to thy seruice yeelds,
Each sight draws on a thought, thought mother of science,
Sweet bird's kindly do graunt harmony vnto thee,
Faire trees shade is enough fortification,
Nor danger to thy selfe if't[91] be not in thy selfe.

O sweete woods the delight of solitarinesse!
O how much I do like your solitarinesse!
Here nor treason is hid, vailed in innocence,
Nor enuies snakie eye, finds any harbor here,
Nor flatterers venimous insinuations,
Nor cunning[92] humorists pudled opinions,[93]
Nor courteous ruine of proffered vsury,
Nor time pratled away, cradle of ignorance,
Nor causelesse dutie, nor comber[94] of arrogance,
Nor trifling title of vanitie dazleth vs,
Nor golden manacles, stand for a paradise,
Here wrongs name is vnheard: slander a monster is,
Keepe thy sprite from abuse, here no abuse doth haunt.
What man grafts in a tree dissimulation?

O sweete woods the delight of solitarinesse!
O how well I do like your solitarinesse!
Yet deare soile, if a soule clos'd in a mansion
As sweete as violets, faire as a lilly is,
Streight as Cedar, a voice staines[95] the Cannary birds,
Whose shade safety[96] doth hold, danger auoideth her:
Such wisedome, that in her liues speculation:
Such goodnesse that in her simplicitie triumphs:
Where enuies snaky eye, winketh[97] or els dyeth,
Slander wants a pretext, flattery gone beyond:
Oh! if such a one haue bent,[98] to a lonely life,
Her steps glad we receiue, glad we receiue her eys.
And thinke not she doth hurt our solitarinesse,
For such company decks such solitarinesse.

---

90 This is an example of Sidney's experiments with classical meters. The meter used here is the lesser (or shorter) asclepiad, named after its inventor, the Greek poet Asclepiades. The normal line scans as follows: – – / – ˘ ˘ – / – ˘ ˘ – / ˘ –

91 *if't* ed. of 1633] *if* STC 22540 (1593), STC 22541.

92 *cunnnng* STC 22544 (1613)]; *comming,* STC 22540, 22541.

93 faddists' confused opinions.

94 cumber.

95 voice that surpasses.

96 *safety* STC 22544]; *safely* STC 22540, 22541.

97 closes.

98 inclination.

My true loue hath my hart, and I haue his,
By iust exchange, one for the other giu'ne.
I hold his deare, and myne he cannot misse:[99]
There neuer was a better bargaine driu'ne.
His hart in me, keepes me and him in one,
My hart in him, his thoughts and senses guides:
He loues my hart, for once it was his owne:
I cherish his, because in me it bides.
His hart his wound receiued from my sight:
My hart was wounded, with his wounded hart,
For as from me, on him his hurt did light,
So still me thought in me his hurt did smart:
Both equall hurt, in this change sought our blisse:
My true loue hath my hart and I haue his.

Lock vp, faire liddes, the treasure of my hart:
Preserue those beames, this ages onely light:
To her sweete sence,[1] sweete sleepe some ease impart,
Her sence too weake to beare her spirits might.
And while O sleepe thou closest vp her sight,
(Her sight where loue did forge his fairest dart)
O harbour all her parts in easefull plight:
Let no strange dreame make her faire body start.[2]
But yet O dreame, if thou wilt not depart
In this rare subiect from thy common right:
But wilt thy selfe in such a seate delight,
Then take my shape, and play a louers part:
Kisse her from me, and say vnto her spirit,
Till her eyes shine, I liue in darkest night.

From CERTAINE SONETS NEUER BEFORE PRINTED[3]

The Nightingale[4] as soone as Aprill bringeth
Vnto her rested sense a perfect waking,
While late bare earth, proud of new clothing springeth,
Sings out her woes, a thorne her song-booke making:[5]
And mournfully bewailing,
Her throate in tunes expresseth
What griefe her breast oppresseth,
For *Thereus* force on her chaste will preuailing,
O *Philomela* faire, O take some gladnesse,
That here is iuster cause of plaintfull sadnesse:
Thine earth now springs, mine fadeth,
Thy thorne without, my thorne my heart inuadeth.

Alas she hath no other cause of anguish

[99] do without.
[1] senses.
[2] disturb.
[3] Under this title the folio of 1598 (STC 22541) includes twenty-seven poems. Eight of these poems had appeared in Henry Constable's *Diana*, 1594, and one in the *Arcadia*.
[4] Tereus, husband of Procne, violated her sister Philomela. The gods turned Philomela into a nightingale and Procne into a swallow.
[5] i.e., by pressing her breast against a thorn.

But *Thereus* loue, on her by strong hand wrokne,[6]
Wherein she suffring all her spirits languish,
Full womanlike complaines her will was brokne.
But I who dayly crauing,
Cannot haue to content me,
Haue more cause to lament me,
Since wanting[7] is more woe then too much hauing.
O *Philomela* faire, O take some gladnesse,
That here is iuster cause of plaintfull sadnesse:
Thine earth now springs, mine fadeth:
Thy thorne without, my thorne my heart inuadeth.

A FAREWELL

Oft haue I musde, but now at length I finde,
Why those that die, men say they do depart:
Depart, a word so gentle to my minde,
Weakely did seeme to paint deaths ougly dart.
But now the starres with their strange course do binde
Me one to leaue, with whome I leaue my hart.
I heare a crye of spirits faint and blinde,
That parting thus my chiefest part I part.
Part of my life, the loathed part to me,
Liues to impart my wearie clay some breath.
But that good part, wherein all comforts be,
Now dead, doth shew departure is a death,
Yea worse then death, death parts both woe and ioy,
From ioy I part still liuing in annoy.

Who hath his fancie pleased,
With fruits of happie sight,
Let here his eyes be raised
On natures sweetest light.
A light which doth disseuer,
And yet vnite the eyes,
A light which dying neuer,
Is cause the looker dyes.

She neuer dies but lasteth
In life of louers hart,
He euer dies that wasteth
In loue, his chiefest part.
Thus is her life still guarded,
In neuer dying faith:
Thus is his death rewarded,
Since she liues in his death.

Looke then and dye, the pleasure
Doth answere well the paine:
Small losse of mortall treasure,
Who may immortall gaine.
Immortall be her graces,
Immortall is her minde:
They fit for heauenly places,
This heauen in it doth binde.

But eyes these beauties see not,
Nor sence that grace descryes:
Yet eyes depriued be not,
From sight of her faire eyes:
Which as of inward glorie
They are the outward seale:
So may they liue still sorie
Which die not in that weale.

But who hath fancies pleased,
With fruits of happie sight,
Let here his eyes be raysed
On natures sweetest light.

[6] wreaked.

[7] lacking.

Ring out your belles, let mourning shewes be spread,
For loue is dead:
All Loue is dead, infected
With plague of deepe disdaine:
Worth as nought worth reiected,
And Faith faire scorne doth gaine,
From so vngratefull fancie,
From such a femall franzie,[8]
From them that vse men thus,
Good Lord deliuer vs.

Weepe neighbours, weepe, do you not heare it said,
That Loue is dead:
His death-bed peacocks follie,
His winding sheete is shame,
His will false-seeming holie,
His sole exectour blame.
From so vngratefull, etc.

Let Dirge be sung, and Trentals[9] rightly read,
For Loue is dead:
Sir Wrong his tombe ordaineth:
My mistresse Marble-heart,[10]
Which Epitaph containeth,
Her eyes were once his dart.
From so vngratefull, etc.

Alas, I lie: rage hath this errour bred,
Loue is not dead.
Loue is not dead, but sleepeth
In her vnmatched mind:
Where she his counsell keepeth,
Till due desert she find.
Therefore from so vile fancie,
To call such wit a franzie,
Who loue can temper thus,
Good Lord deliuer vs.

Thou blind mans marke, thou fooles selfe chosen snare,
Fond fancies scum, and dregs of scattred thought,
Band of all euils, cradle of causelesse care,
Thou web of will, whose end is neuer wrought.
Desire, desire I haue too dearely bought,
With prise of mangled mind thy worthlesse ware,
Too long, too long asleepe thou hast me brought,
Who should my mind to higher things prepare.
But yet in vaine thou hast my ruine sought,
In vaine thou madest me to vaine things aspire,
In vaine thou kindlest all thy smokie fire.
For vertue hath this better lesson taught,
Within my selfe to seeke my onelie hire:
Desiring nought but how to kill desire.

Leaue me O loue, which reachest but to dust,
And thou my mind aspire to higher things:
Grow rich in that which neuer taketh rust:
What euer fades, but fading pleasure brings.
Draw in thy beames, and humble all thy might,
To that sweet yoke, where lasting freedomes be:
Which breakes the clowdes and opens forth the light.
That doth both shine and giue vs sight to see.
O take fast hold, let that light be thy guide,
In this small course which birth drawes out to death,
And thinke how euill becommeth him to slide,
Who seeketh heau'n, and comes of heau'nly breath.
Then farewell world, thy vttermost I see,
Eternall Loue maintaine thy life in me.

Splendidis longum valedico nugis.[11]

---

8 frenzy.
9 Masses for the dead.
10 injustice decrees that the marble of my mistress' heart shall be the tomb of love.
11 A long farewell to glittering trifles.

VPON HIS MEETING WITH HIS TWO WORTHY FRIENDS AND FELLOW-POETS, SIR EDWARD DIER, AND MAISTER FULKE GREUILL[12]

Ioyne Mates in mirth to me,
Graunt pleasure to our meeting:
Let *Pan* our good God see,
How gratefull is our greeting.
Ioyne hearts and hands, so let it be,
Make but one Minde in Bodies three.

Ye Hymnes, and singing skill
Of God *Apolloes* giuing,
Be prest[13] our reedes to fill,
With sound of musicke liuing.
Ioyne hearts and hands, &c.

Sweete *Orpheus* Harpe, whose sound
The stedfast mountaynes moued,
Let heere thy skill abound,
To ioyne sweete friends beloued.
Ioyne hearts and hands, &c.

My two and I be met,
A happy blessed Trinitie;
As three most ioyntly set,
In firmest band of Vnitie.
Ioyne hands, &c.

Welcome my two to me,[14]
The number best beloued,
Within my heart you be
In friendship vnremoued.
Ioyne hands, &c.

Giue leaue your flockes to range,
Let vs the while be playing,
Within the Elmy grange,[15]
Your flockes will not be straying.
Ioyne hands, &c.

Cause all the mirth you can,
Since I am now come hether,
Who neuer ioy, but when[16]
I am with you together.
Ioyne hands, &c.

Like Louers do their Loue,
So ioy I, in you seeing:
Let nothing mee remoue
From alwayes with you beeing.
Ioyne hands, &c.

And as the Turtle-Doue
To mate with whom he liueth,
Such comfort, feruent loue
Of you, to my hart giueth.
Ioyne hands, &c.

Now ioyned be our hands,
Let them be ne'r a sunder,
But linkt in binding bands
By metamorphoz'd wonder.
So should our seuer'd bodies three
As one for euer ioyned bee.

DISPRAYSE OF A COURTLY LIFE[17]

Walking in bright *Phoebus* blaze
Where with heate opprest I was,
I got to a shady wood,
Where greene leaues did newly bud.
And of grasse was plenty dwelling,
Deckt with pyde[18] flowers sweetely smelling.

In this wood a man I met,
On lamenting wholy set:
Rewing change of wonted state,
Whence he was transformed late,
Once to Shepheards God retayning,[19]
Now in seruile Court remayning.

There he wandring malecontent,
Vp and downe perplexed went,
Daring not to tell to mee,
Spake vnto a sencelesse tree,
One among the rest electing
These same words, or this effecting:

My old mates I grieue to see,
Voyde of me in field to bee,
Where we once our louely sheepe,
Louingly like friends did keepe,
Oft each others friendship prouing,
Neuer striuing, but in louing.

But may Loue abiding bee

---

[12] From *A poetical rapsody,* 1602, STC 6373, Folger Library.
[13] ready.
[14] Marginal note: *E.D. F.G. P.S.*
[15] farm buildings.
[16] The rhyme requires the old spelling *whan.*
[17] From *A poetical rapsody,* 1602.
[18] of various colors.
[19] being a retainer.

In poore shepheards base degree?
It belongs to such alone
To whom arte of Loue is knowne:
Seely[20] shepheards are not witting
What in art of Loue is fitting.

Nay, what neede the Arte to those,
To whom we our loue disclose?
It is to be vsed then,
When we doe but flatter men:
Friendship true in hart assured,
Is by natures giftes procured.

Therefore shepheardes wanting skill,
Can Loues duties best fulfill:
Since they know not how to faine,
Nor with Loue to cloake Disdaine,
Like the wiser sorte, whose learning,
Hides their inward will of harming.

Well was I, while vndershade
Oten Reedes me musicke made.
Striuing with my Mates in Song,
Mixing mirth our Songs among,
Greater was that shepheards treasure,
Then this false, fine, Courtly pleasure.

Where, how many Creatures be,
So many pufft in minde I see,
Like to *Iunoes* birdes of pride,[21]
Scarce each other can abide,
Friends like to blacke Swannes appearing,
Sooner these than those in hearing.

Therefore *Pan,* if thou mayst be
Made to listen vnto me,
Grant, I say (if seely man
May make treaty to god *Pan*)
That I, without thy denying,
May be still to thee relying.

Only for my two loues sake,[22]
In whose loue I pleasure take,
Only two do me delight
With their euer-pleasing sight,
Of all men to thee retaining,
Grant me with those two remaining.

So shall I to thee alwayes,
With my reedes, sound mighty praise;
And first Lambe that shall befall,
Yearely decke thine Alter shall:
If it please thee be reflected,[23]
And I from thee not reiected.

So I left him in that place,
Taking pitty on his case,
Learning this among the rest,
That the meane estate is best,
Better filled with contenting,
Voyde of wishing and repenting.

---

[20] simple.
[21] peacocks.

[22] Marginal note: *Sir Ed. D. and M. F. G.* i.e., Dyer and Greville.
[23] highly regarded, worshiped.

Sir Edward Dyer

[1543–1607]

SIR EDWARD DYER was born in Somersetshire, the eldest son of Sir Thomas Dyer, a "gentleman steward" in the household of Henry VIII. It is probable that he attended Oxford, but he took no degree. From about 1565 until the death of Queen Elizabeth Dyer held various minor posts at court. In 1596 he was knighted.

Best known as the friend of Sidney and Greville, he was eleven years older than they, and his extant poetry is more old-fashioned than theirs. Though he was well known as a poet, only a few of his poems (his editor limits the number to fourteen) have survived in early miscellanies and manuscripts.

The standard edition is R. M. Sargent, *At the Court of Queen Elizabeth. The Life and Lyrics of Sir Edward Dyer*, 1935. See also B. M. Wagner, "New Poems by Sir Edward Dyer," *Review of English Studies*, October, 1935, pp. 467–468. The best account of Dyer's life is in Sargent.

ANOTHER OF THE SAME. EXCELLENTLY WRITTEN BY A MOST WOORTHY GENTLEMAN[1]

Silence augmenteth griefe, writing encreaseth rage,
Stald are my thoughts, which lou'd, and lost, the wonder of our age,
Yet quickned now with fire, though dead with frost ere now,
Enrag'de I write, I know not what: dead, quick, I know not how.

Hard harted mindes relent, and rigors teares abound,
And enuie strangely rues his end, in whom no fault she found,
Knowledge hir light hath lost, valor hath slaine hir knight,
Sidney is dead, dead is my friend, dead is the worlds delight.

Place[2] pensiue wailes his fall, whose presence was hir pride,
Time crieth out, my ebbe is come: his life was my spring tide,
Fame mournes in that she lost, the ground of hir reports,
Ech liuing wight laments his lacke, and all in sundry sorts.

[1] From *The phoenix nest*, 1593, STC 21516, Folger Library. The preceding poem in *The Phoenix Nest* is Sir Walter Raleigh's elegy on Sir Philip Sidney. This poem is probably by Dyer.

[2] Men of high rank.

He was (wo worth that word) to ech well thinking minde,
A spotlesse friend, a matchles man, whose vertue euer shinde,
Declaring in his thoughts, his life, and that he writ,
Highest conceits, longest foresights, and deepest works of wit.

He onely like himselfe, was second vnto none,
Whose deth (though life) we rue, and wrong,[3] and al in vain do mone,
Their losse, not him waile they, that fill the world with cries,
Death slue not him, but he made death his ladder to the skies.

Now sinke of sorow I, who liue, the more the wrong,
Who wishing death, whom deth denies, whose thred is al to long,
Who tied to wretched life, who lookes for no reliefe,
Must spend my euer dying daies, in neuer ending griefe.

Harts ease and onely[4] I, like parallels[5] run on,
Whose equall length, keepe equall bredth, and neuer meet in one,
Yet for not wronging him, my thoughts, my sorowes cell,
Shall not run out, though leake they will, for liking him so well.

Farewell to you my hopes, my wonted waking dreames,
Farewell somtimes enioied ioy, eclipsed are thy beames,
Farewell selfe pleasing thoughts, which quietnes brings foorth,
And farewel friendships sacred league, vniting minds of woorth.

And farewell mery hart, the gift of guiltles mindes,
And all sports, which for liues restore,[6] varietie assignes,
Let all that sweete is, voide;[7] in me no mirth may dwell,
Philip, the cause of all this woe, my liues content farewell.

Now rime, the sonne of rage, which art no kin to skill,
And endles griefe, which deads my life, yet knowes not how to kill,
Go seeke that haples tombe, which if ye hap to finde,
Salute the stones, that keepe the lims, that held so good a minde.

Alas my hart, mine eie hath wronged thee,[8]
Presumptious eie, to gaze on Phillis face:
Whose heauenly eie, no mortall man may[9] see,
But he must die, or purchase Phillis grace;
  Poore Coridon, the Nimph whose eie doth moue thee,
  Doth loue to draw, but is not drawne to loue thee.

Hir beautie, Natures pride, and Shepherds praise,
Hir eie, the heauenly Planet of my life,
Hir matchles wit, and grace, hir fame displaies,
As if that Ioue had made hir for his wife;

---

[3] but wrongly.
[4] alone.
[5] *parallels*] *parables* STC 21516.
[6] restoration.
[7] *voide;*] *voide?* STC 21516: avoid, depart.
[8] From *The phoenix nest*, 1593. This poem is reprinted in *England's Helicon*, 1600, where it is entitled *Coridon to his Phillis*.
[9] *may*] *my* STC 21516.

Onely hir eies shoote firie darts to kill,
Yet is hir hart, as cold as Caucase hill.

My wings too weake, to flie against the Sunne,
Mine eies vnable to sustaine hir light,
My hart doth yeeld, that I am quite vndoon,
Thus hath faire Phillis slaine me with hir sight:
My bud is blasted, withered is my leafe,
And all my corne is rotted in the sheafe.

Phillis, the golden fetter of my minde,
My fancies Idoll, and my vitall powre;
Goddesse of Nimphes, and honor of thy kinde,
This Ages Phenix, Beauties brauest bowre;
Poore Coridon for loue of thee must die,
Thy Beauties thrall, and conquest of thine eie.

Leaue Coridon, to plough the barren feeld,
Thy buds of hope are blasted with disgrace;
For Phillis lookes, no hartie loue doe yeeld,
Nor can she loue, for all hir louely face,
Die Coridon, the spoyle of Phillis eie,
She can not loue, and therefore thou must die.

The lowest Trees haue tops, the Ante her gall,[10]
The flie her splene, the little sparkes their heate:
The slender haires cast shadowes, though but small,
And Bees haue stings, although they be not great:
Seas haue their sourse, and so haue shallow springs,
And loue is loue, in Beggars, as in Kings.

Where riuers smoothest run, deepe are the foords,
The Diall stirres, yet none perceiues it mooue:
The firmest faith is in the fewest wordes,
The Turtles cannot sing, and yet they loue:
True Harts haue eyes, and eares, no tongs to speake,
They heare, and see, and sigh, and then they breake.

My mynde to me a kindome is,[11]
Suche preasente ioyes[12] therin I fynde,
That it excells all other blisse
That worlde afords or growes by kynde.[13]
Thoughe muche I wante[14] whiche moste would haue,
Yet still my mynde forbides to craue.

No princlye pompe, no wealthy store,

---

10 From *A poetical rapsody*, 1602, STC 6373, Folger Library.

11 From Bodleian Library, Ms. Rawlinson Poet. 85, ff. 19–19v. The punctuation is the present editor's.

12 Some early manuscripts read *perfect ioy*.

13 nature.

14 lack.

No force to winn the victorye,
No wilye witt to salue a sore,
No shape to feade a louinge eye:
  To none of these I yealde as thrall,
  For why[15] my minde dothe serue for all.

I see how plenty suffers ofte,
And hasty clymers sone do fall:
I see that those whiche are alofte
Myshapp dothe threaten moste of all.
  They get withe toylle, theye keepe withe feare:
  Such cares my mynde coulde neuer beare.

Contente I liue, this is my staye:[16]
I seeke no more than maye suffyse,
I press to beare no haughtye swaye:
Look, what I lack my minde suppliese.
  Lo, thus I tryumphe lyke a kynge,
  Content withe that my mynde doth bringe.

Some haue to muche, yet still do craue:
I litle haue and seeke no more.
They are but poore thoughe muche they haue,
And I am ryche with lytle store.
  They poore, I ryche; they begg, I geue;
  They lacke, I leaue; they pyne, I lyue.

I laughe not at an others loss,
I grudge not at an others gayne:
No worldly waues my mynde cann toss,
My state at one dothe still remayne.
  I feare no foe, I fawne no freende,
  I lothe not lyfe, nor dreade no[17] ende.

Some waye theyre pleasure by theyre luste,
Their wisdom by theyre rage of will:
Theire treasure is theire onlye truste,
A cloked crafte theyre store of skyll:
  But all the pleasure that I fynde
  Is to mayntayne a quiet mynde.

My wealthe is healthe and perfecte ease,
My conscience cleere my choyse defense:
I neither seeke by brybes to please,
Nor by deserte to breede offence.
  Thus do I liue, thus will I dye;
  Would all did so, as well as I.

[15] because.

[16] support.
[17] Two early manuscripts read *my*.

Fulke Greville

[1554–1628]

FULKE GREVILLE, Lord Brooke, friend and biographer of Sir Philip Sidney, was born in the same year as Sidney, and the two boys entered Shrewsbury School on the same day in 1563. After several years at Cambridge, Greville went to court, where under both Queen Elizabeth and King James he held various offices, and was Chancellor of the Exchequer from 1614 to 1622. He was knighted in 1603, and was made the first Baron Brooke in 1621. One of the wealthiest men of his day, he befriended many literary men, among them Daniel, Camden, Speed, and Davenant. On his tomb in St. Mary's Church in the town of Warwick he caused to be cut the inscription: "Fulke Grevill, Servant to Queene Elizabeth, Conceller to King James, Frend to Sir Philip Sidney. Trophaeum Peccati."

Greville probably began to write verse in the 1570's, and he continued to do so until perhaps 1600. A few of his poems appeared in miscellanies and songbooks during his lifetime, and *Mustapha* was printed in 1609, whether with or without his consent we do not know. In 1633 appeared *Certain Learned and Elegant Works of the Right Honorable Fulke, Lord Brooke, written in his Youth and Familiar Exercise with Sir Philip Sidney*, which included short poems under the title *Caelica;* two tragedies in blank verse, *Alaham* and *Mustapha;* a prose letter on the duties of marriage entitled *A Letter to an Honorable Lady;* and his verse "treatises" *Of Human Learning*, *An Inquisition upon Fame and Honor*, and *Of Wars*. Two more "treatises" appeared in *The Remains of Sir Fulk Grevill Lord Brooke: Being Poems of Monarchy and Religion*, 1670. His *Life of the Renowned Sir Philip Sidney*, written about 1610–1612, and perhaps revised later, was first printed in 1652.

Greville seems to have included in *Caelica* all the short poems that he wished to preserve. Only forty-one of them are sonnets. The one hundred nine poems in *Caelica* were probably written over a period of several years. The poems in the beginning of the collection are almost certainly early work, probably dating from about 1577; poems later in the series show greater maturity in thought and style. Only fifty-seven of the poems are in any sense love poems. These are exercises in the Petrarchan convention; at least three women are addressed; Queen Elizabeth is almost certainly celebrated in the eighty-first poem and probably in the third and in a few others. Many of the later poems in the collection deal with religion and politics. It is probable that the earlier poems—perhaps two-thirds of the total—were written before the death of Sidney, and in friendly rivalry with him, though neither poet directly imitates the other.

In the earlier poems in *Caelica* (for example, 1, 3, 7, 16) Greville shared with Sidney, Spenser, and the French and Italian sonnet writers the pseudo-Platonic conception of love, and at times he identifies the beauty of women with Ideal Beauty. When he later writes in this vein in the eighty-fourth poem, the emphasis, as in Spenser's later hymns, is Christian.

Greville's most interesting poetry is in his tragedies and his treatises. In these—and indeed in many of the poems in *Caelica*—he writes as a philosopher and moralist. What he wrote of his tragedies is true of his treatises also: "I found my creeping genius more fixed upon the images of life than the images of wit, and therefore chose not to write to them on whose foot the blacke Oxe had not already trod, as the Proverbe is, but to those only that are weather-beaten in the sea of this world, such as, having lost sight of their gardens and groves, study to sail on a right course among rocks and quick-sands." Interested more in matter than in form, he wrote for those who, like himself, though oppressed by worldly cares, wished "to sail on a right course."

Greville is a Christian humanist. Virtue is submission to God; and learning, without humility and obedience, obscures man's sense of the divine. The disorder in man's soul and in society can be cured only by religious and ethical wisdom and discipline. True learning is wisdom for the conduct of life.

Greville's simple diction and his plain style make his compressed, gnomic, oracular verse conspicuous among the work of his contemporaries.

The one complete edition is *The Works in Verse and Prose Complete of the Lord Brooke*, ed. A. B. Grosart, 4 vols., 1870. A useful edition of the *Life* is *Sir Fulke Greville's Life of Sir Philip Sidney*, ed. Nowell Smith, 1907. The dramas and the poems in the 1633 volume are included in *Poems and Dramas of Fulke Greville*, ed. Geoffrey Bullough, 2 vols., 1939 (with valuable introduction and notes). Commentary is found in M. W. Croll, *The Works of Fulke Greville*, 1903; F. E. Schelling, "An Old-Time Friendship," *The Queen's Progress and Other Elizabethan Sketches*, 1904; A. H. Bullen, "Fulke Greville, Lord Brooke," *Elizabethans*, 1924; J. M. Purcell, "Sidney's *Astrophel and Stella* and Greville's *Caelica*," *PMLA*, l (1935), 413–422.

From CAELICA[1]

1[2]

Loue, the delight of all well-thinking minds;
Delight, the fruit of vertue dearely lov'd;
Vertue, the highest good, that reason finds;
Reason, the fire wherein mens thoughts bee prov'd;[3]
Are from the world by Natures power bereft,
And in one creature, for her glory, left.

Beautie, her couer is, the eyes true pleasure;
In honours fame she liues, the eares sweet musicke,
Excesse of wonder growes from her true measure;
Her worth is passions wound, and passions physicke,
From her true heart, cleare springs of wisdome flow,
Which imag'd in her words and deeds, men know.

Time faine would stay, that she might never leave her,
Place doth reioyce, that she must needs containe her,
Death craues of Heauen, that she may not bereaue her,
The Heauens know their owne, and doe maintaine her,
Delight, Loue, Reason, Vertue let it be,
To set all women light, but only she.

3[4]

More than most faire, full of that heauenly fire,
Kindled aboue to shew the Makers glory,[5]
Beauties first-born, in whom all powers conspire,
To write the *Graces* life, and *Muses* storie.
If in my heart all Saints else be defaced,[6]
Honour the Shrine, where you alone are placed.

Thou window of the skie, and pride of spirits,
True Character of honour in perfection,
Thou heauenly creature, Iudge of earthly merits,
And glorious prison of mans pure affection,
If in my heart all Nymphs else be defaced,
Honour the shrine, where you alone are placed.

4[7]

You little starres that liue in skyes,
And glory in *Apollo's* glorie,
In whose aspects conioined lyes
The Heauens will, and Natures storie,
Ioy to be likened to those eyes,

1 From *Certaine learned and elegant workes,* 1633, STC 12361, Folger Library. The title, meaning "heavenly," was probably suggested by Sidney's title *Astrophel and Stella.*

2 Included in Michael Cavendish's *Ayres in tabletorie,* 1598, and Martin Peerson's *Mottects or graue chamber musique,* 1630.

3 tested.

4 Included in Peerson's *Mottects,* 1630.

5 The first two lines resemble Spenser's *Amoretti,* 8, 1–2.

6 effaced.

7 Included in Peerson's *Mottects,* 1630.

Which eyes make all eyes glad, or sorie,
  For when you force thoughts from aboue,
  These ouer-rule your force by loue.

And thou *O Loue,* which in these eyes
Hast married *Reason* with *Affection,*
And made them Saints of beauties skyes,
Where ioyes are shadowes of perfection,
Lend me thy wings that I may rise
Vp not by worth but thy election;
  For I haue vow'd in strangest fashion,
  To loue, and neuer seeke compassion.

7

The World, that all containes, is euer mouing,
The Starres within their spheres for euer turned,
Nature (*the Queene of Change*) to change is louing,
And Forme to matter new, is still adiourned.[8]

Fortune our *phansie-God,*[9] to varie liketh,
Place is not bound to things within it placed,
The present time vpon time passed striketh,
With *Phoebus* wandring course the earth is graced.

The Ayre still moues, and by its mouing cleareth,[10]
The Fire, vp ascends, and planets feedeth,
The Water passeth on, and all lets[11] weareth,
The Earth stands still, yet change of changes breedeth;

Her plants, which Summer ripes, in Winter fade,
Each creature in vnconstant mother lyeth,[12]
Man made of earth, and for whom earth is made,
Still dying liues, and liuing euer dyeth;
  Onely like fate[13] sweet *Myra* neuer varies,
  Yet in her eyes the doome of all Change carries.

16

Fye foolish Earth, thinke you the heauen wants[14] glory,
Because your shadowes doe your selfe be-night?[15]
All's darke vnto the blind, let them be sory,
The heauens in themselues are euer bright.

Fye fond desire, thinke you that Loue wants glory,
Because your shadowes doe your selfe benight?
The hopes and feares of lust, may make men sorie,
But *loue still in her selfe finds her delight.*

---

[8] deferred, shifted.
[9] capricious god, or god of our caprices.
[10] *cleareth,*] *cleareth* STC 12361.
[11] obstacles.
[12] Every created thing is born of nature's inconstancy.
[13] Destiny, not inconstant Fortune.
[14] lacks.
[15] benight you.

Then Earth stand fast, the skye that you benight
Will turne againe, and so restore your glory;
Desire be steady, hope is your delight,
An orbe wherein no creature can be sorie;
  Loue being plac'd aboue these *middle* regions,[16]
  Where euery passion warres it selfe with legions.[17]

51[18]

Away with these selfe-louing Lads,
Whom *Cupids* arrow neuer glads:
Away poore soules, that sigh and weep,
In loue of those that lye asleepe:
  For *Cupid* is a meadow-God,
  And forceth none to kisse the rod.

Sweet *Cupids* shafts like Destinie
Doe causelesse good or ill decree;
Desert is borne out of his bow,
Reward vpon his wing doth goe;
  What fooles are they that haue not knowne,
  That *Loue likes no Lawes but his owne.*

My songs they be of *Cynthia's* praise,
I weare her Rings on Holy dayes,
In euery Tree I write her name,
And euery Day I read the same.
  Where Honour *Cupids* riuall is
  There miracles are seene of his.

If *Cynthia* craue her Ring of me,
I blot her name out of the Tree,
If doubt doe darken things held deare,
Then well-fare Nothing once a yeare
  For many runne, but one must winne,
  Fooles only hedge the Cuckoe in.

The worth that worthinesse should moue,
Is *Loue,* that is the bow of loue,
And *Loue* as well thee foster can,[19]
As can the mighty Noble-man.
  Sweet Saint 'tis true, you worthy be,
  Yet without Loue nought worth to me.

54

Cynthia, because your Hornes looke diuerse wayes,[20]
Now darkned to the East, now to the West;

---

16 the earth, placed between heaven and hell.

17 of diabolical passions. See Mark v, 9.

18 Included in John Dowland's *The first booke of songes or ayres,* 1597, and in *England's Helicon,* 1600.

19 Love, though poor, can cherish thee as well.

20 It is probable that the poem is addressed to Queen Elizabeth.

Then at Full-glorie once in thirty dayes,
Sense doth beleeue that Change is Natures rest.[21]

Poore earth, that dare presume to iudge the skye;
Cynthia is euer round, and neuer varies,
Shadowes and distance doe abuse[22] *the eye,*
And in abused sense truth oft miscarries:
Yet who this language to the People speaks,
Opinions empire senses idoll breaks.[23]

81

Vnder a Throne[24] I saw a Virgin[25] sit,
The red, and white Rose[26] quarter'd in her face;
Starre of the North, and for true guards[27] to it,
Princes, Church, States, all pointing out her Grace.
The homage done her was not borne of Wit,[28]
Wisdome admir'd, Zeale tooke Ambitions[29] place.
State in her eyes taught Order how to sit,
And fixe Confusions vnobseruing race.[30]
Fortune can here claime nothing truly great,
But that this Princely Creature is her seat.

86

The Earth with thunder torne, with fire blasted,
With waters drowned, with windie palsey shaken
Cannot for this with heauen be distasted,[31]
Since thunder, raine and winds from earth are taken:
Man torne with Loue, with inward furies blasted,
Drown'd with despaire, with fleshly lustings[32] shaken,
Cannot for this with heauen be distasted,
Loue, furie, lustings out of man are taken.
Then Man, endure thy selfe, those clouds will vanish;
Life is a Top which whipping Sorrow driueth;
Wisdome must beare what our flesh cannot banish,
The humble leade, the stubborne bootlesse striueth:
Or Man, forsake thy selfe, to heauen turne thee,
Her flames enlighten Nature, neuer burne thee.[33]

94

Men, that delight to multiply desire,
Like tellers[34] are that take coyne but to pay,

---

[21] The changes of the moon lead us to suppose that change is the law (rest) of nature.

[22] deceive.

[23] Whoever speaks this to the people destroys the rule of mere opinion and the idol that the senses worship, that is, the appearance of things.

[24] under the canopy of a throne.

[25] Queen Elizabeth. This poem is included in Peerson's *Mottects*, 1630.

[26] The roses of Lancaster and York.

[27] Two stars in Ursa Minor.

[28] ingenuity or discretion.

[29] *Ambitions*] *Ambitious* STC 12361.

[30] the tendency to omit dutiful service.

[31] disgusted, offended.

[32] longings.

[33] The last six lines: Man must either endure his fallen human nature or surrender himself to God.

[34] Officers of the Exchequer.

Still tempted to be false, with little hire,
Blacke hands[35] except, which they would haue away:
For, where power wisely Audits her estate,
The Exchequer Mens *best recompense is hate.*

The little Maide that weareth out the day,
To gather flow'rs still couetous of more,
At night when she with her desire would play,
And let her pleasure wanton in her store,
Discernes the first laid vnderneath the last,
Wither'd, and *so is all that we haue past:*

Fixe then on good desire, and if you finde
Ambitious dreames or feares of ouer-thwart;[36]
Changes, temptations, bloomes of earthy minde,
Yet waue[37] not, since earthy change, hath change of smart.
For lest Man should thinke flesh a seat of blisse,
God workes that his ioy mixt with sorrow is.

95

Malice and Loue in their waies opposite,
The one to hurt it selfe for others good;
The other, to haue good by others spite,
Both raging most, when they be most withstood;
Though enemies, yet doe in this agree,
That both still breake the hearts wherein they be.

Malice a habit is, wrought in the spirit,
By intricate opinions information;
Of scornefull wrong or of suppressing merit,
Which either wounds mens states or reputation;
And Tyrant-like, though shew of strength it beare,
Yet is but weakenesse growne, enrag'd by feare.

Loue is the true or false report of sense,
Who sent as spies, returning newes of worth,
With over-wonder breed the hearts offence,[38]
Not bringing in, but carrying pleasure forth,
And child-like must have all things that they see,
So much lesse louers, than things loved be.[39]

Malice, like ruine, with it selfe ouerthrowes
Mankinde, and therefore plaies a diuels part;
Loue puls it self downe, but to build vp those
It loues, and therefore beares an Angels heart.
Tyrants through feare, and malice feed on blood,
Good Kings secure at home, seeke all mens good.

---

[35] Hands soiled by used coins.
[36] rebuffs.
[37] waver.
[38] injury.
[39] Lovers are interested in themselves less than in the things they love (love is unselfish; malice is "tyrant-like" selfish).

97

Eternall Truth, almighty, infinite,
Onely exiled from mans fleshly heart,
Where ignorance and disobedience fight,
In hell and sinne, which shall haue greatest part:
When thy sweet mercy opens forth the light,
Of Grace which giueth eyes vnto the blind,
And with the Law euen plowest vp our sprite
To faith, wherein flesh may saluation finde.
Thou bidst vs pray, and wee doe pray to thee,
But as to power[40] and God without vs plac'd,
Thinking a wish[41] may weare out vanity,
Or habits be by miracles defac'd.[42]
One thought to God wee giue, the rest to sinne,
Quickely vnbent is all desire of good,
True words passe out, but haue no being within,
Wee pray to *Christ,* yet helpe to shed his blood;
For while wee say *beleeve,* and feele it not,
Promise amends, and yet despaire in it,
Heare *Sodom* iudg'd, and goe not out with *Lot,*
Make Law and Gospell riddles of the wit:
We with the *Iewes* euen *Christ* still crucifie,
As[43] not yet come to our impiety.

98

Wrapt vp, O Lord, in mans degeneration;[44]
The glories of thy truth, thy ioyes eternall,
Reflect vpon my soule darke desolation,
And vgly prospects o're the sp'rits infernall.
Lord, I haue sinn'd, and mine iniquity,
Deserues this hell; yet Lord deliuer me.

Thy power and mercy neuer comprehended,
Rest lively imag'd in my Conscience wounded;
Mercy to grace, and power to feare extended,
Both infinite, and I in both confounded;
Lord, I haue sinn'd, and mine iniquity,
Deserues this hell, yet Lord deliver me.

If from this depth of sinne, this hellish graue,
And fatall absence from my Sauiours glory,
I could implore his mercy, who can saue,
And for my sinnes, not paines of sinne, be sorry:
Lord, from this horror of iniquity,
And hellish graue, thou wouldst deliuer me.

99

Downe in the depth of mine iniquity,
That vgly center of infernall spirits;

[40] External power, not inward grace.
[41] A wish without effort.
[42] effaced, removed.
[43] who has.
[44] I, wrapt up in the degeneration of mankind.

Where each sinne feeles her owne deformity,
In these peculiar torments she inherits,
  Depriu'd of humane graces, and diuine,
  Euen there appeares this *sauing God* of mine.

And in this fatall mirrour of transgression,[45]
Shewes man as fruit of his degeneration,
The errours ugly infinite impression,
Which beares the faithlesse downe[46] to desperation;
  Depriu'd of humane graces and diuine,
  Euen there appeares this *sauing God* of mine.

In power and truth, Almighty and eternall,
Which on the sinne reflects strange desolation,
With glory scourging all the Spr'its infernall,
And vncreated hell with vnpriuation;[47]
  Depriu'd of humane graces, not diuine,
  Euen there appeares this *sauing God* of mine.

For on this sp'rituall Crosse condemned lying,
To paines infernall by eternall doome,
I see my Sauiour for the same sinnes dying,
And from that hell I fear'd, to free me, come;
  Depriu'd of humane graces, not diuine,
  Thus hath his death rais'd up this soule of mine.

105

Three things there be in Mans opinion deare,
Fame, many *Friends,* and *Fortunes* dignities:
False visions all, which in our sense appeare,
To sanctifie desires Idolatries.[48]

For what is *Fortune,* but a wat'ry glasse?
Whose chrystall forehead wants a steely backe,
Where raine and stormes beare all away that was,
Whose ship alike both depths and shallowes wracke.

Fame againe, which from blinding power takes light,
Both *Caesars* shadow is, and *Cato's* friend,
The child of humour, not allyed to right,
Liuing by oft exchange of winged end.

And many *Friends,* false strength of feeble mind,
Betraying equals, as true slaues to might;
Like *Ecchoes* still send voyces down the wind,
But neuer in aduersity finde right.

Then Man, though vertue of extremities,
The middle be, and so hath two to one,
By Place and Nature constant enemies,

[45] in this fallen human nature.
[46] *downe* Warwick MS.] *doome* STC 12361.
[47] power and goodness.
[48] *Idolatries.*] *Idolatry.* STC 12361.

And against both these no strength but her owne,
  Yet quit thou for her, Friends, Fame, Fortunes throne;
  Diuels, there many be, and Gods but one.

109

Syon lyes waste, and thy *Ierusalem,*
O Lord, is falne to vtter desolation,
Against thy Prophets, and thy holy men,
The sinne hath wrought a fatall combination,
  Prophan'd thy name, thy worship ouerthrowne,
  And made thee liuing Lord, a God vnknowne.

Thy powerfull lawes, thy wonders of creation,
Thy Word incarnate, glorious heauen, darke hell,
Lye shadowed vnder Mans degeneration,
Thy Christ still crucifi'd for doing well,
  Impiety, O Lord, sits on thy throne,
  Which makes thee liuing light, a God vnknown.

Mans superstition hath thy truths entomb'd,
His Atheisme againe her pomps defaceth,
That sensuall vnsatiable vaste wombe,
Of thy seene Church, thy vnseene Church disgraceth;
  There liues no truth with them that seem thine own,
  Which makes thee liuing Lord, a God vnknowne.

Yet vnto thee, Lord, (mirrour of transgression)
Wee, who for earthly Idols, haue forsaken
Thy heauenly Image (sinlesse pure impression)
And so in nets of vanity lye taken,
  All desolate implore that to thine owne,
  Lord, thou no longer liue a God vnknowne.

Yet Lord let *Israels* plagues not be eternall,
Nor sinne for euer cloud thy sacred Mountaines,
Nor with false flames spirituall but infernall,
Dry up thy mercies euer springing fountaines,
  Rather, sweet *Iesus,* fill vp time and come,
  To yeeld the sinne her euerlasting doome.

CHORVS SACERDOTVM[49]

Oh wearisome Condition of Humanity!
Borne vnder one Law, to another bound:
Vainely begot, and yet forbidden vanity,
Created sicke, commanded to be sound:
What meaneth Nature by these diuerse Lawes?
Passion and Reason, selfe-diuision cause:

[49] From *Mustapha* in *Certaine learned and elegant workes.* In the "Chorus Tartarorum," which precedes this chorus of priests, the Tartars preach reliance on nature. The chorus of priests closes the play with the reflection that man's divided nature can bring him no peace. Nor is peace to be found in ritual and dogma. Man's only stay is the knowledge of God within. Grace alone can save him.

Is it the marke, or Maiesty of Power
To make offences that it may forgiue?
Nature herselfe, doth her owne selfe defloure,
To hate those errors she her selfe doth giue.
For how should man thinke that, he may not doe
If Nature did not faile, and punish too?
Tyrant to others, to her selfe vniust,
Onely commands things difficult and hard.
Forbids vs all things, which it knowes is lust,
Makes easie paines, vnpossible reward.
If Nature did not take delight in blood,
She would have made more easie waies to good.
We that are bound by vowes, and by Promotion,
With pompe of holy Sacrifice and rites,
To teach beleefe in good and still[50] deuotion,
To preach of Heauens wonders, and delights:
Yet when each of vs, in his owne heart lookes,
He findes the God there, farre vnlike his Bookes.

From A TREATIE OF HUMANE LEARNING[51]

143

The chiefe Vse then in man of that he knowes,
Is his paines taking for the good of all,
Not fleshly weeping for our owne made woes,
Not laughing from a Melancholy gall,
Not hating from a soule that ouerflowes
With bitternesse, breath'd out from inward thrall:
  But sweetly rather to ease, loose, or binde,
  As need requires, this fraile fall'n humane kinde.

144

Yet *Some seeke knowledge, meerely but to knowe,*[52]
And idle Curiositie that is;
Some but to *sell,* not freely to bestow,
These gaine and spend both time, and wealth amisse;
Embasing Arts, by basely deeming so,
Some to be knowne, and vanity is this:[53]
  Some to build others, which is Charity,
  But these to build themselues, who wise men be.

145

And to conclude, whether we would erect
Our selves, or others by this choice of Arts;
Our chiefe endeauour must be to effect
A sound foundation, not on sandy parts

---

[50] instill.

[51] From *Certaine learned and elegant workes.* These closing stanzas state Greville's conclusions.

[52] *but to knowe,* Warwick MS.] *to be knowne,* STC 12361.

[53] This line, missing in STC 12361, is from the Warwick MS.

Of light Opinion, Selfenesse, Words of men,
But that *sure rocke of truth, Gods Word, or Penne.*

146

Next that we doe not ouerbuild our states,
In searching secrets of the Deity,
Obscurities of Nature, casualtie of Fates;
But measure first our own Humanity,
Then on our gifts impose an equall rate,
And so seeke wisedome with sobriety:
Not curious what our fellowes ought to doe,
But what our owne creation bindes vs to.

147

Lastly, we must not to the world erect
Theaters,[54] nor plant our Paradise in dust,
Nor build vp *Babels* for the Diuels elect;
Make temples of our hearts to God we must;
And then, as *Godlesse wisedomes follies be,*
So are his heights our true Philosophie.

148

With which faire cautions, Man may well professe
To studie God, whom he is borne to serve,
Nature, t'admire, the greater in the lesse;
Time, but to learne; our selues we may obserue,
To humble vs: Others, to exercise
Our loue and patience, wherein Duty lies.

149

Lastly, the truth and good to loue, and doe them,
The error, onely to destroy, and shunne it,
Our hearts in generall will lead vs to them,
When gifts of Grace, and Faith haue once begun it.
For without these, the minde of man growes numbe,
The body darkenesse, to the soule a tombe.

150

Thus are true Learnings in the humble heart
A *Spirituall worke,* raising Gods Image, rased
By our transgression; a *well-framed art,*
At which the world, and error stand amazed;
A *Light diuine,* where man sees ioy, and smart
Immortall, in this mortall body blazed;
A *wisdome,* which *the Wisedome* vs assureth
With hers euen to the sight of God endureth.

[54] Books or works glorifying worldly life.

151

Hard Characters (I grant) to flesh and blood,
Which in the first perfection of creation
Freely resign'd the state of being good,
To know the euill, where it found priuation;
And lost her being, ere she vnderstood
Depth of this fall, paine of *Regeneration:*
By which she yet must raise her selfe againe,
Ere she can iudge all other knowledge vaine.

AN INQVISITION VPON FAME AND HONOVR[55]

1

What are Mens liues, but *labyrinths of error,*
Shops of deceit, and *Seas of misery?*
Yet Death yeelds so small comfort, so much terror;
Gaine, Honour, Pleasure, such illusions be;
As though against life, each man whet his wit,
Yet all Mens hearts, and sense, take part with it.

2

Of which three baytes, yet *Honour* seemes the chiefe,
And is vnto the world, like goodly weather,
Which giues the spirits life, the thoughts reliefe,
Delight, and trauell[56] reconciles together:
So as the Learn'd, and Great, no more admire it,
Then euen the silly[57] Artisans aspire it.

3

This made the foure rare masters, which begun
Faire *Artemysia's* husbands[58] dainty tombe,
When death tooke her, before their worke was done,
And so bereft them of all hopes to come;
That they would yet their own work perfect make,
Euen for their workes, and their selfe-glories sake.

4

Among the Worthies, *Hercules* is noted,
For *Fame,* to haue neglected Gaine, and Pleasure;
Cleombrotus[59] to haue beene so deuoted,
To pease[60] his deeds, by her nice weights and measure,
As he that to his state, made his life thrall,
Yet to saue both, would not let *Honour* fall.

---

[55] From *Certaine learned and elegant workes.*
[56] travail, pain.
[57] simple.
[58] Mausolus, husband of Artemesia of Caria.
[59] Cleombrotus of Sparta, in order to avoid unjust suspicion of treacherous communication with his opponent Epaminondas, fought him at a disadvantage and was killed.
[60] poise.

5

Which great desire, hatch'd vp in these vast Spirits,
Liues as a relicke of Mans discreation;
When he affected to be Iudge of merits;
Or *eccho,* which giues all Sounds moderation:[61]
An image too sublime for Thrones to beare,[62]
Who all what they command not, euer feare.

6

What was it then, made *Aristotle* raise
These imbound spirits to so high a rate?[63]
Call them ingenious, ciuill, worthy praise?
The Answer's plaine, that neuer any State
Could rise, or stand, without this thirst of *Glory,*
Of noble workes, as well the mould as story.[64]

7

For else, what *Gouernour* would spend his dayes,
In enuious trauell, for the publike good?
Who would in *Bookes,* search after dead mens wayes?
Or in the *Warre,* what Souldier lose his blood?
Liu'd not this *Fame* in clouds, kept as a crowne;
Both for the Sword, the Scepter, and the Gowne.

8

It therefore much concernes each publike State,
To hoyse[65] these costlesse sayles vp to the skye,
For it is held a symptome of ill fate,
When Crownes doe let this thirst of *Glory* dye;
Which doth enlarge States, by enlarging hearts,
And out of deedes teach Schooles to fashion Arts.

9

Thus see we, both the force, and vse of *Fame;*
How States and Men haue honour by her stile,[66]
As *Ecchoes* that enuiron orders frame,
Which disproportion waiteth to beguile.
Fame walls in *Truth,* and cherisheth her end,
Knowes neither why, nor how, yet is her friend.

10

For in the worlds corrupted trafficke here,
Goodnesse puts onely tincture[67] on our gall,

61 Fame, as an echo of real life, alters the original.
62 Others' fame is intolerable to princes.
63 In his *Ethics* Aristotle names the desire for honor as one of man's principal motives.
64 Fame relates great deeds, and it encourages emulation.
65 hoist.
66 titles.
67 A slight infusion of taste.

The light of Truth, doth but in clouds appeare,
Hardly discern'd, and not obey'd at all:
No man yeelds glory vnto him that makes him,
For if he doe, he sees the world forsakes him.

11

Now in this *twilight* of Deliberation,
Where Man is darke, because he will not see:
Must he not trust to his selfe-constellation?[68]
Or else grow confident, he cannot be?[69]
Assuming this, hee makes himselfe his end,
And what he vnderstands, that takes to friend.

12

In which strange oddes, betweene the earth and skie,
Examine but the state of euery heart;
Flesh feeles and feares strong inequality;
Horrors of sinne, cannot be free'd by art:
Humours are mans religion, Power his lawes,
His Wit confusion, and his Will the cause.

13

Nor is it thus, with Man himselfe alone,
His theaters, and trophies, are not free,
I mean all States, all Gouernments, all Thrones
That haue no *basis,* but his Policy;
They all alike feele dissolution ready,
Their owne subsistence failing, and vnsteady.

14

Rebellion in the members to the head,
Aduantage in the head, to keepe them vnder,
The sweet consent of sympathie quite dead,
Selfenesse euen apt to teare it selfe asunder:
All Gouernments, like Man himselfe within,
Being restlesse compositions of the sinne.

15

So as in this estate of Mans defection,
Confus'd amongst the good and ill, he goes;
Both gathers and distributeth infection,
Chuseth and changeth, builds and ouerthrows;
For Truth and Goodnesse, hauing left his heart,
He and his Idols, are but words of Art.

---

[68] his casting his own horoscope, defining his hopes.

[69] or else lose self-confidence.

16

Among which number, men must reckon *Fame,*
Wit, Superstition, Learning, Lawes that binde,
Without our Maker, this worlds crased[70] frame,
All which constraine, but not instruct the minde;
  Gouerne the euils part, with her confusion,
  Which haue no throne or being, but delusion.

17

Then to cast faith on *Fame,* or these foundations,
Or not to thinke, as all these nothing were,
So backe to nothing, they shall haue gradation,[71]
Since *Time must ruine all that she did beare,*
  Were not to know these drams[72] of mortall seed,
  In curing one, still more diseases breed.

18

And yet to part this worlds declining frame,
And let some pillars stand while others fall,
I meane make Vertues bodies vnto *Fame,*
That be indeed hypocrisies of hell;[73]
And smother *Fame* againe with Vertues name,
Must needs exile all hope of doing well:
  God being vnbeleeued, or vnknowne,
  And humane Wisdome, with it selfe o'rethrown.[74]

19

For to be good the world finds it too hard,
And to be nothing to subsistence[75] is
A fatall, and unnaturing[76] award,
So as between perfection, and vnblisse,
  Man, out of man, will make himselfe a frame,[77]
  Seeks outward helpe, and borrowes that of *Fame.*

20

Yet doth there rise from abstract contemplation,
A gilt or painted image, in the braine,
Of humane vertues, *Fames* disestimation,[78]
Which, like an Art, our nature so restraines;
  As while the pride of action[79] wee suppresse,
  Man growes no better, and yet States grow lesse.

---

[70] impaired, unsound.

[71] or not to think that these powers, having no basis in good, must gradually come to nothing.

[72] small draughts of medicine.

[73] To say that fame comes only to the virtuous is hypocrisy.

[74] To condemn fame by insisting on virtue will discourage men lacking both God and wisdom.

[75] to lose hope of survival by fame.

[76] doing violence to human nature.

[77] Man, from the admiration of men, will make himself a support.

[78] A false image of virtue causes contempt for fame.

[79] the pride that leads to action.

21

Hence they that by their words would Gods become,
With pride of thought, depraue[80] the pride of deeds,
Vpon the actiue cast a heauy doome,
And marre weake strengths, to multiply strong weeds:
While they conclude *Fames* trumpets, voice, and pen,
More fit for crafty States, than worthy Men.

22

For *Fame* they still oppose euen from those grounds,
That proue as truely all things else as vaine,
They giue their vertues onely humane bounds,
And without God subuert to build againe
Refin'd *Ideas,* more than flesh can beare,
All foule within, yet speake as God were there.

23

Mans power to make himselfe good, they maintaine,
Conclude that Fate is gouern'd by the wise;
Affections they supplant, and not restraine,
Within our selues, they seat Felicities;
With things as vaine, they vanity beat downe,
And by selfe-ruine, seeke a *Sampsons* crowne:[81]

24

Glory's dispraise, being thus with glory tainted,
Doth not as goodnesse, but as euils doe
Shine, by informing others beauties painted,[82]
Where bashfull Truth vayles neighbours errors too;
All humane pride, is built on this foundation,
And Art on Art, by this seekes estimation.

25

Without his God, Man thus must wander euer,
See *moates* in others, in himselfe no *beames,*
Ill ruines good, and ill erecteth neuer,
Like drowning torrents, not transporting[83] streames:
The vanity from nothing hath her being,
And makes that essence good,[84] by disagreeing.

26

Yet from these grounds, if *Fame* wee ouerthrow,
We lose mans *eccho,* both of wrong and right,
Leaue good and ill, indifferent here below,

---

80 villify, condemn.
81 seek a final honor.
82 seems virtuous by stating that others' ideals are false.
83 fordable.
84 seem good by condemning others.

For humane darkenesse, lacking humane light,
Will easily cancell Natures feare of shame,
Which workes but by intelligence with Fame.

27

And cancell this,[85] before Gods truth be knowne,
Or knowne, but not beleeued, and obeyed;
What seeming good rests in us of our owne?
How is corruption from corrupting staid?
The chaine of Vertues, which the flesh doth boast,
Being since our fall, but *names of Natures lost.*

28

In humane commerce, then let *Fame* remaine,
An outward mirrour of the inward minde,
That what man yeelds, he may receiue againe,
And his ill doing, by ill hearing finde:
For then, though Power erre, though Lawes be lame,
And Conscience dead, yet *ill auoyds not shame.*

29

But let vs leaue these stormy orbs of passion,
Where humours onely ballance one another,
Making our trophies of a mortall fashion,
And vanity of euery act the mother;
For inward peace, being neuer wrought by Fame,
Proues mans worth is no Nature,[86] *but a name.*

30

Therefore let this cleare streame,[87] beare downe together
Fame, and Philosophie her slie opposer;
As hauing nothing of their owne in either,
Worthy to make each by the other loser:
Since if by Christian rules, their depths be taken,
The body and the shadow both are shaken.

31

For where the father of Philosophie,[88]
Vpon the common vertues, but aboue,
Doth raise and build his *Magnanimity,*
A greatnesse not with little *Fame* in loue,
Hard to finde out, as Goodnesse is with vs,
And without Goodnesse, meere[89] ridiculous.

---

85 if fame is destroyed.
86 has no existence.
87 religion.
88 Aristotle, *Ethics* iv. 3.
89 completely.

32

Let Truth examine where this vertue liues,
And hold it vaine, if not produc'd in act;
Man is corrupt, and no perfection giues,
What euer in him others praise enact:
So as if *Fame* be vnto goodnesse due;
It onely can in God, be great and true:

33

For Mans chiefe vertue, is *Humilitie,*
True knowledge of his wants, his height of merit;
This pride of minde, this *Magnanimity;*
His greatest vice, his first seducing spirit;
With venimous infection of his fall,
To *Serpent*-like appearance euer thrall.

34

Further we vrge against this masters grounds,
That our first *Adam,* imag'd is to vs,
In that mixt pride, that worth-exceeding bounds,
Whereon Schooles build their true Magnanimous:[90]
Since to be like his Maker he affected,
And being lesse still thought himselfe neglected.

35

Which spirituall pride (no doubt) possesseth still,
All fleshly hearts, where thirst of *Honour* raues,
For sit vpon the seat of God they will,
As did those Princes, who in stead of graues
Made Idols, Altars, Temples to be rais'd,
Wherein, like gods, they were ador'd and prais'd.

36

And such againe, hath Gods *seene Church* brought forth,
As doe in *Peters* chaire Gods power assume:[91]
Such was *Menecrates*[92] of little worth,
Who *Ioue,* the Sauiour, to be call'd presum'd,
To whom of incense *Phillip* made a feast,
And gaue pride scorne, and hunger to digest.

37

Againe, to take the true Anatomy
Of these, and search in life what sure foundation
For humane good, or greatnesses there be,

---

[90] *Magnanimous:* Warwick MS.] *imaginations:* STC 12361.
[91] The popes.
[92] A Syracusan physician who thought himself Jupiter. Philip of Macedon invited him to a feast and offered him incense instead of food.

In all the swelling stiles of Ostentation;
  What hopes they promise, on what grounds they build,
  What pain they ask, and then what fruit they yeeld.

38

Wee shall discerne the roote of this Ambition
To be conceipt,[93] that glory doth containe
Some supernaturall sparke, or apparition,
More than the common humour can attaine:
  Since to be reuerenc'd, lou'd, obey'd, and knowne,
  Man must effect, with powers aboue his owne.

39

Ah silly Creature, curst Mortality!
What canst thou know, that knowest not Mans estate
To be but *Vice,* gilt with hypocrisie;
Which doth the life it most resembles, hate?
  And yet affects that cleare vnshadow'd light,
  Wherein her darke deformities show bright.

40

So that for thee to passe the piercing eyes,[94]
Light tongues, and listning eares of curious *Fame,*
Were to vse trafficke to thy preiudice,
As with a trumpet publishing thy shame;
  Which all but fooles, who know their own hearts least,
  Rather seeke to conceale, than manifest.

41

Besides, to be well knowne finds out oppressors,
By which the World still honours thee the lesse;
For *who be throughly knowne, are euer loosers,*
If Fame belye not Mans vnworthinesse,
  Where to the iust, in thought, as well as deede;
  What other trumpet, doth the Conscience neede?

42

Yet in Mans youth, perchance, *Fame* multiplies
Courage, and actiue vnderstandingnesse,[95]
Which cooles in Age, and in experience dyes,
Like Fancies smoke,[96] Opinions wantonnesse:
Yet who knowes, whether old age qualifies
This thirst of *Fame,* with vnderstandingnesse,[97]
With selfe-despaire, or disabilities?
Whether experience, which makes *Fame* seeme lesse:

[93] fancy, belief.
[94] *eyes,*] *eyes* STC 12361.
[95] enterprise.
[96] *smoke,*] *smoke* STC 12361.
[97] *vnderstandingnesse,*] *vnderstandingnesse* STC 12361: understanding.

Be wit, or feare, from narrownesse arising,
True noblenesse as none of these despising?

43

Neuerthelesse fraile Man doth still aspire
Vnto this welbeleeuing reuerence,
As helpes, to raise his masked errors higher,
And so by great improuements in the sense,
Extend Mankind unto the bounds of praise,
Farre aboue Order, Law, and Duties wayes.[98]

44

Or if this reuerence be not the fire,
Wherein Mankind affects to mould his state;
Then is it loue which[99] they by *Fame* aspire,
An imposition of the highest rate
Set upon people, by their owne desire,
Not making Powers, but Natures magistrate:
Whether in people, worth, or chance worke this,
Is knowne to them, that know what Mankind is.

45

For true to whom are they, that are vntrue
To God and nothing seriously intend,
But tumult, fury, fancy, hope of new?
Neuer all pleas'd with *Ioue,* if he descend;
Vnconstant, like confusion in a minde,
Not knowing why it hates, nor why 'tis kinde.

46

To proue this by example, take *Camillus,*[1]
Scipio, Solon, Metellus, Aristides,
Themistocles,[2] *Lycurgus,* or *Rutillius,*
And by their change of humors toward these,
Let vs conclude, *All people are vniust,*
And ill affections end in malice must.

47

Besides, the essence of this glorious name,
Is not in him that hath, but him that giues it:
If people onely then distribute *Fame,*
In them that vnderstand it not, yet liues it:
And what can their applause within vs raise,
Who are not conscious of that worth they praise?[3]

[98] Does Age no longer desire fame because of good motives or because of craftiness or fear arising from a narrow mind and blind to true nobility which is neither crafty nor fearful?
[99] to which.

[1] *Camillus,*] *Cmillaus,* STC 12361.
[2] *Themistocles,*] *Themistocles* STC 12361.
[3] *praise?* Warwick MS.]; *praise.* STC 12361. Fame depends on those who do not know when it is deserved.

48

Nor is it by the Vulgar altogether,
That *Fame* thus growes a wonder of nine dayes;
The wise and learned, plucke away her feathers,
With enuious humors, and opposing wayes:
For they depraue[4] each other, and descrie,[5]
Those staues, and beards, these *Augurs* traffick by.

49

Plato (tis true) great *Homer* doth commend,
Yet from his Common-weale did him exile;
Nor is it words, that doe with words contend,
Of deeds they vary, and demurre of[6] stile:
How to please all, as no words yet could tell;
So what one act did all yet censure well?

50

For proofe, what worke more for the Publike good,
Then that rare Librarie of dead mens treasure;
Collected by the *Aegyptian* royall blood?
Which *Seneca* yet censures at his pleasure,
No elegance, nor princely industry,
But rather pompe, and studious luxury.

51

Nay, his owne ephithete *Studious,* he corrected,
Inferring that for pride, not Studies vse,
The luxurie of Kings, had them collected:
So what in scorne of Criticall abuse,
Was said of bookes, of *Fame* will proue the state,
That *Readers censures are the Writers fate.*

52

Thus show our liues, what *Fame* and *Honour* be,
Considered in themselves, or them that gaue them;
Now there remaines a Curiosity,
To know euen what they are, to those that haue them:
Namely vnordinate to get or vse,
Difficult to keepe, and desperate to lose.[7]

53

And for the first, if *Fame* a *monster* be,
As *Virgil* doth describe her, then she must
Come from a monstrous birth and progenie:

---

[4] condemn.

[5] *descrie,* Warwick MS.]; *descrie.* STC 12361: decry, condemn.

[6] debate about.

[7] Greville now discusses the effect of fame and honor on those who seek them.

And if she be the *child of Peoples lust,*
Then must she (without doubt) be basely borne,
And, like her parents, neuer vniforme.

54

For what indeed more monstrous, or more base,
Than these *Chimera's* of distempered mindes,
Borne of Opinion, not of Vertues race,
From whence it growes, that these *Fame*-hunting kindes,
Proue like those Woers, which the Mistris sought,
Yet basely fell, and with the Maids grew naught.

55

They walke not simply good, or euill waies,
But feete of numbers,[8] none of which returne;
As *Polypus*[9] with stones, so they with praise,
Change colours, and like *Proteus* their forme,
Following the Peoples lust,[10] who, like their cloths
Still shift conceit of truth and goodnesse both.

56

These honour none, but such as boast their pride,
And ready heads for all times humours be;
So as not eminent vertue is the tide
Which carries *Fame,* but swolne iniquity,
What shall wee iudge of *Sylla* and *Marius* then?
But Satyrs, Centaures, demi-beasts and men.

57

Such[11] as false *glory* sought by being head,
Of the *Patrician,* or *Plebeian* faction;
By which that mistresse State was ruined,
Diuision euer bringing in contraction;
Among the learn'd, so *Epicurus* wan
His *Fame,* by making Pleasure God of man.

58

Diogenes by mockes, *Heraclitus* by teares,
Democritus by smiles; and by such ladders climes
Each Sect and Heresie, to *Honours* spheares,
With new opinions, in misguided times,
Subuerting nature, grace, ciuillity,
By scandalous, satyricall scurrility.

---

8 They follow a multitude.
9 cuttlefish.
10 wishes, fancies.
11 The same is true of such.

59

Thus *Aretine*[12] of late got reputation,
By scourging Kings, as *Lucian* did of old,
By scorning Gods, with their due adoration;
And therefore to conclude, we may be bold,
That Peoples loue with euill acts is wonne,
And either lost, or kept, as it begunne.

60

What winde then blowes poore Man into this sea,
But Pride of heart, and Singularity?
Which weary of true vertues humble way,
And not enduring Mans equality,
Seeketh by Wit, or Sophistry to rise;
And with good words, put off ill merchandise.

61

Of which *Ambitions,* time obserues three kindes:
Whereof the *first,* and least vnnaturall
Is, when fraile man some good in himselfe findes;
But[13] ouer-priz'd; defects, not peas'd[14] at all:
Like Bankrupts, who in auditing their States,
Of debts, and of expence forget the rates.[15]

62

And of these *Solons* fooles, who their owne wants
Cannot discerne, if there were not too many,
Our inward frailties easily would supplant
Outward ambitions, and not suffer any
To vsurpe these swelling stiles of Domination,
Which are the Godheads true denomination.

63

The *second* wee may terme politicall,
Which value men by place, and not by worth,
Not wisely, thinking we be Counters all,
Which but the summes of Gouernment set forth:
Wherein, euen those that are the highest placed
Not to their owne, but others ends are graced.

64

So that from *Pharoahs* Court to *Iethros* Cell,
If men with *Moyses* could their hearts retire,[16]
In *Honour* they should enuilesse excell,

[12] Pietro Aretino (1492–1557), poet and dramatist.
[13] but this is.
[14] weighed, considered.
[15] amounts.
[16] Exodus ii–iii.

And by an equall ballance of desire,
Liue free from clouds of humane hope, and feare,
Whose troubled circles oft strange Meteors beare.

65

The *last* sort is, that popular vaine pride;
Which neither standeth vpon worth nor place,
But to applause, and selfe-opinion ty'd,
Like *Esops* Iay, whom others feathers grace,
Himselfe as good, and glorious esteemeth,
As in the glasse of Flattery, he seemeth.

66

This makes him fond of *Praise,* that knows it lyes;
The cruell tyrant thinkes his grace renown'd,
Euen while the earth with guiltlesse bloud he dyes;
And his *Magnificence,* euen then resound
When he doth rauine all before his eyes:
Of which vaine minds, it may be truly said,
Who loue false praise, of false scornes are affraid.

67

Besides, as this *Ambition* hath no bound;
So grows it proud, and instantly vniust,
Enforcing short-breath'd *Fame* aloud to sound,
By pardoning debts, and by defrauding trust;
Whence the *Agrarian* mandates[17] had their grounds,
As all veiles else, that couer Soueraigne lust:
For fire and People doe in this agree,
They both good Seruants, both ill Masters be.

68

Thus we discerne what courses they must hold,
That make this humour of applause their end:
They haue no true, and so no constant mould;
Light Change, is both their enemy and friend,
Herostratus shall proue, *Vice gouernes Fame,*
Who built that Church, he burnt, hath lost his name.[18]

69

Yet when this brittle *Glory* thus is gotten,
The keeping is as painefull, more confuse,
Fame liues by doing, is with rest forgotten,
Shee those that would enioy her doth refuse,
Wooed (like a *Lais*) will be and obseru'd;
Euer ill kept, since neuer well deseru'd.

[17] The agrarian laws of Tiberius Gracchus (133 B.C.) distributed land among the poor.

[18] Eratostratus, who burned the temple of Diana at Ephesus, is remembered; the name of the man who built the temple is forgotten.

70

And if true *Fame* with such great paine be wonne,
Wonne, and preseru'd, of false what can we hope?
Since *Ill with greater cost than good is done:*
Againe, what hath lesse Latitude or scope,
To keep, than that which euery Change bereaues,
That times, Mans own heart, or the world receiu's?

71

Lastly, this *Fame* hard gotten, worse to keepe,
Is neuer lost, but with despaire, and shame,
Which makes mans[19] nature, once fallen from this steepe,
Disdaine their being should out-last their name:
Some in self-pitty, some in exile languish,
Others rebell, some kill themselues in anguish.

72

Like Relatiues, thus stand the *World* and *Fame,*
Twinnes of one wombe, that lose, or win together,
With *Vulcan's* nets, they catch each others shame,
Diuide with God, and so are losers euer;
Alone they are but *Nothings,* well disguis'd,
And if compar'd, more worthily despis'd.

73

But now I heare the voice of Power, and Art,
A fatall dissolution straight proclaime,
Closely to be inweau'd in euery heart,
By vndermining thus the World, and Fame;
For wound *Fame* in the world, the world in it,
They aske whats left to stir vp humane Wit.

74

Are God, Religion, Vertue, then but name;
Or need these heauenly beings earthly aid,
To gouerne vnder, as aboue this frame?
Must good Mens deeds, with ill Mens words be payd?
When we are dead, is merit dead with vs?
Shall breath determine God, and Vertue thus?

75

Some Schooles made *Fame* a *Shadow,* some a *Debt,*
To vertue some a *Handmaid,* none her end:
For like a God, she[20] others striues to get,
Affects no honour, needs nor fame, nor friend:

---

19 *Mans* Warwick MS.] *Man* STC 12361.

20 virtue.

Moued, shee moues man to adore her mouer,
And onely giues her selfe to those that loue her.

76

Hence did the *Romanes,* Mountebankes of *Fame,*
Build *Fame,* and *Vertue* temples, so in one,
As thorough *Vertue* all men to it came,
Yet vnto *Vertue,* men might passe alone;
Expressing *Fame,* a consequence, no cause,
A power that speakes, not knowing by what lawes.

77

But let true wisedome carry vp our eyes,
To see how all true vertues figured bee,
Angel-like, passing to and from the skies,
By *Israels ladder,* whose two ends are free
Of Heauen, and Earth; to carry vp, and downe,
Those pure souls, which the Godhead means to crowne.

78

And if you aske them, whether their pure wings,
Be charrets, to beare vp those fleshly prides
Of *Crowne-rooft* Miters, *Church-unroofing* Kings,
Conquest and *Fame,* whose ebbe, and flowing tides,
Bring forth diuiding tytles, captiu'd lawes,
Of Mans distresse, and ignorance the cause?

79

These Vertues answer, they be powers diuine;
Their heauen, faith; obiect, eternity:
Deuised in earth, those ruines to refine,
Vnder whose weight, our Natures buried lye;
Faith making Reason perfect, as before[21]
It fell, for lacke of faith, beleeuing more.

80

Abcees[22] they are, which doe vnteach againe
That knowledge, which first taught vs not to know[23]
The happy state, wherein we did remaine,
When we for lacke of euill, thought not so;
New making Paradise, where we began,
Not in a garden, but the heart of Man.

81

And as to *Serpents,* which put off their skinne,
Nature renewes, a naturall complexion,

[21] *before* Warwick MS.]; *before;* STC 12361.
[22] Spelling books.
[23] *know*] *know.* STC 12361.

So when the goodnesse doth vncase the sinne,
Health so renewed, can neuer take infection:
The World inchants not, Hel hath lost her might,
For *what mist can eclipse the Infinite?*

82

Which pure reflexions, what dimme eye can see?
And after[24] either World, or *Fame* admire?
Comparison[25] expels the vanitie,
Immortall here, is obiect of desire,
Nature abhorres this supernaturall,
And scorn'd of flesh, as God is, they be all.

83

Yet hath the goodnesse, this of Infinite,
That they who hate it, praise, who hurt it, feare,
Who striue to shadow, help to show her light,
Her rootes, not *Fame,* but loue, and wonder beare,
God, that to passe, will haue his Iustice come,
Makes sin the Thiefe, the Hangman, and the doom.

84

These wooe not, but command the voice of *Fame,*
For liue they, dye they, labour they, or rest,
Such glorious lights, are imag'd in their frame;
As Nature feeles not, Art hath not exprest:
All what the world admires comes from within;
A doome, whereby the sinne, condemnes the sinne.

85

Then make the summe of our *Ideas*[26] this,
Who loue the world, giue latitude to *Fame,*
And this Man-pleasing, Gods displeasing is,
Who loue their God, haue glory by his name:
But fixe on Truth, who can, that know it not?
Who fixe on error, doe but write to blot.

86

Who worship *Fame,* commit Idolatry,
Make Men their God, *Fortune* and *Time* their worth,
Forme, but reforme not, meer hypocrisie,
By shadowes, onely shadowes bringing forth,
Which must, as blossomes, fade ere true fruit springs,
(Like voice, and *eccho*) ioyn'd; yet diuers things.

[24] afterwards.

[25] *Comparison*] *Comparisons* STC 12361.
[26] *Ideas*] *Idea's* STC 12361.

Edmund Spenser

[c. 1552–1599]

EDMUND SPENSER was educated at Merchant Taylors' School and at Pembroke Hall, Cambridge. After leaving Cambridge he was in 1578 secretary to John Young, Bishop of Rochester, and in 1579 in the service of Robert Dudley, Earl of Leicester. In 1580 he became secretary to Lord Grey, Lord Deputy of Ireland. Thereafter, except for visits to London, he remained in Ireland as a government official.

Before Spenser entered Cambridge, he made several short verse translations from Petrarch and du Bellay which were printed in Jan van der Noot's *A Theatre for Worldlings*, 1569. Some of these translations were included in revised form, with miscellaneous poems, in Spenser's *Complaints*, 1591. In 1579 he published *The Shepheardes Calender*. In 1590 were published the first three books of *The Faerie Queene*, in 1596 the next three; a fragment of a seventh book, *Two Cantos of Mutabilitie*, was printed in 1609. In 1595 Spenser published *Colin Clout's Come Home Again*, a pastoral written several years earlier. He married Elizabeth Boyle in 1594, and the courtship forms part of the background of his *Amoretti*, a series of eighty-nine sonnets; his *Epithalamion* in the same volume celebrates his marriage. *Prothalamion* (1596) he wrote to celebrate the betrothal of Lady Elizabeth and Lady Katherine, daughters of Edward Somerset, Earl of Worcester. In 1596 he published *Fowre Hymnes*, the first two in praise of earthly love and beauty, the second two in praise of heavenly love and beauty. Late in 1598 Spenser went to London on official business; in January, 1599, he died.

Spenser's *The Shepheardes Calender* is a landmark in the history of English poetry. Since the death of Chaucer in 1400, English poetry had been stiff and awkward both in rhythm and in diction; and though Wyatt, Surrey, and Sackville had restored some of its lost dignity and grace, Spenser in *The Shepheardes Calender* achieved a music and a variety of rhythm that equaled and even surpassed Chaucer's. No less important are Spenser's experiments with diction and his development of style. "He hath laboured," wrote E. K. (probably Edward Kirke, a contemporary at Cambridge), whose explanatory comments were published with *The Shepheardes Calender*, "to restore, as to theyr rightfull heritage such good and naturall English words, as haue ben long time out of vse and almost cleane disherited. Which is the onely cause, that our Mother tonge, which truely of it self is both ful enough for prose and stately enough for verse, hath long time ben counted most bare and barrein of both, which default when as some endeuoured to salue and recure, they patched vp the holes with peces and rags of other languages. . . . So now they haue made our English tongue, a gallimaufray or hodgepodge of al other speches." Spenser employed in *The Shepheardes Calender* and later in *The Faerie Queene* many "olde and obsolete words . . . most vsed of country folke" and many archaic words drawn from Chaucer, Langland, Malory, and Lydgate. Spenser's style is distinctive; it is rich and varied; and, whether plain or ornate, his sentences are fluent, well knit, lucid. E. K. wrote: "For the knitting of sentences . . . and for al the compasse of the speach, it is round without roughnesse, and learned wythout hardnes. . . . For what in most English wryters vseth to be loose, and as it were vngyrt, in this Authour is well grounded, finely framed, and strongly trussed vp together." Spenser's experiments in *The Shepheardes Calender* are within the well-understood convention of Theocritus, Virgil, Mantuan, and many others. His eclogues are allegories; his shepherds are poets, scholars, statesmen, ecclesiastics; his themes are personal, moral, and political. The April eclogue is a panegyric upon Queen Elizabeth. The October eclogue, based on Mantuan's fifth eclogue, tells of Spenser's aspirations as a poet.

In *Amoretti* Spenser borrows from French and Italian sonnet writers, but his sonnets differ from most of the sonnets of the period in the simplicity of the diction and in the linking of the quatrains, as in Marot and in the Scottish poet Alexander Montgomery, by the extension of one rhyme in each quatrain into the next.

Spenser's *magnum opus* is, of course, *The Faerie Queene*. His purpose in this great poem was, as he explained in his famous letter to Raleigh, "to fashion a gentleman or noble person in vertuous and gentle discipline." The poem gives expression both to the idealism of Renaissance Platonism and to the religious and patriotic fervor of Elizabethan England. It is at once a medieval chivalric romance, a romantic epic, an elaborate allegory. Although the allegory deals with sixteenth-century religious and political questions, the underlying theme is the timeless war between good and evil.

For *The Faerie Queene* he invented the "Spenserian stanza," which he probably developed from rhyme royal (rhyming ababcc) and from the eight-line stanza (rhyming ababbcbc) which Chaucer used in *The Monk's Tale* and which Spenser used in the introductory stanzas of the April and November eclogues in *The Shepheardes Calender*. To the eight pentameter lines of the "monk's-tale stanza" he added a hexameter line rhyming with lines six and eight. This beautiful and difficult stanza Spenser used with incomparable skill.

The fragment *Two Cantos of Mutabilitie* is presumably the core of a seventh book of *The Faerie Queene*. It deals with the contest between constancy and inconstancy, permanence and change. The Titaness, "bold Alteration," is the enemy of the gods and of Nature; she seeks to destroy in heaven that divine order which she has already destroyed on earth. When Nature, sitting in judgment, finally speaks, she speaks with the voice of God. Change is the way ordained by God, by which all things grow toward perfection,

> But time shall come that all shall changed bee,
> And from thenceforth, none no more change shall see.

In the last stanzas Spenser turns from "this state of life so tickle" to long for the changeless peace of eternity

> With Him that is the God of Sabbaoth hight.

Spenser concludes in the medieval tradition of *contemptus mundi*. This fragment, one of the great things in English poetry, may have been the last poetry that he wrote.

To his contemporaries Spenser was "the new poet" who surpassed the poets of France and Italy, "our principall poet," "the prince of poets in his tyme." His poetry as a whole shows the great artist's mastery and the idealist's nobility of purpose. He preserved for later generations the best of the medieval Christian tradition; "he saved us," as C. S. Lewis has pointed out, "from the catastrophe of too thorough a renaissance." He is not only the greatest nondramatic poet of the age; he is also the most completely Elizabethan—in his love of England and his pride in the English tongue, in his belief in the ethical function of poetry, in his belief that poetry is a divine gift, a "celestiall inspiration," and that great poetry alone among the works of man can survive the storms of time:

> For deeds doe die, how euer noblie donne,
> And thoughts of man do as themselues decay,
> But wise wordes taught in numbers for to runne,
> Recorded by the Muses, liue for ay;
> Ne may with storming showers be washt away,
> Ne bitter breathing windes with harmfull blast,
> Nor age, nor enuie shall them euer wast.
>
> (*The Ruines of Time*, 400–406)

The standard modern edition is *The Works of Edmund Spenser, a Variorum Edition*, ed. E. Greenlaw, C. G. Osgood, F. M. Padelford, and R. Heffner, 9 vols., 1932–1949. The most useful one-volume edition is that edited by J. C. Smith and E. de Selincourt, 1912. The standard biography is A. C. Judson, *The Life of Edmund Spenser*, 1945. Useful introductions to the study of Spenser are the following: W. L. Renwick, *Edmund Spenser: An Essay on Renaissance Poetry*, 1925; H. S. V. Jones, *A Spenser Handbook*, 1930; B. E. C. Davis, *Edmund Spenser*, 1933; C. S. Lewis, *The Allegory of Love*, 1936; Isabel Elizabeth Rathborne, *The Meaning of Spenser's Fairyland*, 1937; Josephine Waters Bennett, *The Evolution of the Faerie Queene*, 1942; Leicester Bradner, *Edmund Spenser and the "Faerie Queene,"* 1948.

From THE SHEPHEARDES CALENDER[1]

TO HIS BOOKE

Goe little booke: thy selfe present,
As child whose parent is vnkent:[2]
To him that is the president[3]
Of noblesse and of cheualree,
And if that Enuie barke at thee,
As sure it will, for succoure flee
Vnder the shadow of his wing,
And asked, who thee forth did bring,
A shepheards swaine saye did thee sing,
All as his straying flocke he fedde:
And when his honor has thee redde,
Craue pardon for my hardyhedde.
But if that any aske thy name,
Say thou wert base begot with blame:
For thy[4] thereof thou takest shame.
And when thou art past ieopardee,
Come tell me, what was sayd of mee:
And I will send more after thee.

IMMERITO.

APRILL
AEGLOGA QUARTA
ARGVMENT

This Aeglogue is purposely intended to the honor and prayse of our most gracious souereigne, Queene Elizabeth. The speakers herein be Hobbinoll and Thenott, two shepheardes: the which Hobbinoll being before mentioned, greatly to haue loued Colin,[5] is here set forth more largely, complayning him of that boyes great misaduenture in Loue, whereby his mynd was alienate and with drawen not onely from him, who moste loued him, but also from all former delightes and studies, as well in pleasaunt pyping, as conning,[6] ryming and singing, and other his laudable exercises. Whereby he taketh occasion, for proofe of his more excellencie and skill in poetrie, to recorde a songe, which the sayd Colin sometime made in honor of her Maiestie, whom abruptely he termeth Elysa.

THENOT. HOBBINOLL.

Tell me good Hobbinoll, what garres thee greete?[7]
What? hath some Wolfe thy tender Lambes ytorne?

---

1 From *The shepheardes calender. Conteyning twelue Aeglogues proportionable to the twelue monethes. Entitled to the noble and vertvous Gentleman most worthy of all titles both of learning and cheualrie M. Philip Sidney,* 1579, STC 23089, Huntington Library.

2 unknown.

3 precedent, pattern.

4 because.

5 Spenser.

6 *conning,*] *conning* STC 23089: learning by heart.

7 makes you weep.

Or is thy Bagpype broke, that soundes so sweete?
Or art thou of thy loued lasse forlorne?[8]

Or bene thine eyes attempred to the yeare,
Quenching the gasping furrowes thirst with rayne?
Like April shoure, so stremes the trickling teares
Adowne thy cheeke, to quenche thy thristye payne.

Hobbinoll.

Nor thys, nor that, so muche doeth make me mourne,
But for the ladde, whome long I lovd so deare,
Nowe loues a lasse, that all his loue doth scorne:
He plongd in payne, his tressed[9] locks dooth teare.

Shepheards delights he dooth them all forsweare,
Hys pleasaunt Pipe, whych made vs meriment,
He wylfully hath broke, and doth forbeare
His wonted songs, wherein he all outwent.

Thenot.

What is he for a Ladde,[10] you so lament?
Ys loue such pinching payne to them, that proue?[11]
And hath he skill to make[12] so excellent,
Yet hath so little skill to brydle loue?

Hobbinoll.

Colin thou kenst, the Southerne shepheardes boye:
Him Loue hath wounded with a deadly darte.
Whilome[13] on him was all my care and ioye,
Forcing[14] with gyfts to winne his wanton heart.

But now from me hys madding mynd is starte,
And woes the Widdowes daughter of the glenne:
So nowe fayre *Rosalind* hath bredde hys smart,
So now his frend is chaunged for a frenne.[15]

Thenot.

But if hys ditties bene so trimly dight,
I pray thee *Hobbinoll,* recorde some one:
The whiles our flockes doe graze about in sight,
And we close shrowded in thys shade alone.

Hobbinol.

Contented I: then will I singe his laye
Of fayre *Elisa,* Queene of shepheardes all:
Which once he made, as by a spring he laye,
And tuned it vnto the Waters fall.

Ye dayntye Nymphs, that in this blessed Brooke
doe bathe your brest,

---

8 forsaken.
9 curled.
10 what kind of lad is he.
11 experience.
12 write verse.
13 formerly.
14 trying.
15 stranger.

Forsake your watry bowres, and hether looke,
at my request:
And eke you Virgins,[16] that on *Parnasse* dwell,
Whence floweth *Helicon* the learned well,
Helpe me to blaze[17]
Her worthy praise,
Which in her sexe doth all excell.

Of fayre *Eliza* be your siluer song,
that blessed wight:
The flowre of Virgins, may shee florish long,
In princely plight.[18]
For shee is *Syrinx* daughter without spotte,
Which *Pan* the shepheards God of her begot:
So sprong her grace
Of heauenly race,
No mortall blemishe may her blotte.

See, where she sits vpon the grassie greene,
(O seemely sight)
Yclad in Scarlot like a mayden Queene,
And Ermines white.
Vpon her head a Cremosin[19] coronet,
With Damaske roses and Daffadillies set:
Bayleaues betweene,
And Primroses greene
Embellish the sweete Violet.

Tell me, haue ye seene her angelick face,
Like *Phoebe* fayre?
Her heauenly haueour, her princely grace
can you well compare?
The Redde rose medled[20] with the White[21] yfere,[22]
In either cheeke depeincten liuely chere.
Her modest eye,
Her Maiestie,
Where haue you seene the like, but there?

I sawe *Phoebus*[23] thrust out his golden hedde,
vpon her to gaze:
But when he sawe, how broade her beames did spredde,
it did him amaze.
He blusht to see another Sunne belowe,
Ne durst againe his fyrye face out showe:
Let him, if he dare,
His brightnesse compare
With hers, to haue the ouerthrowe.

---

16 The Muses, who dwelt on Mount Parnassus near the spring of Helicon.
17 blazon, publish.
18 condition, state.
19 crimson.
20 mingled.
21 The houses of Lancaster and York.
22 together.
23 The sun.

Shewe thy selfe *Cynthia*[24] with thy siluer rayes,
and be not abasht:
When shee the beames of her beauty displayes,
O how art thou dasht?
But I will not match her with *Latonaes* seede,[25]
Such follie great sorow to *Niobe* did breede.
Now she is a stone,
And makes dayly mone,
Warning all other to take heede.

Pan may be proud, that euer he begot
such a Bellibone,[26]
And *Syrinx* reioyse, that euer was her lot
to beare such an one.
Soone as my younglings cryen for the dam,
To her will I offer a milkwhite Lamb:
Shee is my goddesse plaine,
And I her shepherds swayne,
Albee forswonck and forswatt[27] I am.

I see *Calliope*[28] speede her to the place,
where my Goddesse shines:
And after her the other Muses trace,
with their Violines.
Bene they not Bay braunches, which they doe beare,
All for *Elisa* in her hand to weare?
So sweetely they play,
And sing all the way,
That it a heauen is to heare.

Lo how finely the graces can it foote
to the Instrument:
They dauncen deffly, and singen soote,[29]
in their meriment.
Wants not a fourth grace, to make the daunce euen?
Let that rowme to my Lady be yeuen:[30]
She shalbe a grace,
To fyll the fourth place,
And reigne with the rest in heauen.

And whither rennes this beuie of Ladies bright,
raunged in a rowe?
They bene all Ladyes of the lake behight,[31]
that vnto her goe.
Chloris, that is the chiefest Nympth of al,
Of Oliue braunches beares a Coronall:
Oliues bene for peace,
When wars doe surcease:
Such for a Princesse bene principall.

---

24 The moon.

25 Apollo and Diana, who killed Niobe's children because she boasted of them. Niobe was turned into a stone but continued to weep.

26 fair maid.

27 although exhausted and sweating from work.

28 The Muse of heroic poetry.

29 sweet.

30 given.

31 called.

Ye shepheards daughters, that dwell on the greene,
hye you there apace:
Let none come there, but that Virgins bene,
to adorne her grace.
And when you come, whereas shee is in place,
See, that your rudenesse doe not you disgrace:
Binde your fillets faste,
And gird in your waste,
For more finesse, with a tawdrie lace.[32]

Bring hether the Pincke and purple Cullambine,
With Gelliflowres:
Bring Coronations, and Sops in wine,[33]
worne of Paramoures.
Strowe me the ground with Daffadowndillies,
And Cowslips, and Kingcups, and loued Lillies:
The pretie Pawnce,[34]
And the Cheuisaunce,[35]
Shall match with the fayre flowre Delice.[36]

Now ryse vp *Eliza,* decked as thou art,
in royall aray:
And now ye daintie Damsells may depart
echeone her way.
I feare, I haue troubled your troupes to longe:
Let dame *Eliza* thanke you for her song.
And if you come hether,
When Damsines[37] I gether,
I will part them all you among.

Thenot.

And was thilk[38] same song of *Colins* owne making?
Ah foolish boy, that is with loue yblent:[39]
Great pittie is, he be in such taking,
For naught caren, that bene so lewdly[40] bent.

Hobbinol.

Sicker[41] I hold him, for a greater fon,[42]
That loues the thing, he cannot purchase.[43]
But let vs homeward: for night draweth on,
And twincling starres the daylight hence chase.

Thenots Embleme.
O quam te memorem virgo?[44]
Hobbinols Embleme.
O dea certe.[45]

[32] silk lace or ribbon (originally lace sold at fairs during the festival of Saint Audrey).
[33] pinks.
[34] pansy.
[35] *Cheuisaunce,*] *Cheuisaunce.* STC 23089: an unknown flower.
[36] *Delice.*] *Delice,* STC 23089: iris.
[37] damsons, plums.
[38] the same.
[39] blinded.
[40] foolishly.
[41] surely.
[42] fool.
[43] get.
[44] What name shall I give you, O maiden? (*Aeneid* i, 327.)
[45] O goddess surely. (*Aeneid,* i, 328.)

OCTOBER
AEGLOGLA DECIMA
ARGVMENT

In Cuddie is set out the perfecte paterne of a Poete, which[46] finding no maintenaunce of his state and studies, complayneth of the contempte of Poetrie, and the causes thereof: Specially hauing bene in all ages, and euen amongst the most barbarous alwayes of singular accounpt and honor, and being indede so worthy and commendable an arte: or rather no arte, but a diuine gift and heauenly instinct not to bee gotten by laboure and learning, but adorned with both: and poured into the witte by a certaine ἐνθουσιασμὸς [47] and celestiall inspiration, as the Author hereof els where at large discourseth, in his booke called the English Poete,[48] which booke being lately come to my hands, I mynde also by Gods grace vpon further aduisement to publish.

PIERCE. CUDDIE.

Cvddie, for shame hold vp thy heauye head,
And let vs cast with what delight to chace:
And weary thys long lingring *Phoebus* race.[49]
Whilome thou wont[50] the shepheards laddes to leade,
In rymes, in ridles, and in bydding base:[51]
Now they in thee, and thou in sleepe art dead?

Cuddye.

Piers, I haue pyped erst so long with payne,
That all mine Oten reedes[52] bene rent and wore:
And my poore Muse hath spent her spared store,
Yet little good hath got, and much lesse gayne.
Such pleasaunce makes the Grashopper so poore,[53]
And ligge so layd,[54] when Winter doth her straine:[55]

The dapper ditties, that I wont deuise,
To feede youthes fancie, and the flocking fry,[56]
Delighten much: what I the bett for thy?[57]
They han the pleasure, I a sclender prise.
I beate the bush, the byrds to them doe flye:
What good thereof to Cuddie can arise?

Pires.

Cuddie, the prayse is better, then the price,
The glory eke much greater then the gayne:
O what an honor is it, to restraine
The lust of lawlesse youth with good aduice:
Or pricke them forth with pleasaunce of thy vaine,[58]
Whereto thou list their trayned willes entice.[59]

---

46 *which*] *whishe* STC 23089.

47 enthusiasm, divine inspiration.

48 One of Spenser's lost works.

49 Let us consider with what entertainment we can speed the lingering daylight.

50 formerly you were accustomed.

51 In the game called "bidding base" or "prisoners' base," to "bid the base" meant to challenge a player to run from the base, and hence "to challenge" generally. Here the challenge may be to a wrestling contest as in Mantuan's Fifth Eclogue, which Spenser follows throughout much of this poem.

52 The symbol of pastoral poetry.

53 The allusion is to the grasshopper that sang all summer and laid up no food for the winter.

54 lie so subdued.

55 constrain, force.

56 crowding young people.

57 What was I the better for that?

58 spur them on with your eloquence.

59 to whatever you wish to lead their attracted wills.

Soone as thou gynst to sette thy notes in frame,[60]
O how the rurall routes[61] to thee doe cleaue:
Seemeth thou dost their soule of sence bereaue,
All as[62] the shepheard,[63] that did fetch his dame
From *Plutoes* balefull bowre withouten leaue:
His musicks might the hellish hound did tame.

Cuddie.

So praysen babes the Peacoks spotted traine,[64]
And wondren at bright *Argus* blazing eye:
But who rewards him ere the more for thy?[65]
Or feedes him once the fuller by a graine?
Sike[66] prayse is smoke, that sheddeth[67] in the skye,
Sike words bene wynd, and wasten soone in vayne.

Piers.

Abandon then the base and viler clowne,
Lyft vp thy selfe out of the lowly dust:
And sing of bloody Mars, of wars, of giusts.[68]
Turne thee to those, that weld the awful crowne,[69]
To doubted[70] Knights, whose woundlesse armour rusts,
And helmes vnbruzed wexen[71] dayly browne.

There may thy Muse display her fluttryng wing,
And stretch her selfe at large from East to West:
Whither thou list in fayre *Elisa* rest,[72]
Or if thee please in bigger notes to sing,
Aduaunce the worthy[73] whome shee loueth best,
That first the white beare to the stake did bring.

And when the stubborne stroke of stronger stounds,[74]
Has somewhat slackt the tenor[75] of thy string:
Of loue and lustihead[76] tho[77] mayst thou sing,
And carrol lowde, and leade the Myllers rownde,[78]
All[79] were *Elisa* one of thilke same ring.[80]
So mought[81] our *Cuddies* name to Heauen sownde.

Cuddie.

Indeede the Romish *Tityrus*,[82] I heare,
Through his *Mecaenas* left his Oaten reede,

60 order.
61 crowds.
62 just as.
63 Orpheus, whose music led Pluto, ruler of Hades, to release Eurydice, and even tamed Cerberus, the watchdog of Hades.
64 After the death of the giant Argus, his hundred eyes were transferred to the peacock's tail.
65 that.
66 such.
67 is dispersed.
68 *giusts.*] *guists*, STC 23089: jousts.
69 *crowne,*] *crowne.* STC 23089.
70 dreaded.
71 grow.
72 whether you choose to sing of Queen Elizabeth.
73 Spenser's patron, the Earl of Leicester, whose coat of arms showed a bear chained to a ragged staff.
74 strokes.
75 lowered the pitch.
76 pleasure.
77 then.
78 A country dance.
79 although.
80 group of dancers.
81 might.
82 Virgil, whose patrons were Augustus Caesar and Maecenas, and who wrote pastoral poetry before the *Aeneid*.

Whereon he earst[83] had taught his flocks to feede,
And laboured lands to yield the timely eare,
And eft[84] did sing of warres and deadly drede,
So as the Heauens did quake his verse to here.

But ah *Mecaenas* is yclad in claye,
And great *Augustus* long ygoe is dead:
And all the worthies liggen[85] wrapt in leade,
That matter made for Poets on to play:
For euer, who in derring doe[86] were dreade,
The loftie verse of hem[87] was loued aye.

But after vertue gan for age to stoupe,[88]
And mighty manhode brought a bedde[89] of ease:
The vaunting Poets found nought worth a pease,[90]
To put in preace[91] emong the learned troupe.
Tho[92] gan the streames of flowing wittes to cease,
And sonnebright honour pend in shamefull coupe.[93]

And if that any buddes of Poesie,
Yet of the old stocke gan to shoote agayne:
Or it mens follies mote[94] be forst to fayne,[95]
And rolle with rest in rymes of rybaudrye:
Or as it sprong, it wither must agayne:
Tom Piper[96] makes vs better melodie.

Piers.

O pierlesse Poesye, where is then thy[97] place?
If nor in Princes pallace thou doe sitt:
(And yet is Princes pallace the most fitt)
Ne brest of baser birth doth thee embrace.
Then make thee winges of thine aspyring wit,
And, whence thou camst, flye backe to heauen apace.

Cuddie.

Ah *Percy* it is all to weake and wanne,
So high to sore, and make so large a flight:
Her peeced[98] pyneons bene not so in plight,[99]
For *Colin* fittes such famous flight to scanne:
He, were he not with loue so ill bedight,[1]
Would mount as high, and sing as soote[2] as Swanne.

Pires.

Ah fon,[3] for loue does teach him climbe so hie,

---

83 formerly.
84 later.
85 lie.
86 daring deeds.
87 about them.
88 valor began because of age to fail.
89 to bed.
90 pea.
91 put in press, prepare, put in readiness.
92 then.
93 coop, prison.
94 must.
95 depict imaginatively.
96 Piper for country dances.
97 *thy*] *the* STC 23089.
98 pieced, imperfect.
99 condition.
1 stricken.
2 sweet.
3 fool.

And lyftes him vp out of the loathsome myre:
Such immortall mirrhor,[4] as he doth admire,
Would rayse ones mynd aboue the starry skie,[5]
And cause a caytiue corage[6] to aspire,
For lofty loue doth loath a lowly eye.

Cuddie.[7]

All otherwise the state of Poet stands,
For lordly loue is such a Tyranne fell:[8]
That where he rules, all power he doth expell.
The vaunted verse a vacant head demaundes,[9]
Ne wont with crabbed care the Muses dwell.[10]
Vnwisely weaues,[11] that takes two webbes in hand.

Who euer casts to compasse weightye prise,[12]
And thinks to throwe out thondring words of threate:
Let powre in lauish cups and thriftie bitts of meate,
For *Bacchus* fruite is frend to *Phoebus* wise.
And when with Wine the braine begins to sweate,
The nombers flowe as fast as spring doth ryse.

Thou kenst not *Percie* howe the ryme should rage.
Of if my temples were distaind with wine,
And girt in girlonds of wild Yuie twine,
How I could reare the Muse on stately stage,
And teache her tread aloft in buskin[13] fine,
With queint[14] *Bellona*[15] in her[16] equipage.[17]

But ah my corage[18] cooles ere it be warme,
For thy,[19] content vs in thys humble shade:
Where no such troublous tydes han vs assayde,[20]
Here we our slender pipes may safely charme.[21]

Pires.

And when my Gates shall han their bellies layd:[22]
Cuddie shall haue a Kidde to store his farme.

Cuddies Embleme.

Agitante calescimus illo &c.[23]

---

[4] the beauty of the beloved, which reflects the immortal and heavenly beauty.
[5] *skie,*] *skie.* STC 23089.
[6] base spirit.
[7] The name of the speaker is omitted in STC 23089.
[8] fierce tyrant.
[9] *demaundes,*] *demaundes.* STC 23089.
[10] *dwell.*] *dwell,* STC 23089.
[11] he weaves unwisely.
[12] whoever plans to achieve great things.
[13] High shoe or cothurnus worn by actors in ancient Greek and Roman tragedy.
[14] strange.
[15] Goddess of war.
[16] Bellona's.
[17] retinue.
[18] spirit.
[19] therefore.
[20] times have tested us.
[21] order.
[22] when my goats shall have been delivered of their young.
[23] From Ovid, *Fasti*, vi, 5. The entire verse is: "Est deus in nobis; agitante calescimus illo" (There is a god within us; by his urging we are inspired).

AMORETTI[24]

I

Happy ye leaues[25] when as those lilly hands,
which hold my life in their dead doing[26] might
shall handle you and hold in loues soft bands,
lyke captiues trembling at the victors sight.
And happy lines, on which with starry light,
those lamping eyes will deigne sometimes to look
and reade the sorrowes of my dying spright,[27]
written with teares in harts close bleeding book.
And happy rymes bath'd in the sacred brooke,[28]
of *Helicon* whence she deriued is,
when ye behold that Angels blessed looke,
my soules long lacked foode, my heauens blis.
Leaues, lines, and rymes, seeke her to please alone,
whom if ye please, I care for other none.

3

The souerayne beauty which I doo admyre,
witnesse the world how worthy to be prayzed:
the light wherof hath kindled heauenly fyre,
in my fraile spirit by her from basenesse raysed.
That being now with her huge brightnesse dazed,
base thing I can no more endure to view:
but looking still on her I stand amazed,
at wondrous sight of so celestiall hew.
So when my toung would speak her praises dew,
it stopped is with thoughts astonishment:
and when my pen would write her titles true,
it rauisht is with fancies wonderment:
Yet in my hart I then both speake and write,
the wonder that my wit cannot endite.[29]

5

Rvdely thou wrongest my deare harts desire,
In finding fault with her too portly pride:[30]
the thing which I doo most in her admire,
is of the world vnworthy most enuide.[31]
For in those lofty lookes is close implide,
scorn of base things, and sdeigne[32] of foule dishonor:
thretning rash eies which gaze on her so wide,
that loosely they ne dare to looke vpon her.

---

[24] From *Amoretti and Epithalamion*, 1595, STC 23076, British Museum.
[25] pages of the sonnets.
[26] death-dealing.
[27] spirit.
[28] Stream flowing from Helicon, a mountain in Greece sacred to the Muses; here "Helicon" means "heaven" also, for the lady's beauty is of heavenly origin.
[29] write.
[30] stately dignity.
[31] treated with malice.
[32] disdain.

Such pride is praise, such portlinesse[33] is honor,
that boldned innocence beares in hir eies:
and her faire countenance like a goodly banner,
spreds in defiaunce of all enemies.
Was neuer in this world ought worthy tride,
without some spark of such self-pleasing pride.

15

Ye tradefull Merchants that with weary toyle,
do seeke most pretious things to make your gain:
and both the Indias of their treasures spoile,
what needeth you to seeke so farre in vaine?
For loe my loue doth in her selfe containe
all this worlds riches that may farre be found,
if Saphyres, loe her eies be Saphyres plaine,
if Rubies, loe hir lips be Rubies sound:
If Pearles, hir teeth be pearles both pure and round;
if Yuorie, her forhead yuory weene;
if Gold, her locks are finest gold on ground;
if siluer, her faire hands are siluer sheene,
But that which fairest is, but few behold,
her mind adornd with vertues manifold.

22

This holy season fit to fast and pray,
men to deuotion ought to be inclynd:
therefore, I lykewise on so holy day,
for my sweet Saynt some seruice fit will find.
Her temple fayre is built within my mind,
in which her glorious ymage placed is,
on which my thoughts doo day and night attend
lyke sacred priests that neuer thinke amisse.
There I to her as th'author of my blisse,
will builde an altar to appease her yre:
and on the same my hart will sacrifise,
burning in flames of pure and chast desyre:
The which vouchsafe O goddesse to accept,
amongst thy deerest relicks to be kept.

34

Lyke as a ship that through the Ocean wyde,
by conduct of some star doth make her way,[34]
whenas a storme hath dimd her trusty guyde,[35]
out of her course doth wander far astray.
So I whose star, that wont with her bright ray
me to direct, with cloudes is ouercast,
doe wander now in darknesse and dismay,

---

[33] dignity.

[34] *way,*] *way*. STC 23076.
[35] *guyde,*] *guyde*. STC 23076.

through hidden perils round about me plast.
Yet hope I well, that when this storme is past
my *Helice*[36] the lodestar of my lyfe
will shine again, and looke on me at last,
with louely light to cleare my cloudy grief.
Till then I wander carefull comfortlesse,
in secret sorow and sad pensiuenesse.

37

What guyle is this, that those her golden tresses,
she doth attyre vnder a net of gold:
and with sly skill so cunningly them dresses,
that which is gold or heare, may scarse be told?
Is it that mens frayle eyes, which gaze too bold,
she may entangle in that golden snare:
and being caught may craftily enfold,
theyr weaker harts, which are not wel aware?
Take heed therefore, myne eyes, how ye doe stare
henceforth too rashly on that guilefull net,
in which if euer ye entrapped are,
out of her bands ye by no meanes shall get.
Fondnesse[37] it were for any being free,
to couet fetters, though they golden bee.

55

So oft as I her beauty doe behold,
and therewith doe her cruelty compare:
I maruaile of what substance was the mould
the which her made attonce so cruell faire.
Not earth; for her high thoghts more heauenly are,
not water; for her loue doth burne like fyre:
not ayre; for she is not so light or rare,
not fyre; for she doth friese with faint desire.
Then needs another Element inquire
whereof she mote[38] be made; that is the skye.
for to the heauen her haughty lookes aspire:
and eke her mind is pure immortall hye.
Then sith to heauen ye lykened are the best,
be lyke in mercy as in all the rest.

61

The glorious image of the makers beautie,
my souerayne saynt, the Idoll of my thought,
dare not henceforth aboue the bounds of dewtie,
t'accuse of pride, or rashly blame for ought.
For being as she is diuinely wrought,
and of the brood of Angels heuenly borne:

36 The constellation of the Great Bear.
37 folly.
38 might.

and with the crew of blessed Saynts vpbrought,
each of which did her with theyr guifts adorne;
The bud of ioy, the blossome of the morne,
the beame of light, whom mortal eyes admyre:
what reason is it then but she should scorne,
base things that to her loue too bold aspire?
Such heauenly formes ought rather worshipt be,
then dare be lou'd by men of meane degree.

62

The weary yeare his race now hauing run,
the new begins his compast course anew:
with shew of morning mylde he hath begun,
betokening peace and plenty to ensew,
So let vs, which this chaunge of weather vew,
chaunge eeke our mynds and former liues amend,
the old yeares sinnes forepast let vs eschew,
and fly the faults with which we did offend.
Then shall the new yeares ioy forth freshly send,
into the glooming world his gladsome ray:
and all these stormes which now his beauty blend,[39]
shall turne to caulmes and tymely cleare away.
So likewise loue cheare you your heauy spright,
and chaunge old yeares annoy to new delight.

63

After long stormes and tempests sad assay,[40]
which hardly I endured heretofore:
in dread of death and daungerous dismay,
with which my silly barke was tossed sore:[41]
I doe at length descry the happy shore,
in which I hope ere long for to arryue:
fayre soyle it seemes from far and fraught with store
of all that deare and daynty is alyue.
Most happy he that can at last atchyue
the ioyous safety of so sweet a rest:
whose least delight sufficeth to depriue,
remembrance of all paines which him opprest.
All paines are nothing in respect of this,
all sorrowes short that gaine eternall blisse.

65

The doubt which ye misdeeme, fayre loue, is vaine
that fondly[42] feare to loose your liberty,
when loosing one, two liberties ye gayne,
and make him bond that bondage earst[43] dyd fly.
Sweet be the bands, the which true loue doth tye,

[39] obscure.
[40] trial, assault.
[41] *sore:*] *sore*. STC 23076.
[42] foolishly.
[43] formerly.

without constraynt or dread of any ill:
the gentle birde feeles no captiuity
within her cage, but singes and feeds her fill.
There pride dare not approch, nor discord spill
the league twixt them, that loyal loue hath bound:
but simple truth and mutuall good will,
seekes with sweet peace to salue each others wound:
There fayth doth fearlesse dwell in brasen towre,
and spotlesse pleasure builds her sacred bowre.

67

Lyke as a huntsman after weary chase,
seeing the game from him escapt away:
sits downe to rest him in some shady place,
with panting hounds beguiled of their pray:[44]
So after long pursuit and vaine assay,
when I all weary had the chace forsooke,
the gentle deare returned the selfe-same way,
thinking to quench her thirst at the next[45] brooke.
There she beholding me with mylder looke,
sought not to fly, but fearelesse still did bide:
till I in hand her yet halfe trembling tooke,
and with her owne goodwill hir fyrmely tyde.
Strange thing me seemd to see a beast so wyld,
so goodly wonne with her owne will beguyld.

68

Most glorious Lord of lyfe that on this day,
didst make thy triumph ouer death and sin:
and hauing harrowd hell didst bring away[46]
captiuity thence captiue vs to win:[47]
This ioyous day, deare Lord, with ioy begin,
and grant that we for whom thou diddest dye
being with thy deare blood clene washt from sin,
may liue for euer in felicity.
And that thy loue we weighing worthily,
may likewise loue thee for the same againe:
and for thy sake that all lyke deare didst buy,
with loue may one another entertayne.[48]
So let vs loue, deare loue, lyke as we ought,
loue is the lesson which the Lord vs taught.

69

The famous warriors of the anticke world,
vsed Trophees[49] to erect in stately wize:
in which they would the records haue enrold,

---

[44] *pray:*] *pray.* STC 23076.
[45] nearest.
[46] *away*] *away,* STC 23076.
[47] *win:*] *win.* STC 23076.
[48] treat.
[49] monuments.

of theyr great deeds and valarous emprize.[50]
What trophee then shall I most fit deuize,
in which I may record the memory
of my loues conquest, peerelesse beauties prise,
adorn'd with honour, loue, and chastity.
Euen this verse vowd to eternity,
shall be thereof immortall moniment:
and tell her prayse to all posterity,
that may admire such worlds rare wonderment.
The happy purchase of my glorious spoile,
gotten at last with labour and long toyle.

70

Fresh spring the herald of loues mighty king,[51]
in whose cote armour[52] richly are displayd,
all sorts of flowers the which on earth do spring
in goodly colours gloriously arrayd:[53]
Goe to my loue, where she is carelesse layd,
yet in her winters bowre not well awake:
tell her the ioyous time wil not be staid
vnlesse she doe him by the forelock take.
Bid her therefore her selfe soone ready make,
to wayt on loue amongst his louely crew:
where euery one that misseth then her make,[54]
shall be by him amearst[55] with penance dew.
Make hast therefore sweet loue, whilest it is prime,[56]
for none can call againe the passed time.

71

I ioy to see how in your drawen work,[57]
your selfe vnto the Bee ye doe compare;
and me vnto the Spyder that doth lurke,
in close[58] awayt to catch her vnaware.
Right so your selfe were caught in cunning snare
of a deare foe, and thralled to his loue:
in whose streight bands[59] ye now captiued are
so firmely, that ye neuer may remoue.
But as your worke is wouen all about,
with woodbynd flowers and fragrant Eglantine:
so sweet your prison you in time shall proue,
with many deare delights bedecked fyne.
And all thensforth eternall peace shall see
betweene the Spyder and the gentle Bee.

---

50 enterprises.
51 Cupid.
52 The tabard, the herald's official garment, blazoned with the arms of the sovereign.
53 *arrayd:*] *arrayd.* STC 23076.
54 mate.
55 amerced, punished.
56 *prime,*] *prime.* STC 23076: spring.
57 needlework.
58 secret place.
59 strict bonds.

72

Oft when my spirit doth spred her bolder winges,
in mind to mount vp to the purest sky:
it down is weighd with thoght of earthly things
and clogd with burden of mortality,
Where when that souerayne beauty it doth spy,
resembling heauens glory in her light:
drawne with sweet pleasures bayt, it back doth fly,
and vnto heauen forgets her former flight.
There my fraile fancy fed with full delight,
doth bath in blisse and mantleth[60] most at ease:
ne thinks of other heauen, but how it might
her harts desire with most contentment please.
Hart need not wish none other happinesse,
but here on earth to haue such heuens blisse.

75

One day I wrote her name vpon the strand,
but came the waues and washed it away:
agayne I wrote it with a second hand,
but came the tyde, and made my paynes his pray.
Vayne man, sayd she, that doest in vaine assay,
a mortall thing so to immortalize.
for I my selue shall lyke to this decay,
and eek my name bee wyped out lykewize.
Not so, (quod I) let baser things deuize,[61]
to dy in dust, but you shall liue by fame:
my verse your vertues rare shall eternize,
and in the heuens wryte your glorious name.
Where whenas death shall all the world subdew,
our loue shall liue, and later life renew.

79

Men call you fayre, and you doe credit it,
for that your selfe ye dayly such doe see:
but the trew fayre,[62] that is the gentle wit,[63]
and vertuous mind is much more praysd of me.
For all the rest, how euer fayre it be,
shall turne to nought and loose[64] that glorious hew:
but onely that is permanent and free
from frayle corruption, that doth flesh ensew.
That is true beautie: that doth argue you
to be diuine and borne of heauenly seed:
deriu'd from that fayre Spirit,[65] from whom al true
and perfect beauty did at first proceed.

[60] spreads its wings (a hawking term).
[61] plan.
[62] beauty.
[63] intelligence.
[64] lose.
[65] God.

He onely fayre, and what he fayre hath made,
all other fayre lyke flowres vntymely fade.

80

After so long a race as I haue run
through Faery land, which those six books compile,
giue leaue to rest me being halfe fordonne,[66]
and gather to my selfe new breath awhile.
Then as a steed refreshed after toyle,
out of my prison I will breake anew:
and stoutly will that second worke assoyle,[67]
with strong endeuour and attention dew.
Till then giue leaue to me in pleasant mew,[68]
to sport my muse and sing my loues sweet praise:
the contemplation of whose heauenly hew,
my spirit to an higher pitch[69] will rayse.
But let her prayses yet be low and meane,
fit for the handmayd of the Faery Queene.

EPITHALAMION[70]

Ye learned sisters[71] which haue oftentimes
Beene to me ayding, others to adorne:
Whom ye thought worthy of your gracefull rymes,
That euen the greatest did not greatly scorne
To heare theyr names sung in your simple layes,
But ioyed in theyr prayse.
And when ye list your owne mishaps to mourne,
Which death, or loue, or fortunes wreck[72] did rayse,
Your string could soone to sadder tenor turne,
And teach the woods and waters to lament
Your dolefull dreriment.[73]
Now lay those sorrowfull complaints aside,
And hauing all your heads with girland crownd,
Helpe me mine owne loues prayses to resound,
Ne let the same of any be enuide:[74]
So Orpheus did for his owne bride,
So I vnto my selfe alone will sing,
The woods shall to me answer and my Eccho ring.

Early before the worlds light giuing lampe,
His golden beame vpon the hils doth spred,
Hauing disperst the nights vnchearefull dampe,
Doe ye awake and with fresh lusty hed,[75]
Go to the bowre of my beloued loue,
My truest turtle doue,[76]

---

66 exhausted.
67 accomplish.
68 seclusion; a "mew" is a cage for a hawk that is molting.
69 altitude (a hawking term).
70 From *Amoretti and Epithalamion*, 1595, STC 23076, British Museum.
71 The Muses.
72 violence.
73 sorrow.
74 *enuide:*] *enuide,* STC 23076.
75 vigor.
76 *doue,*] *doue* STC 23076.

Bid her awake; for Hymen[77] is awake,
And long since ready forth his maske[78] to moue,
With his bright Tead[79] that flames with many a flake,[80]
And many a bachelor to waite on him,
In theyr fresh garments trim.
Bid her awake therefore and soone her dight,[81]
For lo the wished day is come at last,
That shall for al the paynes and sorrowes past,
Pay to her vsury of long delight:[82]
And whylest she doth her dight,
Doe ye to her of ioy and solace sing,
That all the woods may answer and your eccho ring.

Bring with you all the Nymphes that you can heare[83]
Both of the riuers and the forrests greene:
And of the sea that neighbours to her neare,
Al with gay girlands goodly wel beseene.[84]
And let them also with them bring in hand,
Another gay girland
For my fayre loue of lillyes and of roses,
Bound trueloue wize with a blew silke riband.
And let them make great store of bridale poses,[85]
And let them eeke bring store of other flowers
To deck the bridale bowers.
And let the ground whereas her foot shall tread,
For feare the stones her tender foot should wrong
Be strewed with fragrant flowers all along,
And diapred[86] lyke the discolored[87] mead.
Which done, doe at her chamber dore awayt,
For she will waken strayt,
The whiles doe ye this song vnto her sing,
The woods shall to you answer and your Eccho ring.

Ye Nymphes of Mulla[88] which with carefull heed,
The siluer scaly trouts doe tend full well,
And greedy pikes which vse therein to feed,
(Those trouts and pikes all others doo excell)
And ye likewise which keepe the rushy lake,
Where none doo fishes take,[89]
Bynd vp the locks the which hang scatterd light,
And in his waters which your mirror make,
Behold your faces as the christall bright,
That when you come whereas my loue doth lie,
No blemish she may spie.
And eke ye lightfoot mayds which keepe the dere,[90]
That on the hoary mountayne vse to towre,[91]

77 The god of marriage.
78 merrymaking procession.
79 torch.
80 flash.
81 adorn herself.
82 *delight:*] *delight,* STC 23076.
83 can hear you.
84 adorned.
85 posies, bouquets.
86 variegated with flowers.
87 many-colored.
88 The Awbeg, the river on Spenser's estate in Ireland.
89 *take,*] *take.* STC 23076.
90 *dere,*] *dore,* STC 23076.
91 climb.

And the wylde wolues[92] which seeke them to deuoure,
With your steele darts doo chace from comming neer,[93]
Be also present heere,
To helpe to decke her and to help to sing,
That all the woods may answer and your eccho ring.

Wake now my loue, awake; for it is time,
The Rosy Morne long since left Tithones[94] bed,
All ready to her siluer coche[95] to clyme,
And Phoebus gins to shew his glorious hed.
Hark how the cheerefull birds do chaunt theyr laies
And carroll of loues praise.
That merry Larke hir mattins[96] sings aloft,
The thrush replyes, the Mauis[97] descant[98] playes,
The Ouzell[99] shrills, the Ruddock[1] warbles soft,
So goodly all agree with sweet consent,[2]
To this dayes merriment.
Ah my deere loue why doe ye sleepe thus long,
When meeter were that ye should now awake,
T'awayt the comming of your ioyous make,[3]
And hearken to the birds louelearned song,
The deawy leaues among.
For they of ioy and pleasance to you sing,
That all the woods them answer and theyr eccho ring.

My loue is now awake out of her dreames,[4]
And her fayre eyes like stars that dimmed were
With darksome cloud, now shew theyr goodly beams
More bright then Hesperus[5] his head doth rere.
Come now ye damzels, daughters of delight,[6]
Helpe quickly her to dight,
But first come ye fayre houres which were begot
In Ioues sweet paradice, of Day and Night,
Which doe the seasons of the yeare allot,
And al that euer in this world is fayre
Doe make and still repayre.
And ye three handmayds[7] of the Cyprian Queene,
The which doe still adorne her beauties pride,
Helpe to addorne my beautifullest bride
And as ye her array, still throw betweene
Some graces to be seene,
And as ye vse[8] to Venus, to her sing,
The whiles the woods shal answer and your eccho ring.

Now is my loue all ready forth to come,
Let all the virgins therefore well awayt,
And ye fresh boyes that tend vpon her groome

[92] There were wolves in Ireland in Spenser's time.
[93] *neer,*] *neer* STC 23076.
[94] In Greek myth, a Trojan prince beloved by Aurora, goddess of the dawn.
[95] coach.
[96] matins, morning songs.
[97] thrush.
[98] melody.
[99] blackbird.
[1] robin.
[2] harmony.
[3] mate.
[4] *dreames,*] *dreame,* STC 23076.
[5] The evening star.
[6] bridesmaids.
[7] The Graces attending Venus.
[8] as you are accustomed to do.

Prepare your selues; for he is comming strayt.
Set all your things in seemely good aray
Fit for so ioyfull day,
The ioyfulst day that euer sunne did see.[9]
Faire Sun, shew forth thy fauourable ray,
And let thy lifull[10] heat not feruent be
For feare of burning her sunshyny face,
Her beauty to disgrace.
O fayrest Phoebus, father of the Muse,
If euer I did honour thee aright,
Or sing the thing, that mote thy mind delight,
Doe not thy seruants simple boone refuse,
But let this day, let this one day be myne,
Let all the rest be thine.
Then I thy soueraype prayses loud wil sing,
That all the woods shal answer and theyr eccho ring.

Harke how the Minstrels gin to shrill aloud[11]
Their merry Musick that resounds from far,
The pipe, the tabor,[12] and the trembling Croud,[13]
That well agree withouten breach or iar.
But most of all the Damzels doe delite,
When they their tymbrels smyte,
And thereunto doe daunce and carrol sweet,
That all the sences they doe rauish quite,
The whyles the boyes run vp and downe the street,
Crying aloud with strong confused noyce,
As if it were one voyce.
Hymen iô Hymen, Hymen[14] they do shout,
That euen to the heauens theyr shouting shrill
Doth reach, and all the firmament doth fill,
To which the people standing all about,
As in approuance doe thereto applaud
And loud aduaunce her laud,[15]
And euermore they Hymen Hymen sing,
That al the woods them answer and theyr eccho ring.

Loe where she comes along with portly pace,[16]
Lyke Phoebe[17] from her chamber of the East,
Arysing forth to run her mighty race,
Clad all in white, that seemes[18] a virgin best.
So well it her beseemes that ye would weene
Some angell she had beene.
Her long loose yellow locks lyke golden wyre,
Sprinckled with perle, and perling flowres a tweene,
Doe lyke a golden mantle her attyre,
And being crowned with a girland greene,

---

[9] *see.*] *see* STC 23076.
[10] life-full.
[11] *aloud*] *aloud,* STC 23076.
[12] Small drum.
[13] Ancient Celtic stringed instrument played with a bow.
[14] In Roman marriage songs a refrain in praise of the god of marriage.
[15] praise.
[16] dignified step.
[17] The moon.
[18] befits.

Seeme lyke some mayden Queene,
Her modest eyes abashed to behold
So many gazers, as on her do stare,
Vpon the lowly ground affixed are.
Ne dare lift vp her countenance too bold,
But blush to heare her prayses sung so loud,
So farre from being proud.
Nathlesse doe ye still loud her prayses sing,
That all the woods may answer and your eccho ring.

Tell me ye merchants daughters did ye see
So fayre a creature in your towne before,
So sweet, so louely, and so mild as she,
Adornd with beautyes grace and vertues store,
Her goodly eyes lyke Saphyres shining bright,
Her forehead yuory white,
Her cheekes lyke apples which the sun hath rudded,
Her lips lyke cherryes charming men to byte,
Her brest like to a bowle of creame vncrudded,[19]
Her paps lyke lyllies budded,
Her snowie necke lyke to a marble towre,
And all her body like a pallace fayre,
Ascending vppe with many a stately stayre,
To honors seat and chastities sweet bowre.
Why stand ye still ye virgins in amaze,
Vpon her so to gaze,
Whiles ye forget your former lay to sing,
To which the woods did answer and your eccho ring.

Bvt if ye saw that which no eyes can see,
The inward beauty of her liuely spright,[20]
Garnisht with heauenly guifts of high degree,
Much more then would ye wonder at that sight,
And stand astonisht lyke to those which red[21]
Medusaes mazeful hed.[22]
There dwels sweet loue and constant chastity,
Vnspotted fayth and comely womanhed,[23]
Regard of honour and mild modesty,
There vertue raynes as Queene in royal throne,
And giueth lawes alone.
The which the base affections doe obay,
And yeeld theyr seruices vnto her will,
Ne thought of thing vncomely euer may
Thereto approch to tempt her mind to ill.
Had ye once seene these her celestial threasures,
And vnreuealed pleasures,
Then would ye wonder and her prayses sing,
That al the woods should answer and your echo ring.

Open the temple gates vnto my loue,
Open them wide that she may enter in,

[19] uncurdled.
[20] spirit, soul.
[21] saw.
[22] In Greek myth, Medusa's head, which had serpents for hair, turned the beholder into stone.
[23] womanhood.

And all the postes adorne as doth behoue,
And all the pillours deck with girlands trim,
For to recyue this Saynt with honour dew,
That commeth in to you.[24]
With trembling steps and humble reuerence,
She commeth in, before th'almighties vew:[25]
Of her ye virgins learne obedience,
When so ye come into those holy places,
To humble your proud faces:[26]
Bring her vp to th'high altar that she may,
The sacred ceremonies there partake,
The which do endlesse matrimony make,
And let the roring Organs loudly play[27]
The praises of the Lord in liuely notes,
The whiles with hollow throates[28]
The Choristers the ioyous Antheme sing,
That al the woods may answere and their eccho ring.

Behold whiles she before the altar stands
Hearing the holy priest that to her speakes
And blesseth her with his two happy hands,
How the red roses flush vp in her cheekes,
And the pure snow with goodly vermill[29] stayne,
Like crimsin dyde in grayne,[30]
That euen th'Angels which continually,
About the sacred Altare doe remaine,
Forget their seruice and about her fly,
Ofte peeping in her face that seemes more fayre,
The more they on it stare.
But her sad[31] eyes still fastened on the ground,
Are gouerned with goodly modesty,
That suffers not one looke to glaunce awry,
Which may let in a little thought vnsownd.[32]
Why blush ye loue to giue to me your hand,
The pledge of all our band?[33]
Sing ye sweet Angels, Alleluya sing,
That all the woods may answere and your eccho ring.

Now al is done; bring home the bride againe,
Bring home the triumph of our victory,
Bring home with you the glory of her gaine,
With ioyance bring her and with iollity.
Neuer had man more ioyfull day then this,
Whom heauen would heape with blis.
Make feast therefore now all this liue long day,
This day for euer to me holy is,
Poure out the wine without restraint or stay,
Poure not by cups, but by the belly[34] full,

---

24 *you.*] *you,* STC 23076.
25 *vew:*] *vew,* STC 23076.
26 *faces:*] *faces* STC 23076.
27 *play*] *play;* STC 23076.
28 *throates*] *throates.* STC 23076.
29 crimson.
30 in the grain, thoroughly.
31 serious.
32 *vnsownd.*] *vnsownd,* STC 23076.
33 *band?*] *band,* STC 23076: bond, union.
34 Bag or skin for holding wine.

Poure out to all that wull,
And sprinkle all the postes and wals with wine,
That they may sweat, and drunken be withall.
Crowne ye God Bacchus with a coronall,
And Hymen also crowne with wreathes of vine,
And let the Graces daunce vnto the rest;
For they can doo it best:
The whiles the maydens doe theyr carroll sing,
To which the woods shal answer and theyr eccho ring.

Ring ye the bels, ye yong men of the towne,
And leaue your wonted labors for this day:
This day is holy; doe ye write it downe,
That ye for euer it remember may.
This day[35] the sunne is in his chiefest hight,
With Barnaby the bright,
From whence declining daily by degrees,
He somewhat loseth of his heat and light,
When once the Crab[36] behind his back he sees.
But for this time it ill ordained was,
To chose the longest day in all the yeare,
And shortest night, when longest fitter weare:[37]
Yet neuer day so long, but late would passe.
Ring ye the bels, to make it weare away,
And bonefiers make all day,
And daunce about them, and about them sing:
That all the woods may answer, and your eccho ring.

Ah when will this long weary day haue end,
And lende me leaue to come vnto my loue?
How slowly do the houres theyr numbers spend?
How slowly does sad Time his feathers moue?
Hast thee O fayrest Planet to thy home
Within the Westerne fome:
Thy tyred steedes long since haue need of rest.
Long though it be, at least I see it gloome,
And the bright euening star with golden creast
Appeare out of the East.
Fayre childe of beauty,[38] glorious lampe of loue
That all the host of heauen[39] in rankes doost lead,
And guydest louers through the nights dread,
How chearefully thou lookest from aboue,
And seemst to laugh atweene thy twinkling light
As ioying in the sight
Of these glad many which for ioy doe sing,
That all the woods them answer and their echo ring.

Now ceasse ye damsels your delights forepast;
Enough is it, that all the day was youres:
Now day is doen, and night is nighing fast:
Now bring the Bryde into the brydall boures.

---

[35] June 11, St. Barnabas' Day, the longest day in the year, according to the old calendar.
[36] The constellation Cancer.
[37] were.
[38] Hesperus, the evening star.
[39] The stars.

Now night is come, now soone her disaray,
And in her bed her lay;
Lay her in lillies and in violets,
And silken courteins ouer her display,
And odourd sheetes, and Arras[40] couerlets.[41]
Behold how goodly my faire loue does ly
In proud humility;
Like vnto Maia,[42] when as Ioue her tooke,
In Tempe, lying on the flowry gras,
Twixt sleepe and wake, after she weary was,
With bathing in the Acidalian[43] brooke.[44]
Now it is night, ye damsels may be gon,
And leaue my loue alone,
And leaue likewise your former lay to sing:
The woods no more shal answere, nor your echo ring.

Now welcome night, thou night so long expected,
That long daies labour doest at last defray,
And all my cares, which cruell loue collected,
Hast sumd in one, and cancelled for eye:
Spread thy broad wing ouer my loue and me,
That no man may vs see,
And in thy sable mantle vs enwrap,
From feare of perrill and foule horror free.
Let no false treason seeke vs to entrap,
Nor any dread disquiet once annoy
The safety of our ioy:
But let the night be calme and quietsome,
Without tempestuous storms or sad afray:
Lyke as when Ioue with fayre Alcmena lay,
When he begot the great Tirynthian groome:[45]
Or lyke as when he with thy selfe[46] did lie,
And begot Maiesty.
And let the mayds and yongmen cease to sing:
Ne let the woods them answer, nor theyr eccho ring.

Let no lamenting cryes, nor dolefull teares,
Be heard all night within nor yet without:
Ne let false whispers breeding hidden feares,
Breake gentle sleepe with misconceiued dout.
Let no deluding dreames, nor dreadful sights
Make sudden sad affrights;
Ne let housefyres, nor lightnings helpelesse harmes,
Ne let the Pouke,[47] nor other euill sprights,
Ne let mischiuous witches with theyr charmes,
Ne let hob Goblins, names whose sence we see not,
Fray[48] vs with things that be not.
Let not the shriech Oule, nor the Storke be heard:

---

[40] Tapestry woven in Arras, France.

[41] *couerlets.*] *couerlets,* STC 23076.

[42] Daughter of Atlas; Jove met her in Tempe, a valley in Thessaly.

[43] from the well Acidalis.

[44] *brooke.*] *brooke* STC 23076.

[45] Hercules, born at Tiryns.

[46] i.e., night; the allusion is puzzling.

[47] In Irish folklore the Pooka or Puck, a malicious fairy.

[48] frighten.

Nor the night Rauen that still deadly yels,
Nor damned ghosts cald vp with mighty spels,
Nor griesly vultures make vs once affeard:
Ne let th'unpleasant Quyre of Frogs still croking
Make vs to wish theyr choking.
Let none of these theyr drery accents sing;
Ne let the woods them answer, nor theyr eccho ring.

But let stil Silence trew night watches keepe,
That sacred peace may in assurance rayne,
And tymely sleep, when it is tyme to sleepe,
May poure his limbs forth on your[49] pleasant playne,
The whiles an hundred little winged loues,
Like diuers fethered doues,
Shall fly and flutter round about your bed,
And in the secret darke, that none reproues,
Their prety stealthes shal worke, and snares shal spread
To filch away sweet snatches of delight,
Conceald through couert night.
Ye sonnes of Venus,[50] play your sports at will,
For greedy pleasure, carelesse of your toyes,
Thinks more vpon her paradise of ioyes,
Then what ye do, albe it good or ill.
All night therefore attend your merry play,
For it will soone be day:
Now none doth hinder you, that say or sing,
Ne will the woods now answer, nor your Eccho ring.

Who is the same, which at my window peepes?
Or whose is that faire face, that shines so bright?[51]
Is it not Cinthia,[52] she that neuer sleepes,
But walkes about high heauen al the night?
O fayrest goddesse, do thou not enuy
My loue with me to spy:
For thou likewise didst loue, though now vnthought,
And for a fleece of woll, which priuily,
The Latmian shephard[53] once vnto thee brought,
His pleasures with thee wrought.
Therefore to vs be fauorable now;
And sith of wemens labours thou hast charge,
And generation goodly dost enlarge,
Encline thy[54] will t'effect our wishfull vow,
And the chast wombe informe with timely seed,
That may our comfort breed:
Till which we cease our hopefull hap[55] to sing,
Ne let the woods vs answere, nor our Eccho ring.

And thou great Iuno, which with awful might
The lawes of wedlock still dost patronize,
And the religion of the faith first plight
With sacred rites hast taught to solemnize:

---

49 night's; but perhaps Spenser wrote *our.*
50 *little winged loues.*
51 *bright?*] *bright,* STC 23076.
52 The moon.
53 Endymion, the shepherd boy from Mount Latmos, beloved by the moon goddess.
54 *thy*] *they* STC 23076.
55 fortune.

And eeke for comfort often called art
Of women in their smart,
Eternally bind thou this louely band,
And all thy blessings vnto vs impart.
And thou glad Genius, in whose gentle hand,
The bridale bowre and geniall[56] bed remaine,
Without blemish or staine,
And the sweet pleasures of theyr loues delight
With secret ayde doest succour and supply,
Till they bring forth the fruitfull progeny,
Send vs the timely fruit of this same night.
And thou fayre Hebe,[57] and thou Hymen free,
Grant that it may so be.
Til which we cease your further prayse to sing,
Ne any woods shal answer, nor your Eccho ring.

And ye high heauens, the temple of the gods,
In which a thousand torches flaming bright
Doe burne, that to vs wretched earthly clods,[58]
In dreadful darknesse lend desired light;
And all ye powers which in the same remayne,
More then we men can fayne,[59]
Poure out your blessing on vs plentiously,
And happy influence vpon vs raine,
That we may raise a large posterity,
Which from the earth, which they may long possesse,
With lasting happinesse,
Vp to your haughty pallaces may mount,
And for the guerdon of theyr glorious merit
May heauenly tabernacles there inherit,
Of blessed Saints for to increase the count.
So let vs rest, sweet loue, in hope of this,[60]
And cease till then our tymely ioyes to sing,
The woods no more vs answer, nor our eccho ring.

Song made in lieu of many ornaments,[61]
With which my loue should duly haue bene dect,
Which cutting off through hasty accidents,[62]
Ye would not stay your dew time to expect,[63]
But promist both to recompens,
Be vnto her a goodly ornament,
And for short time an endlesse moniment.[64]

AN HYMNE IN HONOUR OF BEAUTIE[65]

Ah whither, Loue, wilt thou now carrie mee?
What wontlesse[66] fury dost thou now inspire

[56] nuptial.
[57] Goddess of youth.
[58] *clods,*] *clods:* STC 23076.
[59] imagine.
[60] This is a line without rhyme. Perhaps, as C. G. Osgood suggests, the compositor lost the short line found in all other stanzas before the concluding couplet. He suggests "And of eternall blis."
[61] The meaning of this *envoi* is uncertain.
[62] Perhaps the marriage date had been advanced.
[63] await.
[64] monument.
[65] From *Fowre hymnes,* 1596, STC 23086, Huntington Library.
[66] unaccustomed.

Into my feeble breast, too full of thee?
Whylest seeking to aslake thy raging fyre,
Thou in me kindlest much more great desyre,
And vp aloft aboue my strength doest rayse
The wondrous matter of my fyre to prayse.

That as I earst in praise of thine owne name,
So now in honour of thy Mother deare,[67]
An honourable Hymne I eke should frame,
And with the brightnesse of her beautie cleare,
The rauisht harts of gazefull men might reare,
To admiration of that heauenly light,
From whence proceeds such soule[68] enchaunting might.

Therto do thou great Goddesse, queene of Beauty,
Mother of loue, and of all worlds delight,
Without whose souerayne grace and kindly dewty,
Nothing on earth seemes fayre to fleshly sight,
Doe thou vouchsafe with thy loue-kindling light,
T'illuminate my dim and dulled eyne,
And beautifie this sacred hymne of thyne.

That both to thee, to whom I meane it most,
And eke to her, whose faire immortall beame,
Hath darted fyre into my feeble ghost,[69]
That now it wasted is with woes extreame,
It may so please that she at length will streame
Some deaw of grace, into my withered hart,
After long sorrow and consuming smart.

What time this worlds great workmaister did cast[70]
To make al things, such as we now behold,[71]
It seemes that he before his eyes had plast
A goodly Paterne to whose perfect mould,
He fashioned them as comely as he could,
That now so faire and seemely they appeare,
As nought may be amended any wheare.

That wondrous Paterne wheresoere it bee,
Whether in earth layd vp in secret store,
Or else in heauen, that no man may it see
With sinfull eyes, for feare it to deflore,[72]
Is perfect Beautie which all men adore,
Whose face and feature doth so much excell
All mortall sence, that none the same may tell.

Thereof as euery earthly thing partakes,
Or more or lesse by influence diuine,
So it more faire accordingly it makes,
And the grosse matter of this earthly myne,
Which clotheth it, thereafter doth refyne,

---

67 Venus.
68 *soule* ed. 1617]; *ſoule* STC 23086.
69 spirit.
70 plan.
71 *behold,*] *behold* STC 23086.
72 deflower, desecrate.

Doing away the drosse which dims the light
Of that faire beame, which therein is empight.[73]

For through infusion of celestiall powre,
The duller earth it quickneth with delight,
And life-full spirits priuily doth powre
Through all the parts, that to the lookers sight
They seeme to please. That is thy soueraine might,
O *Cyprian* Queene,[74] which flowing from the beame
Of thy bright starre, thou into them doest streame.

That is the thing which giueth pleasant grace
To all things faire, that kindleth liuely fyre,
Light of thy lampe, which shyning in the face,
Thence to the soule darts amorous desyre,
And robs the harts of those which it admyre,
Therewith thou pointest thy Sons[75] poysned arrow,
That wounds the life, and wastes the inmost marrow.

How vainely then doe ydle wits inuent,
That beautie is nought else, but mixture made
Of colours faire, and goodly temp'rament[76]
Of pure complexions, that shall quickly fade
And passe away, like to a sommers shade,
Or that it is but comely composition
Of parts well measurd, with meet disposition.

Hath white and red in it such wondrous powre,
That it can pierce through th'eyes vnto the hart,
And therein stirre such rage and restlesse stowre,[77]
As nought but death can stint[78] his dolours smart?
Or can proportion of the outward part,
Moue such affection in the inward mynd,
That it can rob both sense and reason blynd?

Why doe not then the blossomes of the field,
Which are arayd with much more orient hew,
And to the sense most daintie odours yield,
Worke like impression in the lookers vew?
Or why doe not faire pictures like powre shew,
In which oftimes, we Nature see of Art
Exceld, in perfect limming[79] euery part.

But ah, beleeue me, there is more then so
That workes such wonders in the minds of men.
I that have often prou'd,[80] too well it know;
And who so list the like assayes to ken,[81]
Shall find by tryall, and confesse it then,

[73] implanted.
[74] Venus, whose favorite dwelling was in Cyprus.
[75] Cupid's.
[76] Perfect combination of the four "humors" in the body.
[77] disturbance.
[78] stop.
[79] painting.
[80] tested.
[81] whoever wishes to discover by the same tests.

That Beautie is not, as fond[82] men misdeeme,
An outward shew of things, that onely seeme.

For that same goodly hew of white and red,
With which the cheekes are sprinckled, shal decay,
And those sweete rosy leaues so fairely spred
Vpon the lips, shall fade and fall away
To that they were, euen to corrupted clay.
That golden wyre, those sparckling stars so bright
Shall turne to dust, and loose their goodly light.

But that faire lampe, from whose celestiall ray
That light proceedes, which kindleth louers fire,
Shal neuer be extinguisht nor decay,
But when the vitall spirits doe expyre,
Vnto her natiue planet shall retyre,
For it is heauenly borne and can not die,
Being a parcell[83] of the purest skie.

For when the soule, the which deriued was
At first, out of that great immortall Spright,
By whom all liue to loue, whilome[84] did pas
Downe from the top of purest heauens hight,
To be embodied here, it then tooke light
And liuely[85] spirits from that fayrest starre,
Which lights the world forth from his firie carre.

Which powre retayning still or more or lesse,
When she in fleshly seede is eft enraced,[86]
Through euery part she doth the same impresse,
According as the heauens haue her graced,
And frames her house, in which she will be placed,
Fit for her selfe, adorning it with spoyle
Of th'heauenly riches, which she robd erewhyle.[87]

Therof it comes, that these faire soules, which haue
The most resemblance of that heauenly light,
Frame[88] to themselues most beautifull and braue[89]
Their fleshly bowre, most fit for their delight,
And the grosse matter by a soueraine might
Tempers so trim,[90] that it may well be seene,
A pallace fit for such a virgin Queene.

So euery spirit, as it is most pure,
And hath in it the more of heauenly light,
So it the fairer bodie doth procure
To habit in, and it more fairely dight[91]
With chearefull grace and amiable sight.

82 foolish.
83 part.
84 formerly.
85 living.
86 again implanted.
87 formerly.
88 make.
89 splendid.
90 controls so perfectly.
91 adorn.

For of the soule the bodie forme doth take:
For soule is forme, and doth the bodie make.

Therefore where euer that thou doest behold
A comely corpse,[92] with beautie faire endewed,
Know this for certaine, that the same doth hold
A beauteous soule, with faire conditions thewed,[93]
Fit to receiue the seede of vertue strewed.[94]
For all that faire is, is by nature good;
That is a signe to know the gentle blood.

Yet oft it falles, that many a gentle mynd
Dwels in deformed tabernacle drownd,
Either by chaunce, against the course of kynd,[95]
Or through vnaptnesse in the substance fownd,
Which it assumed of some stubborne grownd,[96]
That will not yield vnto her formes direction,
But is perform'd[97] with some foule imperfection.

And oft it falles (ay me the more to rew)
That goodly beautie, albe[98] heauenly borne,
Is foule abusd, and that celestiall hew,
Which doth the world with her delight adorne,
Made but the bait of sinne, and sinners scorne;
Whilest euery one doth seeke and sew to haue it,
But euery one doth seeke, but to depraue it.

Yet nathemore[99] is that faire beauties blame,
But theirs that do abuse it vnto ill:
Nothing so good, but that through guilty shame
May be corrupt, and wrested vnto will.
Nathelesse the soule is faire and beauteous still,
How euer fleshes fault it filthy make:
For things immortall no corruption take.

But ye faire Dames, the worlds deare ornaments,
And liuely[1] images of heauens light,
Let not your beames with such disparagements
Be dimd, and your bright glorie darkned quight,
But mindfull still of your first countries sight,
Doe still preserue your first informed grace,
Whose shadow yet shynes in your beauteous face.

Loath that foule blot, that hellish fierbrand,
Disloiall lust, faire beauties foulest blame,
That base affections, which your eares would bland,[2]
Commend to you by loues abused name;
But is indeede the bondslaue of defame,

92 living body.
93 trained, instructed.
94 scattered.
95 nature.
96 reason, cause.
97 Some editors read *deform'd*.
98 although.
99 none the more.
1 living.
2 soothe, flatter.

Which will the garland of your glorie marre,
And quench the light of your bright shyning starre.

But gentle Loue, that loiall is and trew,
Will more illumine your resplendent ray,
And adde more brightnesse to your goodly hew,
From light of his pure fire, which by like way
Kindled of yours, your likenesse doth display,
Like as two mirrours by opposd reflexion,
Doe both expresse the faces first impression.

Therefore to make your beautie more appeare,
It you behoues to loue, and forth to lay
That heauenly riches, which in you ye beare,
That men the more admyre their fountaine[3] may,
For else what booteth[4] that celestiall ray,
If it in darknesse be enshrined euer,
That it of louing eyes be vewed neuer?

But in your choice of Loues, this well aduize,[5]
That likest to your selues ye them select,
The which your forms first sourse may sympathize,[6]
And with like beauties parts be inly deckt:
For if you loosely loue without respect,[7]
It is no loue, but a discordant warre,
Whose vnlike parts amongst themselues do iarre.[8]

For Loue is a celestiall harmonie,
Of likely[9] harts composd of starres concent,
Which ioyne together in sweete sympathie,
To worke ech others ioy and true content,
Which they haue harbourd since their first descent
Out of their heauenly bowres, where they did see
And know ech other here belou'd to bee.

Then wrong it were that any other twaine
Should in loues gentle band combyned bee,
But those whom heauen did at first ordaine,
And made out of one mould the more t'agree:
For all that like the beautie which they see,
Streight[10] do not loue: for loue is not so light,
As streight to burne at first beholders sight.

But they which loue indeede, looke otherwise,
With pure regard and spotlesse true intent,
Drawing out of the obiect of their eyes,
A more refyned forme, which they present
Vnto their mind, void of all blemishment;
Which it reducing to her first perfection,
Beholdeth free from fleshes frayle infection.

[3] spring, source.
[4] avails.
[5] consider.
[6] agree with, harmonize with.
[7] thought.
[8] disagree.
[9] similar.
[10] quickly.

And then conforming it vnto the light,
Which in it selfe it hath remaining still
Of that first Sunne, yet sparckling in his sight,
Thereof he fashions in his higher skill,[11]
An heauenly beautie to his fancies will,
And it embracing in his mind entyre,
The mirrour of his owne thought doth admyre.

Which seeing now so inly faire to be,
As outward it appeareth to the eye,
And with his spirits proportion to agree,
He thereon fixeth all his fantasie,
And fully setteth his felicitie,
Counting it fairer, then it is indeede,
And yet indeede her fairenesse doth exceede.

For louers eyes more sharply sighted bee
Then other mens, and in deare loues delight
See more then any other eyes can see,
Through mutuall receipt of beames bright,
Which carrie priuie message to the spright,[12]
And to their eyes that inmost faire display,
As plaine as light discouers[13] dawning day.

Therein they see through amorous eye-glaunces,
Armies of loues still[14] flying too and fro,
Which dart at them their litle fierie launces,
Whom hauing wounded, backe againe they go,
Carrying compassion to their louely foe;
Who seeing her faire eyes so sharpe effect,
Cures all their sorrowes with one sweete aspect.[15]

In which how many wonders doe they reede[16]
To their conceipt,[17] that others neuer see,
Now of her smiles, with which their soules they feede,
Like Gods with Nectar in their bankets[18] free,
Now of her lookes, which like to Cordials bee;
But when her words embassade[19] forth she sends,
Lord how sweete musicke that vnto them lends.[20]

Sometimes vpon her forhead they behold
A thousand Graces masking in delight,
Sometimes within her eye-lids they vnfold
Ten thousand sweet belgards,[21] which to their sight
Doe seeme like twinckling starres in frostie night:
But on her lips like rosy buds in May,
So many millions of chaste pleasures play.

[11] wisdom.
[12] spirit, soul.
[13] reveals.
[14] always.
[15] look.
[16] perceive.
[17] opinion.
[18] banquets.
[19] on an embassy.
[20] gives.
[21] loving looks.

All those, O *Cytherea,*[22] and thousands more
Thy handmaides be, which do on thee attend
To decke thy beautie with their dainties store,
That may it more to mortall eyes commend,
And make it more admyr'd of foe and frend;
That in mens harts thou mayst thy throne enstall,
And spred thy louely kingdome ouer all.

Then *Iö tryumph,* O great beauties Queene,
Aduance the banner of thy conquest hie,
That all this world, the which thy vassals beene,
May draw to thee, and with dew fealtie,
Adore the powre of thy great Maiestie,
Singing this Hymne in honour of thy name,
Compyld by me, which thy poore liegeman am.

In lieu whereof graunt, O great Soueraine,
That she whose conquering beautie doth captiue
My trembling hart in her eternall chaine,
One drop of grace at length will to me giue,
That I her bounden thrall by her may liue,
And this same life, which first fro me she reaued,[23]
May owe to her, of whom I it receaued.

And you faire *Venus* dearling, my deare dread,
Fresh flowre of grace, great Goddesse of my life,
When your faire eyes these fearefull lines shal read,
Deigne to let fall one drop of dew reliefe,
That may recure[24] my harts long pyning griefe,
And shew what wondrous powre your beauty hath,
That can restore a damned wight from death.

PROTHALAMION[25]

I

Calme was the day, and through the trembling ayre,
Sweete breathing *Zephyrus*[26] did softly play
A gentle spirit, that lightly did delay[27]
Hot *Titans*[28] beames, which then did glyster fayre:
When I whom sullein care,
Through discontent of my long fruitlesse stay
In Princes Court, and expectation vayne
Of idle hopes, which still doe fly away,
Like empty shaddowes, did aflict my brayne,
Walkt forth to ease my payne
Along the shoare of siluer streaming *Themmes,*

22 Venus.
23 took away.
24 heal.
25 From *Prothalamion, or a spousall verse . . . in honour of the double mariage of the two honorable and vertuous ladies, the Ladie Elizabeth and the Ladie Katherine Somerset, daughters to the Right Honourable the Earle of Worcester and espoused to the two worthie gentlemen, M. Henry Gilford, and M. William Peter Esquyers,* 1596, STC 23088, Huntington Library.
26 The west wind.
27 temper.
28 The sun's.

Whose rutty[29] Bancke, the which his Riuer hemmes,
Was paynted all with variable[30] flowers,
And all the meades adornd with daintie gemmes,
Fit to decke maydens bowres,
And crowne their Paramours,
Against[31] the Brydale day, which is not long:[32]
Sweete *Themmes* runne softly, till I end my Song.

2

There, in a Meadow, by the Riuers side,
A Flocke of *Nymphes* I chaunced to espy,
All louely Daughters of the Flood thereby,
With goodly greenish locks all loose vntyde,
As each had bene a Bryde,
And each one had a little wicker basket,
Made of fine twigs entrayled[33] curiously,
In which they gathered flowers to fill their flasket:[34]
And with fine Fingers, cropt full feateously[35]
The tender stalkes on hye.
Of euery sort, which in that Meadow grew,
They gathered some; the Violet pallid blew,
The little Dazie, that at euening closes,
The virgin Lillie, and the Primrose trew,
With store of vermeil[36] Roses,
To decke their Bridegromes posies,
Against the Brydale day, which was not long:
Sweete *Themmes* runne softly, till I end my Song.

3

With that I saw two Swannes[37] of goodly hewe,
Come softly swimming downe along the Lee;[38]
Two fairer Birds I yet did neuer see:
The snow which doth the top of *Pindus*[39] strew,
Did neuer whiter shew,
Nor *Ioue* himselfe when he a Swan would be
For loue of *Leda,*[40] whiter did appeare:
Yet *Leda* was they say as white as he,
Yet not so white as these, nor nothing neare;
So purely white they were,
That euen the gentle streame, the which them bare,
Seem'd foule to them, and bad his billowes spare
To wet their silken feathers, least they might
Soyle their fayre plumes with water not so fayre,
And marre their beauties bright,
That shone as heauens light,

[29] full of ruts or of roots.
[30] various.
[31] in expectation of.
[32] not far hence.
[33] interwoven.
[34] shallow basket.
[35] neatly.
[36] crimson.
[37] The prospective brides.
[38] Perhaps the Lea, a river flowing into the Thames at Greenwich.
[39] Mountains in Thessaly.
[40] Queen of Sparta, wooed by Jove in the form of a swan.

Against their Brydale day, which was not long:
  Sweetė *Themmes* runne softly, till I end my Song.

4

Eftsoones[41] the *Nymphes,* which now had Flowers their fill,
Ran all in haste, to see that siluer brood,
As they came floating on the Christal Flood,
Whom when they sawe, they stood amazed still,
Their wondring eyes to fill.[42]
Them seem'd[43] they neuer saw a sight so fayre,
Of Fowles so louely, that they sure did deeme
Them heauenly borne, or to be that same payre
Which through the Skie draw *Venus* siluer Teeme,
For sure they did not seeme
To be begot of any earthly Seede,
But rather Angels or of Angels breede:
Yet were they bred of *Somers-heat*[44] they say,
In sweetest Season, when each Flower and weede
The earth did fresh aray,
So fresh they seem'd as day,
Euen as their Brydale day, which was not long:
  Sweete *Themmes* runne softly till I end my Song.

5

Then forth they all out of their baskets drew,
Great store of Flowers, the honour of the field,
That to the sense did fragrant odours yeild,
All which vpon those goodly Birds they threw,
And all the Waues did strew,
That like old *Peneus*[45] Waters they did seeme,
When downe along by pleasant *Tempes* shore
Scattred with Flowres, through *Thessaly* they streeme,
That they appeare through Lillies plenteous store,
Like a Brydes Chamber flore:
Two of those *Nymphes,* meane while, two Garlands bound,
Of freshest Flowres which in that Mead they found,
The which presenting all in trim Array,
Their snowie Foreheads therewithall they crownd,
Whil'st one did sing this Lay,
Prepar'd against that Day,
Against their Brydale day, which was not long:
  Sweete *Themmes* runne softly till I end my Song.

6

Ye gentle Birdes, the worlds faire ornament,
And heauens glorie, whom this happie hower

---

[41] soon after.
[42] *fill.*] *fill,* STC 23088.
[43] it seemed to them.
[44] A pun on Somerset, the family name of the prospective brides.
[45] A river in Thessaly; it flows through the valley of Tempe.

Doth leade vnto your louers blisfull bower,
Ioy may you haue and gentle hearts content
Of your loues couplement:[46]
And let faire *Venus,* that is Queene of loue,
With her heart-quelling Sonne vpon you smile,
Whose smile they say, hath vertue to remoue
All Loues dislike, and friendships faultie guile
For euer to assoile.[47]
Let endlesse Peace your steadfast hearts accord,
And blessed Plentie wait vpon your[48] bord,
And let your bed with pleasures chast abound,
That fruitfull issue may to you afford,
Which may your foes confound,
And make your ioyes redound,
Vpon your Brydale day, which is not long:
Sweete *Themmes* run softlie, till I end my Song.

7

So ended she; and all the rest around
To her redoubled that her vndersong,[49]
Which said, their bridale daye should not be long.
And gentle Eccho from the neighbour ground,
Their accents did resound.[50]
So forth[51] those ioyous Birdes did passe along,
Adowne the Lee, that to them murmurde low,
As he would speake, but that he lackt a tong,[52]
Yeat did by signes his glad affection show,
Making his streame run slow.
And all the foule which in his flood did dwell
Gan flocke about these twaine, that did excell
The rest, so far, as *Cynthia*[53] doth shend[54]
The lesser starres. So they enranged well,
Did on those two attend,
And their best seruice lend,
Against their wedding day, which was not long:
Sweete *Themmes* run softly, till I end my song.

8

At length they all to mery *London* came,
To mery London, my most kyndly Nurse,[55]
That to me gaue, this Lifes first natiue sourse:
Though from another place I take my name,
An house of auncient fame.[56]
There when they came, whereas those bricky towres,[57]

---

46 union, marriage.
47 set free.
48 *your*] *you* STC 23088.
49 reëchoed her refrain.
50 *resound.*] *resound?* STC 23088.
51 *forth*] *forth,* STC 23088.
52 *tong,*] *tong* STC 23088.
53 The moon.
54 shame by outshining.
55 Spenser was bred in London and probably born there.
56 An allusion to the Spencers of Althorp, near Northampton.
57 The Temple, first occupied by the Knights Templar, and in Spenser's time and now by students of the common law.

The which on *Themmes* brode aged backe doe ryde,
Where now the studious Lawyers haue their bowers,[58]
There whylome[59] wont the Templer Knights to byde,
Till they decayd through pride:
Next whereunto there standes a stately place,[60]
Where oft I gayned giftes and goodly grace
Of that great Lord, which therein wont to dwell,
Whose want too well, now feeles my freendles case:
But Ah here fits not well
Olde woes but ioyes to tell
Against the bridale daye which is not long:
  Sweete *Themmes* runne softly till I end my Song.

9

Yet therein now doth lodge a noble Peer,[61]
Great *Englands* glory and the Worlds wide wonder,
Whose dreadfull name, late through all *Spaine* did thunder,
And *Hercules* two pillors[62] standing neere,
Did make to quake and feare:
Faire branch of Honor, flower of Cheualrie,
That fillest *England* with thy triumphes fame,
Ioy haue thou of thy noble victorie,
And endlesse happinesse of thine owne name[63]
That promiseth the same:
That through thy prowesse and victorious armes,
Thy country may be freed from forraine harmes:
And great *Elisaes* glorious name may ring
Through al the world, fil'd with thy wide Alarmes,
Which some braue muse may sing
To ages following,
Vpon the Brydale day, which is not long:
  Sweete *Themmes* runne softly till I end my Song.

10

From those high Towers, this noble Lord issuing,
Like Radiant *Hesper*[64] when his golden hayre
In th'*Ocean* billowes he hath Bathed fayre,
Descended to the Riuers open vewing,
With a great traine ensuing.
Aboue the rest were goodly to bee seene
Two gentle Knights[65] of louely face and feature
Beseeming well the bower of anie Queene,
With gifts of wit and ornaments of nature,
Fit for so goodly stature:
That like the twins of *Ioue*[66] they seem'd in sight,

---

58 *bowers,*] bowers STC 23088.
59 formerly.
60 The palace of Spenser's patron, the Earl of Leicester, who died in 1588; in 1596 it was occupied by Robert Devereux, Earl of Essex.
61 In August, 1596, the Earl of Essex returned from the capture of Cadiz.
62 The cliffs at the Straits of Gibraltar.
63 Spenser puns on *Devereux* and *heureux.*
64 Hesperus, the evening star.
65 The prospective bridegrooms.
66 The constellation Gemini.

Which decke the Bauldricke[67] of the Heauens bright.[68]
They two forth pacing to the Riuers side,
Receiued those two faire Brides, their Loues delight,
Which at th'appointed tyde,[69]
Each one did make his Bryde,
Against their Brydale day, which is not long:
Sweete *Themmes* runne softly, till I end my Song.

TWO CANTOS OF MVTABILITIE: WHICH, BOTH FOR FORME AND MATTER, APPEARE TO BE PARCELL OF SOME FOLLOWING BOOKE OF THE FAERIE QVEENE, VNDER THE LEGEND OF CONSTANCIE[70]

CANTO VI

Proud Change (*not pleasd, in mortall things,*
beneath the Moone, to raigne)
Pretends,[71] *as well of Gods, as Men,*
to be the Soueraine.

I

What man that sees the euer-whirling wheele
Of *Change,* the which all mortall things doth sway,
But that therby doth find, and plainly feele,
How *Mvtability* in them doth play
Her cruell sports, to many mens decay?
Which that to all may better yet appeare,
I will rehearse that whylome[72] I heard say,
How she at first her selfe began to reare,
Gainst all the Gods, and th'empire sought from them to beare.

2

But first, here falleth fittest to vnfold
Her antique race and linage ancient,
As I haue found it registred of old,
In *Faery* Land mongst records permanent:
She was, to weet,[73] a daughter by descent
Of those old *Titans,* that did whylome striue
With *Saturnes* sonne[74] for heauens regiment.[75]
Whom, though high *Ioue* of kingdome did depriue,
Yet many of their stemme long after did suruiue.

3

And many of them, afterwards obtain'd
Great power of *Ioue,* and high authority;

67 belt.
68 *bright.*] *bright,* STC 23088.
69 time.
70 From *The Faerie Queene,* 1609, STC 23083, Folger Library.
71 attempts.
72 what formerly.
73 wit.
74 Jove.
75 control.

As *Hecaté,* in whose almighty hand,
He plac't all rule and principality,
To be by her disposed diuersly,
To Gods, and men, as she them list[76] diuide:
And drad[77] *Bellona,*[78] that doth sound on hie
Warres and allarums vnto Nations wide,
That makes both heauen and earth to tremble at her pride.

4

So likewise did this *Titanesse* aspire,
Rule and dominion to her selfe to gaine;
That as a Goddesse, men might her admire,
And heauenly honours yield, as to them twaine.
And first, on earth she sought it to obtaine;
Where she such proofe and sad examples shewed
Of her great power, to many ones great paine,
That not men onely (whom she soone subdewed)
But eke all other creatures, her bad dooings rewed.

5

For, she the face of earthly things so changed,
That all which Nature had establisht first
In good estate, and in meet order ranged,
She did pervert, and all their statutes burst:
And all the worlds faire frame[79] (which none yet durst
Of Gods or men to alter or misguide)
She alter'd quite, and made them all accurst
That God had blest; and did at first prouide
In that still happy state for euer to abide.

6

Ne shee the lawes of Nature onely brake,
But eke of Iustice, and of Policie;
And wrong of right, and bad of good did make,
And death for life exchanged foolishlie:
Since which, all liuing wights haue learn'd to die,
And all this world is woxen[80] daily worse.
O pittious worke of *Mvtabilitie!*
By which, we all are subiect to that curse,
And death in stead of life haue sucked from our Nurse.

7

And now, when all the earth she thus had brought
To her behest, and thralled to her might,
She gan to cast in her ambitious thought,
T'attempt th'empire of the heauens hight,

76 wished.
77 dread.
78 Goddess of war.
79 plan.
80 grown.

And *Ioue* himselfe to shoulder from his right.
And first, she past the region of the ayre,
And of the fire, whose substance thin and slight,
Made no resistance, ne could her contraire,[81]
But ready passage to her pleasure did prepaire.

8

Thence, to the Circle of the Moone she clambe,[82]
Where *Cynthia* raignes in euerlasting glory,
To whose bright shining palace straight she came,
All fairely deckt with heauens goodly story;
Whose siluer gates (by which there sate in hory
Old aged Sire, with hower-glasse in hand,
Hight[83] *Tyme*) she entred, where he liefe[84] or sory:
Ne staide till she the highest stage had scand,[85]
Where *Cynthia* did sit, that neuer still did stand.

9

Her sitting on an Iuory throne shee found,
Drawne of two steeds, th'one black, the other white,
Environd with tenne thousand starres around,
That duly her attended day and night;
And by her side, there ran her Page, that hight
Vesper, whom we the Euening-starre intend:[86]
That with his Torche, still twinkling like twylight,
Her lightened all the way where she should wend,[87]
And ioy to weary wandring trauailers did lend:

10

That when the hardy *Titanesse* beheld
The goodly building of her Palace bright,
Made of the heauens substance, and vp-held
With thousand Crystall pillors of huge hight,
Shee gan to burne in her ambitious spright,
And t'envie her that in such glorie raigned.
Eftsoones[88] she cast[89] by force and tortious might,
Her to displace; and to her selfe to haue gained
The kingdome of the Night, and waters by her wained.[90]

11

Boldly she bid the Goddesse downe descend,
And let her selfe into that Ivory throne;
For, shee her selfe more worthy thereof wend,[91]
And better able it to guide alone:

81 oppose, hinder.
82 climbed.
83 named.
84 willing.
85 climbed.
86 call, name.
87 go.
88 at once.
89 planned.
90 moved.
91 thought.

Whether to men, whose fall she did bemone,
Or vnto Gods, whose state she did maligne,
Or to th'infernall Powers, her need giue lone
Of her faire light, and bounty most benigne,
Her selfe of all that rule shee deemed most condigne.

12

But shee that had to her that soueraigne seat
By highest *Ioue* assign'd, therein to beare
Nights burning lamp, regarded not her threat,
Ne yielded ought for fauour or for feare;
But with sterne countenaunce and disdainfull cheare,[92]
Bending her horned browes, did put her back:
And boldly blaming her for comming there,
Bade her attonce from heauens coast to pack,
Or at her perill bide the wrathfull Thunders wrack.

13

Yet nathemore[93] the *Giantesse* forbare:
But boldly preacing-on, raught forth her hand
To pluck her downe perforce from off her chaire;
And there-with lifting vp her golden wand,
Threatned to strike her if she did with-stand.
Where-at the starres, which round about her blazed,
And eke the Moones bright wagon, still did stand,
All beeing with so bold attempt amazed,
And on her vncouth habit and sterne looke still gazed.

14

Meane-while, the lower World, which nothing knew
Of all that chaunced here, was darkned quite;
And eke the heauens, and all the heauenly crew
Of happy wights,[94] now vnpurvaide[95] of light,
Were much afraid, and wondred at that sight;
Fearing least *Chaos* broken had his chaine,
And brought againe on them eternall night:
But chiefely *Mercury,* that next[96] doth raigne,
Ran forth in haste, vnto the king of Gods to plaine.

15

All ran together with a great out-cry,
To *Ioues* faire Palace, fixt in heauens hight;
And beating at his gates full earnestly,
Gan call to him aloud with all their might,
To know what meant that suddaine lack of light.
The father of the Gods when this he heard,

92 countenance.
93 never the more.
94 creatures.
95 deprived.
96 nearest.

Was troubled much at their so strange affright,
Doubting least *Typhon*[97] were againe vprear'd,
Or other his old foes, that once him sorely fear'd.

16

Eftsoones the sonne of *Maia*[98] forth he sent
Downe to the Circle of the Moone, to knowe
The cause of this so strange astonishment,
And why shee did her wonted course forslowe;[99]
And if that any were on earth belowe
That did with charmes or Magick her molest,
Him to attache, and downe to hell to throwe:
But, if from heauen it were, then to arrest
The Author, and him bring before his presence prest.[1]

17

The wingd-foot God, so fast his plumes did beat,
That soone he came where-as the *Titanesse*
Was striuing with faire *Cynthia* for her seat:
At whose strange sight, and haughty hardinesse,
He wondred much, and feared her no lesse.
Yet laying feare aside to doe his charge,
At last, he bade her (with bold stedfastnesse)
Ceasse to molest the Moone to walke at large,
Or come before high *Ioue,* her dooings to discharge.

18

And there-with-all, he on her shoulder laid
His snaky-wreathed Mace, whose awfull power
Doth make both Gods and hellish fiends affraid:
Where-at the *Titanesse* did sternely lower,
And stoutly answer'd that in euill hower
He from his *Ioue* such message to her brought,
To bid her leaue faire *Cynthias* siluer bower;
Sith shee his *Ioue* and him esteemed nought,
No more then *Cynthia's* selfe; but all their kingdoms sought.

19

The Heauens Herald staid not to reply,
But past away, his doings to relate
Vnto his Lord; who now in th'highest sky,
Was placed in his principall Estate,
With all the Gods about him congregate:
To whom when *Hermes* had his message told,
It did them all exceedingly amate,[2]

---

[97] A monster in Greek myth.
[98] Mercury or Hermes.
[99] delay.

[1] quickly.
[2] dismay.

Saue *Ioue;* who, changing nought his count'nance bold,
Did vnto them at length these speeches wise vnfold;

20

Harken to mee awhile yee heauenly Powers;
Ye may remember since th'Earths cursed seed
Sought to assaile the heauens eternall towers,
And to vs all exceeding feare did breed:
But how we then defeated all their deed,
Yee all doe knowe, and them destroied quite;
Yet not so quite, but that there did succeed
An off-spring of their bloud, which did alite
Vpon the fruitfull earth, which doth vs yet despite.

21

Of that bad seed is this bold woman bred,
That now with bold presumption doth aspire
To thrust faire *Phoebe* from her siluer bed,
And eke our selues from heauens high Empire,
If that her might were match to her desire:
Wherefore, it now behoues vs to advise
What way is best to driue her to retire;
Whether by open force, or counsell wise,
Areed[3] ye soones of God, as best ye can deuise.

22

So hauing said, he ceast; and with his brow
(His black eye-brow, whose doomefull dreaded beck
Is wont to wield the world vnto his vow,
And euen the highest Powers of heauen to check)
Made signe to them in their degrees to speake:
Who straight gan cast[4] their counsell graue and wise.
Meane-while, th'Earths daughter,[5] thogh she nought did reck
Of *Hermes* message; yet gan now aduise,
What course were best to take in this hot bold emprize.[6]

23

Eftsoones she thus resolv'd; that whil'st the Gods
(After returne of *Hermes* Embassie)
Were troubled, and amongst themselues at ods,
Before they could new counsels re-allie,
To set vpon them in that extasie;
And take what fortune time and place would lend:
So, forth she rose, and through the purest sky
To *Ioues* high Palace straight cast to ascend,
To prosecute her plot: Good on-set boads good end.

---

[3] advise.
[4] plan.
[5] The Titaness.
[6] enterprise.

24

Shee there arriuing, boldly in did pass;
Where all the Gods she found in counsell close,
All quite vnarm'd, as then their manner was.
At sight of her they suddaine all arose,
In great amaze, ne wist what way to chose.
But *Ioue,* all fearelesse, forc't them to aby;[7]
And in his soueraine throne, gan straight dispose
Himselfe more full of grace and Maiestie,
That mote encheare his friends, and foes mote terrifie.

25

That, when the haughty *Titanesse* beheld,
All were she fraught with pride and impudence,
Yet with the sight thereof was almost queld;
And inly quaking, seem'd as reft of sense,
And voyd of speech in that drad audience;
Vntill that *Ioue* himselfe, her selfe bespake:
Speake thou fraile woman, speake with confidence,
Whence art thou, and what doost thou here now make?
What idle errand hast thou, earths mansion to forsake?

26

Shee, halfe confused with his great commaund,
Yet gathering spirit of her natures pride,
Him boldly answer'd thus to his demaund:
I am a daughter, by the mothers side,
Of her that is Grand-mother magnifide[8]
Of all the Gods, great *Earth,* great *Chaos* child:
But by the fathers (be it not envide)
I greater am in bloud (whereon I build)
Then all the Gods, though wrongfully from heauen exil'd.

27

For, *Titan*[9] (as ye all acknowledge must)
Was *Saturnes* elder brother by birth-right;
Both, sonnes of *Vranus:* but by vniust
And guilefull meanes, through *Corybantes* slight,[10]
The younger thrust the elder from his right:
Since which, thou *Ioue,* iniuriously[11] hast held
The Heauens rule from *Titans* sonnes by might;
And them to hellish dungeons downe hast feld:
Witnesse ye Heauens the truth of all that I haue teld.

[7] remain.

[8] glorified.

[9] According to one version of the story, Titan, the elder brother of Saturn, agreed to let Saturn rule, on condition that Saturn kill all his children and so leave no descendants to succeed him. This Saturn agreed to do, but at the birth of his son Jove the Corybantes beat shields and rattled helmets to conceal the child's cries from Saturn, and Jove escaped the fate of his brothers and sisters.

[10] trickery.

[11] unjustly, insultingly.

28

Whil'st she thus spake, the Gods that gaue good eare
  To her bold words, and marked well her grace,
  Beeing of stature tall as any there
  Of all the Gods, and beautifull of face,
  As any of the Goddesses in place,
  Stood all astonied,[12] like a sort[13] of Steeres;
  Mongst whom, some beast of strange and forraine race,
  Vnwares is chaunc't, far straying from his peeres:
So did their ghastly gaze bewray[14] their hidden feares.

29

Till hauing pauz'd awhile, *Ioue* thus bespake;
  Will neuer mortall thoughts ceasse to aspire,
  In this bold sort, to Heauen claime to make,
  And touch celestiall seates with earthly mire?
  I would haue thought, that bold *Procrustes* hire,
  Or *Typhons* fall, or proud *Ixions* paine,
  Or great *Prometheus,* tasting of our ire,
  Would haue suffiz'd, the rest for to restraine;
And warn'd all men by their example to refraine:

30

But now, this off-scum of that cursed fry,
  Dare to renew the like bold enterprize,
  And chalenge th'heritage of this our skie;
  Whom what should hinder, but that we likewise
  Should handle as the rest of her allies,
  And thunder-driue to hell? With that, he shooke
  His Nectar-deawed locks, with which the skyes
  And all the world beneath for terror quooke,[15]
And eft[16] his burning levin-brond[17] in hand he tooke.

31

But, when he looked on her louely face,
  In which, faire beames of beauty did appeare,
  That could the greatest wrath soone turne to grace
  (Such sway doth beauty euen in Heauen beare)
  He staide his hand: and hauing chang'd his cheare,[18]
  He thus againe in milder wise began;
  But ah! if Gods should striue with flesh yfere,[19]
  Then shortly should the progeny of Man
Be rooted out, if *Ioue* should doe still what he can:

---

[12] astonished.
[13] group, herd.
[14] reveal.
[15] quaked.
[16] then.
[17] lightning-brand.
[18] expression, mood.
[19] together.

32

But thee faire *Titans* child, I rather weene,[20]
Through some vaine errour or inducement light,
To see that mortall eyes haue neuer seene;
Or through ensample of thy sisters might,
Bellona; whose great glory thou doost spight,
Since thou hast seene her dreadfull power belowe,
Mongst wretched men (dismaide with her affright)
To bandie Crownes, and Kingdomes to bestowe:
And sure thy worth, no lesse then hers doth seem to showe.

33

But wote[21] thou this, thou hardy *Titanesse,*
That not the worth of any liuing wight
May challenge ought in Heauens interesse;[22]
Much lesse the Title of old *Titans* Right:
For, we by Conquest of our soueraine might,
And by eternall doome of Fates decree,
Haue wonne the Empire of the Heauens bright;
Which to our selues we hold, and to whom wee
Shall worthy deeme partakers of our blisse to bee.

34

Then ceasse thy idle claime thou foolish gerle,
And seeke by grace and goodnesse to obtaine
That place from which by folly *Titan* fell;
There-to thou maist perhaps, if so thou faine
Haue *Ioue* thy gratious Lord and Soueraigne.
So, hauing said, she thus to him replide;
Ceasse *Saturnes* sonne, to seeke by proffers vaine
Of idle hopes t'allure mee to thy side,
For to betray my Right, before I haue it tride.

35

But thee, O *Ioue,* no equall[23] Iudge I deeme
Of my desert, or of my dewfull Right;
That in thine owne behalfe maist partiall seeme:
But to the highest him, that is behight
Father of Gods and men by equall might;
To weet, the God of Nature, I appeale.
There-at *Ioue* wexed wroth, and in his spright
Did inly grudge, yet did it well conceale;
And bade *Dan Phoebus* Scribe her Appellation seale.

20 think.
21 know.
22 interest.
23 impartial.

36

Eftsoones the time and place appointed were,
Where all, both heauenly Powers, and earthly wights,
Before great Natures presence should appeare,
For triall of their Titles and best Rights:
That was, to weet, vpon the highest hights
Of *Arlo-hill*[24] (Who knowes not *Arlo-hill?*)
That is the highest head (in all mens sights)
Of my old father *Mole,*[25] whom Shepheards quill
Renowmed hath with hymnes fit for a rurall skill.

37

And, were it not ill fitting for this file,
To sing of hilles and woods, mongst warres and Knights,
I would abate the sternenesse of my stile,
Mongst these sterne stounds[26] to mingle soft delights;
And tell how *Arlo* through *Dianaes* spights
(Beeing of old the best and fairest Hill
That was in all this holy-Islands hights)
Was made the most vnpleasant, and most ill.
Meane while, O *Clio,*[27] lend *Calliope*[28] thy quill.

38

Whylome, when *Ireland* florished in fame
Of wealths and goodnesse, far aboue the rest
Of all that beare the *British* Islands name,
The Gods then vs'd (for pleasure and for rest)
Oft to resort there-to, when seem'd them best:
But none of all there-in more pleasure found,
Then *Cynthia;* that is soueraine Queene profest
Of woods and forrests, which therein abound,
Sprinkled with wholsom waters, more then most on ground.

39

But mongst them all, as fittest for her game,
Either for chace of beasts with hound or boawe,
Or for to shroude in shade from *Phoebus* flame,
Or bathe in fountaines that doe freshly flowe,
Or from high hilles, or from the dales belowe,
She chose this *Arlo;* where shee did resort
With all her Nymphes enranged on a rowe,
With whom the woody Gods did oft consort:
For, with the Nymphes, the Satyres loue to play and sport.

---

24 A mountain near Kilcolman Castle, Spenser's home between Limerick and Cork.
25 The Ballyhoura Hills.
26 assaults, affrays.
27 The Muse of history.
28 The Muse of heroic poetry.

40

Amongst the which, there was a Nymph that hight[29]
Molanna;[30] daughter of old father *Mole,*
And sister vnto *Mulla,*[31] faire and bright:
Vnto whose bed false *Bregog* whylome stole,
That Shepheard *Colin*[32] dearely did condole,
And make her lucklesse loues well knowne to be.
But this *Molanna,* were she not so shole,[33]
Were no lesse faire and beautifull then shee:
Yet as she is, a fairer flood may no man see.

41

For, first, she springs out of two marble Rocks,
On which, a groue of Oakes high mounted growes,
That as a girlond seemes to deck the locks
Of som faire Bride, brought forth with pompous showes
Out of her bowre, that many flowers strowes:
So, through the flowry Dales she tumbling downe,
Through many woods, and shady coverts flowes
(That on each side her siluer channell crowne)
Till to the Plaine she come, whose Valleyes shee doth drowne.

42

In her sweet streames, *Diana* vsed oft
(After her sweatie chace and toilesome play)
To bathe her selfe; and after, on the soft
And downy grasse, her dainty limbes to lay
In couert shade, where none behold her may:
For, much she hated sight of liuing eye.
Foolish God *Faunus,* though full many a day
He saw her clad, yet longed foolishly
To see her naked mongst her Nymphes in priuity.

43

No way he found to compasse his desire,
But to corrupt *Molanna,* this her maid,
Her to discouer[34] for some secret hire:
So, her with flattering words he first assaid;[35]
And after, pleasing gifts for her purvaid,
Queene-apples, and red Cherries from the tree,
With which he her allured and betraid,
To tell what time he might her Lady see
When she her selfe did bathe, that he might secret bee.

---

[29] was named.
[30] The name that Spenser gives to the Behanagh River.
[31] The name that Spenser gives to the Awbeg River.
[32] See Spenser's *Colin Clouts Come Home Again,* lines 104–155.
[33] shallow.
[34] reveal.
[35] tried.

44

There-to hee promist, if shee would him pleasure
  With this small boone, to quit her with a better;
  To weet, that where-as shee had out of measure
  Long lov'd the *Fanchin,*[36] who by nought did set[37] her,
  That he would vndertake, for this to get her
  To be his Loue, and of him liked well:
  Besides all which, he vow'd to be her debter
  For many moe good turnes then he would tell;
The least of which, this little pleasure should excell.

45

The simple maid did yield to him anone;
  And eft him placed where he close might view
  That neuer any saw, saue onely one;[38]
  Who, for his hire to so foole-hardy dew,
  Was of his hounds devour'd in Hunters hew.[39]
  Tho,[40] as her manner was on sunny day,
  Diana, with her Nymphes about her, drew
  To this sweet spring; where, doffing her array,
She bath'd her louely limbes, for *Ioue* a likely pray.

46

There *Faunus* saw that pleased much his eye,
  And made his hart to tickle in his brest,
  That for great ioy of some-what he did spy,
  He could him not containe in silent rest;
  But breaking forth in laughter, loud profest
  His foolish thought. A foolish *Faune* indeed,
  That couldst not hold thy selfe so hidden blest,
  But wouldest needs thine owne conceit[41] areed.[42]
Babblers vnworthy been of so diuine a meed.

47

The Goddesse, all abashed with that noise,
  In haste forth started from the guilty brooke;
  And running straight where-as she heard his voice,
  Enclos'd the bush about, and there him tooke,
  Like darred[43] Larke; not daring vp to looke
  On her whose sight before so much he sought.
  Thence, forth they drew him by the hornes, and shooke
  Nigh all to peeces, that they left him nought;
And then into the open light they forth him brought.

---

[36] The Funcheon River.
[37] esteem.
[38] Actaeon.
[39] According to Ovid, Actaeon was killed by his hounds, not when he was "in hunter's hew," but after he had been changed into a stag.
[40] then.
[41] idea.
[42] make known.
[43] terrified.

48

Like as an huswife, that with busie care
  Thinks of her Dairie to make wondrous gaine,
  Finding where-as some wicked beast vnware[44]
  That breakes into her Dayr'house, there doth draine
  Her creaming pannes, and frustrate all her paine;
  Hath in some snare or gin set close behind,
  Entrapped him, and caught into her traine,
  Then thinkes what punishment were best assign'd,
And thousand deathes deuiseth in her vengefull mind:

49

So did *Diana* and her maydens all
  Vse silly *Faunus,* now within their baile:[45]
  They mocke and scorne him, and him foule miscall;
  Some by the nose him pluckt, some by the taile,
  And by his goatish beard some did him haile:[46]
  Yet he (poore soule) with patience all did beare;
  For, nought against their wils might countervaile:
  Ne ought he said what euer he did heare;
But hanging downe his head, did like a Mome[47] appeare.

50

At length, when they had flouted him their fill,
  They gan to cast what penaunce him to giue.
  Some would haue gelt him, but that same would spill[48]
  The Wood-gods breed, which must for euer liue:
  Others would through the riuer him haue driue,
  And ducked deepe: but that seem'd penaunce light;
  But most agreed and did this sentence giue,
  Him in Deares skin to clad; and in that plight,
To hunt him with their hounds, him selfe saue how hee might.

51

But *Cynthia's* selfe, more angry than the rest,
  Thought not enough, to punish him in sport,
  And of her shame to make a gamesome iest;
  But gan examine him in straighter sort,[49]
  Which of her Nymphes, or other close consort,[50]
  Him thither brought, and her to him betraid?[51]
  He, much affeard, to her confessed short,
  That 'twas *Molanna* which her so bewraid.[52]
Then all attonce their hands vpon *Molanna* laid.

---

[44] suddenly.
[45] custody.
[46] pull, drag.
[47] blockhead.
[48] destroy.
[49] stricter fashion.
[50] companion.
[51] revealed.
[52] betrayed.

52

But him (according as they had decreed)
With a Deeres-skin they couered, and then chast
With all their hounds that after him did speed;
But he more speedy, from them fled more fast
Then any Deere: so sore him dread aghast.[53]
They after follow'd all with shrill out-cry,
Shouting as they the heauens would haue brast:[54]
That all the woods and dales where he did flie.
Did ring againe, and loud reeccho to the skie.

53

So they him follow'd till they weary were;
When, back returning to *Molann'* againe,
They, by commaund'ment of *Diana,* there
Her whelm'd[55] with stones. Yet *Faunus* (for her paine)
Of her beloued *Fanchin* did obtaine,
That her he would receiue vnto his bed.
So now her waues passe through a pleasant Plaine,
Till with the *Fanchin* she her selfe doe wed,
And (both combin'd) themselues in one faire riuer spred.

54

Nath'lesse, *Diana,* full of indignation,
Thence-forth abandoned her delicious brooke;
In whose sweet streame, before that bad occasion,
So much delight to bathe her limbes she tooke:
Ne onely her, but also quite forsooke
All those faire forrests about *Arlo* hid,
And all that Mountaine, which doth over-looke
The richest champian[56] that may else be rid,[57]
And the faire *Shure,* in which are thousand Salmons bred.

55

Them all, and all that she so deare did way,
Thence-forth she left; and parting from the place,
There-on an heauy haplesse curse did lay,
To weet, that Wolues, where she was wont to space,[58]
Should harbour'd be, and all those Woods deface,
And Thieues should rob and spoile that Coast around.
Since which those Woods, and all that goodly Chase,[59]
Doth to this day with Wolues and Thieues abound:
Which too-too true that lands in-dwellers since haue found.

---

53 terrified.
54 burst.
55 overwhelmed.
56 open country.
57 seen.
58 walk.
59 hunting ground.

CANTO VII

Pealing,[60] *from* Ioue, *to* Natur's *Bar,*
bold Alteration[61] *pleades*
Large Euidence: but Nature *soone*
her righteous Doome[62] *areads.*[63]

I

Ah! whither doost thou now thou greater Muse[64]
Me from these woods and pleasing forrests bring?
And my fraile spirit (that dooth oft refuse
This too high flight, vnfit for her weake wing)
Lift vp aloft, to tell of heauens King
(Thy soueraine Sire) his fortunate successe,
And victory, in bigger noates to sing,
Which he obtain'd against that *Titanesse,*
That him of heauens Empire sought to dispossesse.

2

Yet sith I needs must follow thy behest,
Doe thou my weaker wit with skill inspire,
Fit for this turne; and in my feeble[65] brest
Kindle fresh sparks of that immortall fire,
Which learned minds inflameth with desire
Of heauenly things: for, who but thou alone,
That art yborne of heauen and heauenly Sire,
Can tell things doen in heauen so long ygone;
So farre past memory of man that may be knowne.

3

Now, at the time that was before agreed,
The Gods assembled all on *Arlo* hill;
As well those that are sprung of heauenly seed,
As those that all the other world doe fill,
And rule both sea and land vnto their will:
Onely th'infernall Powers might not appeare;
Aswell for horror of their count'naunce ill,
As for th'vnruly fiends which they did feare;
Yet *Pluto* and *Proserpina* were present there.

4

And thither also came all other creatures,
What-euer life or motion doe retaine,
According to their sundry kinds of features;
That *Arlo* scarsly could them all containe;
So full they filled euery hill and Plaine:

---

60 appealing.
61 The Titaness.
62 decree.
63 proclaims.
64 Either Cleo or Calliope.
65 *feeble*] *sable* STC 23083.

And had not Natures *Sergeant* (that is *Order*)
Them well disposed by his busie paine,[66]
And raunged farre abroad in euery border,
They would haue caused much confusion and disorder.

5

Then forth issewed (great goddesse) great dame *Nature,*
With goodly port and gracious Maiesty;
Being far greater and more tall of stature
Then any of the gods or Powers on hie:
Yet certes by her face and physnomy,[67]
Whether she man or woman inly were,
That could not any creature well descry:[68]
For, with a veile that wimpled[69] euery where,
Her head and face was hid, that mote[70] to none appeare.

6

That some doe say was so by skill deuized,
To hide the terror of her vncouth hew,[71]
From mortall eyes that should be sore agrized;[72]
For that her face did like a Lion shew,
That eye of wight could not indure to view:
But others tell that it so beautious was,
And round about such beames of splendor threw,
That it the Sunne a thousand times did pass,[73]
Ne could be seene, but like an image in a glass.

7

That well may seemen true: for, well I weene
That this same day, when she on *Arlo* sat,
Her garment was so bright and wondrous sheene,[74]
That my fraile wit cannot deuize to what
It to compare, nor finde like stuffe to that,
As those three sacred *Saints,*[75] though else most wise,
Yet on mount *Thabor* quite their wits forgat,[76]
When they their glorious Lord in strange disguise
Transfigur'd sawe; his garments so did daze their eyes.

8

In a fayre Plaine vpon an equall Hill,
She placed was in a pauilion;
Not such as[77] Craftes-men by their idle skill
Are wont for Princes states[78] to fashion:

66 pains, care.
67 countenance.
68 perceive.
69 laid in folds
70 might, could.
71 unknown form.
72 horrified.
73 surpass.
74 beautiful.
75 Peter, James, and John. See Mark ix, 2–3.
76 forgot.
77 *as*] *ar* STC 23083.
78 dignity.

But th'earth her self of her owne motion,
Out of her fruitfull bosome made to growe
Most dainty trees; that, shooting vp anon,
Did seeme to bow their blossming heads full lowe,
For homage vnto her, and like a throne did shew.

9

So heard it is for any liuing wight,
All her array and vestiments to tell,
That old *Dan Geffrey*[79] (in whose gentle spright
The pure well head of Poesie did dwell)
In his *Foules parley* durst not with it mel,[80]
But it transferd to *Alane,* who he thought
Had in his *Plaint of kindes*[81] describ'd it well:
Which who will read set forth so as it ought,
Go seek he out that *Alane* where he may be sought.

10

And all the earth for vnderneath her feete
Was dight[82] with flowres, that voluntary grew
Out of the ground, and sent forth odours sweet,
Tenne thousand mores[83] of sundry sent and hew,
That might delight the smell, or please the view:
The which, the Nymphes, from all the brooks thereby
Had gathered, which they at her foot-stoole threw;
That richer seem'd then any tapestry,
That Princes bowres adorne with painted imagery.

11

And *Mole* himselfe, to honour her the more,
Did deck himself in freshest faire attire,
And his high head, that seemeth alwaies hore
With hardned frosts of former winters ire,
He with an Oaken girlond now did tire,[84]
As if the loue of some new Nymph late seene,
Had in him kindled youthfull fresh desire,
And made him change his gray attire to greene;
Ah gentle *Mole!* such ioyance hath thee well beseene.[85]

12

Was neuer so great ioyance since the day,
That all the gods whylome assembled were,
On *Haemus*[86] hill in their diuine array,
To celebrate the solemne bridall cheare,
Twixt *Peleus,*[87] and dame *Thetis* pointed there;

[79] Geoffrey Chaucer's *Parlement of Foules.*
[80] meddle.
[81] *De Planctu Naturae* ("of the plaint of nature or kind"), a treatise by Alanus de Insulis.
[82] adorned.
[83] plants; some editors read *more.*
[84] adorn his head.
[85] provided.
[86] A hill in Thessaly.
[87] *Peleus*] *Pelene* STC 23083.

Where *Phoebus* self, that god of Poets hight,[88]
They say did sing the spousall hymne full cleere,
That all the gods were rauisht with delight
Of his celestiall song, and Musicks wondrous might.

13

This great Grandmother of all creatures bred
Great *Nature,* euer young yet full of eld,
Still moouing, yet vnmoued from her sted;[89]
Vnseene of any, yet of all beheld;
Thus sitting in her throne as I haue teld,
Before her came dame *Mutabilitie;*
And being lowe before her presence feld,[90]
With meek obaysance and humilitie,
Thus gan her plaintif Plea, with words to amplifie;

14

To thee O greatest goddesse, onely great,
An humble suppliant loe, I lowely fly
Seeking for Right, which I of thee entreat;
Who Right to all dost deale indifferently,
Damning all Wrong and tortious[91] Iniurie,
Which any of thy creatures doe to other
(Oppressing them with power, vnequally)
Sith of them all thou art the equall mother,
And knittest each to each, as brother vnto brother.

15

To thee therefore of this same *Ioue* I plaine,
And of his fellow gods that faine to be,
That challenge[92] to themselues the whole worlds raign;
Of which, the greatest part is due to me,
And heauen it selfe by heritage in Fee:
For, heauen and earth I both alike do deeme,
Sith heauen and earth are both alike to thee;
And, gods no more then men thou doest esteeme:
For, euen the gods to thee, as men to gods do seeme.

16

Then weigh, O soueraigne goddesse, by what right
These gods do claime the worlds whole souerainty:
And that is onely dew vnto thy might
Arrogate to themselues ambitiously:
As for the gods owne principality,
Which *Ioue* vsurpes vniustly; that to be

88 is called.
89 place.
90 prostrated.
91 wicked.
92 claim.

My heritage, Ioue's self cannot deny,
From my great Grandsire *Titan,* vnto mee,
Deriv'd by dew descent; as is well knowen to thee.

17

Yet mauger[93] *Ioue,* and all his gods beside,
I doe possesse the worlds most regiment;[94]
As, if ye please it into parts diuide,
And euery parts inholders[95] to conuent,[96]
Shall to your eyes appeare incontinent.[97]
And first, the Earth (great mother of vs all)
That only seems vnmov'd and permanent,
And vnto *Mutability* not thrall;
Yet is she chang'd in part, and eeke in generall.

18

For, all that from her springs, and is ybredde,
How-euer fayre it flourish for a time,
Yet see we soone decay; and, being dead,
To turne again vnto their earthly slime:
Yet, out of their decay and mortall crime,
We daily see new creatures to arize;
And of their Winter spring another Prime,[98]
Vnlike in forme, and chang'd by strange disguise:
So turne they still[99] about, and change in restlesse wise.

19

As for her tenants; that is, man and beasts,
The beasts we daily see massacred dy,
As thralls and vassals vnto mens beheasts:
And men themselues doe change continually,
From youth to eld, from wealth to pouerty,
From good to bad, from bad to worst of all.
Ne doe their bodies only flit and fly:
But eeke their minds (which they immortall call)
Still change and vary thoughts, as new occasions fall.

20

Ne is the water in more constant case;[1]
Whether those same on high, or these belowe.
For, th'Ocean moueth stil, from place to place;
And euery Riuer still doth ebbe and flowe:
Ne any Lake, that seems most still and slowe,
Ne Poole so small, that can his smoothnesse holde,
When any winde doth vnder heauen blowe;

---

93 in spite of.
94 power.
95 tenants.
96 summon together.
97 at once.
98 springtime.
99 always.
1 condition.

With which, the clouds are also tost and roll'd;
Now like great Hills; and, streight, like sluces, them vnfold.

21

So likewise are all watry liuing wights
Still tost, and turned, with continuall change,
Neuer abyding in their stedfast plights.[2]
The fish, still floting, doe at randon[3] range,
And neuer rest; but euermore exchange
Their dwelling places, as the streames them carrie:
Ne haue the watry foules a certaine grange,[4]
Wherein to rest, ne in one stead[5] do tarry;
But flitting still doe flie, and still their places vary.

22

Next is the Ayre: which who feeles not by sense
(For, of all sense it is the middle meane)
To flit still? and, with subtill influence
Of his thin spirit, all creatures to maintaine,
In state of life? O weake life! that does leane
On thing so tickle as th'vnsteady ayre;
Which euery howre is chang'd, and altred cleane[6]
With euery blast that bloweth fowle or faire:
The faire doth it prolong; the fowle doth it impaire.

23

Therein the changes infinite beholde,
Which to her creatures euery minute chaunce;
Now, boyling hot: streight, friezing deadly cold:
Now, faire sun-shine, that makes all skip and daunce:
Streight, bitter storms and balefull countenance,
That makes them all to shiuer and to shake:
Rayne, hayle, and snowe do pay them sad penance,
And dreadfull thunder-claps (that make them quake)
With flames and flashing lights that thousand changes make.

24

Last is the fire: which, though it liue for euer,
Ne can be quenched quite; yet, euery day,
Wee see his parts, so soone as they do seuer,
To lose their heat, and shortly to decay;
So, makes himself his owne consuming pray.
Ne any liuing creatures doth he breed:
But all, that are of others bredd, doth slay;
And, with their death, his cruell life dooth feed;
Nought leauing, but their barren ashes, without seede.

---

[2] conditions.
[3] random.
[4] dwelling place.
[5] place.
[6] completely.

25

Thus, all these fower (the which the ground-work bee
Of all the world, and of all liuing wights)
To thousand sorts of *Change* we subiect see:
Yet are they chang'd (by other wondrous slights)[7]
Into themselues, and lose their natiue mights;
The Fire to Aire, and th'Ayre to Water sheere,[8]
And Water into Earth: yet Water fights
With Fire, and Aire with Earth approaching neere:
Yet all are in one body, and as one appeare.

26

So, in them all raignes *Mutabilitie;*
How-euer these, that Gods themselues do call,
Of them doe claime the rule and souerainty:
As, *Vesta,* of the fire aethereall;
Vulcan, of this, with vs so vsuall;
Ops, of the earth; and *Iuno* of the Ayre;
Neptune, of Seas; and Nymphes, of Riuers all.
For, all those Riuers to me subiect are:
And all the rest, which they vsurp, be all my share.

27

Which to approuen true, as I haue told,
Vouchsafe, O goddesse, to thy presence call
The rest which doe the world in being hold:
As, times and seasons of the yeare that fall:
Of all the which, demand in generall,
Or iudge thy selfe, by verdit of thine eye,
Whether to me they are not subiect all.
Nature did yeeld thereto; and by-and-by,
Bade *Order* call them all, before her Maiesty.

28

So, forth issew'd the Seasons of the yeare;
First, lusty *Spring,* all dight[9] in leaues of flowres
That freshly budded and new bloosmes did beare
(In which a thousand birds had built their bowres
That sweetly sung, to call forth Paramours):
And in his hand a iauelin he did beare,
And on his head (as fit for warlike stoures)[10]
A guilt engrauen morion[11] he did weare;
That as some did him loue, so others did him feare.

29

Then came the iolly *Sommer,* being dight
In a thin silken cassock coloured greene,

[7] devices, tricks.
[8] clear.
[9] adorned.
[10] conflicts.
[11] helmet.

That was vnlyned all, to be more light:
And on his head a girlond well beseene[12]
He wore, from which as he had chauffed[13] been
The sweat did drop; and in his hand he bore
A boawe and shaftes, as he in forrest greene
Had hunted late the Libbard[14] or the Bore,
And now would bathe his limbes, with labor heated sore.

30

Then came the *Autumne* all in yellow clad,
As though he ioyed in his plentious store,
Laden with fruits that made him laugh, full glad
That he had banisht hunger, which to-fore
Had by the belly oft him pinched sore.
Vpon his head a wreath that was enrold
With eares of corne, of euery sort he bore:
And in his hand a sickle he did holde,
To reape the ripened fruits the which the earth had yold.[15]

31

Lastly, came *Winter* cloathed all in frize,[16]
Chattering his teeth for cold that did him chill,
Whil'st on his hoary beard his breath did freese;
And the dull drops that from his purpled bill
As from a limbeck did adown distill.
In his right hand a tipped staffe he held,
With which his feeble steps he stayed still:
For, he was faint with cold, and weak with eld;[17]
That scarse his loosed limbes he hable was to weld.[18]

32

These, marching softly, thus in order went,
And after them, the Monthes all riding came;
First, sturdy *March*[19] with brows full sternly bent,
And armed strongly, rode vpon a Ram,[20]
The same which ouer *Hellespontus* swam:
Yet in his hand a spade he also hent,[21]
And in a bag all sorts of seeds ysame,[22]
Which on the earth he strowed as he went,
And fild her womb with fruitfull hope of nourishment.

---

[12] befitting, of good appearance.
[13] heated.
[14] leopard.
[15] yielded.
[16] coarse woolen cloth.
[17] age.
[18] wield, control.
[19] The legal year began on Lady Day, March 25, until 1753, but January 1 began the year in popular usage. *The Shepheardes Calender* begins with January.
[20] The ram that Helle, daughter of a king of Thessaly, tried to ride across the narrow sea, afterwards called the Hellespont (sea of Helle). The ram is the first sign of the zodiac; the other signs are included in the following description of the months.
[21] took.
[22] together.

33

Next came fresh *Aprill* full of lustyhed,
And wanton as a Kid whose horne new buds:
Vpon a Bull he rode, the same which led
Europa[23] floting through th'*Argolick* fluds:[24]
His hornes were gilden all with golden studs
And garnished with garlonds goodly dight
Of all the fairest flowres and freshest buds
Which th'earth brings forth, and wet he seem'd in sight
With waues, through which he waded for his loues delight.

34

Then came faire *May,* the fayrest mayd on ground,
Deckt all with dainties of her seasons pryde,
And throwing flowres out of her lap around:
Vpon two brethrens[25] shoulders she did ride,
The twinnes of *Leda;* which on eyther side
Supported her like to their soueraine Queene.
Lord! how all creatures laught, when her they spide,
And leapt and daunc't as they had rauisht[26] beene!
And *Cupid* selfe about her fluttred all in greene.

35

And after her, came iolly *Iune,* arrayd
All in greene leaues, as he a Player[27] were;
Yet in his time, he wrought as well as playd,
That by his plough-yrons[28] mote right well appeare:
Vpon a Crab he rode, that him did beare
With crooked crawling steps an vncouth[29] pase,
And backward yode,[30] as Bargemen wont to fare
Bending their force contrary to their face,
Like that vngracious crew[31] which faines demurest grace.

36

Then came hot *Iuly* boyling like to fire,
That all his garments he had cast away:
Vpon a Lyon raging yet with ire
He boldly rode and made him to obay:
It was the beast[32] that whylome did forray
The Nemaean forrest, till th'*Amphytrionide*
Him slew, and with his hide did him array;
Behinde his back a sithe, and by his side
Vnder his belt he bore a sickle circling wide.

---

23 Phoenician princess carried away by Jupiter disguised as a bull; he swam with her to Crete.

24 Waves of the Gulf of Argolis in the Aegean Sea.

25 The Gemini.

26 entranced.

27 actor.

28 colter and plowshare.

29 strange.

30 went.

31 fawning courtiers.

32 The lion that Hercules killed in the valley of Nemea.

37

The sixt was *August,* being rich arrayd
In garment all of gold downe to the ground:
Yet rode he not, but led a louely Mayd
Forth by the lilly hand, the which was cround
With eares of corne, and full her hand was found;
That was the righteous Virgin,[33] which of old
Liv'd here on earth, and plenty made abound;
But, after Wrong was lov'd and Iustice solde,
She left th'vnrighteous world and was to heauen extold.[34]

38

Next him, *September* marched eeke on foote;
Yet was he heauy laden with the spoyle
Of haruests riches, which he made his boot,
And him enricht with bounty of the soyle:
In his one hand, as fit for haruests toyle,
He held a knife-hook; and in th'other hand
A paire of waights, with which he did assoyle[35]
Both more and lesse, where it in doubt did stand,
And equall[36] gaue to each as Iustice duly scann'd.[37]

39

Then came *October* full of merry glee:
For, yet his noule[38] was totty[39] of the must,[40]
Which he was treading in the wine-fats[41] see,
And of the ioyous oyle, whose gentle gust[42]
Made him so frollick and so full of lust:
Vpon a dreadfull Scorpion he did ride,
The same which by *Dianaes* doom[43] vniust
Slew great *Orion:* and eeke by his side
He had his ploughing share, and coulter ready tyde.

40

Next was *Nouember,* he full grosse and fat,
As fed with lard, and that right well might seeme;
For, he had been a fatting hogs of late,
That yet his browes with sweat, did reek and steem,
And yet the season was full sharp and breem;[44]
In planting eeke he took no small delight:
Whereon he rode, not easie was to deeme;
For it a dreadfull *Centaure* was in sight,
The seed of *Saturne,* and faire *Nais, Chiron*[45] hight.

[33] Astraea, goddess of innocence and purity, the constellation Virgo.
[34] raised.
[35] determine.
[36] impartially.
[37] examined.
[38] head.
[39] dizzy.
[40] new wine.
[41] wine vats.
[42] flavor.
[43] decision; Orion was killed by the bite of a scorpion that the jealous Diana had hidden under a stone.
[44] cold.
[45] A wise and beneficent centaur, the constellation Sagittarius.

41

And after him, came next the chill *December:*
Yet he through merry feasting which he made,
And great bonfires, did not the cold remember;
His Sauiours birth his mind so much did glad:
Vpon a shaggy-bearded Goat he rade,[46]
The same wherewith *Dan Ioue* in tender yeares,
They say, was nourisht by th'Idaean mayd;[47]
And in his hand a broad deepe boawle he beares;
Of which, he freely drinks an health to all his peeres.

42

Then came old *Ianuary,* wrapped well
In many weeds to keep the cold away;
Yet did he quake and quiuer like to quell,[48]
And blowe his nayles to warme them if he may:
For, they were numbd with holding all the day
An hatchet keene, with which he felled wood,
And from the trees did lop the needlesse spray:
Vpon an huge great Earth-pot steane[49] he stood;
From whose wide mouth, there flowed forth the Romane floud.[50]

43

And lastly, came cold *February,* sitting
In an old wagon, for he could not ride;
Drawne of two fishes[51] for the season fitting,
Which through the flood before did softly slyde
And swim away: yet had he by his side
His plough and harnesse fit to till the ground,
And tooles to prune the trees, before the pride
Of hasting Prime[52] did make them burgein[53] round:
So past the twelue Months forth, and their dew places found.

44

And after these, there came the *Day,* and *Night,*
Riding together both with equall pase,
Th'one on a Palfrey blacke, the other white;
But *Night* had couered her vncomely face
With a blacke veile, and held in hand a mace,
On top whereof the moon and stars were pight,[54]
And sleep and darknesse round about did trace:[55]
But *Day* did beare, vpon his scepters hight,
The goodly Sun, encompast all with beames bright.

---

46 *rade,*] *rode,* STC 23083.
47 Amalthea, a nymph from Mount Ida who nursed Jove on goat's milk.
48 die.
49 stone.
50 The eleventh sign of the zodiac is Aquarius, the water bearer.
51 Pisces, the twelfth sign of the zodiac.
52 spring.
53 bud.
54 placed.
55 go.

45

Then came the *Howres,* faire daughters of high *Ioue,*
And timely *Night,* the which were all endewed
With wondrous beauty fit to kindle loue;
But they were Virgins all, and loue eschewed,
That might forslack[56] the charge of them fore-shewed
By mighty *Ioue;* who did them Porters make
Of heauens gate (whence all the gods issued)
Which they did dayly watch, and nightly wake
By euen turnes, ne euer did their charge forsake.

46

And after all came *Life,* and lastly *Death;*
Death with most grim and griesly visage seene,
Yet is he nought but parting of the breath;
Ne ought to see, but like a shade to weene,
Vnbodied, vnsoul'd, vnheard, vnseene.
But *Life* was like a faire young lusty boy,
Such as they faine *Dan Cupid* to haue beene,
Full of delightfull health and liuely ioy,
Deckt all with flowres, and wings of gold fit to employ.

47

When these were past, thus gan the *Titanesse;*
Lo, mighty mother, now be iudge and say,
Whether in all thy creatures more or lesse
Change doth not raign and beare the greatest sway:
For, who sees not, that *Time* on all doth pray?
But *Times* do change and moue continually.
So nothing here long standeth in one stay:
Wherefore, this lower world who can deny
But to be subiect still to *Mutabilitie?*

48

Then thus gan *Ioue;* Right true it is, that these
And all things else that vnder heauen dwell
Are chaung'd of *Time,* who doth them all disseise[57]
Of being: But, who is it (to me tell)
That *Time* himselfe doth moue and still compell
To keepe his course? Is not that namely wee
Which poure that vertue from our heauenly cell,
That moues them all, and makes them changed be?
So them we gods doe rule, and in them also thee.

49

To whom, thus *Mutability:* The things
Which we see not how they are mov'd and swayd,
Ye may attribute to your selues as Kings,

---

56 neglect.

57 *disseise*] *disseife* STC 23083: deprive, dispossess.

And say they by your secret powre are made:
But what we see not, who shall vs perswade?
But were they so, as ye them faine to be,
Mov'd by your might, and ordred by your ayde;
Yet what if I can proue, that euen yee
Your selues are likewise chang'd, and subiect vnto mee?

50

And first, concerning her that is the first,
Euen you[58] faire *Cynthia,* whom so much ye make
Ioues dearest darling, she was bred and nurst
On *Cynthus* hill, whence she her name did take:
Then is she mortall borne, how-so ye crake;[59]
Besides, her face and countenance euery day
We changed see, and sundry forms partake,
Now hornd, now round, now bright, now brown and gray:
So that *as changefull as the Moone* men vse to say.

51

Next, *Mercury,* who though he lesse appeare
To change his hew, and always seeme as one;
Yet he his course doth altar euery yeare,
And is of late far out of order gone:
So *Venus* eeke, that goodly Paragone,
Though faire all night, yet is she darke all day;
And *Phoebus* self, who lightsome[60] is alone,
Yet is he oft eclipsed by the way,
And fills the darkned world with terror and dismay.

52

Now *Mars* that valiant man is changed most:
For, he some times so far runs out of square,
That he his way doth seem quite to haue lost,
And cleane without his vsuall sphere to fare;
That euen these Star-gazers stonisht are
At sight thereof, and damne their lying bookes:
So likewise, grim Sir *Saturne* oft doth spare
His sterne aspect, and calme his crabbed lookes:
So many turning cranks[61] these haue, so many crookes.[62]

53

But you *Dan Ioue,* that only constant are,
And King of all the rest, as ye do clame,
Are you not subiect eeke to this misfare?[63]
Then let me aske you this withouten blame,
Where were ye borne? some say in *Crete* by name,

58 Perhaps Spenser wrote *yon.*
59 boast.
60 radiant.
61 windings.
62 bendings.
63 mishap.

Others in *Thebes,* and others other-where;
But wheresoeuer they comment[64] the same,
They all consent that ye begotten were,
And borne here in this world, ne other can appeare.

54

Then are ye mortall borne, and thrall to me,
Vnlesse the kingdome of the sky yee make
Immortall, and vnchangeable to be;
Besides, that power and vertue which ye spake,
That ye here worke, doth many changes take,
And your owne natures change: for, each of you
That vertue haue, or this, or that to make,
Is checkt and changed from his nature trew,
By others opposition or obliquid[65] view.

55

Besides, the sundry motions of your Spheares,
So sundry waies and fashions as clerkes faine,
Some in short space, and some in longer yeares;
What is the same but alteration plaine?
Onely the starrie skie doth still remaine:
Yet do the Starres and Signes therein still moue,
And euen it self is mov'd, as wizards saine.[66]
But all that moueth, doth mutation loue:
Therefore both you and them to me I subiect proue.

56

Then since within this wide great *Vniuerse*
Nothing doth firme and permanent appeare,
But all things tost and turned by transuerse:[67]
What then should let,[68] but I aloft should reare
My Trophee, and from all, the triumph beare?
Now iudge then (O thou greatest goddesse trew!)
According as thy selfe doest see and heare,
And vnto me addoom[69] that is my dew;
That is the rule of all, all being rul'd by you.

57

So hauing ended, silence long ensewed,
Ne *Nature* to or fro spake for a space,
But with firme eyes affixt, the ground still viewed.
Meane while, all creatures, looking in her face,
Expecting[70] th'end of this so doubtfull case,
Did hang in long suspence what would ensew,
To whether side should fall the soueraigne place:

---

[64] devise, invent.
[65] directed obliquely.
[66] say.
[67] in a haphazard way.
[68] prevent.
[69] adjudge.
[70] awaiting.

At length, she looking vp with chearefull view,
The silence brake, and gaue her doome in speeches few.

58

I well consider all that ye haue sayd,
And find that all things stedfastnes doe hate
And changed be: yet being rightly wayd
They are not changed from their first estate;
But by their change their being doe dilate:[71]
And turning to themselues at length againe,
Doe worke their owne perfection so by fate:
Then ouer them Change doth not rule and raigne;
But they raigne ouer change, and doe their states maintaine.

59

Cease therefore daughter further to aspire,
And thee content thus to be rul'd by me:
For thy decay thou seekst by thy desire;
But time shall come that all shall changed bee,
And from thenceforth, none no more change shall see.
So was the *Titaness* put downe and whist,[72]
And *Ioue* confirm'd in his imperiall see.
Then was that whole assembly quite dismist,
And *Natur's* selfe did vanish, whither no man wist.

THE VIII CANTO. VNPERFITE

1

When I bethinke me on that speech whyleare,[73]
Of *Mutability,* and well it way:
Me seemes, that though she all vnworthy were
Of the Heav'ns Rule; yet very sooth to say,
In all things else she beares the greatest sway.
Which makes me loath this state of life so tickle,[74]
And loue of things so vaine to cast away;
Whose flowring pride, so fading and so fickle,
Short *Time* shall soon cut down with his consuming sickle.

2

Then gin I thinke on that which Nature sayd,
Of that same time when no more *Change* shall be,
But stedfast rest of all things firmely stayd
Vpon the pillours of Eternity,
That is contrayr to *Mutabilitie:*
For, all that moueth, doth in *Change* delight:
But thence-forth all shall rest eternally
With Him that is the God of Sabbaoth[75] hight:
O that great Sabbaoth God, graunt me that Sabaoths sight.

---

71 expand, develop.
72 silenced.
73 recently.
74 uncertain.
75 God of Hosts.

Christopher Marlowe

[1564–1593]

CHRISTOPHER MARLOWE is the most brilliant figure among the poets and dramatists of Shakespeare's earliest years in London. He was born in Canterbury, where his father was a shoemaker. He attended Corpus Christi College, Cambridge, and was graduated A.B. in 1584 and M.A. in 1587. Of his six years in London little is known.

He holds an important place in the history of English drama. Two of his nondramatic poems, *The Passionate Shepherd* and *Hero and Leander*, were extremely popular; the former has remained one of the best-known poems in English. At the time of Marlowe's death *Hero and Leander* was unfinished, and George Chapman completed and published it in 1598. Based on a Greek poem by Musaeus, it helped to establish the temporary vogue of the erotic narrative poem on mythological subjects. Marlowe also made verse translations of Ovid's *Amores* and of the first book of Lucan's *Pharsalia.* Marlowe's style in *Hero and Leander* is exuberant and splendid. Despite the faults inherent in the erotic narrative, *Hero and Leander* is a poem of rich and varied beauty.

The most useful editions are *The Works of Christopher Marlowe*, ed. C. F. Tucker Brooke, 1910; *The Works and Life of Christopher Marlowe*, ed. R. H. Case, 6 vols., 1930–1933; *Hero and Leander* (Haslewood Reprints), 1924. For biography and criticism see J. H. Ingram, *Christopher Marlowe and His Associates,* 1904; J. L. Hotson, *The Death of Christopher Marlowe*, 1925; U. M. Ellis-Fermor, *Christopher Marlowe*, 1927; John Bakeless, *Christopher Marlowe, the Man in His Time*, 1937, and *The Tragical History of Christopher Marlowe*, 2 vols., 1942; F. S. Boas, *Marlowe and His Circle*, 1929, and *Christopher Marlowe*, 1940; P. H. Kocher, *Christopher Marlowe: A Study of His Thought, Learning, and Character*, 1946; Tucker Brooke, "Christopher Marlowe," *Essays on Shakespeare and Other Elizabethans*, 1948. For a study of Marlowe's famous lyric, its sources and its influence, see R. S. Forsythe, "*The Passionate Shepherd;* and English Poetry," *PMLA*, xl (1925), 692–742. For bibliography, see S. A. Tannenbaum, *Christopher Marlowe, a Concise Bibliography*, 1937.

From HERO AND LEANDER[1]

On *Hellespont* guiltie of True-loues blood,
In view and opposit two citties stood,
Seaborderers,[2] disioin'd by *Neptunes* might:
The one *Abydos*, the other *Sestos* hight.[3]
At *Sestos*, *Hero* dwelt; *Hero* the faire,
Whom young *Apollo* courted for her haire,
And offred as a dower his burning throne,
Where she should sit for men to gaze vpon.
The outside of her garments were of lawne,
The lining purple silke, with guilt starres drawne,
Her wide sleeues greene, and bordered with a groue,
Where *Venus* in her naked glory stroue,
To please the carelesse and disdainfull eies
Of proud *Adonis* that before her lies.
Her kirtle blew, whereon was many a staine,
Made with the blood of wretched Louers slaine.
Vpon her head she ware a myrtle wreath,
From whence her vaile reacht to the ground beneath.
Her vaile was artificiall flowers and leaues,
Whose workmanship both man and beast deceaues.
Many would praise the sweet smell as she past,
When t'was the odour which her breath foorth cast,
And there for honie bees haue sought in vaine,
And beat from thence, haue lighted there againe.
About her necke hung chaines of peble stone,
Which lightned by her necke, like Diamonds shone.
She ware no gloues, for neither sunne nor wind
Would burne or parch her hands, but to her mind,[4]
Or warme or coole them, for they tooke delite
To play vpon those hands, they were so white.
Buskins of shels all siluered vsed she,
And brancht with blushing corall to the knee;
Where sparrowes pearcht, of hollow pearle and gold,
Such as the world would woonder to behold:
Those with sweet water oft her handmaid fils,
Which as shee went would cherupe through the bils.
Some say, for her the fairest *Cupid* pyn'd,
And looking in her face, was strooken blind.
But this is true, so like was one the other,
As he imagyn'd *Hero* was his mother.
And oftentimes into her bosome flew,
About her naked necke his bare armes threw,
And laid his childish head vpon her brest,
And with still panting rockt, there tooke his rest.
So louely faire was *Hero*, *Venus* Nun,
As nature wept, thinking she was vndone;
Because she tooke more from her than she left,
And of such wondrous beautie her bereft:

---

1 From *Hero and Leander*, 1598, STC 17413, Folger Library. The first 340 lines of the 484 lines of the First Sestiad are included here.

2 *Seaborderers*,] *Seaborders*, STC 17413.

3 called, named.

4 as she wished.

Therefore in signe her treasure suffred wracke,
Since *Heroes* time, hath halfe the world beene blacke.
Amorous *Leander,* beautifull and yoong,
(Whose tragedie diuine *Musaeus*[5] soong)
Dwelt at *Abidus:* since him dwelt there none,
For whom succeeding times make greater mone.
His dangling tresses that were neuer shorne,
Had they beene cut, and vnto *Colchos*[6] borne,
Would have allur'd the vent'rous youth of *Greece*
To hazard more than for the golden Fleece.
Faire *Cinthia*[7] wisht, his armes might be her spheare,[8]
Greefe makes her pale, because she mooves not there.
His bodie was as straight as *Circes* wand,
Ioue might haue sipt out *Nectar* from his hand.
Euen as delicious meat is to the tast,
So was his necke in touching,[9] and surpast
The white of *Pelops* shoulder. I could tell ye,
How smooth his brest was, and how white his bellie,
And whose immortall fingars did imprint
That heauenly path, with many a curious[10] dint,
That rungs along his backe, but my rude pen,
Can hardly blazon foorth the loues of men,[11]
Much lesse of powerfull gods:[12] let it suffise,
That my slacke[13] muse sings of *Leanders* eies,[14]
Those orient[15] cheekes and lippes, exceeding his[16]
That leapt into the water for a kis
Of his owne shadow, and despising many,
Died ere he could enioy the loue of any.
Had wilde *Hippolitus*[17] *Leander* seene,
Enamoured of his beautie had he beene,
His presence made the rudest paisant melt,
That in the vast vplandish countrie dwelt,
The barbarous *Thratian* soldier moou'd with nought,
Was moou'd with him, and for his fauour sought.
Some swore he was a maid in mans attire,
For in his lookes were all that men desire,
A pleasant smiling cheeke, a speaking[18] eye,
A brow for loue to banquet roiallye,
And such as knew he was a man would say,
Leander, thou art made for amorous play:
Why art thou not in loue, and lou'd of all?
Though thou be faire, yet be not thine owne thrall.
  The men of wealthie *Sestos,* euerie yeare,
(For his sake whom their goddesse held so deare,
Rose-cheekt *Adonis*) kept a solemne feast.
Thither resorted many a wandring guest,

---

[5] The reference is to the Greek poem written in the fifth century by Musaeus of Alexandria, who is sometimes confused with a legendary early Musaeus—hence "divine."

[6] Colchis.

[7] The moon.

[8] orbit.

[9] to the touch.

[10] exquisite.

[11] *men,*] *men.* STC 17413.

[12] *gods:*] *gods,* STC 17413.

[13] feeble.

[14] *eies,*] *eies.* STC 17413.

[15] glowing, radiant.

[16] Narcissus.

[17] According to Greek legend, he preferred hunting to love.

[18] expressive.

To meet their loues; such as had none at all,
Came louers home from this great festiuall.
For euerie street like to a Firmament
Glistered with breathing stars, who where they went,
Frighted the melancholie earth, which deem'd
Eternall heauen to burne, for so it seem'd,
As if another *Phaeton* had got
The guidance of the sunnes rich chariot.
But far aboue, the loueliest *Hero* shin'd,
And stole away th' inchaunted gazers mind,
For like Sea-nimphs inueigling harmony,
So was her beautie to the standers by.
Nor that night-wandring pale and watrie starre[19]
(When yawning dragons draw her thirling[20] carre
From *Latmus*[21] mount vp to the glomie skie,
Where crown'd with blazing light and maiestie,
She proudly sits) more ouer-rules the flood,[22]
Than she the hearts of those that neere her stood.
Euen as, when gawdie[23] Nymphs pursue the chace,
Wretched *Ixions* shaggie footed race,[24]
Incenst[25] with sauage heat, gallop amaine,
From steepe Pine-bearing mountains to the plaine:
So ran the people foorth to gaze vpon her,
And all that view'd her, were enamour'd on her.
And as in furie of a dreadfull fight,
Their fellowes being slaine or put to flight,
Poore soldiers stand with fear of death dead strooken,
So at her presence all surpris'd and tooken,
Await the sentence of her scornefull eies:
He whom she fauours liues, the other dies.
There might you see one sigh, another rage,
And some (their violent passions to asswage)
Compile sharpe satyrs, but alas too late,
For faithfull loue will neuer turne to hate.
And many seeing great princes were denied,
Pyn'd as they went, and thinking on her died.
On this feast day, O cursed day and hower,
Went *Hero* thorow[26] *Sestos,* from her tower
To *Venus* temple, where[27] vnhappilye,
As after chaunc'd, they did each other spye.[28]
So faire a church as this, had *Venus* none,
The wals were of discoloured[29] *Iasper* stone,
Wherein was *Proteus* carued, and o'rehead,
A liuelie[30] vine of greene sea agget[31] spread;
Where by one hand light headed *Bacchus* hoong,
And with the other, wine from grapes out wroong.

---

19 The moon.
20 flying, shooting through the air.
21 The mountain where Diana, the moon, visited Endymion.
22 rules over the sea.
23 gaily dressed.
24 Ixion was father of the shaggy-footed centaurs. Because of his love for Juno, Jove caused him to be chained to an eternally revolving wheel.
25 inflamed.
26 through.
27 *where*] *were* STC 17413.
28 *spye.*] *spye,* STC 17413.
29 of various colors.
30 lifelike.
31 sea agate.

Of Christall shining faire the pauement was,
The towne of *Sestos* cal'd it *Venus* glasse.[32]
There might you see the gods in sundrie shapes,
Committing headdie ryots, incest, rapes:
For know, that vnderneath this radiant floure,[33]
Was *Danaes* statue in a brazen tower,
Ioue slylie stealing from his sisters bed,
To dallie with *Idalian Ganimed,*[34]
And for his loue *Europa* bellowing loud,[35]
And tumbling with the Rainbow in a cloud:[36]
Blood-quaffing *Mars* heauing the yron net,[37]
Which limping *Vulcan* and his *Cyclops* set:
Loue kindling fire, to burne such townes as *Troy,*
Syluanus weeping for the louely boy[38]
That now is turn'd into a *Cypres* tree,
Vnder whose shade the Wood-gods loue to bee.
And in the midst a siluer altar stood;
There *Hero* sacrificing turtles[39] blood,
Vailt[40] to the ground, vailing her eie-lids close,
And modestly they opened as she rose:
Thence flew Loues arrow with the golden head,[41]
And thus *Leander* was enamoured.
Stone still he stood, and euermore he gazed,
Till with the fire that from his count'nance blazed,
Relenting *Heroes* gentle heart was strooke,
Such force and vertue[42] *hath an amorous looke.*
  It lies not in our power to loue, or hate,
For will in vs is ouer-rul'd by fate.
When two are stript long ere the course[43] begin,
We wish that one should loose, the other win;
And one especiallie doe we affect,[44]
Of two gold Ingots like in each respect.[45]
The reason no man knowes, let it suffise,
What we behold is censur'd[46] by our eies.
Where both deliberat, the loue is slight,
Who euer lou'd, that lou'd not at first sight?
  He kneel'd, but vnto her devoutly praid;
Chast *Hero* to her selfe thus softly said:
Were I the saint hee worships, I would heare him,
And as shee spake those words, came somewhat nere him.
He started vp, she blusht as one asham'd;
Wherewith *Leander* much more was inflam'd.
He toucht her hand, in touching it she trembled,
Loue deepely grounded, hardly[47] *is dissembled.*[48]
These louers parled[49] by the touch of hands,

---

[32] *glasse.*] *glasse,* STC 17413.
[33] on the floor below.
[34] Jove kidnaped Ganymede from Mount Ida.
[35] Jove took the form of a bull.
[36] *cloud:*] *cloud,* STC 17413.
[37] In which Vulcan trapped Mars.
[38] Cyparissus.
[39] turtledoves (a symbol of constancy in love).
[40] bowed in reverence.
[41] Cupid had blunt arrows also, which caused dislike.
[42] power.
[43] race.
[44] like, prefer.
[45] *respect.*] *respect,* STC 17413.
[46] judged.
[47] with difficulty.
[48] *dissembled.*] *dissembled,* STC 17413.
[49] spoke.

True loue is mute, and oft amazed[50] stands.
Thus while dum signs their yeelding harts entangled,
The aire with sparkes of liuing fire was spangled,
And night deepe drencht in mystie *Acheron*[51]
Heau'd vp her head, and halfe the world vpon[52]
Breath'd darknesse forth (darke night is *Cupids* day).[53]
And now begins *Leander* to display
Loues holy fire, with words, with sighs and teares,
Which like sweet musicke entred *Heroes* eares,
And yet at euerie word shee turn'd aside,
And alwaies cut him off as he replide.[54]
At last, like to a bold sharpe Sophister,[55]
With chearefull hope thus he accosted her.
Faire creature, let me speake without offence,
I would my rude words had the influence,
To lead thy thoughts as thy faire lookes doe mine,
Then shouldst thou bee his prisoner who is thine.
Be not vnkind and faire, mishapen stuffe[56]
Are of behauiour boisterous and ruffe.
O shun me not, but heare me ere you goe,
God knowes I cannot force loue, as you doe.
My words shall be as spotlesse as my youth,
Full of simplicitie and naked truth.
This sacrifice (whose sweet perfume descending,
From *Venus* altar to your footsteps bending)
Doth testifie that you exceed her farre,
To whom you offer, and whose Nunne you are.
Why should you worship her?[57] her you surpasse,
As much as sparkling Diamonds flaring[58] glasse.
A Diamond set in lead his worth retaines,
A heauenly Nimph, belou'd of humane swaines,
Receiues no blemish, but oft-times more grace,
Which makes me hope, although I am but base,
Base in respect of thee, diuine and pure,
Dutifull seruice may thy loue procure,
And I in dutie will excell all other,
As thou in beautie doest exceed loues mother.
Nor heauen, nor thou, were made to gaze vpon,[59]
As heauen preserues all things, so saue thou one.
A stately builded ship, well rig'd and tall,
The Ocean maketh more maiesticall:
Why vowest thou then to liue in *Sestos* here,
Who on Loues seas more glorious wouldst appeare?
Like vntun'd golden strings all women are,
Which long time lie vntoucht, will harshly iarre.
Vessels of Brasse oft handled, brightly shine,
What difference betwixt the richest mine
And basest mold, but vse? for both, not vs'de,

---

50 stunned, bewildered.
51 *Acheron*] *Acheron,* STC 17413. Marginal note: *A periphrasis of night.*
52 *vpon*] *vpon,* STC 17413.
53 Punctuation is crowded off in STC 17413.
54 *replide.*] *replide,* STC 17413.
55 specious reasoner.
56 persons.
57 *her?*] *her,* STC 17413.
58 glaring, gaudy.
59 i.e., merely to gaze upon.

Are of like worth. Then treasure is abus'de,
When misers keepe it; being put to lone,
In time it will returne vs two for one.
Rich robes themselues and others do adorne,
Neither themselues nor others, if not worne.
Who builds a pallace and rams vp the gate,
Shall see it ruinous and desolate.
Ah simple *Hero,* learne thy selfe to cherish,
Lone women like to emptie houses perish.
Lesse sinnes the poore rich man that starues himselfe,
In heaping vp a masse of drossie pelfe,
Than such as you: his golden earth remains,
Which after his disceasse, some other gains.
But this faire iem, sweet in the losse alone,
When you fleet hence, can be bequeath'd to none.
Or if it could, downe from th'enameld skie
All heauen would come to claime this legacie,
And with intestine broiles the world destroy,
And quite confound natures sweet harmony.
Well therefore by the gods decreed it is,
We humane creatures should enioy that blisse.
One is no number,[60] mayds are nothing then,
Without the sweet societie of men.
Wilt thou liue single still? one shalt thou bee,
Though neuer-singling[61] *Hymen* couple thee.
Wild sauages, that drinke of running springs,
Thinke water farre excels all earthly things:
But they that dayly tast neat wine, despise it.
Virginitie, albeit some highly prise it,
Compar'd with marriage, had you tried them both,
Differs as much as wine and water doth.
Base boullion for the stampes[62] sake we allow,
Euen so for mens impression do we you,[63]
By which alone, our reuerend fathers say,
Women receaue perfection euerie way.
This idoll which you terme *Virginitie,*
Is neither essence[64] subiect to the eie,
No, nor to any one exterior sence,
Nor hath it any place of residence,
Nor is't of earth or mold[65] celestiall,
Or capable of any forme at all.
Of that which hath no being, doe not boast,
Things that are not at all, are neuer lost.
Men foolishly doe call it vertuous,
What vertue is it, that is borne with vs?
Much lesse can honour bee ascrib'd thereto,
Honour is purchac'd by the deedes wee do.
Beleeue me *Hero,* honour is not wone,
Vntill some honourable deed be done.
Seeke you for chastitie, immortall fame,

60 Aristotle, *Metaphysics,* xiv, 1.
61 never-separating.
62 i.e., of coinage.
63 *you,*] *you.* STC 17413.
64 something that exists.
65 shape, form.

And know that some haue wrong'd *Dianas* name?[66]
Whose name is it, if she be false or not,
So she be faire, but some vile toongs will blot?
But you are faire (aye me) so wondrous faire,
So yoong, so gentle, and so debonaire,
As *Greece* will thinke, if thus you liue alone,
Some one or other keepes you as his owne.
Then *Hero* hate me not, nor from me flie,
To follow swiftly blasting[67] infamie.
Perhaps, thy sacred Priesthood makes thee loath,
Tell me, to whom mad'st thou that heedlesse oath?
  To *Venus,* answered shee, and as shee spake,
Foorth from those two tralucent cesternes[68] brake,
A streame of liquid pearle, which downe her face
Made milk-white paths, wheron the gods might trace[69]
To *Ioues* high court. Hee thus replide: The rites
In which Loues beauteous Empresse most delites,
Are banquets, Dorick[70] musicke, midnight reuell,
Plaies, maskes, and all that stern age counteth euill.
Thee as a holy Idiot[71] doth she scorne,
For thou in vowing chastitie, hast sworne
To rob her name and honour, and thereby
Commit'st a sinne far worse than periurie,[72]
Euen sacrilege against her Deitie,
Through regular and formall puritie.
To expiat which sinne, kisse and shake hands,
Such sacrifice as this, *Venus* demands.
  Thereat she smild, and did denie him so,
As put[73] thereby, yet might he hope for mo.[74]
Which makes him quickly re-enforce his speech,
And her in humble manner thus beseech.
  Though neither gods nor men may thee deserue,
Yet for her sake whom you haue vow'd to serue,
Abandon fruitlesse cold Virginitie,
The gentle queene of Loues sole enemie.
Then shall you most resemble *Venus* Nun,
When *Venus* sweet rites are perform'd and done.[75]
Flint-brested *Pallas* ioies in single life,
But *Pallas* and your mistresse are at strife.
Loue *Hero* then, and be not tirannous,
But heale the heart, that thou hast wounded thus,
Nor staine thy youthfull years with auarice,
Faire fooles delight to be accounted nice.[76]
The richest corne dies, if it be not reapt,
Beautie alone is lost, too warily kept.
These arguments he vs'de, and many more,
Wherewith she yeelded, that was woon before.[77]

---

66 knowing that some have slandered even Diana.
67 withering.
68 translucent eyes.
69 proceed.
70 Perhaps Marlowe meant "Lydian." Doric music was simple and severe.
71 ignorant person.
72 *periurie,*] *periurie.* STC 17413.
73 repelled.
74 more.
75 *done.*] *done,* STC 17413.
76 shy, reserved.
77 *before.*] *before,* STC 17413.

Heroes lookes yeelded, but her words made warre,
Women are woon when they begin to iarre.[78]
Thus having swallow'd *Cupids* golden hooke,
The more she striu'd, the deeper was she strooke.
Yet euilly faining anger, stroue she still,
And would be thought to graunt against her will.
So hauing paus'd a while, at last shee said:
Who taught thee Rhethoricke to deceiue a maid?
Aye me, such words as these should I abhor,
And yet I like them for the Orator.
With that *Leander* stoopt, to haue imbrac'd her,
But from his spreading armes away she cast her,
And thus bespake him, Gentle youth forbeare
To touch the sacred garments which I weare.
Vpon a rocke, and underneath a hill,
Far from the towne (where all is whist[79] and still,
Saue that the sea playing on yellow sand,
Sends foorth a ratling murmure to the land,
Whose sound allures the golden *Morpheus*
In silence of the night to visite vs.)[80]
My turret stands, and there God knowes I play
With *Venus* swannes and sparrowes all the day.
A dwarfish beldame[81] beares me companie,
That hops about the chamber where I lie,
And spends the night (that might be better spent)
In vaine discourse, and apish merriment.
Come thither.[82] As she spake this, her toong tript,
For vnawares (*Come thither*) from her slipt,
And sodainly her former colour chang'd,
And here and there her eies through anger rang'd.

THE PASSIONATE SHEEPHEARD TO HIS LOUE[83]

Come liue with mee, and be my loue,
And we will all the pleasures proue,
That Vallies, groues, hills and fieldes,
Woods, or steepie mountaine yeeldes.

And wee will sit vpon the Rocks,
Seeing the Sheepheards feede theyr flocks,
By shallow Riuers, to whose falls,
Melodious byrds sings Madrigalls.

And I will make thee beds of Roses,
And a thousand fragrant poesies,
A cap of flowers, and a kirtle,
Imbroydered all with leaues of Mirtle.

78 dispute.

79 silent.

80 *vs.)*] *vs*) STC 17413.

81 old woman.

82 *thither.*] *thither;* STC 17413.

83 From *Englands Helicon,* 1600, STC 3191, Folger Library. This famous poem was first printed in *The passionate pilgrime. By W. Shakespeare,* 1599, STC 22342, where the title, author's name, and the fourth and sixth stanzas are missing. It appeared, with some variations, as a broadside ballad. For the reply, first attributed to Raleigh by Izaak Walton, see page 319. For a discussion of both poems, see *England's Helicon,* ed. H. E. Rollins, 2 vols., 1935, ii, 186–190.

A gowne made of the finest wooll,
Which from our pretty Lambes we pull,
Fayre lined slippers for the cold:
With buckles of the purest gold.

A belt of straw, and Iuie buds,
With Corall clasps and Amber studs,
And if these pleasures may thee moue,
Come liue with mee, and be my loue.

The Sheepheard Swaines shall daunce and sing,
For thy delight each May-morning,
If these delights thy minde may moue;
Then liue with mee, and be my loue.[84]

[84] signed: *Chr. Marlow.*

Sir Walter Raleigh

[c. 1552–1618]

SIR WALTER RALEIGH was born in Devonshire. After leaving Oxford without a degree, he entered upon his amazing career as courtier, soldier, explorer, colonizer, political prisoner, and historian.

Very little of his poetry was written for publication: the scraps of verse in *The History*, his verses in commendation of Gascoigne's *Steel Glass* and of his cousin Sir Arthur Gorges's translation of Lucan's *Pharsalia*, and his two poems in praise of Spenser's *Faerie Queene*. The rest of his poetry was written for Queen Elizabeth, for his friends, or for Queen Anne during his imprisonment. Several of his poems were printed in contemporary anthologies and songbooks, and others were preserved in manuscript. It is probable that many of his poems have been lost or remain unidentified. His longest and most ambitious poem, *Cynthia*, addressed to Queen Elizabeth and praised by Spenser, is lost, except for a rough draft of part of it in Raleigh's handwriting.

Raleigh's poetry is notable for its directness, its nervous and epigrammatic concentration of phrasing. Unlike most sixteenth-century verse, it is intensely personal. Colored by his discontent and bitterness, by his scorn and contempt of the world, it is the expression of a defiant and somber spirit brooding on the vanity and mutability of life. The constant refrain of Raleigh's criticism of life seems to be "Of all which past, the sorow onely staies."

The one complete edition of Raleigh's prose is *The Works of Sir Walter Ralegh*, 8 vols., 1829. The standard edition of *The Discovery of Guiana* is V. T. Harlow's, 1928. For discussion of *The History* see Sir Charles Firth, "Sir Walter Raleigh's 'History of the World,'" *Essays Historical and Literary*, 1928. The best edition of the poetry is *The Poems of Sir Walter Ralegh*, ed. A. M. C. Latham, 1929; revised, 1951. The most useful biographies are E. Edwards, *Life of Sir Walter Raleigh. Together with his Letters*, 2 vols., 1868; W. Stebbing, *Sir Walter Raleigh*, 1891; M. Waldman, *Sir Walter Raleigh*, 1928; Edward Thompson, *Sir Walter Ralegh*, 1935. For discussion of his poetry and literary relationships see Sir Edmund Chambers, "The Disenchantment of the Elizabethans," *Sir Thomas Wyatt and Some Collected Studies*, 1933; E. C. Dunn, *The Literature of Shakespeare's England*, 1936; M. C. Bradbrook, *The School of*

Night, 1936; Tucker Brooke, "Sir Walter Ralegh as Poet and Philosopher," *English Literary History*, v (1938), 93–112, reprinted in *Essays on Shakespeare and Other Elizabethans*, 1948; E. G. Clark, *Ralegh and Marlowe*, 1941; E. A. Strathmann, *Sir Walter Ralegh: A Study in Elizabethan Skepticism*, 1951.

A VISION VPON THIS CONCEIPT OF THE FAERY QUEENE[1]

Me thought I saw the graue, where *Laura*[2] lay,
Within that Temple, where the vestall flame
Was wont to burne, and passing by that way,
To see that buried dust of liuing fame,
Whose tombe faire loue, and fairer vertue kept,
All suddenly I saw the Faery Queene:
At whose approch the soule of *Petrarke* wept,
And from thenceforth those graces were not seene.
For they this Queene attended, in whose steed
Obliuion laid him downe on *Lauras* herse:
Hereat the hardest stones were seene to bleed,
And grones of buried ghostes the heauens did perse.[3]
Where *Homers* spright did tremble all for griefe,
And curst th'accesse of that celestiall theife.

A POEM[4]

Like to an *Hermit* poore in place obscure,[5]
I meane to spende my dayes in endlesse doubt:
To waile such woes as time cannot recure,[6]
Where none but loue shall euer finde me out.
My foode shall be of care and sorrow made,
My drinke nought else but teares falne from mine eyes,
And for my light in such obscured shade,
The flames shall serue that from my heart arise.
A gowne of griefe my bodie shall attire,
And broken hope the staffe of all my stay,
Of late repentance linkt with long desire,
The Couch is made whereon my bones to lay,
And at my gate *Dispaire* shall linger still,
To let in *Death* when *Loue* and *Fortune* will.

A SONET[7]

Her face, her tongue, her wit,
So faire, so sweete, so sharpe:

[1] This sonnet is one of several commendatory poems that Spenser's friends wrote for the first edition of *The Faerie Queene*, 1590, STC 23081, Morgan Library.

[2] To whom Petrarch addressed his sonnets.

[3] pierce.

[4] From *Brittons bowre of delights*, 1591, STC 3633, Huntington Library. This sonnet is largely a translation from Philippe Desportes, *Diane*, ii, 8.

[5] *obscure*,] *obscure*. STC 3633.

[6] restore, remedy.

[7] From *Brittons bowre of delights*, 1591. Although this poem may be the work of Breton or Lodge, it is often attributed to Raleigh. Trick poems were popular in the late sixteenth century.

First bent, then drew, then hit,
Mine eye, mine eare, mine hart.

Mine eye, mine eare, mine heart,
To like, to learne, to loue:
Your face, your tongue, your wit,
Doth lead, doth teach, doth moue.

Her face, her tongue, her wit,
With beame, with sound, with art:
Doth binde, doth charme, doth rule,
Mine eye, mine eare, mine heart.

Mine eye, mine eare, mine heart,
With life, with hope, with skill,
Your face, your tongue, your wit,[8]
Doth feed, doth feast, doth fill.

Oh face, oh tongue, oh wit,
With frownes, with checks, with smart:
Wring not, vex not, moue not,
Mine eye, mine eare, mine hart.

This eye, this eare, this heart,
Shall ioy, shall bind, shall sweare:
Your face, your tongue, your wit,
To serue, to loue, to feare.

AN EPITAPH VPON THE RIGHT HONORABLE SIR PHILIP SIDNEY KNIGHT: LORD GOUERNOR OF FLUSHING[9]

To praise thy life, or waile thy woorthie death,
And want thy wit,[10] thy wit high, pure, diuine,
Is far beyond the powre of mortall line,
Nor any one hath worth that draweth breath.[11]

Yet rich in zeale,[12] though poore in learnings lore,
And friendly care[13] obscurde in secret brest,
And loue that enuie in thy life supprest,
Thy deere life done, and death hath doubled more.

And I, that in thy time and liuing state,
Did onely praise thy vertues in my thought,
As one that seeld the rising sunne hath sought,
With words and teares now waile thy timelesse[14] fate.

Drawne was thy race, aright from princely line,[15]
Nor lesse than such, (by gifts that nature gaue,

[8] *wit,*] *wit.* STC 3633.
[9] From *The phoenix nest*, 1593, STC 21516, Folger Library.
[10] though lacking your wisdom.
[11] nor has any living person merit to do it.
[12] yet one who is rich in zeal.
[13] and who has friendly care.
[14] untimely.
[15] Sidney traced his descent from William the Conqueror.

The common mother that all creatures haue,)
Doth vertue shew, and princely linage shine.

A king gaue thee thy name,[16] a kingly minde,
That God thee gaue, who found it now too deere
For this base world, and hath resumde[17] it neere,[18]
To sit in skies, and sort[19] with powres diuine.

Kent thy birth daies, and Oxford held thy youth,
The heauens made haste, and staide nor yeeres, nor time,
The fruits of age grew ripe in thy first prime,
Thy will, thy words; thy words, the seales of truth.

Great gifts and wisedome rare imploide thee thence,
To treat from kings, with those more great than kings,
Such hope men had to lay the highest things,
On thy wise youth, to be transported hence.

Whence to sharpe wars sweete honor did thee call,
Thy countries loue, religion, and thy friends:
Of woorthy men, the marks, the liues and ends,
And her defence, for whom we labor all.

There didst thou vanquish shame and tedious age,
Griefe, sorow, sicknes, and base fortunes might:
Thy rising day, saw neuer wofull night,
But past with praise, from of this worldly stage.

Back to the campe, by thee that day[20] was brought,
First thine owne death, and after thy long fame;
Teares to the soldiers, the proud Castilians shame;
Vertue exprest, and honor truly taught.

What hath he lost, that such great grace hath woon,
Yoong yeeres, for endles yeeres, and hope vnsure,
Of fortunes gifts, for wealth that still shall dure,[21]
Oh happie race with so great praises run.

England doth hold thy lims[22] that bred the same,
Flaunders thy valure where it last was tried,
The Campe thy sorow where thy bodie died,
Thy friends, thy want; the world, thy vertues fame.

Nations thy wit, our mindes lay vp thy loue,
Letters thy learning, thy losse, yeeres long to come,
In worthy harts sorow hath made thy tombe,
Thy soule and spright enrich the heauens aboue.

Thy liberall hart imbalmd in gratefull teares,[23]
Yoong sighes, sweete sighes, sage sighes, bewaile thy fall,

[16] He was named for Philip II of Spain, who was then husband of Queen Mary of England.
[17] taken back.
[18] nearer.
[19] associate.
[20] He was mortally wounded at Zutphen on September 22, 1586.
[21] endure.
[22] He was buried in St. Paul's Cathedral.
[23] *teares,*] *teares.* STC 21516.

Enuie hir sting, and spite hath left hir gall,
Malice hir selfe, a mourning garment weares.

That day their Haniball died,[24] our Scipio fell,
Scipio, Cicero, and Petrarch of our time,
Whose vertues wounded by my woorthles rime,
Let Angels speake, and heauens thy praises tell.

Praisd be Dianas faire and harmles light,[25]
Praisd be the dewes, wherwith she moists the ground;
Praisd be hir beames, the glorie of the night,
Praisd be hir powre, by which all powres abound.

Praisd be hir Nimphs, with whom she decks the woods,
Praisd be hir knights, in whom true honor liues,
Praisd be that force, by which she moues the floods,
Let that Diana shine, which all these giues.

In heauen Queene she is among the spheares,
In ayr[26] she Mistres like makes all things pure,
Eternitie in hir oft chaunge she beares,
She beautie is, by hir the faire endure.

Time weares hir not, she doth his chariot guide,
Mortalitie belowe hir orbe is plaste,
By hir the vertue of the starrs downe slide,
In hir is vertues perfect image cast.

A knowledge pure it is hir worth to kno,
With Circes let them dwell that thinke not so.

Like truthles dreames, so are my ioyes expired,[27]
And past returne, are all my dandled[28] daies:
My loue misled, and fancie quite retired,
Of all which past, the sorow onely staies.

My lost delights, now cleane from sight of land,
Haue left me all alone in vnknowne waies:
My minde to woe, my life in fortunes hand,
Of all which past, the sorow onely staies.

As in a countrey strange without companion,
I onely waile the wrong of deaths delaies,
Whose sweete spring spent, whose sommer wel nie don,
Of all which past, the sorow onely staies.

Whom care forewarnes, ere age and winter colde,
To haste me hence, to finde my fortunes folde.[29]

[24] Count Hannibal Gonzaga, a Spanish officer, was mortally wounded in the same battle.

[25] From *The phoenix nest*, 1593. This poem, a compliment to Queen Elizabeth, is not certainly by Raleigh.

[26] *ayr*] *ay* STC 21516.

[27] From *The phoenix nest*, 1593.

[28] pampered.

[29] shelter.

THE NIMPHS REPLY TO THE SHEEPHEARD[30]

If all the world and loue were young,
And truth in euery Sheepheards tongue,
These pretty pleasures might me moue,
To liue with thee, and be thy loue.

Time driues the flocks from field to fold,
When Riuers rage, and Rocks grow cold,
And *Philomell* becommeth dombe,
The rest complaines of cares to come.

The flowers doe fade, and wanton fieldes,
To wayward winter reckoning yeeldes,
A honny tongue, a hart of gall,
Is fancies spring, but sorrowes fall.

Thy gownes, thy shooes, thy beds of Roses,
Thy cap, thy kirtle, and thy poesies,
Soone breake, soone wither, soone forgotten:
In follie ripe, in reason rotten.

Thy belt of straw and Iuie buddes,
Thy Corall claspes and Amber studdes,
All these in me no meanes can moue,
To come to thee, and be thy loue.

But could youth last, and loue still breede,
Had ioyes no date,[31] nor age no neede,
Then these delights my minde might moue,
To liue with thee, and be thy loue.

THE PASSIONATE MANS PILGRIMAGE, SUPPOSED TO BE WRITTEN BY ONE AT THE POINT OF DEATH[32]

Giue me my Scallop shell[33] of quiet,
My staffe of Faith to walke vpon,
My Scrip[34] of Ioy, Immortall diet,
My bottle of saluation:
My Gowne of Glory, hopes true gage,[35]
And thus Ile take my pilgrimage.

Blood must be my bodies balmer,[36]
No other balme will there be giuen
Whilst my soule like a white[37] Palmer[38]
Trauels to the land of heauen,
Ouer the siluer mountaines,
Where spring the Nectar fountaines:
And there Ile kisse
The Bowle of blisse,
And drinke my eternall[39] fill
On euery milken hill.
My soule will be a drie before,
But after it, will nere thirst more.

And by the happie blisfull way
More peacefull Pilgrims I shall see,
That haue shooke off their gownes of clay,
And goe appareld fresh like mee.
Ile bring them first
To slake their thirst,
And then to tast those Nectar suckets[40]
At the cleare wells
Where sweetnes dwells,
Drawne vp by Saints in Christall buckets.

And when our bottles and all we,
Are fild with immortalitie:
Then the holy paths weele trauell
Strewde with Rubies thicke as grauell,
Seelings of Diamonds, Saphire floores,
High walles of Corall and Pearle Bowres.

From thence to heauens Bribeles hall
Where no corrupted voyces brall,
No Conscience molten into gold,
Nor forg'd accusers bought and sold,

---

30 From *England's Helicon,* 1600, STC 3191, Folger Library. This poem, here signed *"Ignoto,"* is the reply to Marlowe's *The passionate sheepheard to his loue.*

31 end.

32 From *Daiphantus, or the passions of loue. . . . By An.Sc. Gentleman. Wherevnto is added, The passionate mans pilgrimage,* 1604, STC 21853, Bodleian Library. *Daiphantus,* a long poem conventional in manner and form, is attributed to the almost unknown Anthony Scoloker. *The Passionate Man's Pilgrimage* is attributed to Raleigh in several early-seventeenth century manuscripts and in *Remains of Sir Walter Raleigh,* 1657. On November 17, 1603, Releigh was condemned to death, and on December 6 he was reprieved. He may have written the poem during that interval.

33 Symbol of a pilgrim.

34 The pilgrim's pouch or wallet.

35 pledge.

36 embalmer.

37 *white*] *quiet* in *Remains of Sir Walter Raleigh.*

38 Pilgrim returning from the Holy Land and bearing a palm branch.

39 *eternall*] *everlasting* in *Remains.*

40 sweetmeats.

No cause deferd, nor vaine spent Iorney,
For there Christ is the Kings Atturney:
Who pleades for all without degrees,[41]
And he hath Angells,[42] but no fees.

When the grand twelue million Iury,
Of our sinnes and sinfull[43] fury,
Gainst our soules blacke verdicts giue,
Christ pleades his death, and then we liue,
Be thou my speaker taintles pleader,
Vnblotted[44] Lawyer, true proceeder,
Thou mouest saluation euen for almes:
Not with a bribed Lawyers palmes.

And this is my eternall plea,
To him that made Heauen, Earth and Sea,
Seeing my flesh must die so soone,
And want a head to dine next noone,
Iust at the stroke when my vaines start and spred
Set on my soule an euerlasting head.
Then am I readie like a palmer fit,
To tread those blest paths which before I writ.

THE LIE[45]

Goe soule the bodies guest
vpon a thanklesse arrant,[46]
Feare not to touch the best
the truth shall be thy warrant.
Goe since I needs must die
and giue the world the lie.

Say to the Court it glowes
and shines like rotten wood,
Say to the Church it showes
what's good, and doth noe good.
If Church and Court reply
then giue them both the lie.

Tell potentates they liue
acting by others action,
Not loued vnlesse they giue,
not strong but by affection:[47]
If potentates reply
giue potentates the lie.

Tell men of high condition,
that manage the Estate.[48]
Their purpose is ambition,
their practise[49] only hate,
And if they once reply
then giue them all the lie.

Tell them that braue it most,[50]
they beg for more by spending
Who in their greatest cost
like[51] nothing, but commending.
And if they make reply,
then giue them all the lie.

Tell zeale it wants[52] deuotion
tell loue it is but lust.
Tell time it meets[53] but motion
tell flesh it is but dust.
And wish them not reply
For thou must giue the lie.

Tell age it daily wasteth,
tell honor how it alters.
Tel beauty how she blasteth[54]
tell fauour how it falters
And as they shall reply,
giue euery one the lie.

Tell wit how much it wrangles
In tickle[55] points of nycenesse,[56]
Tell wisedome she entangles
her selfe in ouer wisenesse.
And when they do reply
straight giue them both the lie.

---

41 regardless of rank.

42 A punning reference to the coin called "angel," having as its device the archangel Michael.

43 *sinfull*] *direfull* in *Remains.*

44 unsullied.

45 From Francis Davison, *A poetical rapsody,* 1608, STC 6374, Huntington Library. This poem, almost certainly by Raleigh, was probably written about 1593. The present editor has made no changes in the careless but not misleading punctuation of STC 6374.

46 errand.

47 Some early manuscripts and printed versions read *a faction,* which is probably correct.

48 state.

49 habit; plotting.

50 makes the greatest show.

51 Other early texts read *seek* or *seeks.*

52 lacks.

53 metes, measures.

54 withers.

55 delicate.

56 subtlety, overrefinement.

Tell Phisick of her boldnes,
  tel skill it is preuention[57]
Tell charity of coldnes,
  tell Law it is contention,
And as they doe reply
  so giue them still the lie.

Tell Fortune of her blindnesse,
  tel nature of decay,
Tel friendship of vnkindnesse,
  tel Iustice of delay.
And if they wil reply,
  then giue them all the lie.

Tell Arts they haue no soundnes,
  but vary by esteeming,[58]
Tel schooles they want profoundnes
  and stand to much on seeming.
If Arts and Schooles reply,
  giue arts and schooles the lie.

Tell faith it's fled the Citie,
  tell how the country erreth
Tel manhood shakes of[59] pitty
  tel vertue least preferreth,[60]
And if they doe reply,
  spare not to giue the lie.

So when thou hast as I,
  commanded thee, done blabbing,
Because to giue the lie,
  deserues no lesse then stabbing,
Stab at thee, he that will,
  no stab thy soule can kill.

THE AUTHOURS EPITAPH, MADE BY HIMSELFE[61]

Euen such is Time, which takes in trust
Our Youth, and Ioy's, and all we haue,
And payes vs but with age and dust,
Which in the darke and silent graue,
When we haue wandred all our wayes,
Shuts vp the story of our dayes:
And from which Earth, and Graue, and
  Dust,
The Lord shall raise me vp I trust.

As you came from the holy land[62]
    Of Walsinghame,[63]
Mett you not with my true loue
    By the way as you came?"

"How shall I know your trew loue,
    That have mett many one,
As I went to the holy lande,
    That have come, that have gone?"

"She is neyther whyte nor browne,
    Butt as the heauens fayre;
There is none hathe a forme so diuine
    In the earth or the ayre."

"Such an one did I meet, good Sir,
  Suche an Angelyke face,
Who lyke a queene, lyke a nymph, did
      appere,
    By her gate, by her grace."

"She hath lefte me here all alone,
    All allone, as vnknowne,
Who somtymes did me lead with her
      selfe
    And me loude[64] as her owne."

---

[57] Some early texts read *pretension* or *perversion.*

[58] mere opinion.

[59] off.

[60] *preferreth,*] *preferred,* STC 6374.

[61] From Raleigh, *The prerogative of parliaments in England,* 1628, STC 20648, New York Public Library. According to statements in early-seventeenth-century manuscripts and to John Aubrey, Raleigh wrote these lines in his Bible shortly before he was executed on October 29, 1618. If he did, he merely recast lines that he had written earlier (Latham, pages 21–22, 152–156). John Chamberlain, writing to Sir Dudley Carleton on November 7, 1618, enclosed "halfe a dosen verses he [Raleigh] made the night before his death, to take his farewell of Poetrie wherein he had ben a pidler euen from his youth," but the enclosure is lost (*The Letters of John Chamberlain,* ed. N. E. McClure, 1939, ii, 179).

[62] From Bodleian Library, MS. Rawlinson Poet. 85, f. 123, a late-sixteenth-century manuscript. It is signed "Sr W.R." The punctuation and capitalization are the present editor's. There are no stanza divisions in the manuscript. The poem was first printed in Thomas Deloney, *The garland of good will,* which was entered in the Stationers' Registers in 1593 and contained many ballads that had appeared earlier as broadsides. The unique copy of the first extant edition, 1631 (STC 6554), lacks sheet G, which contains this poem. The poem, written on a ballad framework, is probably Raleigh's. For parallels in poems known to be Raleigh's, see Latham, page 121.

[63] Walsingham in Norfolk was famous as the seat of the shrine of Our Lady of Walsingham. The shrine was destroyed in 1538.

[64] loved.

"Whats the cause that she leaues you alone
And a new waye doth take,
Who loued you once as her owne
And her ioye did you make?"

"I haue loude her all my youth,
Butt now[65] ould, as you see,
Loue lykes not the fallyng frute
From the wythered tree.

"Know that loue is a careless chylld,
And forgets[66] promyse paste;
He is blynd, he is deaff when he lyste,[67]
And in faythe neuer faste.

"His desyre is a dureless[68] contente
And a trustless ioye;
He is wonn with a world of despayre
And is lost with a toye."

"Of women kynde suche indeed is the loue,
Or the word Loue, abused,
Vnder which many chyldysh desyres
And conceytes are excusde.

"But true Loue is a durable fyre
In the mynde euer burnynge;
Neuer sycke, neuer ould, neuer dead,
From itt selfe neuer turnynge."

[65] *now*] *no* MS.
[66] *forgets*] *forgett* MS.
[67] pleases.
[68] brief.

Robert Greene

[c. 1560–1592]

ROBERT GREENE, writer of plays, prose romances, and pamphlets, was one of the best lyric poets of his day. Born at Norwich, he attended St. John's College, Cambridge, and was graduated B.A. in 1578 and M.A. in 1583.

After a few years of great promise in London, he died in poverty and despair. His excesses, repentances, and miseries were recounted in pamphlets either by himself or by others writing soon after his death.

He published no collection of poems, but he included in his romances and pamphlets some graceful and charming lyrics.

The only complete edition is *The Life and Complete Works in Prose and Verse of Robert Greene*, ed. A. B. Grosart, 15 vols., 1881–1886. A useful edition is *The Plays and Poems of Robert Greene*, ed, J. C. Collins, 2 vols., 1905. For biography and criticism see J. C. Jordan, *Robert Greene*, 1915; S. A. Tannenbaum, *Robert Greene, a Concise Bibliography*, 1939.

In tyme we see that siluer drops[1]
  The craggy stones make soft:
The slowest snaile in tyme, we see,
  Doth creepe and clime aloft.

With feeble puffes the tallest pine
  In tract[2] of time doth fall:
The hardest hart in time doth yeelde
  To *Venus* luring call.

Where chilling frost alate did nip,
  There flasheth now a fire:
Where deepe disdaine bred noisome hate,
  There kindleth now desire.

Time causeth hope to haue his hap,
  What care in time not easde,

[1] From *Arbasto*, 1584, STC 12218, Huntington Library.

[2] course.

In time I loathd that now I loue,
In both content and pleasd.

Sweet are the thoughts that sauour of content,[3]
The quiet mind is richer then a crowne,
Sweet are the nights in carelesse slumber spent,
The poore estate scornes fortunes angrie frowne,
Such sweet content, such mindes, such sleep, such blis,
Beggars inioy, when Princes oft do mis.

The homely house that harbors quiet rest,
The cottage that affoords no pride, nor care,
The meane[4] that grees with Countrie musick best,
The sweet consort[5] of mirth and musicks[6] fare,
Obscured life sets downe a type of blis,
A minde content both crowne and kingdome is.

SEPHESTIAS SONG TO HER CHILDE[7]

Weepe not my wanton smile vpon my knee,
When thou art olde ther's grief inough for thee.
Mothers wagge, pretie boy,
Fathers sorrow, fathers ioy:
When thy father first did see
Such a boy by him and mee,
He was glad, I was woe,
Fortune changde made him so,
When he left his pretie boy,
Last his sorowe, first his ioy.

Weepe not my wanton smile upon my knee:
When thou art olde ther's grief inough for thee.
Streaming teares that neuer stint,
Like pearle drops from a flint,
Fell by course from his eyes,
That one anothers place supplies:
Thus he grieud in euerie part,
Teares of bloud fell from his hart,
When he left his pretie boy,
Fathers sorrow, fathers ioy.

Weepe not my wanton smile upon my knee:
When thou art olde ther's griefe inough for thee.
The wanton smilde, father wept;
Mother cride, babie lept:
More he crowde, more we cride;
Nature could not sorowe hide.

[3] From *Greenes farewell to folly*, 1591; registered, 1587, STC 12241, Folger Library.

[4] (1) the middle part in three-part music; (2) the golden mean.

[5] harmony.

[6] Perhaps a misprint for *modest*.

[7] From *Menaphon*, 1589, STC 12272, Folger Library.

He must goe, he must kisse
Childe and mother, babie blisse:
For he left his pretie boy,
Fathers sorowe, fathers ioy.

Weepe not my wanton smile upon my knee:
When thou art olde ther's grief inough for thee.

DORONS DESCRIPTION OF SAMELA[8]

Like to *Diana* in her Summer weede[9]
Girt with a crimson roabe of brightest die,
goes faire *Samela.*
Whiter than be the flockes that straggling feede,
When washt by *Arethusa* faint they lie:
is faire *Samela.*
As faire *Aurora* in her morning gray
Deckt with the ruddie glister of her loue,
is faire *Samela.*
Like lovely *Thetis* on a calmed day,
When as her brightnesse *Neptunes* fancie moue,
shines faire *Samela.*
Her tresses gold, her eyes like glassie streames,
Her teeth are pearle, the breast of yvorie
of faire *Samela.*
Her cheekes like rose and lilly yeeld foorth gleames,
Her browes bright arches framde of ebonie:
thus faire *Samela.*
Passeth faire *Venus* in her brauest[10] hiew,
And *Iuno* in the shew of maiestie,
for she's *Samela.*
Pallas in wit, all three if you will view,
For beautie, wit, and matchlesse dignitie
yeeld to *Samela.*

THE PALMERS ODE[11]

Olde *Menalcas* on a day,
As in field this shepheard lay,
Tuning of his oten pipe,
Which he hit with manie a stripe;
Said to *Coridon* that hee
Once was yong and full of glee,
Blithe and wanton was I then:
Such desires follow men.
As I lay and kept my sheepe,
Came the God that hateth sleepe,
Clad in armour all of fire,
Hand in hand with Queene Desire:
And with a dart that wounded nie,

8 *Ibid.*
9 clothing.
10 most splendid.

11 From *Greenes Neuer too late,* 1590, STC 12253, Huntington Library.

Pearst my heart as I did lie:
That when I wooke I gan sweare,
Phillis beautie palme did beare.
Vp I start, foorth went I,
With hir face to feede mine eye:
There I saw *Desire* sit,
That my heart with *Loue* had hit,
Laying foorth bright *Beauties* hookes
To intrap my gazing lookes.
Loue I did and gan to woe,
Pray and sigh, all would not doe:
Women when they take the toy[12]
Couet to be counted coy.
Coy she was, and I gan court,
She thought *Loue* was but a sport.
Profound Hell was in my thought,
Such a paine *Desire* had wrought,
That I sued with sighes and teares,
Still ingrate she stopt hir eares,
Till my youth I had spent.
Last a passion of *Repent,*
Tolde me flat that *Desire,*
Was a brond[13] of Loues fire,
Which consumeth men in thrall,
Vertue, youth, wit, and all.
At this sawe backe I start,
Bet[14] *Desire* from my hart,
Shooke of *Loue* and made an oth,
To be enemie to both.
Olde I was when thus I fled,
Such fond toyes as cloyde my head.
But this I learnd at Vertues gate,
The way to good is neuer late.

THE SHEPHEARDS WIUES SONG[15]

Ah what is loue it is[16] a pretie thing,
As sweete vnto a Shepheard as a King,
And sweeter too:
For Kinges haue cares that waite vpon a Crowne,
And cares can make the sweetest loue to frowne:
Ah then ah then,
If Countrie loues such sweete desires do gaine,
What Lady would not loue a Shepheard swayne.

His flockes once foulded he comes home at night,
As merry as a King in his delight,
And merrier too:
For Kinges bethinke them what the state require,
Where shepheards carelesse Carroll by the fire.
Ah then, ah then,

[12] whim, notion.
[13] brand.
[14] beat.

[15] From *Greenes Mourning garment,* 1590, STC 12251, Cambridge University Library.
[16] *it is* STC 12252]; *is it* STC 12251.

If countrie loues such sweete desires gaine,
What Ladie would not loue a shepheard swaine.

He kisseth first, then sits as blyth to eate,
His creame and curds, as doth the King his meate,
And blyther too:
For Kinges haue often feares when they do suppe,
Where Shepheards dread no poyson in their cuppe.
Ah then, ah then,
If countrie loues such sweete desires gaine,
What Ladie would not loue a shepheard swaine.

To bed he goes, as wanton then I weene,
As is a King in dalliance with a Queene,
More wanton too:
For Kinges haue many griefes affectes[17] to mooue,
Where Shepheards haue no greater griefe then loue,
Ah then, ah then,
If countrie loues such sweete desires gaine,
What Ladie would not loue a shepheard swaine.

Upon his couch of straw he sleepes as sound,
As doth the King vpon his beds of downe,
More sounder too:
For cares cause Kinges full oft their sleepe to spill,[18]
Where wearie Shepheards lie and snort[19] their fill,
Ah then, ah then,
If country loues such sweete desires gaine,
What Ladie would not loue a Shepheard swayne.

Thus with his wife he spendes the yeare as blyth,
As doth the King at euerie tyde or syth,[20]
And blyther too:
For Kings haue warres and broyles to take in hand,
When shepheards laugh and loue vpon the land.
Ah then, ah then,
If countrie loues such sweete desires gayne,
What Ladie would not loue a shepheard swayne.

PHILOMELAS ODE THAT SHE SUNG IN HIR ARBOUR[21]

Sitting by a riuer side,
Where a silent streame did glide,
Muse I did of many things,
That the mind in quiet brings.
I gan thinke how some men deeme,
Gold their god, and some esteeme
Honour is the cheefe content,
That to man in life is lent.
And some others doe contend,
Quiet none like to a friend.
Others hold there is no welth
Compared to a perfit helth.
Some mans mind in quiet stands,
When he is Lord of many lands.
But I did sigh, and sayd all this
Was but a shade of perfit blis.
And in my thoughts I did approue,
Nought so sweet as is true loue.
Loue twixt Louers passeth these,

[17] affections.
[18] destroy.
[19] snore.
[20] time.
[21] From *Philomela*, 1592, STC 12296, Huntington Library.

When mouth kisseth and hart grees.[22]
With folded armes and lippes meeting,
Each soule another sweetly greeting.
For by the breath the soule fleeteth,
And soule with soule in kissing meeteth.
If Loue be so sweet a thing,
That such happie blisse doth bring,
Happie is Loues sugred thrall,
But vnhappie maidens all,[23]
Who esteeme your Virgins blisses,
Sweeter than a wiues sweet kisses.
No such quiet to the mind,
As true loue with kisses kind.
But if a kisse proue vnchast,
Then is true loue quite disgrast,
Though loue be sweet, learne this of me,
No Loue sweet but honestie.

PHILOMELOES SECOND OADE[24]

It was frostie winters season,
And faire Floras wealth was geason:[25]
Meades that earst with greene were spred,
With choice flowers diapred:[26]
Had tawny vales: Cold had scanted,
What the Springes and Nature planted:
Leauelesse bowes there might you see,
All except faire Daphnes tree,
On their twigges no byrdes pearched,
Warmer couerts now[27] they searched:
And by Natures secret reason;
Framed their voyces to the season:
With their feeble tunes bewraying,[28]
How they greeued the springs decaying:
Frostie Winter thus had gloomed,
Each faire thing that sommer bloomed,
Fieldes were bare and trees vnclad,
Flowers withered, byrdes were sad:[29]
When I saw a shepheard fold,
Sheepe in Coate to shun the cold:
Himselfe sitting on the grasse,
That with frost withered was.
Sighing deepely thus gan say,
Loue is folly when a stray:
Like to loue no passion such,
For tis[30] madnesse if too much:
If too little, then dispaire:
If too high, he beates the ayre:
With bootlesse, if too low:
An Egle matcheth with a Crow.
Thence growes iarres:[31] thus I finde,
Loue is folly if vnkinde:
Yet do men most desire,
To be heated with this fire:
Whose flame is so pleasing hot,
That they burne, yet feele it not.
Yet hath loue another kinde,
Worse than these vnto the minde:
That is when a wantons eie,
Leades desire cleane[32] awrie.
And with the Bee doth reioyce,
Euery minute to change choyce,
Counting he were then in blisse,
If that ech faire fere[33] were his:
Highly thus is[34] loue disgraste
When the louer is vnchaste:
And would tast of fruit forbidden,
Cause the scape[35] is easily hidden.
Though such loue be sweet in brewing,
Bitter is the end insuing:
For the humor of loue he shameth,
And himselfe with lust defameth:
For a minutes pleasure gayning,
Fame and honour euer stayning.
Gazing thus so farre awry,
Last the chip falles in his eie,
Then it burnes that earst but heate him,
And his owne rod gins to beate him:
His choycest sweetes turnes to gall,
He findes lust is sins thrall:
That wanton women in their eyes,
Mens deceiuings do comprise.
That homage done to faire faces,
Doth dishonour other graces:
If lawlesse loue be such a sinne,
Curst is he that liues therein:
For the gaine of Venus game,
Is the downfall vnto shame:
Here he pausd and did stay,
Sighed and rose, and went away.

[22] agrees.
[23] *all,*] *all.* STC 12296.
[24] From *Philomela*, 1592.
[25] scanty.
[26] adorned with a "diaper" pattern, i.e., variegated.
[27] *now*] *none* STC 12296.
[28] revealing.
[29] *Sad:*] *had:* STC 12296.
[30] *tis*] *his* STC 12296.
[31] *iarres:*] *iarres* STC 12296: quarrels.
[32] *cleane*] *cleade* STC 12296.
[33] *fere*] *fall* STC 12296: companion.
[34] *is*] *in* STC 12296.
[35] transgression.

Deceiuing world, that with alluring toyes,[36]
Hast made my life the subiect of thy scorne:
And scornest now to lend thy fading ioyes,
To length my life, whom friends haue left forlorne.
How well are they that die ere they be borne,
And neuer see thy sleights,[37] which few men shun,
Till vnawares they helplesse are vndone.

Oft haue I sung of Loue, and of his fire,
And now I finde that Poet was aduizde;
Which made full feasts increasers of desire,
And proues weake loue was with the poore despizde.
For when the life with foode is not suffizde,
What thoughts of Loue, what motion of delight;
What pleasance can proceede from such a wight?[38]

Witnesse my want, the murderer of my wit,
My rauisht sense of woonted furie reft;
Wants such conceit, as should in Poems fit
Set downe the sorrow wherein I am left:
But therefore haue high heauens their gifts bereft:
Because so long they lent them mee to vse,
And I so long their bountie did abuse.

O that a yeare were graunted me to liue,
And for that yeare my former wits restorde:
What rules of life, what counsell would I giue?
How should my sinne with sorrow be deplorde?
But I must die of euery man abhorde.
Time loosely spent will not againe be wonne,
My time is loosely spent, and I vndone.

---

[36] From *Greenes Groats-worth of witte,* 1592, STC 12245, Folger Library.

[37] tricks.

[38] creature.

Sir John Harington

[c. 1561–1612]

SIR JOHN HARINGTON, a godson of Queen Elizabeth, was educated at Eton, Cambridge, and Lincoln's Inn. His restless energy and versatility are typical of many Elizabethans; he was scholar, courtier, country gentleman, an "undertaker" for the colonizing of Munster, soldier in Ireland, inventor, collector of contemporary plays, and facile writer of both verse and prose. In his own day he was best known as an epigrammatist (though his epigrams were not printed until after his death) and as the translator of Ariosto's *Orlando Furioso.*

Harington's translation appeared in 1591 and was reprinted in 1607 and 1634. He evidently delighted in Ariosto's heroic, satirical, flamboyant poem, with its characters ranging from archangels to flying horses and its scene from the moon to China and the Hebrides. He preserves the *ottava rima*—and much of the vigor and spirit—of the original.

There is no modern reprint of Harington's translation. For Harington's life and work see Sir Walter Raleigh, "Sir John Harington," *The New Review*, xv (1896), reprinted in *Some Authors*, 1923; *The Letters and Epigrams of Sir John Harington*, ed. N. E. McClure, 1930; Townsend Rich, *Harington and Ariosto*, 1940.

From ORLANDO FURIOSO, BOOK XXXIV[1]

49

Soone after he[2] a christall streame espying,
From foote to head he washt himselfe therein,
Then vp he gets him on his courser flying,
And of the ayre he more and more doth win,
Affecting[3] heau'n, all earthly thoughts defying:
As fishes cut the liquid streame with fin,
So cutteth he the ayre and doth not stop,
Till he was come vnto that mountaines top.

[1] From *Orlando Furioso in English heroical verse,* 1607, STC 747, Folger Library. Orlando, one of Charlemagne's knights, has been punished with insanity because of his love for Angelica. Astolfo, an English duke, is carried to Paradise and to the Moon, where he recovers Orlando's lost wits.

[2] Astolfo.

[3] aspiring to.

50

This hill nigh toucht the circle of the Moone,[4]
The top was all a fruitfull pleasant feeld,
And light at night, as ours is here at noone,
The sweetest place that euer man beheeld;
(There would I dwell if God gaue me my boone)
The soyle thereof most fragrant flowres did yeeld,
Like Rubies, Gold, Pearles, Saphyrs, Topas stones,
Crisolits, Diamonds, Iacints for the nones.[5]

51

The trees that there did grow were euer greene,
The fruits that thereon grew were neuer fading,
The sundry colourd birds did sit betweene,
And sing most sweet, the fruitfull boughs them shading:
The riuers cleare as crystall to be seene,
The fragrant smell, the sense and soule inuading,
With ayre so temperate and so delightsome,
As all the place beside was cleare and lightsome.

52

Amid the plaine a pallace passing faire
There stood, aboue conceit[6] of mortall men,
Built of great height into the clearest aire,
And was in circuit twentie mile and ten,
To this faire place the Duke[7] did straight repaire,
And vewing all that goodly country then,
He thought this world, compared with that pallace,
A dunghill vile, or prison voyd of sollace.

53

But when as nearer to the place he came,
He was amazed at the wondrous sight,
The wall was all one precious stone, the same,
And then[8] the carbuncle more sanguine bright;
O workman rare, o most stupendious frame,
What *Dedalus*[9] of this had ouersight?
Peace ye that wont to praise the wonders seau'n
Those earthly kings made, this the King of heau'n.

54

Now while the Duke his eyes with wonder fed,
Behold a faire old man in th'entrie stood,
Whose gowne was white, but yet his iacket red,

---

[4] Marginal note: *The description of Paradise.*
[5] nonce, occasion.
[6] thought, imagination.
[7] Astolfo.
[8] than.
[9] Daedalus, who in Greek myth built the labyrinth for Minos, king of Crete.

The tone[10] as snow, the tother lokt as blood,
His beard was long and white, so was his head,
His countnance was so graue, his grace so good,
A man thereby might at first sight suspect,
He was a Saint, and one of Gods elect.

55

He comming to the Duke with chearfull face,
Who now alighted was for reu'rence sake,
Bold Baron (said the Saint) by speciall grace,
That sufferd wast this voyage strange to make,
And to arriue at this most blessed place,
Not knowing why thou didst this iourny take,
Yet know that not without the will celestiall,
Thou commest here to Paradise terrestiall.

56

The cause you come a iourney of such length,
Is here of me to learne what must be done,
That *Charles*[11] and holy Church may now at length
Be freed, that erst were welnigh ouerrunne,
Wherefore impute it not to thine owne strength,
Nor to thy courage, nor thy wit, my sonne,
For neither could thy horne[12] nor winged steed,
Without Gods helpe stand thee in any steed.[13]

57

But at more leisure hereof we will reason,
And more at large I mind with you to speake,
Now with some meate refresh you, as is reason,
Lest fasting long may make your stomack weake;
Our fruits (said he) be neuer out of season:
The Duke reioyced much, and maruELD eke,
Then chiefe when by his speeches and his cote,
He knew twas he that the fourth Gospell wrote.

58

That holy *Iohn* whom Christ did hold so deare,
That others thought he death should neuer see,
Though in the Gospell it appeares not cleare,
But thus he said, What if it pleased me,
O *Peter,* that thy fellow tarry here,
Vntill my comming, what is that to thee?[14]
So though our Sauiour not directly spake it,
Yet sure it was, so eu'ry one did take it.

---

[10] the one.
[11] Charlemagne.
[12] magic trumpet.
[13] be of any service to you.
[14] John xxi, 22. See Harington's comment at the end of Book xxxiv.

59

He here assumed[15] was in happie houre,
Whereas before *Enoch*[16] the Patriark was,
And where the Prophet[17] bides of mightie powre,
That in the firie coach did thither passe:
These three in that so happie sacred bowre,
In high felicitie their dayes did passe,
Where in such sort to stand they are allowd,
Till Christ returne vpon the burning clowd.

60

These saints him welcome to that sacred seate,
And to a stately lodging him they brought;
And for his horse likewise ordained meate,
And then the Duke himselfe by them was taught,
The daintie fruites of Paradise to eate,
So delicate in tast, as sure he thought
Our first two parents were to be excused,
That for such fruit obedience they refused.

61

Now when the Duke had nature satisfide,
With meate and drinke, and with his due repose,
(For there were lodgings faire, and all beside
That needfull for mans vse man can suppose)
He gets vp early in the morning tide,
What time with vs alow, the Sunne arose,
But ere that he from out his lodging moued,
Came that disciple whom our Sauiour loued.[18]

62

And by the hand the Duke abroade he led,
And said some things to him, I may not name,
But in the end (I thinke) my sonne he sed,
Although that you from France so lately came,
You little know how those in France haue sped,
There your *Orlando* quite is out of frame,[19]
For God his sinne most sharply now rewardeth,
Who most doth punish whom he most regardeth.

63

Know that the champion your *Orlando,* whom
God so great strength and so great courage gaue,
And so rare grace, that from his mothers wome,
By force of steele his skin no hurt might haue,

---

[15] taken into Paradise.
[16] Genesis v, 21–24; Hebrews xi, 5.
[17] Elijah; II Kings ii, 11.
[18] St. John.
[19] out of order, insane.

To th'end that he might fight for his owne home,
And those that hold the Christian faith to saue;
As *Sampson* erst enabled was to stand,
Against Philistins for the Hebrew land.

64

This your *Orlando* hath bin so vngrate,
For so great grace receau'd, vnto his maker,
That when his country was in weakest state,
And needed succor most, he did forsake her
For loue (O wofull loue that breeds Gods hate)
To woo a Pagan wench, with mind to take her,
And to such sinne this loue did him intise,
He would haue kild his kinsman once or twice.

65

For this same cause doth mightie God permit
Him mad to runne, with belly bare and breast,
And so to daze his reason and his wit,
He knowes not others, and himselfe knowes least:
So in times past our Lord did deeme it fit,
To turne the king of Babel[20] to a beast,
In which estate he seu'n whole yeares did passe,
And like an oxe did feed on hay and grasse.

66

But for the Palladins[21] offence is not
So great as was the King of Babels crime,
The mightie Lord of mercie doth allot
Vnto his punishment a shorter time,
Twelue weeks in all he must remaine a sot,[22]
And for this cause you sufferd were to clime
To this high place, that here you may be tought
How to his wits *Orlando* may be brought.

67

Here you shall learne to worke the feate I warrant,
But yet before you can be fully sped,[23]
Of this your great, but not forethought on arrant,
You must with me a more strange way be led,
Vp to the Planet,[24] that of all starrs errant[25]
Is nearest vs, when she comes ouer head,
Then will I bring you where the medcine lies,
That you must haue to make *Orlando* wise.

---

[20] Nebuchadnezzar, king of Babylon; Daniel iv, 25, 33; v, 21.
[21] Orlando's.
[22] madman.
[23] successful.
[24] Marginal note: *The Moone the Lowest Planet*.
[25] moving.

68

Thus all that day they spent in diuers talke,
With solace great, as neuer wanteth there,
But when the Sunne began this earth to balke,[26]
And passe into the tother hemispheare,
Then they prepard to fetch a further walke,
And straight the firie charret that did beare
Elias,[27] when he vp to heau'n was carrid,
Was ready in a trice, and for them tarrid.

69

Foure horses fierce, as red as flaming fire,
Th'Apostle doth into the charret set,
Which when he framed[28] had to his desire,
Astolfo in the carre by him he set,
Then vp they went, and still ascending hire,
Aboue the firie region they did get,
Whose nature so th'Apostle then did turne,
That though they went through fire, they did not burne.

70

I say although the fire were wondrous hot,
Yet in their passage they no heate did feele,
So that it burnd them, nor offends them not;
Thence to the Moon he guides the running wheele,
The Moone was like a glasse all voyd of spot,
Or like a peece of purely burnisht steele,
And lookt, although to vs it seemd so small,
Welnigh as big as earth and sea and all.

71

Here had *Astolfo* cause of double wonder,
One, that that region seemeth there so wide,
That vnto vs that are so farre asunder,
Seems but a little circle, and beside,
That to behold the ground that him lay vnder,
A man had need to haue bin sharply eide,
And bend his browes, and mark eu'n all they might,
It seemd so small, now chiefly wanting light.

72

Twere infinite to tell what wondrous things
He saw, that passed ours not few degrees,
What towns, what hils, what riuers and what springs,
What dales, what pallaces, what goodly trees;
But to be short, at last his guide him brings,

26 leave.
27 Elijah.
28 arranged.

Vnto a goodly valley, where he sees
A mightie masse of things strangely confused,
Things that on earth were lost, or were abused.[29]

73

A store-house strange, that what on earth is lost,
By fault, by time, by fortune, there is found,
And like a merchandize is there ingrost,
In stranger sort then I can well expound;
Nor speake I sole of wealth, or things of cost,
In which blind fortunes powre doth most abound,
But eu'n of things quite out of fortunes powre,
Which wilfully we wast each day and houre.

74

The precious time that fooles mis-spend in play,
The vaine attempts that neuer take effect,
The vowes that sinners make, and neuer pay,
The counsels wise that carelesse men neglect,
The fond[30] desires that leade vs oft astray,
The praises that with pride the heart infect,
And all we loose with folly and mis-spending,
May there be found vnto this place ascending.

75

Now as *Astolfo* by those regions past,
He asked many questions of his guide,
And as he on tone side his eye did cast,
A wondrous hill of bladders he espide;
And he was told they had bin in time past,
The pompous crownes and scepters full of pride,
Of monarks of Assiria, and of Greece,
Of which now scantly[31] there is left a peece.

76

He saw great store of baited hookes with gold,
And those were gifts that foolish men prefard,[32]
To giue to Princes couetous and old,
With fondest hope of future vaine reward;
Then were there ropes all in sweet garlands rold,
And those were all false flatteries he hard,
Then heard he crickets songs like to the verses,
The feruant in his masters praise reherses.

---

[29] Marginal note: *This fiction is agreeing with an English prouerb we vse, that mens wits are beyond the Moone, and they haue layd vp things in the circle of the Moone.*

[30] foolish.

[31] scarcely.

[32] preferred, offered.

77

There did he see fond loues, that men pursew,
To looke like golden giues[33] with stones all set,
Then things like Eagles talents[34] he did vew,
Those offices that fauorites do get:
Then saw he bellows large that much wind blew,
Large promises that Lords make, and forget,
Vnto their Ganimeds[35] in flowre of youth,
But after nought but beggery ensewth.

78

He saw great Cities seated in faire places,
That ouerthrowne quite topsie turuie stood,
He askt and learnd, the cause of their defaces
Was treason, that doth neuer turne to good:
He saw fowle serpents, with faire womens faces,
Of coyners[36] and of thieues the cursed brood,
He saw fine glasses, all in peeces broken,
Of seruice lost in court, a wofull token.

79

Of mingled broth he saw a mightie masse,
That to no vse, all spilt on ground did lye,
He askt his teacher, and he heard it was,
The frutlesse almes that men giue when they dye:
Then by a faire greene mountaine he did passe,
That once smelt sweet, but now it stinks perdye,[37]
This was that gift (be't said without offence)
That *Constantin* gaue *Siluester* long since.[38]

80

Of birdlymd rodds,[39] he saw no little store,
And these (O Ladyes fayre) your bewties be,
I do omit ten thousand things and more
Like vnto these, that there the Duke did see:
For all that here is lost, there euermore
Is kept, and thither in a trise doth flee,
Howbeit more nor lesse there was no folly,
For still that here with vs remaineth wholly.

81

He saw some of his owne lost time and deeds,
But yet he knew them not to be his owne,

33 gyves, fetters.
34 talons.
35 Ganymedes, young attendants.
36 counterfeiters.
37 indeed, truly.
38 Marginal note: *By that gift is vnderstood the Citie of Rome, which Constantin gaue Pope Siluester, which he saith now stinketh because of their sinnes.*
39 Rods covered with a sticky substance to catch birds.

They seemd to him disguisd in so strange weeds,[40]
Till his instructer made them better knowne:
But last, the thing which no man thinks he needs,
Yet each man needeth most, to him was showne,
By name mans wit, which here we leese[41] so fast,
As that one substance, all the other past.

82

It seemd to be a body moyst and soft,
And apt to mount by eu'ry exhalation,
And when it hither mounted was aloft,
It there was kept in pots of such a fashion,
As we call Iarrs, where oyle is kept in oft:
The Duke beheld with no small admiration,[42]
The Iarrs of wit, amongst which one had writ,
Vpon the side thereof, *Orlandos* wit.

83

This vessell bigger was then all the rest,
And eu'ry vessell had ingrau'n with art,
His name, that erst[43] the wit therein possest:
There of his owne the Duke did finde a part,
And much he musd and much himselfe he blest,
To see some names of men of great desart,
That thinke they haue great store of wit, and bost it,
And here it playne appeard they quite had lost it.

84

Some loose their wit with loue, some with ambition,
Some running to the sea, great wealth to get,
Some following Lords, and men of high condition,
And some in fayre iewells rich and costly set:
One hath desire to proue a rare Magicion,
And some with Poetrie their wit forget,
Another thinks to be an Alcumist,
Till all be spent, and he his number mist.

85

Astolfo takes his owne before he goes,
For so th'Euangelist did him permit;
He set the vessels mouth but to his nose,
And to his[44] place, he snuft vp all his wit:
Long after wise he liu'd as *Turpin*[45] shows,

[40] clothing.
[41] lose.
[42] wonder.
[43] formerly.
[44] its.
[45] Some earlier versions of the Orlando stories were attributed to Turpin, whom Charlemagne made archbishop of Rheims in 773.

Vntill one fault he after did commit,
By name the loue of one fayre Northerne lasse,[46]
Sent vp his wit vnto the place it was.

86

The vessell where *Orlandos* wit was closed,
Astolfo tooke, and thence with him did beare,
It was far heauier then he had supposed,
So great a quantitie of wit was theare;
But yet ere backe their iourny they disposed,[47]
The holy Prophet brought *Astolfo,* wheare
A pallace (seldome seene by mortall man)
Was plast, by which a thicke darke riuer ran.

87

Each roome therein was full of diuers fleesis,
Of woll, of lint, of silke, or else of cotten,
An aged women spun the diuers peecis,
Whose looke and hew, did shew her old and rotten:
Not much vnlike vnto that labour, this is,
By which in Sommer, new made silke is gotten,
Where from the silke worme his fine garment taking
They reaue[48] him of the clothes, of his owne making.

88

For first in one large roome a woman span
Threds infinite, of diuers stuffe and hew;
Another doth with all the speed she can,
With other stuffe, the distaues still renew;
The third in feature like, and pale and wan,
Doth seuer faire from foule, and old from new:
Now who be these? the Duke demands his guide.
These be the fatall sisters, he replide;

89

The Parcees[49] that the thred of life do spin,
To mortall men, hence death and nature know
When life must end, and when it must begin:
Now, she that doth deuide them, and bestow
The course from finer, and the thicke from thin,
To that end works, that those that finest grow,
For ornaments in Paradise may dwell,
The course are curst to be consum'd in hell.

---

[46] Marginal note: *This is written in the fourth booke of the fiue Cantos, added to Ariosto, which many thinke were none of his doing, and are verie vnperfect.*

[47] arranged.

[48] rob.

[49] Parcae, the Fates.

90

The Duke did further in the place behold,
That when the threds were spent that had bin spun,
Their names in brasse, in siluer, or in gold,
Were wrote, and so into great heaps were donn;
From which a man that seemed wondrous old,[50]
With whole loads of those names away did run,
And turn'd againe as fast, the way he went,
Nor neuer wearie was, nor euer spent.

91

This aged man did hold his pace so swift,
As though to runne, he onely had bin borne,
Or had it giu'n him as a speciall gift;
And in the lappet of his cloke were borne,
The names of men, with which he made such shift:
But now a while I craue to be forborne,
For in the booke ensewing shalbe showed,
How this old sire his cariage[51] ill bestowed.

[NOTES FOLLOWING BOOK XXXIV]

S.Iohn liued till he was an hundred yeare old, and then made himselfe a tombe, and entred thereinto aliue in presence of many, and on the sodaine, a light shone all about the place, and tooke the tombe for the time, quite from their sights: but the light being gone, the coffin was found empty, and the body of that Saint was no more seene vpon the earth. Whereupon it was certainly thought that he was taken vp into heauen or Paradise, as *Enoch* and *Elias* were. Though this of *S.Iohn* be not recorded in the Scripture (nor no more is the assumption of the blessed virgin) and consequently, no man is bound to beleeue it, as an article of our Creed: Yet for mine owne opinion, I thinke it may be verie true, and I would in such cases beleeue a great deale more then I need, rather then any thing lesse then I ought; for the tone (if it be a sinne) is surely pardonable, but the other doubtles is verye damnable. But I will briefly note the Allegorie that is meant hereby.

First, whereas *Astolfo* washeth himselfe in a christall well of cleare water, before he can fly vp to Paradise, it signifieth, that after a man shall by remorse, and deuout consideration, weigh and behold the filthinesse of his sinne, he must then wash himselfe with the cleare spring water of prayer and repentance; and then and not before, he may mount to Paradise: which may here be vnderstood the comfortable peace of conscience, the onely true Paradise of this world. And whereas *Astolfo* commeth to *S.Iohn* (whose name signifieth grace) to receiue by his helpe *Orlandos* lost wits, for so it is set downe that that was the secret cause why he was guided thither, though vnawares to himselfe: thereby it is to be vnderstood, that no hope nor means is left for any man that hath lost his wit, with following the vanities and pleasures of this world (as diuers carelesse christians do, in forgetting and omitting their duties to God, which is the verie highest point of follie,) I say there is no meane for them to recouer their wit againe, but onely by the helpe of this *S.Iohn,* that is this, grace of God, which can miraculously restore it againe.

50 Time.

51 conduct.

Sonnet Sequences

THE PETRARCHAN sonnet, brought to England by Wyatt and Surrey, had few imitators during the twenty years following the publication of *Tottel's Miscellany*. English poets applied the word "sonnet," in its etymological meaning of "a little song," to almost any short lyric. Gascoigne, however, not only used the word accurately but also wrote "true" sonnets. In *Certayne Notes of Instruction*, 1575, he wrote: "Some thinke that all Poemes (being short) may be called Sonets, . . . but yet I can beste allowe to call those Sonnets whiche are of fouretene lynes, euery line conteyning tenne syllables. The firste twelue do ryme in staues of foure lines by crosse meetre, and the last two ryming togither do conclude the whole." In his *A Hundreth Sundrie Flowers*, 1573, and in his *Posies*, 1575, he included thirty "true" sonnets, seven of them forming a sequence, linked together by the repetition of the last line of one as the first line of the next. Despite Gascoigne's interest few sonnets were written during the 1570's and 1580's. Spenser experimented with the sonnet as early as 1569. In that year appeared *The Theater for Worldlings*, for which he translated several sonnets of du Bellay and Petrarch, the latter from the French of Marot; and although some of Spenser's versions have only twelve lines and others are in blank verse, he rewrote them as true sonnets and included them in his *Complaints*, 1591. The first long sequence with love as theme was Thomas Watson's *Hecatompathia, or Passionate Century of Love*, 1582, but although Watson had gone to Petrarch for models and matter, most of his poems are of eighteen lines. Sidney's sonnets, some of which he probably wrote before 1580, are the first true sonnet sequence in English. Greville probably wrote some of his sonnets at about this time. Two anonymous sonnets were included in Byrd's *Psalms, Sonnets, and Songs*, 1588, and six in his *Songs of Sundry Natures*, 1589. Spenser wrote several sonnets as dedicatory poems for *The Faerie Queene*, 1590.

The publication of Sidney's *Astrophel and Stella*, 1591, was followed by a flood of sonnets and sonnet sequences. In 1592 came Daniel's *Delia* and Constable's *Diana*; in 1593 Lodge's *Phillis*, Barnes's *Parthenophil and Parthenophe*, Fletcher's *Licia*, Watson's *The Tears of Fancy*, and Lok's *Sundry Christian Passions;* in 1594 Drayton's *Idea's Mirror;* in 1595 Spenser's *Amoretti* and Barnes's *Divine Century of Spiritual Sonnets;* in 1596 Griffin's *Fidessa*. It is probable that

Shakespeare wrote most of his sonnets during these years. More than twenty sonnet sequences written during this period survive.

Most of the sequences are amatory, either—like Sidney's and Spenser's—a series telling a more or less connected love story, or a loosely connected series of sonnets praising a lady, real or imaginary. The model was Petrarch's sonnets to Laura or the sonnets of Petrarch's Italian and French imitators. The lady of the conventional sonnet is cruel, golden-haired, ruby-lipped, her cheeks lilies and roses, her teeth pearls, her voice music, her steps lighter than air. The poet hopes and despairs, freezes and burns, invokes sleep, and promises that his verses will bring eternity of fame to the lady. Most of the sonnet writers, despite their avowal of independence and contempt for Petrarchan conventions, accepted these conventions and sought to surpass the ingenuity and extravagance of their models.

The vogue of the amatory sonnet did not long escape satirical attack. It was ridiculed by the epigrammatists and the writers of formal satire; Sir John Davies wrote sonnets that parodied the Petrarchan conventions; Shakespeare's Sonnet 130 mocks the conventional exaggerations. The fashion soon ran its course, and after 1600 few overingenious amatory sonnets were written.

Not all Elizabethan sonnets are in the Petrarchan tradition. Many are complimentary or dedicatory. George Chapman wrote sonnets "to his mistress, Philosophy," and Constable, Lok, Barnes, and many others wrote sonnets—some of them in sequences—on devotional and religious themes.

The best sonnet sequences are those by Sidney, Daniel, Drayton, Spenser, and Shakespeare, but the best—and the most representative—sonnets from the sequences by Constable, Fletcher, Lok, Barnes, and Griffin deserve attention. Elsewhere in this book are sonnets from the sequences by Sidney, Greville, Daniel, Lodge, Barnfield, Spenser, and Shakespeare.

Henry Constable (1562–1613), the son of Sir Robert Constable of Newark, was educated at Cambridge, as a young man became a Catholic, and spent much of his life abroad. In 1592 he published *Diana. The Praises of his Mistress, in certaine sweete Sonnets*, a sequence of twenty-three sonnets. These he reissued in 1594, "augmented with diuers Quatorzains of honorable and lerned personages." The second sequence contains seventy-six sonnets, including eight by Sir Philip Sidney. In 1595 four sonnets by Constable in praise of Sidney appeared in the first edition of *An Apology for Poetry*. Four pastoral poems signed "H. C." in *England's Helicon*, 1600, though sometimes attributed to Constable, are almost certainly the work of Henry Chettle. His religious sonnets were first published in 1815. In his own day Constable was highly regarded as a poet, and was praised by Jonson, Harington, and others.

Giles Fletcher (c. 1549–1611) was the father of the poets Phineas and Giles, and the uncle of the dramatist John Fletcher. Educated at Eton and at King's College, Cambridge, where he proceeded B.A. in 1569, M.A. in 1573, and LL.D.

in 1581, he went on diplomatic missions to Scotland and Russia. In 1593 he published *Licia*, a sequence of fifty-two sonnets, followed by several pastoral poems and "The Rising to the Crown of Richard the third," a poem in the manner of *A Mirror for Magistrates*. Fletcher's sonnets are graceful literary exercises.

Henry Lok or Locke (c. 1553–c. 1608) wrote little but religious verse. His *Sundry Christian Passions*, 1593, contained "a hundred sonnets of meditation, humiliation, and prayer" followed by "a hundred sonnets of comfort, joy, and thanksgiving." These were reprinted in *Ecclesiates; abridged and dilated in English poesie*, 1597, a volume that also included verse translations of some Psalms, more than a hundred "affectionate sonnets of a feeling conscience," twenty-two sonnets entitled "peculiar prayers," and a number of sonnets addressed to important people. His verse is pious, prosaic, and technically skillful.

Michael Drayton (1563–1631) is perhaps the most representative of the Elizabethan poets, and his work reflects the changing fashions in the poetry of four decades. Only his sonnet sequence, however, is within the scope of this book. Drayton probably spent several years as a page in the house of Sir Henry Goodere of Polesworth, whose daughter Anne is the "Idea" of his pastorals and sonnets. The sonnets, which first appeared in *Idea's Mirror*, were often reprinted, with omissions and additions, and many alterations, the final revision being that of 1619. Drayton's sonnets, fresh and lively, are among the best of the period.

Barnabe Barnes (1571–1609), son of Richard Barnes, in turn Bishop of Nottingham, Carlisle, and Durham, attended Brasenose College but took no degree. In 1593 he published *Parthenophil and Parthenophe*, a collection that included not only sonnets but madrigals, sestines, elegies, and other poems in various meters. In 1595 appeared his *Divine Century of Spiritual Sonnets*. His poetry as a whole is notable for energy, extravagant language, and flashes of rare beauty.

Of Bartholomew Griffin's life little is known. His one book, *Fidessa*, 1596, a sequence of sixty-two sonnets which imitate English rather than foreign models, is fairly representative of the minor sonnet sequences of the 1590's.

The most useful modern editions of Elizabethan sonnet sequences are *Elizabethan Sonnets*, ed. Sidney Lee, 2 vols., 1904, and *Elizabethan Sonnet-Cycles*, ed. M. F. Crow, 4 vols., 1896–1898. Constable's *Spiritual Sonnets* and Barnes's *Divine Century of Spiritual Sonnets* are included in *Heliconia*, ed. Thomas Park, 3 vols., 1815. For criticism see J. G. Scott, *Les sonnets élisabéthains*, Paris, 1929, and L. C. John, *The Elizabethan Sonnet Sequences*, 1938. The best account of Constable is in L. I. Guiney, *Recusant Poets*, 1939. The standard edition of Drayton is *The Works of Michael Drayton*, ed. J. W. Hebel, 5 vols., 1931–1941 (completed by K. Tillotson and B. H. Newdigate). For biography and criticism see Oliver Elton, *Michael Drayton, a Critical Study*, 1905; A. H. Bullen, "Michael Drayton," *Elizabethans*, 1924; F. L. Lucas, "Michael Drayton," *Authors Dead and Living*, 1926; B. H. Newdigate, *Michael Drayton and His Circle*, 1941. For biography of Barnes see Mark Eccles, "Barnabe Barnes," in C. J. Sisson, *Thomas Lodge and Other Elizabethans*, 1933.

From DIANA[1]

Mine eye with all the deadly sinnes is fraught,[2]
First *proud,* sith it presum'd to looke so hie:
A watchman being made, stoode gazing by,
And *idle,* tooke no heede till I was caught:
And *enuious,* beares enuie that by thought
Should in his absence be to her so nie:
To kill my hart, mine eye let in her eye,
And so consent gaue to a *murther* wrought:
And *couetous,* it neuer would remoue
From her faire haire, gold so doth please his sight:
Vnchast, a baude between my hart and loue:
A *glutton* eye, with teares drunke euery night.
These sinnes procured haue a Goddesse ire:
Wherfore my hart is damn'd in Loues sweet fire.

My Ladies presence makes the Roses red,
Because to see her lips, they blush for shame:
The Lyllies leaues (for enuie) pale became,
And her white hands in them this enuie bred.
The Marigold the leaues abroad doth spred,
Because the sunnes, and her power is the same:
The Violet of purple cullour came,
Di'd in the blood shee made by hart to shed.
In briefe, all flowers from her their vertue take;
From her sweet breath, their sweet smels do proceede:
The liuing heate which her eye beames doth make,
Warmeth the ground, and quickeneth the seede:
The raine wherewith shee watereth the flowers,
Falls from mine eyes, which she dissolues in showers.

Faire Sunne, if you wold haue me praise your light,
When night approcheth, wherfore doe you flie?
Time is so short, Beauties so many be,
As I haue neede to see them day and night:
That by continuall view, my verses might
Tell all the beames of your diuinitie;
Which praise to you, and ioy should be to mee,
You liuing by my verse, I by your sight.
I by your sight, and not you by my verse:
Neede mortall skill immortall praise rehearse?
No, no, though eyes were blind, and verse were dumb,[3]
Your beautie shold be seene, and your fame known.
For by the winde which from my sighes doe come,
Your praises round about the world is blowne.

---

[1] From Henry Constable, *Diana, or, the excellent conceitful Sonnets of H.C.,* 1594, STC 5638, Huntington Library.

[2] laden, filled.

[3] *dumb,* STC 5637]; *dumb.* STC 5638.

Needes must I leaue, and yet needes must I loue,
In vaine my wit doth tell in verse my woe,
Dispayre in me disdaine in thee dooth shoe,
How by my wit I doe my folly proue:
All this my hart from loue can neuer moue.
Loue is not in my hart, no Lady no,
My hart is loue it selfe, till I forgoe
My hart, I neuer can my loue remoue.
How can I then leaue loue? I doe intend
Not to craue grace, but yet to wish it still.
Not to prayse thee, but beauty to commend,
And so by beauties prayse, prayse thee I will.
For as my hart is loue, loue not in mee,
So beauty thou, beauty is not in thee.

When your perfections to my thoughts appeare,
They say among themselues, O happy wee,
Which euer shall so rare an obiect see:
But happy hart, if thoughts lesse happy were,
For their delights haue cost my hart full dere,
In whom of loue a thousand causes be,
And each cause breeds a thousand loues in me,
And each loue more then thousand harts can beare.[4]
How can my hart so many loues then hold,
Which yet (by heapes) increase from day to day?
But like a shyp that's ouercharg'd with gold,
Must either sinke, or hurle the gold away.
But hurle not loue: Thou canst not feeble hart,
In thine owne blood, thou therefore drowned art.

Ready to seek out death, in my disgrace
My Mistres gan to smooth her gathered browes,
Whereby I am repriued for a space:
O Hope and Feare, who halfe your torments knowes?
It is some mercie in a black-mouth'd Iudge,
To haste his prysoners end, if he must die.
Deere, if all other fauour you shall grudge,
Doe speedie execution with your eye.
With one sole looke, you leaue in me no soule,
Count it a losse to lose a faithfull slaue;
Would God that I might heare my last bell toule,
So in your bosome I might dig my graue.
Doubtfull delay is worse then any feuer,
Or helpe me soone, or cast me off for euer.

---

[4] *beare.* STC 5637]; *beare,* STC 5638.

Hope, like the *Hyenna* comming to be old,
Alters his shape, is turn'd into dispaire:
Pitty my hoarie hopes, maid of cleere mould.
Thinke not that frownes can euer make thee faire.
What harme is it to kisse, to laugh, to play?
Beauties no blosome if it be not vs'd,[5]
Sweet daliance keepeth wrinkles long away,
Repentance followes them that haue refus'd.
To bring you to the knowledge of your good,
I seeke, I sue, O try and then beleeue,
Each Image can be chast thats caru'd of wood:
You show you liue when men you doe releeue.
  Iron with wearing shines, rust wasteth treasure,
  On earth but loue there is no other pleasure.

If euer sorrow spoke from soule that loues,
As speakes a spirit in a man possest,
In mee her spirit speakes, my soule it moues,
Whose sigh-swolne words breed whirlwinds in my brest.
Or like the eccho of a passing bell,
Which sounding on the water, seemes to howle:
So rings my hart a feareful heauie knell,
And keepes all night in consort with the Owle.
My cheekes with a thin Ice of teares is clad,
Mine eyes like morning starres are bleer'd and red:
What resteth[6] then but I be raging mad,
To see that shee, (my cares cheefe conduit head)
  When all streames els help quench my burning hart,
  Shuts vp her springs, and will no grace impart.

Deere to my soule, then leaue me not forsaken,
Flie not, my hart within thy bosome sleepeth:
Euen from my selfe and sence I haue betaken,
Mee vnto thee, for whom my spirit weepeth.
And on the shoare of that salt tearie sea,
Couch'd in a bed of vnseene seeming pleasure,
Where, in imaginarie thoughts thy faire selfe lay,
But being wakt, robd of my liues best treasure.
I call the heauens, ayre, earth, and seas, to heare
My loue, my trueth, and black disdaind estate:
Beating the rocks with bellowings of dispaire,
Which stil with plaints my words reuerberate.
  Sighing, alas, what shall become of me?
  Whilst Eccho cryes, what shal become of me.

---

[5] *vs'd,*] *vs'd* STC 5638.

[6] remains.

Whilst Eccho cryes, what shall become of mee,
And desolate my desolations pitty,[7]
Thou in thy beauties charrack[8] sitt'st to see
My tragick down-fall, and my funerall ditty.
No Tymbrell, but my hart thou play'st vpon,
Whose strings are stretch'd vnto the hiest key,
The dyapazon loue, loue is the vnison,
In loue, my life and labours waft away.
Onely regardlesse, to the world thou leau'st mee,
Whilst slaine hopes, turning from the feast of sorrow,
Vnto Dispaire (their King) which nere deceiues me,
Captiues my hart, whose blacke night hates the morrow,
  And hee, in ruth of my distressed cry,
  Plants mee a weeping starre within mine eye.

To liue in hell, and heauen to behold,
To welcome life, and die a liuing death,
To sweat with heate, and yet be freezing cold,
To graspe at starres, and lye the earth beneath;
To tread a Maze that neuer shall haue end,
To burne in sighes, and starue in daily teares,
To clime a hill, and neuer to discend,
Gyants to kill, and quake at childish feares;
To pyne for foode, and watch th'Hesperian[9] tree,
To thirst for drinke, and Nectar still to draw,
To liue accurst, whom men hold blest to bee,
And weepe those wrongs which neuer creature saw,
  If this be loue, if loue in these be founded,
  My hart is loue, for these in it are grounded.

From LICIA[10]

Sadde all alone, not long I musing satte,
But that my thoughtes compell'd me to aspire,
A Laurell garland in my hande I gatte:
So the Muses I approch'd the nyer.
My sute was this, a Poet to become,
To drinke with them, and from the heavens be fedde:
Phoebus denyed, and sware there was no roome,
Such to be Poets as fonde fancie ledde:
With that I mourn'd; and sat me downe to weepe,
Venus she smil'd, and smyling to me saide,
Come drinke with me, and sitt thee still and sleepe:
This voyce I heard: and Venus I obayde.
  That poyson (sweete), hath done me all this wrong,
  For nowe of love, must needes be all my song.

[7] *pitty,*] *pitty.* STC 5638.
[8] carrack, armed merchant ship.
[9] *th'Hesperian*] *Thesperian* STC 5638.
[10] From Giles Fletcher, *Licia, or poemes of love, in honour of the admirable and singular vertues of his Lady,* 1593? STC 11055, Huntington Library.

First did I feare, when first my love began,
Possest in fittes, by watchfull jealousie,
I sought to keepe, what I by favour wanne,
And brookt no partner in my love to be.
But Tyrant sicknesse, fedde upon my love,
And spred his ensignes, dy'd with colour white,
Then was suspition, glad for to remoove:
And loving much did feare to loose her quite.
Erect (faire sweet) the collours thou didst weare,
Dislodge thy griefes, the shortners of content:
For now of lyfe, not love, is all my feare,
Least lyfe, and love be both together spent.
  Live but (faire love) and banish thy disease:
  And love (kind heart) both when, and whom thou please.

Seven are the lights, that wander in the skies,
And at these seven, I wonder in my love,
To see the Moone, how pale she doeth arise,
Standing amaz'd as though she durst not move:
So is my sweet, much paler than the snowe,
Constant her lookes, those lookes that cannot change,
Mercurie the next, a god sweet tong'd we know,
But her sweet voice, doth woonders speake more strange:
The rising Sunne doeth boast him of his pride,
And yet my love is farre more faire than he.
The warlike Mars, can weildles weapons[11] guide,
But yet that god, is farre more weake than she.
The lovelie Venus, seemeth to be faire,
But at her[12] best, my love is farre more bright.
Saturne for age, with groans doth dimme the aire,
Whereas my love, with smiles doth give it light.
  Gaze at her browes, where heaven ingrafted is:
  Then sigh, and sweare, there is no heaven but this.

I live (sweete love) whereas the gentle winde,
Murmures with sport, in midst of thickest bowes,
Where loving Wood-bine, doth the Harbour[13] binde,
And chirping birdes doe eccho foorth my vowes:
Where strongest elme, can scarce support the vine,
And sweetest flowres enameld have the ground,
Where Muses dwell, and yet hereat repine:
That on the earth so rare a place was found.
But windes delight, I wish to be content:
I praise the Wood-bine, but I take no joye:
I moane the birdes, that musicke thus have spent:
As for the rest, they breede but mine annoye.

[11] weapons that others cannot wield.

[12] Venus's.

[13] arbor.

Live thou (fayre Licia) in this place alone:
Then shall I joye, though all of these were gone.

In tyme the strong and statelie turrets fall,
In tyme the Rose, and silver Lillies die,
In tyme the Monarchs captives are and thrall,
In tyme the sea, and rivers are made drie:
The hardest flint, in tyme doth melt asunder,
Still living fame, in tyme doth fade away,
The mountaines proud, we see in tyme come under,
And earth for age, we see in tyme decay:
The sunne in tyme, forgets for to retire,
From out the east, where he was woont to rise,
The basest thoughtes, we see in time aspire,
And greedie minds, in tyme do wealth dispise,
Thus all (sweet faire) in tyme must have an end:
Except thy beautie, vertues, and thy friend.

Lyke Memnons rocke[14] toucht, with the rising Sunne,
Which yeelds a sownd, and ecchoes foorth a voice:
But when it's[15] drownde, in westerne seas is dunne,[16]
And drousie lyke, leaves off to make a noice.
So I (my love) inlightned with your shyne,
A Poets skill within my soule I shroud,
Not rude lyke that, which finer wittes declyne,
But such as Muses to the best allowde.
But when your figure, and your shape is gone,
I speechlesse am, lyke as I was before:
Or if I write, my verse is fill'd with moane,
And blurd with teares, by falling in such store.
Then muse not (Licia) if my Muse be slacke,
For when I wrote, I did thy beautie lacke.

From SUNDRY CHRISTIAN PASSIONS[17]

It is not Lord the sound of many words,
The bowed knee or abstinence of man,
The filed phrase that eloquence affords,
Or Poets pen that heauens do pearce, or can:
By heauie cheere,[18] of colour pale and wan,
By pined[19] bodie of the Pharisay,
A mortall eye repentance oft doth scan,

---

14 A colossal statue near Thebes which was believed to produce musical sounds when touched by the rays of the rising sun.

15 *it's*] *its'* STC 11055.

16 done; some editors read *dumb*.

17 From Henry Lok, *Ecclesiates; abridged and dilated in English poesie: whereunto are annexed sundrie sonets of christian passions*, 1597, STC 16696, New York Public Library; first printed in *Sundry christian passions contained in two hundred sonnets*, 1593, STC 16697.

18 countenance.

19 starved.

Whose iudgment doth on outward shadows stay,
But thou (O God) doest hearts intent bewray,[20]
For from thy sight Lord nothing is concealed.[21]
Thou formdst the frame fro out the verie clay,
To thee the thoughts of hearts are all reueald,
To thee therefore with hart and mind prostrate,
With teares I thus deplore my sinfull state.

Words may well want,[22] both inke and paper faile,
Wits may grow dull, and will may weary grow,
And worlds affaires may make my pen more slow,
But yet my heart and courage shall not quaile,
Though cares and troubles do my peace assaile,
And driue me to delay thy prayse awhile,
Yet all the world shall not from thoughts exile,
Thy mercies Lord by which my plaints preuaile.
And though the world with face should gratefull smile,
And me her pedlers packe of pleasures show,
No heartie loue on her I would bestow,
Because I know she seekes me to beguile,
Ne will defile my happie peace of mind,
For all the solace I in earth may find.

From IDEA'S MIRROR[23]

To the deere chyld of the Muses, and his euer kind Mecaenas, Master Anthony Cooke, Esquire[24]

Vouchsafe to grace these rude vnpolish'd rymes,
Which long (deer friend) have slept in sable night,
And come abroad now in these glorious tymes,
Can hardly brooke the purenes of the light.

But sith you see their desteny is such,
That in the world theyr fortune they must try,
Perhaps they better shall abide the tuch,
Wearing your name theyr gracious liuery.

Yet these mine owne, I wrong not other men,
Nor trafique further then thys happy Clyme,
Nor filch from *Portes*[25] nor from *Petrarchs* pen,
A fault too common in thys latter tyme.

---

20 reveal.

21 *conceald.*] *conceald* STC 16696.

22 be lacking.

23 From Michael Drayton, *Ideas Mirrour. Amours in quatorzains,* 1594, STC 7203, Folger Library. Drayton's first sequence of sonnets was printed in this edition. In the second edition, 1599, twenty-one of these sonnets were omitted, and twenty-nine others were added. In later editions (1600, 1602, 1605, 1619) there were further omissions, additions, and revisions. The text of the present edition is that of the edition of 1619; seven sonnets that Drayton omitted in 1619 are printed from the editions of 1594 and 1599.

24 Reprinted in all editions before 1619.

25 Philippe Desportes, a French sonneteer, author of *Les Amours de Diane,* often imitated by English poets.

Diuine Syr *Phillip*,[26] I auouch thy writ,
I am no Pickpurse of anothers wit.

My hart imprisoned in a hopeles Ile,[27]
Peopled with Armies of pale iealous eyes,
The shores beset with thousand secret spyes,
Must passe by ayre, or else dye in exile.

He framd him wings with feathers of this thought,
Which by theyr nature learn'd to mount the skye,
And with the same he practised to flye,
Till he himselfe thys Eagles art had taught.

Thus soring still, not looking once below,
So neere thyne eyes celestiall sunne aspyred,
That with the rayes his wafting pyneons fired.
Thus was the wanton cause of hys owne woe.
Downe fell he in thy Beauties Ocean drenched,
Yet there he burnes, in fire thats neuer quenched.

My fayre, looke from those turrets of thine eyes,[28]
Into the Ocean of a troubled minde,
Where my poore soule, the Barke of sorrow lyes,
Left to the mercy of the waues and winde.

See where shee flotes, laden with purest loue,
Which those fayre Ilands of thy lookes affoord,
Desiring yet a thousand deaths to proue,
Then so to cast her Ballast ouer boord.

See how her sayles be rent, her tacklings worne,
Her Cable broke, her surest Anchor lost,
Her Marryners doe leaue her all forlorne,[29]
Yet how shee bends towards that blessed Coast.
Loe where she drownes, in stormes of thy displeasure,
Whose worthy prize should haue enritcht thy treasure.

If chaste and pure deuotion of my youth,[30]
Or glorie of my Aprill-springing yeeres,
Vnfained loue, in naked simple truth,
A thousand vowes, a thousand sighes and teares:

Or if a world of faithful seruice done,

[26] Sidney.

[27] This is in part an imitation of Daniel, *Delia*, 27. It is reprinted in all editions before 1619.

[28] Not reprinted.

[29] *forlorne*,] *forforne*, STC 7203.

[30] Not reprinted.

Words, thoughts, and deeds, deuoted to her honor,
Or eyes that haue beheld her as theyr sunne,
With admiration, euer looking on her.

A lyfe, that neuer ioyd but in her loue,
A soule, that euer hath ador'd her name,
A fayth, that time nor fortune could not moue,
A muse, that vnto heauen hath raisd her fame.
Though these, nor these, deserue to be imbraced,
Yet faire vnkinde, too good to be disgraced.

Blacke pytchy Night, companyon of my woe,[31]
The Inne of care, the Nurse of drery sorrow,
Why lengthnest thou thy darkest howres so,
Still to prolong my long tyme lookt-for morrow?

Thou Sable shadow, Image of dispayre,
Portraite of hell, the ayres black mourning weed,
Recorder of reuenge, remembrancer of care,
The shadow and the vaile of euery sinfull deed.

Death like to thee, so lyue thou still in death,
The graue of ioy, pryson of dayes delight,
Let heauens withdraw their sweet Ambrozian breath,
Nor Moone nor stars lend thee their shining light.
For thou alone renew'st that olde desire,
Which still torments me in dayes burning fire.

Sweet secrecie, what tongue can tell thy worth?[32]
What mortall pen suffyciently can prayse thee?
What curious Pensill serues to lim thee forth?
What Muse hath power, aboue thy height to raise thee?

Strong locke of kindnesse, Closet of loues store,
Harts Methridate,[33] the soules preseruatiue,
O vertue, which all vertues doe adore,
Cheefe good, from whom all good things we deriue.

O rare effect, true bond of friendships measure,
Conceite of Angels, which all wisdom teachest,
O richest Casket of all heauenly treasure,
In secret silence, which such wonders preachest,
O purest merror, wherein men may see
The liuely Image of Diuinitie.

---

[31] Not reprinted.

[32] Not reprinted.
[33] antidote or preservative.

From ENGLAND'S HEROICALL EPISTLES[34]

Many there be excelling in this kind,
Whose well trick'd rimes with all inuention swell,
Let each commend as best shall like his minde,
Some *Sidney, Constable,* some *Daniell.*
That thus theyr names familiarly I sing,
Let none thinke them disparaged to be,
Poore men with reuerence may speake of a King,
And so may these be spoken of by mee;
My wanton verse nere keepes one certaine stay,
But now, at hand; then, seekes inuention far,
And with each little motion runnes astray,
Wilde, madding, iocond, and irreguler;
Like me that lust, my honest mery rimes,
Nor care for Criticke, nor regard the times.

From IDEA[35]

To the Reader of These Sonnets[36]

Into these Loues, who but for Passion lookes,
At this first sight, here let him lay them by,
And seeke else-where, in turning other Bookes,
Which better may his labour satisfie.
No farre-fetch'd Sigh shall euer wound my Brest,
Loue from mine Eye a Teare shall neuer wring,
Nor in *Ah-mees* my whyning Sonnets drest,
(A Libertine) fantastickly I sing:
My Verse is the true image of my Mind,
Euer in motion, still desiring change;
And as thus to Varietie inclin'd,
So in all Humors sportiuely I range:
My Muse is rightly of the *English* straine,
That cannot long one Fashion intertaine.

Like an aduenturous Sea-farer am I,[37]
Who hath some long and dang'rous Voyage beene,
And call'd to tell of his Discouerie,
How farre he sayl'd, what Countries he had seene,
Proceeding from the Port whence he put forth,
Shewes by his Compasse, how his Course he steer'd,
When East, when West, when South, and when by North,
As how the Pole to eu'ry place was rear'd,
What Capes he doubled, of what Continent,
The Gulphes and Straits, that strangely he had past,
Where most becalm'd, where with foule Weather spent,

[34] From Drayton, *Englands heroicall epistles. Newly enlarged: with Idea,* 1599, STC 7195, Folger Library. This sonnet is included in all later editions before 1619.

[35] From Drayton, *Idea, In sixtie three sonnets,* in *Poems, collected into one volume,* 1619, STC 7222, New York Public Library, Berg Collection.

[36] First printed in 1599.

[37] First printed in 1619.

And on what Rocks in perill to be cast?
  Thus in my Loue, Time calls me to relate
  My tedious Trauels, and oft-varying Fate.

Bright starre of Beauty, on whose eye-lids sit[38]
A thousand Nimph-like and inamor'd Graces,
The Goddesses of Memory and Wit,
Which there in order take their seuerall places,
In whose deare Bosome, sweet delicious Loue
Layes downe his Quiuer, which he once did beare:
Since he that blessed Paradise did proue,
And leaues his Mothers lap to sport him there,
Let others striue to entertaine with Words,
My Soule is of a brauer Mettle made,
I hold that vile, which Vulgar wit affords;
In Me's that Faith which Time cannot inuade.
  Let what I praise, be still made good by you:
  Be you most worthy, whilst I am most true.

How many paltry, foolish, painted things,[39]
That now in Coaches trouble eu'ry Street,
Shall be forgotten, whom no Poet sings,
Ere they be well wrap'd in their winding Sheet?
Where I to thee Eternitie shall giue,
When nothing else remayneth of these dayes,
And Queenes hereafter shall be glad to liue
Vpon the Almes of thy superfluous prayse;
Virgins and Matrons reading these my Rimes,
Shall be so much delighted with thy story,
That they shall grieue, they liu'd not in these Times,
To haue seene thee, their Sexes onely glory:
  So shalt thou flye aboue the vulgar Throng,
  Still to suruiue in my immortal Song.

There's nothing grieues me, but that Age should haste,[40]
That in my dayes I may not see thee old,
That where those two cleare sparkling Eyes are plac'd,
Onely two Loope-holes, then I might behold.
That louely, arched, yuorie, pollish'd Brow,
Defac'd with Wrinkles, that I might but see;
Thy daintie Hayre, so curl'd, and crisped now,
Like grizzled Mosse vpon some aged Tree;
Thy Cheeke, now flush with Roses, sunke, and leane,
Thy Lips, with age, as any Wafer thinne,

[38] First printed in 1600.

[39] First printed in 1619.

[40] First printed in 1619.

Thy Pearly Teeth out of thy Head so cleane,[41]
That when thou feed'st, thy Nose shall touch thy Chinne:
  These Lines that now thou scorn'st, which should delight thee,
  Then would I make thee read, but to despight thee.

As other Men, so I my selfe doe Muse,[42]
Why in this sort I wrest Inuention so,
And why these giddy Metaphors I vse,
Leauing the Path the greater part doe goe;
I will resolue you; I am Lunaticke,
And euer this in Mad-men you shall finde,
What they last thought of, when the Braine grew sicke,
In most distraction they keepe that in Minde.
Thus talking idly in this Bedlam fit,
Reason and I (you must conceiue) are twaine,
Tis nine yeeres now since first I lost my Wit,
Beare with Me then, though troubled be my Braine;
  With Diet and Correction, Men distraught,
  (Not too farre past) may to their Wits be brought.

To nothing fitter can I Thee compare,[43]
Then to the Sonne of some rich Penny-father,[44]
Who hauing now brought on his end with Care,
Leaues to his Sonne all he had heap'd together;
This new rich Nouice, lauish of his chest,
To one Man giues, doth on another spend,
Then heere he riots, yet amongst the rest,
Haps to lend some to one true honest Friend.
Thy Gifts thou in Obscuritie doest waste,
False Friends thy kindnesse, borne but to deceiue Thee;
Thy Loue, that is on the vnworthy plac'd,
Time hath thy Beautie, which with Age will leaue thee;
  Onely that little which to Me was lent,
  I giue Thee backe, when all the rest is spent.

TO TIME[45]

Stay, speedy Time, behold, before thou passe,
From Age to Age, what thou hast sought to see,
One, in whom all the Excellencies be,
In whom, Heau'n lookes it selfe as in a Glasse:
Time, looke thou too, in this Tralucent Glasse,
And thy Youth past, in this pure Mirrour see,
As the World's Beautie in his Infancie,
What it was then, and thou before it was;
Passe on, and to Posteritie tell this,

[41] completely.
[42] First printed in 1600.
[43] First printed in 1599.
[44] miser.
[45] First printed in 1594.

Yet see thou tell, but truly, what hath beene:
Say to our Nephewes, that thou once hast seene,
In perfect humane shape, all heau'nly Blisse;
  And bid them mourne, nay more, despaire with thee,
  That she is gone, her like againe to see.

An euill spirit your beautie haunts Me still,[46]
Wherewith (alas) I have beene long possest,
Which ceaseth not to tempt Me to each Ill,
Nor gives Me once, but one poore minutes rest:
In Me it speakes, whether I Sleepe or Wake,
And when by Meanes, to driue it out I try,
With greater Torments, then it Me doth take,
And tortures Me in most extremity;
Before my Face, it layes downe my Despaires,
And hastes Me on vnto a sudden Death;[47]
Now tempting Me, to drowne my Selfe in teares,
And then in sighing, to giue vp my breath;
  Thus am I still prouok'd, to euery Euill,
  By this good wicked Spirit, sweet Angell Deuill.

A witlesse Gallant, a young Wench that woo'd,[48]
(Yet his dull Spirit her not one iot could moue)
Intreated me, as e'r I wish'd his good,
To write him but one Sonnet to his Loue:
When I, as fast as e'r my Penne could trot,
Powr'd out what first from quicke Inuention came;
Nor neuer stood one word thereof to blot,
Much like his Wit, that was to vse the same:
But with my Verses he his Mistress wonne,
Who doted on the Dolt beyond all measure.
But see, for you to Heau'n for Phraze I runne,
And ransacke all *Apollo's* golden Treasure;
  Yet by my Froth, this Foole his Loue obtaines,
  And I lose you, for all my Wit and Paines.

TO THE CRITICKE[49]

Me thinkes I see some crooked Mimicke ieere,
And taxe my Muse with this fantasticke Grace,
Turning my Papers, askes, What haue we heere?
Making withall some filthy Antike[50] Face.
I feare no censure, nor what thou canst say,
Nor shall my Spirit one iot of vigour lose.
Think'st thou, my Wit shall keepe the pack-Horse Way,

---

[46] First printed in 1599. Cf. Shakespeare, Sonnet 144, first printed in *The Passionate Pilgrim*, 1599.

[47] Devils were believed to tempt to suicide.

[48] First printed in 1619.

[49] First printed in 1599.

[50] ugly, grinning.

That eu'ry Dudgen[51] low Inuention goes?
Since Sonnets thus in Bundles are imprest,
And eu'ry Drudge doth dull our satiate Eare;
Think'st thou my Loue shall in those Ragges be drest,
That eu'ry Dowdy, ev'ry Trull doth weare?
Vp, to my Pitch,[52] no common Iudgement flyes,
I scorne all Earthly Dung-bred Scarabies.[53]

TO THE RIUER ANKOR[54]

Our Flouds-Queen *Thames,* for Ships and Swans is crowned,
And stately *Seuerne* for her Shoare is praysed,
The Crystall *Trent,* for Foords and Fish renowned,
And *Auons*[55] Fame, to *Albions* Cliffes is raysed,
Carlegion Chester vaunts her holy *Dee,*
Yorke many Wonders of her *Owse* can tell,
The *Peake* her *Dove,* whose Bankes so fertile be,
And *Kent* will say, her *Medway* doth excell,
Cotswold commends her *Isis* to the *Tame,*
Our Northerne Borders boast of *Tweeds* faire Floud,
Our Westerne Parts extoll their *Wilis* Fame,
And the old *Lea* brags of the *Danish* Bloud;
Ardens sweet *Ankor,* let thy glory bee,
That faire *Idea* onely liues by thee.

TO MIRACLE[56]

Some misbeleeuing, and prophane in Loue,
When I doe speake of Miracles by thee,
May say, that thou art flattered by mee,
Who onely write, my skill in Verse to proue;
See Miracles, ye vnbeleeuing, see,
A dumbe-borne Muse made to expresse the Mind,
A cripple Hand to write, yet lame by Kind,[57]
One by thy Name, the other touching thee;
Blind were mine Eyes, till they were seene of thine,
And my Eares deafe, by thy Fame healed bee,
My Vices cur'd, by Vertues sprung from thee,
My Hopes reuiu'd, which long in Graue had lyne:
All vncleane Thoughts, foule Spirits cast out in mee,
Onely by Vertue that proceeds from thee.

Some Men there be, which like my Method well,[58]
And much commend the strangenesse of my Vaine:
Some say, I haue a passing pleasing Straine,
Some say, That in my Humor[59] I excell;

---

[51] poor, trashy.

[52] The height to which a bird of prey soars before swooping.

[53] beetles. "The kingly Bird . . . did scorne the simple Scarabee." Spenser, *Visions of the worlds vanitie,* 1591, lines 43–44.

[54] First printed in 1594; Polesworth, the home of Anne Goodere, is on the Anker.

[55] Wilton, the Countess of Pembroke's home, is near the Avon in Wiltshire.

[56] First printed in 1594.

[57] nature.

[58] First printed in 1594.

[59] disposition, style.

Some, who not kindly rellish my Conceit,
They say (As Poets doe) I vse to faine,
And in bare words paint out my Passions paine;
Thus sundry Men their sundry Minds repeat:
I passe[60] not, I, how Men affected bee,
Nor who commends, or discommends my Verse;
It pleaseth me, if I my Woes rehearse,
And in my Lines, if she my loue may see:
  Onely my comfort still consists in this,
  Writing her prayse, I cannot write amisse.

Whilst thus my Pen striues to eternize thee,[61]
Age rules my Lines with Wrinkles in my Face,
Where, in the Map of all my Miserie,
Is model'd out the World of my Disgrace;
Whilst in despite of tyrannizing Times,
Medea-like, I make thee young againe,
Proudly thou scorn'st my World-out-wearing Rimes,
And murther'st Vertue with thy coy disdaine:
And though in youth, my Youth vntimely perish,
To keepe Thee from Obliuion and the Graue,
Ensuing Ages yet my Rimes shall cherish,
Where I intomb'd, my better part shall saue;
  And though this Earthly Body fade and die,
  My Name shall mount vpon Eternitie.

In pride of Wit, when high desire of Fame[62]
Gaue Life and Courage to my lab'ring Pen,
And first the sound and vertue of my Name
Wonne grace and credit in the Eares of Men;
With those the thronged Theaters that presse,[63]
I in the Circuit[64] for the Lawrell strove:
Where, the full Prayse I freely must confesse,
In heat of Bloud, a modest Mind might moue.
With Showts and Claps at eu'ry little pawse,
When the proud Round on eu'ry side hath rung,
Sadly I sit, vnmou'd with the Applause,
As though to me it nothing[65] did belong:
  No publike Glorie vainely I pursue,
  All that I seeke, is to eternize you.

Calling to minde since first my Loue begun,[66]
Th'incertaine Times oft varying in their Course,

[60] care.
[61] First printed in 1599.
[62] First printed in 1605.
[63] crowd.
[64] playhouse.
[65] not at all.
[66] First printed in 1605. Drayton mentions the outstanding events of the past six years.

How Things still vnexpectedly haue runne,
As't please the Fates, by their resistlesse force:
Lastly, mine Eyes amazedly haue seene
Essex great fall, *Tyrone* his Peace to gaine,
The quiet end of that Long-liuing Queene,
This Kings faire Entrance, and our Peace with *Spaine,*
We and the *Dutch* at length our Selues to seuer;
Thus the World doth, and euermore shall Reele:
Yet to my Goddesse am I constant euer;
How e're blind Fortune turne her giddie Wheele:
  Though Heauen and Earth, proue both to me vntrue,
  Yet am I still inuiolate to You.

Since ther's no helpe, Come let vs kisse and part,[67]
Nay, I haue done: You get no more of Me,
And I am glad, yea glad with all my heart,
That thus so cleanly,[68] I my Selfe can free,
Shake hands for euer, Cancell all our Vowes,
And when We meet at any time againe,
Be it not seene in either of our Browes,
That We one iot of former Loue reteyne;
Now at the last gaspe, of Loues latest Breath,
When his Pulse fayling, Passion speechlesse lies,
When Faith is kneeling by his bed of Death,
And Innocence is closing vp his Eyes,
  Now if thou would'st, when all haue giuen him ouer,
  From Death to Life, thou might'st him yet recouer.

From SPIRITUAL SONNETS[69]

Gracious, Diuine, and most omnipotent,
  Receiue thy seruants Tallent in good part,
  Which hidde it not, but willing did conuert
  It to best vse hee could when it was lent:
The summe (though slender, yet not all mispent)
  Receiue deare God of grace, from cheerefull hart,
  Of him, that knowes, how mercifull thou art,
  And with what grace to contrite sinners bent:
I know my fault, I did not as I should,
  My sinfull flesh against my soule rebeld,
  But since I did endeuour what I could,
Let not my little nothing bee withheld
  From thy rich treasuries of endlesse grace;
  But (for thy sake) let it procure a place.

A blast of winde, a momentarie breath,
  A watrie bubble simbolizde with ayre,

[67] First printed in 1619.
[68] completely.
[69] From Barnabe Barnes, *A diuine centurie of spirituall sonnets*, 1595, STC 1467, Folger Library.

A sonne blowne Rose, but for a season fayre,
A ghostly glaunce, a skeleton of death,
A morning dew perling the grasse beneath,
Whose moysture Sunnes appearance doth impaire:
A lightning glimse: a Muse of thought and care:
A Planets shot: a shade which followeth:
A voice which vanisheth so soone as heard:
The thriftlesse heire of time: a rowling waue:
A shew no more in action then regard:
A Masse of dust: worlds momentarie slaue
Is man in state of our olde Adam made,
Soone borne to die, soone flourishing to fade.

The worldes bright comforter (whose beamsome light
Poore creatures cheereth, mounting from the deepe)
His course doth in prefixed compasse keepe,
And as courageous Gyant takes delight
To runne his race, and exercise his might:
Till him downe galloping the mountaynes steepe
Cleere Hesperus smooth messenger of sleepe
Viewes: and the siluer ornament of night
Foorth bringes with starres past number in her trayne:
All which with Sunnes long borrowed splendour shine:
The Seas (with full tyde swelling) ebbe agayne:
All yeeres to their olde quarters newe resigne,
The windes forsake their mountayne-chambers wilde,
And all in all thinges with Gods vertue filde.

From FIDESSA[70]

Arraign'd poore captiue at the barre I stand,
The barre of Beautie, barre to all my ioyes,
And vp I hold my euer-trembling hand,
Wishing or life or death to end annoyes.
And when the Iudge doth question of the guilt,
And bids me speake, then sorrow shuts vp words:
Yea though he say, speake boldly what thou wilt,
Yet my confusde affects[71] no speech affoords.
For why (alas) my passions haue no bound,
For feare of death that penetrates so neere.
And still one griefe another doth confound,
Yet doth at length a way to speech appeere.
Then (for I speake too late) the Iudge doth giue
His sentence that in prison I shall liue.

Compare me to the child that plaies with fire,
Or to the flye that dyeth in the flame:

[70] From Bartholomew Griffin, *Fidessa, more chaste then kinde,* 1596, STC 12367, Huntington Library.
[71] affections.

Or to the foolish boy[72] that did aspire,
To touch the glorie of high heauens frame.
Compare me to *Leander* struggling in the waues,
Not able to attaine his safeties shore:
Or to the sicke that doe expect[73] their graues,
Or to the captiue crying euer more.
Compare me to the weeping wounded Hart,
Moning with teares the period[74] of his life:
Or to the Bore that will not feele his smart,
When he is striken with the butchers knife.
  No man to these can fitly me compare:
  These liue to dye: I dye to liue in care.

Care-charmer sleepe, sweet ease in restles miserie,
The captiues libertie, and his freedomes song:
Balme of the brused heart, mans chiefe felicitie,
Brother of quiet death, when life is too too long.
A Comedie it is, and now an Historie,
What is not sleepe vnto the feeble minde?
It easeth him that toyles, and him that's sorrie:
It makes the deaffe to heare, to see the blinde.
Vngentle sleepe, thou helpest all but me,
For when I sleepe my soule is vexed most:
It is *Fidessa* that doth master thee,
If she approach (alas) thy power is lost.
  But here she is: see how he runnes amaine,
  I feare at night he will not come againe.

Flye to her heart, houer about her heart,[75]
With daintie kisses mollifie her heart:
Pierce with thy arrowes her obdurate heart,
With sweet allurements euer moue her heart.
At midday and at midnight touch her heart,
Be lurking closely, nestle about her heart:
With power, (thou art a god) command her heart,
Kindle thy coales of loue about her heart,
Yea euen into thy selfe transforme her heart.
Ah she must loue, be sure thou haue her heart,
And I must dye, if thou haue not her heart.
Thy bed (if thou rest well) must be her heart:
  He hath the best part sure that hath the heart:
  What haue I not, if I haue but her heart?

---

72 Icarus.
73 await.
74 end.
75 Addressed to Cupid. The repetition of a single word or syllable as a substitute for perfect rhyme was called "like loose" (i.e., like endings), a term borrowed from archery (George Puttenham, *The Arte of English Poesie*, 1589, ed. Willcock and Walker, p. 174). For an earlier example, see Wyatt's *Hate whom ye list.*

I haue not spent the Aprill of my time,
The sweet of youth in plotting in the aire:
But doe at first aduenture seeke to clime,
Whil'st flowers of blooming yeares are greene and faire.
I am no leauing of al-withering age,
I haue not suffred many winter lowres:
I feele no storme, vnlesse my Loue doe rage,
And then in griefe I spend both daies and houres.
This yet doth comfort that my flower lasted,
Vntill it did approach my Sunne too neere:
And then (alas) vntimely was it blasted,
So soone as once thy beautie did appeare.
  But after all, my comfort rests in this,
  That for thy sake my youth decaied is.

Faire is my loue that feedes among the Lillies,
The Lillies growing in that pleasant garden,
Where Cupids mount that welbeloued hill is,
And where that little god himselfe is warden.
See where my Loue sits in the beds of spices,
Beset all round with Camphere, Myrrhe and Roses,
And interlac'd with curious deuices,
Which her from all the world apart incloses.
There doth she tune her Lute for her delight,
And with sweet musick makes the ground to moue,
Whil'st I (poore I) doe sit in heauie plight,
Wayling alone my vnrespected loue,
  Not daring rush into so rare a place,
  That giues to her and she to it a grace.

Worke worke apace you blessed Sisters three,[76]
In restles twining of my fatall threed:
Oh let your nimble hands at once agree,
To weaue it out, and cut it off with speed.
Then shall my vexed and tormented ghost
Haue quiet passage to the Elisian rest:
And sweetly ouer death and fortune boast,
In euerlasting triumphs with the blest.
But ah (too well I know) you haue conspired
A lingring death for him that lotheth life:
As if with woes he neuer could be tyred:
For this you hide your all-diuiding knife.
  One comfort yet the heauens haue assign'd me,
  That I must dye and leaue my griefes behind me.

[76] The Fates.

Thomas Lodge

[c. 1558–1625]

THOMAS LODGE was the second son of Sir Thomas Lodge, wealthy merchant and Lord Mayor of London. He attended Merchant Taylors' School, London, and Trinity College, Oxford, where he was graduated B.A. in 1577. In 1578 he became a law student at Lincoln's Inn.

About 1580 he wrote a defense of plays in answer to Stephen Gosson's *School of Abuse*, 1579. He made a voyage to the Canaries about 1585 and a two-year voyage under Thomas Cavendish to South America, 1591–1593. After a busy literary career of fifteen years, he studied medicine, took the degree of M.D. at Avignon about 1600 and at Oxford in 1602, and achieved some reputation as a physician.

Lodge's known contributions to dramatic literature are two plays of uncertain date, one of them written in collaboration with Robert Greene. Much more successful were his prose tales, with a number of lyrics inserted, the best tale being *Rosalynde*, the source of Shakespeare's *As You Like It*. In 1589 he published *Scillaes Metamorphosis*, a mythological narrative poem, and with it a satire and several lyrics. A few other lyrics appeared in the miscellanies *The Phoenix Nest*, 1593, and *England's Helicon*, 1600. In 1593 he published *Phillis*, a collection of sonnets and other short poems, together with a dreary elegiac poem called "The Complaint of Elstred." In 1595 appeared a book of verse entitled *A Fig for Momus*, containing satires, eclogues, and epistles. Late in life he translated Josephus and Seneca's prose works.

He is one of the early imitators of Sidney, especially in *Phillis*, and like Sidney he is fond of metrical experiments, as in his frequent use of feminine rhyme and his varied and unusual rhyme patterns. The best of his lyrics—whether original or translated from the French—are fresh and graceful.

The standard edition is *The Complete Works of Thomas Lodge*, ed. E. W. Gosse, 4 vols., 1883. For biography and criticism, see Gosse's Introduction, reprinted in his *Seventeenth Century Studies*, 1883; N. B. Paradise, *Thomas Lodge. The History of an Elizabethan*, 1931; C. J. Sisson, *Thomas Lodge and Other*

Elizabethans, 1933; E. A. Tenney, *Thomas Lodge*, 1935; S. A. Tannenbaum, *Thomas Lodge, a Concise Bibliography*, 1940.

The earth late choakt with showers[1]
Is now araid in greene:
Her bosome springs with flowers,
The aire dissolues her teene,[2]
The heauens laugh at her glorie:
Yet bide I sad and sorie.

The woods are deckt with leaues,
And trees are cloathed gaie,
And *Flora* crownd with sheues
With oaken boughs dooth play:
Where I am clad in blacke,
The token of my wracke.

The birds vpon the trees
Doo sing with pleasant voices,
And chaunt in their degrees
Their loues and luckie choices:
When I, whilst they are singing,
With sighs mine armes are wringing.

The Thrushes seeke the shade,
And I my fatall graue:
Their flight to heauen is made,
My walke on earth I haue:
They free, I thrall: they iolly,
I sad and pensiue wholly.

THE CONTENTS OF THE SCEDULE WHICH SIR IOHN OF BURDEAUX GAUE TO HIS SONNES[3]

My Sonnes, behold what portion I doe giue:
I leaue you goods, but they are quickly lost:
I leaue aduise, to schoole you how to loue;
I leaue you wit, but wone with little cost:
But keepe it well, for counsel still is one,
When father, friends, and worldly goods are gone.

In choice of thrift, let honour be your gaine,
Winne it by vertue, and by manly might:
In doing good, esteeme thy toile no paine,
Protect the fatherlesse and widdowes right.
Fight for thy faith, thy Countrie and thy King,
For why? this thrift will proue a blessed thing.

In choice of wife, prefer the modest chast,
Lillies are faire in show, but foule in smell:
The sweetest lookes by age are soone defast,
Then choose thy wife by wit, and liuing well.
Who brings thee wealth, and many faults withall,
Presents thee hony mixt with bitter gall.

In choise of friends, beware of light beliefe,
A painted tongue, may shroud a subtill heart:
The *Syrens* teares, doe threaten mickle griefe,
Foresee my sonnes, for feare of sodaine smart,
Chuse in your wants, and he that friends you then,
When richer growen, befriend you him agen.

Learne with the *Ant* in summer to prouide,
Driue with the Bee, the Droane from out the hiue:
Build like the Swallow in the summer tide,
Spare not to much, (my sonnes) but sparing thriue,
Be poore in folly, rich in all but sinne:

---

[1] From *Scillaes metamorphosis*, 1589, STC 16674, Folger Library.
[2] sorrow, trouble.

[3] From *Rosalynde. Euphues golden legacie*, 1596, STC 16666, Huntington Library; written in 1590.

So by your death, your glory shall beginne.

ROSALYNDS MADRIGALL[4]

Loue[5] in my bosome like a Bee,
Doth sucke his sweete:
Now with his wings he plaies with me,
Now with his feete.
Within mine eyes he makes his nest,
His bed amidst my tender breast,
My kisses are his daily feast,
And yet he robs me of my rest,
Ah wanton, will ye?

And if I sleepe, then percheth he,
With pretty flight,
And makes his pillow of my knee,
The liuelong night.
Strike I my lute, he tunes the string,
He musicke plaies if so I singe:
He lends me euery louely thing,
Yet cruel he my heart doth sting:
Whist[6] wanton still yee.

Else I with roses euery day,
Will whip you hence:
And binde you when you long to play,
For your offence.
Ile shut my eyes to keepe you in,
Ile make you fast it for your sinne,
Ile count your powre not worth a pin,
Alas what hereby shall I winne,
If he gaine say me.

What if I beate the wanton boy,
With many a rod?
He will repaie me with anoy,
Because a God.
Then sit thou safely on my knee,
And let thy bower my bosome be:
Lurke in mine eyes I like of thee,
O *Cupid* so thou pittie mee,
Spare not but play thee.

First shall the heauens want starry
light,[7]
The seas be robbed of their waues,[8]
The day want sunne, and sunne want
bright,
The night want shade, the dead men
graues,[9]
The Aprill flowers and leafe and tree,
Before I false my faith to thee:

First shall the tops of highest hils
By humble playnes be ouerpried,
And Poets scorne the Muses quils,
And fish forsake the water glide,[10]
And Iris lose her coloured weede,
Before I fayle thee at thy neede.

First direfull hate shall turne to peace,
And loue relent in deepe disdaine:
And death his fatall stroke shall cease,
And enuie pittie euery paine,
And pleasure mourne, and sorrow
smile,
Before I talke of any guile.

First time shall stay his stailesse race,
And winter blesse his browes with corne,
And snow bemoisten Iulies[11] face,
And winter spring, and summer mourne,
Before my pen by helpe of fame:
Cease to recite thy sacred name.

Phebe sate,[12]
Sweete she sate:
Sweete sate Phebe when I saw her.
White her brow,
Coy her eye:
Brow and eye how much you please
me.
Words I spent,
Sighes I sent:
Sighes and words could neuer draw
her.
Oh my loue,
Thou art lost:
Since no sight could euer ease thee.

Phoebe sate,
By a fount:
Sitting by a fount I spide her.

---

[4] *Ibid.*
[5] Cupid.
[6] be silent.
[7] From *Rosalynde*, 1596.
[8] *waues,*] *waues.* STC 16666.
[9] *men graues,*] *mens graues.* STC 16666.
[10] *glide,*] *glide.* STC 16666.
[11] July's.
[12] From *Rosalynde*, 1596.

Sweete her touch,
Rare her voice:
Touch and voice what may distaine you?[13]
As she sung,
I did sigh,
And by sighes whilst that I tride her,[14]
Oh mine eyes,
You did lose[15]
Her first sight whose want did paine you.[16]

Phebes flocks,
White as wooll:
Yet were Phebes lookes more whiter.
Phebes eyes,
Douelike milde:
Douelike eyes, both milde and cruell.
Montan sweares,
In your lampes:
He will die for to delight her.
Phebe yeeld,
Or I dye:
Shall true hearts be fancies fuell?[17]

SONETTO[18]

Of all chast birdes the Phoenix doth excell,
Of all strong beastes the Lion beares the bell:
Of all sweete flowers the Rose doth sweetest smell,
Of all faire maides my *Rosalynd* is fairest.

Of all pure mettals gold is onely purest,
To all high trees the Pine hath highest crest:
Of all soft sweete, I like my mistris best,
Of all chast thoughts my mistris thoughts are rarest.

Of all proude birdes the Eagle pleaseth *Ioue,*
Of pretty foules kinde *Venus* likes the *Doue:*
Of trees *Minerua* doth the Oliue loue,
Of all sweet Nimphes I honour *Rosalynd.*

Of all her gifts her wisdome pleaseth most,
Of all her graces vertue she doth boast:
For all the gifts my life and ioy is lost,
If *Rosalynd* prooue cruell and vnkinde.

Turne I my lookes vnto the Skies,[19]
Loue with his arrows wounds mine eyes:
If so I looke vpon the ground,
Loue then in euery[20] flower is found.
Search I the shade to flie my paine,
He meets me in the shades againe.
Wend I to walke in secret groue,
Euen there I meet with sacred loue.
If so I baine[21] me in the spring,
Euen on the brinke I heare him sing:
If so I meditate alone,
He will be partner of my mone.
If so I mourne, he weepes with me,
And where I am, there will he be.
When as I talke of *Rosalynd,*
The God from coynesse waxeth kinde:
And seemes in selfe same flame to fry,
Because he loues as well as I.
Sweete *Rosalynd* for pittie rue,
For why[22] than loue[23] I am more true:
He if he speed[24] will quickly flie,
But in thy loue I liue and die.

My mistresse when she goes[25]
To pull the pinke and rose,
Along the riuer bounds,[26]
And trippeth on the grounds
And runnes from rocks to rocks
With lovely scattered locks,[27]
Whilst amarous wind doth play
With haires so golden gay;[28]

13 *you?*] *you.* STC 16666.
14 *her,*] *her.* STC 16666.
15 *lose*] *loose:* STC 16666.
16 *you.*] *you,* STC 16666.
17 *fuell?*] *fuell.* STC 16666.
18 From *Rosalynde*, 1596.
19 *Ibid.*
20 *then in euery*] *then euery* STC 16666.
21 bathe.
22 because.
23 Cupid.
24 succeed.
25 From *The life and death of William Longbeard*, 1593, STC 16659, Harvard Library.
26 *bounds,*] *bounds* STC 16659.
27 *locks,*] *locks* STC 16659.
28 *gay;*] *gay* STC 16659.

The water waxeth cleere,[29]
The fishes draw hir neere,[30]
The *Sirens* sing hir praise,[31]
Sweet flowers perfume hir waies,[32]
And *Neptune* glad and faine
Yeelds vp to hir his raigne.

From PHILLIS[33]

Oh pleasing thoughts, apprentises of loue,
Fore-runners of desire, sweet Methridates[34]
The poison of my sorrowes to remoue,
With whom my hopes and feare full oft debates.
Inritch your selues and me by your selfe riches,
(Which are the thoughts you spend on heauen bred beauty,)
Rowse you my muse beyond our Poets pitches,[35]
And working wonders yet say all is duty.
Vse you no *Eglets* eyes, nor *Phenix* feathers,
To tower[36] the heauen from whence heauens wonder sallies:
For why your sonne singes sweetly to hir wethers:
Making a springe of winter in the vallies.
Show to the world tho poore and scant my skill is,
How sweet thoughts bee, that are but thought on *Phillis*.

The dewie-Roseate morne had with hir haires,
In sundrie sorts the Indian Clime adornd:
And now hir eies apparrailed in teares,
The losse of louely *Memnon*[37] long had moornd.
When as she spide the Nimph whom I admire,[38]
Kembinge hir locks, of which the yelow golde,
Made blush the beauties of hir curled wire,
Which heauen it selfe with wonder might beholde,[39]
Then redd with shame, hir reuerend locks she rent,
And weeping hid the beauty of hir face,
The flower of fancie wrought such discontent:
The sighes which midst the aire she breathd a space,
A three daies stormie tempest did maintaine,
Hir shame a fire, hir eies a swelling raine.

Loue[40] guards[41] the roses of thy lippes,
And flies about them like a bee:
If I approach he forward skippes,
And if I kisse he stingeth me.
Loue in thine eyes doth build his bower,

---

29 *cleere,*] *cleere* STC 16659.
30 *neere,*] *neere* STC 16659.
31 *praise,*] *praise* STC 16659.
32 *waies,*] *waies* STC 16659.
33 From *Phillis: honoured with pastorall sonnets, elegies, and amorous delights*, 1593, STC 16662, Huntington Library.
34 antidotes.
35 heights.
36 soar to.
37 According to Ovid, Aurora's tears for the loss of her son Memnon, slain by Achilles, became the morning dew.
38 *admire,*] *admire*. STC 16662.
39 *beholde,*] *beholde*. STC 16662.
40 Cupid.
41 *guards*] *guides* STC 16662.

And sleepes within their prettie shine:
And if I looke the boy will lower,
And from their orbes shootes shaftes deuine.
  Loue workes thy heart within his fire,
And in my teares doth firme[42] the same:
And if I tempt[43] it will retire,
And of my plaintes doth make a game.
  Loue let me cull hir choycest flowers,
And pittie me, and calme hir eye,
Make soft hir heart, dissolue hir lowers,
Then will I praise thy dietie.
  But if thou do not loue, Ile trulye serue hir,
  In spight of thee, and by firme faith deserue hir.

My *Phillis* hath the morning sunne,
  At first to looke vppon hir.
And *Phillis* hath morne-waking birdes,
  Hir risinges for to honour.
My *Phillis* hath prime-feathered flowers,
  That smile when she treades on them,
And *Phillis* hath a gallant flocke,
  That leapes since she doth owne them.
But *Phillis* hath so hard a heart,
  Ah-las that she should haue it,
As yeeldes no mercie to desart,
  Nor grace to those that craue it:
  Sweet sunne when thou lookest on,
  Pray hir regarde my moane.
  Sweet birdes when you sing to hir,
  To yeeld some pittie wooe hir.
  Sweet flowers when as she treades on,
  Tell hir hir beautie deades one:
And if in life hir loue, she nill[44] agree me,
Pray hir before I die, she will come see me.

Deuoide of reason, thrale to foolish ire,
I walke and chase a sauage fairie still,
Now neere the flood, straight on the mounting hill,
Now midst the woodes of youth, and vaine desire:
  For leash I beare a cord of carefull griefe,
For brach[45] I lead an ouer forward minde,
My houndes are thoughtes, and rage dispairing blind,
Paine, crueltie, and care without reliefe:
  But they perceiuing that my swift pursute,
My flying fairie cannot ouertake,
With open mouthes their pray on me do make,

42 temper, as iron.
43 attempt.
44 will not.
45 Hound that hunts by scent.

Like hungrie houndes that lately lost their suite.[46]
And full of furie on their maister feede,
To hasten on my haplesse death with speede.

AN ODE

Nowe I find thy lookes were fained,
Quickly lost, and quicklie gained:
Soft thy skinne, like wooll of Weathers,
Hart vnstable, light as feathers.
Tongue vntrustie, subtil sighted,
Wanton will, with change delighted:
Siren pleasant, foe to reason,
Cupid plague thee for this treason.

Of thine eyes, I made my mirror,
From thy beautie came mine error,
All thy words I counted wittie,
All thy smiles I deemed pritty.
Thy false teares that me agrieued,
First of all my trust deceiued,
Siren pleasant, foe to reason,
Cupid plague thee for this treason.

Fained acceptance when I asked,
Louely words with cunning masked,
Holy vowes but hart vnholly,
Wretched man my trust was folly:
Lillie white and prettie winking,
Sollemne vowes, but sorry thinking.
Siren pleasant, foe to reason,
Cupid plague thee for this treason.

Now I see O seemely cruell,
Others warme them at my fuell,
Wit shall guide me in this durance,
Since in loue is no assurance.
Change thy pasture, take thy pleasure,
Beautie is a fading treasure.
Siren pleasant, foe to reason,
Cupid plague thee for this treason.

Prime youth lasts not, age will follow,[47]
And make white these tresses yellow,
Wrinckled face for lookes delightfull
Shall acquaint the Dame despightfull:
And when time shall eate thy glory,
Then too late thou wilt be sorry.
Siren pleasant, foe to reason,
Cupid plague thee for thy treason.

---

[46] scent.
[47] *lasts not, age will—The phoenix nest*, 1593, STC 21516]; *lusts not age still* STC 16662.

Accurst be loue and they that trust his traines;[48]
He tastes the fruite, whilst others toyle:
He brings the lampe, we lend the oyle:
He sowes distres, we yeeld him soyle:
He wageth warre, we bide the foyle:[49]

Accurst be Loue, and those that trust his traines:
He laies the trap, we seeke the snare:
He threatneth death, we speake him faire:
He coynes deceits, we foster care:
He fauoreth pride, we count it rare.

Accurst be Loue, and those that trust his traines,
He seemeth blinde, yet wounds with Art:
He vowes content, he paies with smart:
He sweares reliefe, yet kils the hart:
He cals for truth, yet scornes desart.
Accurst be loue, and those that trust his traines,
Whose heauen, is hell; whose perfect ioyes, are paines.[50]

Like desart woods, with darksome shades obscured,[51]
Where dredful beasts, wher hateful horror raigneth,[52]
Such is my wounded hart whom sorrow paineth.

The trees, are fatall shafts, to death inured,
That cruell Loue within my breast maintaineth,
To whet my griefe, when as my sorrow waineth.

The gastly beasts, my thoughts in cares assured,
Which wage me warre, whilst hart no succor gaineth,
With false suspect, and feare that still remaineth.

The horrors, burning sighes by cares procured,
Which forth I send, whilst weeping eie complaineth,
To coole the heate, the helples hart containeth.

But shafts, but cares, sighes, horrors vnrecured,[53]
Were nought esteemde, if for these paines awarded,
My faithfull Loue by you might be rewarded.[54]

For pittie pretie eies surcease,[55]
To giue me warre, and graunt me peace,
Triumphant eies, why beare you Armes,
Against a hart that thinks no harmes,[56]
A hart alreadie quite appalde,

[48] From *The phoenix nest*, 1593, STC 21516, Folger Library. *Traines* means "snares."
[49] foil, defeat.
[50] Signed *T. L. Gent.*
[51] From *The phoenix nest*, 1593.
[52] *raigneth,*] *raigneth* STC 21516.
[53] not remedied.
[54] Signed *T. L. Gent.*
[55] From *The phoenix nest*, 1593.
[56] *harmes,*] *harmes.* STC 21516.

A hart that yeelds, and is enthrald?[57]
Kill Rebels prowdly that resist,
Not those that in true faith persist,[58]
And conquered serue your Deitie.[59]
Will you alas commaund me die?
Then die I yours, and death my crosse,
But vnto you pertains the losse.[60]

OLDE DAMONS PASTORALL[61]

From Fortunes frownes and change remou'd,
  Wend silly Flocks in blessed feeding:
None of *Damon* more belou'd,
  Feede gentle Lambs while I sit reading.

Carelesse worldlings, outrage quelleth
  All the pride and pompe of Cittie:
But true peace with Sheepheards dwelleth,
  (Sheepheards who delight in pittie.)
Whether grace of heauen betideth,
  On our humble minds such pleasure:
Perfect peace with Swaines abideth,
  Loue and faith is Sheepheards treasure.
On the lower Plaines the thunder
  Little thriues, and nought preuaileth:
Yet in Citties breedeth wonder,
  And the highest hills assaileth.

Enuie of a forraigne Tyrant
  Threatneth Kings, not Sheepheards humble:
Age makes silly Swaines delirant,[62]
  Thirst of rule garres[63] great men stumble.
What to other seemeth sorrie,
  Abiect state and humble biding:
Is our ioy and Country glorie,
  Highest states haue worse betiding.
Golden cups doo harbour poyson,
  And the greatest pompe, dissembling:
Court of seasoned words hath foyson,[64]
  Treason haunts in most assembling.

Homely breasts doo harbour quiet,
  Little feare, and mickle solace:
States[65] suspect their bed and diet,
  Feare and craft doo haunt the Pallace.
Little would I, little want I,
  Where the mind and store agreeth,
Smallest comfort is not scantie,
  Least he longs that little seeth.

---

57 *enthrald?*] *enthrald,* STC 21516.
58 *persist,*] *persist.* STC 21516.
59 *Deitie.*] *Deitie,* STC 21516.
60 Signed *T. L. Gent.*
61 From *Englands Helicon,* 1600, STC 3191, Folger Library.
62 foolish.
63 makes.
64 plentiful crop.
65 Persons of rank.

Time hath beene that I haue longed,
  Foolish I, to like of follie:
To conuerse where honour thronged,
  To my pleasures linked wholy.

Now I see, and seeing sorrow
  That the day consum'd, returnes not:
Who dare trust vpon to morrow,
  When nor time, nor life soiournes not?[66]

[66] Signed *Thom. Lodge*.

Nicholas Breton

[c. 1545–c. 1625]

NICHOLAS BRETON was the son of William Breton, a wealthy London merchant who died in 1559. After several years at Oxford Breton published a volume of verse in 1575. During the next forty years he published some forty volumes of verse and prose, satirical, religious, pastoral. His prose is notable for his quiet and kindly interest in character and for his pleasant pictures of Elizabethan life. His best poetry is in his lyrics, which in their simplicity, sweetness, and grace resemble the best of Greene, Lodge, and Barnfield.

A comprehensive but incomplete edition is *The Works in Verse and Prose of Nicholas Breton*, ed. A. B. Grosart, 2 vols., 1875–1879. Useful editions of Breton's verse are *The Passionate Shepheard*, ed. F. Ouvry, 1877; *No Whippinge nor Trippinge*, ed. Charles Edmonds, 1895; *Brittons Bowre of Delights*, ed. H. E. Rollins, 1933; *The Arbour of Amorous Devises*, ed. H. E. Rollins, 1936. For criticism see A. H. Bullen, "Nicholas Breton," *Elizabethans*, 1924; S. A. Tannenbaum, *Nicholas Breton, a Concise Bibliography*, 1947.

A PRAYER FOR GENTLEWOMEN AND OTHERS TO VSE, WHEREBY THROUGH THE HELPE OF THE DEUINE GRACE, THEY MAY ATTEYNE THE RIGHT SENTE OF THIS POSIE OF GODLY FLOWERS[1]

Vouchsafe, O Lorde, to be our guyde,
  thy spirite of grace into vs powre:
Defende our cause on euery side,
  that we may passe into the bowre:
Whereas those heauenly Flowres do growe:
By Christ that Garden first dyd sowe.

Illuminate our inwarde minde,
  to seeke to thee continually:
From worldly Errours that be blind,
  preserue vs for thy Maiestie.
Teache vs as we in wordes professe,
In deedes eache one to do no lesse.

Assist vs dayly to begin,
  spiritually to enterfight[2]
Agaynst the worlde, the flesh, and sinne,
  that we may shunne the duskie nyght.
In whiche our enimie the deuill,
Doth watche to worke eache Christian euyll.

[1] From *A smale handfull of fragrant flowers, selected and gathered out of the louely garden of sacred scriptures, fit for any honorable or woorshipfull gentlewoman to smell vnto*, 1575, STC 3695, Huntington Library.

[2] fight.

Arme vs with fayth to beare the shielde,
and sworde of heauenly puritie:
Crowne vs with Helmet in the fielde,
of thy surpassing veritie.
Graunt this O bounteous Jesu sweete,
That we with thee at last may meete.

A SWEETE PASTORALL[3]

Good Muse rocke me asleepe with some sweet harmonie,
This weary eie is not to keepe, thy warie companie.
Sweet Loue be gone a while, thou knowst my heauines,
Bewtie is borne but to beguile my heart of happines.
See how my litle flocke that lou'd to feed on hie,
Do head-long tumble downe the rocke, and in the vally die.
The bushes and the trees, that weare so fresh and greene,
Do all their daintie colours leese,[4] and not a leafe is seene.
The *Black-bird,* and the *Thrush,* that made the woods to ring
With all the rest are now at hush, and not a note they sing.
Sweet *Philomele* the bird, that hath the heauenly throte,
Doth now (alas) not once afoord recording of a note.
The flowers have had a frost, each hearbe hath lost her sauor,
And *Phillida* the faire hath lost, the comfort of her fauor.[5]
Now all these carefull sights, so kill me in conceit,
That how to hope vpon delights, it is but meere deceit.
And therefore my sweet *Muse,* that knowst what help is best,
Do now thy heauenly cunning use to set my heart at rest.
And in a dreame bewray,[6] what fate shall be my friend,
Whether my life shall still decay, or when my sorow end.

[3] From *Brittons bowre of delights,* 1591, STC 3633, Huntington Library. This poem was reprinted in *The Arbor of Amorous Devices,* 1597, and in *England's Helicon,* 1600, where the long lines are broken in two.

[4] lose.

A PASTORALL OF PHILLIS AND CORIDON[7]

On a hill there growes a flower,
Faire befall the daintie sweete:
By that flower there is a bower,
Where the heauenly *Muses* meete.

In that Bower there is a Chaire,
Fringed all about with golde:
Where doth sit the fairest faire,
That did euer eye beholde.

It is *Phyllis* faire and bright,
She that is the shepheards ioy:
She that *Venus* did dispight,
And did blind her little boy.

This is she the wise, the rich,
And the world desires to see,
This is *Ipsa quae* the which,
There is none but onely shee.

Who would not this face[8] admire,
Who would not this Saint adore,
Who would not this sight desire
Though he thought to see no more:

Oh faire eyes yet let me see,
One good looke, and I am gone,
Looke on me for I am hee,
Thy poore sillie *Corridon.*

Thou that art the shepheards Queene,
Looke vpon thy sillie Swaine:
By thy comfort haue beene seene,
Dead men brought to life againe.

A SONET TO THE TUNE OF A HONE A HONE[9]

Come solemne *Muse* and helpe me sing,
A dolefull note, a dying song,
What wretched cares my heart do wring,
To see howe death hath done me wrong.

For I haue lost (oh deadly wo)
My iem, my ioy, my life, my loue,

[5] beauty.

[6] reveal.

[7] From *Brittons bowre of delights,* 1591.

[8] *face*] *fact* STC 3633.

[9] From *Brittons bowre of delights,* 1591. This poem was obviously a broadside ballad.

And in the world their is no mo,
Can heale the paine that I do proue.

My sweete affections all are fled,
Desires, delights, and all are gone,
My heart is sicke, my hope is dead,
And onely death to looke vpon.

These secrete cares so kill my heart,
With inward gripes[10] of endlesse griefe,
That how can sorrow euer part,[11]
Where is no hope to haue reliefe.

But helpelesse hopelesse still I lie.
Consuming so in secret care:
That who doth liue and would not die,
To looke vpon my heauie fare.

But all in vaine I make this mone,
Where nothing can my griefe release,
For I am onely left alone,
To sorrow still and neuer cease.

But sorrow now euen do thy wurst,
For death in fine[12] will be a friend:
For I do know my heart will burst,
And then thy force will haue an end.

A PASTORALL[13]

Sweet birds that sit and sing amid the shadie vallies,
And see how sweetly *Phillis* walks amid her garden allies:
Go round about her bower and sing, as ye are bidden,
To her is only knowne his faith, that from the world is hidden.
And she among you all that hath the sweetest voice,
Go chirpe of him that neuer told, yet neuer changd his choise.
And not forget his faith, that liu'd and[14] euer lou'd,
Yet neuer made his fancie knowne, nor euer fauour mou'd.
And euer let your ground of all your grace be this,
To you, to you, to you, the due of loue and honour is.
On you, on you, on you, our musicke all attendeth,
For as on you our *Muse* begun, in you all musicke endeth.

[10] pains.
[11] *part,*] *part.* STC 3633.
[12] in the end.
[13] From *Brittons bowre of delights,* 1591.
[14] *and*] *for* STC 3633.

CORIDONS SUPPLICATION TO PHILLIS[15]

Sweet *Phillis* if a sillie Swaine,
May sue to thee for grace:
See not thy louing shepheard slaine,
With looking on thy face.
But thinke what power thou hast got,
Upon my flocke and mee:
Thou seest they now regard me not,
But all doe follow thee.

And if I haue so farre presumed,
With prying in thine eyes:
Yet let not comfort be consumed,
That in thy pitie lyes.
But as thou art that *Phillis* faire,
That Fortune fauour giues,
So let not loue die in dispaire,
That in thy fauour liues.

The Deere do browse[16] upon the brier,
The birds do picke[17] the cheries,
And will not Bewtie graunt[18] Desire,
One handfull of her berries.
If so it be that thou hast sworne,
That none shall looke on thee:
Yet let me know thou dost not scorne,
To cast a looke on mee.

But if thy Bewtie make thee prowde,
Thinke then what is ordained:
The heauens haue neuer yet allowed,
That Loue should be disdained.
Then least the Fates that fauour Loue,
Should curse thee for vnkinde.
Let me report for thy behoue,
The honour of thy minde.

Let *Coridon* with full content,
Set downe what he hath seene:
That *Phillida* with Loues consent,
Is sworne the Shepheards Queene.

[15] From *Brittons bowre of delights,* 1591.
[16] *browse*] *bruise* STC 3633.
[17] *picke*] *pricke* STC 3633.
[18] *graunt* STC 3634]; *grunnt* STC 3633.

A SWEET LULLABIE[19]

Come little babe, come silly[20] soule,
Thy fathers shame, thy mothers griefe,
Borne as I doubt[21] to all our dole,
And to thy selfe vnhappie chiefe:
  Sing Lullabie and lap it warme,
  Poore soule that thinkes no creature harme.

Thou little thinkst and lesse doost knowe,
The cause of this thy mothers moane,
Thou wantst the wit to waile her woe,
And I my selfe am all alone:
  Why doost thou weepe? Why doost thou waile?
  And knowest not yet what thou doost ayle.

Come little wretch, ah silly heart,
Mine onely ioy, what can I more?
If there be any wrong thy smart,
That may the destinies implore:
  Twas I, I say, against my will,
  I wayle the time, but be thou still.

And doest thou smile, oh thy sweete face,
Would God himselfe he might thee see,
No doubt thou wouldst soone purchace grace,
I know right well for thee and mee:
  But come to mother babe and play,
  For father false is fled away.

Sweet boy if it by fortune chance,
Thy father home againe to send,
If death do strike me with his launce,
Yet mayst thou me to him commend:
  If any aske thy mothers name,
  Tell how by loue she purchast blame.

Then will his gentle heart soone yeeld,
I know him of a noble minde.
Although a Lyon in the field,
A Lamb in towne thou shalt him finde:
  Aske blessing babe, be not afrayde,
  His sugred words hath me betrayde.

Then mayst thou ioy and be right glad,
Although in woe I seeme to moane.
Thy father is no Rascall[22] lad,
A noble youth of blood and boane:
  His glancing lookes if he once smile,
  Right honest women may beguile.

Come little boy and rocke a sleepe,
Sing lullabie and be thou still,
I that can doe nought else but weepe,
Wil sit by thee and waile my fill:
  God blesse my babe and lullabie,
  From this thy fathers qualitie.

[19] From *The arbour of amorous deuises,* 1594, STC 3631, Huntington Library.
[20] innocent.
[21] fear.
[22] Lean or inferior deer.

From MELANCHOLIC HUMORS[23]

A SOLEMNE CONCEIPT

Doth loue liue in beauties eyes?
  Why then are they so vnlouing?
  Patience in her passion prouing:
There his sorrowe chiefely lies.

Liues beliefe in louers hearts?
  Why then are they vnbelieuing,
  Hourely so the spirit grieuing,
With a thousand iealous smarts?

Is there pleasure in loues passion?
  Why then is it so vnpleasing,
  Heart and spirit both diseasing,[24]
Where the wits are out of fashion?

No: loue sees, in beauties eyes:
  He hath only lost his seeing:
  Where in sorrowes only being,
All his comfort wholly dies.

Faith, within the heart of loue,
  Fearefull of the thing it hath,
  Treading of a trembling path,
Doth but iealousie approue.[25]

In loues passion then what pleasure?
  Which is but a lunacy:
  Where griefe, feare, and iealousie
Plague the senses out of measure.

[23] From *Melancholike humours, in verses of diuerse natures,* 1600, STC 3666, Huntington Library.
[24] disturbing.
[25] prove to be.

Farewell then (vnkindly) fancy,
In thy courses all too cruell:
Woe, the price of such a iewell,
As turnes reason to a franzy.

A DISPLEASURE AGAINST LOUE[26]

Loue is witty, but not wise,
When he stares on beauties eyes,
Finding wonders in conceit,[27]
That doe fall out but deceit.

Wit is stable, but not staied,
When his senses are betraied:
Where, too late sorrow doth proue,
Beauty makes a foole of loue.

Youth is forward,[28] but too fond,[29]
When he falles in *Cupids* bond:
Where repentance lets him see,
Fancy fast is neuer free.

Age is cunning,[30] but vnkinde,
When he once growes *Cupid*-blinde.
For, when beauty is vntoward,[31]
Age can neuer be but froward.

So that I doe finde in briefe,
In the grounds of natures griefe,
Age, and youth, and wit doe proue,
Beauty makes a foole of loue.

AN ODDE CONCEIPT[32]

Louely kinde, and kindly louing,
Such a minde were worth the mouing:
Truly faire, and fairely true,
Where are all these, but in you?

Wisely kinde, and kindely wise,
Blessed life, where such loue lies.
Wise, and kinde, and faire, and true,
Louely liue all these in you.

Sweetely deare, and dearely sweete,
Blessed where these blessings meete.
Sweete, faire, wise, kinde, blessed, true,
Blessed be all these in you.

The worldly prince doeth in his Septer hold[33]
A kind of heauen in his authorities:
The wealthy miser, in his masse of gold,
Makes to his soule a kind of Paradice:

The Epicure, that eates and drinkes all day,
Accounts no Heauen, but in his hellish rowtes:
And she, whose beauty seemes a sunny day,
Makes vp her heauen, but in her babies clowtes.

But, my sweete God, I seeke no Princes power,
No misers wealth, nor beauties fading glosse,
Which pamper sin, whose sweetes are inward sowre,
And sorry gaynes, that breed the Spirits losse.

No, my deare Lord, let my Heauen onely bee
In my Loues seruice, but to liue to thee.

What is the gold of all this world but drosse;[34]
The ioy, but sorrow, and the pleasure, payne,
The wealth, but beggery, and the gayne but losse,
The wit, but folly, and the vertue vayne;

The power, but weakenesse, and but death the life,
The hope, but feare, and the assurance dout,
The trust, deceit, the concord but a strife,
Where one conceit doth put another out;

---

26 From *Melancholike humours*, 1600.
27 imagination.
28 eager.
29 foolish.
30 knowing.
31 perverse.
32 From *Melancholike humours*, 1600.
33 From *The soules harmony*, 1602, STC 3699, Huntington Library.
34 *Ibid.*

Time but an instant, and the vse a toyle,
The knowledge, blindnesse, and the care a madnesse,
The siluer, lead, the diamond, but a foyle,
The rest, but trouble, and the mirth but sadnesse.

Thus since to heauen compar'd, the earth is such,
What thing is man, to loue the world so much?

Who can liue in heart so glad,[35]
As the merrie countrie lad?
Who vpon a faire greene balke[36]
May at pleasures sit and walke?
And amidde the Azure skies,
See the morning Sunne arise?
While hee heares in euery spring,[37]
How the Birdes doe chirpe and sing:
Or, before the houndes in crie,
See the Hare goe stealing by:
Or along the shallow brooke,
Angling with a baited hooke:
See the fishes leape and play,
In a blessed Sunny day:
Or to heare the Partridge call,
Till shee haue her Couye all:
Or to see the subtill foxe,
How the villaine plies the box:[38]
After feeding on his pray,
How he closely[39] sneakes away,
Through the hedge and downe the furrow,
Till he geets into his burrowe.
Then the Bee to gather honey,
And the little blacke-haird Cony,
On a banke for Sunny place,
With her fore-feete wash her face:
Are not these with thousandes moe,
Then the Courts of Kinges doe knowe?
The true pleasing spirits sights,
That may breede true loues delightes,
But with all this happinesse,
To beholde that Shepheardesse,
To whose eyes all Shepheards yeelde,
All the fairest of the fielde.
Faire *Aglaia* in whose face,
Liues the Shepheards highest Grace:
In whose worthy wonder praise,
See what her true Shepheard saies.
Shee is neither proude nor fine,
But in spirit more diuine:
Shee can neither lower nor leere,
But a sweeter smiling cheere:[40]
She had neuer painted face,
But a sweeter smiling grace:
Shee can neuer loue dissemble,
Truth doth so her thoughts assemble:
That where wisdome guides her will,
Shee is kind and constant still,
All in summe she is that creature,
Of that truest comfortes Nature,
That doth shewe (but in exceedinges)
How their praises had their breedings:
Let then poetts faine their pleasure,
In their fictions of loues treasure:
Proud high spirits seeke their graces,
In their Idoll painted faces:
My loues spirits lowlinesse,
In affections humblenesse,
Vnder heau'n no happines
Seekes but in this Shepheardesse.
For whose sake I say and sweare,
By the passions that I beare,
Had I got a Kinglie grace,
I would leaue my Kinglie place.
And in heart be truelie glad:
To become a Country Lad.
Hard to lie, and goe full bare,
And to feede on hungry fare:
So I might but liue to bee,
Where I might but sit to see,
Once a day, or all day long,
The sweet subiect of my song:
In *Aglaiaes* onely eyes,
All my worldly paradise.

[35] From *The passionate shepheard,* 1604, STC 3682, Huntington Library.
[36] Strip of unplowed ground that serves as a boundary.
[37] tree, grove.
[38] dodges, plays a trick.
[39] covertly.
[40] countenance.

Robert Southwell

[c. 1561–1595]

ROBERT SOUTHWELL was the one poet of his day who wrote verse entirely religious or devotional. Born in Norfolk, he was educated in Douay, Paris, and Rome. In 1578 he entered the Society of Jesus, and in 1584 he was ordained. Although a law passed in 1584 made it a treasonable offense for an English subject ordained as priest after 1557 to remain in England for more than forty days, Father Southwell in 1586 returned to England as a Jesuit missionary. In 1592 he was arrested, and after nearly three years of imprisonment he was executed.

Immediately after his death two volumes of his verse were published: *Saint Peter's Complaint*, a poem of some six hundred lines, with a supplement of short lyrics, and *Moeoniae,* a collection of short lyrics. He also wrote devotional works in prose. It is upon his short lyrics that his literary fame rests.

All his poetry, like his life, was dedicated to devotion. Probably much of his work was written in prison. Though some of his lyrics reveal his suffering and loneliness, the best are illuminated by the faith and radiant joy of a pure and gentle soul. At times his verse is marred by extravagant conceits and by the rhetoric and diction and versification of the outmoded tradition of poets like Gascoigne and Turberville, but in his best poems the homely simplicity of his language and rhythms gives admirable expression to his thought and emotion.

The modern edition is *The Complete Works of Robert Southwell*, ed. A. B. Grosart, 1872. Some of the poems are included, with biographical and critical matter, in C. M. Hood, *The Book of Robert Southwell*, 1926, and in L. I. Guiney, *Recusant Poets*, 1929. See also Sister Rosa Anita Morgan, *An Appreciation of Robert Southwell*, 1929; P. Janelle, *Robert Southwell, the Writer*, 1935; Joseph B. Collins, *Christian Mysticism in the Elizabethan Age with Its Background in Mystical Methodology*, 1940.

DECEASE, RELEASE
DUM MORIOR, ORIOR[1]

The pounded spise both tast and sent doth please;
In fadinge smoke the force doth incense showe;
The perisht kernell springeth with increase;
The lopped tree doth best and soonest growe.

Gods spice I was, and poundinge was my due;
In fadinge breath my incense savoured best;
Death was my meane my kernell to renewe;
By lopping shott I vpp to heavenly rest.

Some thinges more perfit are in their decaye,
Like sparke that going out geeves clerest light;
Such was my happe, whose dolefull dying daye
Begane my ioye and termed[2] fortunes spight.

Alive a Queene, now dead I am a Saint;
Once *Mary* cald, my name now Martyr is;
From earthly raigne debarred by restrainte,
In liew wherof I raigne in heavenly blis.

My life my griefe, my death hath wrought my ioye;
My freendes my foyle,[3] my foes my weale procurd;
My speedie death hath scorned longe annoye,[4]
And losse of life an endles life assurd.

My scaffolde was the bedd where ease I fownde;
The blocke a pillow of eternall rest.
My headman cast mee in in a blesfull sownde;[5]
His axe cutt of my cares from combred[6] brest.

Rue not my death; reioyce at my repose;
It was no death to mee but to my woe;
The budd was opened to let owt the rose;
The cheynes vnloosed to let the captive goe.

A Prince by birth, a prisoner by mishappe,
From crowne to crosse, from throne to thrall, I fell.
My right my ruth, my tytles wrought my trapp,
My weale my woe, my worldly heaven my hell.

By death from prisoner to a prince enhaunced,
From crosse to crowne, from thrall to throne againe;

---

[1] From Br. Mus. Addit. MS. 10422, ff. 32v–33, where it is unsigned. In MS. 655, Lambeth Palace Library, it is attributed to Southwell. This poem "represents faithfully the English Catholic tradition, then forming, in regard to the cause for which Mary, Queen of Scots died, and her right to be considered a martyr" (Louise Imogen Guiney, *Recusant Poets,* pp. 247–248). Miss Guiney gives the poem the title "At Fotheringay," where Mary was executed in 1587. The punctuation is the present editor's.

[2] ended.

[3] overthrow.

[4] woe.

[5] swoon, sleep.

[6] cumbered, afflicted.

My ruth my righte, my trappe my styll[7] advaunced,
From woe to weale, from hell to heavenly raigne.

In the wrackes of Walsingam[8]
  Whom should I chuse
But the Queene of Walsingham
  To be guide to my muse.

Then, thou Prince of Walsingham,
  Graunt me to frame
Bitter plaintes to rewe thy wronge,
  Bitter wo for thy name.

Bitter was it oh to see
  The seely[9] sheepe
Murdred by theraueninge wolues
  While the sheephardes did sleep.

Bitter was it oh to vewe
  The sacred vyne,
Whiles the gardiners plaied all close,
  Rooted vp by the swine.

Bitter, bitter, oh to behould
  The grasse to growe
Where the walles of Walsingam
  So statly did sheue.

Such were the workes of Walsingam
  While shee did stand;
Such are the wrackes as now do shewe
  Of that holy land.

Levell, levell with the ground,
  The towres doe lye,
Which with their golden glitteringe tops
  Pearsed once to the skye.

Wher weare gates no gates ar nowe;
  The waies unknowen
Wher the presse of peares[10] did passe
  While her fame far was blowen.

Oules do scrike wher the sweetest himnes
  Lately weer songe;
Toades and serpentes hold ther dennes
  Wher the Palmers did thronge.

---

[7] style, honorable state.

[8] From Bodleian MS. Rawlinson Poet. 219, ff. 16–16v. Walsingham in Norfolk was the seat of the famous shrine of Our Lady of Walsingham. In 1538 the shrine was stripped and the building was allowed to decay. This poem is probably by Southwell. The punctuation is the present editor's.

[9] innocent.

[10] throng of peers.

Weepe, weepe, O Walsingam,
Whose dayes are nightes,
Blessings turned to blasphemies,
Holy deedes to dispites.

Sinne is wher our Ladie sate;
Heauen turned is to hell;
Sathan sittes wher our Lord did swaye.
Walsingam, oh farewell.

TIMES GOE BY TURNES[11]

The lopped tree in time may grow againe,
Most naked plants renew both fruite and flower:
The sorriest wight may find release of paine,
The dryest soyle sucke in some moystning shower.
Times goe by turnes, and chaunces change by course,
From foule to faire: from better hap to worse.

The sea of Fortune doth not euer flow,
Shee drawes her fauours to the lowest ebbe;
Her tides haue equall times to come and goe,
Her Loome doth weaue the fine and coursest webbe.
No ioy so great, but runneth to an end:
No hap so hard, but may in fine[12] amend.

Not alwaies fall of leafe, nor euer spring,
No endlesse night, nor yet eternall day:
The saddest Birds a season find to sing,
The roughest storme a calme may soone allay.
Thus with succeeding turnes God tempereth all:
That man may hope to rise, yet feare to fal.

A chaunce may winne that[13] by mischaunce was lost,
That net that holds no great, takes little fish;
In some things all, in all things none are crost,
Fewe all they neede: but none haue all they wish,
Vnmeddled[14] ioyes heere to no man befall:
Who least, hath some, who most, hath neuer all.

SCORNE NOT THE LEAST[15]

Where wards[16] are weak, and foes encountring strong,
Where mightier doe assault then doe defend,
The feebler part puts vp[17] enforced wrong,
And silent sees, that[18] speech could not amend;
Yet higher powers must thinke, though they repine,
When sunne is set, the little starres will shine.

---

[11] From *Saint Peters complaint, newly augmented with other poems*, n.d., STC 22961, Huntington Library.
[12] end.
[13] win that which.
[14] unmixed.
[15] From *Saint Peters complaint*, 1605(?).
[16] defenses.
[17] suffers quietly.
[18] what.

While Pike doth range, the silly[19] Tench doth flie,
And crouch in priuie creekes, with smaller fish:
Yet Pikes are caught when little fish goe by,[20]
These fleete aflote,[21] while those doe fill the dish;
There is a time euen for the wormes to creepe,
And sucke the deaw while all their foes doe sleepe.

The Marline[22] cannot euer soare on high,
Nor greedie Grey-hound still[23] pursue the chase,
The tender Larke will finde a time to flie,
And fearefull Hare to runne a quiet race.
He that high growth on Cedars did bestow,
Gaue also lowly Mushrumps[24] leaue to growe.

In Hamans pompe poore Mardocheus[25] wept,
Yet God did turne his fate vpon his foe.
The Lazar pinde,[26] while Diues feast was kept,
Yet he to heauen, to hell did Diues goe.
We trample grasse, and prize the flowers of May,
Yet grasse is greene, when flowers doe fade away.

A CHILD MY CHOICE[27]

Let follie prayse that fancie loues: I prayse and loue that child,
Whose hart no thought, whose tongue no word, whose hand no deede defil'd.
I praise him most, I loue him best, all prayse and loue is his:
While him I loue, in him I liue, and cannot liue amisse.

Loues sweetest marke, lawdes[28] highest theme, mans most desired light,
To loue him, life; to leaue him, death; to liue in him, delight.
He mine by gift, I his by debt, thus each to other's due,
First friend hee was, best friend he is, all times will try him true.

Though young, yet wise, though small, yet strong, though man, yet God he is.
As wise, he knowes, as strong he can, as God he loues to blisse:[29]
His knowledge rules, his strength defends, his loue doth cherrish all,
His birth our ioy, his life our light, his death our end of thrall.

Alas, hee weepes, he sighes, he pants, yet doe his Angels sing,
Out of his teares, his sighes and throbs, doth bud a ioyfull spring,
Almightie babe, whose tender armes can force all foes to flie,
Correct my faults, protect my life, direct mee when I die.

CONTENT AND RICH[30]

I dwell in graces Court,
  Enricht with vertues rights;
Faith guides my wit, loue leades my will
  Hope all my minde delights.

In lowly vales I mount
  To pleasures highest pitch:
My seely shroude[31] true honour brings,
  My poore estate is rich.

My conscience is my crowne,

[19] harmless.
[20] escape.
[21] swim at liberty.
[22] merlin, a small falcon.
[23] always.
[24] mushrooms.
[25] Mordecai. *Mardochaeus* is the spelling in the Vulgate, the Bible that Southwell read.
[26] suffered from hunger. See Luke xvi, 19–31.
[27] From *Saint Peters complaint,* 1605(?).
[28] laud's.
[29] bless, rejoice.
[30] From *Saint Peters complaint,* 1605(?).
[31] simple shelter.

Contented thoughts, my rest,
My hart is happie in it selfe,
My blisse is in my brest.

Enough, I reckon wealth,
A meane, the surest lot,
That lyes too high for base contempt,
Too low, for enuies shot.

My wishes are but few,
All easie to fulfill:
I make the limits of my power,
The bounds vnto my will.

I haue no hopes but one
Which is of heauenly raigne:
Effects attaind, or not desir'd
All lower hopes refraine.

I feele no care of coyne,
Well-doing is my wealth,
My mind to me an Empire is
While grace affoordeth health.

I clyp high-climing thoughts,
The wings of swelling pride,
Their fall is worst that from the height
Of greatest honour slide.

Sith[32] sayles of largest size
The storme doth soonest teare,
I beare so low and small a saile
As freeth mee from feare.

I wrastle not with rage
While furies flame doth burne,
It is in vaine to stop the streame
Vntill the tide doth turne.

But when the flame is out,
And ebbing wrath doth end,
I turne a late enraged foe
Into a quiet friend.

And taught with often proofe,
A tempered calme I finde
To be most solace to it selfe,
Best cure for angrie mind.

Spare dyet is my fare,
My clothes more fit then fine,
I know I feede and clothe a foe,
That pamp'red, would repine.

I enuie not their hap
Whom fauour doth aduance;
I take no pleasure in their paine
That haue lesse happie chaunce.

To rise by others fall,
I deeme a loosing gaine;
All states with others ruines built,
To ruine runne a maine.

No change of Fortunes calmes
Can cast my comforts downe,
When Fortune smiles, I smile to thinke
How quickly shee will frowne.

And when in froward moode
Shee proues an angrie foe,
Small gaine I found to let her come,
Lesse losse to let her goe.

32 since.

LOSSE IN DELAYES[33]

Shun delayes: they breede remorse,
Take thy time while time doth serue thee,
Creeping Snayles haue weakest force,
Flie their fault, least thou repent thee,
Good is best when soonest wrought,
Lingring labours come to nought.

Hoyse vp saile while gale doth last,
Tide and wind stay no mans pleasure;
Seeke not time, when time is past,
Sober speede is wisedoms leysure:
After wits are dearely bought,
Let thy fore-wit guide thy thought.

Time weares all his locks before,
Take thou hold vpon his fore-head,
When he flyes, he turnes no more,
And behind his scalpe is naked,
Workes adiournd,[34] haue many stayes,
Long demurres breede new delayes.

Seeke thy salue while soare is greene,
Festered wounds aske deeper launcing;
After cures are sildome seene,

33 From *Saint Peters complaint,* 1605(?).
34 postponed.

Often sought scarce euer chauncing,
Time and place giue best aduise,
Out of season, out of price.

Crush the Serpent in the head,
Breake ill egges ere they be hatched.
Kill bad Chickins in the tread;[35]
Fligge,[36] they hardly can be catched,
In the rising, stifle ill,
Least it grow against thy will.

Drops doe pearce the stubborne flint,
Not by force but often falling,
Custome kils with feeble dint,[37]
More by vse then strength preuailing.
Single sands haue little waight,
Many make a drowning fraight.

Tender twigs are bent with ease,
Aged trees doe breake with bending,
Young desires make little prease,[38]
Growth doth make them past amending.
Happie man that soone doth knock,
Babel[39] babes against the rocke.

LOUES SERUILE LOT[40]

Loue, mistresse is of many minds,
Yet few know whom they serue,
They reckon least how little loue
Their seruice doth deserue.

The will she robbeth from the wit,
The sense from reasons lore,
She is delightfull in the rine,[41]
Corrupted in the core;

Shee shroudeth vice in vertues vaile,
Pretending good in ill,
She offereth ioy, affordeth griefe,
A kisse where she doth kill.

A honey shower raines from her lips,
Sweet lights shine in her face.
She hath the blush of virgine mind,
The mind of Vipers race.

Shee makes thee seeke, yet feare to find,
To finde, but not enioy;
In many frownes some gliding smiles,
Shee yeelds,[42] to more annoy.

Shee wooes thee to come neere her fire,
Yet doth she draw it from thee,
Farre off she makes thy hart to fry,[43]
And yet to freeze within thee.

Shee letteth fall some luring baits
For fooles to gather vp:
Too sweet, too sowre, to euerie taste
Shee tempereth her cup.

Soft soules she binds in tender twist,
Small Flyes in spinners webbe,
She sets afloate some luring streames,
But makes them soone to ebbe.

Her watrie eyes haue burning force:
Her floods and flames conspire:
Teares kindle sparks, sobs fuell are:
And sighs doe blow her fire.

May neuer was the Month of loue,
For May is full of flowers,
But rather Aprill wet by kind,[44]
For loue is full of showers.

Like tyrant cruell wounds she giues,
Like Surgeon salue she lends,
But salue and sore haue equall force,
For death is both their ends.

With soothing words, inthralled soules
Shee chaines in seruile bands,
Her eye in silence hath a speach,
Which eye best vnderstands.

Her little sweet hath many sowres,
Short hap immortall harmes,
Her louing lookes, are murdring darts,
Her songs bewitching charmes.

Like winter rose, and sommer Ise
Her ioyes are still vntimely,
Before her hope, behind remorse,
Faire first, in fine[45] vnseemely.

---

35 egg.
36 fledged.
37 blow.
38 pressure.
39 babel (turbulent) or bauble (foolish).
40 From *Saint Peters complaint*, 1605 (?).
41 rind.
42 *yeelds,*] *yeelds* STC 22961.
43 burn.
44 nature.
45 end.

Moodes, passions, fancies,[46] iealous fits,
Attend vpon her traine:
Shee yeeldeth rest without repose,
A heau'n in hellish paine.

Her house is sloth, her doore deceite,
And slipperie hope her staires,
Vnbashfull boldness bids her guests,
And euerie vice repaires.[47]

Her dyet is of such delight,
As please till they be past,
But then the poyson kils the hart,
That did entise the taste.

Her sleepe in sinne, doth end in wrath,
Remorse rings her awake,
Death cals her vp, shame driues her out,
Despaires her vp-shot make.

Plow not the Seas, sowe not the sands,
Leaue off your idle paine,
Seeke other mistresse for your mindes,
Loues seruice is in vaine.

LIFE IS BUT LOSSE[48]

By force[49] I liue, in will I wish to dye,
  In plaint I passe the length of lingring dayes,
Free would my soule from mortall bodie flye,
  And tread the tracke of deaths desired wayes;
Life is but losse, where death is deemed gaine,
And loathed pleasures breede displeasing paine.

Who would not dye to kill all murdering greeues,
  Or who would liue in neuer dying feares:
Who would not wish his treasure safe from theeues,
  And quit his hart from pangs, his eyes from teares?
Death parteth but two, euer fighting foes,
Whose ciuill strife, doth worke our endlesse woes.

Life is a wandring course to doubtfull rest,
  As oft a cursed ryse to damning leape;
As happie race to winne a heauenly crest,
  None being sure, what finall fruits to reape.
And who can like in such a life to dwell,
Whose wayes are straite[50] to heau'n, but wide to hell.

Come cruell death why lingrest thou so long,
  What doth withhold thy dint[51] from fatall stroke?
Now prest[52] I am: alas thou doest me wrong,
  To let me liue more anger to prouoke:
Thy right is had, when thou hast stopt my breath,
Why should'st thou stay, to work my double death?

If *Saules* attempt in falling on his blade,
  As lawfull were, as ethe[53] to put in vre:[54]
If *Sampsons* leaue, a common law were made,
Of *Abels* lot if all that would were sure,
Then cruell death thou should'st the tyrant play,
With none but such as wished for delay.

---

46 *Moodes, passions, fancies*] *Moodes passions, fancies* STC 22961.
47 goes (as guest).
48 From *Saint Peters complaint*, 1605 (?).
49 of necessity.
50 narrow.
51 blow.
52 ready.
53 easy.
54 use, practice.

Where life is lou'd, thou readie art to kil,
And to abbridge with sodaine pangs their ioy,
Where life is loath'd thou wilt not work their will,
But dost adiourne[55] their death to their annoy.
To some thou art a fierce vnbidden guest:
But those that craue thy helpe thou helpest least.

Auant O viper, I thy spight defie,
There is a God that ouer-rules thy force,
Who can thy weapons to his will apply,
And shorten or prolong our brittle course:
I on his mercie, not thy might relye,
To him I liue, for him I hope to dye.

I DIE ALIUE[56]

O life what lets[57] thee from a quick decease?
O death what drawes thee from a present pray?
My feast is done, my soule would be at ease,
My grace is said, O death come take away.

I liue, but such a life as euer dies:
I die, but such a death, as neuer ends,
My death to end my dying life denies,
And life my liuing death no whit amends.

Thus still I dye, yet still I doe reuiue,
My liuing death by dying life is fed:
Grace more then Nature keepes my hart aliue,
Whose idle hopes and vaine desires are dead.

Not where I breath, but where I loue I liue,
Not where I loue, but where I am I die:
The life I wish, must future glorie giue,
The deaths I feele, in present dangers lie.

NEW PRINCE, NEW POMPE[58]

Behold a silly[59] tender Babe,
In freesing Winter night;
In homely manger trembling lies,
Alas a pittious sight:

The Innes are full, no man will yeeld
This little Pilgrime bed;
But forc't he is with sillie beasts,
In Crib to shrowd his head.

Despise him not for lying there,
First what he is enquire:

[55] postpone.
[56] From *Saint Peters complaint,* 1605(?).
[57] delays, hinders.
[58] From *Saint Peters complaint,* 1605 (?).
[59] innocent, helpless.

An orient pearle is often found,
In depth of dirtie mire.

Waigh not his Crib, his wodden dish,
Nor beasts that by him feede:
Waight not his Mothers poore attire,
Nor Iosephs simple weede.[60]

This stable is a Princes Court,
The Crib his chaire of state:
The beasts are parcell of his Pompe,
The wodden dish his plate.

The persons in that poore attire,
His royall liueries weare,
The Prince himselfe is com'n from heauen,
This pompe is prized there.

With ioy approach O Christian wight,[61]
Doe homage to thy King;
And highly prayse his humble pompe,
Which he from heauen doth bring.

THE BURNING BABE[62]

As I in hoarie Winters night stood shiuering in the snowe,
Surpris'd I was with sodaine heate, which made my hart to glowe;
And lifting vp a fearefull eye, to view what fire was neere,
A prettie Babe all burning bright did in the ayre appeare;
Who, scorched with excessiue heate, such floods of teares did shed,
As though his floods should quench his flames, which with his teares were bred:
Alas, (quoth he) but newly borne, in fierie heates I frie,
Yet none approach to warme their harts, or feele my fire but I;
My faultlesse breast the furnace is, the fuell wounding thornes:
Loue is the fire, and sighes the smoake, the ashes shames and scornes;
The fewell Iustice layeth on, and Mercie blowes the coales,
The metall in this furnace wrought, are mens defiled soules:
For which, as now on fire I am to worke them to their good,
So will I melt into a bath, to wash them in my blood.
With this he vanisht out of sight, and swiftly shrunk away,
And straight I called vnto minde, that it was Christmasse day.

TO THE CHRISTIAN READER[63]

If vertue be thy guide,
True comfort is thy path,
And thou secure from erring steps,
That leade to vengeance wrath.

Not widest open doore,
Nor spacious wayes she goes,

[60] clothing.
[61] man.

[62] From *Saint Peters complaint,* 1605(?).
[63] From *St. Peters complaint,* 1620, STC 22965, Folger Library.

To straight and narrow gate and way,
She cals, she leads, she shewes.

She cals, the fewest come,
She leades the humble sprited,
She shews them rest at rases end,
Soules rest to heauen inuited.

Tis she that offers most,
Tis she that most refuse,
Tis she preuents the broad way plagues,
Which most do wilfull chuse.

Do chuse the wide, the broad,
The left-hand way and gate:
These vice applauds, these vertue loaths
And teacheth hers to hate.

Her wayes are pleasant wayes,
Vpon the right hand side,
And heauenly happie is that soule,
Takes vertue for her guide.

From MOEONIAE[64]

VPON THE IMAGE OF DEATH

Before my face the picture hangs,
That daily should put me in mind,
Of those cold qualms[65] and bitter pangs,
That shortly I am like to find:
But yet alas full little I
Do thinke hereon that I must die.

I often looke vpon a face
Most vgly, grisly, bare and thinne,
I often view the hollow place,
Where eies and nose, had sometimes bin,
I see the bones acrosse that lie:
Yet little thinke that I must die.

I reade the Labell vnderneath
That telleth me whereto I must,
I see the sentence eake[66] that saith,
Remember man that thou art dust:
But yet alas but seldome I,
Doe thinke indeede that I must die.

Continually at my beds head,
A hearse[67] doth hang which doth me tel,

[64] From *Moeoniae, Or certaine excellent poems and spirituall hymnes,* 1595, STC 22955, Huntington Library. The title is usually spelled *Maeoniae* (i.e., "Lydian Muses").

[65] *qualms* Simon Wastell, *Microbiblion,* 1629, STC 25102]; *names* STC 22955.

[66] eke, also.

[67] Canopy to be placed over a coffin.

That I ere morning may be dead,
  Though now I feele my selfe ful well:
But yet alas, for all this I
Haue little mind that I must die.

The gowne which I do vse to weare,
  The knife wherewith I cut my meate,
And eke that old and ancient chaire,
  Which is my onely vsuall seate:
All those do tel me I must die,
And yet my life amend not I.

My ancestors are turnd to clay,
  And many of my mates are gone,
My yongers[68] daily drop away,
  And can I thinke to scape alone?
No, no, I know that I must die,
And yet my life amend not I.

Not *Salomon* for al his wit,
  Nor *Samson* though he were so strong,
No king nor person euer yet
  Could scape, but death laid him along:
Wherefore I know that I must die,
And yet my life amend not I.

Though all the East did quake to heare,
  Of *Alexanders* dreadfull name,
And all the West did likewise feare,
  To heare of *Iulius Caesars* fame,
Yet both by death in dust now lie,
Who then can scape but he must die?

If none can scape deaths dreadfull dart,
  If rich and poore his becke obey,
If strong, if wise, if all do smart,
  Then I to scape shall haue no way.
Oh grant me grace O God that I,
My life may mend sith[69] I must die.

MANS CIUILL WARRE[70]

My houering thoughts would flie to heauen, and quiet nestle in the skie,
Faine would my ship in vertues shore without remoue[71] at anchor lie:
But mounted thoughts are hailed[72] downe with heauie poise[73] of mortall load,
And blustring stormes denie my ship in vertues hauen sure aboade.
When inward eie to heauenly sights doth draw my longing harts desire,
The world with iesses[74] of delight, would to her pearch my thought retire,

68 younger persons.
69 since.
70 From *Moeoniae,* 1595.
71 removal.
72 hauled.
73 weight.
74 *iesses*] *lesses* STC 22955. In falconry, jesses straps are the short straps fastened to the legs of the hawk and attached to the leash.

Fond fancie traines to pleasures lure,[75] though reason stiffely do repine.
Though reason wooe me to the saint, yet sense would win me to the shrine:
Where wisdome loathes, there fancie loues, and euer rules the captiue will.[76]
Foes senses are[77] to vertues lore,[78] they draw the wit their wish to fill.
Neede craues consent of soule to sense, yet diuers bents breeds ciuill fray,[79]
Hard hap where halues must disagree, or trust of halues the whole betray.
O cruell fight where fighting frend with loue doth kill a fauoring foe,
Where peace with sense is warre with God, and selfe delight the seed of woe,
Dame pleasures drugges are steept in sinne, their sugred taste doth breede anoy,
O fickle sense beware her ginne,[80] sell not thy soule for brittle ioy.

75 In training the hawk, the falconer uses as "the lure" either a dead bird or a feathered decoy.

76 *will.*] *will* STC 22955.

77 *senses are*] *senses, and* STC 22955.

78 Our senses are foes to the lessons of reason.

79 propensities.

80 snare.

Richard Barnfield

[1574–1627]

RICHARD BARNFIELD was born in Shropshire and was graduated B.A. at Oxford in 1592. After a few years in London he retired to his country home. His three books of verse, published before he was twenty-five, are the work of a gifted and scholarly amateur. In 1594 appeared *The Affectionate Shepherd*, in 1595 *Cynthia*, and in 1598 *The Encomion of Lady Pecunia*, a satire on the power of wealth. Especially interesting are his generous tributes to contemporary writers. Barnfield's best lyrics are simple and graceful.

Modern editions are *The Complete Poems of Richard Barnfield*, ed. A. B. Grosart, 1876; *Some Longer Elizabethan Poems*, ed. A. H. Bullen, 1903; *The Poems of Richard Barnfield*, ed. Montague Summers, n.d. (1936?).

TO HIS MYSTRESSE[1]

Bright Starre of beauty, fayrest Fayre aliue,
Rare president[2] of peerelesse chastitie;
(In whom the Muses and the Graces striue,
Which shall possesse the chiefest part of thee;)
Oh let these simple lines accepted bee:
Which here I offer at thy sacred shrine;
Sacred, because sweete Beauty is diuine.

And though I cannot please each curious eare,
With sugred Noates of heauenly Harmonie;
Yet if my loue shall to thy selfe appeare,
No other Muse I will inuoke but thee;
And if thou wilt my faire *Thalia* bee,
I'le sing sweet Hymnes and prayses to thy Name,
In that cleare Temple of eternall Fame.

But ah (alas) how can myne infant Muse
(That neuer heard of *Helicon* before)
Performe my promise past: when they refuse
Poore Shepheards Playnts? yet will I still adore

[1] From *Cynthia, with certaine Sonnets and the legend of Cassandra*, 1595, STC 1483, Huntington Library.

[2] guardian; sometimes the modern "precedent" is so spelled.

Thy sacred Name, although I write no more:
Yet hope I shall, if this accepted bee;
If not, in silence sleepe eternally.

TO HIS FRIEND MAISTER R.L. IN PRAISE OF MUSIQUE AND POETRIE[3]

If Musique and sweet Poetrie agree,
As they must needes (the Sister and the Brother)
Then must the Loue be great, twixt thee and mee,
Because thou lou'st the one, and I the other.
Dowland[4] to thee is deare; whose heauenly tuch
Vpon the Lute, doeth rauish humaine sense:
Spenser to mee; whose deepe Conceit is such,
As passing all Conceit, needs no defence.
Thou lou'st to heare the sweete melodious sound,
That *Phoebus* Lute (the Queene of Musique) makes:
And I in deepe Delight am chiefly drownd,
When as himselfe to singing he betakes.
One God is God of Both (as Poets faigne)
One Knight loues Both, and Both in thee remaine.

AGAINST THE DISPRAYSERS OF POETRIE[5]

Chaucer is dead; and *Gower* lyes in grave;
The Earle of *Surrey*, long agoe is gone;
Sir *Philip Sidneis* soule, the Heauens haue;
George Gascoigne him beforne, was tomb'd in stone.
Yet, tho their Bodies lye full low in ground,
(As euery thing must dye, that earst[6] was borne)
Their liuing fame, no Fortune can confound;
Nor euer shall their Labours be forlorne.
And you, that discommend sweete Poetrie,
(So that the Subiect of the same be good)
Here may you see, your fond simplicitie;
Sith[7] Kings haue fauord it, of royall Blood.
The King of *Scots*[8] (now liuing) is a Poet,
As his *Lepanto*, and his *Furies* shoe it.

A REMEMBRANCE OF SOME ENGLISH POETS[9]

Liue *Spenser* euer, in thy *Fairy Queene:*
Whose like (for deepe Conceit) was neuer seene.
Crownd mayst thou bee, vnto thy more renowne,
(As King of Poets) with a Lawrell Crowne.

---

3 From *Poems in diuers humors*, 1598, STC 1488, printed with *The encomion of lady Pecunia*, 1598, STC 1485, Huntington Library. "R.L." is perhaps the poet Richard Lynche.

4 John Dowland, a celebrated lutanist.

5 From *Poems in diuers humors*, 1598.

6 formerly.

7 since.

8 James VI of Scotland, who in 1603 became James I of England, published in 1584 *The essayes of a prentise in the diuine art of poesie* (STC 14373) and in 1591 *His Maiesties poeticall exercises*, which contained the poems Barnfield mentions.

9 From *Poems in diuers humors*, 1598.

And *Daniell,* praised for thy sweet-chast Verse:
Whose Fame is grav'd on *Rosamonds* blacke Herse.[10]
Still mayst thou liue: and still be honored,
For that rare Worke, *The White Rose and the Red.*[11]

And *Drayton,* whose wel-written Tragedies,
And sweete Epistles, soare thy fame to skies.
Thy learned Name, is aequall with the rest;
Whose stately Numbers are so well addrest.

And *Shakespeare* thou, whose hony-flowing Vaine,
(Pleasing the World) thy Praises doth containe.
Whose *Venus,* and whose *Lucrece* (sweete, and chaste)
Thy Name in fames immortall Booke haue plac't.
Liue euer you, at least in Fame liue euer:
Well may the Bodye dye, but Fame die neuer.

AN ODE[12]

As it fell vpon a Day,
In the merrie Month of May,
Sitting in a pleasant shade,
Which a groue of Myrtles made,
Beastes did leape, and Birds did sing,
Trees did grow, and Plants did spring:
Euery thing did banish mone,
Saue the Nightingale alone.
Shee (poore Bird) as all forlorne,
Leand her Breast vp-till[13] a Thorne;
And there sung the dolefulst Ditty,
That to heare it was great Pitty.
Fie, fie, fie; now would the cry
Teru Teru, by and by:
That to heare her so complaine,
Scarce I could from Teares refraine:
For her griefes so liuely showne,
Made me thinke vpon mine owne.
Ah (thought I) thou mournst in vaine;
None takes Pitty on thy paine:
Senslesse Trees, they cannot heere thee;
Ruthlesse Beares, they wil not cheer thee.
King *Pandion,*[14] hee is dead:
All thy friends are lapt in Lead.
All thy fellow Birds doe singe,
Carelesse of thy sorrowing.
Whilst as fickle Fortune smilde,
Thou and I, were both beguilde.
Euerie one that flatters thee,
Is no friend in miserie:
Words are easie, like the winde;
Faithfull friends are hard to finde:
Euerie man will bee thy friend,
Whilst thou hast wherewith to spend:
But if store of Crownes be scant,
No man will supply thy want.
If that one be prodigall,
Bountifull, they will him call:
And with such-like flattering,
Pitty but hee were a King.
If he bee adict to vice,
Quickly him, they will intice.
If to Woemen hee be bent,
They haue at Commaundement.
But if Fortune once doe frowne,
Then farewell his great renowne:
They that fawnd on him before,
Vse his company no more.
Hee that is thy friend indeed,
Hee will helpe thee in thy neede:
If thou sorrow, hee will weepe;
If thou wake, hee cannot sleepe:
Thus of euerie griefe, in hart
Hee, with thee, doeth beare a Part.
These are certaine Signes, to knowe
Faithfull friend, from flatt'ring foe.

---

10 Samuel Daniel, *The Complaint of Rosamund,* 1592, STC 6253; 1594, STC 6254.

11 *The first fowre bookes of the ciuile wars between the two houses of Lancaster and Yorke,* 1595, STC 6244.

12 From *Poems in diuers humors,* 1598.

13 against.

14 In Greek legend, Pandion was the father of Philomela and Procne, whom the gods, in pity for their sorrows, turned into a nightingale and a swallow.

A COMPARISON OF THE LIFE OF MAN[15]

Mans life is well compared to a feast,
Furnisht with choice of all Varietie:
To it comes Tyme; and as a bidden guest
Hee sets him downe, in Pompe and Maiestie;
The three-folde Age of Man, the Waiters bee:
Then with an earthen voyder[16] (made of clay)
Comes Death, and takes the table clean away.

[15] From *Poems in diuers humors,* 1598.
[16] Basket or tray for removing food after a meal.

William Shakespeare

[1564–1616]

WILLIAM SHAKESPEARE, the greatest English dramatist, would hold an honored place among the poets even if he had written no plays. His nondramatic poems, most of them written during the first half of his career, belong in four groups: the narrative poems, *Venus and Adonis* and *The Rape of Lucrece;* the sonnets; *The Phoenix and the Turtle;* and the songs included in the plays.

Venus and Adonis, 1593, Shakespeare dedicated to the young Earl of Southampton (1573–1626), and in his dedication he called the poem "the first heir of my invention." It is an erotic narrative poem of the kind fashionable in the 1590's, other examples of the type being Lodge's *Scilla's Metamorphosis* (or *Glaucus and Scilla*), Marlowe's *Hero and Leander,* Barnfield's *Cassandra,* and Drayton's *Endimion and Phoebe.* Lodge, Shakespeare, and Barnfield use the same verse form.

Shakespeare, retelling a story in Ovid's *Metamorphoses,* deals with a pagan theme in a pagan spirit. Lodge's *Scilla's Metamorphosis,* 1589, tells a somewhat similar story: a nymph courts an unwilling swain much as Venus courts Adonis in Shakespeare's poem. Although the story is "rather indecent and rather absurd," the poem is notable for what Barnfield called Shakespeare's "honey-flowing vein," for the graceful, fluent, melodious verse of his earliest manner, and for the vivid pictures of hunting scenes which seem to have been drawn from personal observation.

The Rape of Lucrece, 1594, is no doubt the "graver labor" promised to the Earl of Southampton in the dedication of *Venus and Adonis.* The principal sources of the poem are Livy, Ovid, and Chaucer's *Legend of Good Women.* In tone and in the rhetorical dialogues and soliloquies, *Lucrece* resembles Daniel's *Complaint of Rosamund,* 1592, and other poems in the medieval tradition of *A Mirror for Magistrates.* The verse form is rhyme royal as in Daniel and the *Mirror* poems.

Both of Shakespeare's poems became very popular at once; by 1616 there were at least ten editions of *Venus and Adonis* and at least six of *Lucrece.*

Shakespeare's two poems—ornate, rhetorical, prolix—are apprentice work, exercises done to test his craftsmanship. In them one sees the painstaking artist's love of beauty before it was transformed into the dramatist's understanding love of humanity.

Shakespeare's sonnets were published in 1609 by an obscure publisher, Thomas Thorpe, who added a dedication: "To the onlie begetter of these insving sonnets Mr. W. H. all happinesse and that eternitie promised by ovr ever-living poet wisheth the well-wishing adventvrer in setting forth. T.T." In simple language this means: "Thomas Thorpe, the well-meaning publisher, hopes that Master W. H., the sole begetter of the following sonnets, may have all happiness and that eternity of fame which Shakespeare promised." We do not know what "begetter" means, or who "Mr. W. H." was, or how Thorpe obtained the manuscript or manuscripts that he printed, or whether Shakespeare wrote all of the one hundred fifty-four sonnets in Thorpe's volume, or whether the arrangement of the sonnets is Thorpe's or Shakespeare's or some other's, or when the sonnets were written, or to whom any of them were addressed, or whether any of them were addressed to anyone, or to what extent they are autobiographical. The value of the sonnets as great poetry is quite independent of all such knowledge.

Although Shakespeare's name on the title page is not proof of his authorship, most critics and scholars believe that Shakespeare wrote all, or nearly all, of the one hundred fifty-four sonnets in Thorpe's volume. The exact date of composition has never been determined. In *Palladis Tamia*, 1598, Francis Meres mentions Shakespeare's "sugred Sonnets among his private friends," but from Meres's statement we cannot know whether any of the sonnets that he had seen or heard of are included in Thorpe's volume. A distinguished scholar has recently found in three sonnets (107, 123, 124) topical allusions that have led him to believe that these sonnets, and by implication others, were written before the end of 1589; it is almost certain, however, that the sonnets were written at different times from about 1592 to 1609, and most of them before 1600.

Shakespeare's sonnets exhibit many of the characteristics of the conventional sonnet. He adopted a conventional form. Many English poets—Sidney and Constable, for example—used the Italian form; others, notably Spenser and Drummond, devised rhyme patterns of their own; Shakespeare used the form developed by Surrey—three quatrains, with alternate rhyme, followed by a couplet. Some of Shakespeare's sonnets treat the conventional themes of the sonnet writers: the promise of immortality through verse, the "then and now" contrast, the pain of absence. But his sonnets as a whole are strikingly original in subject and in tone. Many are vibrant and glowing with emotion. The creator of Othello and Lear made many of his sonnets sound like autobiography.

As a consequence, many have read them as autobiography and have concluded that Sonnets 1–126 form a coherent series about an aristocratic young man, and that 127–154 form a less coherent series about a dark woman. Such a conclusion depends on the hypothesis that Shakespeare arranged his sonnets in approximately the order in which they are printed in Thorpe's edition. This arrangement is almost certainly neither the order in which they were written nor the order in which Shakespeare intended them to stand if published. It is probable that whoever arranged the sonnets, whether he found them in a commonplace book or in loose sheets, put the longest series at the beginning of the collection and grouped together elsewhere pairs and trios and single sonnets on related themes, leaving for the end of the collection the sonnets that seemed less closely related than the others. Many attempts have been made to revise Thorpe's arrangements; but even the best, Tucker Brooke's *Shakespeare's Sonnets*, 1936, is unconvincing.

Whatever the arrangement of the sonnets and however mixed their contents, they are bound together by one general theme: the triumph of time over youth and beauty, over all human ambitions, a triumph against which man's sole defense is a love that knows no change or defeat.

Whether any of the sonnets are addressed to real persons or allude to real persons, no one knows. The friend or friends, the dark woman or women, the rival poet or poets, all—though they seem to be sketches from life—may be creatures of the imagination like characters in the plays.

Some of the sonnets are coarse, brutal, sardonic; some are flat and conventional; a few of them are the best sonnets in our language.

Shakespeare's *The Phoenix and the Turtle* is included in a group of poems appended to Robert Chester's *Love's Martyr, or Rosalin's Complaint. Allegorically shadowing the truth of Loue, in the constant Fate of the Phoenix and Turtle*, 1601. Chester's poem is in honor of Sir John Salisbury or Salusbury (c. 1566–1612) of Lleweni, Denbighshire, and his wife Ursula. Salisbury, a poet and patron of poets, is described in the preface as "one of the esquires of the bodie to the Queenes most excellent Maiestie." The appended poems are preceded by a title page that states: "Hereafter Follow Diuerse Poeticall Essaies on the former Subiect; viz: the Turtle and Phoenix. Done by the best and chiefest of our moderne writers, with their names subscribed to their particular workes: neuer before extant." The poems added are "subscribed" Shakespeare, Chapman, Jonson, Marston, "Vatum Chorus," and "Ignoto." The poem ascribed to Shakespeare is generally accepted as his, although there is nothing else like it in his acknowledged works. Shakespeare's poem, which in Chester's book has no title, seems to use the phoenix to symbolize love and the turtledove constancy. Masefield writes: "This strange, very beautiful poem . . . in dark and noble verse . . . describes a spiritual marriage, suddenly ended by death." The exact meaning and the circumstances that led Shakespeare to write the poem remain a mystery.

Shakespeare included in his plays more than one hundred songs. Unlike many Elizabethan dramatists, he usually employed a song to serve a definite dramatic purpose. Several of the songs in his plays are among the most beautiful lyrics in English.

The indispensable book of reference is E. K. Chambers, *William Shakespeare, a Study of Facts and Problems*, 2 vols., 1930. The standard edition of the poems is *A New Variorum Edition of Shakespeare: The Poems*, ed. H. E. Rollins, 1938. See also Douglas Bush, *Mythology and the Renaissance Tradition.* The standard edition of the sonnets is *A New Variorum Edition of Shakespeare: The Sonnets*, ed. H. E. Rollins, 2 vols., 1944. See also *Shakespeare's Sonnets*, ed. Tucker Brooke, 1936; Leslie Hotson, *Shakespeare's Sonnets Dated and Other Essays*, 1949; Alfred Harbage, "Dating Shakespeare's Sonnets," *The Shakespeare Quarterly*, i (1950), 57–63; S. A. Tannenbaum, *Shakspere's Sonnets, a Concise Bibliography*, 1940. For the songs, see Richmond Noble, *Shakespeare's Use of Song. With the Text of the Principal Songs*, 1923; *The Shakespeare Songs*, ed. Tucker Brooke, with an introduction by Walter de la Mare, 1929.

From VENUS AND ADONIS[1]

To the Right Honorable
Henrie Wriothesley, Earle of Southampton,
and Baron of Titchfield

Right Honourable, I know now how I shall offend in dedicating my vnpolisht lines to your Lordship, nor how the world will censure mee for choosing so strong a proppe to support so weake a burthen, onelye if your Honour seeme but pleased, I account my selfe highly praised, and vowe to take aduantage of all idle houres, till I haue honoured you with some grauer labour. But if the first heire of my inuention proue deformed, I shall be sorie it had so noble a god-father; and neuer after eare so barren a land, for feare it yeeld me still so bad a haruest, I leaue it to your Honourable suruey, and your Honor to your hearts content, which I wish may alwaies answere your owne wish, and the worlds hopefull expectation.

Your Honors in all dutie,
William Shakespeare.

But if thou needs wilt hunt, be rul'd by me,[2]
Vncouple[3] at the timerous flying hare,
Or at the foxe which liues by subtiltie,
Or at the Roe which no incounter dare:
  Pursue these fearfull[4] creatures o're the downes,
  And on thy wel breathd[5] horse keep with thy hounds

And when thou hast on foote the purblind[6] hare,
Marke the poore wretch to ouer-shut[7] his troubles,

[1] From *Venus and Adonis*, 1593, STC 22354, Bodleian Library.
[2] Shakespeare describes hunting the hare.
[3] set loose the hounds.
[4] timid.
[5] sound in wind.
[6] dim-sighted.
[7] overshoot, run beyond.

How he outruns the wind, and with what care,
He crankes[8] and crosses with a thousand doubles,
The many musits[9] through the which he goes,
Are like a laberinth to amaze his foes.

Sometime he runnes among a flocke of sheepe,
To make the cunning hounds mistake their smell,
And sometime where earth-deluing Conies keepe,[10]
To stop the loud pursuers in their yell:
And sometime sorteth with[11] a heard of deare,
Danger deuiseth shifts, wit waites on feare.

For there his smell with others being mingled,
The hot sent-snuffing hounds are driuen to doubt,
Ceasing their clamorous cry, till they haue singled
With much ado the cold fault[12] cleanly out,
Then do they spend their mouth's,[13] eccho replies,
As if an other chase were in the skies.

By this poore wat[14] farre off vpon a hill,
Stands on his hinder-legs with listning eare,
To hearken if his foes pursue him still,
Anon their loud alarums he doth heare,
And now his griefe may be compared well,
To one sore sicke, that heares the passing bell.[15]

Then shalt thou see the deaw-bedabbled wretch,
Turne, and returne, indenting[16] with the way,
Ech enuious[17] brier, his wearie legs do scratch,
Ech shadow makes him stop, ech murmour stay,
For miserie is troden on by manie,
And being low, neuer releeu'd by anie.

. . . .

Lo here the gentle larke wearie of rest,[18]
From his moyst cabinet[19] mounts vp on hie,
And wakes the morning, from whose siluer brest,
The sunne ariseth in his maiestie,
Who doth the world so gloriously behold,
That Ceader tops and hils, seeme burnisht gold.

Venus salutes him with this faire good morrow,
Oh thou cleare god, and patron of all light,
From whom ech lamp, and shining star doth borrow,
The beautious influence that makes him bright,
There liues a sonne that suckt an earthly mother,
May lend thee light, as thou doest lend to other.

---

8 zigzags.
9 Gaps in hedge or fence.
10 dwell.
11 consorts with, accompanies.
12 cold scent, loss of scent.
13 bark.
14 Wat, familiar name for the hare.
15 A bell rung for prayers for the dying.
16 moving in a zigzag line.
17 malicious.
18 Shakespeare describes hunting the boar.
19 nest.

This sayd, she hasteth to a mirtle groue,
Musing[20] the morning is so much ore-worne,[21]
And yet she heares no tidings of her loue;
She harkens for his hounds, and for his horne,
Anon she heares them chaunt it lustily,
And all in hast she coasteth[22] to the cry.

And as she runnes, the bushes in the way,
Some catch her by the necke, some kisse her face,
Some twin'd about her thigh to make her stay,
She wildly breaketh from their strict imbrace,
Like a milch Doe, whose swelling dugs do ake,
Hasting to feed her fawne, hid in some brake,

By this she heares the hounds are at a bay,[23]
Whereat she starts like one that spies an adder,
Wreath'd vp in fatall folds iust in his way,
The feare whereof doth make him shake, and shudder,
Euen so the timerous yelping of the hounds,
Appals her senses, and her spirit confounds.

For now she knowes it is no gentle chase,
But the blunt[24] boare, rough beare, or lyon proud,
Because the crie[25] remaineth in one place,
Where fearefully the dogs exclaime aloud,
Finding their enemie to be so curt,[26]
They all straine curt'sie[27] who shall cope[28] him first.

This dismall crie rings sadly in her eare,
Through which it enters to surprise her hart,
Who ouercome by doubt, and bloodlesse feare,
With cold-pale weakenesse, nums ech feeling part,
Like soldiers when their captain once doth yeeld,
They basely flie, and dare not stay[29] the field.

Thus stands she in a trembling extasie,[30]
Till cheering vp her senses all dismayd,
She tels them tis a causlesse fantasie,
And childish error that they are affrayd,
Bids them leaue quaking, bids them feare no more,
And with that word, she spide the hunted boare.

Whose frothie mouth bepainted all with red,
Like milke, and blood, being mingled both togither,
A second feare through all her sinewes spred,
Which madly hurries her, she knowes not whither,
This way she runs, and now she will no further,
But backe retires, to rate[31] the boare for murther.

20 wondering.
21 passed away.
22 hovers, skirts the thickets.
23 i.e., surrounding the boar.
24 rough.
25 baying of the hounds.
26 savage, vicious.
27 stand upon ceremony, are punctiliously polite.
28 encounter.
29 offer resistance to.
30 excitement.
31 berate.

A thousand spleenes[32] beare her a thousand wayes,
She treads the path, that she vntreads[33] againe;
Her more then hast, is mated[34] with delayes,
Like the proceedings of a drunken braine,
Full of respects, yet naught at all respecting,[35]
In hand with all things,[36] naught at all effecting.

Here kenneld in a brake, she finds a hound,
And askes the wearie caitiffe for his maister,
And there another licking of his wound,
Gainst venimd sores, the onely soueraigne plaister.
And here she meets another, sadly skowling,
To whom she speaks, and he replies with howling.

When he hath ceast his ill resounding noise,
Another flapmouthd mourner, blacke, and grim,
Against the welkin, volies out his voyce,
Another, and another, answer him,
Clapping their proud tailes to the ground below,
Shaking their scratcht-eares, bleeding as they go.

. . . .

She lookes vpon his lips, and they are pale,[37]
She takes him by the hand, and that is cold,
She whispers in his eares a heauie tale,
As if they heard the wofull words she told:
She lifts the coffer-lids that close his eyes,
Where lo, two lamps burnt out in darknesse lies.

Two glasses where her selfe, her selfe beheld
A thousand times, and now no more reflect,
Their vertue lost, wherein they late exceld,
And euerie beautie robd of his effect;
Wonder of time (quoth she) this is my spight,[38]
That thou being dead, the day shuld yet be light.

Since thou art dead, lo here I prophecie,
Sorrow on loue hereafter shall attend:
It shall be wayted on with iealousie,
Find sweet beginning, but vnsauorie end.
Nere setled equally, but high or lo,
That all loues pleasure shall not match his wo.

It shall be fickle, false, and full of fraud,
Bud, and be blasted, in a breathing while,
The bottome poyson, and the top ore-strawd[39]
With sweets, that shall the truest sight beguile,
The strongest bodie shall it make most weake,
Strike the wise dumbe, and teach the foole to speake.

---

32 caprices.
33 retraces.
34 confounded.
35 full of cautious consideration, and yet really considering nothing.
36 attempting, occupied with.
37 Venus, lamenting the death of Adonis, comments on love.
38 vexation, grievance.
39 overstrewed.

It shall be sparing, and too full of ryot,
Teaching decrepit age to tread the measures,[40]
The staring[41] ruffian shall it keepe in quiet,
Pluck down the rich, inrich the poore with treasures,
It shall be raging mad, and sillie milde,
Make the yoong old, and the old become a childe.

It shall suspect where is no cause of feare,
It shall not feare where it should most mistrust,
It shall be mercifull, and too seueare,
And most deceiuing, when it seemes most iust,
Peruerse it shall be, where it showes most toward,[42]
Put feare to valour, courage to the coward.

It shall be cause of warre, and dire euents,
And set dissention twixt the sonne, and sire,
Subiect, and seruill to all discontents:
As drie combustious matter is to fire,
Sith in his prime, death doth my loue destroy,
They that loue best, their loues shall not enioy.

By this the boy that by her side laie kild,
Was melted like a vapour from her sight,
And in his blood that on the ground laie spild,
A purple floure sproong vp, checkred with white,
Resembling well his pale cheekes, and the blood,
Which in round drops, vpon their whitenesse stood.

She bowes her head, the new-sprong floure to smel,
Comparing it to her Adonis breath,
And saies within her bosome it shall dwell,
Since he himselfe is reft from her by death;
She crop's the stalke, and in the breach appeares,
Green-dropping sap, which she compares to teares.

Poore floure (quoth she) this was thy fathers guise,[43]
Sweet issue of a more sweet smelling sire,
For euerie little griefe to wet his eies,
To grow vnto himselfe was his desire;
And so tis thine, but know it is as good,
To wither in my brest, as in his blood.

Here was thy fathers bed, here in my brest,
Thou art the next of blood, and tis thy right.
Lo in this hollow cradle take thy rest,
My throbbing hart shall rock thee day and night;
There shall not be one minute in an houre,
Wherein I wil not kisse my sweet loues floure.

Thus weary of the world, away she hies,
And yokes her siluer doues, by whose swift aide,
Their mistresse mounted through the emptie skies,

[40] to dance.
[41] bold-eyed(?), furious.
[42] willing.
[43] way, custom.

In her light chariot, quickly is conuaide,
Holding their course to Paphos,[44] where their queen,
Meanes to immure her selfe, and not be seen.

From LUCRECE[45]

To the Right Honovrable, Henry Wriothesley, Earle of Southampton, and Baron of Titchfield

The loue I dedicate to your Lordship is without end: wherof this Pamphlet without beginning is but a superfluous Moity. The warrant I haue of your Honourable disposition, not the worth of my vntutord Lines makes it assured of acceptance. What I haue done is yours, what I haue to doe is yours, being part in all I haue, deuoted yours. Were my worth greater, my duety would shew greater, meane time, as it is, it is bound to your Lordship; To whom I wish long life still lengthned with all happinesse.

Your Lordships in all duety.

William Shakespeare.

The Argvment

Lvcius Tarquinius (for his excessive pride surnamed *Superbus*) after hee had caused his owne father in law *Seruius Tullius* to be cruelly murdred, and contrarie to the Romaine lawes and customes, not requiring or staying for the peoples suffrages, had possessed himselfe of the kingdome: went accompanyed with his sonnes and other Noble men of Rome, to besiege *Ardea,* during which siege, the principall men of the Army meeting one euening at the Tent of *Sextus Tarquinius* the Kings sonne, in their discourses after supper euery one commended the vertues of his owne wife: among whom *Colatinus* extolled the incomparable chastity of his wife *Lucretia.* In that pleasant humor they all posted to Rome, and intending by theyr secret and sodaine arrivall to make triall of that which euery one had before auouched, onely *Colatinus* finds his wife (though it were late in the night) spinning amongest her maides, the other Ladies were all found dauncing and reuelling, or in seuerall disports: whereupon the Noble men yeelded *Colatinus* the victory, and his wife the Fame. At that time *Sextus Tarquinius* being enflamed with *Lucrece* beauty, yet smoothering his passions for the present, departed with the rest backe to the Campe: from whence he shortly after priuily withdrew himselfe, and was (according to his estate) royally entertayned and lodged by *Lucrece* at *Colatium.* The same night he tretcherouslie stealeth into her Chamber, violently rauisht her, and early in the morning speedeth away. *Lucrece* in this lamentable plight, hastily dispatcheth Messengers, one to Rome for her father, another to the Campe for *Colatine.* They came, the one accompanyed with *Iunius Brutus,* the other with *Publius Valerius:* and finding *Lucrece* attired in mourning habite, demanded the cause of her sorrow. She first taking an oath of them for her reuenge, reuealed the Actor, and whole maner of his dealing, and withall sodainely stabbed her selfe. Which done, with one consent they all vowed to roote out the whole hated family of the *Tarquins:* and bearing the dead body to Rome, *Brutus* acquainted the people with the doer and

[44] A city of Cyprus, chief seat of the worship of Venus.

[45] From *Lucrece,* 1594, STC 22345, Folger Library.

manner of the vile deede: with a bitter inuectiue against the tyranny of the King, wherewith the people were so moued, that with one consent and a general acclamation, the *Tarquins* were all exiled, and the state gouernment changed from Kings to Consuls.

The lockes between her chamber and his will,[46]
Ech one by him inforst retires his ward:[47]
But as they open they all rate his ill,[48]
Which driues the creeping theefe to some regard,
The threshold grates[49] the doore to haue him heard,
Night-wandring weezels shreek to see him there,
They fright him, yet he still pursues his feare.[50]

As each vnwilling portall yeelds him way,
Through little vents and cranies of the place,
The wind warres with his torch, to make him staie,
And blowes the smoake of it into his face,
Extinguishing his conduct[51] in this case.
But his hot heart, which fond desire doth scorch,
Puffes forth another wind that fires the torch.

And being lighted, by the light he spies
Lucrecias gloue, wherein her needle sticks,
He takes it from the rushes where it lies,
And griping it, the needle his finger pricks.
As who should say, this gloue to wanton trickes
Is not inur'd; returne againe in hast,
Thou seest our mistresse ornaments are chast.

But in all these poore forbiddings could not stay him,
He in the worst sence consters[52] their deniall:
The dores, the wind, the gloue that did delay him,
He takes for accidentall things of triall.
Or as those bars which stop the hourely diall,[53]
Who with a lingring staie his course doth let,[54]
Till euerie minute payes the howre his debt.

So so, quoth he, these lets attend the time,[55]
Like little frosts that sometime threat the spring,
To ad a more reioysing to the prime,[56]
And giue the sneaped[57] birds more cause to sing.
Pain payes the income of ech precious thing,
Huge rocks, high winds, strong pirats, shelues[58] and sands
The marchant feares, ere rich at home he lands.

Now is he come vnto the chamber dore,
That shuts him from the Heauen of his thought,

[46] Tarquin approaches Lucrece's bedroom.
[47] draws back its protection.
[48] berate his evil deed by creaking.
[49] makes to creak.
[50] the cause of his fear.
[51] guide (i.e., the torch).
[52] construes.
[53] clock or watch.
[54] hinder.
[55] These hindrances are incidental to the occasion.
[56] spring.
[57] pinched with cold.
[58] sandbanks.

Which with a yeelding latch, and with no more,
Hath bard him from the blessed thing he sought.
So from himselfe impiety hath wrought,
That for his pray to pray he doth begin,
As if the Heauens should countenance his sin.

But in the midst of his vnfruitfull prayer,
Hauing solicited th'eternall power,
That his foule thoughts might compasse his fair faire,[59]
And they[60] would stand auspicious to the howre.
Euen there he starts, quoth he, I must deflowre;
The powers to whom I pray abhor this fact,[61]
How can they then assist me in the act?

Then Loue and Fortune be my Gods, my guide,
My will is backt with resolution:
Thoughts are but dreames till their effects be tried,
The blackest sinne is clear'd with absolution.
Against loues fire, feares frost hath dissolution.[62]
The eye of Heauen is out, and mistie night
Couers the shame that followes sweet delight.

This said, his guiltie hand pluckt vp the latch,
And with his knee the dore he opens wide,
The doue sleeps fast that this night Owle will catch.
Thus treason workes ere traitors be espied.
Who sees the lurking serpent steppes aside;
But shee sound sleeping fearing no such thing,
Lies at the mercie of his mortall sting.

. . . .

Why should the worme intrude[63] the maiden bud?[64]
Or hatefull Kuckcowes hatch in Sparrows nests?
Or Todes infect faire founts with venome mud?
Or tyrant follie lurke in gentle brests?
Or Kings be breakers of their owne behestes?
But no perfection is so absolute,[65]
That some impuritie doth not pollute.

The aged man that coffers vp his gold,
Is plagu'd with cramps, and gouts, and painefull fits,
And scarce hath eyes his treasure to behold,
But like still pining *Tantalvs* he sits,
And vselesse barnes[66] the haruest of his wits:
Hauing no other pleasure of his gaine,
But torment that it cannot cure his paine.

So then he hath it when he cannot vse it,
And leaues it to be maistred by his yong:
Who in their pride do presently abuse it,

[59] beauty.
[60] the powers.
[61] deed.
[62] is compelled to melt.
[63] enter forcibly.
[64] Lucrece, lamenting her misfortune, apostrophizes Opportunity and Time.
[65] complete.
[66] stores in a barn.

Their father was too weake, and they too strong
To hold their cursed-blessed Fortune long.
  The sweets we wish for, turne to lothed sowrs,
  Euen in the moment that we call them ours.

Vnruly blasts wait on the tender spring,
Vnholsome weeds take roote with precious flowrs,
The Adder hisses where the sweete birds sing,
What Vertue breedes Iniquity deuours:
We haue no good that we can say is ours,
  But ill annexed opportunity
  Or kils his[67] life, or else his quality.[68]

O opportunity thy guilt is great,
Tis thou that execut'st the traytors treason:
Thou sets the wolfe where he the lambe may get,
Who euer plots the sinne thou poinst[69] the season.
Tis thou that spurn'st at right, at law, at reason,
  And in thy shadie Cell where none may spie him,
  Sits sin to ceaze the soules that wander by him.

Thou makest the vestall violate her oath,
Thou blowest the fire when temperance is thawd,
Thou smotherst honestie, thou murthrest troth,
Thou fowle abbettor, thou notorious bawd,
Thou plantest scandall, and displacest lawd.
  Thou rauisher, thou traytor, thou false theefe,
  Thy honie turnes to gall, thy ioy to greefe.

Thy secret pleasure turnes to open shame,
Thy priuate feasting to a publicke fast,
Thy smoothing[70] titles to a ragged[71] name,
Thy sugred tongue to bitter wormwood tast,
Thy violent vanities can neuer last.
  How comes it then, vile opportunity
  Being so bad, such numbers seeke for thee?

When wilt thou be the humble suppliants friend
And bring him where his suit may be obtained?
When wilt thou sort[72] an howre great strifes to end?
Or free that soule which wretchednes hath chained?
Giue phisicke to the sicke, ease to the pained?
  The poore, lame, blind, hault,[73] creepe, cry out for thee,
  But they nere meet with oportunitie.

The patient dies while the Phisitian sleepes,
The Orphane pines while the oppressor feedes.
Iustice is feasting while the widow weepes.
Aduise is sporting while infection breeds.
Thou graunt'st no time for charitable deeds.

---

67 its (referring to *good*).
68 nature, character.
69 appoints.
70 flattering.
71 wretched.
72 choose.
73 halt, limp.

Wrath, enuy, treason, rape, and murthers rages,
Thy heinous houres wait on them as their Pages.

When Trueth and Vertue haue to do with thee,
A thousand crosses keepe them from thy aide:
They buie thy helpe, but sinne nere giues a fee,
He gratis comes, and thou art well apaide,[74]
As well to heare, as graunt what he hath saide.
My *Colatine* would else haue come to me,
When *Tarqvin* did, but he was staied by thee.

Guilty thou art of murther, and of theft,
Guilty of periurie, and subornation,
Guilty of treason, forgerie, and shift,[75]
Guilty of incest that abhomination,
An accessarie by thine inclination.
To all sinnes past and all that are to come,
From the creation to the generall doome.

Misshapen time, copesmate[76] of vgly night,
Swift subtle post, carrier of grieslie care,
Eater of youth, false slaue to false delight:
Base watch of woes,[77] sins packhorse, vertues snare.
Thou noursest all, and murthrest all that are.
O heare me then, iniurious shifting time,
Be guiltie of my death since of my crime.

Why hath thy seruant opportunity
Betraide the howres thou gau'st me to repose?
Canceld my fortunes, and inchained me
To endlesse date[78] of neuer-ending woes?
Times office is to fine[79] the hate of foes,
To eate vp errours by opinion bred,
Not spend the dowrie of a lawfull bed.

Times glorie is to calme contending Kings,
To vnmaske falshood, and bring truth to light,
To stampe the seale of time in aged things,
To wake the morne, and Centinell the night,
To wrong the wronger till he render right,
To ruinate proud buildings with thy[80] howres,
And smeare with dust their glitring golden towrs.

To fill with worme-holes stately monuments,
To feede obliuion with decay of things,
To blot old bookes, and alter their contents,
To plucke the quils from auncient rauens wings,
To drie the old oakes sappe, and cherish[81] springs:

---

[74] pleased.
[75] trick.
[76] companion.
[77] divided and marked only by woes.
[78] duration.
[79] end or (more probably) soften and refine.
[80] Perhaps *thy* should read *his*.
[81] Many emendations have been suggested: *tarish* (dry up), *sere its, perish, cheerish* (cheering), but *cherish* may be correct.

To spoile Antiquities of hammerd steele,
And turne the giddy round of Fortunes wheele.

To shew the beldame[82] daughters of her daughter,
To make the child a man, the man a childe,
To slay the tygre that doth liue by slaughter,
To tame the Vnicorne, and Lion wild,
To mocke the subtle in themselues beguild,
To cheare the Plowman with increasefull[83] crops,
And wast huge stones with little water drops.

Why work'st thou mischiefe in thy Pilgrimage,
Vnlesse thou could'st returne to make amends?
One poore retyring[84] minute in an age
Would purchase thee a thousand thousand friends,
Lending him wit that to bad detters lends,
O this dread night, would'st thou one howr come backe,
I could preuent this storme, and shun thy wracke.

Thou ceaselesse lackie to Eternitie,
With some mischance crosse *Tarquin* in his flight.
Deuise extreames beyond extremitie,
To make him curse this cursed crimefull night:
Let gastly shadowes his lewd eyes affright,
And the dire thought of his committed euill,
Shape euery bush a hideous shapelesse deuill.

Disturbe his howres of rest with restlesse trances,
Afflict him in his bed with bedred grones,
Let there bechaunce him pitifull mischances,
To make him mone, but pitie not his mones:
Stone him with hardned hearts harder then stones,
And let milde women to him loose their mildnesse,
Wilder to him then Tygers in their wildnesse.

Let him haue time to teare his curled haire,
Let him haue time against himselfe to raue,
Let him haue time of times helpe to dispaire,
Let him haue time to liue a lothed slaue,
Let him haue time a beggers orts[85] to craue,
And time to see one that by almes doth liue,
Disdaine to him disdained scraps to giue.

Let him haue time to see his friends his foes,
And merrie fooles to mocke at him resort:
Let him haue time to marke how slow time goes
In time of sorrow, and how swift and short
His time of follie, and his time of sport.
And euer let his vnrecalling[86] crime
Haue time to waile th'abusing of his time.

---

82 grandmother, old woman.
83 productive, fruitful.
84 returning.
85 fragments (of food).
86 irrevocable.

O time thou tutor both to good and bad,
Teach me to curse him that thou taught'st this ill:
At his owne shadow let the theefe runne mad,
Himselfe, himselfe seeke euerie howre to kill,
Such wretched hands such wretched blood shuld spill.
For who so base would such an office haue,
As sclandrous[87] deaths-man[88] to so base a slaue.

The baser is he comming from a King,
To shame his hope[89] with deedes degenerate,
The mightier man the mightier is the thing
That makes him honord, or begets him hate:
For greatest scandall waits on greatest state.
The Moone being clouded, presently[90] is mist,
But little stars may hide them when they list.

The Crow may bath his coaleblacke wings in mire,
And vnperceau'd flie with the filth away,
But if the like the snow-white Swan desire,
The staine vppon his siluer Downe will stay.
Poore grooms are sightles[91] night, kings glorious day,
Gnats are vnnoted wheresoere they flie,
But Eagles gaz'd vppon with euerie eye.

Out idle wordes, seruants to shallow fooles,
Vnprofitable sounds, weake arbitrators,
Busie your selues in skill contending schooles,
Debate where leysure serues with dull debators:
To trembling Clients be you mediators,
For me, I force[92] not argument a straw,
Since that my case is past the helpe of law.

In vaine I raile at oportunitie,
At time, at *Tarqvin,* and vnchearfull night,
In vaine I cauill with mine infamie,
In vaine I spurne at my confirm'd despight,
This helpelesse smoake of words doth me no right:
The remedie indeede to do me good,
Is to let forth my fowle defiled blood.

. . . .

At last shee cals to mind where hangs a peece[93]
Of skilfull painting, made for *Priams* Troy,
Before the which is drawn[94] the power of Greece,
For *Helens* rape, the Cittie to destroy,
Threatning cloud-kissing *Illion* with annoy,
Which the conceipted[95] Painter drew so prowd,
As Heauen (it seem'd) to kisse the turrets bow'd.

---

87 despicable.
88 executioner.
89 Person or thing that is the center of one's hopes.
90 at once.
91 blind, dark.
92 esteem.
93 Lucrece remembers a picture of Troy.
94 arrayed.
95 imaginative.

A thousand lamentable obiects there,
In scorne of Nature, Art gaue liuelesse life,
Many a dry drop seem'd a weeping teare,
Shed for the slaughtred husband by the wife.
The red bloud reek'd to shew the Painters strife,[96]
And dying eyes gleem'd forth their ashie lights,
Like dying coales burnt out in tedious nights.

There might you see the labouring Pyoner[97]
Begrim'd with sweat, and smeared all with dust,
And from the towres of Troy, there would appeare
The verie eyes of men through loop-holes thrust,
Gazing vppon the Greekes with little lust,[98]
Such sweet obseruance[99] in this worke was had,
That one might see those farre of[1] eyes looke sad.

In great commaunders, Grace, and Maiestie,
You might behold triumphing in their faces,
In youth quick-bearing and dexteritie,
And here and there the Painter interlaces
Pale cowards marching on with trembling paces.
Which hartless peasaunts did so wel resemble,
That one would swear he saw them quake and tremble.

In *Aiax* and *Vlysses,* o what Art
Of Phisiognomy might one behold!
The face of eyther cypher'd eythers heart,
Their face, their manners most expreslie told,
In *Aiax* eyes blunt rage and rigour rold,
But the mild glance that slie *Vlysses* lent,
Shewed deepe regard[2] and smiling gouernment.[3]

There pleading might you see graue *Nestor* stand,
As 'twere incouraging the Greekes to fight,
Making such sober action with his hand,
That it beguild attention, charm'd the sight,
In speech it seemd his beard, all siluer white,
Wagg'd vp and down, and from his lips did flie,
Thin winding breath which purl'd[4] vp to the skie.

About him were a presse[5] of gaping faces,
Which seem'd to swallow vp his sound aduice,
All ioyntlie listning, but with seuerall graces,
As if some Marmaide did their eares intice,
Some high, some low, the Painter was so nice.[6]
The scalpes of manie almost hid behind,
To iump vp higher seem'd to mocke the mind.

Here one mans hand leand on anothers head,

---

96 effort, art's strife with nature.
97 pioneer, digger, miner.
98 pleasure.
99 observant care.
1 far-off.
2 thoughtful consideration.
3 self-control.
4 curled.
5 crowd.
6 precise, accurate.

His nose being shadowed by his neighbours eare,
Here one being throng'd,[7] bears back all boln,[8] and red,
Another smotherd, seemes to pelt[9] and sweare,
And in their rage such signes of rage they beare,
  As but for losse of *Nestors* golden words,
  It seem'd they would debate with angrie swords.

For much imaginarie[10] worke was there,
Conceipt deceitfull, so compact,[11] so kinde,[12]
That for *Achilles* image stood his speare
Grip't in an Armed hand, himselfe behind
Was left vnseene, saue to the eye of mind,
  A hand, a foote, a face, a leg, a head
  Stood for the whole to be imagined.

And from the wals of strong besieged *Troy,*
When their braue hope, bold *Hector* march'd to field,
Stood manie Troian mothers sharing ioy,
To see their youthfull sons bright weapons wield,
And to their hope[13] they such odde action yeeld,
  That through their light[14] ioy seemed to appeare,
  (Like bright things staind) a kind of heauie feare.

And from the strond of *Dardan*[15] where they fought,
To *Simois*[16] reedie bankes the red bloud ran,
Whose waues to imitate the battaile sought
With swelling ridges, and their rankes began
To breake vppon the galled[17] shore, and than
  Retire againe, till meeting greater ranckes
  They ioine, and shoot their fome at *Simois* bancks.

. . . .

And now this pale Swan in her watrie nest,[18]
Begins the sad Dirge of her certaine ending,
Few words (quoth shee) shall fit the trespasse best,
Where no excuse can giue the fault amending.
In me moe woes then words are now depending,[19]
  And my laments would be drawn out too long,
  To tell them all with one poore tired tong.

Then be this all the taske it hath to say,
Deare husband in the interest of[20] thy bed
A stranger came, and on that pillow lay,
Where thou wast wont to rest thy wearie head,
And what wrong else may be imagined,
  By foule inforcement might be done to me,
  From that (alas) thy *Lvcrece* is not free.

---

7 crowded.
8 swollen.
9 rage, curse.
10 fanciful.
11 *compact,*] *compact* STC 22345.
12 natural.
13 Hector.
14 cheerful.
15 Troy.
16 A river near Troy.
17 chafed.
18 Lucrece tells her tale and dies.
19 impending.
20 seeking.

For in the dreadfull dead of darke midnight,
With shining Fauchion in my chamber came
A creeping creature with a flaming light,
And softly cried, awake thou Romaine Dame,
And entertaine my loue, else lasting shame
  On thee and thine this night I will inflict,
  If thou my loues desire do contradict.

For some hard fauour'd Groome of thine, quoth he,
Vnlesse thou yoke thy liking to my will
Ile murther straight, and then ile slaughter thee,
And sweare I found you where you did fulfill
The lothsome act of Lust, and so did kill
  The lechors in their deed, this Act will be
  My Fame, and thy perpetuall infamy.

With this I did begin to start and cry,
And then against my heart he set his sword,
Swearing, vnlesse I tooke all patiently,
I should not liue to speake another word.
So should my shame still rest vpon record,
  And neuer be forgot in mightie Roome
  Th' adulterat death of *Lvcrece,* and her Groome.

Mine enemy was strong, my poore selfe weake,
(And farre the weaker with so strong a feare)
My bloudie Iudge forbod[21] my tongue to speake,
No rightfull plea might plead for Iustice there.
His scarlet Lust came euidence to sweare
  That my poore beautie had purloin'd his eyes,
  And when the Iudge is rob'd, the prisoner dies.

O teach me how to make mine owne excuse,
Or (at the least) this refuge let me finde,
Though my grosse bloud be staind with this abuse,
Immaculate, and spotlesse is my mind,
That was not forc'd, that neuer was inclind
  To accessarie yeeldings, but still pure
  Doth in her poyson'd closet yet endure.

Lo heare the hopelesse Marchant of this losse,[22]
With head declin'd, and voice dam'd vp with wo,
With sad set eyes and wretched armes acrosse,
From lips new waxen pale, begins to blow
The griefe away, that stops his answer so.
  But wretched as he is he striues in vaine,
  What he breaths out, his breath drinks vp again.

As through an Arch, the violent roaring tide,
Outruns the eye that doth behold his hast:
Yet in the Edie boundeth in his pride,

21 forbade.
22 Collatine, Lucrece's husband, hopeless about his loss.

Backe to the strait that forst him on so fast:
In rage sent out, recald in rage being past,
  Euen so his sighes, his sorrowes make a saw,[23]
  To push griefe on, and back the same grief draw.

Which speechlesse woe of his poore she attendeth,
And his vntimelie frenzie thus awaketh,
Deare Lord, thy sorrow to my sorrow lendeth
Another power, no floud by raining slaketh,
My woe too sencible thy passion maketh
  More feeling painfull, let it than suffice
  To drowne on[24] woe, one paire of weeping eyes.

And for my sake when I might charme thee so,
For shee that was thy *Lvcrece,* now attend me,
Be sodainelie[25] reuenged on my Foe.
Thine, mine, his own, suppose thou dost defend me
From what is past, the helpe that thou shalt lend me
  Comes all too late, yet let the Traytor die,
  For sparing Iustice feeds iniquitie.

But ere I name him, you faire Lords, quoth shee,
(Speaking to those that came with *Colatine*)
Shall plight your Honourable faiths to me,
With swift pursuit to venge this wrong of mine,
For 'tis a meritorious faire designe,
  To chase iniustice with reuengefull armes,
  Knights by their oaths should right poore Ladies harmes.

At this request, with noble disposition,
Each present Lord began to promise aide,
As bound in Knighthood to her imposition,[26]
Longing to heare the hatefull Foe bewraide.[27]
But shee that yet her sad taske hath not said,
  The protestation stops, O speake quoth shee,
  How may this forced staine be wip'd from me?

What is the qualitie of my offence
Being constrayn'd with dreadfull circumstance?
May my pure mind with the fowle act dispence
My low declined Honor to aduance?
May anie termes acquit me from this chance?
  The poysoned fountaine cleares it selfe againe,
  And why not I from this compelled staine?

With this they all at once began to saie,
Her bodies staine, her mind vntainted cleares,
While with a ioylesse smile, shee turnes awaie
The face, that map which deepe impression beares
Of hard misfortune, caru'd it in[28] with tears.

---

[23] move back and forth like a saw.
[24] one.
[25] immediately.
[26] demand.
[27] revealed.
[28] in it.

No no, quoth shee, no Dame hereafter liuing,
By my excuse shall claime excuses giuing.

Here with a sigh as if her heart would breake,
Shee throwes forth *Tarquins* name: he he, she saies,
But more then he, her poore tong could not speake,
Till after manie accents and delaies,
Vntimelie breathings, sicke and short assaies,
Shee vtters this, he he faire Lords, tis he
That guides this hand to giue this wound to me.

Euen here she sheathed in her harmlesse breast
A harmfull knife, that thence her soule vnsheathed,
That blow did baile it from the deepe vnrest
Of that polluted prison, where it breathed:
Her contrite sighes vnto the clouds bequeathed
Her winged sprite, and through her wounds doth flie
Liues lasting date,[29] from cancel'd destinie.

SONNETS[30]

1

From fairest creatures we desire increase,
That thereby beauties *Rose* might neuer die,
But as the riper should by time decease,
His tender heire might beare his memory:
But thou contracted[31] to thine owne bright eyes,
Feed'st thy lights flame with selfe substantiall fewell,[32]
Making a famine where aboundance lies,
Thy selfe thy foe, to thy sweet selfe too cruell:
Thou that art now the worlds fresh ornament,
And only herauld to the gaudy[33] spring,
Within thine owne bud buriest thy content,[34]
And tender chorle[35] makst wast in niggarding:
Pitty the world, or else this glutton be,
To eate the worlds due, by the graue and thee.[36]

2

When fortie Winters shall beseige thy brow,
And digge deep trenches in thy beauties field,
Thy youthes proud liuery[37] so gaz'd on now,
Wil be a totter'd weed[38] of smal worth held:
Then being askt, where all thy beautie lies,
Where all the treasure of thy lusty daies;
To say within thine owne deepe sunken eyes,
Were an all-eating shame, and thriftlesse praise.

---

29 duration (i.e., life itself).

30 From *Shakes-peares sonnets. Neuer before imprinted*, 1609, STC 22353a, Folger Library.

31 betrothed (the sense of "limited," "confined," also is present).

32 you burn your own substance.

33 joyful, showy.

34 potential fatherhood.

35 miser.

36 The grave and you consume what is due the world, i.e., children.

37 dress.

38 tattered garment.

How much more praise deseru'd thy beauties vse,[39]
If thou couldst answere this faire child of mine
Shall sum my count, and make my old excuse[40]
Proouing his beautie by succession thine,
This were to be new made when thou art ould,
And see thy blood warme when thou feel'st it could.[41]

3

Looke in thy glasse and tell the face thou vewest,
Now is the time that face should forme an other,
Whose fresh repaire[42] if now thou not renewest,
Thou doo'st beguile the world, vnblesse[43] some mother.
For where is she so faire whose vn-eard[44] wombe
Disdaines the tillage of thy husbandry?
Or who is he so fond[45] will be the tombe,
Of his selfe loue to stop posterity?
Thou art thy mothers glasse[46] and she in thee
Calls backe the louely Aprill of her prime,
So thou through windowes of thine age shalt see,
Dispight of wrinkles this thy goulden time.
But if thou liue remembred not to be,[47]
Die single and thine Image dies with thee.

5

Those howers that with gentle worke did frame,[48]
The louely gaze[49] where euery eye doth dwell
Will play the tirants to the very same,
And that vnfaire[50] which fairely[51] doth excell:
For neuer resting time leads Summer on,
To hidious winter and confounds[52] him there,
Sap checkt with frost and lustie leau's quite gon,[53]
Beauty ore-snow'd and barenes euery where.[54]
Then were not summers distillation left
A liquid prisoner pent in walls of glasse,
Beauties effect with beauty were bereft,[55]
Nor it nor noe remembrance what it was.
But flowers distil'd though they with winter meete,
Leese[56] but their show, their substance still liues sweet.

6

Then let not winters wragged[57] hand deface,
In thee thy summer ere thou be distil'd:

[39] investment.
[40] sum up my account and be an excuse for my old age.
[41] *could.*] *could,* STC 22353a.
[42] healthful state.
[43] refuse happiness to.
[44] unplowed.
[45] foolish.
[46] mirror.
[47] if you live only to be forgotten.
[48] form, plan.
[49] sight.
[50] deprive of beauty.
[51] in beauty.
[52] destroys.
[53] *gon,*] *gon.* STC 22353a.
[54] *where.*] *where,* STC 22353a.
[55] Beauty and its fruit would be destroyed.
[56] lose.
[57] rugged, rough.

Make sweet some viall; treasure[58] thou some place,
With beauties[59] treasure ere it be selfe kil'd:
That vse[60] is not forbidden vsery,
Which happies those that pay the willing lone;[61]
That's for thy selfe to breed an other thee,
Or ten times happier be it ten for one.[62]
Ten times thy selfe were happier then thou art,
If ten of thine ten times refigur'd thee,[63]
Then what could death doe if thou should'st depart,
Leauing thee liuing in posterity?
Be not selfe-wild for thou art much too faire,
To be deaths conquest and make wormes thine heire.

7

Loe in the Orient when the gracious light,
Lifts vp his burning head, each vnder eye[64]
Doth homage to his new appearing sight,
Seruing with lookes his sacred maiesty,
And hauing climb'd the steepe vp heauenly hill,
Resembling strong youth in his middle age,
Yet mortall lookes adore his beauty still,
Attending on his goulden pilgrimage:
But when from high-most pich[65] with wery car,
Like feeble age he reeleth from the day,
The eyes (fore dutious) now conuerted[66] are
From his low tract[67] and looke an other way:
So thou, thy selfe out-going in thy noon:[68]
Vnlock'd on diest vnlesse thou get a sonne.

12

When I doe count the clock that tels the time,
And see the braue[69] day sunck in hidious night,
When I behold the violet past prime,
And sable curls all[70] siluer'd ore with white:
When lofty trees I see barren of leaues,
Which erst[71] from heat did canopie the herd
And Sommers greene all girded vp in sheaues
Borne on the beare with white and bristly beard:
Then of thy beauty do I question make[72]
That thou among the wastes of time must goe,
Since sweets and beauties do them-selues forsake,
And die as fast as they see others grow,
And nothing gainst Times sieth[73] can make defence
Saue breed[74] to braue[75] him, when he takes thee hence.

[58] enrich.
[59] *beauties*] *beautits* STC 22353a.
[60] Interest on borrowed money.
[61] makes happy those who willingly pay the loan.
[62] *one.*] *one,* STC 22353a.
[63] copied you.
[64] each eye below.
[65] height.
[66] turned away.
[67] course.
[68] passing beyond your noon of beauty.
[69] splendid.
[70] *all*] *or* STC 22353a.
[71] formerly.
[72] consider.
[73] scythe.
[74] children.
[75] defy.

13

O that you were your selfe,[76] but loue you are
No longer yours, then[77] you your selfe here liue:[78]
Against this cumming end you should prepare,
And your sweet semblance to some other giue.
So should that beauty which you hold in lease
Find no determination,[79] then you were
Your[80] selfe again after your selfes decease,
When your sweet issue your sweet forme should beare.
Who lets so faire a house fall to decay,
Which husbandry[81] in honour might vphold,
Against the stormy gusts of winters day
And barren rage of deaths eternall cold?
O none but vnthrifts,[82] deare my loue you know,
You had a Father, let your Son say so.

14

Not from the stars do I my iudgement plucke,[83]
And yet me thinkes I haue Astronomy,[84]
But not to tell of good, or euil lucke,
Of plagues, of dearths, or seasons quallity,
Nor can I fortune to breefe mynuits tell;
Pointing[85] to each his thunder, raine and winde,
Or say with Princes if it shal go wel
By oft predict[86] that I in heauen finde.
But from thine eies my knowledge I deriue,
And constant stars in them I read such art[87]
As truth and beautie shal together thriue
If from thy selfe, to store thou wouldst conuert:[88]
Or else of thee this I prognosticate,
Thy end is Truthes and Beauties doome and date.[89]

15

When I consider euery thing that growes
Holds in perfection but a little moment,[90]
That this huge stage presenteth nought but showes[91]
Whereon the Stars in secret influence comment;[92]
When I perceiue that men as plants increase,
Cheared and checkt euen by the selfe-same skie:
Vaunt in their youthfull sap, at height decrease,
And were[93] their braue state out of memory;[94]

---

76 unchangeably yourself.
77 than.
78 *liue:*] *liue,* STC 22353a.
79 end.
80 *Your*] *You* STC 22353a.
81 thrift; marriage.
82 wastrels.
83 derive.
84 understand astrology.
85 appointing.
86 by frequent prediction.
87 knowledge.
88 if you would turn from living for yourself and would have children.
89 end.
90 *moment,*] *moment.* STC 22353a.
91 spectacles.
92 *comment;*] *comment* STC 22353a.
93 wear.
94 *memory;*] *memory.* STC 22353a: outlive the memory of their prime.

Then the conceit[95] of this inconstant stay,[96]
Sets you most rich in youth before my sight,
Where wastfull time debateth with decay
To change your day of youth to sullied night,
  And all in war with Time for loue of you
  As he takes from you, I ingraft you new.[97]

17

Who will beleeue my verse in time to come
If it were fild with your most high deserts?
Though yet heauen knowes it is but as a tombe
Which hides your life, and shewes not halfe your parts:
If I could write the beauty of your eyes,
And in fresh numbers[98] number all your graces,
The age to come would say this Poet lies,
Such heauenly touches nere toucht earthly faces.
So should my papers (yellowed with their age)
Be scorn'd, like old men of lesse truth then tongue,
And your true rights be termd a Poets rage,[99]
And stretched miter[1] of an Antique song.
  But were some childe of yours aliue that time,
  You should liue twice in it, and in my rime.

18

Shall I compare thee to a Summers day?
Thou art more louely and more temperate:
Rough windes do shake the darling buds of Maie,
And Sommers lease[2] hath all too short a date:[3]
Sometime too hot the eye of heauen shines,
And often is his gold complexion dimm'd,
And euery faire[4] from faire some-time declines,
By chance, or natures changing course vntrim'd:[5]
But thy eternall Sommer shall not fade,
Nor loose possession of that faire thou ow'st,[6]
Nor shall death brag thou wandr'st in his shade,
When in eternall lines to time thou grow'st.[7]
  So long as men can breath or eyes can see,
  So long liues this, and this giues life to thee.

19

Deuouring time blunt thou the Lyons pawes,
And make the earth deuoure her owne sweet brood,
Plucke the keene teeth from the fierce Tygers iawes,[8]
And burne the long liu'd Phænix in her blood,

---

95 idea.
96 continuance.
97 renew your youth (by my verse).
98 verses.
99 due praise be termed poetic enthusiasm.
1 stretched meter (overstrained poetry, exaggeration).
2 allotted time.
3 duration.
4 beauty.
5 stripped of adornment.
6 you possess.
7 *grow'st.*] *grow'st,* STC 22353a.
8 *iawes,*] *yawes,* STC 22353a.

Make glad and sorry seasons as thou fleet'st,
And do what ere thou wilt swift-footed time
To the wide world and all her fading sweets:
But I forbid thee one most hainous crime,
O carue not with thy howers my loues faire brow,
Nor draw noe lines there with thine antique pen.[9]
Him in thy course vntainted[10] doe allow,
For beauties patterne to succeding men.
Yet doe thy worst ould Time:[11] dispight thy wrong,
My loue shall in my verse euer liue young.

21

So is it not with me as with that Muse,[12]
Stird by a painted beauty to his verse,
Who heauen it selfe for ornament doth vse,
And euery faire[13] with his faire doth reherse,[14]
Making a coopelment of proud compare[15]
With Sunne and Moone, with earth and seas rich gems:
With Aprills first borne flowers and all things rare,
That heauens ayre in this huge rondure[16] hems.[17]
O let me true in loue but truly write,
And then beleeue me, my loue is as faire,
As any mothers childe, though not so bright
As those gould candells fixt in heauens ayer:
Let them say more that like of heare-say well,
I will not prayse that purpose not to sell.

23

As an vnperfect[18] actor on the stage,
Who with his feare is put besides his part,
Or some fierce thing repleat with too much rage,
Whose strengths abondance weakens his owne heart;
So I for feare of trust,[19] forget to say,
The perfect ceremony of loues right,[20]
And in mine owne loues strength seeme to decay,
Ore-charg'd with burthen of mine owne loues might:
O let my looks[21] be then the eloquence,
And domb presagers of my speaking brest,
Who pleade for loue, and look for recompence,
More then that tonge that more hath more exprest.[22]
O learne to read what silent loue hath writ,
To heare with[23] eies belongs to loues fine wit.[24]

---

[9] *pen.*] *pen,* STC 22353a.
[10] uninjured.
[11] *Time:*] *Time* STC 22353a.
[12] poet.
[13] beauty.
[14] relate.
[15] joining in proud comparison.
[16] sphere.
[17] *hems.*] *hems,* STC 22353a.
[18] not knowing his lines.
[19] fearing to trust myself.
[20] rite.
[21] *looks*] *books* STC 22353a.
[22] more than that tongue that has expressed more praises and more often.
[23] *with*] *wit* STC 22353a.
[24] *wit.*] *wiht.* STC 22353a.

25

Let those who are in fauor with their stars,
Of publike honour and proud titles bost,
Whilst I whome fortune of such tryumph bars
Vnlookt for[25] ioy in that I honour most;
Great Princes fauorites their faire leaues spread,
But[26] as the Marygold at the suns eye,
And in them-selues their pride lies buried,
For at a frowne they in their glory die.
The painefull warrier famosed[27] for fight,[28]
After a thousand victories once foild,
Is from the booke of honour rased quite,
And all the rest forgot for which he toild:
Then happy I that loue and am beloued
Where I may not remoue, nor be remoued.

27

Weary with toyle, I hast me to my bed,
The deare repose for lims with trauaill tired,
But then begins a iourny in my head
To worke[29] my mind, when boddies work's expired.
For then my thoughts (from far where I abide)
Intend[30] a zelous pilgrimage to thee;
And keep my drooping eye-lids open wide,
Looking on darknes which the blind doe see.
Saue that my soules imaginary[31] sight
Presents thy[32] shaddoe[33] to my sightles view,
Which like a iewell (hunge in gastly night)
Makes blacke night beautious, and her old face new.
Loe thus by day my lims, by night my mind,
For[34] thee, and for my selfe, noe quiet finde.

29

When in disgrace with Fortune and mens eyes,
I all alone beweepe my out-cast state,
And trouble deafe heauen with my bootlesse cries,
And looke vpon my selfe and curse my fate,[35]
Wishing me like to one more rich in hope,
Featur'd like him, like him with friends possest,
Desiring this mans art,[36] and that mans skope,[37]
With what I most inioy contented least,
Yet in these thoughts my selfe almost despising,
Haplye I thinke on thee, and then my state,
(Like to the Larke at breake of daye arising)
From sullen[38] earth sings himns at Heauens gate,

[25] unexpectedly.
[26] only.
[27] renowned.
[28] *fight,*] *worth,* STC 22353a.
[29] act upon.
[30] plan or set out upon.
[31] imaginative.
[32] *thy*] *their* STC 22353a.
[33] image.
[34] because of.
[35] *fate,*] *fate.* STC 22353a.
[36] knowledge, skill.
[37] range of ability (or of opportunity).
[38] dark, dull.

For thy sweet loue remembred such welth brings,
That then I skorne to change my state with Kings.

30

When to the Sessions[39] of sweet silent thought,
I sommon vp remembrance of things past,
I sigh the lacke of many a thing I sought,
And with old woes new waile my deare times waste:[40]
Then can I drowne an eye (vn-vs'd to flow)
For precious friends hid in deaths dateles night,
And weepe a fresh loues long since canceld woe,
And mone th'expence[41] of many a vannisht sight.
Then can I greeue at greeuances fore-gon,[42]
And heauily from woe to woe tell ore[43]
The sad account of fore-bemoned mone,
Which I new pay, as if not payd before.
But if the while I thinke on thee (deare friend)
All losses are restord, and sorrowes end.

32

If thou suruiue my well contented daie,[44]
When that churle death my bones with dust shall couer
And shalt by fortune once more re-suruay[45]
These poore rude lines of thy deceased Louer:[46]
Compare them with the bett'ring of the time,[47]
And though they be out-stript by euery pen,
Reserue[48] them for my loue, not for their rime,
Exceeded by the hight of happier men.[49]
Oh then vouchsafe[50] me but this louing thought,
Had my friends Muse growne with this growing age,
A dearer birth then this his loue had brought
To march in ranckes of better equipage:[51]
But since he died and Poets better proue,
Theirs for their stile ile read, his for his loue.

33

Full many a glorious morning haue I seene,
Flatter the mountaine tops with soueraine eie,
Kissing with golden face the meddowes greene;
Guilding pale streames with heauenly alcumy:
Anon permit the basest[52] cloudes to ride,
With ougly rack[53] on his celestiall face,

---

39 sittings (of a court of justice).
40 lament again the ravages which time has inflicted on things dear to me.
41 loss.
42 past griefs.
43 count over.
44 the day that I shall be contented with.
45 *re-suruay*] *re-suruay:* STC 22353a.
46 friend.
47 better works of a later time.
48 preserve, retain.
49 more fortunate, more gifted.
50 *vouchsafe*] *voutsafe* STC 22353a.
51 richer equipment.
52 darkest.
53 clouds.

And from the for-lorne world his visage hide
Stealing vnseene to west with this disgrace:[54]
Euen so my Sunne one early morne did shine,
With all triumphant splendor on my brow,
But out alack, he was but one houre mine,
The region cloude[55] hath mask'd him from me now.
  Yet him for this, my loue no whit disdaineth,
  Suns of the world may staine,[56] when heauens sun staineth.[57]

50

How heauie[58] doe I iourney on the way,
When what I seeke (my wearie trauels end)
Doth teach that ease and that repose to say
Thus farre the miles are measurde from thy friend.
The beast that beares me, tired with my woe,
Plods dully[59] on, to beare that waight in me,
As if by some instinct the wretch did know
His rider lou'd not speed being made from thee:
The bloody spurre cannot prouoke him on,
That some-times anger thrusts into his hide,
Which heauily he answers with a grone,
More sharpe to me then spurring to his side,
  For that same grone doth put this in my mind,
  My greefe lies onward and my ioy behind.

54

Oh how much more doth beautie beautious seeme,
By that sweet ornament which truth[60] doth giue![61]
The Rose lookes faire, but fairer we it deeme
For that sweet odor, which doth in it liue:
The Canker bloomes[62] haue full as deepe a die,
As the perfumed tincture[63] of the Roses,
Hang on such thornes, and play as wantonly,
When sommers breath their masked buds discloses:[64]
But for[65] their virtue only is their show,
They liue vnwoo'd, and vnrespected[66] fade,
Die to themselues. Sweet Roses doe not so,
Of their sweet deathes, are sweetest odors made:
  And so of you, beautious and louely youth,
  When that shall vade,[67] by verse distils[68] your truth.

55

Not marble, nor the guilded monuments,[69]
Of Princes shall out-liue this powrefull rime,

54 disfigurement.
55 clouds of the upper air.
56 grow dim, be obscured.
57 *staineth.*] *stainteh.* STC 22353a.
58 gloomy.
59 *dully*] *duly* STC 22353a.
60 fidelity.
61 *giue!*] *giue,* STC 22353a.
62 dog roses, scentless wild roses.
63 color.
64 opens.
65 because.
66 unnoticed.
67 perish.
68 preserves its essence.
69 *monuments,*] *monument,* STC 22353a.

But you shall shine more bright in these contents[70]
Then vnswept stone,[71] besmeer'd with sluttish time.
When wastefull warre shall *Statues* ouer-turne,
And broiles roote out the worke of masonry,
Nor *Mars* his sword, nor warres quick fire shall burne:
The liuing record of your memory.
Gainst death, and all obliuious enmity[72]
Shall you pace forth, your praise shall stil find roome,
Euen in the eyes of all posterity
That weare this world out to the ending doome.
So til the iudgement that[73] your selfe arise,
You liue in this, and dwell in louers eyes.

60

Like as the waues make towards the pibled[74] shore,
So do our minuites hasten to their end,
Each changing place with that which goes before,
In sequent toile all forwards do contend.
Natiuity once in the maine of light,[75]
Crawles to maturity, wherewith being crown'd,
Crooked[76] eclipses gainst his glory fight,
And time that gaue, doth now his gift confound.[77]
Time doth transfixe[78] the florish[79] set on youth,
And delues the paralels in beauties brow,
Feedes on the rarities of natures truth,
And nothing stands but for his sieth[80] to mow.
And yet to times in hope,[81] my verse shall stand
Praising thy worth, dispight his cruell hand.

63

Against[82] my loue shall be as I am now
With times iniurious hand crusht[83] and ore-worne,
When houres haue dreind his blood and fild his brow
With lines and wrincles, when his youthfull morne
Hath trauaild on to Ages steepie night,
And all those beauties whereof now he's King
Are vanishing, or vanisht out of sight,
Stealing away the treasure of his Spring—[84]
For such a time do I now fortifie
Against confounding[85] Ages cruell knife,
That he shall neuer cut from memory
My sweet loues beauty, though my louers life.
His beautie shall in these blacke lines be seene,
And they shall liue, and he in them still greene.

---

70 what is contained in these verses.
71 than in neglected stone.
72 *enmity*] *emnity* STC 22353a.
73 Judgment Day when.
74 pebbled.
75 main body of light, ocean of light.
76 perverse, malignant.
77 ruin, destroy.
78 destroy.
79 outer adornment, bloom.
80 scythe.
81 future times.
82 in expectation of the time when.
83 *crusht*] *chrusht* STC 22353a.
84 *Spring*—] *Spring*. STC 22353a.
85 destroying.

64

When I haue seene by times fell hand defaced
The rich proud cost[86] of outworne buried age;[87]
When sometime loftie towers I see downe rased,
And brasse eternall slaue to mortall rage;[88]
When I haue seene the hungry Ocean gaine
Aduantage on the Kingdome of the shoare,
And the firme soile win of the watry maine,
Increasing store[89] with losse, and losse with store;[90]
When I haue seene such interchange of state,[91]
Or state[92] it selfe confounded, to decay,
Ruine hath taught me thus to ruminate
That Time will come and take my loue away.
  This thought is as a death which cannot choose
  But weepe to haue, that which it feares to loose.

65

Since[93] brasse, nor stone, nor earth, nor boundlesse sea,
But sad mortallity ore-swaies their power,
How with this rage shall beautie hold a plea,
Whose action is no stronger then a flower?
O how shall summers hunny breath hold out,
Against the wrackfull[94] siedge of battring dayes,
When rocks impregnable are not so stoute,
Nor gates of steele so strong but time decayes?
O fearefull meditation, where alack,
Shall times best Iewell from times chest lie hid?[95]
Or what strong hand can hold his swift foote back,
Or who his spoile[96] of[97] beautie can forbid?
  O none, vnlesse this miracle haue might,
  That in black inck my loue[98] may still shine bright.

66

Tyr'd with all these[99] for restfull death I cry,
As to behold desert a begger borne,
And needie Nothing trimd in iollitie,[1]
And purest faith vnhappily forsworne,
And gilded honor shamefully misplast,
And maiden vertue rudely strumpeted,
And right perfection wrongfully disgrac'd,
And strength by limping sway[2] disabled,
And arte made tung-tide by authoritie,

---

[86] ornament, pomp.
[87] *age;*] *age* STC 22353a.
[88] *rage;*] *rage.* STC 22353a: deadly power of time (or of men's rage that destroys).
[89] supply.
[90] *store;*] *store.* STC 22353a.
[91] condition.
[92] greatness.
[93] since there is neither.
[94] destructive.
[95] Where can Time's best jewel (the friend) be hidden so as to escape being locked up in Time's chest?
[96] destruction.
[97] *of*] *or* STC 22353a.
[98] friend.
[99] the evils mentioned in the lines that follow.
[1] the unworthy dressed in finery.
[2] misrule.

And Folly (Doctor-like)[3] controuling skill,
And simple-Truth miscalde Simplicitie,[4]
And captiue-good attending[5] Captaine ill.
Tyr'd with all these, from these would I be gone,
Saue that to dye,[6] I leaue my loue alone.

67

Ah wherefore with infection should he liue,[7]
And with his presence grace impietie,
That sinne by him aduantage should atchiue,
And lace[8] it selfe with his societie?
Why should false painting immitate his cheeke,
And steale dead seeing[9] of his liuing hew?
Why should poore beautie indirectly seeke,
Roses of shaddow,[10] since his Rose is true?
Why should he liue, now nature banckrout is,
Beggerd of blood to blush through liuely vaines,[11]
For she hath no exchecker now but his,
And proud of many, liues vpon his gaines?[12]
O him she stores,[13] to show what welth she had,
In daies long since, before these last so bad.

71

Noe Longer mourne for me when I am dead,
Then you shall heare the surly sullen[14] bell
Giue warning to the world that I am fled
From this vile world with vildest wormes to dwell:
Nay if you read this line, remember not,
The hand that writ it, for I loue you so,
That I in your sweet thoughts would be forgot,
If thinking on me then should make you woe.
O if (I say) you looke vpon this verse,
When I (perhaps) compounded am with clay,
Do not so much as my poore name reherse;
But let your loue euen with my life decay.
Least the wise world should looke into your mone,
And mocke you with me after I am gon.

73

That time of yeare[15] thou maist in me behold,
When yellow leaues, or none, or few doe hange
Vpon those boughes which shake against the could,
Bare ruin'd[16] quiers, where late the sweet birds sang.

3 with the air of one who knows.
4 ignorance.
5 serving, obeying.
6 by dying.
7 why should my friend live in this evil world.
8 adorn.
9 lifeless appearance.
10 painted roses.
11 *vaines?*] *vaines*, STC 22353a.
12 what he can provide her.
13 Nature hoards his beauty.
14 mournful.
15 *yeare*] *yeeare* STC 22353a.
16 *ruin'd*] *rn'wd* STC 22353a.

In me thou seest the twi-light of such day,
As after Sun-set fadeth in the West,
Which by and by blacke night doth take away,
Deaths second selfe that seals vp all in rest.
In me thou seest the glowing of such fire,
That on the ashes of his youth doth lye,
As the death bed, whereon it must expire,
Consum'd with that which it was nurrisht by.[17]
This thou perceu'st, which makes thy loue more strong,
To loue that well, which thou must leaue ere long.

76

Why is my verse so barren of new pride?[18]
So far from variation or quicke change?
Why with the time[19] do I not glance aside
To new found methods, and to compounds strange?
Why write I still all one, euer the same,
And keepe inuention in a noted weed,[20]
That euery word doth almost tel[21] my name,
Shewing their birth, and where they did proceed?
O know sweet loue I alwaies write of you,
And you and loue are still[22] my argument:[23]
So all my best is dressing old words new,
Spending againe what is already spent:
For as the Sun is daily new and old,
So is my loue still telling what is told.[24]

80

O how I faint when I of you do write,
Knowing a better spirit[25] doth vse your name,
And in the praise thereof spends all his might,
To make me toung-tide speaking of your fame.
But since your worth (wide as the Ocean is)
The humble as[26] the proudest saile doth beare,
My sawsie barke (inferior farre to his)
On your broad maine doth wilfully[27] appeare.
Your shallowest helpe will hold me vp a floate,
Whilst he vpon your soundlesse[28] deepe doth ride,
Or (being wrackt) I am a worthlesse bote,
He of tall building, and of goodly pride.
Then if[29] he thriue and I be cast away,
The worst was this, my loue was my decay.[30]

---

[17] choked by the ashes of what was once the fuel.
[18] novelty.
[19] following the fashion.
[20] keep my poems in a familiar dress.
[21] *tel*] *fel* STC 22353a.
[22] always.
[23] subject matter.
[24] *told.*] *told,* STC 22353a.
[25] a greater poet.
[26] as well as.
[27] venturously.
[28] unfathomable.
[29] *if*] *If* STC 22353a.
[30] because it prompted me to write.

86

Was it the proud full saile of his great verse,
Bound for the prize of (all to precious) you,
That did my ripe thoughts in my braine inhearce,[31]
Making their tombe the wombe wherein they grew?
Was it his spirit, by spirits taught to write,
Aboue a mortall pitch, that struck me dead?
No, neither he, nor his compiers by night
Giuing him ayde, my verse astonished.[32]
He nor that affable familiar ghost
Which nightly gulls[33] him with intelligence,[34]
As victors of my silence cannot boast;[35]
I was not sick of any feare from thence;[36]
  But when your countinance[37] fild vp his line,
  Then lackt I matter, that infeebled mine.[38]

87

Farewell thou art too deare for my possessing,
And like enough thou knowst thy estimate.[39]
The Charter of thy worth giues thee releasing:
My bonds in thee are all determinate.[40]
For how do I hold thee but by thy granting,
And for that ritches where is my deseruing?
The cause of this faire guift in me is wanting,
And so my pattent back again is sweruing.[41]
Thy selfe thou gau'st, thy owne worth then not knowing,
Or mee to whom thou gau'st it, else mistaking;[42]
So thy great guift vpon misprision growing,[43]
Comes home againe, on better iudgement making.[44]
  Thus haue I had thee as a dreame doth flatter,
  In sleepe a King, but waking no such matter.

89

Say that thou didst forsake mee for some falt,
And I will comment vpon[45] that offence.[46]
Speake of my lamenesse, and I straight will halt:[47]
Against thy reasons making no defence.
Thou canst not (loue) disgrace me halfe so ill,
To set a forme vpon desired change,[48]
As ile my selfe disgrace, knowing thy wil,

---

31 enclose as in a coffin.
32 dismayed, struck dumb.
33 deceives.
34 talk.
35 *boast;*] *boast,* STC 22353a.
36 *thence;*] *thence,* STC 22353a.
37 approval.
38 The foregoing allusions to the rival poet and his associates, despite much speculation, remain unexplained.
39 *estimate.*] *estimate,* STC 22353a: worth.
40 ended.
41 the grant of your friendship returns to you.
42 *mistaking;*] *mistaking,* STC 22353a.
43 the mistake of overestimating my worth or of underestimating your own.
44 when you make a better judgment.
45 discuss.
46 *offence.*] *offence,* STC 22353a.
47 limp.
48 give an appearance to the change that you desire.

I will acquaintance strangle[49] and looke strange:[50]
Be absent from thy walkes[51] and in my tongue,
Thy sweet beloued name no more shall dwell,
Least I (too much prophane) should do it wronge:
And haplie of our old acquaintance tell.
For thee, against my selfe ile vow debate,[52]
For I must nere loue him whom thou dost hate.

98

From you haue I beene absent in the spring,
When proud pide[53] Aprill (drest in all his trim)[54]
Hath put a spirit of youth in euery thing:
That heauie *Saturne*[55] laught and leapt with him.
Yet nor the laies of birds, nor the sweet smell
Of different flowers in odor and in hew,
Could make me any summers story tell:
Or from their proud lap pluck them where they grew:
Nor did I wonder at the Lillies white,
Nor praise the deepe vermillion in the Rose;[56]
They weare[57] but sweet, but figures of delight:
Drawne after you, you patterne of all those.
Yet seem'd it Winter still, and you away,
As with your shaddow I with these did play.

102

My loue is strengthened though more weake in seeming;[58]
I loue not lesse, thogh lesse the show appeare.[59]
That loue is marchandiz'd, whose ritch esteeming,[60]
The owners tongue doth publish euery where.
Our loue was new, and then but in the spring,
When I was wont to greet it with my laies,
As *Philomell* in summers front[61] doth singe,
And stops her[62] pipe in growth of riper daies:
Not that the summer is lesse pleasant now
Then when her mournefull himns did hush the night,
But that wild musick burthens euery bow,
And sweets growne common loose their deare delight,
Therefore like her, I some-time hold my tongue:
Because I would not dull[63] you with my songe.

104

To me faire friend you neuer can be old,
For as you were when first your eye I eyde,

[49] put an end to.
[50] act like a stranger.
[51] haunts.
[52] pledge a quarrel.
[53] splendidly variegated.
[54] ornamental dress.
[55] The god Saturn was cold and austere.
[56] *Rose;*] *Rose,* STC 22353a.
[57] were.
[58] *seeming;*] *seeming* STC 22353a.
[59] *appeare.*] *appeare,* STC 22353a.
[60] worth.
[61] beginning.
[62] *her*] *his* STC 22353a.
[63] make gloomy.

Such seemes your beautie still: Three Winters colde,
Haue from the forrests shooke three summers pride,
Three beautious springs to yellow *Autumne* turn'd,
In processe of the seasons haue I seene,
Three Aprill perfumes in three hot Iunes burn'd,
Since first I saw you fresh which yet are greene.
Ah yet doth beauty like a Dyall hand,
Steale from his figure, and no pace perceiu'd;[64]
So your sweete hew, which me thinkes still doth stand
Hath motion, and mine eye may be deceaued.
For feare of which, heare this thou age vnbred,[65]
Ere you were borne was beauties summer dead.

106

When in the Chronicle of wasted[66] time,
I see discriptions of the fairest wights,[67]
And beautie making beautifull old rime,
In praise of Ladies dead, and louely Knights,
Then in the blazon[68] of sweet beauties best,
Of hand, of foote, of lip, of eye, of brow,
I see their antique Pen would haue exprest,
Euen such a beauty as you maister[69] now.
So all their praises are but prophesies
Of this our time, all you prefiguring,
And for[70] they look'd but with deuining eyes,[71]
They had not skill[72] enough your worth to sing:
For we[73] which now behold these present dayes,
Haue eyes to wonder, but lack toungs to praise.

107

Not mine owne feares, nor the prophetick soule,
Of the wide world, dreaming on things to come,
Can yet the lease of my true loue controule,[74]
Supposde as forfeit to a confin'd doome.[75]
The mortall Moone[76] hath her eclipse indur'de,[77]
And the sad Augurs mock their owne presage;[78]
Incertenties now crowne them-selues assur'de,
And peace proclaimes Oliues of endlesse age.
Now with the drops of this most balmie time,
My loue[79] lookes fresh, and death to me subscribes,[80]

---

64 *perceiu'd;*] *perceiu'd,* STC 22353a.
65 generations unborn.
66 past.
67 men or women.
68 description.
69 possess.
70 because.
71 eyes that try to see into the future.
72 *skill*] *still* STC 22353a.
73 for even we.
74 can limit the duration of our friendship.
75 supposed doomed to forfeiture at a set time.
76 Queen Elizabeth.
77 If *endured* here means "safely passed through," the reference may be to the defeat of the Armada, or to the Peace of Vervins, 1598, or to the revolt of Essex, 1601, or to some other danger. If *endured* means "undergone," the reference may be to Queen Elizabeth's death in 1603, and lines 6–8 may refer to the accession of King James.
78 *presage;*] *presage,* STC 22353a: are mocked by their predictions.
79 This may mean the person addressed, or it may mean "my love for you."
80 submits.

Since spight of him Ile liue in this poore rime,
While he insults ore dull and speachlesse tribes.
  And thou in this shalt finde thy monument,
  When tyrants crests and tombs of brasse are spent.

109

O neuer say that I was false of heart,
Though absence seem'd my flame to quallifie;[81]
As easie might I from my selfe depart,
As from my soule which in thy brest doth lie:
That is my home of loue, if I have rang'd,[82]
Like him that trauels I returne againe,
Iust to the time,[83] not with the time exchang'd,[84]
So that my selfe bring water for my staine.[85]
Neuer beleeve though in my nature raign'd,
All frailties that besiege all kindes of blood,[86]
That it could so preposterouslie be stain'd,
To leaue for nothing all thy summe of good:
  For nothing this wide Vniverse I call,
  Saue thou my Rose, in it thou art my all.

110

Alas 'tis true, I haue gone here and there,
And made my selfe a motley[87] to the view,
Gor'd mine own thoughts, sold cheap what is most deare,[88]
Made old offences of affections new.[89]
Most true it is, that I haue lookt on truth[90]
Asconce[91] and strangely: But by all aboue,
These blenches[92] gaue my heart an other youth,
And worse essaies[93] prou'd thee my best of loue.[94]
Now all is done, haue what shall haue no end:[95]
Mine appetite I neuer more will grin'de[96]
On newer proofe,[97] to trie an older friend,
A God in loue,[98] to whom I am confin'd.
  Then giue me welcome, next my heauen the best,
  Euen to thy pure and most most louing brest.

111

O for my sake doe you with[99] fortune chide,
The guiltie goddesse of my harmfull deeds,

---

81 *quallifie;*] *quallifie,* STC 22353a: moderate.
82 wandered.
83 punctually.
84 altered.
85 *staine.*] *staine,* STC 22353a.
86 temperament.
87 dress of the professional fool; here, actor's costume.
88 his friend's regard.
89 offended old friends and made new ones.
90 constancy.
91 askance.
92 swervings.
93 experiments (in friendship).
94 *loue.*] *loue,* STC 22353a.
95 *end:*] *end,* STC 22353a: my constant friendship.
96 whet.
97 further experiment.
98 i.e., his friend.
99 *with*] *wish* STC 22353a.

That did not better for my life prouide,
Then publick meanes[1] which public manners[2] breede.
Thence comes it that my name receiues a brand,
And almost thence my nature is subdu'd
To[3] what it workes in, like the Dyers hand.[4]
Pitty me then, and wish I were renu'de,[5]
Whilst like a willing pacient I will drinke,
Potions of Eysell[6] gainst my strong infection;[7]
No bitternesse that I will bitter thinke,
Nor double pennance to correct correction.[8]
  Pittie me then deare friend, and I assure yee,
  Euen that your pittie is enough to cure mee.

115

Those lines that I before haue writ doe lie,
Euen those that said I could not loue you deerer,
Yet then my iudgement knew no reason why,
My most full flame should afterwards burne cleerer.
But reckening[9] time, whose milliond[10] accidents
Creepe in twixt vowes, and change decrees of Kings,
Tan[11] sacred beautie, blunt the sharp'st intents,
Diuert strong mindes to th' course of altring things:[12]
Alas why fearing of times tiranie,
Might I not then say now I loue you best,
When I was certaine ore[13] in-certainty,
Crowning[14] the present, doubting of the rest:
  Loue is a Babe;[15] then might I not say so
  To giue full growth to that which still doth grow.

116

Let me not to the marriage of true mindes
Admit impediments;[16] loue is not loue
Which alters when it alteration findes,
Or bendes[17] with the remouer[18] to remoue.
O no, it is an euer fixed marke
That lookes on tempests and is neuer shaken;
It is the star to euery wandring barke,
Whose worths vnknowne, although his height[19] be taken.[20]
Lou's not Times foole,[21] though rosie lips and cheeks
Within his bending sickles compasse come.[22]
Loue alters not with his breefe houres and weekes,

1 work dependent on the approval of the public.
2 conduct no better than that of the crowd.
3 brought into conformity with.
4 *hand.*] *hand,* STC 22353a.
5 restored.
6 vinegar (used as antiseptic and remedy).
7 *infection;*] *infection,* STC 22353a.
8 nor will I refuse double penance to complete the correction of my conduct.
9 reckoning with.
10 millionfold.
11 deprive of the freshness of youth.
12 changeableness.
13 o'er.
14 glorifying.
15 *Babe;*] *Babe,* STC 22353a.
16 *impediments;*] *impediments,* STC 22353a.
17 changes its course.
18 inconstant one.
19 *height*] *higth* STC 22353a.
20 Although the altitude of a star is known, its influence is unknowable.
21 the sport of time.
22 *come.*] *come,* STC 22353a.

But beares it out[23] euen to the edge of doome:[24]
If this be error and vpon me proued,
I neuer writ, nor no man euer loued.

123

No! Time, thou shalt not bost that I doe change;[25]
Thy pyramyds[26] buylt vp with newer might
To me are nothing nouell, nothing strange;[27]
They are but dressings of a former sight:[28]
Our dates[29] are breefe, and therefor we admire,[30]
What thou dost foyst vpon vs that is ould,
And rather make[31] them borne to our desire,
Then thinke that we before haue heard them tould:
Thy registers and thee I both defie,
Not wondring at the present, nor the past,
For thy records, and what we see doth lye,
Made more or les by thy continuall hast:[32]
This I doe vow and this shall euer be,
I will be true dispight thy syeth[33] and thee.

130

My Mistres eyes are nothing[34] like the Sunne,
Currall[35] is farre more red, then her lips red,
If snow be white, why then her brests are dun:
If haires be wiers,[36] black wiers grow on her head:
I haue seene Roses damaskt,[37] red and white,
But no such Roses see I in her cheekes,
And in some perfumes is there more delight,
Then in the breath that from my Mistres reekes.[38]
I loue to heare her speake, yet well I know,
That Musicke hath a farre more pleasing sound:
I graunt I neuer saw a goddesse goe,[39]
My Mistres when shee walkes treads on the ground.
And yet by heauen I thinke my loue as rare,
As any she[40] beli'd with false compare.

132

Thine eies I loue, and they as pittying me,
Knowing thy heart torments[41] me with disdaine,
Haue put on black, and louing mourners bee,
Looking with pretty ruth[42] vpon my paine.

---

23 survives.
24 doomsday.
25 *change;*] *change,* STC 22353a.
26 any massive structures.
27 *strange;*] *strange,* STC 22353a.
28 New marvels of architecture are only refashionings of what has been seen before.
29 years.
30 wonder at.
31 think.
32 magnified or dwarfed by the flight of time.
33 scythe.
34 not at all.
35 coral.
36 This is an allusion to the conventional description of ladies' hair as golden wire.
37 of mingled red and white.
38 is exhaled.
39 walk.
40 woman.
41 *torments*] *torment* STC 22353a.
42 pity.

And truly not the morning Sun of Heauen
Better becomes the gray cheeks of th' East,
Nor that full Starre that vshers in the Eauen
Doth halfe that glory to the sober West
As those two morning eyes become thy face:
O let it then as well beseeme thy heart
To mourne for me since mourning doth thee grace,
And sute[43] thy pitty like[44] in euery part.
Then will I sweare beauty her selfe is blacke,
And all they foule that thy complexion lacke.

146

Poore soule the center of my sinfull earth,[45]
Thrall to[46] these rebbell powres that thee array,[47]
Why dost thou pine within and suffer dearth
Painting thy outward walls so costlie gay?
Why so large cost[48] hauing so short a lease,
Dost thou vpon thy fading mansion spend?
Shall wormes inheritors of this excesse
Eate vp thy charge?[49] is this thy bodies end?
Then soule liue thou vpon thy seruants losse,
And let that[50] pine to aggrauat[51] thy store;
But tearmes diuine[52] in selling houres of drosse:
Within be fed, without be rich no more,
So shalt thou feed on death, that feeds on men,
And death once dead, ther's no more dying then.

THE PHOENIX AND THE TURTLE[53]

Let the bird of lowdest lay,[54]
On the sole *Arabian* tree,[55]
Herauld sad[56] and trumpet be:
To whose sound chaste wings obay.

But thou shriking harbinger,[57]
Foule precurrer[58] of the fiend,
Augour of the feuers end,[59]
To this troupe come thou not neere.

From this Session interdict
Euery foule of tyrant wing,
Saue the Eagle feath'red King,
Keepe the obsequie so strict.

Let the Priest in Surples white,
That defunctiue[60] Musicke can,[61]
Be the death-deuining Swan,
Lest the *Requiem* lacke his right.[62]

And thou treble dated[63] Crow,
That thy sable gender[64] mak'st,
With the breath thou giu'st and tak'st,[65]
Mongst our mourners shalt thou go.

Here the Antheme doth commence,
Loue and Constancie is dead,

43 dress.
44 similarly.
45 body.
46 *Thrall to*] *My sinfull earth* STC 22353a.
47 afflict (or clothe).
48 expense.
49 expenditure.
50 the servant, the body.
51 increase.
52 eternity.
53 From Robert Chester, *Loues Martyr*, 1601, STC 5119.1, Folger Library.
54 The identity of the bird is not clear.
55 the tree of the phoenix.
56 serious, dignified.
57 i.e., the screech owl.
58 forerunner.
59 i.e., of death.
60 funereal.
61 knows, is skilled in.
62 its rite or its due.
63 long-lived.
64 race.
65 Crows and ravens were believed to conceive and lay their eggs at the bill.

Phoenix[66] and the *Turtle*[67] fled,
In a mutuall flame from hence.

So they loued as[68] loue in twaine,
Had the essence but in one,
Two distincts,[69] Diuision none,
Number there in loue was slaine.

Hearts remote, yet not asunder;
Distance and no space was seene,
Twixt this *Turtle* and his Queene;
But in them[70] it were a wonder.

So betweene them Loue did shine,
That the *Turtle* saw his right,[71]
Flaming in the *Phoenix* sight;[72]
Either was the others mine.[73]

Propertie[74] was thus appalled,
That the selfe was not the same:[75]
Single Natures double name,
Neither two nor one was called.

Reason in it selfe confounded,
Saw Diuision[76] grow together,
To themselues yet either neither,
Simple were so well compounded.[77]

That it[78] cried, how true a twaine,
Seemeth this concordant one,
Loue hath Reason, Reason none,
If what parts, can so remaine.[79]

Whereupon it made this *Threne,*[80]
To the *Phoenix* and the *Doue,*
Co-supremes and starres of Loue,
As *Chorus* to their Tragique Scene.

THRENOS

Beautie, Truth, and Raritie,
Grace in all simplicitie,
Here enclosde, in cinders lie.

Death is now the *Phoenix* nest,
And the *Turtles* loyall brest,
To eternitie doth rest.

Leauing no posteritie,
Twas not their infirmitie,
It was married Chastitie.

Truth may seeme, but cannot be,
Beautie bragge, but tis not she,
Truth and Beautie buried be.

To this vrne let those repaire,
That are either true or faire,
For these dead Birds, sigh a prayer.

SONGS FROM THE PLAYS

Who is Siluia? what is she?[81]
That all our Swaines commend her?
Holy, faire, and wise is she,
The heauen such grace did lend her,
That she might admired be.

Is she kinde as she is faire?
For beauty liues with kindnesse:
Loue doth to her eyes repaire,
To helpe him of his blindnesse:
And being help'd, inhabits there.

Then to Siluia, let vs sing,
That Siluia is excelling;
She excels each mortall thing
Vpon the dull earth dwelling.
To her let vs Garlands bring.

When Dasies pied,[82] and Violets blew,[83]
And Ladie-smockes all siluer white,[84]

66 here symbolizing love or beauty.
67 turtledove, symbolizing constancy.
68 that.
69 separate persons.
70 except in them, in any but them.
71 i.e., the love due him.
72 i.e., eyes.
73 treasure.
74 essential quality, personality.
75 that identity was lost.
76 separate persons.
77 simples or elements were so well blended.
78 Reason.
79 Love is right, and Reason is mistaken if two persons can remain so united.
80 lament.
81 From *The Two Gentlemen of Verona,* written in 1594–1595 (?). The text of the songs, except where other editions are mentioned, is that of the First Folio, 1623, STC 22273, Morgan Library.
82 spotted, touched with color.
83 From *Love's Labour's Lost,* written in 1594–1595 (?).
84 All early editions transpose lines 2–3. Theobald corrected this error in 1733.

And Cuckow-buds[85] of yellow hew:
  Do paint the Medowes with delight.
The Cuckow then on euerie tree,
Mockes married men, for thus sings he,
    Cuckow,
Cuckow, Cuckow: O word of feare,
Vnpleasing to a married eare.

When Shepheards pipe on Oaten strawes,
  And merrie Larkes are Ploughmens clockes:
When Turtles[86] tread, and Rookes and Dawes,
  And Maidens bleach their summer smockes:
The Cuckow then on euerie tree
Mockes married men; for thus sings he,
    Cuckow.
Cuckow, Cuckow: O word of feare,
Vnpleasing to a married eare.

When Isicles hang by the wall,[87]
  And Dicke the Shepheard blowes his naile;[88]
And Tom beares Logges into the hall,
  And Milke comes frozen home in paile:
When blood is nipt, and waies be fowle,[89]
Then nightly sings the staring Owle
Tu-whit, to-who. A merrie note,
While greasie Ione doth keele[90] the pot.

When all aloud the winde doth blow,
  And coffing drownes the Parsons saw:
And birds sit brooding in the snow,
  And Marrians nose lookes red and raw:
When roasted Crabs[91] hisse in the bowle,
Then nightly sings the staring Owle,
Tu-whit, to who: a merrie note,
While greasie Ione doth keele the pot.

[FAIRY SONG][92]

Ouer hil, ouer dale,
  Thorough[93] bush, thorough briar,
Ouer parke, ouer pale,
  Thorough flood, thorough fire,
I do wander euerie where,
Swifter then the Moons sphere;
And I serue the Fairy Queene,
To dew her orbs vpon the green.
The Cowslips tall, her pensioners bee,
In their gold coats, spots you see,
Those be Rubies, Fairie fauours:[94]
In those freckles, liue their sauours.[95]
I must go seeke some dew drops heere,
And hang a pearle in euery cowslips eare.

[FAIRY LULLABY][96]

You spotted[97] Snakes with double tongue,
  Thorny Hedgehogges be not seene,
Newts and blinde wormes do no wrong,
  Come not neere our Fairy Queene.

    Philomele[98] with melodie,
    Sing in our[99] sweet Lullaby.
Lulla, lulla, lullaby, lulla, lulla, lullaby,
    Neuer harme,
    Nor spell, nor charme,
    Come our louely Lady nye.
    So good night with Lullaby.

Weauing Spiders come not heere,
  Hence you long leg'd Spinners, hence.
Beetles blacke approach not neere;
  Worme nor Snayle doe no offence.

    Philomele with melodie,
    Sing in our sweet Lullaby.
Lulla, lulla, lullaby, lulla, lulla, lullaby,
    Neuer harme,
    Nor spell, nor charme,
    Come our louely Lady nye.
    So good night with Lullaby.

Hence away, now all is well,
One aloofe, stand Centinell.

---

85 cowslip buds.
86 turtledoves.
87 From *Love's Labour's Lost.*
88 blows on his fingertips to warm them.
89 muddy.
90 cool by stirring.
91 crab apples.
92 From *A Midsummer Night's Dream,* written in 1595–1596 (?).
93 *Thorough* STC 22302]; *Through* STC 22273.
94 *fauours:* STC 22302]; *fauors,* STC 22273.
95 *sauours.* STC 22302]; *sauors,* STC 22273.
96 From *A Midsummer Night's Dream.*
97 *spotted* STC 22302]; *spotied* STC 22273.
98 nightingale.
99 *our* STC 22302]; *your* STC 22273.

[PUCK'S SONG][1]

Now the hungry Lyon[2] rores,
And the Wolfe behowls[3] the Moone;
Whilest the heauy ploughman snores,
All with wearie taske fore-done.
Now the wasted brands doe glow,
Whilst the scritch-owle, schritching loud,
Puts the wretch, that lies in woe,
In remembrance of a shrowd.
Now it is the time of night,
That the graues, all gaping wide,
Euery one lets forth his spright,
In the Church-way paths to glide.
And we Fairies, that doe runne,
By the triple *Hecates* teame,
From the presence of the Sunne,
Following darkenesse like a dreame,
Now are frollicke: not a Mouse
Shall disturbe this hallowed house.
I am sent, with broome before,
To sweep the dust behinde the doore.

Enter King and Queene of Fairies, with their traine[4]

Oberon

Through the house giue glimmering light,
By the dead and drowsie fier,
Euerie Elfe and Fairie spright,
Hop as light as bird from brier.
And this Ditty after me,
Sing and dance it tripping lie.

Titania

First rehearse your[5] song by roate,
To each word a warbling note.
Hand in hand, with Fairie grace,
Will we sing and blesse this place.

Oberon[6]

Now vntill the breake of day,
Through this house each Fairy stray.

Oberon and Fairies

To the best Bride-bed will we,
Which by vs shall blessed be:
And the issue there create,[7]
Euer shall be fortunate:
So shall all the couples three,
Euer true in louing be:
And the blots of Natures hand,
Shall not in their issue stand.
Neuer mole, harelip, nor scarre,
Nor marke prodigious, such as are
Despised in Natiuitie,[8]
Shall vpon their children be.

Oberon

With this field dew consecrate,[9]
Euery Fairie take his gate,[10]
And each seuerall chamber blesse,
Through this Pallace with sweet peace,
And the owner of it blest,[11]
Euer shall in safety rest.
Trip away, make no stay;
Meet me all by breake of day.

A SONG THE WHILST BASSANIO COMMENTS ON THE CASKETS TO HIMSELFE[12]

Tell me where is fancie[13] bred,
Or in the heart, or in the head:
How begot, how nourished.
Replie, replie.

It is engendred in the eyes,
With gazing fed, and Fancie dies,
In the cradle where it lies:
Let vs all ring Fancies knell.
Ile begin it. Ding dong, bell.
All. Ding, dong, bell.

Sigh no more Ladies, sigh no more,[14]
Men were deceiuers euer,

[1] From *A Midsummer Night's Dream.*
[2] *Lyon*] *Lyons* STC 22273.
[3] *behowls* Theobald] *beholds* STC 22273.
[4] From *A Midsummer Night's Dream.*
[5] *your* STC 22302]; *this* STC 22273.
[6] In the First Quarto (STC 22302) lines 11–32 are assigned to Oberon; in the First Folio (STC 22273) they are headed *The Song,* and assigned to no one.
[7] created.
[8] birth.
[9] *consecrate,* STC 22302]; *consecrate.* STC 22273; consecrated.
[10] gait, i.e., make his way.
[11] In all the early editions lines 29–30 are printed in the reverse order. Singer suggested the correction, and Staunton adopted it.
[12] From *The Merchant of Venice,* written in 1596–1597 (?).
[13] love.
[14] From *Much Ado About Nothing,* written in 1598– 1599 (?).

One foote in Sea, and one on shore,
To one thing constant neuer,
Then sigh not so,
But let them goe,
And be you blithe and bonnie,[15]
Conuerting all your sounds of woe,
Into hey nony nony.

Sing no more ditties, sing no moe,
Of dumps[16] so dull and heauy,[17]
The fraud of men was[18] euer so,
Since summer first was leauy.
Then sigh not so,
But let them goe,
And be you blithe and bonnie,
Conuerting all your sounds of woe,
Into hey nony nony.

Pardon goddesse of the night,[19]
Those that slew thy virgin knight,
For the which with songs of woe,
Round about her tombe they goe:
Midnight assist our mone,
Helpe vs to sigh and grone.
Heauily, heauily.
Graues yawne and yeelde your dead,
Till death be vttered,[20]
Heauily, heauily.[21]

Vnder the greene wood tree,[22]
Who loues to lye with mee,
And turne[23] his merrie Note,[24]
Vnto the sweet Birds throte,
Come hither, come hither, come hither:
Heare shall he see
No enemie,
But Winter and rough Weather.

Who doth ambition shunne,
And loues to liue i'th Sunne:[25]
Seeking the food he eates,
And pleas'd with what he gets:
Come hither, come hither, come hither,
Heere shall he see
No enemie,
But Winter and rough Weather.

Blow, blow, thou winter wind,[26]
Thou art not so vnkinde,
As mans ingratitude:[27]
Thy tooth is not so keene,
Because thou art not seene,
Although thy breath be rude.
Heigh ho, sing heigh ho, vnto the greene holly,
Most frendship, is fayning; most Louing, meere folly:
Then[28] heigh ho, the holly,
This Life is most iolly.

Freize, freize, thou bitter skie
That does not bight so nigh
As benefitts forgot:
Though thou the waters warpe,[29]
Thy sting is not so sharpe,
As freind remembred not.[30]
Heigh no, sing heigh no, vnto the greene holly,
Most frendship, is fayning; most Louing, meere folly:
Then heigh ho, the holly,
This Life is most iolly.

It was a Louer, and his lasse,[31]
With a hey, and a ho, and a hey nonino,[32]

---

15 cheerful.

16 mournful tunes, sorrowful moods.

17 mournful.

18 *was* STC 22304]; *were* STC 22273.

19 From *Much Ado About Nothing.* The "goddesse" is Diana.

20 sent forth.

21 *Heauily, heauily.* STC 22304]; *Heauenly, heauenly.* STC 22273.

22 From *As You Like It,* written in 1599–1600 (?).

23 adapt or compose (music). Many editors substitute *tune.*

24 tune.

25 in the open air.

26 From *As You Like It. wind,*] *winds,* STC 22273.

27 *ingratitude:*]; *ingratitude* STC 22273.

28 *Then*] *The* STC 22273.

29 freeze.

30 *not.*] *not* STC 22273.

31 From *As You Like It.* This song, with music, is printed in Thomas Morley's *The first booke of ayres,* 1600, STC 18116a, Folger Library.

32 *nonino,*] *nonino.* STC 22273.

That o're the greene corne feild did passe,
In the spring time,
The onely pretty ring[33] time.
When Birds do sing,
Hey ding a ding, ding,
Sweet Louers loue the spring.

Between the acres[34] of the Rie,
With a hey, and a ho, and a hey nonino:
These prettie Countrie folks[35] would lie.
In spring time,
The onely pretty ring time.
When Birds do sing,
Hey ding a ding, ding,
Sweet Louers loue the spring.

This Carroll they began that houre,
With a hey and a ho, and a hey nonino:
How that a life was but a Flower,
In spring time,
The onely pretty ring time.
When Birds do sing,
Hey ding a ding, ding,
Sweet Louers loue the spring.

And therefore take the present time.[36]
With a hey, and a ho, and a hey nonino,
For loue is crowned with the prime.[37]
In spring time,
The onely pretty ring time.
When Birds do sing,
Hey ding a ding, ding,
Sweet Louers loue the spring.

O Mistris mine where are you roming?[38]
O stay and heare, your true loues coming,
That can sing both high and low.
Trip no further prettie sweeting.
Iourneys end in louers meeting,[39]
Euery wise mans sonne doth know.

What is loue, tis not heereafter,
Present mirth, hath present laughter:
What's to come, is still[40] vnsure.
In delay there lies no plentie,
Then come kisse me sweet and twentie:[41]
Youths a stuffe will not endure.

Come away, come away death,[42]
And in sad cypresse[43] let me be laide.
Flye away, flie[44] away breath,
I am slaine by a faire cruell maide:
My shrowd of white, stuck all with Ew,
O prepare it.
My part of death[45] no one so true
Did share it.[46]

Not a flower, not a flower sweete
On my blacke coffin, let there be strewne:
Not a friend, not a friend greet
My poore corpes, where my bones shall be throwne:
A thousand thousand sighes to saue,
Lay me O where
Sad true louer neuer find my graue,
To weepe there.

When that I was and a little tine boy,[47]
With hey, ho, the winde and the raine:

[33] *ring* STC 18116a]; *rang* STC 22273.
[34] on the balks or strips of unplowed turf between the fields.
[35] *folks* STC 22273]; *fooles* STC 18116a.
[36] This stanza is printed as the fourth stanza in STC 18116a and as the second in STC 22273.
[37] spring.
[38] From *Twelfth Night,* written in 1599–1600 (?).
[39] when lovers meet.
[40] always.
[41] sweet and twenty times sweet.
[42] From *Twelfth Night.* In this sentimental song Feste playfully satirizes the love grief of the self-pitying Orsino. *Come away* means *come hither.*
[43] Crepe-like fabric used as mourning, or, perhaps, a coffin made of cypress wood or a bier strewn with branches of cypress.
[44] *Flye away, flie*] *fye away, fie* STC 22273.
[45] my allotted portion—death.
[46] No one who has died for love was as true as I am.
[47] From *Twelfth Night.* Cf. the Fool's song in *King Lear,* III, ii, 74–77:
He that has and a little-tyne wit,

A foolish thing was but a toy,[48]
  For the raine it raineth euery day.

But when I came to mans estate,
  With hey ho, the winde and the raine:
Gainst Knaues and Theeues men shut their gate,
  For the raine it raineth euery day.

But when I came alas to wiue,
  With hey, ho, the winde and the raine:
By swaggering[49] could I neuer thriue,
  For the raine it raineth euery day.

But when I came vnto my beds,
  With hey, ho, the winde and the raine:
With[50] tospottes[51] still had drunken heades,
  For the raine it raineth euery day.

A great while ago the world begon,
  Hey ho, the winde and the raine:
But that's all one,[52] our Play is done,
  And wee'l striue to please you euery day.[53]

Take, oh take those lips away,[54]
  That so sweetly were forsworne,
And those eyes: the breake of day,[55]
  Lights that do mislead the Morne;[56]
But my kisses bring againe, bring againe,
Seales of loue, but seal'd in vaine, seal'd in vaine.

Hearke, hearke, the Larke at Heauens gate sings,[57]
  And Phoebus[58] gins arise,
His Steeds to water at those Springs
  On chalic'd[59] Flowres that lyes:
And winking Mary-buds[60] begin
  To ope their Golden eyes,[61]
With euery thing that pretty is,
  My Lady sweet arise:
    Arise, arise.

Guid.

Feare no more the heat o' th' Sun,[62]
  Nor the furious Winters rages,
Thou thy worldly task hast don,
  Home art gon, and tane thy wages.
Golden Lads, and Girles all must,
As Chimney-Sweepers come to dust.

Arui.

Feare no more the frowne o' th' Great,
  Thou art past the Tirants stroake,
Care no more to cloath and eate,
  To thee the Reede is as the Oake:

With heigh-ho, the Winde and the Raine,
Must make content with his Fortunes fit,
Though the Raine it raineth euery day.

"When the play is over, the Duke plighted to his page, Olivia rightly married to the wrong man and the whole ravel of sentiment begins to be attached to the serious conditions of life, Feste is left alone upon the stage. Then he sings a song which conveys to us his feelings of the world's impartiality; all things proceed according to law; nobody is humoured; people must abide the consequences of their actions, 'for the rain it raineth every day.' A little boy may have his toy; but a man must guard against knavery and thieving; marriage itself cannot be sweetened by swaggering; whoso drinks with 'toss-pots' will get a 'drunken head'; it is a very old world and began so long ago that no change in its habits can be looked for" (John Weiss, *Wit, Humour, and Shakespeare,* 1876, as quoted by Richmond Noble, *Shakespeare's Use of Song,* 1923, p. 86). Many critics, however, consider Feste's song a clumsy development of the Fool's song in *King Lear,* added about 1606 to the playhouse version of *Twelfth Night* by a hand other than Shakespeare's.

[48] trifle.

[49] bullying.

[50] Perhaps *With* is a misprint for *We.*

[51] toss-pots, drunkards.

[52] but never mind about that.

[53] Such promises were usual in epilogues.

[54] From *Measure for Measure,* written in 1604–1605 (?). This song, the only one in the play, is sung by a boy "to give colour effect to the desolate situation of the jilted Mariana on the occasion of her first presentation to the audience" (Richmond Noble, *Shakespeare's Use of Song,* p. 88).

[55] *day,*] *day* STC 22273; i.e., like the dawn.

[56] *Morne;*] *Morne* STC 22273: mislead one to expect the morning.

[57] From *Cymbeline,* written in 1609–1610 (?).

[58] the sun.

[59] cup-shaped.

[60] sleeping marigold buds.

[61] *eyes,*] *eyes* STC 22273.

[62] From *Cymbeline.* Guiderius and Arviragus recite this dirge over the supposedly dead Imogen.

The Scepter, Learning, Physicke must,
All follow this and come to dust.

Guid.
Feare no more the Lightning flash.

Arui.
Nor th' all-dreaded Thunderstone.[63]

Guid.
Feare not Slander, Censure rash.

Arui.
Thou hast finish'd Ioy and mone.

Both
All Louers young, all Louers must,
Consigne[64] to thee and come to dust.

Guid.
No Exorcisor[65] harme thee,

Arui.
Nor no witch-craft charme thee.

Guid.
Ghost vnlaid forbeare thee.

Arui.
Nothing ill come neere thee.

Both
Quiet consumation[66] haue,
And renowned be thy graue.

When Daffadils begin to peere,[67]
With heigh the Doxy[68] ouer the dale,
Why then comes in the sweet o' the yeere,
For the red blood raigns in the winters pale.[69]
The white sheete bleaching on the hedge,
With hey the sweet birds, O how they sing:
Doth set my pugging[70] tooth an edge,[71]
For a quart of Ale is a dish for a King.[72]

The Larke, that tirra Lyra chaunts,
With heigh, the Thrush and the Iay:
Are Summer songs for me and my Aunts[73]
While we lye tumbling in the hay.

I have serued Prince *Florizell,* and in my time wore three pile,[74] but now I am out of seruice.

But shall I go mourne for that (my deere)
The pale Moone shines by night:
And when I wander here, and there
I then do most go right.

If Tinkers may haue leaue to liue,
And beare the Sow-skin Bowget,[75]
Then my account I well may giue,
And in the Stockes auouch-it.

Iog-on, Iog-on, the foot path way,[76]
And merrily hent[77] the Stile-a:
A merry heart goes all the day,
Your sad tyres in a Mile-a.

Lawne as white as driuen Snow,[78]
Cypresse[79] blacke as ere was Crow,
Gloues as sweete as Damaske Roses,
Maskes for faces, and for noses:

---

63 *Thunderstone.*] *Thunderstone* STC 22273.
64 submit.
65 conjuror.
66 conclusion, death.
67 From *The Winter's Tale,* written in 1610–1611 (?). The stage is empty, and Autolycus enters singing. His gay, rascally nature is instantly revealed by this song. The songs that follow are also his.
68 mistress (slang).
69 (a) pallor, (b) fenced area, enclosure.
70 thieving (slang).
71 on edge.
72 *King.*] *King* STC 22273.
73 light women.
74 rich velvet.
75 leather pouch or tool kit.
76 From *The Winter's Tale.* Autolycus leaves.
77 take, leap over.
78 From *The Winter's Tale.* Autolycus enters as a peddler.
79 crepe.

Bugle-bracelet,[80] Necke-lace Amber,
Perfume for a Ladies Chamber:
Golden Quoifes,[81] and Stomachers[82]
For my Lads, to giue their deers:
Pins, and poaking-stickes[83] of steele.
What Maids lacke from head to heele:
Come buy of me, come: come buy, come buy,
Buy Lads, or else your Lasses cry: Come buy.

Will you buy any Tape[84]
Or Lace for your Cape?
My dainty Ducke, my deere-a?
Any Silke, and Thred,
Any Toyes for your head
Of the news't, and fins't, fins't weare-a.
Come to the Pedler,
Money's a medler,[85]
That doth vtter[86] all mens ware-a.

Come vnto these yellow sands[87]
And then take hands:
Curtsied when you have, and kist,[88]
The wilde waues whist:[89]
Foote it featly[90] heere, and there,
And sweete Sprights the burthen[91] beare.[92]
Harke, harke.
Burthen dispersedly.[93] Bowgh wawgh.
The watch-Dogges barke
(*Burthen*) Bowgh-wawgh.
Hark, hark, I heare,
The straine of strutting Chanticlere
Cry cockadidle-dowe.

Full fadom fiue thy Father lies,[94]
Of his bones are Corrall made:
Those are pearles that were his eies,
Nothing of him that doth fade,
But doth suffer a Sea-change
Into something rich, and strange:
Sea-Nimphs hourly ring his knell.
(*Burthen*) Ding dong.
Harke now I heare them, ding-dong bell.

Where the Bee sucks, there suck I,[95]
In a Cowslips bell, I lie,
There I cowch[96] when Owles doe crie,
On the Batts backe I doe flie
After Sommer merrily.
Merrily, merrily, shall I liue now[97]
Vnder the blossom that hangs on the Bow.

Orpheus with his Lute made Trees,[98]
And the Mountaine tops that freeze,
Bow themselues when he did sing.
To his Musicke, Plants and Flowers
Euer sprung; as Sunne and Showers,
There had made a lasting Spring.

Euery thing that heard him play,
Euen the Billowes of the Sea,
Hung their heads, and then lay by.
In sweet Musicke is such Art,
Killing care, and griefe of heart,
Fall asleepe, or hearing dye.

---

[80] made of long black beads.
[81] close-fitting caps.
[82] Ornamental coverings worn by women.
[83] Rods for stiffening the plaits of ruffs.
[84] From *The Winter's Tale*.
[85] (a) thing of no value, like the fruit of the medlar, (b) meddler.
[86] put to sale.
[87] From *The Tempest*, written in 1611–1612 (?). Ariel sings to Prince Ferdinand. The arrangement of the lines of this song in the only early text, that of the First Folio, has perplexed editors. The present editor follows in general the rearrangement suggested by Capell in 1768.
[88] *kist,*] *kist* STC 22273: when you have curtsied and kissed (formalities before some Elizabethan dances.)
[89] the wild waves being whist, i.e., silent.
[90] gracefully.
[91] refrain.
[92] *The burthen beare*. quarto of 1674]; *beare the burthen*. STC 22273.
[93] coming from different directions.
[94] From *The Tempest*. Ariel sings to Ferdinand.
[95] From *The Tempest*. Ariel's song of freedom.
[96] lie.
[97] *Now*] *Now*. STC 22273.
[98] From *Henry VIII*, written in 1612–1613 (?). This song is possibly by Shakespeare but probably by John Fletcher.

Songs from Plays and Masques

THE TRADITION of song in English drama is unbroken from the medieval liturgical play through the plays of the sixteenth and seventeenth centuries. The principal purpose of the song was to entertain. Although Shakespeare and some of his contemporaries used songs with greater dramatic propriety and usually for a specific purpose—to reveal character, to create atmosphere, to bridge a time interval, to increase suspense—many songs in Elizabethan drama were included solely because the audience enjoyed them.

Some of the plays contain no songs; others have from one to a dozen. Sometimes the songs are assigned to one actor, sometimes to several, sometimes to a singer who is not an actor. Hundreds of the songs are extant; others have been lost, for the stage directions in some printed plays call for songs that are not included in the text.

The songs in Elizabethan plays and masques reflect the changing fashions in poetry throughout the period. The best of these songs are in every respect the equal of lyrics not included in plays—the equal in variety of subject, in diversity of metrical design, in artistry. Peele, Dekker, and Fletcher wrote almost no lyric poetry except the songs in their plays. Nashe's best poetry is in the songs in *Summer's Last Will and Testament.* Many of Jonson's best lyrics are in his plays.

The most useful collections are *Lyrics from the Dramatists of the Elizabethan Age*, ed. A. H. Bullen, 1892; *Songs from the British Drama*, ed. E. B. Reed, 1925. Many songs from plays are included in *A Book of Elizabethan Lyrics*, ed. F. E. Schelling, 1895; *Elizabethan Lyrics*, ed. Norman Ault, 1925, and revised, 1949; *Elizabethan and Seventeenth-Century Lyrics*, ed. M. W. Black, 1938. The following articles are of special interest: L. B. Wright, "Extraneous Song in Elizabethan Drama After the Advent of Shakespeare," *Studies in Philology*, xxiv (1927), 261–274; J. R. Moore, "The Songs of the Public Theaters in the Time of Shakespeare," *Journal of English and Germanic Philology*, xxviii (1929), 162–202; W. J. Lawrence, "The Problem of Lyly's Songs," *Times Literary Supplement*, London, December 20, 1923; J. R. Moore, "The Songs in Lyly's Plays," *PMLA*, xlii (1927), 623–640.

Here entreth lusty Iuuentus, or youth singinge as foloweth.[1]

In a herber[2] grene aslepe[3] where as I laye,
The byrdes sang swete in the myddes[4] of the daye;
I dreamed fast of myrth and play:
  In youth is pleasur, in youth is pleasure.

Me thought I walked stil to and fro,
And from her company I could not go,
But when I waked it was not so:
  In youth is pleasure, in youth is pleasure.

Therfore my harte is surely pyght[5]
Of her alone to haue a sight,
Whiche is my ioy and hartes delyght:
  In youth is pleasure, in youth is pleasure.

Backe and syde go bare, go bare,[6]
  booth foote and hande go colde:
But Bellye god sende thee good ale ynoughe,
  whether it be newe or olde.

I can not eate, but lytle meate,
  my stomacke is not good:
But sure I thinke, that I can drynke[7]
  with him that weares a hood.
Though I go bare, take ye no care,
  I am nothinge[8] a colde:
I stuffe my skyn, so full within,
  of ioly good Ale and olde.
Backe and syde go bare, go bare,
  booth foote and hand go colde:
But belly god send the good ale inoughe
  whether it be new or olde.

I loue no rost, but a nut browne toste
  and a Crab[9] layde in the fyre,
A lytle bread, shall do me stead[10]
  much breade I not desyre:
No froste nor snow, no winde I trowe[11]
  can hurte mee if I wolde,
I am so wrapt, and throwly[12] lapt
  of ioly good ale and olde.
    Backe and syde go bare. &c.

And Tyb my wyfe, that as her lyfe
  loueth well good ale to seeke,
Full ofte drynkes shee, tyll ye may see
  the teares run downe her cheeke:[13]
Then dooth she trowle,[14] to mee the bowle
  euen as a mault worme shuld,
And sayth sweete hart, I tooke my part
  of this ioly good ale and olde.
    Backe and syde go bare. &c.

Now let them drynke, tyll they nod and winke,[15]
  euen as good felowes shoulde doe
They shall not mysse, to haue the blisse,
  good ale doth bringe men to:
And all poore soules that haue scowred[16] boules
  or haue them lustely trolde,
God saue the lyues, of them and theyr wyues
  whether they be yonge or olde.
    Backe and syde go bare. &c.

Tom Tyler commeth in singing[17]

The Proverb reporteth, no man can deny,
That wedding and hanging is destiny.

I am a poor *Tyler*[18] in simple aray,
And get a poor living, but eight pence a day,

[1] From Robert Weaver, *An enterlude called lusty Iuuentus,* c.1565, STC 25147, Huntington Library; written before 1553.
[2] arbor.
[3] *aslepe*] *a slope* STC 25147.
[4] midst.
[5] fixed, determined.
[6] From William Stevenson, *A ryght pithy, pleasaunt and merrie comedie; intytuled Gammer gurtons nedle,* 1575, STC 23263, New York Public Library, Berg Collection. The play was written about 1555; this song may be older. A longer version appears in E. K. Chambers, *The Oxford Book of Sixteenth Century Verse.*
[7] *drynke*] *drytke* STC 23263.
[8] not at all.
[9] crab apple.
[10] fill my need.
[11] think.
[12] thoroughly.
[13] *cheeke:*] *cheekes:* STC 23263.
[14] pass.
[15] close the eyes.
[16] emptied.
[17] From the anonymous *Tom Tyler and his wife,* 1661, Folger Library; written about 1558.
[18] tiler.

My wife as I get it, doth spend it away;
  And I cannot help it, she saith; wot ye why,
  For wedding and hanging is destiny.

I thought when I wed her, she had been a sheep,
At boord to be friendly, to sleep when I sleep.
She loves so unkindly, she makes me to weep;
  But I dare say nothing god wot, wot ye why?
  For wedding and hanging is destiny.

Besides this unkindnesse whereof my grief grows,
I think few *Tylers* are matcht with such shrows;[19]
Before she leaves brawling, she falls to deal blows
  Which early and late doth cause me cry,
  That wedding and hanging is destiny.

The more that I please her, the worse she doth like me,
The more I forbear her, the more she doth strike me,
The more that I get her the more she doth glike[20] me;
  Wo worth[21] this ill Fortune that maketh me crie
  That wedding and hanging is destinie.

If I had been hanged when I had been married,
My torments had ended, though I had miscarried;[22]
If I had been warned, then would I have tarried;
  But now all to lately I feel and crie,
  That wedding and hanging is destinie.

Here entreth the Mariners with a song[23]

  Lustely, lustely, lustely, let vs saile forthe,
  The winde trim[24] doth serue vs, it blowes at the North.

All thinges we haue ready, and nothing we want,
  To furnishe our Ship that rideth hereby:
Victals and weapons thei be nothyng skant,
  Like worthie Mariners our selues we will trie.
    Lustely, lustely, &c.

Her Flagges be newe trimmed set flantyng[25] alofte,
  Our ship for swift swimmyng oh she doeth excell:
Wee feare no enemies, wee haue escaped them ofte,
  Of all ships that swimmeth she bareth the bell.[26]
    Lustely, lustely, &c.

And here is a Maister excelleth in skill,
  And our Maisters mate he is not to seeke:[27]
And here is a Boteswane will doe his good will,
  And here is a ship Boye, wee neuer had the leeke.[28]
    Lustely, lustely, &c.

If fortune then faile not, and our next voiage proue,[29]
  Wee will retourne merely,[30] and make good cheare:
And holde all together, as freends linkt in loue,
  The Cannes shalbe filled, with wine Ale and Beare.
    Lustely, lustely, &c.

Oenone

Faire and fayre and twise so faire,[31]
  As fayre as any may be:

19 shrews.
20 flout, scoff.
21 woe betide.
22 perished.
23 From the anonymous *An excellent and pleasant comedie termed after the name of the vice Common Conditions*, c. 1576, STC 5592a, Huntington Library.
24 good, suitable.
25 flaunting.
26 is the best.
27 is not lacking.
28 like.
29 prove successful.
30 merrily.
31 From George Peele, *The araygnement of Paris, a pastorall*, 1584, STC 19530, Huntington

The fayrest sheepeherd on our grene,
  A loue for anie Ladie.

Paris

Faire and faire and twise so fayre,
  As fayre as anie may bee:
Thy loue is fayre for thee alone,
  And for no other Ladie.

Oenone

My loue is faire, my loue is gaie,
As fresh as bine[32] the flowers in May,
And of my loue my roundylaye,
My merrie merrie[33] roundelaie
  Concludes with Cupids curse:
They that do chaunge olde loue for newe,
  Pray Gods they chaunge for worse.

Ambo simul[34]

They that do chaunge olde loue for newe,
  Pray Gods they chaunge for worse.

Oenone

Faire and faire and twise so faire,
  As fayre as any may be:
The fayrest sheepeherd on our grene,
  A loue for anie Ladie.

Paris

Faire and faire and twise so fayre,
  As fayre as anie may bee:
Thy loue is faire for thee alone,
  And for no other Ladie.

Oenone

My loue can pype, my loue can sing,
My loue can manie a pretie thing,
And of his louelie prayses ring
My merry merry roundelayes:
  Amen to Cupids curse:
They that do chaunge olde loue for newe,
  Pray Gods they chaunge for worse.

Library; written about 1581. In Greek legend Oenone is the nymph whom Paris deserted for Helen, the wife of Menelaus.

32 are.

33 In STC 19530 a third *merrie* follows.

34 both together.

35 From John Lyly, *Alexander and Campaspe*, 1584, in *Sixe court comedies*, 1632, STC 17088, Folger Library. The songs in the 1632 edition of Lyly's comedies are not included in the edi-

Paris

They that do chaunge olde loue for newe,
  Pray Gods they chaunge for worse.

Ambo

Faire and fayre and twise so faire,
  As fayre as any may be:
The fayrest sheepeherd on our grene,
  A loue for anie Ladie.

Cupid and my Campaspe playd,[35]
At Cardes for kisses, Cupid payd;
He stakes his Quiuer, Bow, and Arrows,
His Mothers[36] doues, and teeme of sparrows,
Looses them too, then, downe he throwes
The corrall of his lippe, the rose
Growing on's cheek, (but none knows how)
With These, the cristall of his Brow,
And then the dimple of his chinne,
All These did my Campaspe[37] winne,
At last, hee set[38] her, both his eyes
She won, and *Cupid* Blind did rise.
  O Loue! has shee done this to Thee?
  What shall (Alas!) become of Mee?

What Bird so sings, yet so does wayle?[39]
O tis the Rauish'd Nightingale.
Iug, Iug, Iug, Iug, tereu shee cryes.
And still her woes at Midnight rise.
Braue[40] prick song![41] Who is't now we heare?
None but the Larke so shrill and cleare,
How at heauens gats she claps her wings,
The Morne not waking till shee sings.
Heark, heark, with what a pretty throat,
Poore Robin red-breast tunes his note;

tions printed during his lifetime (c. 1554–1606), and they may have been written by another poet, perhaps Thomas Dekker.

36 Venus's.

37 *Compaspe*] *Compasse* STC 17088.

38 wagered.

39 From John Lyly, *Alexander and Campaspe*, 1584.

40 fine.

41 written music, so called from the "pricks" or notes.

Heark how the Iolly Cuckoes sing
Cuckoe, to welcome in the spring,
Cuckoe, to welcome in the spring.

O Cupid! Monarch ouer Kings,[42]
Wherefore hast thou feete and wings?
Is it to shew how swift thou art,
When thou wound'st a tender heart,
Thy wings being clip'd, and feete hel'd[43] still,
Thy Bow so many could not kill.

It is all one in *Venus* wanton schoole,
Who highest sits, the wiseman or the foole:
Fooles in loues colledge
Have farre more knowledge,
To Reade a woman ouer,
Than a neate prating louer.
Nay, tis confest,
That fooles please women best.

[*Apollo sings*][44]

My *Daphne's* Haire is twisted Gold,
Bright starres a-piece her Eyes doe hold,
My *Daphne's* Brow inthrones the Graces,
My *Daphne's* Beauty staines all Faces,[45]
My *Daphne's* Cheeke grow Rose and Cherry
On *Daphne's* Lip a sweeter Berry,
Daphne's snowy Hand but touch'd does melt,
And then no heauenlier Warmth is felt,
My *Daphne's* Musick charmes all Eares.
Fond[46] am I thus to sing her prayse,
These glories now are turn'd to Bayes.

[*Pan sings*][47]

Pan's Syrinx was a Girle indeede,
Though now shee's turn'd into a Reed,
From that deare Reed *Pan's* Pipe does come,
A Pipe that strikes *Apollo* dumbe;
Nor Flute, nor Lute, nor Gitterne can,
So chant it, as the Pipe of *Pan;*
Crosse-gartred Swaines, and Dairie girles,
With faces smug, and round as Pearles,
When *Pans* shrill Pipe begins to play,
With dancing weare out Night and Day:
The Bag-pipes Drone his Hum layes by,
When *Pan* sounds vp his Minstrelsie,
His Minstrelsie! O Base! This Quill
Which at my mouth with winde I fill,
Puts me in minde though Her I misse,
That still my *Syrinx* lips I kisse.

A SONET[48]

His Golden lockes, Time hath to Siluer turn'd,
O Time too swift, O Swiftnesse neuer ceasing:
His Youth gainst Time and Age hath euer spurn'd
But spurn'd in vain, Youth waineth by increasing.
  Beauty Strength, Youth, are flowers, but fading seen,
  Dutie, Faith, Loue are roots, and euer greene.

His Helmet now, shall make a hiue for Bees,
And Louers Sonets, turn'd to holy Psalmes:
A man at Armes must now serue on his knees,
And feede on praiers, which are Age his almes.
  But though from Court to Cottage he depart,
  His Saint is sure of his vnspotted heart.

---

[42] From Lyly, *Mother Bombie*, c. 1587, STC 17088.
[43] held.
[44] From Lyly, *Midas*, c. 1589, STC 17088.
[45] obscures their beauty by contrast.
[46] foolish.
[47] From Lyly, *Midas*.
[48] From *Polyhymnia, describing the honourable triumph at Tylt*, 1590, STC 19546, Huntington Library. This book describes in blank verse the tilt on the thirty-second anniversary of Queen Elizabeth's accession, November 17, 1590. The occasion marked the retirement of Sir Henry Lee (1533–1611) as Queen Elizabeth's champion. At the end of the tournament this song was sung by Robert Hales, royal lutanist from 1568 to 1603. It is usually ascribed to Peele, but Lee may have written it (E. K. Chambers, *Sir Henry Lee*, 1936, pp. 135–140; D. H. Horne, *The Life and Minor Works of George Peele*, 1952, pp. 169–173).

And when he saddest sits in homely Cell,
Heele teach his Swaines this Carroll for a Song,
Blest be the heartes that wish my Soueraigne well,
Curst be the soules that thinke her any wrong.
Goddesse, allow this aged man his right,
To be your Beads-man now, that was your Knight.

THE DITTIE OF THE SIX VIRGINS SONG[49]

With fragrant flowers we strew the way
And make this our chiefe hollidday:
For though this clime were blest of yore,
Yet was it neuer proud[50] before,
O beauteous Queene of second Troy,[51]
Accept of our vnfained ioy.

Now th'ayre is sweeter then sweet balme,
And *Satyrs* daunce about the palme:
Now earth with verdure newly dight,
Giues perfect signe of her delight.
O beauteous Queene of second Troy,
Accept of our vnfained ioy.

Now birds record new harmonie,
And trees doe whistle melodie:
Now euerie thing that nature breeds,
Doth clad it selfe in pleasant weeds.
O beauties Queene of second Troy,
Accept of our vnfained ioy.

THE PLOWMANS SONG[52]

In the merrie moneth of May,
In a morne, by breake of day,
Forth I walked by the woodside,
Where as *May* was in his pride.
There I spied all alone
Phyllida and *Corydon.*
Much adoe there was God wot,
He would loue, and she would not.
She said, neuer man was true:
He said, none was false to you.
He said, he had loued her long:
She said, loue should haue no wrong.
Coridon would kisse her then:
She said, maides must kisse no men,[53]
Till they did for good and all.
Then she made the shepheard call
All the heauens to witnesse truth,
Neuer lou'd a truer youth.
Thus with many a pretie oath,
Yea and nay, and faith and troth,
Such as silly[54] shepheards vse,
When they will not loue abuse.
Loue, which had beene long deluded,
Was with kisses sweet concluded:
And *Phyllida* with garlands gay,
Was made the Lady of the May.

Enter Ver[55] with his trayne, ouerlayde with suites of greene mosse, representing short grasse, singing[56]

THE SONG

Spring, the sweete spring, is the yeres pleasant King,
Then bloomes eche thing, then maydes daunce in a ring,
Cold doeth not sting, the pretty birds doe sing,
Cuckow, iugge, iugge, pu we, to witta woo.[57]

The Palme[58] and May[59] make countrey houses gay,
Lambs friske and play, the Shepherds pype all day,
And we heare aye, birds tune this merry lay,
Cuckow, iugge, iugge, pu we, to witta woo.

---

[49] From *The honorable entertainment gieuen to the Queenes Maiestie in progresse, at Eluetham in Hampshire, by the right Honorable the Earle of Hertford,* 1591, STC 7583, Huntington Library. This song is included in *England's Helicon,* 1600, and is there attributed to Thomas Watson.

[50] Perhaps the reading should be *provd,* proved.

[51] London.

[52] From *The honorable entertainment,* etc. In *England's Helicon* this song is attributed to Nicholas Breton.

[53] *men,*] *men.* STC 7583.

[54] simple.

[55] spring.

[56] From Thomas Nashe, *A pleasant comedie, called Summers last will and testament,* 1600, STC 18376, Folger Library; written about 1593.

[57] the call of the cuckoo, nightingale, lapwing, and owl, respectively.

[58] branches of trees and shrubs.

[59] blossoms of the hawthorn.

The fields breathe sweete, the dayzies
kisse our feete,
Young louers meete, old wiues a sunning
sit:
In euery streete, these tunes our eares
doe greete,
Cuckow, iugge, iugge, pu we, to witta
woo.
Spring the sweete spring.

Adieu, farewell earths blisse,[60]
This world vncertaine is,
Fond[61] are lifes lustfull[62] ioyes,
Death proues them all but toyes,
None from his darts can flye,
I am sick, I must dye.
Lord haue mercy on vs.

Rich men, trust not in wealth,
Gold cannot buy you health,
Phisick himselfe must fade.
All things, to end are made,
The plague full swift goes bye,
I am sick, I must dye,
Lord haue mercy on vs.

Beauty is but a flowre,
Which wrinckles will deuoure,
Brightnesse falls from the ayre,
Queenes have died yong, and faire,
Dust hath closde *Helens* eye.
I am sick, I must dye,
Lord haue mercy on vs.

Strength stoopes vnto the graue,
Wormes feed on *Hector* braue,
Swords may not fight with fate,
Earth still holds ope her gate,
Come, come, the bells do crye.
I am sick, I must dye,
Lord haue mercy on vs.

Wit with his wantonesse,
Tasteth deaths bitternesse,
Hels executioner,
Hath no eares for to heare,
What vaine art can reply.
I am sick, I must dye,
Lord haue mercy on vs.

Haste therefore eche degree,
To welcome destiny:
Heauen is our heritage,
Earth but a players stage,
Mount wee vnto the sky.
I am sick, I must dye,
Lord haue mercy on vs.

He [the Prologue] drawes a curtaine, and discouers Bathsabe with her maid bathing ouer a spring: she sings, and Dauid sits aboue vewing her[63]

SONG

Hot sunne, coole fire, tempered with
sweete aire,
Black shade, fair nurse, shadow my
white[64] haire
Shine sun, burne fire, breath aire, and
ease mee,
Black shade, fair nurse, shroud me and
please me
Shadow (my sweet nurse) keep me from
burning
Make not my glad cause, cause of
mourning.
Let not my beauties fire,
Enflame vnstaied[65] desire,
Nor pierce any bright eye,
That wandreth lightly.

Vertues braunches wither, vertue
pines,[66]
O pittie, pittie, and alacke the time,
Vice doth florish, Vice in glorie shines,
Her gilded boughes aboue the Cedar
clime.
Vice hath golden cheekes, O pittie, pittie,
She in euery land doth monarchize.

---

60 From Thomas Nashe, *A pleasant comedie*, 1600.

61 foolish.

62 pleasant, delightful.

63 From George Peele, *The loue of king David and fair Bethsabe*, 1599, STC 19540, Bodleian Library; written about 1594.

64 fair.

65 unrestrained.

66 From Thomas Dekker, *The pleasant comedie of Old Fortunatus*, 1600, STC 6517, New York Public Library, Berg Collection.

Vertue is exilde from euery Cittie,
Vertue is a foole, Vice onely wise.
O pittie, pittie, Vertue weeping dies.
Vice laughs to see her faint (alacke the time)
This sinckes: with painted wings the other flies,
Alacke that best should fall, and bad should clime,
O pittie, pittie, pittie, mourne, not sing,
Vice is a Saint, Vertue an vnderling.
Vice doth florish, Vice in glorie shines,
Vertues braunches wither, Vertue pines.

Art thou poore yet hast thou golden Slumbers?[67]
Oh sweet content!
Art thou rich yet in thy minde perplexed?
Oh punnishment.
Dost thou laugh to see how fooles are vexed?
To ad to golden numbers, golden numbers.
O sweet content, O sweet &c.

Work apace, apace, apace, apace:
Honest labour beares a louely face,
Then hey noney, noney: hey noney, noney.

Canst drinke the waters of the Crisped[68] spring,
O sweet content!
Swim'st thou in wealth, yet sinck'st in thine owne teares,
O punnishment.
Then hee that patiently want's[69] burden beares,
No burden beares, but is a King, a King.
O sweet content, &c.

Worke apace, apace, &c.

Golden slumbers kisse your eyes,[70]
Smiles awake you when you rise:
Sleepe pretty wantons doe not cry,
And I will sing a lullabie,
Rocke them rocke them lullabie.

Care is heauy therefore sleepe you,
You are care and care must keep you:
Sleepe pretty wantons doe not cry,
And I will sing a lullabie,
Rocke them rocke them lullabie.

Slow, slow, fresh fount, keepe time with my salt teares;[71]
Yet slower, yet, O faintly gentle springs:
List to the heauy part the musique beares,
Woe weepes out her diuision,[72] when shee sings.
Droupe hearbs, and flowres;
Fall griefe in showres;
Our beauties are not ours:
O, I could still
(Like melting snow vpon some craggie hill,)
Drop, drop, drop, drop,
Since natures pride is, now, a wither'd daffodill.

[THE SONG OF HESPERUS][73]

Qveene, and *Huntresse,*[74] chaste, and faire,
Now the *Sunne* is laid to sleepe.
Seated, in thy siluer chaire,
State in wonted manner keepe:
Hespervs intreats thy light,
Goddesse, excellently bright.

Earth, let not thy enuious shade
Dare it selfe to interpose;

---

67 From Thomas Dekker, *The pleasant comodie of Patient Grissill,* 1603, STC 6518, Folger Library; written about 1599.

68 rippled, (?) clear.

69 *want's*] *wants,* STC 6518.

70 From Dekker, *Patient Grissill,* 1603.

71 From Ben Jonson, *The fountaine of selfe-loue. Or Cynthias reuells* in *The workes of Beniamin Jonson,* 1616, STC 14751, Morgan Library; written 1600.

72 rapid passage of melody.

73 From Ben Jonson, *Cynthia's Revels.*

74 This song to Cynthia or Diana, the virgin huntress and goddess of the moon, is a compliment to Queen Elizabeth.

Cynthias shining orbe was made
Heauen to cleere,[75] when day did close:
Blesse vs then with wished sight,
Goddesse, excellently bright.

Lay thy bow of pearle apart,
And thy cristall-shining quiuer;
Giue vnto the flying hart
Space to breathe, how short soeuer:
Thou that mak'st a day of night,
Goddesse, excellently bright.

This is *Mab* the mistris-Faerie,[76]
That doth nightly rob the dayrie,
And can hurt, or helpe the cherning,
(As shee please) without discerning.[77]
Shee, that pinches countrey wenches,
If they rub not cleane their benches,
And with sharper nayles remembers,[78]
When they rake not vp their embers:
But if so they chance to feast her,
In a shooe shee drops a tester.[79]
This is shee, that empties cradles,
Takes out children, puts in ladles:
Traynes[80] forth mid-wiues in their slumber,
With a siue the holes to number.
And then leads them, from her borroughs
Home through ponds, and water furrowes.
Shee can start our *Franklins*[81] daughters,
In their sleepe, with shrikes, and laughters,
And on sweet Saint *Anne's* night,
Feed them with a promis'd sight,
Some of husbands, some of louers,
Which an emptie dreame discouers.[82]

[VOLPONE'S SONG][83]

Come, my Celia, let vs proue,[84]
While we can, the sports of loue;
Time will not be ours, for euer,
He, at length, our good will seuer;
Spend not then his gifts, in vaine.
Sunnes, that set, may rise againe:
But if, once, we lose this light,
'Tis with vs perpetuall night.
Why should we deferre our ioyes?
Fame, and rumor are but toies.[85]
Cannot we delude the eyes
Of a few poore houshold-spies?
Or his easier eares beguile,
Thus remooued, by our wile?
'Tis no sinne, loues fruits to steale;
But the sweet thefts to reueale:
To be taken, to be seene,
These haue crimes accounted beene.

[CLERIMONT'S SONG][86]

Still[87] to be neat, still to be drest,
As,[88] you were going to a feast;
Still to bee pou'dred, still perfum'd:
Lady, it is to be presum'd,
Though arts hid causes are not found,
All is not sweet, all is not sound.

Giue me a looke, giue me a face,
That makes simplicity a grace;
Robes loosely flowing, haire as free:
Such sweet neglect more taketh me,
Then all th'adulteries of art.
Thy strike mine eyes, but not, my heart.

See the Chariot at hand here of Love[89]
Wherein my Lady rideth!
Each that drawes, is a Swan, or a Dove
And well the Carre Love guideth.
As she goes, all hearts doe duty
Unto her beauty;
And enamour'd, doe wish, so they might

---

75 illuminate.

76 From Jonson, *A particular entertainment of the Queen and Prince at Althorpe* in *The Works*, STC 14751; written in 1603.

77 being seen.

78 reminds.

79 sixpence.

80 lures.

81 farmers'.

82 reveals.

83 From Ben Jonson, *Volpone or the foxe* in *Works*, STC 14751; written about 1605.

84 try, test.

85 trifles.

86 From Jonson, *Epicoene, or the silent woman* in *Works*, STC 14751; written about 1609.

87 always.

88 as if.

89 The first two stanzas are printed in *The*

But enjoy such a sight,
That they still were, to run by her side,
Through Swords, through Sees, whether she would ride.

Doe but looke on her eyes, they do light
All that Loves world compriseth!
Doe but looke on her Haire, it is bright
As Loves starre when it riseth!
Doe but marke her forhead's smoother
Then words that sooth her!
And from her arched browes, such a grace
Sheds it selfe through the face,
As alone there triumphs to the life
All the Gaine, all the Good, of the Elements strife.

Have you seene but a bright Lillie grow,
Before rude hands have touch'd it?
Ha' you mark'd but the fall o' the Snow
Before the soyle hath smutch'd it?
Ha' you felt the wooll of Bever?
Or Swans Downe ever?
Or have smelt o' the bud o' the Brier?
Or the Nard in the Fire?
Or have tasted the bag of the Bee?
O so white! O so soft! O so sweet is she!

Come sleepe, and with thy sweet deceiuing,[90]
Lock me in delight a while,
Let some pleasing Dreames beguile
All my fancies that from thence,
I may feele an influence,
All my powers of care bereauing.

Though but a shaddow, but a sliding,
Let me know some little Ioy,
We that suffer long anoy
Are contented with a thought
Through an idle fancie wrought,
O let my ioyes, haue some abiding.

divell is an asse, 1631, STC 14755; written about 1616. The third stanza was first printed in *Underwoods* in *The workes of Benjamin Jonson. The second volume*, 1640, STC 14754, New York Public Library.

[90] From Francis Beaumont and John Fletcher, *The woman hater*, 1607, STC 1693, Folger Library; written about 1606.

Tis mirth that fils the veines with bloud,[91]
More than wine, or sleepe, or food.
Let each man keepe his heart at ease,
No man dies of that disease.
He that would his body keepe
From diseases, must not weepe,
But who euer laughes and sings,
Neuer he his body brings
Into feuers, gouts, or rhumes,
Or lingringly his longs consumes:
Or meets with aches in the bone,
Or Catharhes, or griping stone:
But contented liues for aye,
The more he laughes, the more he may.

Come you whose loues are dead,[92]
And whiles I sing
Weepe and wring
Euery hand and euery head,
Bind with Cipres and sad Ewe,[93]
Ribands blacke, and candles blew,
For him that was of men most true.

Come with heauy moaning,[94]
And on his graue
Let him haue
Sacrifice of sighes and groaning,
Let him haue faire flowers enow,
White and purple, greene and yellow,
For him that was of men most true.

Better Musicke nere was knowne,[95]
Then a quire of hearts in one.
Let each other that hath beene,
Troubled with the gall or spleene:
Learne of vs to keepe his brow,
Smoth and plaine as ours are now.
Sing though before the houre of dying
He shall rise and then be crying.

[91] From Beaumont and Fletcher, *The knight of the burning pestle*, 1613, STC 1674, Folger Library; written about 1607.

[92] *Ibid.*

[93] yew.

[94] *moaning,*] *morning*, STC 1674.

[95] From Beaumont and Fletcher, *The knight of the burning pestle*, 1613.

Hey ho, 'tis nought but mirth.
That keepes the body from the earth.

Lay a garland on my hearse[96]
Of the dismall Yew,
Maidens willow branches beare,
Say I died true.

My loue was false, but I was firme,
From my houre of birth,
Vpon my buried body lay
Lightly gently earth.

His Body lies interr'd within this mould;[97]
Who dyed a young man, yet departed old.
And in all strength of youth that Man can haue,
Was ready still to drop into his graue.
For ag'd in vertue with a youthfull eye,
He welcom'd it being still prepar'd to dye;
And liuing so, though young depriu'd of breath,
He did not suffer an vntimely death.
But we may say of his braue bless'd decease:
He dyed in warre; and yet hee dyed in peace.

Are they shadowes that we see?[98]
And can shadowes pleasure giue?
Pleasures onely shadowes bee
Cast by bodies we conceiue,[99]
And are made the thinges we deeme,
In those figures which they seeme.
But these pleasures vanish fast,
Which by shadowes are exprest.[1]
Pleasures are not, if they last,
In their passing, is their best.
Glory is most bright and gay
In a flash, and so away.

Feed apace then greedy eyes
On the wonder you behold.
Take it sodaine[2] as it flies
Though you take it not to hold:
When your eyes haue done their part,
Thought must length it in the hart.

Loue is a sicknesse full of woes,[3]
All remedies refusing:
A plant that with most cutting growes,
Most barren with best vsing
Why so?
More we enioy it, more it dyes,
If not enioy'd, it sighing cries,
Hey ho.

Loue is a torment of the minde,
A tempest euerlasting;
And Ioue hath made it of a kinde,
Not well, nor full nor fasting.
Why so?
More we enioy it, more it dies,
If not enioyd, it sighing cries,
Hey ho.

[*Six satyrs sing to Diana and Jupiter*][4]

Haile beauteous *Dian,* Queene of shades,
That dwels beneath these shadowie glades,
Mistresse of all those beauteous maids
That are by her allowed.
Virginitie we all professe,
Abiure the worldlie vaine excesse,
And will to *Dyan* yeeld no lesse

[96] From Beaumont and Fletcher, *The maides tragedy*, 1622, STC 1678, Folger Library; written about 1611.

[97] From Cyril Tourneur, *The atheist's tragedie*, 1612, STC 24147, New York Public Library, Berg Collection; written in 1607–1611.

[98] From Samuel Daniel, *Tethys festival. The order and solemnitie of the creation of Prince Henrie, Prince of Wales*, 1610, STC 13161, Morgan Library.

[99] imagine.

[1] *exprest.*] *exprest* STC 13161.

[2] quickly.

[3] From Samuel Daniel, *Hymens triumph; a pastoral tragicomaedie* in *The whole workes of S. Daniel Esquire in poetrie*, 1623, STC 6238, Morgan Library; written in 1614.

[4] From Thomas Heywood, *The golden age*, 1611, STC 13325, Folger Library.

Then we to her haue vowed.
The Shepheards, Satirs, Nimphs, and Fawnes,
For thee will trippe it ore the lawnes.

Come to the Forrest let vs goe,
And trip it like the barren Doe,
The Fawnes and Satirs still do so,
And freelie thus they do.
The Fairies daunce, and Satirs sing,
And on the grasse tread manie a ring,
And to their caues their ven'son bring,
And we will do as they do.
The Shepheards, Satirs, Nimphs, and Fawnes,
For thee will trippe it ore the lawnes.

Our food is honie from the Bees,
And mellow fruits that drop from trees,
In chace we clime the high degrees,
Of euerie steepie mountaine,
And when the wearie day is past,
We at the euening hie vs fast,
And after this our field repast,
We drinke the pleasant fountaine.
The Shepheards, Satirs, Nimphs, and Fawnes,
For thee will trippe it ore the lawnes.

Call for the Robin-Red-brest and the wren,[5]
Since ore shadie groues they houer,
And with leaues and flowres doe couer
The friendlesse bodies of unburied men.
Call vnto his funerall Dole[6]
The Ante, the field-mouse, and the mole
To reare him hillockes, that shall keepe him warme,
And (when gay tombes are rob'd) sustaine no harme,
But keepe the wolfe far thence: that's foe to men,
For with his nailes hee'l dig them vp agen.
Let holie Church receiue him duly,
Since hee payd the Church tithes truly.

[THE MADMAN'S SONG][7]

O let vs howle, some heauy note,
Some deadly-dogged howle,
Sounding, as from the threatning throat,
Of beastes, and fatall fowle.
As Rauens, Scrich-owles, Bulls, and Beares,
We'll bill,[8] and bawle our parts,
Till yerk-some[9] noyce haue cloy'd your eares,
And corasiu'd[10] your hearts.
At last when as our quire wants breath,
Our bodies being blest,
We'll sing like Swans, to welcome death,
And die in loue and rest.

Harke, now euery thing is still,[11]
The Scritch-Owle, and the whistler shrill,
Call vpon our Dame, aloud,
And bid her quickly don her shrowd:
Much you had of Land and rent,
Your length in clay's now competent.[12]
A long war, disturb'd your minde,
Here your perfect peace is signed,
Of what is't, fooles make such vaine keeping?
Sin their conception, their birth, weeping:
Their life, a generall mist of error,
Their death, a hideous storme of terror,
Strew your haire, with powders sweete:
D'on cleane linnen, bath your feete,
And (the foule feend more to checke)
A crucifixe let blesse your necke,
'Tis now full tide, 'tweene night, and day,
End your groane, and come away.

---

[5] From John Webster, *The white divel*, 1612, STC 25178, Folger Library; written in 1609–1612. Stage directions: *Cornelia doth this in seuerall formes of distraction.* She sings while her son's body is being prepared for burial.

[6] mourning.

[7] From Webster, *The tragedy of the Dutchesse of Malfy*, 1623, STC 25176, Folger Library; written in 1613–1614.

[8] bellow, roar.

[9] irksome.

[10] corrosived, corroded.

[11] From Webster, *The . . . Dutchesse of Malfy*, 1623.

[12] sufficient for you.

All the Flowers of the Spring,[13]
Meet to perfume our burying:
These haue but their growing prime,
And man does flourish but his time.
Suruey our progresse from our birth,
We are set, we grow, we turne to earth.
Courts adieu, and all delights,
All bewitching appetites;
Sweetest Breath, and clearest eye,
Like perfumes goe out and dye;
And consequently this is done,
As shadowes wait vpon the Sunne.
Vaine the ambition of Kings,
Who seeke by trophies and dead things,
To leaue a liuing name behind,
And weaue but nets to catch the wind.

Welcome to this flowrie place,[14]
Faire Goddesse and sole Queene of
grace:
All eyes triumph in your sight,
Which through all this emptie space
Casts such glorious beames of light.

Paradise were meeter farre
To entertaine so bright a Starre:
But why erres my folly so?
Paradise is where you are
Heau'n aboue, and heau'n below.

Could our powers and wishes meete,
How well would they your graces greete,
Yet accept of our desire,
Roses of all flowers most sweete
Spring out of the silly brier.

Can you the Author of our ioy[15]
So soone depart?
Will you reuiue, and straight destroy,
New mirth to teares conuert?
O that euer cause of gladnesse
Should so swiftly turne to sadnesse!

Now as we droupe, so will these flowers
Bard of your sight.
Nothing auaile them heau'nly showres
Without your heau'nly light.
When the glorious Sunne forsakes vs,
Winter quickly ouer-takes vs.

Yet shall our praiers your waies attend,
When you are gone;
And we the tedious time will spend,
Remembring you alone.
Welcome here shall you heare euer,
But the word of parting neuer.

[A BRIDAL SONG][16]

Roses their sharpe spines being gon,
Not royall in their smels alone,
But in their hew.
Maiden Pinckes, of odour faint,
Dazies smel-lesse, yet most quaint
And sweet Time[17] true.

Prim-rose first borne, child of Ver,[18]
Merry Spring times Herbinger,
With her bels dimme.
Oxlips, in their Cradles growing,
Mary-golds, on death beds blowing,
Larkes-heeles trymme.[19]

All deere natures children sweete[20]
Ly fore Bride and Bridegroomes feete
Blessing their sence.
Not an angle[21] of the aire,
Bird melodious, or bird faire,
Is absent hence.

The Crow, the slaundrous Cuckoe, nor
The boding Raven, nor Chough hoar[22]
Nor chattring Pie,
May on our Bridehouse pearch or sing,
Or with them any discord bring
But from it fly.

---

[13] From Webster, *The deuils law-case*, 1623, STC 25173, Morgan Library; written about 1619.

[14] From Thomas Campion, *A relation of the late royall entertainment given by the Lord Knowles*, 1613, STC 4545, Harvard College Library.

[15] *Ibid.* This song was sung as Queen Anne left.

[16] From John Fletcher and William Shakespeare, *The two noble kinsmen*, 1634, STC 11075, Morgan Library; written about 1613.

[17] thyme.

[18] spring.

[19] trim, beautiful.

[20] *children sweete*] *children:sweete*—STC 11075.

[21] angel.

[22] *hoar*] *hee* STC 11075.

Vrnes, and odours, bring away,[23]
Vapour, sighes, darken the day;
Our dole more deadly lookes than dying;[24]
Balmes, and Gummes, and heavy cheeres,
Sacred vials fill'd with teares,
And clamors through the wild ayre flying.

Come all sad, and solempne Showes,
That are quick-eyd pleasures foes;
We convent[25] nought else but woes.
We convent nought else but woes.

[THE PASSIONATE MAN'S SONG][26]

Hence all you vaine Delights,
As short as are the nights,
Wherein you spend your folly,
Ther's nought in this life sweet,
If man were wise to see't,
But onely Melancholy,
O sweetest melancholy.

Welcome folded Armes, and fixed eyes,
A sigh that piercing mortifies,[27]
A look that's fastned to the ground,
A tongue chain'd up without a sound.

Fountaine heads, and pathlesse Groves,
Places which pale passion loves:
Moon-light walkes, when all the fowles
Are warmly hous'd, save Bats and Owles;
A mid-night Bell, a parting groane,
These are the sounds we feed upon;
Then stretch our bones in a still gloomy valley,
Nothing's so daintie sweet as lovely melancholy.

Cast our Caps and cares away: this is Beggars Holli-day,[28]
At the Crowning of our King, thus we ever dance and sing.
In the world looke out and see: where so happy a Prince as he?
Where the nation live so free, and so merry as do we?
Be it peace, or be it war, here at liberty we are,
And enjoy our ease and rest; To the field we are not prest;
Nor are called into the Towne, to be troubled with the Gowne.
Hang all Officers[29] we cry, and the Magistrate too, by;
When the Subsidies encreast, we are not a penny ceast.[30]
Nor will any goe to law, with the Beggar for a straw.
All which happinesse he brags, he doth owe unto his rags.

---

[23] From John Fletcher and William Shakespeare, *The two noble kinsmen,* 1634.
[24] *dying;*] *dying* STC 11075.
[25] summon.
[26] From John Fletcher, *The nice valour,* in Beaumont and Fletcher, *Comedies and Tragedies,* 1647, Morgan Library; written about 1613.
[27] numbs, deadens.
[28] From John Fletcher, *Beggars' Bush,* in Beaumont and Fletcher, *Comedies and Tragedies,* 1647, Morgan Library; written about 1622.
[29] *Officers* ed. of 1679]; *Offices* ed. of 1647.
[30] assessed, taxed.

Miscellaneous Poems

[1575–1602]

THE POEMS in this section are of many kinds, drawn from several books, some of them from the three important late Elizabethan verse miscellanies —*The Phoenix Nest*, 1593; *England's Helicon*, 1600; and *A Poetical Rhapsody*, 1602.

In an age when many of her subjects wrote verse it is not surprising to find Queen Elizabeth (1533–1603) included among the poets. The few poems, some imperfectly authenticated, attributed to her hardly deserve George Puttenham's superlatives in *The Arte of English Poesie*, 1589: "Last in recitall and first in degree is the Queene our soueraigne Lady, whose learned, delicate, noble Muse, easily surmounteth all the rest that haue written before her time or since, for sence, sweetnesse and subtillitie, be it in Ode, Elegie, Epigram, or any other kinde of poeme Heroick or Lyricke, wherein it shall please her Maiestie to employ her penne, euen by as much oddes as her owne excellent estate and degree exceedeth all the rest of her most humble vassalls." Puttenham selected the poem included here as an example of the figure *Exargasia* or *Expolitio*, "the polished" or "the gorgeous" or ornamental amplification. He writes: "I finde none example in English meetre, as well maintayning this figure as that dittie of her Maiesties owne making. . . . This was the occasion: our soueraigne Lady perceiuing how by the Sc. Q. [Mary, Queen of Scots] residence within this Realme at so great libertie and ease (as were skarce meete for so great and daungerous a prysoner) bred secret factions among her people, and made many of the nobilitie incline to her partie . . . writeth this dittie most sweet and sententious, not hiding from all such aspiring minds the daunger of their ambition and disloyaltie." The date of this poem in poulter's measure is unknown.

Of Humphrey Gifford, whose *A Posy of Gillyflowers* appeared in 1580, little is known. *A Posy* contains prose translations of Italian tales and poems imitative of Surrey and his followers. Some of his verse is fresh and spirited. The poem beginning "A womans face is full of wiles" is a song from a poem entitled *A Delectable Dream.*

Thomas Watson (c. 1557–1592) probably attended Oxford, but he took no degree. His *Hekatompathia, or Passionate Century of Love*, 1582, was influential in establishing the vogue of the Petrarchan sonnet, though Watson's "sonnets" were of eighteen lines. His *Italian Madrigals Englished*, 1590, was one of the earliest of the long series of songbooks. In the year after his death appeared his *Tears of Fancy*, a sequence of sixty conventional sonnets.

Bartholomew Yong or Yonge or Young (fl. 1577–1598) published in 1598 his translation of Jorge de Montemayor's Spanish romance, *Diana*, an immense storehouse of pastoral prose narrative and pastoral songs. Twenty-five of Yong's poems are included in *England's Helicon*, 1600.

Edward de Vere, seventeenth Earl of Oxford (1550–1604) succeeded to the earldom in 1562 and throughout his youth and early manhood was one of Queen Elizabeth's favorites. Praised by his contemporaries as a court poet, he published nothing, although about twenty-two of his poems were printed in several miscellanies. His plays, mentioned by Puttenham and Meres, are either lost or not identified.

During the last decade of Queen Elizabeth's reign three important poetic miscellanies were printed. The first, *The Phoenix Nest*, 1593, compiled by an unidentified "R. S. of the Inner Temple," contains some of the best and most characteristic poetry of the period. Although not one of the authors is named, authors' initials are given to about a third of the poems. Among the poets represented are Oxford, Peele, Breton, Dyer, Raleigh, and others. Sixteen of Lodge's poems are included, thirteen of which are not preserved elsewhere.

England's Helicon, 1600, contains one hundred fifty poems attributed by the compiler to some thirty authors, including several of the greatest poets of the period, Sidney, Spenser, Marlowe, Shakespeare. Twenty-four of the poems are not preserved elsewhere. The miscellany was projected by John Bodenham and was compiled, Professor Rollins believes, by Nicholas Ling, a prominent publisher. *England's Helicon* is an anthology of pastoral poetry and the most beautiful of the Elizabethan miscellanies.

A Poetical Rhapsody, 1602, the last of the Elizabethan verse miscellanies, contains one hundred seventy-six poems; it was reprinted in 1608, 1611, and 1621, each time with additional poems. The book has three main divisions: forty poems by the editor, Francis Davison (c. 1575–c. 1619), son of William Davison, Secretary of State to Queen Elizabeth, 1586–1587; eighteen by his brother Walter (1581–c. 1608), who was "not 18. yeeres olde when he writt these Toyes"; sixty-five poems by "Anomos," whom the editor describes as his dear friend, and whose contributions he says were written "almost twentie yeers since, when Poetry was farre from that perfection, to which it hath now attained." It is possible that "Anomos" means "anonymous," and that the poems so assigned are the work of more than one writer. There are fifty-three other poems that Davison says were added by the printer; these include additional poems by the

Davisons and "Anomos," together with poems by Sidney, Raleigh, Campion, Constable, and others.

If we are to believe Francis Davison, most of his own poems in the *Rhapsody* were written six or seven years before 1602, and those of "Anomos" in the early 1580's. The volume contains a wide variety of verse—sonnets, experiments in classical meters, madrigals, epigrams.

The poems of Gifford and Oxford are included in *Miscellanies of the Fuller Worthies' Library*, ed. A. B. Grosart, 1870. *A Posy of Gillyflowers* has been edited by F. J. H. Darton, 1933. Watson's *Tears of Fancy* is included in *Elizabethan Sonnets*, ed. Sir Sidney Lee, 2 vols., 1904. The definitive editions of the miscellanies are *The Phoenix Nest*, ed. H. E. Rollins, 1931; *England's Helicon*, ed. H. E. Rollins, 2 vols., 1935; *A Poetical Rhapsody*, ed. H. E. Rollins, 2 vols., 1932. A convenient edition of *England's Helicon* is that by Hugh Macdonald, 1925; revised, 1950.

The doubt of future foes, exiles my present ioy,[1]
And wit me warnes to shun such snares as threaten mine annoy.
For falshood now doth flow, and subiect faith doth ebbe,
Which would not be, if reason rul'd or wisdome weu'd the webbe.
But clowdes of tois[2] vntried, do cloake aspiring mindes,
Which turne to raigne of late repent,[3] by course of changed windes.
The toppe of hope supposed, the roote of ruth[4] wil be,
And frutelesse all their graffed[5] guiles, as shortly ye shall see.
Then dazeld eyes with pride, which great ambition blinds,
Shalbe vnseeld[6] by worthy wights,[7] whose foresight falshood finds.
The daughter of debate, that eke discord doth sowe
Shall reap no gaine where formor rule hath taught stil peace to growe.
No forreine bannisht wight shall ancre in this port,
Our realme it brookes no strangers force, let them elswhere resort.
Our rusty sworde with rest, shall first his edge employ,
To polle[8] their toppes that seeke, such change and gape for ioy.

FOR SOULDIERS[9]

Ye buds of Brutus land[10] couragious youths, now play your parts,
Unto your tackle stand, abide the brunt with valiant hearts.
For newes is carried too and fro, that we must forth to warfare goe:
Men muster now in euery place, and souldiers are prest forth apace.
Faynt not, spend blood, to doe your Queen and country good.
Fayre wordes, good pay, wil make men cast al care away.

The time of warre is come, prepare your corslet, speare, and shield,

[1] From George Puttenham, *The arte of English poesie*, 1589, STC 20519, Folger Library. This poem is by Queen Elizabeth.
[2] toys, idle (or dangerous) fancies.
[3] from late repentance.
[4] grief.
[5] engrafted.
[6] enabled to see clearly.
[7] persons.
[8] cut off.
[9] From Humphrey Gifford, *A posie of gilloflowers*, 1580, STC 11872, Folger Library.
[10] England.

Me thinks I heare the drumme, strike doleful marches to the field,
Tantara, tantara, the trumpets sound, which makes our harts with ioy abound,
The roring guns are heard a far, and euery thing denounceth[11] warre.
Serue God, stand stoute, bold courage brings this geare about.[12]
Feare not; forth run; faint heart, faire Lady neuer woonne.

Yee curious Carpet knights,[13] that spende the time in sport and play
Abrode and see new sights, your countries cause cals you away:
Doe not to make your Ladies game, bring blemish to your worthy name.
Away to field, and win renoune, with courage beat your enimies down.
Stoute hearts gaine praise, when Dastards sayle in slaunders seas:
Hap what hap shall, we sure, shal die but once for all.

Alarme me thinkes they cry, be packing mates, be gone with speed,
Our foes are very nigh, shame haue that man that shrinks at need.
Unto it boldly let vs stand, God wil geue right the vpper hand.
Our cause is good, we need not doubt, in signe of courage geue a showte,
March forth, be strong, good hap wil come ere it be long.
Shrinke not, fight well, for lusty lads must beare the bell.[14]

All you that wil shun euil, must dwel in warfare euery day,
The world, the flesh and Diuel, alwayes do seeke our soules decay.
Striue with these foes with al your might, so shal you fight a worthy fight.
That conquest doth deserue most praise, wher vice do yeeld to vertues wayes.
Beat down foule sin, a worthy crown then shal ye win.
If we liue wel, in heauen with Christ our soules shal dwell.

A womans face is full of wiles,[15]
Her teares are like the Crocadill:
With outward cheere on thee shee smiles,
When in her heart shee thinkes thee ill.

Her tongue still chattes of this and that,
Then aspine leafe it wagges more fast:
And as she talkes shee knowes not what,
There yssues many a troathlesse blast.

Thou farre doest take thy marke amisse,
If thou thinke fayth in them to finde:
The Wethercocke more constant is,
Which turnes about with every winde.

O, how in pittie they abound!
Their heart is milde, like marble stone,
If in thyselfe no hope bee found,
Be sure of them thou gettest none.

---

11 announces.
12 finish this work.
13 fastidious knights whose activity has been limited to peaceful pursuits.
14 conquer.
15 From Humphrey Gifford, *A posie of gillo-flowers,* 1580.

I know some pepernosed dame
 Will tearme mee foole and sawcie iack,
That dare their credit so defame,
 And lay such slaunders on their backe.

What though on mee they powre their spite?
 I may not vse the glosers[16] trade,
I cannot say the crow is white,
 But needes must call a spade a spade.

Come gentle Death; who cals? one thats opprest:[17]
What is thy will? that thou abridge my woe,
By cutting of my life; cease thy request,
I cannot kill thee yet: alas, why soe?
 Thou want'st thy Hart. Who stoale the same away?
 Loue, whom thou seru'st, intreat him if thou may.

Come, come, come *Loue:* who calleth me so oft?
Thy Vassall true, whome thou should'st know by right.
What makes thy cry so faint? my voyce is softe,
And almost spent by wayling day and night.
 Why then, whats thy request? that thou restore
 To me my Hart, and steale the same no more.

And thou O Death, when I possesse my *Hart,*
Dispatch me then at once: why so?
By promise thou art bound to end my smart.
Why, if thy *Hart* returne, then whats thy woe?
 That brought from colde, It neuer will desire
 To rest with me, which am more hot then fire.

Time wasteth yeeres, and month's, and howr's:[18]
Time doth consume fame, honour, witt, and strength:
Time kills the greenest Herbes and sweetest flowr's:
Time weares out youth and beauties lookes at length:
 Time doth conuey to ground both foe and friend,
 And each thing else but Loue, which hath no end.

Time maketh eu'ry tree to die and rott:
Time turneth ofte our pleasures into paine:
Time causeth warres and wronges to be forgott:
Time cleares the skie, which first hung full of rayne:
 Time makes an end of all humane desire,
 But onely this, which settes my heart on fire.

16 flatterer's.

17 From Thomas Watson, *The hekatompathia or passionate centurie of love,* 1582, STC 25118a, Morgan Library. In the first and third stanzas the speakers are the lover and Death; in the second stanza, the lover and Cupid. Watson states that in this poem and the next he imitates Serafino.

18 *Ibid.*

Time turneth into naught each Princely state:
Time brings a fludd from newe resolued[19] snowe:
Time calmes the Sea where tempest was of late:
Time eates what ere the Moone can see belowe:
And yet no time preuailes in my behoue,[20]
Nor any time can make me cease to loue.

Shepherd, who can passe such wrong[21]
And a life in woes so deepe?
Which to liue is to too long,
As it is too short to weepe.

Greeuous sighes in vaine I waste,
Leesing my affiance,[22] and
I perceiue my hope at last
With a candle in the hand.[23]

What time then to hope among
Bitter hopes, that euer sleepe?
When this life is to too long,
As it is too short to weepe.

This greefe which I feele so rife,[24]
(Wretch) I do deserue as hire,
Since I came to put my life
In the handes of my desire.

Then cease not my plaints so strong,
For (though life her course doth keepe)
It is not to liue so long,
As it is too short to weepe.

OF THE BIRTH AND BRINGING VP OF DESIRE[25]

When wert thou born Desire? in pompe and prime of May:
By whom sweet boy wert thou begot? by good conceit men say.[26]
Tell me who was thy nurse? fresh youth in sugred ioy:
What was thy meat and dayly food? sore sighes with great annoy.
What had you then to drinke? vnfained louers teares:
What cradle were you rocked in? in hope deuoide of feares.
What brought you then a sleepe? sweet speach that liked[27] men best:
And where is now your dwelling place? in gentle hearts I rest.
Doth companie displease? it doth in many one:

[19] melted.
[20] behoof.
[21] From Bartholomew Yong, translation of Montemayor's *Diana,* 1598, STC 18044, New York Public Library. Selvagia sings the song as she and Sirenus and Sylvanus are "going on softly towardes the towne."
[22] losing my confidence.
[23] my hope decreasing.
[24] abundantly.
[25] From *Brittons bowre of delights,* 1591, STC 3633, Huntington Library.
[26] *say.*] *say* STC 3633.
[27] pleased.

Where would *Desire* then choose to be? he likes to muse alone.
What feedeth most your sight? to gaze on fauour[28] still:
Who find you most to be your foe? Disdaine of my good will.
Will euer age or death bring you vnto decay?
No, no, *Desire* both liues and dies ten thousand times a day.[29]

What cunning can expresse[30]
The fauor[31] of hir face,
To whom in this distresse,
I doe appeale for grace,
A thousand Cupids flie,
About hir gentle eie.

From whence each throwes a dart,
That kindleth soft sweete fier:
Within my sighing hart,
Possessed by desire:
No sweeter life I trie,
Than in hir loue to die.

The Lillie in the fielde,
That glories in his white:
For purenes now must yeelde,
And render vp his right:
Heau'n pictur'de in hir face,
Doth promise ioy and grace.

Faire Cinthias siluer light,
That beates on running streames;
Compares not with hir white,
Whose haires are all sunbeames;
Hir vertues so doe shine,
As daie vnto mine eine.

With this there is a Red,
Exceeds the Damaske Rose;
Which in hir cheekes is spred;
Whence euery fauor groes,
In skie there is no starre,
That she surmounts not farre.

When Phoebus from the bed,
Of Thetis doth arise,
The morning blushing red,
In faire carnation wise,
He shewes it in hir face,
As Queene of euery grace.

---

28 beauty.
29 Signed "*E. of Ox.*," i.e., Earl of Oxford.
30 From *The phoenix nest*, 1593, STC 21516, Folger Library.
31 beauty.

This pleasant Lillie white,
This taint of roseat red,
This Cinthias siluer light,
This sweete faire Dea[32] spread[33]
These sunbeames in mine eie,
These beauties make me die.[34]

Crabbed age and youth cannot liue together,[35]
Youth is full of pleasance,[36] Age is full of care,
Youth like summer morne, Age like winter weather,
Youth like summer braue,[37] Age like winter bare,
Youth is full of sport, Ages breath is short,
Youth is nimble, Age is lame,
Youth is hot and bold, Age is weake and cold,
Youth is wild, and Age is tame.
Age I doe abhor thee, Youth I doe adore thee,
O my loue my loue is young:
Age I doe defie[38] thee. Oh sweet Shepheard hie thee:
For me thinks thou staies too long.

Those eies which set my fancie on a fire,[39]
Those crisped[40] haires, which hold my hart in chains,
Those daintie hands, which conquer'd my desire,
That wit, which of my thoughts doth hold the rains.
Those eies for cleernes doe the starrs surpas,
Those haires obscure the brightnes of the Sunne,
Those hands more white, than euer Iuorie was,
That wit euen to the skies hath glorie woon.
O eies that pearce our harts without remorse,[41]
O haires of right that weares a roiall crowne,
O hands that conquer more than Cæsars force,
O wit that turns huge kingdoms vpside downe.
Then Loue be Iudge, what hart may thee withstand:
Such eies, such haire, such wit, and such a hand.

A PALINODE[42]

As withereth the Primrose by the riuer,
As fadeth Sommers-sunne from gliding fountaines;
As vanisheth the light blowne bubble euer,

[32] goddess.
[33] *spread*] *spread,* STC 21516.
[34] Signed *"E.O.,"* i.e., Earl of Oxford.
[35] From *The passionate pilgrime,* 1599, STC 22342.1, Folger Library. Four additional stanzas are included in the earliest extant edition of Thomas Deloney's *The garland of good will,* 1631 (STC 6554), which was published by 1596. See F. O. Mann, *The Works of Thomas Deloney,* 1912, pp. 363–365; H. E. Rollins, *Shakespeare: The Poems,* 1938, pp. 548–549. This poem is possibly by Shakespeare.
[36] gaiety.
[37] beautiful.
[38] despise.
[39] From *The phoenix nest,* 1593, STC 21516, Folger Library. The author is unknown. The woman described may be Queen Elizabeth.
[40] curled.
[41] compassion.
[42] From *England's Helicon,* 1600, STC 3191, Folger Library.

As melteth snow vpon the mossie Mountaines.
So melts, so vanisheth, so fades, so withers,
The Rose, the shine, the bubble and the snow,
Of praise, pompe, glorie, ioy (which short life gathers,)
Faire praise, vaine pompe, sweet glory, brittle ioy.
The withered Primrose by the mourning riuer,
The faded Sommers-sunne from weeping fountaines:
The light-blowne bubble, vanished for euer,
The molten snow vpon the naked mountaines,
Are Emblems that the treasures we vp-lay,
Soone wither, vanish, fade, and melt away.

For as the snowe, whose lawne did ouer-spread
Th' ambitious hills, which Giant-like did threat
To pierce the heauen with theyr aspiring head,
Naked and bare doth leaue their craggie seate.
When as the bubble, which did emptie flie
The daliance of the vndiscerned winde:
On whose calme rowling waues it did relie,
Hath shipwrack made, where it did daliance finde:
And when the Sun-shine which dissolu'd the snow,
Cullourd the bubble with a pleasant varie,[43]
And made the rathe[44] and timely[45] Primrose grow,
Swarth clowdes with-drawne (which longer time doe tarie)
Oh what is praise, pompe, glory, ioy, but so
As shine by fountaines, bubbles, flowers or snow?[46]

A NIMPHS DISDAINE OF LOUE[47]

Hey downe a downe did *Dian* sing,
amongst her Virgins sitting:
Then[48] loue there is no vainer thing,
for Maydens most vnfitting,
And so think I, with a downe downe derrie.

When women knew no woe,
but liu'd them-selues to please:
Mens fayning guiles they did not know,
the ground of their disease.[49]
Vnborne was false suspect,
no thought of iealousie:
From wanton toyes and fond affect,[50]
the Virgins life was free.
Hey downe a downe did *Dian* sing,
amongst her Virgins sitting:
Then loue there is no vainer thing,
for Maydens most vnfitting,

43 variation.
44 early.
45 early.
46 Signed "*E.B.*," i.e., Edmund Bolton.
47 From *England's Helicon*, 1600. The author is unknown.
48 than.
49 discomfort.
50 foolish affection.

And so think I, with a downe downe derrie.

At length men vsed charmes,
to which what Maides gaue eare:
Embracing gladly endlesse harmes,
anone enthralled were.
Thus women welcom'd woe,
disguis'd in name of loue:
A iealous hell, a painted show,
so shall they finde that proue.[51]
Hey downe a downe did *Dian* sing,
amongst her Virgins sitting:
Then loue there is no vainer thing,
for Maydens most vnfitting.
And so thinke I, with a downe downe derrie.

MADRIGAL I. TO CUPID[52]

Loue, if a God thou art,
Then euermore thou must,
Be mercifull and iust.
If thou be iust; O wherefore doth thy Dart,
Wound mine alone, and not my Ladies Hart?

If mercifull, then why
Am I to paine reseru'd,[53]
Who haue thee truely seru'd:
While she that by thy powre sets not a flie.
Laughs thee to scorne, and liues in libertie?[54]

Then, if a God thou would'st accounted be,
Heale me like her, or else wound her like me.

ODE II[55]

A DIALOGUE BETWEENE HIM AND HIS HART

At her faire hands how haue I grace intreated,
With prayers oft repeated,
Yet still my loue is thwarted:
Hart let her goe, for shee'le not be conuarted.
Say, shal shee goe?
Oh no, no, no, no, no.
Shee is most faire, though shee be marble harted.

How often haue my sighs declar'de mine anguish?
Wherein I dayly languish,
Yet doth shee still procure it:

[51] test.

[52] From *A poetical rapsody*, 1602, STC 6373, Folger Library. The author of this poem is Francis Davison.

[53] singled out for.

[54] *libertie?*] *libettie?* STC 6373.

[55] From *A poetical rapsody*, 1602. By Walter Davison.

Hart let her goe, for I can not endure it.
Say, shal shee goe?
Oh no, no, no, no, no.
Shee gaue the wound, and shee alone must cure it.

The trickling tears that down my cheeks haue flowed,
My loue haue often showed;
Yet still vnkind I proue her:
Hart, let her goe, for nought I do can moue her.
Say, shall shee goe?
Oh no, no, no, no, no.
Though mee shee hate, I can not chuse but loue her.

But shall I still a true affection owe her,
Which prayers, sighs, teares do shew her:
And shall shee still disdaine mee?
Hart, let her goe, if they no grace can gaine mee.
Say, shal shee goe?
Oh no, no, no, no, no.
Shee made mee hers, and hers shee will retaine mee.

But if the Loue that hath, and still doth burne mee,
No loue at length returne mee,
Out of my thoughts Ile set her:
Hart, let her goe, oh hart, I pray thee let her.
Say, shal shee goe?
Oh no, no, no, no, no.
Fixt in the hart, how can the hart forget her.

But if I weepe and sigh, and often waile mee,
Till teares, sighes, prayers fayle mee,
Shall yet my Loue perseuer?
Hart, let her goe, if shee will right thee neuer.
Say, shal shee goe?
Oh no, no, no, no, no.
Teares, sighs, praiers faile, but true loue lasteth euer.

PHALEVCIAKS I[56]

Time nor place did I want,[57] what held me tongtide?
What Charmes, what magicall abused Altars?
Wherefore wisht I so oft that hower vnhappy,
When with freedome I might recount my torments,
And pleade for remedy by true lamenting?
Dumbe, nay dead in a trance I stood amazed,
When those looks I beheld that late I long'd for;
No speech, no memory, no life remained,
Now speech prateth apace, my griefe bewraying,

---

[56] *Ibid.* By "Anomos." In Phaleuciac verse (named from the ancient Greek poet Phalaecus), the line is made up of a spondee or trochee, followed by a dactyl and three trochees.

[57] lack.

Now bootlesse memory my plaints remembreth,
Now life moueth againe, but al auailes not.
Speech, life, and memory die altogether,
With speech, life, memory, Loue onely dies not.

The golden Sunne that brings the day,[58]
And lends men light to see withall,
In vaine doth cast his beames away,
Where they are blinde on whom they fall.
There is no force in all his light,
To giue the Mole a perfect sight.

But thou, my Sunne, more bright then hee,
That shines at noone in Summer tide,
Hast giuen me light and power to see,
With perfect skill my sight to guide.
Till now I liu'de as blinde as Mole,
That hides her head in earthly hole.

I heard the praise of beauties grace,
Yet deem'd it nought but Poets skill.
I gaz'de on many a louely face,
Yet found I none to binde my will.
Which made me thinke, that beauty bright,
Was nothing else but red and white.

But now thy beames haue cleer'd my sight,
I blush to thinke I was so blinde.
Thy flaming Eies affoord me light,
That Beauties blaze each where I finde:
And yet these Dames that shine so bright,
Are but the shadow of thy light.

PHALEVCIAKS II[59]

Wisdome warns me to shun that once I sought for,
And in time to retire my hasty footsteps:
Wisdome sent from aboue, not earthly wisdome,
No such thoughts can arise from earthly wisdome.
Long, too long haue I slept in ease vneasie,
On falce worldly releefe my trust reposing;
Health and wealth in a bote, no sterne nor ankor,
(Bold and blinde that I was) to Sea be taking:[60]
Scarce from shore had I lancht, when all about mee,
Waues like hilles did arise, till help from heauen,
Brought my Ship to the Porte of late repentence.

O nauis, referent in mare te noui Fluctus.[61]

---

[58] From *A poetical rapsody*, 1602. By "Anomos."

[59] *Ibid.* By "Anomos."

[60] betaking.

[61] Horace, *Carmina*, I, xiv, 1–2: "O ship, new waves will bear you back to sea again."

BEING SCORNED, AND DISDAINED, HEE INUEIGHS AGAINST HIS LADY[62]

Since iust disdaine began to rise,
And cry reuenge for spitefull wrong:
What erst I praisde, I now despise,
And thinke my Loue was all too long.
I tread in durt that scornefull pride,
Which in thy lookes I haue descride:
Thy beautie is a painted skin,
For fooles to see their faces in.

Thine Eyes that some as Starres esteeme,
From whence themselues, they say, take light,
Like to thee[63] foolish fire I deeme,
That leades men to their death by night.
Thy words and othes are light as winde,
And yet farre lighter is thy minde:
Thy friendship is a broken reede,
That failes thy friends in greatest neede.

Vitys patientia victa est.[64]

AN ALTARE AND SACRIFICE TO DISDAINE, FOR FREEING HIM FROM LOUE[65]

My Muse by thee restor'd to life,
To thee Disdaine, this Altare reares,
Whereon she offers causlesse strife,
Self-spending sighs, and bootlesse teares,

Long Sutes in vaine,
Hate for Good will:
Still-dying paine,
Yet liuing still.
Selfe-louing pride,
Lookes coyly strange,
Will Reasons guide,
Desire of change.
And last of all,
Blinde Fancies fire;
False Beauties thrall,
That bindes desire.

All these I offer to Disdaine,
By whome I liue from fancie free.

---

62 From *A poetical rapsody,* 1602. By "Anomos."

63 the.

64 Ovid, *Amores,* III, xi, 1: "My patience has been conquered by my wrongs."

65 From *A poetical rapsody,* 1602. By "Anomos." Puttenham in *The Arte of English Poesie,* 1589, includes a chapter entitled "Of Proportion in figure." Many poets of the sixteenth and seventeenth centuries wrote poems in the shape of altars, crosses, pyramids, eggs, wings, etc.

With vow, that if I loue againe,
My life the sacrifice shall bee.

Vicimus et domitum pedibus calcamus amorem.[66]

A SONG, IN PRAISE OF A BEGGERS LIFE[67]

Bright shines the Sun, play Beggers play,
Here's scraps enough to serue to day.
What noyse of Vials is so sweete,
As when our merry clappers[68] ring?
What mirth doth want where Beggers meete?
A Beggers life is for a King.
Eate, drinke, and play, sleepe when wee list,
Go where wee will, so stocks be mist.
Bright shines, &c.

The world is ours, and ours alone,
For wee alone haue world at will,
Wee purchase not, all is our owne,
Both fields and streetes wee Beggers fill.
Nor care to get, nor feare to keepe,
Did euer breake a Beggers sleepe.
Bright shines, &c.

A hundred head of blacke and white,[69]
Vpon our downes securely feede,
If any dare his master bite,
He dies therefore as sure as Creede.
Thus Beggers Lord it as they please,
And none but Beggers liue at ease.
Bright shines the Sun, &c.

ODE. OF CYNTHIA[70]

Th' Ancient Readers of Heauens Booke,
Which with curious eye did looke
Into Natures story;
All things vnder *Cynthia* tooke
To bee transitory.

This the learned only knew,
But now all men finde it true,
Cynthia is descended:
With bright beames, and heauenly hew,
And lesser starres attended.

---

[66] Ovid, *Amores*, III, xi, 5: "We have conquered, and we tread under foot the conquered love."

[67] From *A poetical rapsody*, 1602. By "Anomos."

[68] Rattles used by beggars to attract attention.

[69] Fleas and lice are the beggars' "sheep."

[70] From *A poetical rapsody*, 1602. The author is unknown.

Landes and Seas shee rules below,
Where things change, and ebbe, and flowe,
Spring, waxe olde, and perish;
Only Time which all doth mowe,
Her alone doth cherish.

Times yong howres attend her still,
And her Eyes and Cheekes do fill,
With fresh youth and beautie:
All her louers olde do grow,
But their hartes, they do not so
In their Loue and duty.

This Song was sung before her sacred Maiestie at a shew on horsebacke, wherwith the right Honorable the Earle of Cumberland presented her Highnesse on Maie day last.[71]

[71] In 1600, when Queen Elizabeth was sixty-seven years old.

Songs from Songbooks

THE LATER Elizabethan period was the golden age of English music. Not only was it the time of the greatest English composers—William Byrd, John Bull, Orlando Gibbons, Thomas Morley, and many others scarcely inferior to them—but it was also the time when a knowledge of music and a taste for music were more widespread than ever before or since. In *Popular Music of the Olden Time* William Chappell writes: "Tinkers sang catches; milk-maids sang ballads. . . . Each trade, and even the beggars, had their special song," and he adds that the musical ability of boys was emphasized in recommending them for employment "as servants, apprentices, and husbandmen," and that the lute, cittern, and virginals were supplied for the waiting customers in the barber shop. A knowledge of music was regarded as an essential part of a gentleman's education. In Thomas Morley's *A Plaine and Easie Introduction to Practicall Musicke, set down in Forme of a Dialogue*, 1597, the reader meets an embarrassed young man who says: "Supper being ended, and Musicke bookes, according to the custome being brought to the table: the mistresse of the house presented mee with a part; earnestly requesting mee to sing. But when after manie excuses, I protested vnfainedly that I could not: euerie one began to wonder. Yea, some whispered to others, demaunding how I was brought vp." In *The Compleat Gentleman*, 1622, Henry Peacham writes: "I desire no more in you than to sing your part sure, at the first sight, withall, to play the same upon your Violl, or the exercise of the Lute, privately to your selfe."

This love of music and especially of song gave impetus to the writing of poems to be set to music. Many of the most beautiful lyrics of the period survive only in the ninety songbooks published between 1588 and 1630.

Elizabethan songbooks were of two kinds: books of madrigals and books of airs. The madrigal was an unaccompanied song for at least three, but rarely more than six, voice parts. It consisted of short musical phrases treated contrapuntally, all voice parts being of equal melodic interest, the various voice parts taking up the musical phrases in turn rather than simultaneously, and the verbal phrases being repeated several times. The true madrigal was seldom set to more than one stanza of poetry. The air was sung as a solo accompanied by a lute and usually a bass viol, or as a part song with the highest voice carrying the melody and the other voices accompanying. The air was a song of several stanzas with the same music for each stanza. The madrigals were printed in small quartos, each book containing the music for only one voice part. When the composer adapted airs as part songs, all the voice parts were printed in one book with the parts so arranged on the page that each of the singers seated at a table could face his part.

Most of the hundreds of songs in the songbooks are of unknown authorship. Some composers wrote music for suitable poems that came to their hands; some poets wrote lyrics for tunes already familiar. At times perhaps a single composer and a single poet worked together. It is possible that some composers, like Thomas Campion, wrote both the music and the words, but he is the only man who is known to have done so.

The most comprehensive editions of the lyrics in Elizabethan songbooks is *English Madrigal Verse, 1588–1632*, ed. E. H. Fellowes, 1920, which includes both madrigals and lute songs; and *Some Shorter Elizabethan Poems*, ed. A. H. Bullen (Arber's English Garner, 1903). Useful collections are *Lyrics from the Song-Books of the Elizabethan Age*, ed. A. H. Bullen, 1887, and *More Lyrics from the Song-Books*, ed. A. H. Bullen, 1888. Editions of the lyrics with the musical settings are *The English Madrigal School*, ed. E. H. Fellowes, 36 vols., 1913–1924, and *The English School of Lutenist Song-Writers*, ed. E. H. Fellowes, 1920 ff. For accounts of Elizabethan music and musicians see William Chappell, *Popular Music of the Olden Time*, 2 vols., 1855, revised by H. E. Wooldridge, 1893; a short account of Elizabethan music by W. B. Squire in *Shakespeare's England*, 1916, ii, 15–31; E. H. Fellowes, *The English Madrigal Composers*, 1921, and his *William Byrd*, 1923; *The English Madrigal*, 1925; Peter Warlock (i.e., Philip Heseltine), *The English Ayre*, 1926; M. C. Boyd, *Elizabethan Music and Musical Criticism*, 1940. For Elizabethan music and poetry see Bruce Pattison, *Music and Poetry of the English Renaissance*, 1948; Catherine Ing, "Elizabethan Lyrics Influenced by Music," *Elizabethan Lyrics*, 1951.

I ioy not in no earthly blisse,[1]
  I force[2] not Cressus[3] welth a straw:
For care I know not what it is,
  I fear not Fortunes fatall law.
My mind is such as may not moue,
For beautie bright nor force of loue.

I wish but what I haue at will,
  I wander not to seeke for more:
I like the plaine,[4] I clime no hill,
  In greatest stormes I sitte on shore:
And laugh at them that toyle in vaine,
To get what must be lost againe.

I kisse not where I wish to kill,
  I faine not loue where most I hate:
I breake no sleepe to winne my will,
  I wayte not at the mighties gate:
I scorne no poor, nor feare no ritch,
I feele no want not haue to much.

The Court and cart I like nor loath,
  Extreames are counted worst of all:
The golden meane betweene them both,
  Doth surest sit and feare no fall:
This is my choyce, for why[5] I finde,
No wealth is like the quiet minde.

[1] From William Byrd, *Psalmes, sonets, and songs of sadnes and pietie*, 1588, STC 4253, Folger Library. This song is sometimes attributed to Sir Edward Dyer.

[2] care for.

[3] Croesus.

[4] *plaine,*] *plaine* STC 4253.

[5] because.

Though *Amarillis* daunce in greene,[6]
  Like Fayrie Queene,
  And sing full cleere,
Corina can with smiling cheere:
Yet since their eyes make heart so sore,
Hey ho, hey ho, chill[7] loue no more.

My sheepe are lost for want of foode,
  And I so wood:[8]
  That all the day,
I sit and watch a heardmaid gaye:
Who laughes to see me sigh so sore,
Hey ho, hey ho, chill loue no more.

Her louing lookes, her beautie bright,
  Is such delight:
  That all in vaine,
I loue to like, and lose my gaine:
For her that thankes me not therefore,
Hey ho, hey ho, chill loue no more.

Ah wanton eyes my friendlie foes,
  And cause of woes:
  Your sweete desire,
Breeds flames of Ise and freese in fire:
Ye skorne to see me weepe so sore,
Hey ho, hey ho, chill loue no more.

Loue ye who list, I force him not,
  Sith God it wot,
  The more I wayle,
The lesse my sighs and teares preuaile:
What shall I doe but say therefore,
Hey ho, hey ho, chill loue no more.

What pleasure haue great princes,[9]
  More daintie to their choice,
Then heardmen wyld, who carelesse
  In quiet life reioyce,
And fortunes fate not fearing,
Sing sweet in Sommer morning.

Their dealings plaine and rightfull,
  Are voyd of all disceit:
They neuer know how spitefull,
  It is to kneele and waite
On fauorite presumptious,
Whose pride is vaine and sumptious.

All day their flocks ech tendeth,
  At night they take their rest,
More quiet then who sendeth
  His ship into the East,
Where gold and pearle are plentie,
But getting very daintie.

For Lawiers and their pleading
  The'steeme it not a straw,
They think that honest meaning
  Is of it selfe a law,
Where conscience iudgeth plainely
They spend no mony vainely.

O happie who thus liueth,
  Not caring much for gold,
With clothing which suffiseth
  To keepe him from the cold,
Though poore and plaine his diet,
Yet merry it is and quiet.

Constant *Penelope,* sends to thee carelesse *Vlisses,*[10]
Write not againe, but come sweet mate thy selfe to reuiue me.
Troy we doe much enuie, we desolate lost ladies of *Greece:*
Not *Priamus,* nor yet all Troy, can vs recompence make.
Oh, that he had when he first took shipping to Lacedaemon,
That adulter I meane, had been o'rewhelmed with waters:
Then had I not line[11] now all alone, thus quiuering for cold,
Nor vsed this complaint, nor haue thought the day to be so long.

---

[6] From William Byrd, *Psalmes, sonets,* etc., 1588.
[7] I will.
[8] distracted.
[9] From William Byrd, *Psalmes, sonets,* etc., 1588.
[10] *Ibid.* These lines, as E. H. Fellowes points out, are classical hexameters, a translation of Ovid's First Epistle: *Hanc tua Penelope lento tibi mittit Ulysse.*
[11] lain.

Whyle that the Sunne with his beames hot,[12]
Scorched the fruits in vale and mountaine,
Philon the shepherd late forgot,
Sitting besides a Cristall fountaine,
In shadow of a greene Oke tree,
Vppon his pipe this song plaid hee:
Adew loue, adew loue, vntrue loue,
Your minde is light, soone lost for new loue.

So long as I was in your sight,
I was as your hart, your soul, your treasure;
And euermore you sob'd and sigh'd,
Burning in flames beyond all measure.
Three days endur'd your Loue to mee,
And it was lost in other three.
Adew loue, adew loue, vntrue loue,
Your minde is light, soone lost for new loue.

Another shepherd you did see,
To whome your hart was soone enchayned,
Full soone your loue was leapt from mee,
Full soon my place he had obtained,
Soone came a third your loue to winne,
And wee were out and he was in.
Adew loue, adew loue, vntrue loue,
Your minde is light, soone lost for new loue.

Sure you have made me passing glad,
That you your mind so soon remoued,
Before that I the leisure had
To choose you for my best beloued.
For all my loue was past and done
Two days before it was begun.
Adew loue, adew loue, vntrue loue,
Your minde is light, soone lost for new loue.

Blow, Shepherds, blow your pipes, with gladsome glee resounding,[13]
See where the faire *Eliza* comes with loue and grace abounding.
Runne, Nimphes, apace, goe meet hir,
With flowers and garlands greet hir.
All haile *Eliza* faire, the countries pride and goddesse,
Long mayst thou liue the shepherds Queen and louely mistresse.

Aprill is in my Mistris face,[14]
And Iuly in hir eyes hath place.
Within hir bosom is September,
But in hir heart a could December.

[12] From William Byrd, *Songs of sundrie natures, some of grauite, and others of myrth,* 1589, STC 4256a, Folger Library.

[13] From Thomas Morley, *Canzonets, or little short songs to three voyces,* 1593, STC 18121, Folger Library.

[14] From Thomas Morley, *Madrigalls to foure voices, the firste booke,* 1594, STC 18127, Folger Library.

Hoe who comes here along with bagpiping and drumming?[15]
O the Morris, tis I see, the Morris daunce a comming.
Come Ladies come come quickly,
Come away come I say, O come come quickly,
And see about how trim they daunce and trickly.
  Hey ther again! how the bells they shake it!
  Hey ho, now for our town;[16] and take it!
Soft awhile, piper, not away so fast! They melt them.
Be hanged, knaue,[17] see'st thou not the dauncers swelt them.[18]
  Stand out awhile! you come to far, I say in.
  There give the hobby-horse more room to play in.

Deare if you change Ile neuer chuse againe,[19]
  Sweete if you shrinke Ile neuer thinke of loue,
Fayre if you faile, Ile iudge all beauty vaine,
  Wise if to weake moe wits Ile neuer proue.
Deare, sweete, faire, wise, change shrink nor be not weake,
And on my faith, my faith shall neuer breake.

Earth with her flowers shall sooner heau'n adorne,
  Heauen her bright stars through earths dim globe shall moue,
Fire heate shall loose and frosts of flames be borne,
  Aire made to shine as blacke as hell shall proue.
Earth, heauen, fire, ayre, the world transform'd shall vew,
E're I proue false to faith, or strange to you.

Take time while Time doth last,[20]
Marke how faire[21] fadeth fast;
Beware if enuy raigne,
Take heede of proude disdaine.
Hold fast now in thy youth;
Regard thy vowed truth,
Least when thou waxeth old
Friends faile and loue growe cold.

A Womans looks[22]
Are barbed hooks,
That catch by art
The strongest hart,
When yet they spend no breath,
  But let them speake
  And sighing break,
  Forth into teares,
  Their words are speares,
That wound our souls to death.

  The rarest wit
  Is made forget,
  And like a child
  Is oft beguild,
With loues sweete seeming baite:
  Loue with his rod
  So like a God,
  Commands the mind

15 *Ibid.* The morris dance was a grotesque dance in fancy costume.

16 E. H. Fellowes suggests that spectators shout encouragement to the dancers representing their town.

17 The piper.

18 make themselves very warm.

19 From John Dowland, *The first booke of songes or ayres,* 1597, STC 7091, Folger Library.

20 From John Farmer, *The first set of English madrigals,* 1599, STC 10697, Folger Library.

21 beauty.

22 From Robert Jones, *The first booke of songes and ayres,* 1600, STC 14732, Folger Library.

We cannot find,
Faire shewes hide fowle deceit.

Time that all thinges
In order bringes,
Hath taught me now
To be more slow,
In giuing faith to speech:
Since womens wordes
No truth affordes,
And when they kisse
They thinke by this,
Vs men to ouer-reach.

Once did I loue and yet I liue,[23]
Though loue and truth be now forgotten.
Then did I ioy nowe doe I grieue,
That holy vowes must needs be broken.

Here be the blame that causd it so,
Mine be the griefe though it be little,
Shee shall haue shame,[24] I cause to know[25]
What tis to loue a dame so fickle.

Loue her that list I am content,
For that Camelion like shee changeth,
Yeelding such mistes as may preuent[26]
My sight to view her when she rangeth.

Let him not vaunt that gaines my losse,
For when that he and time hath prou'd her,
Shee may him bring to weeping crosse:
I say no more because I lou'd her.

Life is a Poets fable,[27]
And al her daies are lies
Stolne from deaths reckoning table,
For I die, for I die, as I speake
Death times the notes that I doe breake.

Childhood doth die in youth,
And youth in old age dies.
I thought I liv'd in truth:
But I die, but I die, now I see.
Each age of death makes one degree.

Farewell the doting score,
Of worlds arithmeticke,
Life, ile trust thee no more,
Till I die, till I die, for thy sake
Ile go by deaths new almanacke.

This instant of my song,
A thousand men lie sicke,
A thousand knels are rong:
And I die and I die as they sing,
They are but dead and I dying.

Death is but lifes decay,
Life time, time wastes away,
Then reason bids me say
That I die, that I die, though my breath
Prolongs this space of lingring death.

Weepe you no more sad fountaines,[28]
What need you flowe so fast,
Looke how the snowie mountaines,
Heau'ns sun doth gently waste.
But my sunnes heau'nly eyes
View not your weeping,
That nowe lies sleeping
Softly now softly lies
Sleeping.

Sleepe is a reconciling,
A rest that peace begets:
Doth not the sun rise smiling,
When fair at eu'n he sets,
Rest you, then rest sad eyes,
Melt not in weeping,
While she lies sleeping
Softly, now softly lies
Sleeping.

---

23 *Ibid.*
24 *shame,*] *shame* STC 14732.
25 *know*] *know:* STC 14732.
26 *preuent*] *preuent:* STC 14732.
27 From Robert Jones, *The first booke of songes and ayres,* 1600.
28 From John Dowland, *The third and last booke of songs or aires,* 1603, STC 7096, Folger Library.

Beautie is a louely sweet,[29]
Where pure white and crimson meet:
Ioyn'd with fauour of the face,
Chiefest flour of femall race.
But if vertue might be seene,
It would more delight the eine.[30]

If I could shut the gate against my thoughts,[31]
And keepe out sorrow from this roome with-in,
Or memory could cancell all the notes,
Of my misdeeds, and I vnthink my sinne,
How free, how cleare, how cleane my soule should lye,
Discharg'd of such a loathsome company.

Or were there other roomes with-out my hart,
That dyd not to my conscience ioyne so neare,
Where I might lodge the thoughts of sin apart,
That I might not their claim'rous crying heare.
What peace, what Ioy, what ease should I possesse,
Free'd from their horrors that my soule oppresse.

But O my Sauiour, who my refuge art,
Let thy deare mercies stand twixt them and mee:
And be the wall to seperate my hart,
So that I may at length repose mee free:
That peace, and Ioy, and rest may be within,
And I remaine deuided from my sinne.

Loue me not for comely grace,[32]
For my pleasing eye or face,
Nor for any outward part,
No, nor for my constant heart:
For those may faile or turne to ill,
So thou and I shall seuer:
Keepe therfore a true womans eye,
And loue me still, but know not why,
So hast thou the same reason still
To dote vpon me euer.

In Christall Towres, and turrets richly set[33]
With glittring gems, that shine against the Sunne,
In regall roomes of Iasper and of Iet,
Content of minde not alwayes likes to woon:[34]
But oftentimes, it pleaseth her to stay,
In simple cotes,[35] enclosde with wals of clay.

This sweet and merry month of May,[36]
While nature wantons in her Prime,
And birds do sing, and beasts do play
For pleasure of the ioyful time,
I choose the first for holy day,
And greet *Eliza*[37] with a rime.
O beauteous Queene of second Troy,
Take wel in worth a simple toy.

Crowned with flowres, I saw faire *Amarillis*,[38]
By Thirsis sit, hard by a fount of Christall,

---

[29] From Thomas Bateson, *The first set of English madrigales*, 1604, STC 1586, Folger Library.

[30] eyes.

[31] From John Danyel, *Songs for the lute, viol and voice*, 1606, STC 6268, Folger Library.

[32] From John Wilbye, *The second set of English madrigals*, 1609, STC 25619a, Folger Library.

[33] From William Byrd, *Psalmes, songs and sonnets*, 1611, STC 4255, Folger Library. This stanza is from a poem in Geffrey Whitney, *A choice of emblemes and other deuises*, 1586, STC 25438, Folger Library.

[34] dwell.

[35] cottages.

[36] From William Byrd, *Psalmes, songs and sonnets*, 1611. This song was first printed in Thomas Watson, *The first sett of Italian madrigalls Englished*, 1590, STC 25119, Folger Library. Watson is probably the author.

[37] Queen Elizabeth.

[38] From William Byrd, *Psalmes, songs and sonnets*, 1611.

And with her hand, more white than snow or Lillies,
  On sand she wrote my faith shall be immortall.
And sodainly a storme of winde and weather
Blew all her faith and sand away together.

The siluer Swanne, who liuing had no Note,[39]
When death approacht vnlockt her silent throat,
Leaning her breast against the reedie shore,
Thus sung her first and last, and sung no more,
Farewell all ioyes, O death come close mine eyes,
More Geese then Swannes now liue, more fooles then wise.

39 From Orlando Gibbons, *The first set of madrigals and mottets,* 1612, STC 11826, Folger Library.

Thomas Campion

[1567–1620]

THOMAS CAMPION, musician and poet, studied at Cambridge and Gray's Inn, later took a degree in medicine, probably abroad, and thereafter practiced in London.

Five of his poems appeared anonymously in the unauthorized edition of Sidney's *Astrophel and Stella* in 1591. In 1595 he published a volume of Latin epigrams. In 1601, in collaboration with Philip Rosseter, he published *A Book of Airs*, for at least the first half of which he wrote both the lyrics and the musical settings. Within the next few years he published two more volumes of airs for which he wrote both words and music. In 1602 appeared his prose treatise, *Observations in the Art of English Poesy*, in which he protested against "the vulgar and vnartificiall custome of riming," and advocated more flexibility in the rhythms of English poetry. About 1618 he published a short treatise entitled *A New Way of Making Four Parts in Counterpoint*. He wrote also at least four masques, one in 1607 and three in 1613.

Campion is the only song writer of his day who is known to have written both music and words for his airs. "Short Ayres," he wrote, "if they be skilfully framed, and naturally exprest, are like quicke and good Epigrammes in Poesie, many of them shewing as much artifice, and breeding as great difficultie as a larger Poeme. . . . In these *English* Ayres I haue chiefely aymed to couple my Words and Notes louingly together, which will be much for him to doe that hath not power ouer both."

Campion's songs are notable for their artistic structure, for the effective simplicity of their diction, word order, and rhymes, and for the variety of their cadence and rhythm. He had learned the best lessons that Horace and Catullus could teach; in his verse there is nothing awkward or excessive. His range is wide. In his hundred-odd songs he caught the joy and pain of living, the darkness of death, the hope of heaven. Though most of his "divine and moral songs" are quiet and meditative, a few reveal an intensely personal relationship with God and a vision of heaven that suggest Henry Vaughan. In his "light conceits of lovers" he writes usually with detachment and serenity, but now and then there is deeper feeling as in "Follow thy fair sun, unhappy shadow" and "When thou must home to shades of under ground." There are few songs in English so artistic as the best of Campion's.

The standard edition of Campion is *Campion's Works*, ed. Percival Vivian, 1909. For commentary see A. H. Bullen, "Dr. Thomas Campion," *Elizabethans,* 1924; M. M. Kastendieck, *England's Musical Poet: Thomas Campion*, 1938; R. W. Berringer, "Thomas Campion's Share in *A Book of Ayres*," *PMLA*, lviii (1943), 938–948; R. W. Short, "The Metrical Theory and Practice of Thomas Campion," *PMLA*, lix (1944), 1003–1018; Catherine Ing, "The Lyrics of Thomas Campion," *Elizabethan Lyrics*, 1951.

From A BOOKE OF AYRES[1]

My sweetest Lesbia let vs liue and loue,[2]
And though the sager sort our deedes reproue,
Let vs not way them: heau'ns great lampes doe diue
Into their west, and strait againe reuiue,
But soone as once set is our little light,
Then must we sleepe one euer-during night.

If all would lead their liues in loue like mee,
Then bloudie swords and armour should not be,
No drum nor trumpet peaceful sleepes should moue,
Vnles alar'me came from the campe of loue:
But fooles do liue, and wast their little light,
And seeke with paine their euer-during night.

When timely death my life and fortune ends,
Let not my hearse[3] be vext with mourning friends,
But let all louers rich in triumph come,
And with sweet pastimes grace my happie tombe;
And Lesbia close vp thou my little light,
And crowne with loue my euer-during night.

Though you are yoong and I am olde,
Though your vaines hot and my bloud colde,
Though youth is moist and age is drie,
Yet embers liue when flames doe die.

The tender graft is easely broke,
But who shall shake the sturdie Oke?
You are more fresh and faire then I,
Yet stubs do liue, when flowers doe die.

---

[1] From *A booke of ayres, set foorth to be song to the lute, orpherian, and base violl, by Philip Rosseter, lutenist,* 1601, STC 21332, Huntington Library. Campion wrote the twenty-one songs in Part I.

[2] This poem is in part a translation of Catullus, v, *Vivamus, mea Lesbia, atque amemus.*

[3] Canopy to be placed over a coffin.

Thou that thy youth doest vainely boast,
Know buds are soonest nipt with frost,
Thinke that thy fortune still doth crie,
Thou foole tomorrow thou must die.

Followe thy faire sunne vnhappy shaddowe
Though thou be blacke as night
And she made all of light,
Yet follow thy faire sunne vnhappie shaddowe.

Follow her whose light thy light depriueth,[4]
Though here thou liu'st disgrac't,
And she in heauen is plac't,
Yet follow her whose light the world reuiueth.

Follow those pure beames whose beautie burneth,
That so haue scorched thee,
As thou still blacke must bee,
Til her kind beames thy black to brightnes turneth.

Follow her while yet her glorie shineth,
There comes a luckles night,
That will dim all her light,
And this the black vnhappie shade deuineth.

Follow still since so thy fates ordained,
The Sunne must haue his shade,
Till both at once doe fade,
The Sun still proud the shadow still disdained.

When to her lute Corrina sings,
Her voice reuiues the leaden stringes,
And doth in highest noates appeare
As any challeng'd eccho cleere,
But when she doth of mourning speake,
Eu'n with her sighes, the strings do breake.

And as her lute doth liue or die,
Led by her passion, so must I,
For when of pleasure she doth sing,
My thoughts enioy a sodaine spring,
But if she doth of sorrow speake,
Eu'n from my hart the strings doe breake.

The man of life vpright
Whose guiltlesse hart is free,
From all dishonest deedes
Or thought of vanitie.

[4] takes away.

The man whose silent dayes,
In harmeles ioys are spent,
Whome hopes cannot delude,
Nor sorrow discontent.

That man needes neither towers
Nor armour for defence,
Nor secret vautes to flie
From thunders violence.

Hee onely can behold
With vnafrighted eyes,
The horrours of the deepe
And terrours of the Skies.

Thus, scorning all the cares
That fate, or fortune brings,
He makes the heau'n his booke,
His wisedome heeu'nly things,

Good thoughts his onely friendes,
His wealth a well-spent age,
The earth his sober Inne,
And quiet Pilgrimage.

When thou must home to shades of vnder ground,
And there ariu'd a newe admired guest,
The beauteous spirits do ingirt thee round,
White Iope, blith Hellen, and the rest,
To heare the stories of thy finisht loue,
From that smoothe toong whose musicke hell can moue.

Then wilt thou speake of banqueting delights,
Of masks and reuels which sweete youth did make,
Of Turnies and great challenges of knights,
And all these triumphes for thy beauties sake,
When thou hast told these honours done to thee,
Then tell, O tell how thou didst murther mee.

Come let vs sound with melody the praises[5]
Of the kings king, th'omnipotent creator,
Author of number, that hath all the world in
Harmonie framed.

Heau'n is His throne perpetually shining,
His deuine power and glorie thence he thunders,
One in all, and all still in one abiding,
Both Father, and Sonne.

[5] This is an example of Sapphic verse.

O sacred sprite inuisible, eternall,
Eu'ry where, yet vnlimited, that all things
Canst in one moment penetrate, reuiue me
O holy Spirit.

Rescue, O rescue me from earthly darknes,
Banish hence all these elementall obiects,
Guide my soule, that thirsts, to the liuely Fountaine
Of thy deuinenes.

Cleanse my soule, O God, thy bespotted Image,
Altered with sinne, so that heau'nly purenes
Cannot acknowledge me but in thy mercies
O Father of grace.

But when once thy beames do remoue my darknes,
O then I'le shine forth as an Angell of light,
And record with more than an earthly voice thy
Infinite honours.

Rose-cheekt *Lawra,* come[6]
Sing thou smoothly with thy beawties
Silent musick, either other
Sweetely gracing.

Louely formes do flowe
From concent[7] deuinely framed,
Heau'n is musick, and thy beawties
Birth is heauenly.

These dull notes we sing
Discords neede for helps to grace them,
Only beawty purely louing
Knowes no discord:

But still mooues delight
Like cleare springs renu'd by flowing,
Euer perfet, euer in them-
selues eternall.

From TWO BOOKES OF AYRES[8]

Author of light reviue my dying spright,
Redeeme it from the snares of all-confounding night.
Lord, light me to thy blessed way:

[6] From *Observations in the arte of English poesie*, 1602, STC 4543, Bodleian Library. This song is one that Campion wrote to illustrate his principles of quantitative versification. His comment on this poem follows: "The second kinde consists of *Dimeter*, whose first foote may either be a *Sponde* or a *Trochy:* The two verses following are both of them *Trochaical,* and consist of foure feete, the first of either of them being a *Spondee* or *Trochy*, the other three only *Trochyes*. The fourth and last verse is made of two *Trochyes*. The number is voluble and fit to expresse any amorous conceit."

[7] Singing or playing in harmony.

[8] From *Two bookes of ayres. The first contayning diuine and morall songs: the second, light conceits of louers,* c. 1610, STC 4547, Huntington Library.

For blinde with worldly vaine desires I wander as a stray.[9]
Sunne and Moone, Starres and vnderlights I see,
But all their glorious beames are mists and darknes being compar'd to thee.

Fountaine of health my soules deepe wounds recure,
Sweet showres of pitty raine, wash my vncleannesse pure.
One drop of thy desired grace
The faint and fading hart can raise, and in ioyes bosome place.
Sinne and Death, Hell and tempting Fiends may rage;
But God his owne will guard, and their sharp paines and griefe in time asswage.

View mee Lord, a worke of thine;
Shall I then lye drown'd in night?
Might thy grace in mee but shine,
I should seeme made all of light.

But my soule still surfets so
On the poysoned baytes of sinne,
That I strange and vgly growe,
All is[10] darke and foule within.

Clense mee, Lord, that I may kneele
At thine Altar, pure and white,
They that once thy Mercies feele,
Gaze no more on earths delight.

Worldly ioyes like shadowes fade,
When the heau'nly light appeares,
But the cou'nants thou hast made
Endlesse, know nor dayes, nor yeares.

In thy word Lord is my trust,
To thy mercies fast I flye,
Though I am but clay and dust,
Yet thy grace can lift me high.

To Musicke bent is my retyred minde,
And faine would I some song of pleasure sing:
But in vaine ioyes no comfort now I finde:
From heau'nly thoughts all true delight doth spring.
Thy power O God, thy mercies to record,
Will sweeten eu'ry note, and eu'ry word.

All earthly pompe or beauty to expresse,
Is but to carue in snow, on waues to write.
Celestiall things though men conceiue them lesse,
Yet fullest are they in themselues of light:
Such beames they yeeld as know no meanes to dye:
Such heate they cast as lifts the Spirit high.

[9] vagabond.

[10] *is*] *in* STC 4547.

Wise men patience neuer want,[11]
Good men pitty cannot hide:
Feeble spirits onely vant
Of reuenge, the poorest pride.
Hee alone forgiue that can
Beares the true soule of a man.

Some there are debate that seeke
Making trouble their content,
Happy if they wrong the meeke,
Vexe them that to peace are bent;
Such vndooe the common tye
Of mankinde, societie.

Kindnesse growne is, lately, colde,
Conscience hath forgot her part:
Blessed times were knowne of old,
Long ere Law became an Art.
Shame deterr'd, not Statutes then,
Honest loue was law to men.

Deedes from loue and words that flowe
Foster like kinde *Aprill* showres;
In the warme Sunne all things grow,
Wholsome fruits and pleasant flowres.
All so thriues his gentle rayes,
Where on humane loue displayes.

Neuer weather-beaten Saile more willing bent to shore,
Neuer tyred Pilgrims limbs affected[12] slumber more;
Then my wearied spright now longs to flye out of my troubled brest.
O come quickly sweetest Lord, and take my soule to rest.

Euer-blooming are the ioyes of Heau'ns high paradice,
Cold age deafes not there our eares, nor vapour dims our eyes;
Glory there the Sun out-shines, whose beames the blessed onely see:
O come quickly glorious Lord, and raise my spright to thee.

Loe, when backe mine eye,
Pilgrim-like, I cast,
What fearefull wayes I spye,
Which blinded I securely past?

But now heau'n hath drawne
From my browes that night;
As when the day doth dawne,
So cleares my long imprison'd sight.

[11] lack.

[12] desired.

Straight the caues of hell
Drest with flowres I see:
Wherein false pleasures dwell,
That winning most, most deadly be.

Throngs of masked Feinds,
Wing'd like Angels flye,
Euen in the gates of Friends;
In faire disguise blacke dangers lye.

Straight to Heau'n I rais'd
My restored sight:
And with loud voyce I prais'd
The Lord of euer-during light.

And since I had stray'd
From his wayes so wide,
His grace I humble pray'd
Hence-forth to be my guard and guide.

Awake, awake thou heauy spright,
That sleep'st the deadly sleepe of sinne;
Rise now and walke the waies of light:
'Tis not too late yet to begin.
Seeke heauen earely, seeke it late;
True Faith still findes an open gate.

Get vp, get vp, thou leaden man,
Thy tracks to endlesse ioy, or paine,
Yeelds but the modell of a span;
Yet burnes out thy lifes lampe in vaine.
One minute bounds thy bane, or blisse,
Then watch and labour, while time is.

Come chearfull day, part of my life, to mee:
For while thou view'st me with thy fading light,
Part of my life doth still depart with thee,
And I still onward haste to my last night.
Times fatall wings doe euer forward flye,
Soe eu'ry day we liue, a day wee dye.

But O yee nights ordain'd for barren rest,
How are my dayes depriu'd of life in you,
When heauy sleepe my soule hath dispossest,
By fayned death life sweetly to renew?
Part of my life in that you life denye:
So eu'ry day we liue a day wee dye.

Iacke and *Ione* they thinke no ill,
But louing liue, and merry still:
Doe their weeke dayes worke, and pray
Deuotely on the holy day:
Skip and trip it on the greene,
And help to chuse the Summer Queene:
Lash out[13] at a Country Feast
Their siluer penny with the best.

Well can they iudge of nappy Ale,
And tell at large a Winter tale:
Climbe vp to the Apple loft,
And turne the Crabs[14] till they be soft.
Tib is all the fathers ioy,
And little *Tom* the mothers boy:
All their pleasure is content,
And care to pay their yearely rent.

Ione can call by name her Cowes,
And decke her windowes with greene boughs:
Shee can wreathes and tuttyes[15] make,
And trimme with plums a Bridall Cake.
Iacke knowes what brings gaine or losse,
And his long Flaile can stoutly tosse,
Make the hedge which others breake,
And euer thinkes what he doth speake.

Now you Courtly Dames and Knights,
That study onely strange delights;
Though you scorne the home-spun gray,
And reuell in your rich array,
Though your tongues dissemble deepe,
And can your heads from danger keepe;
Yet for all your pompe and traine,
Securer liues the silly Swaine.

Giue beauty all her right,
  Shees not to one forme tyed:
  Each shape yeelds faire delight
  Where her perfections bide.
Hellen I grant might pleasing be,
And *Ros'mond*[16] was as sweet as shee.

  Some the quicke eye commends,
  Some swelling[17] lips and red:
  Pale lookes haue many friends,
  Through sacred sweetnesse bred.
Medowes haue flowres that pleasure moue,
Though Roses are the flowres of loue.

[13] spend freely.
[14] crab apples.
[15] nosegays.

[16] See Samuel Daniel's *The Complaint of Rosamond.*
[17] *swelling*] *smelling* STC 4547.

Free beauty is not bound
To one vnmoued clime,
She visits eu'ry ground,
And fauours eu'ry time.
Let the old loues with mine compare,
My sou'raigne is as sweet, and fayre.

From THE THIRD AND FOURTH BOOKE OF AYRES[18]

Now winter nights enlarge
The number of their houres,
And clouds their stormes discharge
Upon the ayrie towres,
Let now the chimneys blaze,
And cups o'erflow with wine:
Let well-tun'd words amaze
With harmonie diuine.
Now yellow waxen lights
Shall waite on hunny Loue
While youthfull Reuels, Masks, and Courtly sights,
Sleepes leaden spels remoue.

This time doth well dispence
With louers long discourse;
Much speech hath some defence,
Though beauty no remorse.
All doe not all things well;
Some measures comely tread;
Some knotted Ridles tell;
Some Poems smoothly read.
The Summer hath his ioyes,
And Winter his delights;
Though Loue and all his pleasures are but toyes,
They shorten tedious nights.

Come, O come my lifes delight;
Let me not in langour, pine:
Loue loues no delay: thy sight,
The more enioy'd, the more diuine.
O come and take from mee
The paine of being depriu'd of thee.

Thou all sweetnesse dost enclose,
Like a little world of blisse:
Beauty guards thy lookes, the Rose
In them pure and eternall is.
Come then and make thy flight
As swift to me as heau'nly light.

---

[18] From *The third and fourth booke of ayres,* c. 1612, STC 4548, Huntington Library.

Silly boy, 'tis ful Moone yet, thy night as day shines clearely;
Had thy youth but wit to feare, thou couldst not loue so dearely:
Shortly wilt thou mourne when all thy pleasures are bereaued;
Little knowes he how to loue that neuer was deceiued.

This is thy first mayden flame that triumphes yet vnstayned;
All is artlesse now you speake, not one word yet is fayned;
All is heau'n that you behold, and all your thoughts are blessed:
But no Spring can want his Fall, each *Troylus* hath his *Cresseid.*

Thy well-order'd lockes ere long shall rudely hang neglected;
And thy liuely pleasant cheare,[19] reade griefe on earth deiected:
Much then wilt thou blame thy Saint that made thy heart so holy,
And with sighs confesse, in loue, that too much faith is folly.

Yet be iust and constant still, Loue may beget a wonder;
Not vnlike a Summers frost, or Winters fatall thunder:
He that holds his Sweet-hart true vnto his day of dying,
Liues of all that euer breath'd most worthy the enuying.

Neuer loue vnlesse you can
Beare with all the faults of man:
Men sometimes will iealous bee,
Though but little cause they see,
And hang the head as discontent,
And speake what straight they will repent.

Men that but one Saint adore,
Make a shew of loue to more:
Beauty must be scorn'd in none,
Though but truely seru'd in one;
For what is courtship but disguise?
True hearts may haue dissembling eyes.

Men when their affaires require,
Must a while themselues retire;
Sometimes hunt, and sometimes hawke,
And not euer sit and talke.
If these and such like you can beare,
Then like, and loue, and neuer feare.

So sweet is thy discourse to me,
And so delightfull is thy sight,
As I taste nothing right but thee.
O why inuented Nature light?
Was it alone for beauties sake,
That her grac't words might better take?

---

[19] countenance.

No more can I old ioyes recall,
They now to me become vnknowne,
Not seeming to haue beene at all.
Alas, how soone is this loue growne
To such a spreading height in me,
As with it all must shadowed be?

There is a Garden in her face,
Where Roses and white Lillies grow;
A heau'nly paradice is that place,
Wherein all pleasant fruits doe flow.
There Cherries grow which none may buy,
Till Cherry ripe[20] themselues doe cry.

Those Cherries fayrely doe enclose
Of Orient Pearle a double row,
Which when her louely laughter showes,
They look like Rose-buds fill'd with snow.
Yet them nor Peere, nor Prince can buy,
Till Cherry ripe themselues doe cry.

Her Eyes like Angels watch them still;
Her Browes like bended bowes doe stand,
Threatning with piercing frownes to kill
All that attempt with eye or hand
Those sacred Cherries to come nigh,
Till Cherry ripe themselues doe cry.

[20] The call of the London street venders.

Samuel Daniel

[c. 1562–1619]

SAMUEL DANIEL, the son of a musician, was born in Somersetshire. He was a student at Oxford, but he took no degree. As tutor to William Herbert, later the third Earl of Pembroke and son of Sir Philip Sidney's sister Mary, Countess of Pembroke, he was admitted to the literary circle at Wilton, which he later called his "best school." He was afterward tutor to Lady Anne Clifford, and to her and to her mother, the Countess of Cumberland, he addressed verse epistles. Another early patron was Fulke Greville, to whom he dedicated *Musophilus*. After the accession of King James, Queen Anne appointed him one of her grooms of the privy chamber, and he held various offices in her household until 1618. In 1619 he died at Beckington, in Somersetshire. At some time after 1650 that formidable old lady who a half-century earlier had been his pupil erected in Beckington Church a mural monument with the inscription: "Here lies, expecting the second coming of our Lord and Saviour Jesus Christ, the dead body of Samuel Daniel, Esq., that excellent poet and historian who was tutor to the Lady Anne Clifford in her youth, she that was sole daughter and heir to George Clifford, Earl of Cumberland; who in gratitude to him erected this monument to his memory a long time after when she was Countess Dowager of Pembroke, Dorset and Montgomery. He died in October, 1619."

In the unauthorized editions of Sidney's *Astrophel and Stella*, 1591, were included twenty-eight of Daniel's sonnets, all but five of which were retained in the sequence of fifty sonnets that Daniel published in 1592 under the title *Delia*. The "Delia" of the sonnets was almost certainly the Countess of Pembroke, who would consider them as conventional compliments in the Petrarchan tradition. They are notable for their grace and finish and for their purity of diction.

With *Delia* was printed *The Complaint of Rosamond*, a narrative in the manner of Thomas Churchyard's *Shore's Wife*, written for the 1563 edition of *A Mirror for Magistrates*, and republished, with additions, in *Churchyard's Challenge*, 1593. Rosamond's ghost tells her story in rhyme royal, but the style resembles that of Marlowe rather than of Churchyard. Daniel adds to the erotic narrative a moral emphasis that is repeated in later poems of this kind, notably in Shakespeare's *Lucrece* and in Drayton's *Matilda* and *England's Heroical Epistles*.

In 1594 Daniel published a Senecan tragedy, *Cleopatra*, written to accompany the Countess of Pembroke's *Antonie*, and several years later he wrote a second play similar in form, *Philotas*, that was published in 1605.

In 1595 he published *The First Four Books of the Civil Wars between the Two Houses of Lancaster and York*. This ambitious undertaking, inspired by his passion for order and for the welfare of England, contains much admirable political and moral reflection. In fourteen years *The Civil Wars* grew to eight books, about seven thousand lines in all, but remained unfinished. In 1612 appeared the first part of his prose *History of England*. Though in 1618 the *History* was continued through the reign of Edward III, it was, like *The Civil Wars*, never completed. For many years it was his most popular work. His masques and pastoral plays for performance at court were written from 1604 to 1614.

In 1603 Daniel published *A Defence of Ryme* in reply to Thomas Campion's *Observations in the Art of English Poesie*. Daniel's little treatise is a clear, reasonable, temperate, and courteous statement in defense of rhyme in English poetry and a warning against arrogance and affectation in poets and critics.

Daniel's best and most characteristic poetry is in his *Musophilus*, 1599, a dialogue between Musophilus ("lover of learning") and Philocosmus ("lover of the world," the unlettered man of action); in the Horatian epistles, published in 1603, especially in the epistles addressed to Margaret, Countess of Cumberland, and to Lucy, Countess of Bedford; and in *Ulysses and the Siren*, published in 1605.

Daniel's best work is marked by simple diction, by a style spare and precise, and by high seriousness. Like Sidney, Greville, and Spenser, he was a Christian humanist who in learning sought discipline of the heart and mind, wisdom for the conduct of life. Instead of the turbulent, passionate spirit that inspired so many Elizabethans, one finds in him moderation, an appreciation of the dignity of the scholar and poet, an ardent devotion to England. To him poetry was "the speech of heaven"; and the English poet must write poetry "bettered by the patience of the North," poetry worthy of England's greatness, so that "the treasure of our tongue" may reach "worlds in the yet unformed Occident." This quiet, manly scholar, living in a time of valiant action, is a true Elizabethan when he asks

> What good is like to this,
> To do worthy the writing, and to write
> Worthy the reading, and the world's delight?

He was proud to be an English poet, and he believed that his poetry would be read

> So long as men speak English, and so long
> As verse and vertue shall be in request.

In his own time he was admired and imitated, and in later periods he was praised by poets as diverse as Gray, Coleridge, Wordsworth, and Housman.

The most useful modern editions are *The Complete Works in Verse and Prose of Samuel Daniel*, ed. A. B. Grosart, 5 vols., 1885–1896; *Samuel Daniel, Poems and a Defence of Ryme*, ed. A. C. Sprague, 1930. For biography and criticism see the excellent Introduction in Sprague's edition; G. K. Brady, *Samuel Daniel*, 1923; A. H. Bullen, "Samuel Daniel," *Elizabethans*, 1924; S. A. Tannenbaum, *Samuel Daniel, a Concise Bibliography*, 1942.

From DELIA[1]

To the Right Honourable the Ladie Mary, Countesse of Pembroke[2]

Right honorable, although I rather desired to keep in the priuate passions of my youth, from the multitude, as things vtterd to my selfe, and consecrated to silence: yet seeing I was betraide by the indiscretion of a greedie Printer,[3] and had some of my secrets bewraide[4] to the world, vncorrected: doubting[5] the like of the rest, I am forced to publish that which I neuer ment. But this wrong was not onely doone to mee, but to him[6] whose vnmatchable lines haue indured the like misfortune; Ignorance sparing not to commit sacriledge vpon so holy Reliques. Yet *Astrophel,* flying with the wings of his own fame, a higher pitch[7] then the gross-sighted can discerne, hath registred his owne name in the Annals of eternitie, and cannot be disgraced, howsoeuer disguised. And for my selfe, seeing I am thrust out into the worlde, and that my vnboldned Muse, is forced to appeare so rawly in publique; I desire onely to bee graced by the countenance of your protection: whome the fortune of our time hath made the happie and iudiciall Patronesse of the Muses, (a glory hereditary to your house) to preserue them from those hidious Beastes, Obliuion, and Barbarisme. Whereby you doe not onely possesse the honour of the present, but also do bind posterity to an euer gratefull memorie of your vertues, wherein you must suruiue your selfe. And if my lines heereafter better laboured, shall purchase grace in the world, they must remaine the monuments of your honourable fauour, and recorde the zealous duetie of mee, who am vowed to your honour in all obseruancy for euer,

Samuel Danyell.

To the right honorable, the Lady Mary, Countesse of Pembrooke[8]

Wonder of these, glory of other times,
O thou whom Enuy eu'n is forst t'admyre:
Great Patroness of these my humble Rymes,
Which thou from out thy greatnes doost inspire:
Sith onely thou hast deign'd to rayse them higher

---

1 From *Delia, contayning certayne sonnets: with the complaint of Rosamond*, 1592, STC 6253, Huntington Library.

2 Sister of Sir Philip Sidney.

3 Twenty-eight of Daniel's sonnets had appeared in the unauthorized editions of Sidney's *Astrophel and Stella* in 1591.

4 revealed.

5 fearing.

6 Sidney.

7 height.

8 From *Delia and Rosamond augmented,* 1594, STC 6254, Morgan Library.

Vouchsafe now to accept them as thine owne,
Begotten by thy hand, and my desire,
Wherein my Zeale, and thy great might is showne.
And seeing this vnto the world is knowne,
O leaue not, still to grace thy worke in mee:
Let not the quickning seede be ouer-throwne,
Of that which may be borne to honour thee.
Whereof, the trauaile I may challenge mine,
But yet the glory, (Madam) must be thine.

1[9]

Vnto the boundles Ocean of thy beautie
Runs this poore riuer, charg'd with streames of zeale:
Returning thee the tribute of my dutie,
Which heere my loue, my youth, my playnts reueale.
Heere I vnclaspe the booke of my charg'd soule,
Where I haue cast th'accounts of all my care:
Heere haue I summ'd my sighes, heere I enroule
Howe they were spent for thee; Looke what they are.
Looke on the deere expences of my youth,
And see how iust I reckon with thyne eyes:
Examine well thy beautie with my trueth,
And crosse[10] my cares ere greater summes arise.
Reade it sweet maide, though it be doone but slightly;
Who can shewe all his loue, doth loue but lightly.

4

These plaintiue verse,[11] the Posts[12] of my desire,
Which haste for succour to her slowe regarde:[13]
Beare not report of any slender fire,
Forging a griefe to winne a fames rewarde.
Now are my passions limnd[14] for outward hewe,
For that no collours can depaynt my sorrowes:
Delia her selfe, and all the world may viewe
Best in my face, how cares hath til'd deepe forrowes.
No Bayes I seeke to deck my mourning brow,
O cleer-eyde Rector of the holie Hill:[15]
My humble accents craue the Olyue bow,
Of her milde pittie and relenting will.
These lines I vse, t'unburthen mine owne hart;
My loue affects[16] no fame, nor steemes[17] of art.

6

Faire is my loue, and cruell as sh'is faire;
Her brow shades frownes, although her eyes are sunny;
Her Smiles are lightning, though her pride dispaire;[18]

---

9 From *Delia*, 1592.
10 cross off or cancel (as a debt).
11 This is the plural form.
12 couriers.
13 attention.
14 drawn, painted.
15 ruler (Apollo) of Parnassus.
16 aspires to.
17 esteems.
18 cause despair.

And her disdaines are gall; her fauours hunny.
  A modest maide, deckt with a blush of honour,
Whose feete doe treade greene pathes of youth and loue,
The wonder of all eyes that looke vppon her:
Sacred on earth, design'd a Saint aboue.
  Chastitie and Beautie, which were deadly foes,
Liue reconciled friends within her brow:
And had she pittie to conioine with those,
Then who had heard the plaints I vtter now.
  O had she not beene faire, and thus vnkinde,
  My Muse had slept, and none had knowne my minde.

9

  If this be loue, to drawe a weary breath,
Painte on flowdes,[19] till the shore, crye to th'ayre:
With downward lookes, still reading on the earth;
The sad memorials of my loues despaire.
  If this be loue, to warre against my soule,
Lye downe to waile, rise vp to sigh and grieue me:
The neuer-resting stone of care to roule,
Still to complaine my greifes, and none releiue me.
  If this be loue, to cloath me with darke thoughts,
Haunting vntroden pathes to waile apart;
My pleasures horror, Musique tragicke notes,
Teares in my eyes, and sorrowe at my hart.
  If this be loue, to liue a liuing death;
  O then loue I, and drawe this weary breath.

12

  My spotles loue hoouers with white wings:
About the temple of the proudest frame:
Where blaze those lights fayrest of earthly things,
Which cleere[20] our clouded world with brightest flame.
  M'ambitious thoughts confined in her face,
Affect no honour, but what she can giue mee:
My hopes doe rest in limits of her grace,
I weygh no comfort vnlesse she releeue mee.
  For she that can my hart imparadize,
Holdes in her fairest hand what deerest is:
My fortunes wheele, the circle of her eyes,
Whose rowling grace deigne once a turne of blis.
  All my liues sweete consists in her alone,
  So much I loue the most vnlouing one.

31

  Looke *Delia* how wee steeme[21] the half-blowne Rose,
The image of thy blush and Summers honor:
Whilst in her tender greene she doth inclose

[19] floods.

[20] illuminate.
[21] esteem.

That pure sweete beautie, Time bestowes vppon her.
No sooner spreades her glorie in the ayre,
But straight her ful-blowne pride is in declyning;
She then is scorn'd that late adorn'd the fayre:
So clowdes thy beautie, after fayrest shining.
No Aprill can reuiue thy withred flowers,
Whose blooming grace adornes thy glorie now:
Swift speedy Time, feathred with flying howers,
Dissolues the beautie of the fairest brow.
O let not then such riches waste in vaine;
But loue whilst that thou maist be lou'd againe.

32

But loue whilst that thou maist be lou'd againe,
Now whilst thy May hath fill'd thy lappe with flowers;
Now whilst thy beautie beares without a staine;
Now vse thy Summer smiles ere winter lowres.
And whilst thou spread'st vnto the rysing sunne,
The fairest flowre that euer sawe the light:
Now ioye thy time before thy sweete be dunne,
And *Delia,* thinke thy morning must haue night.
And that thy brightnes sets at length to west:
When thou wilt close vp that which now thou showest:
And thinke the same becomes thy fading best,
Which then shall hide it most, and couer lowest.
Men doe not weigh the stalke for that it was,
When once they finde her flowre, her glory passe.

33

When men shall finde thy flowre, thy glory passe,
And thou with carefull brow sitting alone:
Receiued hast this message from thy glasse,[22]
That tells thee trueth, and saies that all is gone.
Fresh shalt thou see in mee the woundes thou madest,
Though spent thy flame, in mee the heate remayning:
I that haue lou'd thee thus before thou fadest,
My faith shall waxe, when thou art in thy wayning.
The world shall finde this miracle in mee,
That fire can burne, when all the matter's spent:
Then what my faith hath beene thy selfe shalt see,
And that thou wast vnkinde thou maiest repent.
Thou maist repent, that thou hast scorn'd my teares,
When Winter snowes vppon thy golden[23] heares.

45

Care-charmer sleepe, sonne of the Sable night,
Brother to death, in silent darknes borne:
Relieue my languish, and restore the light,
With darke forgetting of my cares returne.

---

[22] mirror.

[23] *sable* in 1601 and later editions.

And let the day be time enough to morne,
The shipwrack of my ill-aduentred youth:
Let waking eyes suffice to wayle theyr scorne,
Without the torment of the nights vntruth.
Cease dreames, th'ymagery of our day desires,
To modell foorth the passions of the morrow:
Neuer let rysing Sunne approue you lyers,
To adde more griefe to aggrauat my sorrow.
Still let me sleepe, imbracing clowdes in vaine;
And neuer wake, to feele the dayes disdayne.

46

Let others sing of Knights and Palladines,
In aged accents, and vntimely[24] words:
Paint shadowes in imaginary lines,
Which well the reach of their high wits records;
But I must sing of thee and those faire eyes,
Autentique shall my verse in time to come,
When yet th'vnborne shall say, loe where she lyes,
Whose beautie made him speake that els was dombe.
These are the Arkes the Tropheis I erect,
That fortifie thy name against old age,
And these thy sacred vertues must protect,
Against the Darke and times consuming rage.
Though th'error of my youth they shall discouer,[25]
Suffice they shew I liu'd and was thy louer.

48

None other fame myne vnambitious Muse,
Affected[26] euer but t'eternize thee:
All other honours doe my hopes refuse,
Which meaner priz'd and momentarie bee.
For God forbid I should my papers blot,
With mercynary lines, with seruile pen:
Praising vertues in them that haue them not,
Basely attending on[27] the hopes of men.
No no my verse respects nor Thames nor Theaters,
Nor seekes it to be knowne vnto the Great:
But *Auon*[28] rich in fame, though poore in waters,
Shall haue my song, where *Delia* hath her seate.
Auon shall be my Thames, and she my Song;
Ile sound her name the Ryuer all along.

AN ODE

Nowe each creature ioyes the other,
Passing happy daies and howers:
One byrd reports[29] vnto another,

24 archaic or obsolete.
25 reveal.
26 aspired to.
27 serving.
28 Not the famous river in Warwickshire, but the Wiltshire Avon, which flows near Wilton, the seat of the Countess of Pembroke.
29 answers.

In the fall of siluer showers,
Whilst the earth our common mother,
Hath her bosome deckt with flowers.

Whilst the greatest torch of heauen,
With bright rayes warmes *Floras*[30] lappe:
Making nights and dayes both euen,
Cheering plants with fresher sappe:
My field of flowers quite be-reauen,[31]
Wants refresh of better happe.[32]

Eccho daughter of the ayre,
Babbling gheste of Rocks and Hills,
Knowes the name of my fearce[33] Fayre,
And soundes the accents of my ills:
Each thing pitties my dispaire,
Whilst that she her Louer kills.

Whilst that she O cruell Maide,
Doth me, and my true loue dispise:
My liues florish is decayde
That depended on her eyes:
But her will must be obaide,
And well he ends for loue who dies.

From THE COMPLAINT OF ROSAMOND[34]

Ovt from the horror of infernall deepes,
My poore afflicted ghost comes heere to plaine it:[35]
Attended with my shame that neuer sleepes,
The spot[36] wherewith my kinde,[37] and youth did staine it:
My body found a graue where to containe it,
A sheete could hide my face, but not my sin,
For Fame finds neuer tombe t'inclose it in.

And which is worse, my soule is nowe denied,
Her transport to the sweet Elisean rest,
The ioyfull blisse for ghosts repurified,
Th'euer springing Gardens of the blest,
Caron denies my waftage with the rest.
And sayes my soule can neuer passe that Riuer,
Till Louers sighes on earth shall it deliuer.

So shall I neuer passe; for how should I
Procure this sacrifice amongst the liuing?
Time hath long since worne out the memorie,
Both of my life, and liues vniust depriuing:
Sorrow for me is dead for aye reuiuing.

---

30 The Roman goddess of flowers.
31 robbed of its beauty.
32 lacks the refreshing of better fortune.
33 fierce, proud, haughty.
34 From *Delia,* 1592. Rosamond was the mistress of Henry II, who reigned from 1154 to 1189.
35 complain.
36 stain, disgrace.
37 nature.

Rosamond hath little left her but her name,
And that disgrac'd, for time hath wrong'd the same.

No Muse suggests the pittie of my case,[38]
Each penne dooth ouerpasse my iust complaint,
Whilst others are preferd, though farre more base:
Shores wife[39] is grac'd, and passes for a Saint;
Her Legend iustifies her foule attaint;
Her well-told tale did such compassion finde,
That she is pass'd, and I am left behinde.

Which seene with griefe, my myserable ghost,
(Whilome[40] inuested in so faire a vaile,
Which whilst it liu'd, was honoured of the most,
And being dead, giues matter to bewaile)
Comes to sollicit thee, since others faile,
To take this taske, and in thy wofull Song
To forme[41] my case, and register my wrong.

Although I knowe thy iust lamenting Muse,
Toylde[42] in th'affliction of thine owne distresse,
In others cares hath little time to vse,
And therefore maist esteeme of mine the lesse:
Yet as thy hopes attend happie redresse,
Thy ioyes depending on a womans grace,
So moue thy minde a wofull womans case.

Delia[43] may happe to deygne to read our story,
And offer vp her sigh among the rest,
Whose merit would suffice for both our glorie,
Whereby thou might'st be grac'd, and I be blest,
That indulgence would profit me the best;
Such powre she hath by whom thy youth is lead,
To ioy the liuing and to blesse the dead.

So I through beautie made the wofull'st wight,[44]
By beautie might haue comfort after death:
That dying fayrest, by the fayrest might
Finde life aboue on earth, and rest beneath:
She that can blesse vs with one happy breath,
Giue comfort to thy Muse to doe her best.
That thereby thou maist ioy, and I might rest.

Thus saide: forthwith mou'd with a tender care
And pittie, which my selfe could neuer finde:
What she desir'd, my Muse deygn'd to declare,
And therefore will'd her boldly tell her minde:
And I more willing tooke this charge assignd,
Because her griefes were worthy to be knowne,
And telling hers, might hap forget mine owne.

[38] situation.

[39] Jane Shore, mistress of Edward IV, who reigned from 1461 to 1483. Thomas Churchyard's poem *Shore's Wife* was added to *The Mirror for Magistrates* in 1563.

[40] formerly.

[41] inform, report.

[42] your strength taxed; or ensnared.

[43] The "Delia" of the sonnets.

[44] creature.

Then write quoth shee the ruine of my youth,
Report the downe-fall of my slippry state:
Of all my life reueale the simple truth,
To teach to others, what I learnt too late:
Exemplifie my frailtie, tell howe Fate
  Keepes in eternall darke our fortunes hidden,
  And ere they come, to know them tis forbidden.

For whilst the sunn-shine of my fortune lasted,
I ioy'd the happiest warmth, the sweetest heat
That euer yet imperious beautie tasted,
I had what glory euer flesh could get:
But this faire morning had a shamefull set;
  Disgrace darkt honor, sinne did clowde my brow,
  As note the sequel, and Ile tell thee how.

The blood I staind was good and of the best,
My birth had honor, and my beautie fame:
Nature and Fortune ioyn'd to make me blest,
Had I had grace t'haue knowne to vse the same:
My education shew'd from whence I came,
  And all concur'd to make me happy furst,
  That so great hap might make me more accurst.

Happie liu'd I whilst Parents eye did guide,
The indiscretion of my feeble wayes:
And Country home kept me from being eyde,
Where best vnknowne I spent my sweetest dayes;
Till that my frindes mine honour sought to rayse,
  To higher place, which greater credite yeeldes,
  Deeming such beauty was vnfit for feeldes.

From Country then to Court I was preferr'd,
From calme to stormes, from shore into the deepes:
There where I perish'd, where my youth first err'd;
There where I lost the Flowre which honour keepes;
There where the worser thriues, the better weepes;
  Ah me poore wench, on this vnhappy shelfe[45]
  I grounded me, and cast away my selfe.

For thither com'd,[46] when yeeres had arm'd my youth
With rarest proofe of beautie euer seene:
When my reuiuing eye had learnt the truth,
That it had powre to make the winter greene,
And flowre affections whereas none had beene:
  Soone could I teach my browe to tyrannize,
  And make the world do homage to mine eyes.

For age I saw, though yeeres with cold conceit,[47]
Congeald theyr thoughts against a warme desire:
Yet sigh their want, and looke at such a baite,
I saw how youth was waxe before the fire:

[45] sandbank.
[46] having come,
[47] thought,

I saw by stealth, I fram'd my looke a lire,[48]
Yet well perceiu'd how Fortune made me then,
The enuy of my sexe, and wonder vnto men.

Looke how a Comet at the first appearing,
Drawes all mens eyes with wonder to behold it:
Or as the saddest tale at suddaine hearing,
Makes silent listning vnto him that told it:
So did my speech when rubies did vnfold it;
So did the blasing of my blush appeere,
T'amaze the world, that holds such sights so deere.

Ah beauty Syren, fayre enchaunting good,
Sweet silent rethorique of perswading eyes:
Dombe eloquence, whose powre doth moue the blood,
More then the words, or wisedome of the wise:
Still harmonie, whose diapason lyes
Within a brow, the key which passions moue,
To rauish sence, and play a world in loue.

What might I then not doe whose powre was such?
What cannot women doe that know theyr powre?
What woman[49] knowes it not I feare too much,
How blisse or bale lyes in theyr laugh or lowre?
Whilst they enioy their happy blooming flowre,
Whilst nature decks her with her proper fayre[50]
Which cheeres the worlde, ioyes each sight, sweetens th'ayre.

Such one was I, my beautie was mine owne,
No borrowed blush which banck-rot[51] beauties seeke:
The new-found shame, a sinne to vs vnknowne,
Th'adulterate beauty of a falsed cheeke:
Vild[52] staine to honor and to women eeke,
Seeing that time our fading must detect,
Thus with defect to couer our defect.

Impiety of times, chastities abator,
Falshod, wherein thy selfe, thy selfe deniest:
Treason, to counterfeit the seale of nature,
The stampe of heauen, impressed by the hiest.
Disgrace vnto the world, to whom thou lyest,
Idol vnto thy selfe, shame to the wise,
And all that honors thee idolatrise.

Farre was that sinne from vs whose age was pure,
When simple beautie was accounted best,
The time when women had no other lure
But modestie, pure cheekes, a vertuous brest:
This was the pompe wherewith my youth was blest;
These were the weapons which mine honour wunne
In all the conflicts that mine eyes begunne.

[48] liar.
[49] *woman* ed. 1607, STC 6240]; *women* STC 6253.
[50] beauty.
[51] bankrupt.
[52] vile.

Which were not small, I wrought on no meane obiect;
A Crowne was at my feete, Scepters obaide mee:
Whom Fortune made my King, Loue made my Subiect,
Who did commaund the Land, most humbly praid mee:
Henry the second, that so highly weigh'd mee,
Founde well by proofe[53] the priuiledge of Beautie,
That it hath powre to counter-maund all duetie.

For after all his victories in Fraunce,
Tryumphing in the honour of his deedes:
Vnmatch'd by sword, was vanquisht by a glaunce,
And hotter warres within his bosome breedes:
Warres whom whole Legions of desires feedes,
Against all which my chastity opposes,
The fielde of honour, vertue neuer loses.[54]

. . . .

And safe mine honor stoode till that in truth,
One of my Sexe, of place, and nature bad:
Was set in ambush to intrap my youth,
One in the habit of like frailtie clad,
One who the liu'ry of like weakenes had.
A seeming Matrone, yet a sinfull monster,
As by her words the chaster sort may conster.[55]

Shee set vpon me with the smoothest speech,
That Court and age could cunningly deuise:
Th'one autentique[56] made her fit to teach,
The other learnt her how to subtelise:
Both were enough to circumuent the wise.
A document that well may teach the sage,
That there's no trust in youth, nor hope in age.[57]

. . . .

Now did I find my selfe vnparadis'd,
From those pure fieldes of my so cleane beginning:
Now I perceiu'd how ill I was aduis'd,
My flesh gan loathe the new-felt touch of sinning:
Shame leaues vs by degrees, not at first winning.
For nature checks a new offence with lothing:
But vse of sinne doth make it seeme as nothing.

And vse of sinne did worke in me a boldnes,
And loue in him, incorporates such zeale:
That iealosie increas'd with ages coldnes,
Fearing to loose the ioy of all his weale.
Or doubting[58] time his stealth might else reueale,
H'is driuen to deuise some subtile way,
How he might safeliest keepe so rich a pray.

[53] test.
[54] Six stanzas are omitted.
[55] interpret, understand.
[56] authoritative.
[57] Thirty-two stanzas are omitted. The "sinfull monster" persuades Rosamond to grant King Henry's request.
[58] fearing.

A stately Pallace he foorthwith did buylde,
Whose intricate innumerable wayes,
With such confused errors[59] so beguil'd
Th'vnguided entrers with vncertaine strayes,[60]
And doubtfull turnings kept them in delayes,
With bootlesse labor leading them about,
Able to finde no way, nor in, nor out.

Within the closed bosome of which frame,
That seru'd a Center to that goodly round:
Were lodgings, with a garden to the same,
With sweetest flowers that eu'r adorn'd the ground,
And all the pleasures that delight hath found,
T'entertaine the sence of wanton eyes,
Fuell of loue, from whence lusts flames arise.

Heere I inclos'd from all the world a sunder,
The Minotaure[61] of shame kept for disgrace:
The monster of fortune, and the worlds wonder,
Liu'd cloystred in so desolate a case:
None but the King might come into the place.
With certaine maides that did attend my neede,
And he himselfe came guided by a threed.[62]

O Iealousie, daughter of enuy, and loue
Most wayward issue of a gentle Syer;
Fostred with feares, thy Fathers ioyes t'improue,
Myrth-marring Monster, borne a subtile lyer;
Hatefull vnto thy selfe, flying thine owne desier:
Feeding vpon suspect that dooth renue thee,
Happie were Louers if they neuer knewe thee.

Thou hast a thousand gates thou enterest by,
Conducting trembling passions to our hart:
Hundred eyed *Argos,* euer waking Spye,
Pale hagge, infernall fury, pleasures smart,
Enuious Obseruer, prying in euery part;
Suspicious, fearefull, gazing still[63] about thee,
O would to God that loue could be without thee.

Thou didst depriue (through false suggesting feare)
Him of content, and me of libertie:
The onely good that women holde so deare,
And turnst my freedome to captiuitie,
First made a Prisoner, ere an enemy:
Enioynd the raunsome of my bodies shame,
Which though I paide could not redeeme the same.

What greater torment euer could haue beene,
Then to inforce the fayre to liue retired:

[59] wandering ways.
[60] straying.
[61] The Minotaur, a legendary monster that was kept in a labyrinth in Crete.
[62] thread.
[63] always.

For what is Beautie if it be not seene,
Or what is't to be seene vnlesse admired?
And though admyred, vnlesse in loue desired?
  Neuer were cheekes of Roses, locks of Amber,
  Ordayn'd to liue imprisoned in a Chamber.

Nature created Beautie for the view,
Like as the fire for heate, the Sunne for light:
The Faire doe holde this priuiledge as due,
By auncient Charter, to liue most in sight,
And she that is debarr'd it, hath not right.
  In vaine our friends in this vse their dehorting,[64]
  For Beautie will be where is most resorting.

Witnes the fayrest streets that Thames doth visit,
The wondrous concourse of the glittering Faire:
For what rare woman[65] deckt with Beautie is it,
That thither couets not to make repaire.
The solitary Country may not stay her,
  Heere is the center of all beauties best,
  Excepting *Delia,* left to adorne the West.

Heere doth the curious with iudiciall eyes,
Contemplate beauty gloriously attired:
And heerein all our cheefest glory lyes,
To liue where we are prais'd and most desired.
O how we ioy to see our selues admired,
  Whilst niggardly our fauours we discouer,[66]
  We loue to be belou'd, yet scorne the Louer.

Yet would to God my foote had neuer moued
From Countrey safety, from the fields of rest:
To know the danger to be highly loued,
And lyue in pompe to braue[67] among the best,
Happy for me, better had I beene blest;
  If I vnluckely had neuer strayde:
  But liu'd at home a happy Country mayde.

Whose vnaffected innocencie thinks
No guilefull fraude, as doth the Courtly liuer:
She's deckt with trueth, the Riuer where she drinks
Doth serue her for her glasse, her counsell giuer:
She loues sincerely, and is loued euer.
  Her dayes are peace, and so she ends her breath,
  True life that knowes not what's to die till death.

So should I neuer haue been registred,
In the blacke booke of the vnfortunate:
Nor had my name enrold with Maydes misled,
Which bought theyr pleasures at so hie a rate.
Nor had I taught through my vnhappy fate,

---

64 dissuading.
65 *woman*] *women* STC 6253.
66 reveal.
67 be splendid.

This lesson which my selfe learnt with expence,
How most it hurts that most delights the sence.

Shame followes sinne, disgrace is duly giuen,
Impietie will out, neuer so closely doone:
No walles can hide vs from the eyes of heauen,
For shame must end what wickednesse begun:
Forth breakes reproch when we least thinke thereon.
And thys is euer propper vnto Courts:
That nothing can be doone but Fame[68] reports.

Fame doth explore what lyes most secrete hidden,
Entring the closet of the Pallace dweller:
Abroade reuealing what is most forbidden,
Of trueth and falshood both an equall teller:
Tis not a guarde can serue for to expell her,
The sword of iustice cannot cutte her wings,
Nor stop her mouth from vtt'ring secrete things.

And this our stealth she could not long conceale,
From her whom such a forfeit most concerned:
The wronged Queene, who could so closely deale:
That she the whole of all our practise[69] learned,
And watcht a time when least it was discerned,
In absence of the King, to wreake her wrong,
With such reuenge as she desired long.

The Laborinth she entred by that threed
That seru'd a conduct to my absent Lord:
Left there by chaunce, reseru'd for such a deede,
Where she surpriz'd me whom she so abhord.
Enrag'd with madnes, scarce she speakes a word,
But flyes with eger fury to my face,
Offring me most vnwomanly disgrace.

Looke how a Tygresse that hath lost her whelpe,
Runs fearcely raging through the woods astray:
And seeing her selfe depriu'd of hope or helpe,
Furiously assaults what's in her way,
To satisfie her wrath, not for a pray:
So fell she on me in outragious wise,
As could Disdaine and Iealousie deuise.

And after all her vile reproches vsed,
She forc'd me take the poyson she had brought:
To end the lyfe that had her so abused,
And free her feares, and ease her iealous thought.
No crueltie her wrath would leaue vnwrought,
No spightfull act that to reuenge is common:
For no beast fearcer then a iealous woman.[70]

[68] rumor, gossip.
[69] trickery, intrigue.
[70] Here in the edition of 1594 (STC 6254) the following three stanzas are added.

Heere take (saith shee) thou impudent vncleane,
Base graceles strumpet, take this next your hart;
Your loue-sick hart, that ouer-charg'd hath beene
With pleasures surfeite, must be purg'd with arte.
This potion hath a power, that will conuart
To nought those humors that oppresse you so.
And (Gerle,) Ile see you take it ere I goe.

What stand you now amaz'd, retire you back?
Tremble you (minion?) come dispatch with speed.
There is no helpe, your Champion now you lack,
And all these teares you shed will nothing steed;
Those dainty fingers needes must doe the deed.
Take it, or I will drench you[71] els by force,
And trifle not, least that I vse you worse.

Hauing this bloody doome from hellish breath,
My wofull eyes on euery side I cast:
Rigor about me, in my hand my death,
Presenting mee the horror of my last;
All hope of pitty and of comfort past.
No meanes, no powre, no forces to contend,
My trembling hands must giue my selfe my end.

Those handes that beauties ministers had bin,
Must now gyue death, that me adorn'd of late:
That mouth that newly gaue consent to sin,
Must now receiue destruction in there-at.
That body which my lusts did violate,
Must sacrifice it selfe t'appease the wrong,
So short is pleasure, glory lasts not long.[72]

And shee no sooner saw I had it taken,
But foorth shee rushes, (proude with victory,)
And leaues m'alone, of all the world forsaken,
Except of Death, which shee had left with me.
(Death and my selfe alone together be.)
To whom shee did her full reuenge refer.
Ah poore weake conquest both for him and her.

Then straight my Conscience summons vp my sin,
T'appeare before me, in a hideous face;
Now doth the terror of my soule begin,
When eu'ry corner of that hatefull place
Dectates[73] mine error, and reueales disgrace;
Whilst I remaine opprest in euery part,
Death in my bodie, horror at my hart.

Downe on my bed my lothsome selfe I cast,
The bed that likewise giues in euidence

[71] make you drink.

[72] Here in the edition of 1594 (STC 6254) are added the following five stanzas and also fifteen additional stanzas telling of Rosamond's repentance.

[73] dictates, utters.

Against my soule, and tells I was vnchast,
Tells I was wanton, tells I followed sence.
And therefore cast, by guilt of mine offence,
  Must heere the right of heauen needes satis-fie.
  And where I wanton lay, must wretched die.

Heere I began to waile my hard mishap,
My suddaine, strange vnlookt for misery.
Accusing them that did my youth intrap,
To gyue me such a fall of infamie.
And poore distressed *Rosamond,* (said I,)
  Is this thy glory got, to die forlorne
  In Dezarts, where no eare can heare thee morne?

Nor any eye of pitty to behold
The wofull end of thy sad tragedie;
But that thy wrongs vnseene, thy tale vntold,
Must heere in secrete silence buried lie.
And with thee, thine excuse together die.
  Thy sin reueal'd, but thy repentance hid,
  Thy shame aliue, but dead what thy death did.

The poyson soone disperc'd through all my vaines,
Had dispossess'd my liuing sences quite:
When naught respecting Death,[74] the last of paines,
Plac'd his pale collours, th'ensigne of his might,
Vpon hys new-got spoyle before his right;
  Thence chac'd my soule, setting my day ere noone,
  When I least thought my ioyes could end so soone.

And as conuaid t'vntimely funerals,
My scarce colde corse not suffred longer stay:
Behold the King (by chance) returning, falls
T'incounter with the same vpon the way,
As he repaird to see his deerest ioy.
  Not thinking such a meeting could haue beene,
  To see his loue, and seeing beene vnseene.

Iudge those whom chaunce depriues of sweetest treasure,
What tis to lose a thing we hold so deare:
The best delight, wherein our soule take pleasure,
The sweet of life, that penetrates so neare.
What passions feeles that hart, inforce'd to beare
  The deepe impression of so strange a sight?
  Tongue, pen, nor art, can neuer shew aright.

Amaz'd he standes, nor voyce nor body steares,[75]
Words had no passage, teares no issue found:
For sorrow shut vp words, wrath kept in teares,
Confus'd affects[76] each other doe confounde:
Oppress'd with griefe his passions had no bounde:

---

[74] *respecting Death,* STC 6254]; *respecting, death* STC 6253.

[75] controls.

[76] emotions, inclinations.

Striuing to tell his woes, wordes would not come;
For light cares speake, when mightie griefes are dombe.

At length extremitie breakes out a way,
Through which th'imprisoned voice with teares attended,
Wayles out a sound that sorrowes doe bewray:[77]
With armes a crosse and eyes to heauen bended,
Vauporing out sighes that to the skyes ascended.
Sighes, the poore ease calamitie affords,
Which serue for speech when sorrow wanteth words.

O heauens (quoth he) why doe myne eyes behold,
The hatefull rayes of this vnhappy sonne?
Why haue I light to see my sinnes controld,[78]
With blood of mine owne shame thus vildly[79] donne?
How can my sight endure to looke thereon?
Why doth not blacke eternall darknes hide,
That from myne eyes my hart cannot abide?

What saw my life, wherein my soule might ioy?
What had my dayes, whom troubles still afflicted?
But onely this, to counterpoize annoy,
This ioy, this hope, which death hath inderdicted:[80]
This sweete, whose losse hath all distresse inflicted.
This that did season all my sowre of life,
Vext still at home with broyles, abroade in strife.

Vext styll at home with broyles, abrode in strife,
Dissention in my blood, iarres[81] in my bed:
Distrust at boord, suspecting still my life,
Spending the night in horror, dayes in dred;
Such life hath tyrants, and thys lyfe I led.
These myseries goe mask'd in glittering showes,
Which wisemen see, the vulgar little knowes.

Thus as these passions doe him ouer-whelme,
He drawes him neere my bodie to behold it:
And as the Vine maried vnto the Elme
With strict[82] imbraces, so doth he infold it;
And as he in hys carefull armes doth hold it,
Viewing the face that euen death commends,
On sencelesse lips, millions of kysses spends.

Pittifull mouth (quoth he) that liuing gauest
The sweetest comfort that my soule could wish:
O be it lawfull now, that dead thou hauest,
Thys sorrowing farewell of a dying kisse.
And you fayre eyes, containers of my blisse,
Motiues of loue, borne to be matched neuer:
Entomb'd in your sweet circles sleepe for euer.

---

77 reveal.
78 rebuked.
79 vilely.
80 excluded.
81 quarrels.
82 close.

Ah how me thinks I see death dallying seekes,
To entertaine it selfe in loues sweet place:
Decayed Roses of discoloured cheekes,
Doe yet retaine deere notes of former grace:
And ougly death sits faire within her face;
Sweet remnants resting of vermilion red,
That death it selfe, doubts whether she be dead.

Wonder of beautie, oh receiue these plaints,
The obsequies, the last that I shall make thee:
For loe my soule that now already faints,
(That lou'd thee lyuing, dead will not forsake thee,)
Hastens her speedy course to ouer-take thee.
Ile meete my death, and free my selfe thereby,
For ah what can he doe that cannot die?

Yet ere I die, thus much my soule doth vow,
Reuenge shall sweeten death with ease of minde:
And I will cause posterity shall know,
How faire thou wert aboue all women kind.
And after ages monuments shall find,
Shewing thy beauties title not thy name,
Rose of the world that sweetned so the same.

This said, though more desirous yet to say,
(For sorrow is vnwilling to giue ouer)
He doth represse what griefe would els bewray,
Least that too much his passions might discouer:[83]
And yet respect scarce bridles such a Louer.
So farre transported that he knowes not whether,
For loue and Maiestie dwell ill together.

Then were my funerals not long deferred,
But doone with all the rites pompe could deuise:
At *Godstow,*[84] where my body was interred,
And richly tomb'd in honorable wise.
Where yet as now scarce any note descries[85]
Vnto these times, the memory of me,
Marble and Brasse so little lasting be.

For those walles which the credulous deuout,
And apt-beleeuing ignorant did found:
With willing zeale that neuer call'd in doubt,
That time theyr works should euer so confound,
Lye like confused heapes as vnder-ground.
And what their ignorance esteem'd so holy,
The wiser ages doe account as folly.

And were it not thy fauourable lynes,
Reedified[86] the wracke of my decayes:
And that thy accents willingly assignes,
Some farther date, and giue me longer daies,

[83] reveal.
[84] A nunnery near Oxford.
[85] describes.
[86] rebuilt.

Fewe in this age had knowne my beauties praise.
  But thus renewd by fame, redeemes some time,
  Till other ages shall neglect thy rime.

Then when confusion in her course shall bring,
Sad desolation on the times to come:
When myrth-lesse Thames shall haue no Swan to sing,
All Musique silent, and the Muses dombe.
And yet euen then it must be known to some,
  That once they florisht, though not cherisht so,
  And Thames had Swannes as well as euer Po.

But heere an end, I may no longer stay thee,
I must returne t'attend[87] at *Stigian* flood:
Yet ere I goe, thys one word more I pray thee,
Tell *Delia* now her sigh may doe me good,
And will her note the frailtie of our blood.
  And if I passe vnto those happy banks,
  Then she must haue her praise, thy pen her thanks.

So vanisht shee, and left me to returne,
To prosecute the tenor of my woes:
Eternall matter for my Muse to mourne,
But ah the worlde hath heard too much of those,
My youth such errors must no more disclose.
  Ile hide the rest, and greeue for what hath beene,
  Who made me knowne, must make me liue vnseene.

[RICHARD II AS CAPTIVE][88]

71

Now *Isabell* the young afflicted Queene,
Whose yeares had neuer shew'd her but delights,
Nor louely eies before had euer seene
Other then smiling ioies and ioyfull sights:
Borne great, matcht great, liu'd great and euer beene
Partaker of the worlds best benefits,
Had plac'd her selfe, hearing her Lord should passe
That way where shee vnseene in secret was.

72

Sicke of delay and longing to behold
Her long mist loue in fearfull ieoperdies,
To whom although it had in sort beene told
Of their proceeding, and of his surprize,
Yet thinking they would neuer be so bold
To lead their Lord in any shamefull wise,

[87] to wait.

[88] From *The first fowre bookes of the ciuile wars between the two houses of Lancaster and Yorke*, 1595, STC 6244, Morgan Library. The following stanzas from Book II tell of Richard II's entry into London and of his interview with Queen Isabel. See Shakespeare, *Richard II*, v, i.

But rather would conduct him as their king,
As seeking but the states reordering.

73

And foorth shee looks: and notes the formost traine
And grieues to view some there she wisht not there,
Seeing the chiefe not come, staies, lookes againe,
And yet she sees not him that should appeare:
Then backe she stands, and then desires as[89] faine
Againe to looke to see if hee were nere,
At length a glittring troupe farre off she spies,
Perceiues the thronge and heares the shoots and cries.

74

Lo yonder now at length he comes (saith shee)
Looke my good women where he is in sight:
Do you not see him? yonder that is hee
Mounted on that white courser all in white,
There where the thronging troupes of people bee,
I know him by his seate, he sits s'vpright:
Lo, now he bows: deare Lord with what sweet grace:
How long haue I longd to behold that face?

75

O what delight my hart takes by mine eie?
I doubt me when he comes but something neere
I shall set wide the window: what care I
Who doth see me, so him I may see cleare?
Thus doth false ioy delude her wrongfully
Sweete lady in the thing she held so deare;
For nearer come, shee findes shee had mistooke,
And him she markt was *Henrie Bullingbrooke.*

76

Then *Enuie* takes the place of her sweet eies
Where sorrow had prepard her selfe a seat,
And words of wrath from whence complaints should rise,
Proceed from egar[90] lookes, and browes that threat:
Traytor saith she; i'st thou that in this wise
To braue thy Lord and king art made so great?
And haue mine eies done vnto me this wrong
To looke on thee? for this staid I so long?

77

O haue they grac'd a periur'd rebell so?
Well for their error I will weepe them out,

[89] *as* STC 6245]; *was* STC 6244.

[90] sharp, severe.

And hate the tongue defilde that praisde my fo,
And loath the minde that gaue me not to doubt:
O haue I added shame vnto my woe?
Ile looke no more; *Ladies* looke you about,
And tell me if my Lord bee in this traine,
Least my betraying eies should erre againe.

78

And in this passion turnes her selfe away:
The rest looke all, and carefull note each wight;[91]
Whilst she impatient of the least delay
Demaunds againe, and what not yet in sight?
Where is my Lord? what gone some other way?
I muse at this, O God graunt all go right.
Then to the window goes againe at last
And sees the chiefest traine of all was past.

79

And sees not him her soule desir'd to see,
And yet hope spent makes her not leaue to looke,
At last her loue-quicke eies which ready be,
Fastens on one whom though she neuer tooke
Could be her Lord: yet that sad cheere[92] which he
Then shew'd, his habit and his wofull looke,
The grace he doth in base attire retaine,
Causd her she could not from his sight refraine.

80

What might he be she said that thus alone
Rides pensiue in this vniuersall ioy:
Some I perceiue as well as we do mone,
All are not pleasd with euery thing this day,
It maie be he laments the wronge is done
Vnto my Lord, and grieues as well he may,
Then he is some of ours, and we of right
Must pitty him, that pitties our sad plight.

81

But stay, ist not my Lord himselfe I see?
In truth if twere not for his base araie,
I verily should thinke that it were he;
And yet his basenes doth a grace bewray:[93]
Yet God forbid, let me deceiued be;
O be it not my Lord although it may:
And let desire make vowes against desire,
And let my sight approue my sight a liar.

---

[91] person.
[92] countenance.
[93] reveal.

82

Let me not see him, but himselfe, a king;
For so he left me, so he did remoue:
This is not he, this feeles some other thing,
A passion of dislike or else of loue:
O yes tis he, that princely face doth bring
The euidence of maiestie to proue:
That face I haue conferr'd[94] which now I see
With that within my hart, and they agree.

83

Thus as shee stoode assur'd and yet in doubt,
Wishing to see, what seene she grieud to see,
Hauing beliefe, yet faine would be without;
Knowing, yet striuing not to know twas he:
Her hart relenting, yet her hart so stout
As would not yeeld to thinke what was, could be:
Till quite condemnd by open proofe of sight
She must confesse or else denie the light.

84

For whether loue in him did sympathize
Or chance so wrought to manifest her doubt,
Euen iust before, where she thus secret prize,[95]
He staies[96] and with cleare[97] face lookes all about:
When she: tis o too true, I know his eies
Alas it is my owne deare Lord, cries out:
And with that crie sinkes downe vpon the flore,
Abundant griefe lackt words to vtter more.

85

Sorrow keepes full possession in her soule,
Lockes him within, laies vp the key of breath,
Raignes all alone a *Lord* without controule[98]
So long till greater horror threatneth:
And euen in daunger brought, to loose the whole
H'is forst come forth or else to stay with death,
Opens a sigh and lets in sence againe,
And sence at length giues words leaue to complaine.

86

Then like a torrent had beene stopt before,
Teares, sighes, and words, doubled togither flow,
Confusdly striuing whether[99] should do more,
The true intelligence of[1] griefe to show:

[94] compared.
[95] pries.
[96] stops.
[97] serene.
[98] restraint.
[99] which.
[1] information about.

Sighes hindred words, words perisht in their store,
Both intermixt in one together grow:
One would do all, the other more then's[2] part
Being both sent equall agents from the hart.

87

At length when past the first of sorrowes worst,
When calm'd confusion better forme affords
Her heart commands her words should pass[3] out first,
And then her sighes should interpoint[4] her words;
The whiles her eies out into teares should burst,
This order with her sorrow she accords,
Which orderles all forme of order brake,
So then began her words and thus she spake.

88

O dost thou thus returne againe to mee?
Are these the triumphs for thy victories?
Is this the glory thou dost bring with thee,
From that vnhappie Irish enterprise?[5]
O haue I made so many vowes to see
Thy safe returne, and see thee in this wise?
Is this the lookt for comfort thou dost bring,
To come a captiue that wentst out a king?

89

And yet deare Lord though thy vngratefull Land
Hath left thee thus, yet I will take thy part,
I doo remaine the same vnder thy hand,
Thou still dost rule the kingdome of my hart;
If all be lost, that gouernment doth stand
And that shall neuer from thy rule depart:
And so thou bee, I care now how thou be,
Let greatnes goe, so it goe without thee.

90

And welcome come, how so vnfortunate,
I will applaud what others do dispise,
I loue thee for thy selfe not for thy state,[6]
More then thy selfe is what without thee, lies:
Let that more goe, if it be in thy fate,
And hauing but thy selfe it will suffize:
I married was not to thy crowne but thee,
And thou without a crowne all one to mee.

---

2 than his.
3 *pass*] *past* STC 6244.
4 punctuate.
5 His military campaign in Ireland.
6 rank, majesty.

91

But what doe I heere lurking idlie mone
And waile apart, and in a single part
Make seuerall[7] griefe which should be both in one,
The touch[8] being equall of each others hart?
Ah no sweet Lord thou must not mone alone,
For without me thou art not all thou art,
Nor my teares without thine are fullie teares,
For thus vnioyn'd, sorrow but halfe appeares.

92

Ioine then our plaints and make our griefe ful griefe,
Our state being one, o lets not part our care,
Sorrow hath only this poore bare reliefe,
To be bemon'd of such as wofull are:
O should I rob thy griefe and be the thiefe
To steale a priuate part, and seuerall share,
Defrauding sorrow of her perfect due?
No no my Lord I come to helpe thee rue.

93

Then forth she goes a close concealed way
As grieuing to be seene not as she was;
Labors t'attaine his presence all shee maie,
Which with most hard a doe was brought to passe:
For that night vnderstanding where he laie
With earnest treating she procur'd her passe
To come to him. Rigor could not deny
Those teares, so poore a suite or put her by.

94

Entring the chamber where he was alone
As one whose former fortune was his shame,
Loathing th'obraiding[9] eie of anie one
That knew him once and knowes him not the same:
When hauing giuen expresse commaund that none
Should presse to him, yet hearing some that came
Turnes angerly about his grieued eies;
When lo his sweete afflicted Queene he spies.

95

Straight cleeres his brow and with a borrowed smile
What my deare Queene, o welcome deare he saies?
And striuing his owne passion to beguile
And hide the sorrow which his eie betraies,
Could speake no more but wrings her hands the while,

[7] separate.

[8] emotion.

[9] upbraiding.

And then (sweet lady) and againe he staies:
Th' excesse of ioy and sorrow both affords
Affliction none, or but poore niggard words.

96

Shee that was come with a resolued hart
And with a mouth full stoor'd, with words wel chose,
Thinking this comfort will I first impart
Vnto my Lord, and thus my speach dispose:
Then thus ile say, thus looke, and with this art
Hide mine owne sorrow to relieue his woes,
When being come all this prou'd nought but winde,
Teares, lookes, and sighes doe only tell her minde.

97

Thus both stood silent and confused so,
Their eies relating how their harts did morne
Both bigge with sorrow, and both great with woe
In labour with what was not to be borne:
This mightie burthen wherewithall they goe
Dies vndeliuered, perishes vnborne;
Sorrow makes silence her best oratore
Where words may make it lesse not shew it more.

98

But he whom longer time had learn'd the art
T'indure affliction as a vsuall touch:
Straines forth his wordes, and throwes dismay apart
To raise vp her, whose passions now were such
As quite opprest her ouerchardged hart,
Too small a vessell to containe so much,
And cheeres[10] and mones, and fained hopes doth frame
As if himselfe belieu'd, or hop'd the same.

TO THE RIGHT WORTHIE AND IUDICIOUS FAUOURER OF VERTUE, MAISTER FULKE GREUILL[11]

I do not here vpon this hum'rous Stage,
Bring my transformed verse apparailed
With others passions, or with others rage;
With loues, with wounds, with factions furnished:
But here present thee, onelie modelled
In this poore frame, the forme of mine owne heart:
Here to reuiue my selfe my Muse is lead
With motions of her owne, t'act her owne part
Striuing to make, her nowe contemned arte

[10] cheering words.

[11] The dedication of *Musophilus: Containing a generall defence of learning*, from *The poeticall essayes of Sam. Danyel. Newly corrected and augmented*, 1599, STC 6261, New York Public Library, Berg Collection.

As faire t'her selfe as possiblie she can;
Least seeming of no force, of no desart
She might repent the course that she began,
And, with these times of dissolution, fall
From goodnes, vertue, glorie, fame and all.

From MUSOPHILUS

Philocosmvs.

Fond[12] man *Musophilus,* that thus dost spend
In an vngainefull arte thy deerest daies,
Tyring thy wits and toiling to no end,
But to attaine that idle smoake of praise;
Now when this busie world cannot attend
Th'vntimely musicke of neglected layes.
Other delights then these, other desires
This wiser profit-seeking age requires.

Musophilus.

Friend *Philocosmus,* I confesse indeed,
I loue this sacred arte thou sett'st so light,
And though it neuer stand my life in steed,
It is inough, it giues my selfe delight,
The whiles my vnafflicted minde doth feed
On no vnholy thoughts for benefit.
Be it that my vnseasonable song
Come out of time, that fault is in the time,
And I must not do vertue so much wrong
As loue her ought the worse for others crime;
And yet I find some blessed spirits among,
That cherish me, and like and grace my rime.
Againe[13] that I do more in soule esteeme
Then al the gain of dust, the world doth craue;
And if I may attaine but to redeeme
My name from dissolution and the graue,
I shall haue done enough, and better deeme
T'haue liu'd to be, then to haue dyde to haue.
Short-breath'd mortalitie would yet extend
That span of life so far forth as it may,
And rob her fate, seeke to beguile her end
Of some few lingring daies of after staie,
That all this little All, might not descend
Into the darke a vniuersall pray.
And giue our labors yet this poore delight,
That when our daies do end they are not done;
And though we die we shall not perish quite,
But liue two liues where other haue but one.

Philocosmus.

Sillie desires of selfe-abusing[14] man,
Striuing to gaine th'inheritance of ayre

[12] foolish.

[13] *A gaine* STC 6240]; *Againe* STC 6261.

[14] self-deceiving.

That hauing done the vttermost he can
Leaues yet perhaps but beggerie to his heir;
Al that great purchase[15] of the breath he wan,
Feeds not his race, or makes his house more faire.
And what art thou the better thus to leaue
A multitude of words to small effect,
Which other times may scorn and so deceiue
Thy promis'd name of what thou dost expect,
Besides some viperous Creticke may bereaue[16]
Th'opinion of thy worth for some defect,
And get more reputation of his wit
By but controlling[17] of some word or sence,
Then thou shalt honor for contriuing it,
With all thy trauell,[18] care and diligence;
Being learning now enough to contradict
And censure others with bold insolence.
Besides so many so confusedlie sing,
Whose diuers discords haue the musick mar'd,
And in contempt that mysterie[19] doth bring,
That he must sing alowd that will be heard;
And the receiu'd opinion of the thing,
For some vnhallowed strings that vildly iar'd,[20]
Hath so vnseason'd[21] now the eares of men,
That who doth touch the tenor of that vaine
Is held but vaine, and his vnreck'ned[22] pen
The title but of leuitie doth gaine.
A poore light gaine to recompence their toile,
That thought to get eternitie the while.
And therefore leaue the left and out-worne course
Of vnregarded wayes, and labour how
To fit the times with what is most in force,
Be new with mens affections that are now;
Striue not to run an idle counter-course
Out from the sent of humours, men allow.
For not discreetly to compose our parts
Vnto the frame of men (which we must be)
Is to put off our selues, and make our artes
Rebles to Nature and societie,
Whereby we come to burie our desarts,
In th'obscure graue of singularitie.

Musophilus.

Do not profane the worke of doing well,
Seduced man, that canst not looke so hie
From out that mist of earth as thou canst tell
The wayes of right, which vertue doth descrie,
That ouer-lookes the base, contemptible,
And low-laid follies of mortalitie:
Nor meate out truth and right-deseruing prayse,
By that wrong measure of confusion

[15] acquisition.
[16] impair, spoil.
[17] censuring.
[18] labor.
[19] art, craft.
[20] were vilely discordant.
[21] displeased.
[22] unvalued.

The vulgar foote: that neuer takes his wayes
By reason, but by imitation;
Rowling[23] on with the rest, and neuer way's
The course which he should go, but what is gone.
Well were it with mankind, if what the most
Did like were best, but ignorance will liue
By others square,[24] as by example lost;
And man to man must th'hand of errour giue
That none can fall alone at their owne cost,
And all because men iudge not, but beleeue.
For what poore bounds haue they whom but th'earth bounds,
What is their end whereto their care attaines,
When the thing got relieues not, but confounds
Hauing but trauaile to succeed their paines?
What ioy hath he of liuing that propounds
Affliction but his end, and griefe his gaines?
Gath'ring, incroching, wresting, ioining to,
Destroying, building, decking, furnishing,
Repairing, altring, and so much a do
To his soules toile, and bodies trauailing:
And all this doth he little knowing who
Fortune ordaines to haue th'inheriting.
And his faire house rais'd hie in enuies eie,
Whose pillars rear'd perhaps on blood and wrong
The spoyles and pillage of Iniquitie,
Who can assure it to continue long?
If rage spar'd not the walls of pietie,
Shal the profanest piles[25] of sinne keepe strong?
How manie proude aspiring pallaces
Haue we known made the pray of wrath and pride,
Leuell'd with th'earth, left to forgetfulnes,
Whilest titlers[26] their pretended[27] rights decide,
Or ciuill tumults, or an orderles
Order pretending change of some strong side?
Then where is that proude title of thy name,
Written in yce of melting vanitie?
Where is thine heire left to possesse the same?
Perhaps not so well as in beggerie.
Some thing may rise to be beyond the shame
Of vile and vnregarded pouertie.
Which, I confesse, although I often striue
To cloth in the best habit of my skill,
In all the fairest colours I can giue;
Yet for all that me thinks she lookes but ill,
I cannot brooke that face, which dead-aliue
Shewes a quicke bodie, but a buried will.
Yet oft we see the barres of this restraint
Holds goodnes in, which loose wealth would let flie,
And fruitlesse riches barrayner then want,
Brings forth small worth from idle libertie:[28]

---

[23] rolling.
[24] rule.
[25] strongholds.
[26] Those who claim or assert a legal title.
[27] claimed.
[28] *libertie:*] *libertie?* STC 6261.

Which when disorders shal againe make scant,
It must refetch her state from pouertie.
But yet in all this interchange of all,
Virtue we see, with her faire grace, stands fast;
For what hy races hath there come to fall,
With low disgrace, quite vanished and past,
Since *Chaucer* liu'd who yet liues and yet shall,
Though (which I grieue to say) but in his last.[29]
Yet what a time hath he wrested from time,
And won vpon the mighty waste of daies,
Vnto th'immortall honor of our clime,
That by his meanes came first adorn'd with Baies,
Vnto the sacred Relicks of whose rime
We yet are bound in zeale to offer praise?
And could our lines begotten in this age
Obtaine but such a blessed hand[30] of yeeres,
And scape the fury of that threatning rage,
Which in confused clowdes gastly appeares,
Who would not straine his trauailes to ingage,
When such true glory should succeed his cares?
But whereas he came planted in the spring,
And had the Sun, before him, of respect;
We set in th'Autumne, in the withering,
And sullen season of a cold defect,[31]
Must taste those soure distastes the times do bring,
Vpon the fulnesse of a cloid[32] neglect,
Although the stronger constitutions shall
Weare out th' infection of distempred daies,
And come with glory to out-liue this fall,
Recouring[33] of another spring of praise,
Cleer'd from th' oppressing humors, wherewithall
The idle multitude surcharge their laies.
When as perhaps the words thou scornest now
May liue, the speaking picture of the mind,
The extract of the soule that laboured how
To leaue the image of her selfe behind,
Wherein posteritie that loue to know
The iust proportion of our spirits may find.
For these lines are the vaines, the Arteries,
And vndecaying life-strings of those harts
That still shall pant, and still shall exercise
The motion spirit and nature both imparts,
And shall, with those aliue so sympathize
As nourisht with their powers inioy their parts.
O blessed letters that combine in one
All ages past, and make one liue with all,
By you we do confer with who are gone,
And the dead liuing vnto councell call:
By you th'vnborne shall haue communion
Of what we feele, and what doth vs befall.

---

[29] *last.*] *last* STC 6261.
[30] measure.
[31] deficiency.
[32] burdened, surfeited.
[33] recovering.

Soule of the world, knowledge, without thee,
  What hath the earth that truly glorious is?
  Why should our pride make such a stir to be,
  To be forgot? what good is like to this,
  To do worthy the writing, and to write
  Worthy the reading, and the worlds delight?
And let th' vnnaturall and waiward race
  Borne of one wombe with vs, but to our shame,[34]
  That neuer read t'obserue but to disgrace,
  Raise all the tempest of their powre to blame;
  That puffe of follie neuer can deface,
  The worke a happy *Genius* tooke to frame.
Yet why should ciuill learning seeke to wound
  And mangle her own members with despight?
  Prodigious wits that study to confound
  The life of wit, to seeme to know aright,
  As if themselues had fortunately found
  Some stand from of the earth beyond our sight,
  Whence ouerlooking all as from aboue,
  Their grace is not to worke, but to reproue.
But how came they plac'd in so high degree
  Aboue the reach and compasse of the rest?
  Who hath admitted them onely to be
  Free-denizons[35] of skill, to iudge the best?
  From whom the world as yet could neuer see
  The warrant of their wit soundly exprest.
T'acquaint our times with that perfection
  Of high conceipt, which only they possesse,
  That we might haue things exquisitely done
  Measur'd with all their strict obseruances:
  Such would (I know) skorne a translation,
  Or bring but others labors to the presse;
  Yet oft these monster-breeding mountains wil
  Bring forth small Mice of great expected skill.
Presumption euer fullest of defects,
  Failes in the doing to performe her part;
  And I haue known proud words and poore effects,
  Of such indeed as do condemne this Arte:
  But let them rest, it euer hath beene knowne,
  They others vertues skorn, that doubt their owne:
And for the diuers disagreeing cordes,
  Of interiangling ignorance that fill
  The dainty eares, and leaue no roome for words,
  The worthier mindes neglect, or pardon will;
  Knowing the best he hath, he frankly[36] foords[37]
  And skornes to be a niggard of his skill.
And that the rather since this short-liu'd race,
  Being fatallie the sonnes but of one day,
  That now with all their powre ply it apace,
  To hold out with the greatest might they may
  Against confusion that hath all in chace,
  To make of all a vniuersall pray.

[34] *shame,*] *shame* STC 6261.
[35] those privileged to judge.
[36] generously.
[37] affords, supplies.

For now great *Nature* hath laid down at last
That mighty birth, wherewith so long she went
And ouerwent the times of ages past,
Here to lie in, vpon our soft content,
Where fruitfull she, hath multiplied so fast,
That all she hath on these times, seem'd t'haue spent.
All that which might haue many ages grac'd,
Is borne in one, to make one cloid with all;
Where plenty hath imprest a deepe distast,
Of best and worst, and all in generall:[38]
That goodnes seems, goodnes to haue defac't,
And virtue hath to virtue giuen the fall.
For emulation, that proud nurse of wit,
Skorning to stay below or come behind,
Labors vpon that narrow top to sit
Of sole perfection in the highest kind;
Enuie and wonder looking after it,
Thrust likewise on the selfe same blisse to find:
And so long striuing till they can no more,
Do stuffe the place or others hopes shut out,
Who doubting to ouertake those gone before
Giue vp their care, and cast no more about;
And so in skorne leaue al as fore-possest,
And will be none where they may not be best.
Euen like some empty Creek that long hath lain,
Left or neglected of the Riuer by,
Whose searching sides pleas'd with a wandring vaine,
Finding some little way that close did lie,
Steale in at first, then other streames againe
Second the first, then more then all supplie,
Till all the mighty maine hath borne at last
The glory of his chiefest powre that way,
Plying this new-found pleasant roome so fast
Till all be full, and all be at a staie;
And then about, and backe againe doth cast,
Leauing that full to fall another way:
So feares[39] this humorous[40] world, that euermore
Rapt with the Current of a present course,
Runs into that which laie contemnd before;
Then glutted leaues the same, and fals t'a worse:
Now zeale holds all, no life but to adore;
Then cold in spirit, and faith is of no force.
Straight all that holie was vnhallowed lies,
The scattered carcasses of ruind vowes:
Then truth is false, and now hath blindnes eies,
Then zeale trusts al, now scarcely what it knows:
That euermore to follish or to wise,
It fatall is to be seduc'd with showes.
Sacred *Religion,* mother of forme and feare,
How gorgeously somtimes dost thou sit deckt?
What pompous vestures do we make thee weare?
What stately piles we prodigall erect?

[38] *in generall:*] *ingenerall:* STC 6261.
[39] fares.
[40] changeable.

How sweet perfum'd thou art, how shining cleare?
How solemnly obseru'd, with what respect?
Another time all plaine, and quite threed bare,
Thou must haue all within and nought without,
Sit poorely without light, disrob'd, no care
Of outward grace, to amuze[41] the poore deuout,
Powrelesse vnfollowed, scarcely men can spare
Thee necessary rites to set thee out.
Either truth, goodnes, vertue are not still[42]
The selfe same which they are, and alwaies one,
But alter to the proiect of our will,
Or we our actions make them waite vpon,[43]
Putting them in the liuery of our skill,
And cast them off againe when we haue done.
You mighty Lords, that with respected grace
Do at the sterne of faire example stand,
And all the body of this populace
Guide with the onely turning of your hand,
Keepe a right course, bear vp from al disgrace,
Obserue the point of glory to our land:
Hold vp disgraced knowledge from the ground,
Keepe vertue in request, giue worth her due,
Let not neglect with barbarous means confound
So faire a good to bring in night anew.
Be not, o be not accessary found
Vnto her death that must giue life to you.
Where wil you haue your vertuous names safe laid,
In gorgeous tombes, in sacred Cels secure?
Do you not see those prostrate heapes betraid
Your fathers bones, and could not keepe them sure?
And will you trust deceitfull stones faire laid:
And thinke they will be to your honor truer?
No, no, vnsparing time will proudly send
A warrant vnto wrath that with one frown
Wil al these mock'ries of vaine glory rend,
And make them as before, vngrac'd, vnknown,
Poore idle honors that can ill defend
Your memories, that cannot keepe their own.
And whereto serue that wondrous *trophei*[44] now,
That on the goodly plaine neare *Wilton* stands?
That huge domb heap, that cannot tel vs how,
Nor what, nor whence it is, nor with whose hands,
Nor for whose glory, it was set to shew
How much our pride mockes that of other lands?
Whereon when as the gazing passenger[45]
Hath greedy lookt with admiration,[46]
And faine would know his birth, and what he were,
How there erected, and how long agone:
Enquires and askes his fellow trauailer
What he hath heard and his opinion:
And he knowes nothing. Then he turnes againe

[41] cause to muse.
[42] always.
[43] *vpon,*] *vpon* STC 6261.
[44] Stonehenge, on Salisbury Plain.
[45] passer-by.
[46] wonder.

And looks and sighs, and then admires afresh,
And in himselfe with sorrow doth complaine
The misery of darke forgetfulnesse;
Angrie with time that nothing should remain,
Our greatest wonders-wonder to expresse.
Then ignorance with fabulous discourse
Robbing faire arte and cunning of their right,
Tels how these stones were by the diuels force
From Affricke brought to Ireland in a night,
And thence to Britannie by Magicke course,
From giants hand redeem'd by *Merlins* sleight.[47]
And then neare *Ambri*[48] plac'd in memorie
Of all those noble Britons murthred there[49]
By *Hengist*[50] and his Saxon trecherie,
Comming to parle in peace at vnaware.
With this old Legend then credulitie
Holdes her content, and closes vp her care:
But is antiquitie so great a liar,
Or, do her yonger sonnes her age abuse,
Seeing after commers still so apt t'admire
The graue authoritie that she doth vse,
That reuerence and respect dares not require
Proofe of her deeds, or once her words refuse?
Yet wrong they did vs to presume so far
Vpon our easie credit and delight:
For once found false they straight became[51] to mar
Our faith, and their owne reputation quite:
That now her truths hardly beleeued are,
And though sh'auouch the right, she scarce hath right.
And as for thee, thou huge and mightie frame
That stands corrupted so with times despight,
And giu'st false euidence against their fame
That set thee there to testifie their right:
And art become a traitor to their name
That trusted thee with all the best they might;
Thou shalt stand still belide and slandered,
The onely gazing stocke of ignorance,
And by thy guile the wise admonished
Shal neuer more desire such heapes t'aduance,[52]
Nor trust their liuing glorie with the dead
That cannot speak, but leaue their fame to chance;
Considering in how small a roome do lie
And yet lie safe, as fresh as if aliue
All those great worthies of antiquitie,
Which long foreliu'd thee, and shal long suruiue,
Who stronger tombs found for eternitie,
Then could the powres of al the earth contriue.
Where they remaine these trifles to obraid[53]
Out of the reach of spoile, and way of rage,
Though time with all his power of yeares hath laid

[47] cunning.
[48] Mt. Ambrius, near Salisbury.
[49] The story is told by Nennius, *Historia Britonum*.
[50] leader of the Jutes (d. 488).
[51] came.
[52] raise.
[53] upbraid, reproach.

Long batterie, back'd with vndermining age,
Yet they make head onely with their own aide
And war, with his all conquering forces, wage.
Pleading the heauens prescription[54] to be free
And t'haue a grant t'indure as long as he.

Philocosmus.

Beholde how euery man drawne with delight
Of what he doth, flatters him in his way;
Striuing to make his course seeme onely right
Doth his owne rest, and his owne thoughts betray;
Imagination bringing brauely dight[55]
Her pleasing images in best aray,
With flattering glasses that must shew him faire
And others foule; his skill and his wit best,
Others seduc'd, deceiu'd and wrong in their;
His knowledge right, all ignorant the rest,
Not seeing how these minions[56] in the aire
Present a face of things falsely exprest,
And that the glimmering of these errors showne,
Are but a light to let him see his owne.
Alas poore Fame, in what a narrow roome
As an incaged Parrot, art thou pent
Here amongst vs; where euen as good be domb
As speake, and to be heard with no attent?
How can you promise of the time to come
When as the present are so negligent?
Is this the walke[57] of all your wide renowne,
This little point, this scarce discerned Ile,
Thrust from the world, with whom our speech vnknown
Made neuer any traffike of our stile.
And is this all where all this care is showne,
T'inchant your fame to last so long a while?
And for that happier tongues haue woon so much
Think you to make your barbarous language such?
Poore narrow limits for so mightie paines,
That cannot promise any forraine vent:
And yet if here to all your wondrous vaines
Were generally knowne, it might content:
But lo how many reads not, or disdaines
The labors of the chiefe and excellent.
How many thousands neuer heard the name
Of *Sydney*, or of *Spencer*, or their bookes?
And yet braue fellowes, and presume of fame
And seem to beare downe all the world with lookes:
What then shall they expect of meaner frame,
On whose indeuours few or none scarse looks?
Do you not see these *Pamphlets, Libels, Rymes,*
These strange confused tumults of the minde,
Are growne to be the sicknes of these times,

[54] right, title (a legal term).
[55] splendidly adorned.
[56] the *pleasing images* in the fifth line preceding.
[57] limited area.

The great disease inflicted on mankind?
Your vertues, by your follies, made your crimes,
Haue issue with your indiscretion ioin'd.[58]
Schooles, arts, professions, all in so great store,
Passe the proportion of the present state,
Where being as great a number as before,
And fewer roomes them to accommodate;
It cannot be but they must throng the more,
And kicke, and thrust, and shoulder with debate.
For when the greater wittes cannot attaine
Th'expected good, which they account their right,
And yet perceiue others to reape that gaine
Of far inferiour vertues in their sight;
They present with the sharpe of *Enuie* straine
To wound them with reproches and despight:
And for these[59] cannot haue as well as they,[60]
They scorne their faith should daigne to looke that way.
Hence discontented Sects, and Schismes arise,
Hence interwounding controuersies spring,
That feed the simple, and offend the wise,
Who know the consequence of cauilling:
Disgrace that these to others do deuise,
Contempt and scorne on all in th'end doth bring
Like scolding wiues reckning each others fault
Make standers by imagin both are naught.
For when to these rare dainties time admits,
All commers, all Complexions,[61] all that will,
Where none should be let in, but choisest wits,
Whose milde discretion could comport with skill,
For when the place their humor neither fits,
Nor they the place: who can expect but ill?
For being vnapt for what they tooke in hand,
And for ought else whereto they shal b'addrest
They euen become th'incombrance of the land
As out of ranke disordring all the rest:
This grace of theirs to seeme to vnderstand,
Marres all their grace to do, without their rest.
Men find that action is another thing
Then what they in discoursing papers reade,
The worlds affaires require in managing
More arts then those wherin you Clearks proceed,
Whilst timorous knowledge stands considering,
Audacious ignorance hath done the deed.
For who knowes most, the more he knows to doubt,[62]
The least discourse is commonly most stout.[63]
This sweet inchaunting knowledge turnes you cleene
Out from the fields of naturall[64] delight,
And makes you hide vnwilling to be seene
In th'open concourse of a publike sight:
This skill wherewith you haue so cunning beene,
Vnsinewes all your powres, vnmans you quite.

[58] *ioin'd.*] *ioin'd* STC 6261.
[59] *these*] *these,* STC 6261.
[60] *they,*] *they* STC 6261.
[61] temperaments.
[62] *doubt,*] *doubt* STC 6261.
[63] strong, sound.
[64] *naturall*] *natur all* STC 6261.

Publike societie and commerce of men
Require another grace, another port:
This eloquence, these rymes, these phrases then
Begot in shades, do serue vs in no sort,
Th'vnmateriall swellings of your pen
Touch not the spirit that action doth import:
A manly stile fitted to manlie eares
Best grees[65] with wit,[66] not that which goes so gay,
And commonly the gaudie liu'rie weares
Of nice[67] corruptions which the times do sway,
And waites on th'humor of his pulse that beares
His passions set to such a pleasing kay;[68]
Such dainties serue onely for stomacks weake,
For men do fowlest when they finest speake.
Yet do I not dislike that in some wise
Be sung the great heroycall deserts
Of braue renowned spirits, whose exercise
Of worthy deedes may call vp others hearts,
And serue a modell for posterities
To fashion them fit for like glorious parts:
But so that all our spirits may tend hereto
To make it not our grace, to say, but do.

Musophilus.

Much thou hast said, and willingly I heare,
As one that am not so possest with loue
Of what I do, but that I rather beare
An eare to learne, then a toong to disproue:
I know men must as caried in their spheare
According to their proper motions moue.
And that course likes[69] them best which they are on,
Yet truth hath certaine bounds, but falshood none.
I do confesse our limits are but small
Compar'd with all the whole vaste earth beside,
All which againe rated to that great All,
Is likewise as a point scarcelie discride;
So that in these respects we may this call
A point but of a point where we abide.
But if we shall descend from that high stand
Of ouer-looking Contemplation,
And cast our thoughts but to, and not beyond
This spatious circuit which we tread vpon,
We then may estimate our mightie land
A world within a world standing alone.
Where if our fame confind cannot get out,
What,[70] shall we then imagine it is pen'd
That hath so great a world to walke about,
Whose bounds with her reports haue both one end:
Why shall we not rather esteeme her stout
That farther then her owne scorne to extend?
Where being so large a roome both to do well

[65] agrees.
[66] sound sense, wisdom.
[67] subtle.
[68] key.
[69] pleases.
[70] *What,*] *What* STC 6261.

And eke to heare th'applause of things well done,
That farther if men shall our vertues tell
We haue more mouthes, but not more merit won,
It doth not greater make that which is laudable,
The flame is bigger blowne, the fire all one.
And for the few that onely lend their eare,
That few is all the world, which with a few
Doth euer liue, and moue, and worke and stirre,
This is the heart doth feele, and onely know
The rest of all, that onely bodies beare
Rowle vp and downe, and fill but vp the row.
And serue as others members not their own,
The instruments of those that do direct.
Then what disgrace is this not to be known
To those know not to giue themselues respect?
And thogh they swel with pomp of folly blown,
They liue vngrac'd, and die but in neglect.
And for my part if onely one allow
The care my labouring spirits take in this,
He is to me a Theater large ynow,
And his applause only sufficient is:
All my respect is bent but to his brow,
That is my all, and all I am is his.
And if some worthy spirits be pleased to,
It shall more comfort breed, but not more will;
But what if none; it cannot yet vndo
The loue I beare vnto this holy skill:
This is the thing that I was borne to do,
This is my Scene, this part must I fulfill.[71]

. . . .

Powre aboue powres, O heauenly *Eloquence,*
That with the strong reine of commanding words,
Dost manage, guide, and master th'eminence
Of mens affections, more then all their swords:
Shall we not offer to thy excellence
The richest treasure that our wit affoords?
Thou that canst do much more with one poor pen
Then all the powres of princes can effect:
And draw, diuert, dispose, and fashion men
Better then force or rigour can direct:
Should we this ornament of glorie then
As th'vnmateriall fruits of shades, neglect?
Or should we carelesse come behind the rest
In powre of wordes, that go before in worth,
When as our accents equall to the best
Is able greater wonders to bring forth:
When all that euer hotter spirits exprest
Comes bettered by the patience of the North?
And who in time knowes whither we may vent
The treasure of our tongue, to what strange shores
This gaine of our best glorie shal be sent,

[71] The next 363 lines are omitted. Musophilus continues; Philocosmus does not speak again.

T'inrich vnknowing Nations with our stores?
What worlds in th'yet vnformed Occident
May come refin'd with th'accents that are ours?
Or who can tell for what great worke in hand
The greatnes of our stile is now ordain'd?
What powres it shall bring in, what spirits command,
What thoughts let out, what humors keep restrain'd,[72]
What mischiefe it may powrefully withstand,
And what faire ends may thereby be attain'd.
And as for Poesie (mother of this force)
That breeds, brings forth, and nourishes this might,
Teaching it in a loose, yet measured course,
With comely motions how to go vpright:
And fostring it with bountifull discourse
Adorns it thus in fashions of delight,
What should I say? since it is well approu'd
That speech of heauen, with whom they haue commerce
That only seeme out of themselues remou'd,
And do with more then humane skils conuerse:
Those numbers wherewith heauen and earth are mou'd,
Shew, weakenes speaks in prose, but powre in verse.
Wherein thou likewise seemest to allow
That th'acts of worthy men shuld be preseru'd;
As in the holiest tombes we can bestow
Vpon their glory that haue well deseru'd,
Wherein thou dost no other virtue show
Then what most barbrous countries haue obseru'd:
When all the happiest nations hitherto
Did with no lesser glory speake then do.
Now to what else thy malice shall obiect,
For schooles, and Arts, and their necessitie:
When from my Lord, whose iudgement must direct
And forme, and fashion my abilitie
I shall haue got more strength: thou shalt expect
Out of my better leasure, my reply.
And if herein the curious sort shall deeme
My will was caried far beyond my force,
And that it is a thing doth ill beseeme
The function of a *Poem,* to discourse:
Thy learned iudgement which I most esteeme
(Worthy *Fulke Greuil*)[73] must defend this course.
By whose mild grace, and gentle hand at first
My Infant Muse was brought in open sight
From out the darkenesse wherein it was nurst,
And made to be partaker of the light;
Which peraduenture neuer else had durst
T'appeare in place, but had beene smothered quite.
And now herein incourag'd by thy praise,
Is made so bold and ventrous to attempt
Beyond example, and to trie those waies,
That malice from our forces thinkes exempt:
To see if we our wronged lines could raise
Aboue the reach of lightnesse and contempt.

[72] *restrain'd,*] *restrain'd* STC 6261.

[73] The poem is dedicated to Fulke Greville.

TO THE LADY MARGARET COVNTESSE OF CVMBERLAND[74]

He that of such a height hath built his minde,
And rear'd the dwelling of his thoughts so strong
As neither Feare nor Hope can shake the frame
Of his resolued powres, nor al the winde
Of Vanitie or Malice, pierce to wrong
His setled peace, or to disturbe the same,
What a faire seate hath he from whence hee may
The boundlesse wastes, and weilds[75] of man suruay.

And with how free an eye doth he looke downe,
Vpon these lower Regions of turmoyle,
Where all these stormes of passions mainely[76] beate
On flesh and blood, where honor, power, renowne
Are onely gay afflictions, golden toyle,
Where Greatnesse stands vpon as feeble feete
As Frailtie doth, and only great doth seeme
To little mindes, who do it so esteeme.

He lookes vpon the mightiest Monarchs warres
But onely as on stately robberies,
Where euermore the fortune that preuailes
Must be the right, the ill-succeeding marres
The fairest and the best-fac't enterprize:
Great Pyrat *Pompey* lesser Pyrates quailes,
Iustice, he sees, as if seduced, still
Conspires with powre, whose cause must not be ill.

He sees the face of *Right* t'appeare as manyfold
As are the passions of vncertaine man,
Who puts it in all coulours, all attires
To serue his ends, and make his courses hold:
He sees that let Deceit worke what it can,
Plot and contriue base wayes to high desires,
That the all-guiding Prouidence doth yet
All disappoint, and mockes this smoake of wit.

Nor is he moou'd with all the thunder crackes
Of Tyrants threats, or with the surly brow
Of power, that prowdly sits on others crimes,
Chardg'd with more crying sinnes, then those he checks:
The stormes of sad confusion that may grow
Vp in the present, for the cumming times,
Appall not him, that hath no side at all
But of himselfe, and knowes the worst can fall.[77]

Although his hart so neere allied to earth,
Cannot but pittie the perplexed State

---

[74] From *A panegyrike congratulatorie to the King's Maiestie; also certaine epistles,* 1603, STC 6258, Morgan Library.

[75] wilds.

[76] strongly.

[77] befall.

Of troublous, and distrest mortalitie,
That thus make way vnto the ougly birth
Of their owne sorrowes, and doe still beget
Affliction vpon imbecilitie:
Yet seeing thus the course of things must run,
He lookes thereon, not strange, but as foredun.

And whilst distraught Ambition compasses
And is incompast, whil'st as craft deceiues
And is deceiu'd, whil'st man doth ransack man
And builds on bloud, and rises by distresse,
And th'inheritance of desolation leaues
To great expecting hopes, he lookes thereon
As from the shore of peace with vnwet eye
And beares no venture in impietie.

Thus, Madame, fares the man that hath prepar'd
A rest for his desires, and sees all things
Beneath him, and hath learn't this booke of man,
Full of the notes of frailtie, and compar'd
The best of glory with her sufferings,
By whom I see you labour all you can
To plant your heart, and set your thought as neere
His glorious mansion, as your powres can beare.

Which, Madame, are so soundly fashioned,
By that cleere iudgement that hath caried you
Beyond the feeble limits of your kinde,[78]
As they can stand against the strongest head
Passion can make, invr'd to any hew
The world can cast, that cannot cast that minde
Out of her forme of goodnesse, that doth see
Both what the best and worst of earth can bee.

Which makes, that whatsoeuer here befalles,
You in the region of your selfe remaine,
Where no vaine breath of th'impudent molests,
That hath secur'd within the brasen walls
Of a cleere conscience, that without all staine
Rises in peace, in innocencie rests:
Whilst all what malice from without procures,
Shews her owne ougly heart, but hurts not yours.

And whereas none reioyce more in reuenge
Then women vse to doe, yet you well know,
That wrong is better checkt, by being contemn'd,
Then being pursu'd, leauing to him t'auenge
To whom it appertaines, wherein you show
How worthily your Clearenesse hath condemn'd
Base malediction, liuing in the darke,
That at the raies of goodnesse still doth barke.

---

[78] nature, sex.

Knowing the heart of man is set to be
The centre of his world, about the which
These reuolutions of disturbances
Still roule, where all th'aspects of miserie
Predominate, whose strong effects are such
As he must beare, being powrelesse to redresse,
And that vnlesse aboue himselfe he can
Erect himselfe, how poore a thing is man?[79]

And how turmoyld they are that leuell lie
With earth, and cannot lift themselues from thence,
That neuer are at peace with their desires,
But worke beyond their yeares, and euen deny
Dotage her rest, and hardly will dispence
With Death: that when ability expires,
Desire liues still, so much delight they haue
To carry toile, and trauaile to the graue.

Whose ends you see, and what can be the best
They reach vnto, when they haue cast the summe
And recknings of their glory, and you know
This floting life hath but this Port of rest,
A heart prepar'd that feares no ill to come:
And that mans greatnesse rests but in his show;
The best of all those dayes consumed are,
Eyther in warre, or peace conceiuing warre.

This Concord (Madame) of a wel-tun'd minde
Hath beene so set by that all-working hand
Of heauen, that though the world hath done his worst,
To put it out, by discords most vnkinde,
Yet doth it still in perfect vnion stand
With God and Man, nor euer will be forc't
From that most sweete accord, but still agree
Equall in Fortunes inequalitie.

And this note (Madame) of your Worthines
Remaines recorded in so many Hearts
As time nor malice cannot wrong your right
In th'inheritance of Fame you must possesse,
You that haue built you by your great desarts,
Out of small meanes, a farre more exquisite
And glorious dwelling for your honoured name
Then all the gold of leaden mindes can frame.

TO THE LADY LVCIE, COVNTESSE OF BEDFORD[80]

Though virtue be the same when low she stands
  In th'humble shadowes of obscuritie
  As when she either sweats in martiall bands,
Or sits in Court, clad with authoritie:

[79] Wordsworth, in *The Excursion* (Book IV, lines 323–331), quotes this stanza and in a note he quotes stanzas 5–8, which, he says, "contain an admirable picture of the state of a wise man's mind in a time of public commotion."

[80] From STC 6258.

Yet Madame, doth the strictnesse[81] of her roome
Greatly detract from her abilitie:
For as inwalld within a liuing tombe
Her handes and armes of action, labour not;
Her thoughts as if abortiue from the wombe,
Come neuer borne, though happily begot.
But there she hath mounted in open sight
An eminent, and spacious dwelling got.
Where shee may stirre at will, and vse her might,
There is she more her selfe, and more her owne:
There in the faire attyre of honour dight,[82]
She sits at ease and makes her glory knowne,
Applause attends her hands, her deedes haue grace,
Her worth new-borne is straight as if ful growne,
With such a goodly and respected face
Doth vertue looke, that's set to looke from hie,
And such a faire aduantage by her place
Hath state and greatnesse to doe worthily.
And therefore well did your high fortunes meete
With her, that gracing you, comes grac't thereby,
And well was let into a house so sweete
So good, so faire; so faire, so good a guest,
Who now remaines as blessed in her seate,
As you are with her residencie blesst.
And this faire course of knowledge whereunto
Your studies, learned Lady, are addrest,
Is th'onely certaine way that you can goe
Vnto true glory, to true happines:
All passages on earth besides, are so
Incumbred with such vaine disturbances,
As still we loose our rest, in seeking it,
Being but deluded with apparances.
And no key had you else that was so fit
T'vnlocke that prison of your Sex, as this,
To let you out of weakenesse, and admit
Your powers into the freedome of that blisse
That sets you there where you may oversee
This rowling world, and view it as it is,
And apprehend how th'outsides do agree
With th'inward being of the things, we deeme
And hold in our ill-cast accounts, to be
Of highest value, and of best esteeme.
Since all the good we haue rests in the mind,
By whose proportions onely we redeeme
Our thoughts from out confusion, and do finde
The measure of our selues, and of our powres.
And that all happinesse remaines confind
Within the Kingdome of this breast of ours.
Without whose bounds, all that we looke on, lies
In others Iurisdictions, others powres,
Out of the circuit of our liberties.

81 narrowness.

82 dressed.

All glory, honor, fame, applause, renowne,
Are not belonging to our royalties,[83]
But t'others wills, wherein th'are onely growne.
And that vnlesse we finde vs all within,
We neuer can without vs be our owne:
Nor call it right our life,[84] that we liue in:[85]
But a possession held for others vse,
That seeme to haue most int'rest therein.
Which we do so disseuer, parte, traduce,
Let out to custome, fashion, and to shew
As we enioy but onely the abuse,
And haue no other Deed at all to shew.
How oft are we constrained to appeare
With other countenance then that we owe,[86]
And be our selues farre off, when we are neere?
How oft are we forc't on a clowdie hart,
To set a shining face, and make it cleere.[87]
Seeming content to put our selues apart,
To beare a part of others weaknesses:
As if we onely were compos'd by Arte,
Not Nature, and did all our deedes addresse
T'opinion, not t'a conscience what is right:
As fram'd b'example, not aduisednesse
Into those formes that intertaine our sight.
And though Bookes, Madame, cannot make this minde,
Which we must bring apt to be set aright,
Yet do they rectifie it in that kinde,
And touch it so, as that it turnes that way
Where iudgement lies: And though we cannot finde
The certaine place of truth, yet doe they stay,
And intertaine vs neere about the same.
And giue the Soule the best delights that may
Encheere it most, and most our spirits inflame
To thoughts of glory, and to worthy ends.
And therefore in a course that best became
The cleerenesse of your heart, and best commends
Your worthy powres, you runne the rightest way
That is on Earth, that can true glory giue,
By which when all consumes, your fame shal liue.

VLISSES AND THE SYREN[88]

Syren. Come worthy Greeke, *Vlisses* come
Possesse these shores with me:
The windes and Seas are troublesome,
And heere we may be free.
Here may we sit, and view their toile
That trauaile in the deepe,
And ioy the day in mirth the while,
And spend the night in sleepe.

[83] rights.
[84] *right our life,* STC 6259]; *right, our life* STC 6258.
[85] *in:*] *in.* STC 6258.
[86] own.
[87] serene.
[88] From *Certaine small poems,* 1605, STC 6239, Morgan Library.

Vlis. Fair Nimph, if fame, or honor were
To be attaynd with ease
Then would I come, and rest me there,[89]
And leaue such toyles as these.
But here it dwels, and here must I
With danger seeke it forth,
To spend the time luxuriously
Becomes not men of worth.

Syr. *Vlisses,* O be not deceiu'd
With that vnreall name:
This honour is a thing conceiu'd,[90]
And rests on others fame.[91]
Begotten onely to molest
Our peace, and to beguile[92]
(The best thing of our life) our rest,
And giue vs vp to toile.

Vlis. Delicious Nimph, suppose there were
Nor honour, nor report,
Yet manlines would scorne to weare
The time in idle sport.
For toyle doth giue a better touch,[93]
To make vs feele our ioy;
And ease findes tediousnesse as much
As labour yeelds annoy.

Syr. Then pleasure likewise seemes the shore,
Whereto tends all your toyle,
Which you forgo to make it more,
And perish oft the while.
Who may disporte them diuersly,
Finde neuer tedious day,
And ease may haue varietie,
As well as action may.

Vlis. But natures of the noblest frame
These toyles, and dangers please,
And they take comfort in the same,
As much as you in ease.
And with the thought of actions past
Are recreated still;
When pleasure leaues a touch at last,
To shew that it was ill.

Sy. That doth opinion onely cause,
That's out of custome bred,
Which makes vs many other lawes
Then euer Nature did.
No widdowes waile for our delights,

---

[89] *me there,* H. C. Beeching]; *with thee,* STC 6239 and other early editions.
[90] imagined.
[91] report.
[92] cheat.
[93] touchstone.

Our sportes are without bloud,
The world we see by warlike wights[94]
Receiues more hurt then good.

Vlis. But yet the state of things require
These motions of vnrest,
And these great Spirits of high desire,
Seeme borne to turne them best.
To purge the mischiefes that increase,
And all good order mar:
For oft we see a wicked peace
To be well chang'd for war.

Sy. Well, well *Vlisses* then I see,
I shall not haue thee heere,
And therefore I will come to thee,
And take my fortunes there.
I must be wonne that cannot win,
Yet lost were I not wonne:
For beauty hath created bin,
T'vndoo, or be vndonne.

TO THE READER[95]

Behold once more with serious labor here
Haue I refurnisht out this little frame,[96]
Repaird some parts defectiue here and there,
And passages new added to the same,
Some rooms inlargd, made some les then they were
Like to the curious builder who this yeare
Puls downe, and alters what he did the last,[97]
As if the thing in doing were more deere
Then being done, and nothing likes thats past,[98]

For that we euer make the latter day
The scholler of the former, and we find
Something is still amisse that must delay
Our busines, and leaue worke for vs behinde,[99]
As if there were no saboath of the minde.[1]
And howsoeuer be it well or ill
What I haue done, it is mine owne;[2] I may
Do whatsoeuer therewithall I will.[3]

I may pull downe, raise, and reedifie;[4]
It is the building of my life,[5] the fee
Of Nature, all th'inheritance that I
Shal leaue to those which must come after me

---

94 *wights*] *wights.* STC 6239.
95 From *Certaine small workes heretofore divulged by Samuel Daniel . . . and now againe by him corrected and augmented,* 1607, STC 6240, New York Public Library, Berg Collection.
96 structure.
97 *last,*] *last* STC 6240.
98 *past,*] *past* STC 6240.
99 *behinde,*] *behinde.* STC 6240.
1 *minde.*] *minde* STC 6240.
2 *owne;*] *owne* STC 6240.
3 *will.*] *will* STC 6240.
4 *reedifie;*] *reedifie* STC 6240.
5 *life,*] *life* STC 6240.

And all the care I haue is but to see
These lodgings of m'affections neatly drest
Wherein so many noble friends there be
Whose memories with mine must therin rest.[6]

And glad I am that I haue liud to see
This edifice renewd, who doo but long
To liue t'amend. For man is a tree
That hath his fruite late ripe, and it is long
Before he come t'his taste, there doth belong
So much t'experience, and so infinite
The faces of things are, as hardly we
Discerne which lookes the likest vnto right.

Besides these curious times stuf'd with the store
Of compositions in this kind, do driue
Me to examine my defects the more,
And oft would make me not my self belieue
Did I not know the world wherein I liue,
Which neither is so wise, as that would seeme
Nor certaine iudgement of those things doth giue
That it disliks, nor that it doth esteeme.

I know no work from man yet euer came
But had his marke,[7] and by some error shewd
That it was his, and yet what in the same
Was rare, and[8] worthy, euermore allowd
Safe conuoy for the rest: the good thats sow'd
Thogh rarely paies our cost, and who so looks
T'haue all thinges in perfection, and in frame[9]
In mens inuentions, neuer must read books.

And howsoeuer here detraction may
Disvalew this my labour, yet I know
There wilbe found therin, that which wil pay
The reckning for the errors which I owe[10]
And likewise will sufficiently allow
T'an vndistasted iudgement fit delight,[11]
And let presumptuous selfe-opinion say
The worst it can, I know I shall haue right.

I know I shalbe read, among the rest
So long as men speake English,[12] and so long
As verse and vertue shalbe in request
Or grace to honest industry belong:
And England since I vse thy present tongue
Thy forme of speech thou must be my defence
If to new eares, it seemes not well exprest
For though I hold not accent I hold sence.[13]

---

6 *rest.*] *rest* STC 6240.
7 distinguishing characteristic.
8 *and*] *an* STC 6240.
9 perfect order.
10 own.
11 *delight,*] *delight* STC 6240.
12 *English,*] *english* STC 6240.
13 *sence.*] *sence* STC 6240.

And since the measures of our tong we see
Confirmd by no edict of power doth rest
But onely vnderneath the regencie
Of vse and fashion, which may be the best
Is not for my poore forces to contest
But as the Peacock, seeing himselfe to weake
Confest the Eagle fairer farre to be
And yet not in his feathers but his beake.

Authoritie of powerfull censure may
Preiudicate the forme wherein we mould
This matter of our spirite, but if it pay
The eare with substance, we haue what wee wold,[14]
For that is all which must our credit hold.
The rest (how euer gay, or seeming rich
It be in fashion, wise men will not wey)
The stamp will not allow it, but the touch.[15]

And would to God that nothing falty were
But only that poore accent in my verse
Or that I could all other recknings cleere
Wherwith my heart stands charg'd, or might revers
The errors of my iudgment passed here
Or else where, in my bookes, and vnrehearce
What I haue vainely said, or haue addrest
Vnto neglect mistaken in the rest.

Which I do hope to liue yet to retract
And craue that England neuer wil take note
That it was mine. Ile disavow mine act,
And wish it may for euer be forgot.[16]
I trust the world will not of me exact
Against my will, that hath all els I wrote.[17]
I will aske nothing therein for my paine
But onely to haue in mine owne againe.

---

[14] *wold,*] *wold* STC 6240.
[15] *touch.*] *touch* STC 6240: test (of coin).
[16] *forgot.*] *forgot,* STC 6240.
[17] *els I wrote.*] *els, I wrote* STC 6240.

Sir John Davies

[1569–1626]

SIR JOHN DAVIES was born in Wiltshire, was educated at Winchester and Queen's College, Oxford, studied law at the Middle. Temple, and was called to the bar in 1595. In 1594 his *Orchestra* was entered in the Stationers' Registers, but the earliest edition bears the date 1596. He wrote his epigrams probably in the early 1590's. From 1598 until 1601 Davies was disbarred on account of an assault made upon his former friend, Richard Martin. In 1599 he published *Hymns of Astraea* and *Nosce Teipsum.* After he was readmitted to the Middle Temple in 1601, he wrote almost no verse. In 1603 he was knighted and appointed Solicitor General for Ireland; from 1606 to 1619 he was Attorney General for Ireland; in 1626 he was appointed Lord Chief Justice of the King's Bench in England but died before he could take office. His prose *Discovery of the State of Ireland* was printed in 1612 and 1613.

Davies's epigrams are among the earliest and wittiest of those of the period. His *Hymns of Astraea* is a series of twenty-six ingenious acrostic poems in praise of Queen Elizabeth. His fame rests upon *Orchestra* and *Nosce Teipsum.*

Orchestra, or a poeme of dauncing is typically Elizabethan in its fusion of the serious with the fanciful. Davies borrows his characters from the *Odyssey*. The scene is Penelope's palace at Ithaca. Antinous, most courtly of Penelope's suitors, invites her to dance, and upon her refusal they begin a discussion of dancing—and of the organization of the universe.

The medieval conception of a rigidly ordered universe was generally accepted by the Elizabethans. In expressing this view or in alluding to it they usually employed one of three metaphors: (1) a chain linking all created things to God, each in his place, from highest to lowest; (2) a series of planes, one below another, from highest to lowest, but related by many correspondences, with God and the angelic hierarchy as the highest plane, below it the universe or macrocosm, next kings and their subjects of all ranks, next man or the microcosm, next the several planes of beasts and inanimate objects; (3) a dance. Davies chose dancing as the symbol of the measured harmony established by God (creative love) throughout the universe. All created things from the highest to the lowest

—angels, men, beasts, inanimate objects—have like dancers their appointed places, and they move like dancers in ordered rhythm, in accordance with the plan of the Creator. These commonplaces Davies with his ingenuity and exuberant fancy made into a most unusual poem, thoroughly Elizabethan in spirit and expression.

In *Nosce Teipsum* Davies expresses the orthodox Elizabethan view, first, of the vanity and peril of man's desire for scientific knowledge without knowledge of self and of God, and, second, of the nature of the soul and the grounds for belief in immortality. The verse is clear and graceful. Davies uses the difficult pentameter quatrain, with alternate rhyme, the stanza of Gray's *Elegy*.

The most useful modern editions are *The Complete Poems of Sir John Davies*, ed. A. B. Grosart, 2 vols., 1876; *The Poems of Sir John Davies. Reproduced in Facsimile from the First Editions in the Henry E. Huntington Library and Art Gallery*, ed. Clare Howard, 1941; *Orchestra*, ed. E. M. W. Tillyard, 1945. *Silver Poets of the Sixteenth Century*, ed. Gerald Bullett, Everyman's Library, 1947, includes *Orchestra*, *Nosce Teipsum*, and other poems. For biography and criticism see Margarete Seeman, *Sir John Davies, sein Leben und seine Werke*, 1913; E. M. W. Tillyard, *The Elizabethan World Picture*, 1943, and "Sir John Davies, *Orchestra*, 1594," *Five Poems, 1470–1870*, 1948.

From NOSCE TEIPSUM[1]

To my most graciovs dread Soueraigne

To that *cleare Maiestie*, which in the North,
Doth like another Sunne in glorie rise,
Which standeth fixt, yet spreds her heauenly worth,
Loadstone to Hearts, and Loadstarre to all Eyes;

Like Heau'n in all; like th'Earth in this alone,
That though great States[2] by her support do stand,
Yet she her selfe supported is of none,
But by the Finger of th'Almighties hand;

To the diuinest and the richest minde,
Both by Arts purchase,[3] and by Natures Dower,
That euer was from Heauen to Earth confin'd,
To shew the vtmost of a Creatures power;

To that great Spirit, which doth great Kingdomes moue,
The sacred Spring, whence *Right* and *Honor* streames,
Distilling *Vertue*, shedding *peace* and *Loue*,
In euery place, as *Cynthia* sheds her beames;

I offer vp some sparkles of that fire,
Whereby we *reason, liue, and moue, and bee:*

[1] From *Nosce teipsum. This oracle expounded in two elegies. 1. Of humane knowledge. 2. Of the soule of man, and the immortalitie thereof,* 1599, STC 6355, Huntington Library.
[2] persons of high rank.
[3] acquired by learning.

These sparkes by nature euermore aspire,
Which makes them to so *high* an *Highnesse* flee.

Faire *Soule,* since to the fairest bodie knit,
You giue such liuely life, such quickning power,
Such sweete celestiall influence to it,
As keepes it still in youths immortall flower,

(As where the Sunne is present all the yeare,
And neuer doth retire his golden ray,
Needes must the Spring be euerlasting there,
And euery season like the Mon'th of May)

O many, many yeares may you remaine,
A happie Angell to this happie Land:
Long, long, may you on earth our Empresse raigne,
Ere you in Heauen a glorious Angell stand;

Stay long (sweet Spirit) ere thou to Heauen depart,
Which mak'st each place a Heauen wherin thou art.

Her Maiesties least and
vnworthiest Subiect,

John Dauies.

OF HUMANE KNOWLEDGE

Why did my parents send me to the schooles
That I with knowledg might enrich my mind?
Since the *desire to know* first made men fooles,
And did corrupt the roote of all mankind?

For when Gods hand had written in the harts
Of the first Parents all the rules of good,
So that their skill enfusde did passe all Arts
That euer were, before, or since the Flood;

And when their reasons eye was sharpe and cleere,
And (as an Eagle can behold the Sunne,)
Could haue approch't th'eternall light as neere,
As the intellectual Angels could haue done;

Euen then to them the *Spirit of lies* suggests,
That they were blind, because they saw not Ill:
And breathes into their incorrupted breasts,
A curious *wish,* which did corrupt their *will.*

For that same Ill they straight desir'd to know:
Which Ill being nought but a defect[4] of good,
And all Gods workes the Diuell could not show,
While Man their Lord in his perfection stood.

So that them selues were first to do the Ill,
Ere they thereof the knowledge could attaine;

[4] lack.

Like him, that knew not poisons power to kill,
Vntill (by tasting it) himselfe was slaine.

Euen so by tasting of that Fruite forbid,
Where they sought *knowledge,* they did *error* find,
Ill they desir'd to know, and Ill they did;
And to giue *Passion* eyes, made *Reason* blind.

For then their minds did first in passion see,
Those wretched shapes of *Miserie* and *Woe,*
Of *Nakednesse,* of *Shame,* of *Pouertie,*
Which then their owne experience made them know.

But then grew *Reason* darke, that *she* no more
Could the faire Formes of *God* and *Truth* discerne;
Battes they became that *Eagles* were before,
And this they got by their *desire to learne.*

But we their wretched Offspring, what do we?
Do not wee still tast of the fruite forbid?
Whiles with fond,[5] fruitelesse curiositie,
In bookes prophane we seeke for knowledge hid.

What is this *knowledge?* but the Skie-stolne[6] fire,
For which the *Thiefe*[7] still chaind in Ice doth sit?
And which the poore rude *Satyre* did admire,
And needs would kisse, but burnt his lips with it?

What is it? but the cloud of emptie Raine
Which when *Ioues* Guest[8] embrac't, he Monsters got?
Or the false *Pailes,* which oft being fild with paine,
Receiu'd the water, but retained it not?[9]

Shortly what is it? but the fierie Coach,
Which the *Youth*[10] sought, and sought his death withall?
Or the *Boyes* wings,[11] which when he did approch
The *Sunnes* hote beames, did melt and let him fall?

And yet, alas, when all our Lampes are burnd,
Our Bodies wasted, and our Spirits spent;
When we haue all the learned *volumes* turnd,
Which yeeld mens wits both helpe and ornament;

What can we know? or what can we discerne?
When *Error* chokes the windowes of the mind;
The diuerse formes of things, how can we learne,
That haue bene euer from our birth-day blind?

When *Reasons* lampe which (like the *Sunne* in skie)
Throughout *Mans* litle world her beams did spread;

5 foolish.
6 *Skie-stolne*] *Shie-stolne* STC 6355.
7 Prometheus.
8 Ixion.
9 For killing their husbands, the Danaides, daughters of Danaus, were condemned in Hades to pour water forever into perforated pails.
10 Phaëthon.
11 the wings of Icarus.

Is now become a Sparkle, which doth lie
Vnder the Ashes, halfe extinct, and dead;

How can we hope, that through the Eye and Eare,
This dying Sparkle, in this cloudie place,
Can recollect these beames of knowledge cleare,
Which were enfus'd in the first minds by grace?

So might the heire, whose father hath in play,
Wasted a thousand pounds of auncient rent,
By painfull earning of one grote a day,
Hope to restore the patrimonie spent.

The wits that div'd most deepe, and soar'd most hie,
Seeking Mans powers, haue found his weaknes such.
Skill[12] comes so slow, and life so fast doth flie,
We learne so litle, and forget so much.

For this the wisest[13] of all Mortall men
Said *he knew nought, but that he nought did know:*
And the great mocking Maister[14] mockt not then,
When he said, *Truth was buried deepe below.*

For how may we to others things attaine,
When none of vs his owne soule vnderstands?
For which the Diuell mockes our curious braine,
When *know thy selfe* his oracle commands.[15]

For why should we the busie Soule beleeue,
When boldly she concludes of that, and this,
When of her selfe she can no iudgement geue,
Nor how, nor whence, nor where, nor what she is?

All things without, which round about we see,
We seeke to know, and how therewith to do:
But that whereby we *reason, liue, and be,*
Within our selues, we strangers are thereto.

We seeke to know the mouing of each spheare,
And the straunge cause of th'ebs and flouds of Nile:
But of that clocke within our breasts we beare,
The subtill motions we forget the while.

We that acquaint our selues with euery *Zoane,*
And passe both *Tropikes,* and behold the *Poles,*
When we come home, are to our selues vnknowne,
And vnacquainted still with our owne *Soules.*

We studie *Speech,* but others we perswade;
We *Leech-craft* learne, but others Cure with it;

---

12 knowledge.

13 Socrates.

14 Democritus.

15 In *Phaedrus* Plato quotes Socrates: "I must first know myself, as the Delphian oracle says." To Christians the oracle of Apollo at Delphi was the mouthpiece of the devil.

We interpret *Lawes,* which other men haue made;
But reade not those which in our harts are writ.

Is it because the minde is like the eye,
(Through which it gathers knowledge by degrees,)
Whose rayes reflect not, but spread outwardly,
Not seeing it selfe, when other things it sees?

No doubtlesse, for the minde can backward cast
Vpon her selfe, her vnderstanding light;
But she is so corrupt, and so defac't,
As her owne image doth her selfe affright.

As is the fable of that Ladie faire,[16]
Which for her lust was turnd into a Cow,
When thirstie to a streame she did repaire,
And saw her selfe transformd she wist not how,

At first she startles,[17] then she stands amaz'd,
At last with terror she from thence doth flie,
And loathes the watrie glasse wherein she gaz'd,
And shunnes it still, though she for thirst do die.

Euen so *Mans soule* which did Gods Image beare,
And was at first faire, good, and spotlesse pure,
Since with her *sinnes* her beauties blotted were,
Doth of all sights her owne sight least endure.

For euen at first reflection she espies,
Such strange *Chymeraes,* and such Monsters there,
Such Toyes, such *Antikes,* and such Vanities,
As she retires, and shrinks for shame and feare;

And as the man loues least at home to bee,
That hath a sluttish house haunted with *Sprites,*
So she impatient her owne faults to see,
Turnes from her selfe, and in strange things delites.

For this few *know themselues:* for merchants broke[18]
View their estate with discontent, and paine;
And *Seas* are troubled when they do reuoke[19]
Their flowing waues, into themselues againe.

And while the face of outward things we find,
Pleasing, and faire, agreable, and sweete;
These things transport, and carrie out the mind,
That with her selfe her selfe can neuer meete.

Yet if *Affliction* once her warres begin,
And threat[20] the feeble *Sense* with sword and fire,

[16] Io.
[17] starts in alarm.
[18] bankrupt.
[19] call back.
[20] *threat* STC 6357]; *thereat* STC 6355.

The *Mind* contracts her selfe, and shrinketh in,
And to her selfe she gladly doth retire;

As *Spiders* toucht, seeke their webs inmost part;
As *Bees* in stormes vnto their hiues returne:
As Blood in danger gathers to the hart;
As Men seeke Towns when foes the Country burne.

If ought can teach vs ought, *Afflictions* lookes,
(Making vs looke into our selues so neare)
Teach vs to *know our selues,* beyond all bookes,
Or all the learned *Schooles* that euer were.

This *Mistresse*[21] lately pluckt me by the Eare,
And many a golden lesson hath me taught;
Hath made my *Senses* quicke, and Reason cleare,
Reformd my Will, and rectifide my Thought;

So do the *Winds and Thunders* cleanse the Aire,
So working lees settle and purge the wine;
So lopt and pruned Trees do florish faire;
So doth the fire the drossie Gold refine.

Neither *Minerua,* nor the learned *Muse,*
Nor Rules of *Art,* nor *Precepts* of the wise,
Could in my braine those beames of skill enfuse,
As but the glaunce of this *Dames*[22] angrie eyes.

She within *Listes*[23] my raunging minde hath brought,
That now beyond my selfe I list not go;
My selfe am *Center* of my circling thought,
Onely *my selfe* I studie, learne, and know.

I know my Bodi's of so fraile a kinde,
As force without, feauers within can kill;
I know the heauenly nature of my minde,
But tis corrupted both in wit and will:

I know my *Soule* hath power to know all things,
Yet is she blind and ignorant in all;
I know I am one of *Natures* litle kings,
Yet to the least and vilest things am thrall.

I know my life's a paine, and but a span,
I know my *Sense* is mockt with euery thing;
And to conclude, I know my selfe a *Man,*
Which is a *proud* and yet a *wretched* thing.[24]

. . . .

21 affliction (Davies refers to his recent disbarment).
22 affliction's.
23 Palisades enclosing a space set apart for tilting.
24 Here ends the section entitled "Of humane knowledge." The second section, entitled "Of the soule of man, and the immortalitie thereof," is more than 1700 lines in length and is divided into many subsections, seven of which are given here.

This substance and this *spirit of Gods owne making*,[25]
Is in the bodie plac't, and planted here,
That both of God, and of the world partaking,
Of all that is, man might the image beare.

God first made Angels bodilesse pure minds,
Then other things, which mindlesse bodies bee;
Last he made Man th'*Horizon* twixt both kinds,
In whom we do the worlds abridgement see.

Besides, this world below did need *one wight*,[26]
Which might thereof distinguish euery part,
Make vse thereof, and take therein delight
And order things with industrie, and Art.

Which also God might in his works admire,
And here beneath, yeeld him both prayer and praise,
As there, aboue, the holy Angels Quire
Doth spread his glorie, with spirituall layes.

Lastly, the bruite vnreasonable wights,
Did want a *visible king* on them to raigne;
And God himselfe thus to the world vnites,
That so the world might endlesse blisse obtain.

But how shall we this *vnion* well expresse?[27]
Nought tyes the *Soule*, her subtiltie is such;
She moues the bodie, which she doth possesse,
Yet no part toucheth, but by *vertues* touch.

Then dwels she not therein as in a tent,
Nor as a Pilot in his Ship doth sit;
Nor as a Spider in her Web is pent;
Nor as the Waxe retaines the print in it;

Nor as a Vessell water doth containe;
Nor as one Liquor in another shed;
Nor as the heate doth in the fire remaine,
Nor as a voice throughout the aire is spred.

But as the faire, and cheerefull *morning light*,
Doth here and there her siluer beames impart,
And in an instant doth her selfe vnite
To the transparent Aire, in all and part:

Still resting whole, when blowes the Aire deuide;
Abiding pure, when th'Aire is most corrupted;
Throughout the Aire her beames dispersing wide,
And, when the Aire is tost, not interrupted;

So doth the piercing *Soule* the bodie fill,
Being all in all, and all in part diffus'd,

---

25 Marginal note: *Why the soule is vnited to the body.*

26 creature.

27 Marginal note: *In what maner the soule is vnited to the body.*

Indiuisible, vncorruptible still,
Not forc't, encountred, troubled, or confus'd.

And as the *Sunne* aboue the light doth bring,
Though we behold it in the Aire below;
So from th'eternall light the *Soule* doth spring,
Though in the Bodie she her powers do show.

. . . .

Will puts in practise what the *wit* deuiseth;[28]
Will euer acts, and *wit* contemplates still,
And as from *wit* the power of *wisdome* riseth,
All other vertues daughters are of *will.*

Will is the *Prince,* and *wit* the Counsellour,
Which doth for common good in Councell sit;
And when *wit* is resolu'd, *will* lends her power,
To execute, what is aduisd by *wit.*

Wit is the minds chief Iudge, which doth Comptroule
Of *fancies* Court the iudgements false and vaine;
Will holds the royall Scepter in the *Soule,*
And on the passions of the hart doth raigne.

Will is as Free as any Emperour;
Nought can restraigne her *gentle* libertie:
No Tyrant, nor no Torment hath the powre,
To make vs *will,* when we *vnwilling* bee.

To these high powers a Store-house doth pertaine,[29]
Where they all Arts and generall Reasons lay,
Which in the *Soule,* euen after death remaine,
And no *Lethæan* Flud can wash away.

This is the *Soule,* and those her vertues bee,
Which though they haue their sundry proper ends,
And one exceeds another in degree,
Yet each on other mutually depends.

Our wit is geuen, *Almightie* God to *know;*
Our *will* is giuen to *loue* him being *knowne;*
But God could not be *knowne* to vs below,
But by his *works,* which through the *sense* are shown;

And as the *wit* doth reape the fruits of *sense,*
So doth the *quickning* powre the *senses feed;*
Thus while they do their sundrie gifts dispence,
The best the seruice of the least doth need.

Euen so the King his Magistrats do serue;
Yet commons feede both Magistrate and King;

---

[28] Marginal note: *The Relations betwixt wit and will.*

[29] Marginal note: *The intellectuall memorie.*

The commons peace the Magistrats preserue,
By borrowed power, which from the Prince doth spring.

The *quickning* power would *be,* and so would rest;
The *sense* would not *be* only, but *be well;*
But *wits* ambition longeth to be *best,*
For it desires in endlesse blisse to dwell.

And these three powers three sorts of men do make;
For some like plants their veines do only fill;
And some like beasts their senses pleasure take;
And some like Angels do Contemplate still.[30]

Therefore the fables turnd some men to flowers,
And others did with brutish formes inuest,
And did of others make Celestiall powers,
Like Angels, which still trauell,[31] yet still rest.

Yet these three powrs are not three *Soules,* but one;
As one and two are both containd in *three,*
Three being one number by it selfe alone;
A shadow of the blessed Trinitie.

O what is man (great maker of mankind)[32]
That thou to him so great respect[33] dost beare?
That thou adornst him with so bright a mind,
Mak'st him a king, and euen an Angels peere?

O what a liuelie life, what heauenly power,
What spreading vertue, what a sparkling Fire,
How great, how plentifull, how rich a dowre,
Do'st thou within this dying Flesh inspire.

Thou leau'st thy print in other workes of thine,
But thy whole image thou in man hast writ;
There cannot be a creature more diuine,
Except (like thee) it should be infinit.

But it exceeds mans thought, to think how high
God hath raizd *man,* since *God a man* became;
The Angels do admire[34] this *mysterie,*
And are astonisht when they view the same.

Nor hath he giuen these blessings for a day,[35]
Nor made them on the bodies life depend;
The *Soule,* though made in time, *Suruiues for aye,*
And though it hath beginning, sees no end.

Her onely *end,* is *neuer ending* blisse;
Which is, *th'eternall Face of God to see;*

[30] always.
[31] labor.
[32] Marginal note: *An Acclamation.*
[33] consideration.
[34] wonder at.
[35] Marginal note: *That the soule is immortall, and cannot die.*

Who *last of ends*, and *first of causes is*,
And to do this, she must *eternall* bee.

How senslesse then and dead a *Soule* hath hee,
Which *thinks* his *Soule* doth with his bodie dye?
Or *thinks* not so, but so would haue it bee,
That he might sinne with more securitie?

For though these light and vicious persons *say*,
Our *Soule* is but a smoke, or aiery blast,
Which during life doth in our nosthrils play,
And when we die, doth turne to wind at last;

Although they *say*, come, *let vs eate and drinke*,
Our life is but a sparke, which quicklie dyes;
Though thus they *say*, they know not what *to thinke*,
But in their minds ten thousand doubts arise.

Therefore no heretikes desire to spread
Their light opinions, like these *Epicures*;[36]
For so their staggering thoughts are comforted,
And other mens assent their doubt assures.

Yet though these men against their conscience striue,
There are some sparkles in their flintie breasts
Which cannot be extinct, but still reuiue,
That though they would, they cannot quite be *beasts*.

But who so makes a mirror of his mind,
And doth with patience view himselfe therein,
His *Soules* eternitie shall cleerly find,
Though th'other beauties he defac't with sinne.

. . . .

O *ignorant* poore man, what doost thou beare,[37]
Lock't vp within the Casket of thy breast?
What Iewels, and what riches hast thou there?
What heauenly treasure in so weake a cheast?

Looke in thy *Soule*, and thou shalt *beauties* find,
Like those which drownd *Narcissus* in the floud,
Honor, and *Pleasure* both are in thy mind,
And all that in the world is counted *good*.

Thinke of her worth, and thinke that God did meane,
This worthy mind should worthy things embrace;
Blot not her beauties with thy thoughts vncleane,
Nor her dishonor with thy passions base;

Kill not her *quickning power* with surfettings,
Mar not her *sense* with Sensualitie,
Cast not her serious *wit* on idle things,
Make not her free *will* slaue to vanitie.

[36] Epicureans.

[37] Marginal note: *An Acclamation.*

And when thou thinkst of her *eternitie,*
Thinke not that *death* against her nature is;
Thinke it a *birth:* and when thou goest to die,
Sing like a Swan, as if thou wentst to blisse.

And if thou like a Child didst feare before,
Being in the darke, where thou didst nothing see;
Now I haue brought the *torch light,* feare no more,
Now when thou Diest, thou canst not hudwinkt bee.

And thou my *Soule,* which turnst thy Curious eye,
To view the beames of thine owne forme diuine,
Know, that thou canst know nothing perfectly,
While thou art Clouded with this flesh of mine.

Take heed of *ouer-weening,* and compare
Thy Peacocks feet with thy gay Peacocks traine:
Studie the best, and highest things that are,
But of thy selfe an humble thought retaine;

Cast downe thy selfe, and onely striue to raise
The glorie of thy Makers sacred name;
Vse all thy powers, that blessed power to praise,
Which giues thee power to *be,* and *vse the same.*

From HYMNS OF ASTRAEA[38]

OF ASTRAEA

Early before the day doth spring,
Let vs awake my Muse, and sing;
It is no time to slumber,
So many Ioyes this time doth bring,
As time will faile to number.

But whereto shall we bend our Layes?
Euen vp to Heauen, againe to raise
The Mayde, which thence descended
Hath brought againe the golden dayes,
And all the world amended.

Rudenesse it selfe she doth refine,
Euen like an Alchymist diuine,
Grosse times of Iron[39] turning
Into the purest forme of gold:
Not to corrupt till heauen waxe old,
And be refin'd with burning.

TO ASTRAEA

Eternall Virgin, *Goddesse* true,
Let me presume to sing to you.
Ioue, euen great *Ioue* hath leisure
Sometimes to heare the vulgar crew,
And heares them oft with pleasure.

Blessed *Astraea,* I in part
Enioy the blessings you impart,
The Peace, the milke and hony,
Humanity, and ciuill *Art,*
A richer *Dower* then money.

Right glad am I that now I liue,
Euen in these daies whereto you giue
Great happinesse and glorie;
If after you I should be borne,
No doubt I should my birth day scorne,
Admiring your sweete storie.

TO THE SPRING

Earth now is greene, and heauen is blew,
Liuely Spring which makes all new

[38] From *Hymnes of Astraea, in acrosticke verse,* 1599, STC 6351, Huntington Library. Astraea is the goddess of justice, the constellation Virgo, and Queen Elizabeth. The first letters of the lines, if read downward, spell "Elisabetha Regina."

[39] Astraea left the earth in the Iron Age, the age of evil.

Iolly Spring doth enter,
Sweete young Sun-beames do subdue
Angry, aged winter.

Blasts are mild, and Seas are calme,
Euery medow flowes with Balme,
The earth weares all her riches,
Harmonious birdes sing such a Psalme
As eare and hart bewitches.

Reserue (sweete Spring) this Nymph of ours
Eternall garlands of thy flowers,
Greene garlands neuer wasting;
In her shall last our *states* faire spring,
Now and for euer flourishing,
As long as heauen is lasting.

TO THE LARKE

Early chearfull, mounting Larke,
Lights gentle Vsher, mornings clarke,
In merrie Notes delighting:
Stint[40] awhile thy Song, and harke,
And learne my new Inditing.[41]

Beare vp this Hymme, to heau'n it beare,
Euen vp to heau'n, and sing it there,
To heau'n each morning beare it;
Haue it set to some sweete Sphere,
And let the Angels heare it.

Renownd *Astraea,* that great name,
Exceeding great in worth and fame,
Great worth hath so renownd it,
It is *Astraeas* name I praise,
Now then, sweete Larke, do thou it raise,
And in high Heauen resound it.

TO THE NIGHTINGALE

Euery night from Euen till Morne
Loues Quirister amidde the thorne
Is now so sweet a Singer,
So sweete, as for her Song I scorne
Apollos voice, and finger.

But Nightingale since you delight
Euer to watch the Starrie night,
To all the Starres of heauen,
Heauen neuer had a Starre so bright,
As now to earth is giuen.

Royall *Astraea* makes our Day
Eternall with her beames, nor may
Grosse darkenesse ouercome her;
I now perceiue why some do write,
No countrie hath so short a night,
As England hath in sommer.

TO THE ROSE

Eye of the garden, Queene of flowers,
Loues Cuppe wherein he Nectar poures,
Ingendred first of Nectar:
Sweete nurse-child of the Springs young howres,
And Beauties faire Character.[42]

Best Iewell that the earth doth weare,
Euen when the braue yong Sun drawes neare,
To her hoate Loue pretending;[43]
Himselfe likewise like forme doth beare,
At rising and descending.

Rose of the Queene of loue belou'd;
England's great Kings diuinely mou'd,
Gaue Roses in their Banner;[44]
It shewed that Bewties Rose indeede,
Now in this age should them succeede,
And raigne in more sweet manner.

TO ENUIE

Enuie go weepe, my Muse and I
Laugh thee to scorne; thy feeble Eye
Is dazled with the glorie
Shining in this gay poesie,
And litle golden Storie.

Behold how my proud quil doth shed
Eternall *Nectar* on her head:
The pompe of Coronation
Hath not such power her fame to spread,
As this my admiration.

Respect my Pen as free and franke,
Expecting not Reward nor Thanke;
Great wonder onely moues it;
I neuer made it mercenary;
Nor should my Muse this burthen carie
As hyr'd, but that she loues it.

[40] stop.
[41] writing.
[42] face, appearance.
[43] asserting.
[44] The red rose of Lancaster and the white rose of York.

Satires

SATIRE is both a form and a mode. As a mode it is common in English literature from Chaucer onward. In the burlesque of Barclay's *Ship of Fools*, in Skelton's verse, in Gascoigne's *Steel Glass*, in the satirical fable of Spenser's *Mother Hubberd's Tale,* there is satire of the medieval kind. Satire as a form in English literature is derived from Horace, Persius, and Juvenal. Horace's satires and epistles are pleasant narratives of personal experiences, with his kindly, witty, urbane comment on human follies. The satires of Persius and Juvenal are direct and severe rebukes, harsh and bitter in tone, involved and obscure in style.

Sir Thomas Wyatt is the first English writer to imitate classical satire. His three epistles or satires are Horatian in form, matter, and tone. After Wyatt no formal satire was written in English until Thomas Drant translated Horace's satires in 1577. The satirists of the 1590's followed Juvenal and Persius rather than Horace.

Thomas Lodge, Joseph Hall, and John Donne probably began to write formal satire at about the same time. Donne's satires, some of them written probably in 1593 or 1594 though not printed until 1633, are outside the scope of this book. Lodge, already known as a writer of prose romances, lyrics, and plays (see page 363), published in *A Fig for Momus*, 1595, four satires and several verse epistles to Daniel, Drayton, and other friends. He is indebted to all three Roman satirists but chiefly to Juvenal. His satires lack local color and contemporary allusions and are dull and flat, and the epistles have little of Horace's urbanity and grace.

Two years later Joseph Hall (1574–1656), then a Fellow of Emmanuel College, Cambridge, and later to become Bishop of Exeter and of Norwich, published three books of *Virgidemiarum* and in 1598 three more books. The title is the genitive plural of "virgidemia" or "virgindemia," meaning "a harvest of rods." The first three books he calls "toothless satires," for they deal with literature and minor social abuses; the second three he calls "biting satires," for they deal severely with serious evils. His satires are concise, spirited, witty, and sometimes obscene. In 1642 John Milton, in controversy with Hall, then Bishop of Norwich, reproved him: "A Satyr . . . ought . . . to strike high, and adventure dangerously at the most eminent vices among the greatest persons, and not to creepe into every blinde Taphouse that fears a Constable more than a Satyr."

In 1598 Everard (or Edward) Guilpin published anonymously *Skialetheia, or a Shadow of Truth, in certain Epigrams and Satires.* Little is known about him; he tells us that he is a Cambridge man and at the time of writing at one of the Inns of Court. In his six satires he gives vivid glimpses of London life. He is especially vehement in his comments on contemporary poetry, which he condemns as "food to sinnes," and insists that satire and epigram alone can help an age addicted to "whimpring Sonnets, puling Elegies," and "lewd ballad stuffe." His satires are marred by obscurity and obscenity.

The last of the important satirists of the 1590's is John Marston (1576–1634). Educated at Brasenose College, Oxford, and at the Middle Temple, he turned from the study of law to write poetry and, after 1600, plays. He was ordained in 1609, and from 1616 to 1631 he was rector of Christ Church in Hampshire. In 1598 he published *The Metamorphosis of Pygmalion's Image and Certain Satires. The Metamorphosis* is an erotic poem in the manner of *Venus and Adonis* and *Hero and Leander*. Later in the same year he published *The Scourge of Villanie*, which contains nine satires; a tenth is added in the second edition, 1599. Marston's satires are turgid, pretentious, cynical, foul. The best is the tenth with its caricatures of some familiar types of Elizabethan gallant.

The formal satires of the 1590's are poor indeed when contrasted with those of Dryden and Pope, but they are interesting for several reasons: they contain illuminating comment on contemporary poetry; they reveal something of the rivalry and the friendship among the writers of the period; they depict, though with some distortion, the manners and morals of Londoners; they are early experiments in the use of the decasyllabic couplet for satire.

Probably to lessen the danger of libelous attacks and of disturbing comment on social and political problems, and perhaps to discourage the publication of erotic verse, the Archbishop of Canterbury and the Bishop of London, the censors of the press, on June 1, 1599, prohibited the further printing of satires and epigrams, and ordered the Stationers' Company to call in and burn a number of books, including among others the satires of Hall, Guilpin, and Marston. But the prohibition was not long enforced, for some fifty new collections of satires and epigrams were printed during the next fifteen years.

The most convenient modern editions are the following: *Complete Works of Thomas Lodge*, ed. E. Gosse, 4 vols., 1883; *The Collected Poems of Joseph Hall*, ed. A. Davenport, 1949; Everard Guilpin, *Skialetheia*, ed. G. B. Harrison, 1932; *The Works of John Marston*, ed. A. H. Bullen, 3 vols., 1887; John Marston, *The Scourge of Villanie*, ed. G. B. Harrison, 1925. For discussion see R. M. Alden, *The Rise of Formal Satire in England*, 1899; Arnold Stein, "Donne's Obscurity and the Elizabethan Tradition," *English Literary History*, xiii (1946), 98–118; T. F. Kinloch, *The Life and Works of Joseph Hall*, 1952; M. S. Allen, *The Satire of John Marston*, 1920; T. Spencer, "John Marston," *Criterion*, xiii (1934), 581–599.

From Lodge's A FIG FOR MOMUS[1]

SATIRE 4

To a deere friend lately giuen ouer to couetousnesse

I heare of late (but hould it verie strange)
(That such vaine newes is common in the change)[2]
How being old, and drawing to the graue,
Thou waxest greedie, and desir'st to saue:
As if thy life of sorrowes had no store,
But thou in policie[3] shouldst purchase more?
Alas for thee, that at thy iournies end
Art growne so neere[4] and carefull what to spend.
Looke on thy selfe, age hath thee by the backe,
Thy haires are white, which erst were frisseld[5] blacke:
Thine eies are suncke, thy cheeks are leane and pale,
Thy lips are blew, thy breath is stincking stale,
Thy grinders gone, thy ghastlie gout, and murre;[6]
Do breake thy sleepes, and scarcely let thee sturre:
Thy memorie is dul, and wel nie dead,
Thy tongue alreadie faulters in thy head:
Where al these torments make thee loth thy self,
Why art thou now enamored with thy pelfe?
Think'st thou the purchase of a niggards name
Is not a preiudice vnto thy fame?
Marke me a miserable[7] mysing[8] wretch,
That liues by others losse, and subtle fetch,[9]
He is not onely plagu'd with heauines,[10]
For that which other happie men possesse,
But takes no tast of that himselfe partakes,
And sooner life, then miserie[11] forsakes:
And what in most aboundance, he retaines
In seeming little, doth augment his paines:
His trauailes,[12] are suspitions backt by feare,
His thoughts distraught incessant troubles leare,[13]
He doubts[14] the raine, for feare it raise a floud
And beare away his houses, and his good,
He dreads his neighbours cattle as they passe,
For feare they stay and feed vpon his grasse,
He hides his treasures vnder locke and kay,
Lest theeues breake in, and beare his bags away:
Onely vnto himselfe, for whom he spares,
He gathers nothing but continuall cares:
His eie disdaines[15] his hungrie bellie meate,

---

1 From *A fig for Momus: containing pleasant varietie, included in satyres, eclogues, and epistles*, 1595, STC 16658, Folger Library.

2 The Royal Exchange, a place where Londoners congregated.

3 intentionally.

4 niggardly.

5 frizzled, curled.

6 catarrh.

7 miserly.

8 miserly.

9 trick.

10 sadness (envy).

11 miserliness.

12 labors, troubles.

13 study, learn.

14 fears.

15 scorns (for needing).

Himselfe repines, at that himselfe doth eate,
Though rents increase, he lets his body lacke,
And neither spares his bellie nor his backe:
What on himselfe he laies, he houlds it lost,
What on his wife, he deemes vnthriftie cost,
What on his heires, his miserie and misse;
What on his seruants, ryotting it is.
Thus from himselfe, his couetous desire
Doth draw himselfe, and on his hart doth tire:
So liues he to the wretched world alone,
Lothsome to all that long to see him gone:
If such he be, (as such he is indeede)
And fare more worse, (if wealth more worse may breed)
For shame from such a sinne thy life exempt,
That makes thee rich in nothing but contempt,
They say the many packs before thy doore,
Are but the pawnes,[16] and wages of the poore,
They say the buildings which thou dost begin,
Are rich without, but yeeld no rest within;
They say thy deerest friends are sure to pay
Great forfeitures, and if they misse their day:
They say the interest of tenne a yeere
Is held too little to maintaine thy cheere,
And yet thy selfe, thy wife, thy maid, thy knaue,[17]
Scarce butter'd turneps vpon Sundaies haue,
They say at New-yeares-tide men giue thee cakes,
And thou the next day sels them for their sakes,
They say thou sel'st the chipping of thy bred
For feare thy seruants should be ouer fed,
They say one horse may beare thy houshould stuffe,
Where for thy coyne three carts are not enough;
They say thy welted[18] gowne, and ruffes of lawne,
When thou wert warden last was but a pawne:[19]
They say thy plate is forfeited and lost
For halfe the money that at first it cost,
They say thy wiues cast kertle is become
A paire of breeches to enskonce thy bum.
Briefly, they say that for the world thou art
Too wretched,[20] and for God too false in hart.
All these reports thou knowest as well as I
Spring from some grounds, things sould by common cry
Are quickly sould, men hardly stop the noice
Of slanders published by common voice:
If these be true, reforme them; if vntrue,
Take them for warnings what thou shouldst eschue:
What ere they be, now thinke vpon thy graue,
And leaue thy worldly drudging to thy knaue,
And let him carrie fier vnto thy stils,
And tend thy brewhouse, watch, and ward thy mils,
Looke to thine apples, lest they rotte away,
Set vp thy hop-powles, and thy champions lay.[21]

[16] things forfeited.
[17] boy.
[18] with ornamental seams.
[19] borrowed or rented.
[20] hateful.
[21] prepare thy fields.

And thou thy selfe safe wrapt in cloth and furre,
Fall to thy prayers, desire no more to sturre,
Giue to the poore, what thou hast got by wrong,
For be assur'd thy daies cannot be long:
Follow this frendly counsell which I giue,
Or els in shame, and hatred thou shalt liue,
Or dead, those passengers[22] that spie thy graue,
Shall say here lies a broking[23] bribing knaue.

From Hall's VIRGIDEMIARVM[1]

Book I

PROLOGUE

I first aduenture, with fool-hardy might,
To tread the steps of perilous despight:
I first aduenture: follow me who list,
And be the second English Satyrist.
Enuy wayts on my backe, Truth on my side:
Enuy will be my Page, and Truth my Guide.
Enuy the margent[2] holds, and Truth the line:
Truth doth approue, but Enuy doth repine.
For in this smoothing[3] age who durst indite,
Hath made his pen an hyred Parasite,
To claw the back[4] of him that beastly liues,
And pranck[5] base men in proud Superlatiues.
Whence damned vice is shrouded quite from shame
And crown'd with Vertues meed, immortall Name:
Infamy dispossest of natiue due,
Ordain'd of olde on looser life to sue:
The worlds eye bleared with those shamelesse lies,
Mask'd in the shew of meal-mouth'd Poesies.
Goe daring Muse on with thy thanklesse taske,
And do the vgly face of vice vnmaske:
And if thou canst not thine high flight remit,
So as it mought[6] a lowly Satyre fit,
Let lowly Satyres rise aloft to thee:
Truth be thy speed, and Truth thy Patron bee.

SATIRE 1

Nor Ladies wanton loue, nor wandring knight,
Legend I out in rymes all richly dight.[7]
Nor fright the Reader with the Pagan vaunt
Of mightie Mahound, or great Termagaunt.[8]
Nor list[9] I Sonnet of my Mistresse face,

---

[22] those who pass by.
[23] bargaining.
[1] From *Virgidemiarum, sixe bookes*, 1597, STC 12716, Folger Library.
[2] margin.
[3] flattering.
[4] to stroke the back, to flatter.
[5] adorn.
[6] might.
[7] adorned.
[8] Mohammed and Termagaunt, a mythical goddess believed to be worshiped by the Saracens, appeared in many romances of chivalry.
[9] wish.

To paint some Blowesse[10] with a borrowed grace.
Nor can I bide to pen some hungry *Scene*[11]
For thick-skin[12] eares, and vndiscerning eyne.
Nor euer could my scornfull Muse abide
With Tragick shooes[13] her ankles for to hide.
Nor can I crouch, and writhe my fauning tayle
To some great Patron, for my best auaile.
Such hunger-staruen, Trencher-Poetry,[14]
Or let it neuer liue, or timely die:
Nor vnder euery banke, and euery Tree,
Speake rymes vnto my oten Minstralsie:
Nor caroll out so pleasing liuely laies,
As mought the *Graces* moue my mirth to praise.
Trumpet, and reeds, and socks, and buskins fine,
I them bequeath: whose statues wandring Twine
Of Yuy, mixt with Bayes, circlen around
Their liuing Temples likewise *Laurell-bound.*
Rather had I, albee[15] in carelesse rymes,
Check the mis-ordred world, and lawlesse Tymes.
Nor need I craue the Muses mid-wifry,
To bring to light so worth-lesse Poetry:
Or if we list, what baser Muse can bide,
To sit and sing by *Grantaes*[16] naked side.
They haunt the tyded *Thames* and salt *Medway,*
Ere since the fame of their late Bridall day.[17]
Nought haue we here but willow-shaded shore,
To tell our *Grant* his banks are left forlore.

SATIRE 3

With some Pot-fury rauisht from their wit,
They[18] sit and muse on some no-vulgar writ:
As frozen Dung-hils in a winters morne,
That voyd of Vapours seemed all beforne,[19]
Soone as the Sun, sends out his piercing beames,
Exhale out filthy smoke and stinking steames:
So doth the base, and the fore-barren braine,
Soone as the raging wine begins to raigne.
One higher pitch'd doth set his soaring thought
On crowned kings that Fortune hath low brought:
Or some vpreared, high-aspiring swaine
As it might be the Turkish *Tamberlaine.*[20]
Then weeneth he his base drink-drowned spright,
Rapt to the threefold loft of heauens hight,[21]
When he conceiues vpon his fained stage
The stalking steps of his great personage,[22]

[10] trull.
[11] "a scene penned . . . to satisfy the writer's hunger" (Grosart).
[12] dull.
[13] buskins.
[14] Verse written in the hope of entertainment by a patron or, possibly, verse written to be carved on trenchers.
[15] albeit, although.
[16] Granta, river at Cambridge.
[17] The Muses haunt the Thames and Medway ever since Spenser celebrated their wedding (*The Faerie Queene,* IV, xi, 8 ff.).
[18] The "wondrous rablements of Rimsters new" that Hall mentions in the preceding satire.
[19] before.
[20] The reference is to Marlowe's play.
[21] elevation.
[22] This perhaps describes Edward Alleyn's manner in playing the part of Tamburlaine.

Graced with huf-cap termes,[23] and thundring threats,
That his poore hearers hayre quite vpright sets.
Such soone, as some braue-minded hungry youth,[24]
Sees fitly frame to his wide-strained mouth,
He vaunts his voyce vpon an hyred stage,
With high-set[25] steps, and princely carriage:
Now sooupinG[26] in side robes of Royaltie,
That earst did skrub[27] in lowsie brokerie.[28]
There if he can with termes Italianate,
Big-sounding sentences, and words of state,
Faire patch me vp his pure *Iambick* verse,
He rauishes the gazing Scaffolders:[29]
Then certes was the famous *Corduban*[30]
Neuer but halfe so high *Tragedian*.
Now, least such frightfull showes of Fortunes fall,
And bloody Tyrants rage, should chance appall
The dead stroke audience, mids the silent rout,[31]
Comes leaping in a selfe-misformed lout,
And laughes, and grins, and frames his Mimik face,
And iustles straight into the princes place.
Then doth the *Theatre Eccho* all aloud,
With gladsome noyse of that applauding croud.
A goodly *hoch-poch;*[32] when vile *Russettings,*[33]
Are match't with monarchs, and with mighty kings.
A goodly grace to sober *Tragike Muse,*
When each base clown, his clumbsie fist doth bruise,
And show his teeth in double rotten-row,
For laughter at his selfe-resembled show.[34]
Meane while our Poets in high Parliament,
Sit watching euery word, and gesturement,
Like curious Censors of some doughtie geare,[35]
Whispering their verdit in their fellowes eare.
Wo to the word whose margent in their scrole,
Is noted with a blacke condemning Cole.
But if each periode might the Synode please,
Ho, bring the Iuy boughs, and bands of Bayes.
Now when they part and leaue the naked stage,
Gins the bare hearer in a guiltie rage,
To curse and ban,[36] and blame his likerous[37] eye,
That thus hath lauisht his late halfe-peny.
Shame that the Muses should be bought and sold,
For euery peasants brasse, on each scaffold.[38]

23 blustering.
24 This and the next five lines perhaps describe the spectator who dreams of emulating Alleyn in the role of Tamburlaine.
25 pompous.
26 sweeping.
27 go in poor attire.
28 second-hand clothes.
29 spectators in the galleries.
30 Seneca, who was born in Cordova.
31 throng.
32 hodgepodge.
33 rustics wearing russet clothes.
34 The clown on the stage makes himself resemble, in appearance and conduct, the clown in the audience.
35 important activity.
36 curse.
37 eager.
38 stage.

SATIRE 4

Too popular is *Tragick Poesie,*
Strayning his tip-toes for a farthing fee,
And doth besides on *Rimelesse* numbers tread,
Vnbid *Iambicks* flow from carelesse head.
Some brauer braine in high *Heroick* rimes
Compileth worm eate stories of olde times:
And he like some imperious *Maronist,*[39]
Coniures the *Muses* that they him assist.
Then striues he to bumbast[40] his feeble lines
With farre-fetcht phraise:
And maketh vp his hard-betaken tale[41]
With strange enchantments, fetcht from darksom vale
Of some *Melissa,* that by Magicke doome
To *Tuscans* soyle transporteth *Merlins toombe:*
Painters and *poets* hold your auncient right:[42]
Write what you wil, and write not what you might:
Their limits be their *List,*[43] their reason will.
But if some painter in presuming skill
Should paint the stars in center of the earth,
Could ye forbeare some smiles, and taunting mirth.
But let no rebell *Satyre* dare traduce
Th'eternall *Legends* of thy *Faery Muse,*
Renowmed *Spencer:* whome no earthly wight
Dares once to emulate, much lesse dares despight.
Salust[44] of *France* and *Tuscan Ariost,*
Yeeld vp the *Lawrell girlond* ye haue lost:
And let all others willow weare with mee,
Or let their vndeseruing *Temples* bared bee.

SATIRE 6

Another[45] scorns the home-spun threed of rimes,
Match'd with the loftie feet of elder times:
Giue him the numbred verse that *Virgil* sung,
And *Virgill* selfe shall speake the English tung:
Manhood and garboiles[46] *shall be chaunt* with chaunged feete,
And head-strong *Dactils* making musicke meete.
The nimble *Dactils* striuing to out-go
The drawling *Spondees* pacing it below.
The lingring *Spondees,* labouring to delay,
The breath-lesse *Dactils* with a sudden stay.[47]
Who euer saw a colt wanton and wilde,
Yok'd with a slow-foote oxe on fallow field?
Can right areed[48] how handsomly besets[49]

---

39 disciple of Virgil.

40 pad, stuff.

41 This and the next three lines refer to Ariosto's *Orlando Furioso,* translated by Sir John Harington in 1591.

42 In this and the next five lines Hall borrows from the first few lines of Horace's *Ars Poetica.*

43 pleasure.

44 Guillaume de Saluste, Sieur du Bartas, some of whose verse Joshua Sylvester had recently translated into English.

45 another poet.

46 commotion. Hall is ridiculing the hexameters of Richard Stanyhurst's translation of the *Aeneid,* 1582: "Now manhod and garbroyls I chaunt, and martial horror."

47 stop.

48 determine.

49 accords with.

Dull *Spondees* with the English *Dactilets?*
If *Ioue* speake English in a thundring cloud,
Thwick thwack, and *rif raf,*[50] rores he out aloud.
Fie on the forged mint that did create
New coyne of words neuer articulate.

SATIRE 8

Hence ye profane: mell[51] not with holy things
That *Sion* Muse from *Palestina* brings.
Parnassus is transform'd to *Sion-hill,*
And *Iury-palmes*[52] her steep ascents done fill.
Now good Saint *Peter*[53] weeps pure *Helicon,*
And both the *Maries*[54] make a Musick mone:
Yea and the Prophet of the heauenly Lire,
Great *Salomon,*[55] sings in the English Quire,
And is become a newfound Sonetist,
Singing his loue, the holy spouse of Christ:
Like as she were some light-skirts of the rest,
In mightiest Ink-hornismes[56] he can thither wrest.
Ye *Sion* Muses shall by my deare will,
For this your zeale, and far-admired skill,
Be straight transported from *Ierusalem,*
Vnto the holy house of *Betleem.*[57]

Book 2

SATIRE 6

A Gentle Squire woulde gladly intertayne
Into his house, some trencher-Chaplaine:
Some willing man that might instruct his sons,
And that would stand to good conditions.
First that He lie vpon the Truckle-bed,
Whiles his yong maister lieth ore his hed.
Secondly, that he doe, on no default,
Euer presume to sit aboue the salt.
Third, that he neuer change his trencher twise.
Fourth, that he vse all comely courtesies:
Sit bare at meales, and one halfe rise and wait.
Last, that he neuer his yong master beat,
But he must aske his mother to define,
How many ierkes she would his breech should line.
All these obseru'd, he could contented bee,
To giue fiue markes, and winter liuerye.

---

50 Cf. Stanyhurst: "Of ruffe raffe roaring, mens herts with terror agrysing. With peale meale ramping, with thwick thwack sturdilye thundring."

51 meddle.

52 the palms of Jewry.

53 A reference to Robert Southwell's *St. Peters complaint,* 1595.

54 Perhaps a reference to Southwell's *Marie Magdalens funeral teares,* 1591, and to Thomas Lodge's *Prosopopeia: containing the teares of the holy Marie,* 1596.

55 Perhaps a reference to Gervase Markham's *The poem of poems: or Sion's muse,* 1596.

56 pedantic words.

57 A reference to Bethlehem Hospital, or Bedlam, the famous lunatic asylum in London.

Book 3

PROLOGUE

Some say my Satyrs ouer-loosely flow,
Nor hide their gall inough from open show:
Not riddle-like obscuring their intent:
But packe-staffe[58] plaine vttring what thing they ment:
Contrarie to the Roman ancients,
Whose wordes were short, and darkesome was their sence.
Who reads one line of their harsh poesies,
Thrise must he take his wind, and breath him thrise.
My Muse would follow them that haue fore-gone,
But cannot with an English pineon,
For looke how farr the ancient Comedie
Past former Satyrs in her libertie:
So farre must mine yeeld vnto them of old.
'Tis better be too bad, then be to bold.

SATIRE 1

Time was, and that was term'd the time of Gold,
When world and time were yong, that now are old.
(When quiet *Saturne* swaid[59] the mace of lead,
And Pride was yet vnborne, and yet vnbred.)
Time was, that whiles the Autumne fall did last,
Our hungry sires gap't for the falling mast
of the *Dodonian*[60] okes.
Could no vnhusked Akorne leaue the tree,
But there was chalenge made whose it might bee.
And if some nice and likorous[61] appetite,
Desir'd more daintie dish of rare delite,
They scal'd the stored *Crab*[62] with clasped knee,
Till they had sated their delicious eie:
Or search'd the hopefull thicks of hedgy-rowes,
For brierie berries, or hawes, or sowrer sloes:
Or when they meant to fare the fin'st of all,
They lickt oake-leaues besprint[63] with hony fall.
As for the thrise three-angled beech-nut shell,
Or chesnuts armed huske, and hid kernell,
No *Squire* durst touch, the law would not afford,[64]
Kept for the Court, and for the Kings owne bord.
Their royall Plate was clay, or wood, or stone:
The vulgar, saue his hand, else had he none.
Their onely seller was the neighbour brooke:
None did for better care, for better looke.
Was then no playning of the Brewers scape,[65]
Nor greedie *Vintner* mixt the strained grape.
The kings pauilion, was the grassy green,
Vnder safe shelter of the shadie treen.
Vnder each banke men layd their lims along,

[58] Staff on which a peddler supports his pack when standing to rest himself.
[59] wielded.
[60] of the ancient Greek town of Dodona.
[61] greedy.
[62] crab-apple tree.
[63] covered.
[64] permit.
[65] complaining about the brewer's deceit.

Not wishing any ease, not fearing wrong:
Clad with their owne, as they were made of old,
Not fearing shame, not feeling any cold.
But when by *Ceres* huswifrie and paine,
Men learn'd to bury the reuiuing graine:
And father *Ianus* taught the new found vine,
Rise on the *Elme,* with many a friendly twine,[66]
And base desire bad men to deluen low,[67]
For needlesse mettals: then gan mischiefe grow.
Then farewell fayrest age, the worlds best dayes,
Thriuing in ill, as it in age decaies.
Then crept in *Pride,* and peeuish Couetise:[68]
And men grew greedy, discordous and nice.
Now man, that earst *Haile-fellow* was with beast,
Woxe on to weene[69] himselfe a God at least.
No aery foule can take so high a flight,
Tho she her daring wings in clouds haue dight:
Nor fish can diue so deepe in yeelding Sea,
Tho *Thetis-selfe* should sweare her safetie:
Nor fearefull beast can dig his caue so lowe,
All[70] could he further then *Earths* center goe:
As that the ayre, the earth, or *Ocean,*
Should shield them from the gorge of greedy man.
Hath vtmost *Inde* ought better then his owne?
Then vtmost *Inde* is neare, and rife to gone.[71]
O *Nature:* was the world ordain'd for nought,
But fill mans maw, and feed mans idle thought:
Thy *Grandsires* words sauord of thriftie Leekes,
Or manly Garlicke: But thy furnace[72] reekes
Hote steams of wine: and can aloofe descrie
The drunken draughts of sweet *Autumnitie.*
They naked went: or clad in ruder hide:
Or home-spun *Russet,* void of forraine pride:
But thou canst maske in garish gauderie,
To suit a fooles far-fetched liuery.
A *French* head ioynd to necke *Italian:*
Thy thighs from *Germanie,* and brest fro *Spaine:*
An *Englishman* in none, a foole in all:
Many in one, and one in seuerall.
Then men were men, but now the greater part
Bestes are in life, and women are in heart.
Good *Saturne* selfe, that homely Emperour,
In proudest pompe was not so clad of yore,
As is the vnder-groome of the Ostlerie,
Husbanding it[73] in work-day yeomanrie.
Lo the long date of those expired dayes,
Which the inspired *Merlins* word fore-sayes:
When dunghill Pesants shall be dight as kings,
Then one confusion another brings:

66 *twine,*] *twine.* STC 12716.
67 dig deep.
68 covetousness.
69 grew to consider.
70 although.
71 easy to go to.
72 mouth.
73 doing farm or household work.

Then farewell fairest age, the worlds best dayes,
Thriuing in ill, as it in age decayes.

SATIRE 7

Seest thou how gayly my yong maister goes,
Vaunting himselfe vpon his rising toes,
And pranks[74] his hand vpon his dagger side,
And picks his glutted teeth since late Noon-tide?
T's *Ruffio:* Trow'st thou where he dind to day:
In sooth I sawe him sit with Duke *Humfray*.[75]
Many good welcoms, and much *Gratis* cheere,
Keepes he for euery stragling *Caualiere:*
An open house haunted with great resort,
Long seruice mixt with Musicall disport.
Many a fayre yonker with a fether'd crest,
Chooses much rather be his shot free[76] guest,
To fare so freely with so little cost,
Then stake his *Twelue-pence* to a meaner host.
Hadst thou not tould me, I should surely say,
He touch't no meat of all this liue-long day.
For sure me thought, yet that was but a ghesse,
His eyes seeme sunke for very hollownesse.
But could he haue (as I did it mistake)
So little in his purse, so much vpon his backe:
So nothing in his maw: yet seemeth by his belt,
That his gaunt gut, no too much stuffing felt.
Seest thou how side[77] it hangs beneath his hip,
Hunger, and heauie Iron makes girdles slip,
Yet for all that how stifly strits[78] he by,
All trapped in the new-found brauerie.[79]
The *Nuns* of new-woon *Cales*[80] his bonnet lent,
In lieu of their so kinde a Conquerment.
What neded he fetch that from farthest *Spaine,*
His *Grandame* could haue lent with lesser paine?
Tho he perhaps neuer past the English shore;
Yet faine would counted be a Conquerour.
His haire *French-like;* stares[81] on his frighted hed,
One locke *Amazon-like* disheueled:
As if he ment to weare a natiue cord,[82]
If chance his *Fates* should him that bane afford.[83]
All *Brittish* bare vpon the bristled skin,
Close noched[84] is his beard both lip and chin.
His linnen coller *Labyrinthian*-set,
Whose thousand double turnings neuer met:
His sleeues halfe hid with elbow-*Pineonings,*
As if he meant to flye with linnen wings.
But when I looke and cast mine eyes below,

[74] makes a display of.

[75] "To dine with Duke Humphrey" was to spend the dinner hour walking in the south aisle of St. Paul's, where it was believed Humphrey, Duke of Gloucester, had been buried.

[76] free from having to pay a tavern reckoning.

[77] low.

[78] struts.

[79] finery.

[80] Cadiz, captured in 1596.

[81] stands on end.

[82] to be hanged with a native cord of hemp.

[83] give.

[84] cut unevenly.

What monster meets mine eyes in humane show?
So slender wast with such an Abbots loyne,
Did neuer sober Nature sure conioyne:
Lik'st a strawne[85] scar-crow in the new-sowne field,
Reard on some sticke, the tender corne to shield:
Or if that semblance sute not euery deale,[86]
Like a broad shak-forke[87] with a slender steale.
Despised Nature suit them once aright,
Their body to their cote: both now mis-dight:
Their body to their clothes might shapen bee,
That nill[88] their clothes shape to their body.
Meane while I wonder at so proud a backe,
Whiles th'emptie guts loud rumblen for long lacke.
The belly enuieth the backs bright glee,
Aud murmurs at such inequalitie.
The backe appeales vnto the partiall eine,
The plaintiue belly pleades they bribed beene:
And he for want of better Aduocate,
Doth to the eare his iniurie relate.
The backe insulting ore the bellies need,
Saies: thou thy selfe, I others eyes must feed.
The maw, the guts, all inward parts complaine
The backs great pride, and their owne secret paine.
Ye witlesse gallants, I beshrew your harts,
That set such discord twixt agreeing parts,
Which neuer can be set at onement more,
Vntill the mawes wide mouth be stopt with store.

From Guilpin's SKIALETHEIA[1]

SATYRE PRELUDIUM

Fie on these *Lydian* tunes[2] which blunt our sprights
And turne our gallants to Hermaphrodites:[3]
Giue me a Doricke touch, whose Semphony,[4]
And dauncing aire may with affinity
Moue our light vaulting spirits and capering,[5]
Woo Alexander from lewd banquetting
To armes, bid[6] *Haniball* remember *Cannas,*[7]
And leaue *Salapian Tamyras* embrace.
Hence with these fidlers, whose oyle-buttred lines,
Are Panders vnto lusts, and food to sinnes,
Their whimpring Sonnets, puling Elegies
Slaunder the Muses; make the world despise,
Admired poesie, marre *Resolutions* ruffe,[8]
And melt true valour with lewd ballad stuffe.
Heere one's Elegiack pen patheticall,

---

[85] stuffed with straw.
[86] part.
[87] pitchfork.
[88] do not wish.
[1] From *Skialetheia. Or a shadowe of truth, in certaine epigrams and satyres,* 1598, STC 12504, Huntington Library.
[2] sweet or amatory verse.
[3] Here the meaning is "weaklings."
[4] harmony.
[5] *capering,*] *capering.* STC 12504.
[6] *armes, bid*] *armes. Bid* STC 12504.
[7] Hannibal defeated the Romans at Cannae in 216 B.C.
[8] excitement, strength.

His parting from his Mistris doth bewaile:
Which when young gallant *Mutio* hath perus'd,
His valour's crestfalne, his resolues abusd,[9]
For whatsoe're his courage erst did moue,
He'le goe no voyage now to leaue his Loue.
  Another with his supple passion
Meaning to moue his Pigsney[10] to compassion,
Makes puisne[11] *Lucius* in a simpathy
In loue with's pibald Laundres by and by.

. . . .

  The Satyre onely and Epigramatist,
(Concisde[12] Epigrame, and sharpe Satyrist)
Keepe diet from this surfet of excesse,
Tempring themselues from such licenciousnes.
The bitter censures of their Critticke spleenes,
Are Antidotes to pestilentiall sinnes,
They heale with lashing, seare luxuriousnes,[13]
They are Philosophicke true *Cantharides*[14]
To vanities dead flesh. An Epigrame
Is popish displing,[15] rebell flesh to tame:
A plaine dealing lad, that is not afraid
To speake the truth, but calls a iade,[16] a iade.
And *Mounsieur Guulard*[17] was not much too blame,
When he for meat mistooke an Epigrame,
For though it be no cates,[18] sharpe sauce it is,
To lickerous[19] vanitie, youths sweet amisse.[20]
But oh the Satyre hath a nobler vaine,
He's the Strappado,[21] rack,[22] and some such paine
To base lewd vice; the Epigram's Bridewell,[23]
Some whipping cheere:[24] but this is follies hell.

. . . .

These critique wits which nettle vanitie,
Are better farre then foode to foppery:
And I dare warrant that the hangingst brow,
The sowrest Stoicke that will scarce allow
A riming stone vpon his fathers graue,
(Though he no reason haue no rime to haue:)
The stricktest (*Plato*) that for vertues health:
Will banish Poets forth his common-wealth,[25]
Will of the two affoord the Satyre grace,
Before the whyning loue-song shall haue place:
And by so much his night-cap's ouer awde,
As a Beadle's better states-man then a Bawde.

---

9 deceived, injured.
10 darling.
11 puny.
12 concised, cut off, terse.
13 lust.
14 irritant.
15 discipline.
16 rascal.
17 The editor cannot explain this allusion.
18 delicacy.
19 greedy, lustful.
20 fault.
21 An instrument of torture.
22 An instrument of torture.
23 The epigram is Bridewell, a prison in London.
24 welcome, entertainment.
25 *common-wealth,*] *common-wealth.* STC 12504.

SATIRE 5

Let me alone I prethee in thys Cell,
Entice me not into the Citties hell;
Tempt me not forth this *Eden* of content,
To tast of that which I shall soone repent:
Prethy excuse me, I am not alone,[26]
Accompanied with meditation,
And calme content, whose tast more pleaseth me
Then all the Citties lushious vanity.
I had rather be encoffin'd in this chest
Amongst these bookes and papers I protest,
Then free-booting abroad purchase offence,
And scandale my calme thoughts with discontents.
Heere I conuerse with those diuiner spirits,
Whose knowledge, and admire[27] the world inherits:
Heere doth the famous profound *Stagarite,*[28]
With Natures mistick harmony delight
My rauish'd contemplation: I heere see
The now-old worlds youth in an history:
Heere may I be graue *Platos* auditor;
And learning of that morrall Lecturer,
To temper mine affections, gallantly
Get of my selfe a glorious victory:
And then for change, as we delight in change,[29]
(For this my study is indeede m'Exchange)
Heere may I sit, yet walke to *Westminster*
And heare *Fitzherbert, Plowden, Brooke,* and *Dier*[30].
Canuas a law-case: or if my dispose[31]
Perswade me to a play, I'le to the *Rose,*[32]
Or *Curtaine,*[33] one of *Plautus* Comedies,
Or the *Patheticke Spaniards*[34] Tragedies:
If my desire doth rather wish the fields,
Some speaking Painter, some Poet straitway yeelds
A flower bespangled walk, where I may heare
Some amorous Swaine his passions declare
To his sun-burnt Loue. Thus my books little case,
My study, is mine All, mine euery place.[35]

From Marston's THE SCOURGE OF VILLAINY[1]

TO DETRACTION I PRESENT MY POESIE

Foule canker of faire vertuous action,
Vile blaster of the freshest bloomes on earth,
Enuies abhorred child *Detraction,*
I heare expose, to thy all-taynting breath
The issue of my braine, snarle, raile, barke, bite,
Know that my spirit scornes *Detractions* spight.

---

[26] *alone,*] *alone* STC 12504.
[27] admiration.
[28] Aristotle, who was born in Stagira, a city of ancient Macedonia.
[29] *change,*] *change.* STC 12504.
[30] The standard writers on English law.
[31] disposition, mood.
[32] A theater in London.
[33] A theater in London.
[34] Seneca's.
[35] In 138 lines that follow Guilpin attacks the evils of London.
[1] From *The scourge of villanie,* 1599, STC 17486, Folger Library.

Know that the *Genius,* which attendeth on,
And guides my powers intellectuall,
Holds in all vile repute *Detraction,*
My soule an essence metaphisicall,
That in the basest sort scornes *Critickes* rage,
Because he knowes his sacred parentage.

My spirit is not puft vp with fatte fume
Of slimie Ale, nor *Bacchus* heating grape.
My minde disdaines the dungie muddy scum
Of abiect thoughts, and *Enuies* raging hate.
True iudgement, slight regards Opinion,
A sprightly wit, disdaines Detraction.

A partiall prayse shall neuer eleuate
My setled censure, of mine owne esteeme.
A cankered verdit of malignant Hate
Shall nere prouoke me, worse my selfe to deeme.
  Spight of despight, and rancors villanie,
  I am my selfe, so is my poesie.

SATIRE 10

Humours[2]

Sleep grim *Reproofe,* my iocond Muse doth sing
In other keyes, to nimbler fingering.
Dull sprighted *Melancholy,* leaue my braine
To hell *Cimerian* night, in liuely vaine
I striue to paint, then hence all darke intent
And sullen frownes, come sporting meriment,
Cheeke dimpling laughter, crowne my very soule
With iouisance, whilst mirthfull iests controule
The goutie humours of these pride-swolne dayes,
Which I doe long vntill my pen displaies.
O I am great with mirth, some midwifrie,
Or I shall breake my sides at vanitie.
  Roome for a capering mouth, whose lips nere stur,
But in discoursing of the gracefull slur:[3]
Who euer heard spruce skipping *Curio*
Ere prate of ought, but of the whirle on toe.
The turne aboue ground, *Robrus* sprauling kicks,
Fabius caper, *Harries* tossing tricks?
Did euer any eare, ere heare him speake
Vnlesse his tongue of crosse-poynts did intreat?
His teeth doe caper whilst he eates his meate,
His heeles doe caper, whilst he takes his seate,
His very soule, his intellectuall
Is nothing but a mincing capreall.[4]
He dreames of toe-turnes, each gallant hee dooth meete

[2] Chapman's *An Humourous Day's Mirth* and Jonson's *Every Man in His Humour* established the vogue of the "comedy of humours," comedy that satirizes a person's predominant characteristic or affectation. Satire of this kind was popular for several years after 1597.

[3] A gliding movement in dancing.

[4] capriole, caper.

He fronts him with a trauers[5] in the streete,
Prayse but *Orchestra,*[6] and the skipping art,
You shall commaund him, faith you haue his hart
Euen capring in your fist. A hall, a hall,
Roome for the Spheres, the Orbes celestiall
Will daunce *Kemps Iigge.*[7] They'le reuel with neate iumps
A worthy Poet hath put on their Pumps?

. . . .

Luscus what's playd to day? fayth now I know
I set thy lips abroach, from whence doth flow
Naught but pure *Iuliet* and *Romeo.*
Say, who acts best? *Drusus,* or *Roscio?*
Now I haue him, that nere of ought did speake
But when of playes or Plaiers he did treate.
H'ath[8] made a common-place booke out of playes,
And speakes in print, at least what ere he sayes
Is warranted by Curtaine[9] *plaudities,*[10]
If ere you heard him courting *Lesbias* eyes;
Say (Curteous Sir) speakes he not mouingly
From out some new pathetique Tragedie?
He writes, he railes, he iests, he courts, what not,
And all from out his huge long scraped stock
Of well penn'd playes.

. . . .

But roome for *Tuscus,* that iest-mounging youth,
Who nere did ope his Apish gerning[11] mouth
But to retaile and broke anothers wit.
Discourse of what you will, he straight can fit
Your present talke, with, *Sir, I'le tell a iest,*
(Of some sweet Lady, or graund Lord at least)
Then on he goes. And nere his tongue shall lie
Till his ingrossed[12] iests are all drawne dry;
But then as dumbe as *Maurus,* when at play
H'ath lost his crownes, and paun'd his trim aray.
He doth naught but retaile iests, breake but one,
Out flies his table-booke, let him alone,
He'le haue't i-fayth; Lad, hast an Epigram,
Wilt haue it put into the chaps of Fame?
Giue *Tuscus* coppies, sooth as his owne wit
His propper issue he will father it.
O that this Eccho, that doth speake, spet, write
Naught but the excrements of others spright,
This ill-stuft trunck of iests, whose very soule
Is but a heape of Iibes, should once inroule
His name mong creatures termed rationall,
Whose chiefe repute, whose sence, whose soule and all

---

5 traverse, a dance step.
6 These lines refer to Davies' poem.
7 Will Kemp, famous dancer and comedian, acted in Shakespeare's earlier plays.
8 He hath.
9 A London theater.
10 Appeals for applause at the end of plays; epilogues. Cf. *As You Like It.*
11 grinning.
12 written and memorized.

Are fed with offall scraps, that somtimes fall
From liberall wits, in their large festiuall.

. . . .

O spruce! How now *Piso, Aurelius* Ape,
What strange disguise, what new deformed shape
Doth hold thy thoughts in contemplation?
Faith say, what fashion art thou thinking on?
A stitch'd Taffata cloake, a payre of slops[13]
Of Spanish leather? O who heard his chops
Ere chew of ought, but of some strange disguise,
This fashion-mounger, each morne fore he rise
Contemplates sute shapes, and once from out his bed,
He hath them straight full liuely portrayed.
And then he chukes,[14] and is as proud of this,
As *Taphus* when he got his neighbours blisse.
All fashions since the first yeere of this Queene,
May in his studdy fairely drawne be seene,
And all that shall be to his day of doome,
You may peruse within that little roome.
For not a fashion once dare show his face,
But from neate *Pyso* first must take his grace.
The long fooles coat, the huge slop, the lugg'd[15] boot
From mimick *Pyso,* all doe claime their roote.
O that the boundlesse power of the soule
Should be coop'd vp in fashioning some roule!
But O, *Suffenus,* (that dooth hugge, imbrace
His propper selfe, admires his owne sweet face,
Prayseth his owne faire limmes proportion,
Kisseth his shade, recounteth all alone
His owne good parts) who enuies him? not I,
For well he may, without all riualrie.
Fie, whether's fled my sprights alacritie?
How dull I vent this humorous poesie.
In faith I am sad, I am possest with ruth,
To see the vainenes of faire *Albions* youth;
To see their richest time euen wholy spent
In that which is but Gentries ornament.
Which being meanly done, becomes them well,
But when with deere times losse they doe excell,
How ill they doe things well. To daunce and sing,
To vault, to fence, and fairely trot a ring
With good grace, meanely done. O what repute
They doe beget, but being absolute,
It argues too much time, too much regard
Imploy'd in that which might be better spard,
Then substance should be lost. If one should sew
For *Lesbias* loue, hauing two dayes to woe
And not one more, and should imploy those twaine
The fauour of her wayting-wench to gaine,
Were he not mad? Your apprehension,
Your wits are quicke in application.[16]

---

[13] loose breeches.
[14] chuckles.
[15] having lugs or ears.
[16] The concluding thirty-six lines are omitted.

TO EUERLASTING OBLIUION

Thou mighty gulfe, insatiat cormorant,
Deride me not, though I seeme petulant
To fall into thy chops. Let others pray
For euer their faire Poems flourish may.
But as for mee, hungry *Obliuion*
Deuoure me quick, accept my orizon:
  My earnest prayers, which doe importune thee,
  With gloomy shade of thy still Emperie,
  To vaile both me and my rude poesie.[17]

Farre worthier lines in silence of thy state
Doe sleepe securely free from loue or hate,
From which this liuing, nere can be exempt,
But whilst it breathes will hate and fury tempt.
Then close his eyes with thy all-dimming hand,
Which not right glorious actions can with-stand.
Peace hatefull tongues, I now in silence pace.[18]
Vnlesse some hound doe wake me from my place,
  I with this sharpe, yet well meant poesie,
  Will sleepe secure, right free from iniurie
  Of cancred hate, or rankest villanie.

[17] *poesie.*] *poesie,* STC 17486.

[18] *pace.*] *pace,* STC 17486.

Epigrams

THE EPIGRAM was one of the favorite genres of the European Renaissance, and in England epigrams were written in large numbers throughout the Elizabethan period, especially in the 1590's and the early years of the seventeenth century. During the period the word "epigram" was used inaccurately to describe almost any short poem; when the word is used accurately it means a short poem ending in a witty or ingenious turn or in a sententious comment. In English schools the composition of Latin epigrams was required as an exercise in rhetoric. Almost every educated Englishman wrote Latin epigrams, and many published collections of them.

The epigram in English developed slowly. In the middle of the century John Heywood wrote several hundred homespun English epigrams, and though they were reprinted at intervals until the end of the century few writers imitated them. In Robert Crowley's *One and Thirty Epigrams*, 1550, we find short type-satires rather than epigrams. In 1567 Turberville published a number of epigrams derived from neo-Latin sources and from the Greek anthology. In 1577 Timothy Kendall included in his *Flowers of Epigrams* a great many translations from Greek and Latin epigrams, among the latter some by Sir Thomas More and other sixteenth-century writers. Most of the epigrams are Kendall's own rather clumsy translations from Martial. Kendall assures the reader that he has avoided all that is objectionable in Martial: "I have left the lewde, I have chosen the chaste: I have weeded away all wanton and woorthlesse woordes: I have pared away all pernicious patches: I have chipt and chopt of all beastly boughes and branches, all filthy and fulsom phrases." It was perhaps Martial's lack of moral earnestness that so long delayed Elizabethan imitation of his epigrams. This consideration did not deter Harington and Davies. Their epigrams, many of them translations and imitations of Martial, did much to establish the vogue of the epigram in the 1590's.

At Queen Elizabeth's court Sir John Harington (see page 330) was a privileged jester. She called him "that merry poet, my godson." She liked his epigrams and read them to the court. When she had but a few months to live, he read her "some verses, whereat she smilede once, and was pleasede to saie, 'When thou doest feele creepinge tyme at thye gate, these fooleries will please thee lesse.'" Some of Harington's epigrams are drawn directly from Martial; a few come from the Renaissance Latin epigrammatists; many of them appear to be suggested by his everyday experiences and conversations. Although many of his epigrams are satires in little, his mood has none of the bitterness of Hall and Marston. Instead of savage indignation one finds urbanity and even gaiety. During his lifetime there are many references to his epigrams, although no collection was printed until after his death. In 1613 a few were printed in J. C.'s *Alcilia* and in Henry Parrot's *Springes for Woodcocks.* There are one hundred sixteen in the edition of 1615, and three hundred forty-six in the edition of 1618, which was reprinted in 1625 and 1633; some eighty additional epigrams from his manuscripts are included in *The Letters and Epigrams of Sir John Harington,* 1930. His epigrams date from about 1585 to 1603. He was the best known of the Elizabethan epigrammatists, and he probably did more than anyone else to make the English epigram fashionable.

After Harington came a long line of epigrammatists. The epigrams of Sir John Davies (see page 540), forty-eight in number, are social satire in the manner of Martial, witty and coarse. Davies's *Epigrams* was one of the books burned by order of the Archbishop of Canterbury in 1599. *Skialetheia,* 1598, by Everard Guilpin (see page 565) contains seventy epigrams which, like his satires, give us glimpses of the London taverns and theaters and inns of court. Thomas Bastard (1566–1618) was educated at Winchester and New College, Oxford, and was for a time vicar of Bere Regis in his native Dorsetshire. In 1598 he published *Chrestoleros,* a collection of about two hundred epigrams, some of which were written several years earlier. In his Dedication he writes: "I haue taught Epigrams to speake chastlie; besides I haue acquainted them with more grauitie of sence, and barring them of their olde libertie, not onlie forbidden them to be personall, but turned all their bitternesse rather into sharpnesse." He addressed two pleasant epigrams to Henry (later Sir Henry) Wotton, whom he had known at Winchester and New College. John Weever (1576–1632) was educated at Queen's College, Cambridge. His one volume of epigrams was published in 1599; in 1600 appeared his satirical *Faunus and Melliflora,* and in 1601 two volumes of more serious verse. He then became an antiquary, made a study of the tombs of England, and in 1631 published his *Ancient Funeral Monuments.* Samuel Rowlands (c. 1570–c. 1630), popular satirist and pamphleteer, wrote many volumes in verse and prose from 1600 to 1627. John Heath, Fellow of New College, Oxford, from 1609 to 1616, is remembered chiefly for his one volume of epigrams, 1610. Of Thomas Freeman little is known. Soon after leaving Oxford he published the one volume for which he is remembered, a collection of epigrams in two parts, the first entitled *Rub and a Great Cast,* and the second, *Run and a Great Cast,* 1614. Their special interest is in their reference to contemporary writers. John Davies of Hereford (c. 1565–1618) was known as a writing master and as a prolific writer of many kinds of nondramatic poetry, especially religious and moralistic verse. His *Scourge of Folly,* 1611, and *Wit's Bedlam,*

1617, are collections of epigrams. John Taylor (c. 1578–1653), "the water poet," was for some years a Thames water-man and a collector of wine duties from ships in the port of London. From 1612 on he wrote a large number of popular pamphlets in verse and prose. His books are a rich mine of information about the lower levels of English society. Richard Brathwait (1588–1673) attended both Oxford and Cambridge, and entered Gray's Inn in 1609. During his long life as a country gentleman he wrote verse and prose of many kinds: sonnets, epigrams, satires, characters, pastorals, courtesy books, burlesque, literary criticism, religious essays. His best-known books are a courtesy book, *The English Gentleman*, 1630, and the famous burlesque, *Barnaby's Journal*, 1638. His *Strappado for the Devil*, 1615, is a collection of fifty-six epigrams, most of them satiric. Henry Parrot (fl. 1606–1626) is perhaps the most prolific epigrammatist of the period. Nothing of his life is known. He published in his five collections nearly one thousand epigrams. Brief, clear, lively, they are examples of the Elizabethan epigram at its best and worst.

During the quarter-century from 1585 to 1615 the epigram was fashionable wherever gallants met. In addition to the thousands of epigrams that were printed, many were circulated in manuscript and by word of mouth. Most of the epigrams, like the formal satires, were written by young men who were recently from the universities or from the Inns of Court, and who were eager to display their wit. Rowlands, Taylor, Parrot, and Davies of Hereford were notable exceptions; they wrote for a larger public. By 1616, when Ben Jonson's epigrams were printed, the English epigram at its worst was formless, obscene, and scurrilous, and at its best retained little of Martial's artistry. Jonson gave to the writing of his epigrams the same scholarly care that he gave to his best poetry; with him the epigram became established as a form.

The most useful modern editions are the following: Timothy Kendall, *Flowers of Epigrams*, Spenser Society, 1874; *The Letters and Epigrams of Sir John Harington*, ed. N. E. McClure, 1930; *Ovid's Elegies translated by Christopher Marlowe, together with the Epigrams of Sir John Davies*, 1925; *The Poems of Sir John Davies*, ed. Clare Howard, 1941; Everard (or Edward) Guilpin, *Skialetheia*, ed. G. B. Harrison, 1932; Thomas Bastard, *Chrestoleros*, ed. G. B. Harrison, 1932; John Weever, *Epigrammes*, ed. R. B. McKerrow, 1911; Samuel Rowlands, *Complete Works*, ed. E. Gosse, 3 vols., Hunterian Club, 1874–1880; John Davies of Hereford, *The Complete Works*, ed. A. B. Grosart, 2 vols., 1878; Richard Brathwait, *A Strappado for the Divell*, ed. J. B. Ebsworth, 1878; John Taylor, *Works of John Taylor, 1630*, Spenser Society, 1869; *Works not included in the Folio Volume of 1630*, Spenser Society, 1870. The following are illuminating accounts: T. K. Whipple, *Martial and the English Epigram from Sir Thomas More to Ben Jonson*, 1925; H. H. Hudson, *The Epigram in the English Renaissance*, 1947; John Wilcox, "Informal Publication of Late Sixteenth-Century Verse Satire," *The Huntington Library Quarterly*, xiii (1950), 191–200;

Clay Hunt, "The Elizabethan Background of Neo-Classic Polite Verse," *English Literary History*, viii (1941), 273–304; M. W. Black, *Richard Brathwait, an Account of His Life and Works*, 1928; F. B. Williams, Jr., "Henry Parrot's Stolen Feathers," *PMLA*, lii (1937), 1019–1030, and "The Epigrams of Henry Parrot," *Harvard Studies and Notes in Philology and Literature*, xx (1938), 15–28.

From Sir John Harington's ELEGANT AND WITTY EPIGRAMS[1]

COMPARISON OF THE SONNET, AND THE EPIGRAM

Once, by mishap, two Poets fell a-squaring,
The Sonnet, and our Epigram comparing;
And *Faustus,* hauing long demurd vpon it,
Yet, at the last, gaue sentence for the Sonnet.
Now, for such censure, this his chiefe defence is,
Their sugred taste best likes his likresse senses.
Well, though I grant Sugar may please the taste,
Yet let my verse haue salt to make it last.

OF DON PEDRO AND HIS POETRY[2]

Sir, I shall tell you newes, except you know it,
Our noble friend *Don Pedro,* is a Poet.
His verses all abroad are read and showne,
And he himselfe doth sweare they are his owne.
His owne? tis true, for he for them hath paid
Two crownes a Sonnet, as I heard it said.
So *Ellen* hath faire teeth, that in her purse
She keepes all night, and yet sleepes ne're the worse.
So widdow *Lesbia,* with her painted hide,
Seem'd, for the time, to make a handsome bride.
If *Pedro* be for this a Poet cald,
So you may call one hairie that is bald.

A COMFORT FOR POORE POETS

Poets, hencefoorth for pensions need not care,
Who call you beggers, you may call them lyers,
Verses are growne such merchantable ware,
That now for Sonnets, sellers are, and buyers.

AN EPITAPH IN COMMENDATION OF GEORGE TURBERUILL, A LEARNED GENTLEMAN

When rimes were yet but rude, thy pen endeuored
To pollish Barbarisme with purer stile:
When times were grown most old, thy heart perseuered
Sincere and iust, vnstaind with gifts or guile.
Now liues thy soule, though from thy corps disseuered,

[1] From *The most elegant and wittie epigrams of Sir J. Harrington. Digested into foure bookes,* 1618, STC 12776, Folger Library.

[2] Suggested by Martial, ii, 20.

There high is blisse, here cleare in fame the while;
To which I pay this debt of due thanks-giuing,
My pen doth praise thee dead, thine grac'd me liuing.

AGAINST PAULUS

Because in these so malecontented times,
I please my selfe with priuate recreation;
In reading or in sweetest contemplation,
Or writing sometime prose, oft pleasant rimes:
Paulus, whom I haue thought my friend sometimes,
Seekes all he may to taint my reputation:
Not with complaints, nor any haynous crimes,
But onely saying in his scoffing fashion,
These writers that still sauour of the schooles,
Frame to themselues a Paradice of fooles.
But while he scornes our mirth and plaine simplicitie,
Himselfe doth sayle to *Affricke* and to *Ind.*
And seekes with hellish paines, yet doth not finde
That blisse, in which he frames his wise felicitie.
Now which of twaine is best, some wise man tell,
Our Paradice, or else wise *Paulus* hell.

OF CINNA'S ELECTION

Pvre *Cinna* makes no question he's elect,
Yet lewdly liues: I might beleeue him better,
If he would change his life, or change one letter,
And say that he is sure he is eiect.
An holy, true, and long preserued purity,
May hap, and but perhap breede such securitie.

THE AUTHOR TO A DAUGHTER OF NINE YEERE OLDE[3]

Though pride in Damsels is a hatefull vice,
Yet could I like a Noble-minded Girle,
That would demand me things of costly price,
Rich Veluet gownes, pendents, and chaines of Pearle,
Carknets[4] of Aggats, cut with rare deuice,
Not that hereby she should my minde entice
To buy such things against both wit and profit.
But I like well she should be worthy of it.

TO THE LADY ROGERS,[5] OF HER VNPROFITABLE SPARING

When I to you sometimes make friendly motion,
To spend vp your superfluous prouision,
Or sell the same for coyne, or for deuotion,
To make thereof among the poore diuision;
Straight you answere me, halfe in derision,
And bid me speake against your course no more:
For plenty you doe loue, store is no sore.
But ah, such store is enemy to plenty,

[3] The source is Martial, xi, 27.

[4] A carcanet is a collar or necklace set with jewels.

[5] Harington's mother-in-law.

You waste for feare to want, I dare assume it:
For, while to sell, spend, giue, you make such dainty,
Keepe corne and cloth, till rat and rot consume it,
Let meat so mould, till muske cannot perfume it,
And by such sparing, seeke to mend such store,
Sore is such store, and God offending sore.

AGAINST AN ATHEIST[6]

That heau'ns are voide, and that no gods there are,
Rich *Paulus* saith, and all his proofe is this:
That while such blasphemies pronounce he dare,
He liueth here in ease, and earthly blisse.

OF FAUSTUS, A STEALER OF VERSES

I heard that *Faustus* oftentimes reherses,
To his chaste Mistris, certain of my Verses:
In which with vse, so perfect he is growne,
That she poore foole, now thinkes they are his owne.
I would esteeme it (trust me) grace, not shame,
If *Dauis,* or if *Daniel* did the same.
For would I thanke, or would I quarrell pike?[7]
I, when I list, could doe to them the like.
But who can wish a man a fowler spight,
Then haue a blinde man take away his light?
A begging Theefe, is dangerous to my purse:
A baggage Poet to my Verse is worse.

AGAINST FEASTING

Kinde *Marcus,* me to supper lately bad,
And to declare how well to vs he wishes,
The roome was strow'd with Roses, not[8] with Rushes,
And all the cheere was got, that could be had.
Now in the midst of all our dainty dishes,
Me thinke, said he to me, you looke but sad.
Alas (said I) 'tis to see thee so mad,
To spoile the skies of Fowles, the seas of fishes,
The land of beasts, and be at so much cost,
For that which in one houre will all be lost.
That entertainment that makes me most glad,
Is not the store of stew'd, boyl'd, bak't and rost.
But sweet discourse, meane fare; and then beleeue me,
To make to thee like cheere, shall neuer grieue me.

OF HONEST THEFT. TO MY GOOD FRIEND MASTER SAMUEL DANIEL

Proud *Paulus* late my secrecies reuealing,
Hath told I got some good conceits by stealing.
But where got he those double Pistolets,
With which good clothes, good fare, good land he gets?
Tush, those, he saith, came by a man of warre,

---

[6] The source is Martial, iv, 21.
[7] *pike?*] *pike,* STC 12776.
[8] *Roses, not* Addit. Ms. 12049]; *Roses and* STC 12776.

That brought a Prize of price, from countries farre.
Then fellow Thiefe, let's shake together hands,
Sith both our wares are filcht from forren lands.
  You'le spoile the Spaniards, by your writ of Mart:
  And I the Romanes rob, by wit, and Art.

TO MASTER BASTARD,[9] A MINISTER THAT MADE A PLEASANT BOOKE OF ENGLISH EPIGRAMS

Though dusty wits of this vngratefull time,
Carpe at thy booke of Epigrams, and scoffe it:
Yet wise men know, to mix the sweet with proffit[10]
Is worthy praise, not onely void of crime.
Then let not enuy stop thy veine of Rime:
Nor let thy function make thee shamed of it:
A Poet is one step vnto a Prophet:
And such a step, as 'tis no shame to clime.
You must in Pulpit treat of matters serious:
As best beseemes the person, and the place,
There preach of Faith, Repentance, hope and grace,
Of Sacraments, and such high things mysterious.
But they are too seuere, and too imperious,
That vnto honest sports will grant no space:
For these our minds refresh, when those weary vs,
And spurre our dulled[11] spirit to swifter pace.
The wholsom'st meates that are, will breed satietie,[12]
Except we should admit of some varietie.
In musike notes must be some high, some base.
And this I note, your Verses haue intendment,
Still kept within the lists of good sobrietie,
To work in mens ill manners, good amendment.
Wherefore if any thinke such verse vnseasonable:
Their Stoicke mindes are foes to good societie,
And men of reason may thinke them vnreasonable.
It is an act of vertue and of pietie,
  To warne vs of our sinnes in any sort,
  In prose, in verse, in earnest, or in sport.

OF GALLA'S GOODLY PERIWIGGE

You see the goodly hayre that *Galla* weares,[13]
'Tis certain her own hair, who would haue thought it?
She sweares it is her owne: and true she sweares:
For hard by Temple-barre last day she bought it.
  So faire a haire, vpon so foule a forehead,
  Augments disgrace, and showes the grace is borrowed.

TO MASTER BASTARD, TAXING HIM OF FLATTERY

It was a saying vs'd a great while since,
The subiects euer imitate the Prince,

---

[9] Thomas Bastard, author of *Chrestoleros,* 1598.

[10] *proffit* Addit. Ms. 12049]; *profit.* STC 12776.

[11] *dulled* Addit. Ms. 12049]; *doubled* STC 12776.

[12] *satietie* Addit. Ms. 12049]; *sacietie* STC 12776.

[13] The source is Martial, vi, 12.

A vertuous Master, makes a good Disciple,
Religious Prelates breede a godly people.
And euermore the Rulers inclination,
Workes in the time the chawnge and alteration.
Then what's the reason, *Bastard,* why thy Rimes
Magnifie Magistrates, yet taunt the times?
I thinke that he to taunt the time that spares not,
Would touch the Magistrate, saue that he dares not.

LESBIAS RULE OF PRAISE

Lesbia, whom some thought a louely creature,
Doth sometimes praise some other womans feature:
Yet this I do obserue, that none she praises,
Whome worthy fame by bewties merrits rayses.[14]
But onely of their seemely parts she tels,
Whom she doth sure beleeue, her self excels.
So, *Linus* praises *Churchyard* in his censure,
Not *Sydney, Daniel, Constable,* nor *Spencer.*

OF LYNUS, BORROWING

When *Lynus* meets me, after salutations,
Courtsies, and complements, and gratulations,
He presseth me, euen to the third deniall,
To lend him twenty shillings, or a royall:
But of his purpose, of his curtsie fayling,
He goes behind my backe, cursing and rayling.
Foole, thy kind speeches cost not thee a penny,
And more foole I, if they should cost me any.

OF SUMMUM BONUM

While I of *summum bonum* was disputing,
Propounding some positions, som confuting,
Old *Sextus* sayes that we were all deluded,
And that not one of vs aright concluded.
Knowledge, sayth he, is only true felicity,
Straightwayes a stranger askt me in simplicity,
Is *Sextus* learned? no quoth I, by this light.[15]
Then without light, how iudgeth he so right?
He doth but ayme, as poore men vallew wealth,
The feeble value strength, the sicke man health.

OF GOOD SAUCE

I went to suppe with *Cinna* tother night,
And to say true (for giue the diuell his right)
Though scant of meat we could a morsell get,
Yet here with store of passing sauce we met.
You aske what sauce, where pittance was so small?
This, Is not hunger the best sauce of all?

---

[14] *rayses.* Addit. Ms. 12049]; *praises.* STC 12776.

[15] *light.* Addit. Ms. 12049]; *light,* STC 12776.

OF TREASON

Treason doth neuer prosper, what's the reason?
For if it prosper, none dare call it Treason.

THE AUTHOR TO QUEENE ELIZABETH, IN PRAISE OF HER READING

For euer deare, for euer dreaded Prince,
You read a verse of mine a little since,
And so pronounst each word, and euery letter,
Your gracious reading, grac't my verse the better:
Sith then your Highnes doth by gift exceeding,
Make what you read, the better in your reading,
Let my poore Muse your paines thus far importune,
To leaue to read my verse, and read my fortune.

OF A CERTAINE MAN

There was (not certain when) a certaine preacher,
That neuer learn'd, and yet became a Teacher,
Who hauing read in Latine thus a Text
Of *erat quidam homo*, much perplext,
He seem'd the same with study great to scan
In English thus; *there was a certaine man.*
But now (quoth he) good people, note you this,
He saith there was, he doth not say there is:
For in these daies of ours, it is most certaine,
Of promise, oth, word, deed, no man is certaine:
Yet by my text you see it comes to passe,
That surely once a certaine man there was.
But yet I thinke, in all your Bible no man
Can finde this text; *there was a certaine woman.*

OF THE PILLARS OF THE CHURCH

In old time they were Call'd the Churches pillars,
That did excell in learning and in piety,
And were to youth examples of sobriety,
Of Christ's faire field the true and painefull tillers:
But where are now the men of that society?
Are all those tillers dead? those pillars broken?
No, God forbid such blasphemy be spoken;
I say, to stop the mouthes of all ill-willers,
God's field hath harrowers still, his Church hath pillars.[16]

A RULE TO PLAY

Lay down your stake at play, lay down your passion:
A greedy gamester still[17] hath some mis-hap.
To chafe at luck proceeds of foolish fashion.
No man throws still the dice in fortunes lap.

OF A FAIRE SHREW[18]

Faire, rich, and yong? how rare is her perfection,
Were it not mingled with one foule infection?
I meane, so proud a heart, so curst a tongue,
As makes her seeme, nor faire, nor rich, nor yong.

---

[16] robbers.

[17] always.

[18] The source is Martial, i, 64.

OF FRIENDSHIP[19]

New friends are no friends; how can that be true?
The oldest friends that are, were sometimes new.

OF INCLOSING A COMMON

A Lord, that purpos'd for his more auaile,
To compasse in a Common with a rayle,
Was reckoning with his friend about the cost
And charge of euery reule, and euery post:
But he (that wisht his greedy humour crost)
Said, Sir, prouide you posts, and without fayling,
Your neighbors round about wil find you rayling.

From ADDITIONAL MS. 12049[20]

TO JAMES THE VI KING OF SCOTLAND. THE DEDICACION OF THE COPY SENT BY CAP. HUNTER

Joy to the present, hope of future ages,
Bright Northern starre, whose oryent lyght infused,
In sowth and west stayed[21] myndes that stood amused,[22]
Accept a present heer of skribled pages,
A work whose method ys to be confused,
A work in which my pen yt self engages
To vse them right that have the world abused.
Yf I, whear sin ys wrought, pay shame for wages,
Let your ritch grace hold my poor zeall excused;
Enormous acts move modest mindes to rages,
Which strayght a tart reproofe well gev'n asswages,
And dewly gev'n yt cannot be refused.
We do but poynt out vices and detect them;
Tis you, great prince, that one day must correct them.

AGAINST AN EXTREAM FLATTERER THAT PREACHED AT BATH ON THE QUEENS DAY THE FORTETH YEER OF HER RAIGN

You that extoll the bliss of this our nation,
And lade our ears with stale and lothsom praise
Of forty yeares sweet peace and restfull dayes,
Which you advance with fayned admiration,
Much better would it sewt your high vocation
To beat down that[23] your flattring tongues do raise,
And rather seeke som words of Commination
For tymes abounding with abhomination.
Say that Gods wrath against vs is provoked,
And tell vs tis to vs the scripture saies,
"I forty yeers have brookt this generation."
And said, "Theis people have not known my wayes."
For law with lust, and rule with rape is yoked,
And zeall with schisme and Symony is choked.

---

[19] The source is Martial, i, 54.
[20] The punctuation is the present editor's.
[21] supported.
[22] distracted, bewildered.
[23] that which.

OF TWO RELIGIONS

One by his father kept long time to schoole,
And prooving not vnlearned nor a foole,
Was earst by him demaunded one occasion
Which was the sounder Church in his perswasion,
If this Church of *Geneua* late reformed,
Or that old Catholick that theis have skorned.
Both do cyte doctors, Councells both alleadge,
Both bost the word truths everlasting pleadge.
"Then say, my sonn," quoth he. "Fear no controule.
Which of the two is safest for my soule?"
"Sure," quoth the sonn, "a man had needs be crafty
To keepe his soule and body both in safty.
But both to save, this is best way to houlde:
Live in the new, dy yf you can in th'olde."

MISACMOS[24] OF HIMSELFE THAT LOVES TO BE WORST IN THE COMPANY

When I from schooles came to the citty first,
My Syre advisde me warely to chuse
All such as for compannions I would vse
So if I could as I might be the worst,
For why the graver and the wiser sorte
Men like their chief compannions do esteeme,
And such they doe their inclination deeme,
And theirs ys known with whome they do consorte.
Now while I thought I had som praise deserved,
To daunt my pride heerin, I have been tolde
Faustus as strict as I this rule doth holde;
Nay, more: he cannot break it yf he would.

TO MASTER IOHN DAUYS[25]

My deer friend *Davys,* some against vs partiall
Have found we steall some good conceits from Martiall;
So though they graunt our verse hath some Acumen,
Yet make they fooles suspect we skant ar trew men.
But *Surrey* did the same, and worthy *Wyatt,*
And they had praise and reputation by it;
And *Heywood,* whome your putting down hath raised,[26]
Did vse the same and with the same is praised.
Wherfore yf they had witt that soe did trace[27] vs,
They must again for their own creddits grace vs;
Or else to our more honour and their greevs
Match vs at least with honorable theevs.

OF HIS MUSE

I near desearvd that gloriows name of Poet;
No Maker I, nor do I care who know it.
Occasion oft my penn doth entertayn
With trew discourse; let others Muses fayn;

[24] A pseudonym that Harington sometimes used.

[25] Later Sir John Davies.

[26] See page 584.

[27] follow.

Myne never sought to set to sale her wryting;
In part her frends, in all her selfe delighting,
She cannot beg applause of vulgar sort,
Free born and bred, more free for noble sport.
My Muse hath one still bids her in her eare;
Yf well disposd, to write; yf not, forbear.

A GRATULATORY ELEGY OF THE PEACEABLE ENTRY OF KING IAMES GEV'N TO HIS MAIESTIE AT BURLEGH 1603

Come, triumphe, enter Church, courte, citty, towne;
Heer Iames the sixt, now Iames the first proclaymed.
See how all harts ar healld that earst wear maymed:
The peer is pleasd, the Knight, the clarck, the clowne;
The mark at which the mallcontent had aymed
Ys mist; succession stablisht in the crowne.
Ioy, protestaunt; let papists be reclaymed;
Leave, puritan, your supercilliows frowne,
Ioyn voice, hart, hande; all discorde be disclaymed.
Make all one flock by one great sheppard guided.
No forren woolfe can force a fould so fenced.
God for his house this *Steward* hath provided,
Right to dispose what earst was wrong dispenced.
But in my loyall love and long prepensed,
With all, yet more than all, reioyce do I
To conster[28] *Iames primus et non vi.*

From Sir John Davies' EPIGRAMS[29]

AD MUSAM

Flie merry Muse vnto that merry towne,
Where thou maist playes, reuel, and triumphs see
The house of fame, and theatre of renowne,
Where all good wittes and spirites loue to be.

Fall in betweene their hands that praise and loue thee
And be to them a laughter and a iest:
But as for them which scorning shall reprooue thee,
Disdaine their wittes, and thinke thine owne the best.

But if thou find any so grosse and dull,
That thinke I do to priuate taxing[30] leane,
Bid him go hang, for he is but a gull,
And knowes not what an Epigramme doth meane:
Which taxeth vnder a particular name,
A generall vice that merites publike blame.

OF A GULL[31]

Oft in my laughing rimes I name a gull,
But this new terme will many questions breede;

[28] construe.

[29] From *Epigrammes and elegies by J.D. and C.M.*, c. 1592, STC 6350, Huntington Library.

[30] censuring.

[31] Suggested by Martial, iii, 63.

Therefore at first I will expresse at full
Who is a true and perfect gull indeede.

A gull is he who feares a veluet gowne,
And when a wench is braue,[32] dares not speake to her:
A gull is he which trauerseth the towne,
And is for marriage knowne a common wooer.

A gull is he, which while he prowdly weares
A siluer hilted rapier by his side,
Indures the lies and knockes about the eares,
Whilst in his sheathe his sleeping sword doth bide.

A gull is he which weares good hansome cloathes,
And stands in presence stroking vp his haire,
And filles vp his vnperfect speech with othes,
But speakes not one wise word throughout the yeare:
But to define a gull in termes precise,
A gull is he which seemes, and is not wise.

IN CIPRIUM[33]

The fine youth Ciprius is more tierse[34] and neate,
Then the new garden of the old temple is,
And still the newest fashion he doth get,
And with the time doth change from that to this,
He weares a hat now of the flat crowne blocke,
The treble ruffes, long cloake, and doublet French,
He takes tobacco, and doth weare a locke,[35]
And wastes more time in dressing then a wench,
Yet this new-fangled youth made for these times,
Doth aboue all prayse old Gascoins rime.[36]

IN HAYWODUM

Haywood which did in Epigrams excell,
Is now put down since my light muse arose,
As buckets are put downe into a well,
Or as a Schoole-boy putteth downe his hose.

MEDITATIONS OF A GULL

See yonder melancholy Gentleman,
Which hoodwinck'd with his hat, alone doth sit,
Thinke what he thinkes, and tel me if you can,
What great affaires troubles his little wit:
He thinkes not of the warre twixt France and Spain,
Whether it be for Europes good or ill,
Nor whether the Empire can it selfe maintaine
Against the Turkish powre encroching still.
Nor what great towne in all the nether lands,
The States determine to besiege this spring,

[32] finely dressed.
[33] Suggested by Martial, ii, 29.
[34] neat.
[35] Lovelock worn over the forehead.
[36] The verse of George Gascoigne, who died in 1577.

Nor how the Scottish pollicie now standes,
Nor what becomes of th'Irish mutining:
But he doth seriouslie bethinke him whether
Of the guld people he be more esteemde,
For his long cloake, or for his great blacke feather,
By which each gull is now a gallant deemde.
Or of a Iourney he deliberates,
To Paris garden cock pit, or the play,
Or how to steale a dogge he meditates,
Or what he shall vnto his mistris say:
Yet with these thoughts he thinks himselfe most fit
To be of counsell with a King for wit.

From Everard Guilpin's SKIALETHEIA[37]

As in the greatest of societies,
The first beginners, like good natur'd soules,
Beare with their neighbors poore infirmities:
But after, when ambition controules
Theyr calme proceedings, they imperiously
(As great things still orewhelme themselues with weight)
Enuy their countrimens prosperity,
And in contempt of poorer fates delight.
So *Englands* wits (now mounted the full height,)
Hauing confounded monstrous barbarismes,
Puft vp by conquest, with selfe-wounding spight,
Engraue themselues in ciuill warres *Abismes,*[38]
Seeking by all meanes to destroy each other,
The vnhappy children of so deere a mother.

OF TITUS

Titus oft vaunts his gentry euery where,
Blazoning his coate, deriuing's pedegree;
What needest thou daily *Titus* iade mine eare?
I will beleeue thy houses auncestry;
If that be auncient which we doe forget,
Thy gentry is so; none can remember it.

OF ZENO

Zeno desirous of the idle fame
Of Stoicke resolution, recklesly
Seemes to esteeme of good report or blame;
So prouing himselfe dull, most foolishly,
To euery thing he heares, he saith he cares not:
He cares not for his booke, nor yet for wit,
For pleasant catch-fooles[39] in like sort he spares not
To sweare hee's carelesse, carelesse to forget
Or thinke vpon his dutie, soules comfort;
Carelesse to thriue, or liue in decencie;
Carelesse of vertuous, and a good consort,[40]

[37] From *Skialetheia. Or a shadowe of truth, in certaine epigrams and satyres,* 1598, STC 12504, Huntington Library.

[38] abysses.

[39] statements to deceive fools.

[40] company.

Carelesse of wisedome, and of honestie;
To all this carelesnes, should one declare
His fathers death, I am sure he would not care.

TO LICUS

Licus, thou art deceau'd in saying, that
I'me a fine man: thou saist thou knowst not what.
He's a fine fellow who is neate and fine,
Whose locks are kem'd,[41] and neuer a tangled twine,
Who smels of Musk, Ciuet, and Pomander,
Who spends, and out-spends many a pound a yeare,
Who piertly iets,[42] can caper, daunce, and sing,
Play with his Mistris fingers, her hand wring,
Who companying with wenches nere is still:
But either skips[43] or mowes,[44] or prates[45] his fill,
Who is at euery play, and euery night
Sups with his *Ingles,*[46] who can well recite,
Whatsoeuer rimes are gracious (*Licus*) leaue,
Iniure not my content then, to bereaue
My fortune of her quiet: I am I,
But a fine fellow in my fantasie
Is a great trouble, trouble me not then,
For a fine fellow, is a fine foole mongst men.

TO THE READER

Excuse me (Reader) though I now and than,
In some light lines doe shew my selfe a man,
Nor be so sowre, some wanton words to blame,
They are the language of an Epigrame.

OF CORNELIUS

See you him yonder, who sits o're the stage,
With the Tobacco-pipe now at his mouth?
It is *Cornelius* that braue gallant youth,
Who is new printed to this fangled[47] age:
He weares a Ierkin[48] cudgeld[49] with gold lace,
A profound slop,[50] a hat scarce pipkin[51] high,
For boots, a paire of dagge cases;[52] his face,
Furr'd with *Cads*-beard:[53] his poynard on his thigh.
He wallows in his walk his slop to grace,
Sweares by the *Lord,* daines no salutation
But to some iade[54] that's sick of his owne fashion,
As *farewell sweet Captaine,* or (*boy*) *come apace:*
Yet this Sir *Beuis,* or the fayery Knight,
Put vp the lie[55] because he durst not fight.

---

[41] combed.
[42] briskly struts.
[43] gambols.
[44] grimaces.
[45] talks foolishly.
[46] favorites.
[47] fond of foppery.
[48] close-fitting jacket.
[49] heavily trimmed.
[50] wide, loose breeches.
[51] small earthen pot.
[52] pistol cases.
[53] a Cadiz beard, a Spanish beard.
[54] contemptible person.
[55] submitted quietly to being called a liar.

From Thomas Bastard's CHRESTOLEROS[56]

DE SUBIECTO OPERIS SUI

I speake of wants, of frauds, of policies,
Of manners, and of vertues and of times,
Of vnthrifts and of frends, and enimies,
Poets, Physitions, Lawyers, and Diuines,
Of vsurers, buyers, borrowers, ritch and poore,
Of theeues, of murtherers by sea and land,
Of pickthankes,[57] lyers, flatterers lesse and more,
Of good and bad, and all that comes to hand,
I speake of hidden and of open things:
Of strange euents, of countries farre and wide,
Of warres, of captaynes, Nobles, Princes, kings,
Asia, Europe, and all the world beside.
This is my subiect reader I confesse,
From which I thinke seldom I doe digresse.

AD LECTOREM

Reader, my booke flies low, and comes not neere,
The higher world, and the celestiall spheare.
Yet not so low, but that it doth despise
The earthes round lumpe, and farre aboue it flies.
This is the middle labour of my pen,
To drawe thee forth (Reader) a mappe of men.

DE MICROCOSMO

Man is a little world and beares the face,
And picture of the Vniuersitie:[58]
All but resembleth God, all but his glasse,
All but the picture of his maiestie.
Man is the little world (so we him call,)
The world the little God, God the great All.

AD CURIOSUM LECTOREM

Me thinks some curious Reader, I heare say,
What Epigrams in english? tis not fit.
My booke is plaine, and would haue if it may,
An english Reader but a latine witt.

DE POETA MARTIALI

Martiall, in sooth none should presume to write,
Since time hath brought thy Epigrams to light:
For through our writing, thine so prais'de before
Haue this obteinde, to be commended more:
Yet to our selues although we winne no fame,
Wee please, which gets[59] our maister a good name.

[56] From Thomas Bastard, *Chrestoleros. Seven bookes of epigrames written by T.B.*, 1598, STC 1559, Morgan Library.

[57] flatterers.

[58] universe.

[59] *gets*] *get* STC 1559.

They which reade *Horace, Virgill* and the rest,
Of ancient Poets; all new wits detest:
And say O times; what happy wits were then,
I say, O fooles; rather what happy men.

Nisus writes Epigrams and so doe I,
Matter he hath enough, but I haue lesse,
Yet but in one poynt the ods doth lie,
He may speake of lewde loues and wantonnesse.
Is not this ods? am not I in a streight,
His matter pleaseth more, then my conceipt.

AD LECTOREM

How quickly doth the Reader passe away,
My pens long taske and travaile of the day?
Foure lines, which hold me tug[60] an howre or twaine
He sups vp[61] with a breath and takes no paine.
Yet vse me well Reader, which to procure
Thy one short pleasure two long paines endure:
The one of writing when it is begonne:
Th'other of shame, if't please not when tis done.

AD HENRICUM WOTTONUM[62]

Wotton, the country and the country swayne,
How can they yeelde a Poet any sense?
How can they stirre him vp, or heat his vaine?
How can they feede him with intelligence?[63]
You haue that fire which can a witt enflame,
In happy London Englands fayrest eye:
Well may you Poets haue of worthy name,
Which haue the foode and life of poetry.
And yet the country or the towne may swaye,
Or beare a part, as clownes doe in a play.

DE MENSE IANUARII QUAE FUIT AN. DO. 1595

When coldes and frosts and snowes were wont to reigne,
As in their time of prime in *Ianiuere.*
Then calme and milde and pleasant was the yeare,
Like to the spring which maketh all things feyne.[64]
The little sparrowes these I sawe deceiue,
Which cherped merily and built their nest.
Pore birds, the frost will come when you think lest,[65]
And you of pleasure sodainlye bereaue.
And this poore birds let me your errour rue;
But let the yeare deceiue no more then you.

[60] fully occupied.
[61] consumes.
[62] Knighted in 1603.
[63] news.
[64] glad.
[65] least.

IN CACUM

Cacus, if any chance on him to call,
Drawes forth the loafe and cheese, but if they eate
A golden sentence he drawes forth withall,
Friendship consisteth not in drinke and meate.
This is a goolden sentence I dare sweare.
This sentence saues him many pound's a yeare.

Heywood goes downe saith *Dauie,* sikerly,[66]
And downe he goes, I can it not deny.
But were I happy, did not fortune frowne,
Were I in heart, I would sing *Dauy* downe.

AD LECTOREM

Reader, there is no biting in my verse;
No gall, no wormewood, no cause of offence.
And yet there is a biting I confesse
And sharpenesse tempred to a wholsome sense.
Such are my Epigrams well vnderstood,
As salt which bites the wound, but doth it good.

AD REGINAM ELIZABETHAM

Liue long *Elisa,* that the wolfe of *Spayne,*
In his owne thirst of blood consumde may be,[67]
That forraine princes may enuie thy reigne,
That we may liue and florish vnder thee,
And though the bended force of mighty kings,
Ayme at thy royall Scepter, purposing
Confusion to thy country and thy state,[68]
Heauen fights for thee, and thou shalt have thy will
Of all thy foes, for thy Sunne standeth still.

IN CAIUM

So thy rare vertues fixed in mine eyes,
Thy gentle nature *Caius,* and thy minde[69]
So fraught with learning and good qualities:
That thou art ritch this onely fault I finde.
When thou wast poore thy vertues me releeued.
Since thou are ritch, of both I am depriued.

IN PHILONEM

Phylo is richly rayde,[70] and beareth hye
His great reuenues dated in[71] his coate.
Coyne, iewels, plate and land: loa heere they lie.

---

66 certainly; see page 584.
67 *be,*] *be.* STC 1559.
68 *state,*] *state.* STC 1559.
69 *minde*] *minde.* STC 1559.
70 arrayed.
71 limited to.

That is their last[72] which lately so did floate.
First in his bely shipt, they suffred wracke.
Now they are landed all vpon his backe.

AD REGINAM ELIZABETHAM

Mother of *England,* and sweete nurse of all,
Thy countries good which all depends on thee,
Looke not that countries father I thee call,
A name of great and kingly dignitie,
Thou dost not onely match old kings but rather,
In thy sweete loue to vs, excell a father.

AD EANDEM

I know where is a thiefe, and long hath beene,
Which spoyleth euery place where he resortes.
He steales away both subiectes from the Queene,[73]
And men from his owne country of all sortes.
Howses by three, and seauen, and ten he raseth,
To make the common gleabe, his priuate land.
Our country Cities cruell he defaceth,
The grasse grows greene where litle *Troy* did stand,
The forlorne father hanging downe his head,
His outcast company drawne vp and downe.
The pining[74] labourer doth begge his bread.
The plowswayne seek's his dinner from the towne.
O Prince, the wrong is thine, for vnderstand:
Many such robbries will vndoe thy land.

Our fathers did but vse the world before,
And hauing vsde did leaue the same to vs.
We spill[75] what euer resteth[76] of their store.
What can our heyres inherit but our curse?
For we haue suckt the sweete and sappe away,
And sowd consumption[77] in the fruitfull ground:
The woods and forests cladd in rich aray,
With nakednesse and baldnesse we confounde.
We haue defast the lasting monymentes
And caus'd all honour to haue ende with vs:
The holy temples feele our rauishments.
What can our heyres inherit but our curse?
The world must ende, for men are so accurst,
Vnlesse God ende it sooner: they will furst.

AD HENRICUM WOTTONEM

Wotton my little Beere[78] dwels on a hill,
Vnder whose foot the siluer Trowt doth swim,

[72] load, weight carried.
[73] *Queene,*] *Queene.* STC 1559.
[74] starving.
[75] destroy.
[76] remains.
[77] waste.
[78] Bastard was vicar of Bere Regis in Dorsetshire.

The Trowt siluer without and goold within,
Bibbing[79] cleere *Nectar,* which doth aye destill
From *Nulams* lowe head;[80] there the birds are singing
And there the partiall Sunne still giues occasion,
To the sweete dewes eternall generation:
There is greene ioy and pleasure euer springing,
O iron age of men, O time of rue.
Shame ye not that all things are goold but you?

A wonderfull scarsety will shortly ensue,
Of Butchers, of Bakers, of all such as brewe,
Of Tanners, of Taylors, of Smithes and the rest,[81]
Of all occupations that can be expres'd,
In the year of our Lorde, six hundred and ten,[82]
I thinke: for all these will be Gentlemen.

AD SAMUELEM DANIELEM

Daniell, beside the subiect of thy verse,
With thy rich vaine and stile adorned so,[83]
Besides that sweetnes with which I confesse,
Thou in thy proper kinde doth ouerflowe,[84]
Me thinkes thou steal'st my Epigrams away,
And this small glory for which now I waite.
For reading thee me thinks thus would I say,[85]
This hits my vaine, this had beene my conceipt.
But when I come my selfe to doe the like,
Then pardon me, for I am farre to seeke.

AD LECTOREM

If my bookes easie of digestion be,
Thanke not my matter reader but thanke me,
How many verses haue I cancelled?
How many lompes of meaning seasoned.
I suffer Epigrams to sprowte forth, when
I vse mine arte, and prune them with my pen.
For he that will write Epigrams indeed,
Must vse[86] to wring the meaning till it bleede.

From John Weever's EPIGRAMS[87]

IN RUDIONEM

Yon goes a gallant which will get repute,
From head to heele in his Carnation sute,
Slops, dublet, stockings, shooes, hat, band, and fether,

[79] drinking.
[80] The present editor cannot explain the allusion.
[81] *rest,*] rest. STC 1559.
[82] *ten,*] *ten.* STC 1559.
[83] *so,*] *so.* STC 1559.
[84] *overflowe,*] *ouerflowe.* STC 1559.
[85] *say,*] *say.* STC 1559.
[86] be accustomed.
[87] From John Weever, *Epigrammes in the oldest cut, and newest fashion,* 1599, STC 25224, Harvard College Library.

Red yard-long ribbin, see the youth coms hither,
Who lest his Dutchman hose should be vnseene
Aboue his mid-thigh he his cloake doth pin:
O that he had to his Carnation hose,
(I wish him well) a faire rich crimson nose.

AD GULIELMUM SHAKESPEARE

Honie-tong'd *Shakespeare* when I saw thine issue
I swore *Apollo* got them and none other,
Their rosie-tainted features cloth'd in tissue,
Some heauen born goddesse said to be their mother:
Rose-checkt *Adonis* with his amber tresses,
Faire fire-hot *Venus* charming him to loue her,
Chaste *Lucretia* virgine-like her dresses,
Prowd lust-stung *Tarquine* seeking still to proue her:
Romea,[88] *Richard;* more whose names I know not,
Their sugred tongues, and power attractiue beuty
Say they are Saints althogh that Saints they shew not
For thousands vowes to them subiectiue dutie:
They burn in loue thy children *Shakespear* het them,[89]
Go, wo[90] thy Muse,[91] more Nymphish brood beget them.

AD IO: MARSTON, ET BEN: IOHNSON

Marston, thy Muse enharbours *Horace* vaine,
Then some *Augustus* giue thee *Horace* merit,
And thine embuskin'd *Iohnson* doth retaine
So rich a stile, and wondrous gallant spirit,
That if to praise your Muses I desired,
My Muse would muse. Such wittes must be admired.

IN TUMULUM AUARI

Here lieth he who neuer aught
To man or woman gaue:
And now it grieues him that thou read'st
For nought this on his graue.

IN TUMULUM ABRAHAMI SIMPLE

Within this place lies *Abraham* the *Ciuil,*
Who neuer did good, who neuer did euill:
Too ill then for God, too good for the deuill.

From Samuel Rowlands's THE LETTING OF HUMOUR'S BLOOD[92]

Politique *Peter* meetes his friend a shore,
That came from Seas but newly tother day:
And giues him French embracements by the score,

[88] *Romea,*] *Romea* STC 25224.

[89] they (thousands of readers) burn in love; the children of your brain, Shakespeare, heated them.

[90] woo.

[91] *Muse,*] *Muse* STC 25224.

[92] From Samuel Rowlands, *Humors ordinarie,* 1607, STC 21395, New York Public Library, Arents Collection. This book is the third edition of *The letting of humours blood in the head-vaine,* 1600, STC 21393.

Then followes: *Dicke,* Hast made good voyage, say?
But hearing *Richards* shares be poore and sicke:
Peter ha's haste and cannot drinke with *Dicke.*

Well, then he meetes an other Caualeere,
Whom he salutes about the Knees and Thighes:
Welcom sweet *Iames,* now by the Lord what cheer?
Ner'e better *Peter,* We haue got rich prize.
Come, come (sayes *Peter*) euen a welcome quart,
For by my faith weele drinke before we part.

Bid me go sleepe: I scorne it with my heeles,
I know my selfe as good a man as thee:
Let goe mine arme I say, lead him that reeles,
I am a right good fellow; doest thou see?
I know what longes to drinking, and I can
Abuse my selfe as well as any man.

I care no more for twentie hundred pound,
(Before the Lord) then for a verie straw:
Ile fight with any hee aboue the ground,
Tut, tell not me whats what; I know the law,
Rapier and Dagger: hey a kingly fight,
Ile now trie falles with any by this light.

From Rowlands's LOOK TO IT[93]

VP-START COURTIER

Courtier, whose hart with pride, so mighty growes,
Thou wilt not to thy Father moue thy Hat,
Because he weares a paire of russet Hose:
Thy Veluet Breeches looke awry at that:
Nay, ere he shall disgrace thee, thou wilt rather
Sweare by the Lord, that he is not thy Father.

You that deny the stocke from whence you came,
Thrusting your selfe into some Gentle kin.
You that will giue your selfe another name,
Which must not from an old Thatcht-house begin.
You that will haue an Armes shall grace you too,
Though your poore Father cobled many a Shoo.
Ile Stabbe yee.

MISERABLE[94] MERCHANT

Marchant, that doest endeuour all thy dayes
To get commodities for priuate gaine:
Caring no whit by what synister wayes,

93 From Samuel Rowlands, *Looke to it: for Ile stabbe ye,* 1604, STC 21399, New York Public Library, Arents Collection.

94 miserly.

Nor by what hazard, trauell, toyle, or paine:
Neuer respecting other mens hard crosses,
So thou mayst sell deere pen-worths by their losses.

Thou that doest couet all in thine owne hand,
And for a nother let him sincke or swim:
Thou that hast blessinges both by sea and land,
Giuen by God, yet neuer thankest him:
Thou that with careful nights doest breake thy sleepe
To gather wealth, which long thou canst not keepe.
Ile Stabbe yee.

IDLE-HUSWIFE

Fine, neate, and curious mistris Butterflie,
The Idle-toy to please an Idiots eyes.
You that wish all Good-huswiues hang'd; for why,
Your dayes-work's done each morning when you rise,
Put on your Gowne, your Ruffe, your Maske, your Chaine,
Then dine and sup, and go to bed againe.

You that will call your Husband Gull and Clowne,
If he refuse to let you haue your will:
You that will poute and lowre, and fret and frowne
Vnlesse his purse be lauish open still.
You that will haue it, get it how he can
Or he shall weare a *Vulcans* brow, poore man.
Ile Stabbe thee.

GLUTTONE

You goodman Glutton, bellyed like a Butt,
Fac'd like the North-windes picture in a Map:
Thou with the neuer satisfied gutt,
Whose life is eate, and drinke, and take a nap.
Thou that if *Wolner*[95] were aliue againe,
Would'st eate more at a meale, then he in twaine.

Thou most vnhealthy lothsome rauenous beast,
That tak'st delight in nothing but excesse:
And hast a nose to smell out any Feast:
A brazen face to ceaze on euery messe,
That vndertakest nothing with good-will,
Vnlesse it be thy Pudding-house to fill.
Ile Stabbe thee.

From John Heath's TWO CENTURIES OF EPIGRAMS[96]

A Parson hauing a tithe Pigge or two,
To supper did his neighb'ring friends inuite:
Telling them briefly without more a dooe,

[95] A famous glutton.
[96] From John Heath, *Two centuries of epigrammes*, 1610, STC 13018, New York Public Library, Arents Collection.

A sp'rituall pigge was all their cheere that night.
And well he styl'd his pigge spirituall,
For spirit-like it had no flesh at all.

AD MODERNOS EPIGRAMMATISTAS

Heywood, th'old English Epigrammatist
Had wit at will, and art was all he mist:
But now a daies we of the moderne frie
Haue art, and labour with wits penurie.
Wit is the substance, art the polishment:
Art does adorne, and wit it does inuent.
Since then they are so ioyntly link't, that neither
Can well subsist without the helpe of either:
I gladly could haue wisht with all my hart,
That we had had his wit, or he our art.

DE GELU DIUTINO, ANNO DOM. 1607

When the frost did so long a time perseuer,
Nought was there scap't the rigour of the wether,
Except our hearts frozen so hard before,
That they could hardly then be frozen more.

Those which have traueld o're the earths round ball,
Tell vs of men that have no heads at all,
Who so belieue what euer they haue writ,
Heads they may haue, but sure they haue no wit.

IN SENECAM

Who so thy wittie writings throughly knowes,
Will iudge them to be Epigrams in prose.

VOLUCRE FERRUM

Iron long time hid in our mother earth,
And now brought forth by an vnhappy birth,
What hauocke hath it made since of our liues,
By rapyers, poniards, daggers, swords, and kniues.[97]
Yet more to hasten on our destinie,
We make it wings, and teach it how to flie.

Health is a iewell; true. Which when we buy,
Physitians value it accordingly.

IN PORCUM

Porcus that foule vnsociable hogge,
Grunts me out this still: *Loue me, loue my dog.*
And reason is there why we should so doe,
Since that his dog's the louelier of the two.

---

[97] *kniues.*] *kniues* STC 13018.

IN ARIOSTUM ORLANDI FURIOSI AUTOREM

He that could so well expresse those frantike fits,
Shewes that himselfe was passing well in's wits.

From Thomas Freeman's RUB AND A GREAT CAST[98]

LECTORI QUOMODO LEGAT

Reader remember that I doe fore-warne thee,
Pry not into the secrets of my Pen.
See not; if thou seest ought, that seemes to harme thee,
Wrong not thy selfe; if I doe, blame me then:
Looke on, laugh on, and if I touch thy griefe,
Or tell the fault wherein thou hast beene filthy,
Let not thy knowledge cause thy mis-beliefe,
I name thee not, what need'st thou then cry *Guilty?*
The Cholericke descry[99] their owne offence,
When like a gald-backt Iade scarce touch't they wince.

ME QUOQUE VATEM

Why am I not an *Epigrammatist?*
I write in couert, and conceale their names,
Whose liues I burden with some bitter iest,
Themselues I cloake, and yet vn-clowd their shames.
Againe, me thinkes I am not shallow sprighted,
Nor seemes my wit so insufficient
(Although not like to others deepe-conceited)[1]
It can indite,[2] although not excellent.
The Reader laughes, this reason he rehearses,
The Ape likes her owne whelpes, and I my verses.

O TEMPORA! O MORES!

Had I an hundred mouthes, as many tongues,
An Iron voyce; then should this Iron Age
Be mou'd, or I would thunder out their wrongs,
And breath out boysterous accents full of rage.
I would inueigh against fowle *Vsurers,*
As those that liue by causing others wants;
I would defie the filthy *Flatterers,*
That shew themselues dissembling Sycophants.
The *Lawyer* too my lauish tongue should lash,
And *Auarice* should not auoid the scourge,
And with the *Courtier* would I haue a crash:
And most of all the *Atheist* would I vrge.[3]
Yea euery one (as euery one is faulty)
Should bide the brunt of my all-biting tongue,
It should be no excuse t'alledge their frailty,

---

[98] From Thomas Freeman, *Rubbe, and a great cast: Epigrams. Runne, and a great cast. The second bowle,* 1614, STC 11370, Huntington Library. The titles are taken from the sport of bowling.

[99] reveal.

[1] imaginative.

[2] write.

[3] speak (against).

Suffiz'd, they sin'd, and I must tell the wrong.
  Yet well I wot, when words had done their worst
  Lewd men (like *Foxes*) fare best when th'are curst.

IN SUPERBUM

Superbus sold a gallant Mannor place,
Himselfe with a new-fashion'd sute to grace.
Meant he himselfe an Elephant to make,
In carrying such a Castle on his backe.

QUO RUIS AB DEMENS?
LONDONS PROGRESSE

Why how now *Babel,* whither wilt thou build?
I see old *Holborne, Charing-crosse,* the *Strand,*
Are going to St. *Giles* his in the field;
Saint *Katernes* she shakes *Wapping* by the hand:
And *Hoggesdon* will to *Hy-gate* ere't be long.
London is got a great way from the streame,
I thinke she meanes to goe to *Islington,*
To eate a messe of straw-berries and Creame.
The Citty's sure in *Progresse* I surmise,
Or going to reuell it in some disorder
Without the Walles, without the Liberties,
Where she need feare nor *Mayor* nor *Recorder.*
  Well, say she do; 'twere pretty, but 'twere pitty
  A *Middlesex Bayliffe* should arrest the Citty.

IN MARCELLUM

Marcellus if you marke how he doth go
Is nothing else but imitation,
By his apparell you can hardly know
What Countriman he is, or of what Nation,
For note you him; he weares a *Spanish felt,*
A *French-craw'd*[4] *Doublet,* and a *Dutch* deep *Slop:*
A *Turky Blade,* a Crosse-bar'd *Irish* Hilt,
Hangers guilt-wrought with *Indian* pearle a top,
And girdle too, wherein (ware the stabbado)
His Poyniard in a swaggering skarfe is got:
His stocking silke of *Naples* or *Granado,*
His Garter tyed with a *Switzers* knot,
Beside a long *French* locke, a *Sarazens* head,
A big *Gades*[5] Beard, a grim *Swartruttres*[6] looke:
By these what Countriman, who can aread?
Nay of what Country may hee not bee tooke?
  Sure if a man a μικροκοσμος[7] bee,
  Marcellus seemes that little world to mee.

---

[4] *craw'd* seems to mean "stuffed or distended like a bird's craw."
[5] Cadiz.
[6] A swartrutter was "one of a class of irregular troopers, with black dress and armour and blackened faces, who infested the Netherlands in the 16th and 17th centuries." *O.E.D.*
[7] Marginal note: *Microcosmus.*

QUOT BIPEDES AURUM

What ordinary Gallant now but goes
On *Spanish* leather haltred with a Rose,
Circling with gold, or siluer-spangled lace:
'Tis strange how times haue altered the case.
Lesse cost, then's now bestow'd on either foote,
Did buy K. *William Rufus* a whole sute.

IN CHRISTOPHORUM

Kits conscience shal ne're bring him in trouble
'Tis like an Osier any way 'twill double:
And for the oath, no touching of him there,
You shall haue him, what you wil haue him, swear:
Nor for Religion; for to tell you true,
Hee's neither of the Old nor of the New.

Pitty O pitty, death had power
Ouer *Chaucer, Lidgate, Gower:*
They that equal'd all the Sages
Of these, their owne, of former Ages,
And did their learned Lights aduance
In times of darkest ignorance,
When palpable impurity
Kept knowledge in obscurity,
And all went Hood-winkt in this Ile,
They could see and shine the while:
Nor Greece nor Rome could reckon vs,
As then, among the Barbarous:
Since these three knew to turne perdy
The Scru-pin of Phylosophy
As well as they; and left behind
As rich memorials of the mind:
By which they liue, though they are dead,
As all may see that will but read;
And on good workes will spend good howres,
In *Chaucers, Lidgates,* and in *Gowers.*

TO THE STATIONER

I tell thee *Stationer,* why neuer feare,
They'll sell yfaith, and't be but for their Title,
Thou canst not lose, nay, I dare warrant cleare,
They'l get thee twenty nobles, not so little:
Why reade this Epigram, or that, or any,
Do they not make thee itch, and moue thy bloud;
Of all thou hast had (and thou hast had many)
Hast e're read better? nay, hast read so good?
Dost laugh? they'l make the rigidst *Cato* doe it;
Besides smooth verse, quaint phrase, come, what wilt giue?
No more but so: Ah! what shall I say to it?
I pitty *Poetrie,* but curse the time,
When none will bid vs Reason for our Rime.

OF SPENCERS FAIERY QUEENE

Virgil from *Homer,* th'*Italian* from him,
Spenser from all, and all of these I weene,
Were borne when *Helicon* was full to th'brim,
Witnes their works, witnes our *Faiery Queene:*
That lasting monument of *Spensers* wit,
Was n'er come neare to, much lesse equal'd yet.

IN OWENNI EPIGRAMMATA[8]

Owen, not to vse flattery (as they
That tune mens praises in too high a kay)
Thus far, in troth, I thinke I may commend thee,
The *Latines* al (saue one) must come behind thee,
Adde yet one little, but a louely fault,
Thou hast: too little gall, but full of salt.

TO GEORGE CHAPMAN

George, it is thy *Genius* innated,
Thou pick'st not flowers from anothers field,
Stolne *Similies* or *Sentences* translated,
Nor seekest, but what thine owne soile doth yield:
Let barren wits go borrow what to write,
'Tis bred and borne with thee what thou inditest,
And our Comedians thou out-strippest quite,
And all the Hearers more then all delightest,
With vnaffected Stile and sweetest Straine,
Thy in-ambitious Pen keeps on her pace,
And commeth near'st the ancient Commicke vaine,
Thou hast beguilde vs all of that sweet grace:
And were *Thalia*[9] to be sold and bought,
No *Chapman* but thy selfe were to be sought.

TO MASTER W: SHAKESPEARE

Shakespeare, that nimble *Mercury* thy braine,
Lulls many hundred *Argus*-eyes asleepe,
So fit, for all thou fashionest thy vaine,
At th'*horse-foote* fountaine thou hast drunk full deepe,
Vertues or vices theame to thee all one is:
Who loues chaste life, there's *Lucrece* for a Teacher:
Who list read lust there's *Venus* and *Adonis,*
True modell of a most lasciuious leatcher.
Besides in plaies thy wit windes like *Meander:*
Whence needy new-composers borrow more
Then *Terence* doth from *Plautus* or *Menander.*
But to praise thee aright I want thy store:
Then let thine owne works thine owne worth vpraise,
And help t'adorne thee with deserued Baies.

---

[8] on the epigrams of Owen, i.e., John Owen, whose Latin epigrams, first printed in 1607, were often reprinted.

[9] The Muse of comedy and idyllic poetry.

From John Davies's THE SCOURGE OF FOLLY[10]

AGAINST GAUDY-BRAGGING VNDOUGHTY DACCUS

Daccus is all bedawb'd with golden lace,
Hose, Doublet, Ierkins; and *Gamashes*[11] too;
Yet is he foolish, rude, and beastly-base,
Crowes like a Cocke, but like a Crauen does:
Then hee's (to prise him nought his worth beneath)
A leaden Rapier in a golden sheath.

TO OUR ENGLISH TERENCE MR. WILL: SHAKE-SPEARE

Some say good *Will* (which I, in sport, do sing)
Hads't thou not plaid some Kingly parts in sport,
Thou hadst bin a companion for a *King;*
And, beene a King among the meaner sort.
Some others raile; but raile as they thinke fit,
Thou hast no rayling, but, a raigning Wit:
And honesly *thou sow'st, which they do reape;*
So, to increase their Stocke *which they do keepe.*

AGAINST MUSTOLPHUS HIS LYING

Where now lies *Mustolphus?* Eueriewhere. Why?
Wheresoeuer he goes, he doth nothing but lye.

TO OLD IOHN HEYWOOD THE EPIGRAMMATIST, WHERESOEUER

Olde *Heywood,* haue with thee, in *His od vaine*[12]
That yet with Booke-sellers, as new, doth remaine.
New *Poets* sing riming; but thy rymes aduance
Themselues in light *Measures;* for, thus they do dance.
Ile gather some Prouerbes thou gatherdst before,
To descant vpon them, as thou didst of yore:
But yet not as thou didst, for now that were sin;
But as my Muse prompteth; and thus I begin.

Little or nothing said, soone mended is:
But they that nothing do, do most amisse.

Lyes haue short wings. He lyes that so sings:
For, farre do they flye, when they be on their wings.

Spend and God will send, but wot ye what followes?
A Staffe and Wallet, the Gaile or the Gallowes.

---

[10] From John Davies of Hereford, *The scourge of folly,* 1611, STC 6341, Folger Library.

[11] leggins or gaiters.

[12] Marginal note: *An Annagram.*

From Davies's WIT'S BEDLAM[13]

OF A FLATTERER

A flatterer (like a Wrastler) stoupeth low
To him he flatters; so, to ouerthrow:
God blesse good *Princes* from such stoupers; and,
Place such about them as doe vpright stand.

OF THE SMALL RESPECT HAD OF LEARNED MEN IN GENERALL

Caligula, enuying the bright fames
Of *Homer, Virgill,* and graue *Liuius,*
Or'ethrew their *statuaes,* to or'ethrow their Names,
But would these times had none more barbarous,
For, in this *age, Caligulaes* we find
That let them starue, that shine in either kind.[14]

AGAINST THE FANTASTICALL ATTIRE THAT MANY LADIES WEARE NOWADAIES

If *Ladies Maners* with their *Gauds* agree;
Then they *Seeme* such, they would not seeme to *Bee;*
But if they would not *Bee* as th'are in sight,
Let them not weare what makes them seeme so light.

From John Taylor's THE SCULLER[15]

Walking along the streets the other day,
A ragged Souldier crost me on the way;
And though my purses lyning was but scant,
Yet somewhat I bestow'd to ease his want.
For which he kindly thankt me with his heart,
And tooke his leaue, and friendly we did part.
When straight mine eyes a Horse and Footcloth spy'd,
Vpon whose backe in pompous state did ride,
One, whom I thought was deputie to *Ioue,*
Yet not this Souldiers wants could pitty moue,
But with disdainefull lookes and tearmes of scorne,
Commands him trauaile whether he was borne.
'Twill almost make a Puritan to sweare,
To see an Asses Horse a cloake to weare.
When Christians must goe naked bare and thin,
Wanting apparell t'hide their mangled skin.
Vaine world vnto thy Chaos turne agen,
Since brutish beasts are more esteem'd then men.

---

[13] From *Wits Bedlam where is had whipping-cheer to cure the mad,* 1617, STC 6343, Folger Library.

[14] either in poetry or in history.

[15] From *The sculler,* 1612, in *All the workes of J. Taylor the Water Poet,* 1630, STC 23725, New York Public Library, Berg Collection.

From Richard Brathwait's A STRAPPADO FOR THE DEVIL[16]

TO THE PRECISION

For the Precision that dares hardly looke,
(Because th'art pure forsooth) on any books
Saue Homilies, and such as tend to th' good
Of thee, and of thy zealous brother-hood:
Know my Time-noting lines ayme not at thee,
For thou art too too curious for mee.
I will not taxe that man that's wont to slay
His Cat for killing mise on th' Sabboth day:
No; know my resolution it is thus,
I'de rather be thy foe then be thy pus:[17]
And more should I gaine by't: for I see,
The daily fruits of thy fraternity.
Yea, I perceiue why thou my booke should shun,
Because there's many faultes th'art guiltie on:
Therefore with-drawe, by me thou art not call'd,
Yet do not winch (good iade) when thou art gall'd,
I to the better sort my lines display,
I pray thee then keep thou thy selfe away.

From Henry Parrot's THE MOUSE-TRAP[18]

11

Brutus, that braue and compleat Caualier,
Who thus of late in Fleet-street flourished:
Thought then no pleasure or expence too deare,
But see how soone the case is altered.
As that constrained to diuide the streete,
He now betakes himselfe vnto the Fleete.[19]

14

Faunus for feates of Fencing beares the Bell.
for skill in musick on each instrument:
For dancing, caruing, and discoursing well,
with other sundry gifts more excellent.
But striuing still to make his credit stronger,
The Taylor will not trust him any longer.

20

Tvsh hang it: haue at all (sayes *Curio,*)
Comes not deuce ace, assoone as six and three?
Who would not rather, halfe his lands forgo,

[16] From Richard Brathwait, *A strappado for the divell*, 1615, STC 3588, New York Public Library, Berg Collection.

[17] cat.

[18] From Henry Parrot, *The mous-trap*, 1606, STC 19334, Huntington Library.

[19] A prison.

Then be out dar'd, by such a one as he.
But thus he speakes (his father scant yet cold,)
And neuer meanes to liue, till he be old.

30

Would any deeme *Dacus* were now the man,
who was not worth of late a wooden Can?
Doubtlesse his skill in something doth surpasse,
but his Red nose is still the same it was.

34

I cry you mercy sir, I knew you not,
thus Courtly Metamorphised of late:
The Country questionlesse hath you forgot,
you braue it out with that maiestick state.
As (but I now recall whose sonne you were)
You might haue passed for some Nobles heyre.

36

Rufus is wondrous rich, but what of that?
he liues obscurely like a water Rat:
And his apparell, which he seldome buies,
are such as Houns-dich and Long-lane[20] supplies.

40

A knot of Knaues are early met together,
consulting where to breake their fast that day:
Each well prepared, said no matter whether,
for none amongst them had wherewith to pay.
At length an honest gull, that knew them not,
Came in by chance, and needs would pay the shot.

41

Cutbert our Cobler can no more forbeare,
to take Tobacco, then to liue vnknowne:
He drinkes[21] all whiffes at least, and learnes to sweare,
by Heauens: his othes and humors are his owne.
But adding herevnto a pot or more,
He stands to nothing which he spake before.

46

Such were those Epigrams of elder times,
done by that rare and matchlesse *Martiall:*
As whats now written, are but idle rimes,

[20] London streets where old clothes were sold. [21] smokes.

(compar'd to him) that did surpasse them all.
  Not *Virgil, Homer, Horace, Iuuenal,*
  Nor all the rest were like to *Martial.*

50

What tell you me of such a Pesant Groome,
that scrapeth vp together so much thrift:
Which he obscures within some desart roome,
and basely liues vnknowne by any shift.
His lookes as Characters of his discent,
sprung from the loynes of some mechanick Syre:
That neuer knew what ciuill vsage ment,
but to be only rich doth still aspire:
  Spurre such a one in ought but in his trade,
  And you shall soone perceiue hele proue a Iade.

57

Haue you not heard of *Mounseir Maximus,*
that liues by lending without interest:
Yes, yes: but (*Prouiso* tels you thus)
you must assure your lands, for such request.
  Which done, youle finde that inconuenience,
  As better 'twere the Deuill had fetcht him hence.

63

Heard yee not yet of Captaine *Ferdinand?*
that was so wont to swagger and carowse:
He lodgeth now no longer in the *Strand,*
but is remoued thence to such a house:
  Where all his best acquaintance that he knowes,
  Will not redeeme th'one halfe of what he owes.

66

Shall *Simon Suckegge,* simple *Simkins* sonne,
be matcht with beauty for his little pelfe?
Much better were the Lobcock[22] lost then wonne,
vnlesse he knew how to behaue himselfe.
  But this hath euer beene the plague of it:
  That such are lou'd more for their wealth then wit.

77

Sir, can you tell where my young maister liues,
that was surnamed here the Prodigall,
He that so much for his silke Stockings giues,
till nought is left him to buy bootes withall.
  Oh blame him not to make what show he can,
  How should he else be thought a Gentleman.

[22] lubber, bumpkin.

81

Silus hath sold his Crimsen Satten sute,
and needs would learne to play vpon the Lute:
'Tis well done (*Silus*) for such sutes soone wast,
whereas thy skill in Lutes will euer last.

85

The humour of *Tobacco* (and the rest,)
wherein our gallants tooke their chiefe delight:
Is dayly had (methinkes) in lesse request,
and will (I feare) in time be worne out quite.
For now ech Pesant puffes it through his nose:
As well as he that's clad in veluet hose.

88

Musco, that alwayes kept with pollicy,
what he had scraped since his infancie:
Scarce one yere wedded (for he needs would marry)
hath taken Ludgate[23] for his Sanctuarie.

97

Magus would needs forsooth this other day,
vpon an idle humor see a play:
When asking him at dore, that held the box,
What might you call the play? (quoth he) the Fox.[24]
In goes my Gen-man (who could iudge of wit)
And being asked how he liked it:
Said all was ill, both Fox and him that playd it,
But was not he thinke you a Goose that said it?

EPILOGUS

Thus haue I waded through a worthlesse taske,
Whereto (I trust) ther's no exceptions tane:
For (meant to none) I answer such as aske,
'tis like apparell made in *Birchin* lane.[25]
If any please to sute themselues and weare it,
The blame's not mine, but theirs that needs will beare it.

From Parrot's EPIGRAMS[26]

TO THE VNGENTILIZED CENSURER

If my ill-tuned Rimes content the wise,
Whose deeper iudgements I desire to please:
Let not the ruder sort be so precise,[27]

---

23 A prison.
24 Ben Jonson's *Volpone.*
25 Where old clothes were sold.
26 From Henry Parrot, *Epigrams,* 1608, STC 19330, Huntington Library.
27 puritanical.

That (*Critticke* seeming) cannot censure these.
I write not to the rusticke rablement,
Nor fawne vpon the curious kinde of men,
But hold it more then bootlesse labour spent
To begge their poore applause: nor care I then
If such repine, whose enuy cannot hurt,
Though like a raging sea they foame their durt.

SIC ARS DILUDITUR ARTE

Marke but the semblance of *Fucatas* face,
How to the life her picture doth excell:
For louely feature, sweete and comely grace,
(Surely the Painter hath done wondrous well):
But heer's the doubt, (both faces made by Art)
Which you would choose to be of best desert.

PERDAT QUI CAUEAT EMPTOR

Nor lesse meant *Promus* when that vow he made,
Then to giue ore his cousening Tapsters trade:
Who checkt for short and frothy measure, swore,
He neuer would from thenceforth fill pot more.

OLIM HAEC MEMINISSE IUUABIT

Grunto lies groaning of a grieuous gout,
And would giue thousands to be soundly cured:
But all the cunning that his coyne findes out,
Cannot expell his paines so long endured:
Oh *Grunto* thou hast liu'd so vnrepenting
As scarce two helles sufficeth thy tormenting.

ASPERIUS NIHIL EST HUMILI CUM SURGAT IN ALTUM

The world is well amended with Sir *Hugh,*
Since from the time he was a Shepherd swain,
And little dreamed then (I may tell you)
He should be made one of the knightly traine:
But (for his substance answeres not his will)
As good haue dreamt, or been a Shepheard still.

IMPAR IMPARES ODIT

Sotus hates wise-men, for himselfe is none:
And fooles he hates because himselfe is one.

From Parrot's SPRINGES FOR WOODCOCKS[28]

VIDEANTUR QUAE NON SUNT

Saltus goes booted to the dauncing schoole,
As if from thence his meaning were to ride;
But *Saltus* says they keepe his legs more coole,

[28] From Henry Parrot, *Laquei ridiculosi: or springes for woodcocks*, 1613, STC 19332, Folger Library.

And which for ease he better may abide:
Tut, that's a cold excuse. It rather seem'd
Saltus silke stockings were not yet redeem'd.

VENIUNT SPECTENTUR VT IPSI

When yong *Rogero* goes to see a play,
His pleasure is you place him on the Stage,
The better to demonstrate his aray,
And how he sits attended by his Page,
That onely serues to fill those pipes with smoke,
For which he pawned hath his riding Cloke.

A country Farmer had a friend at Court,
That for his Coine procur'd him to the Knighted;
On whom his neighbours now giues worse report,
Saying, that since all house-keeping is slighted,
Therefore, in truth, they did him much vnright,
To spoile so good a Clowne for such a Knight.

NEMO NASCITUR ARTIFEX

If these (quoth *Potus*) proue not things admir'd,
When poore *Mechannick* toyling Water-men,[29]
Shall with *Apolloes* Muse be straight inspir'd,
To leaue their Sculls, and deale with Poets-pen:
Let *Hercules* be henceforth tearm'd a Dwarfe,
And Paules-Church-yard[30] exchang'd for Puddle-Wharfe.[31]

DUPLICITER BEATUS

A freeman once of London made a Knight,[32]
Would in that Order still maintain his Trade,
And trafficke as before, taking delight
To say, his wealth would grow when Titles fade.
T'was wisely thought vpon, so let it be,
Thy sonne shall braue it for himselfe and thee.

From Parrot's THE MASTIVE[33]

TEMPUS EDAX RERUM

Heywood was held for *Epigrams* the best,
What time old *Church-yard* dealt in verse and prose,
But fashions since are growne out of request,
As Bombast-Dublets, Bases,[34] and Round-hose.
Or as your Lady, may it now be saide,
That looks lesse lovely then her *Chamber-maide*.

[29] A reference to John Taylor.
[30] The center of the book trade.
[31] Where scullers met their passengers.
[32] Perhaps Sir Baptist Hicks, later Viscount Campden.
[33] From Henry Parrot, *The mastive, or young-whelpe of the olde-dogge,* 1615, STC 19333, Folger Library.
[34] Pleated skirt attached to the doublet and reaching to the knee.

NUPTIAE POST NUMMOS

There was a *Time* when Men for loue did marrie,
And not for Lucre sake, as now we see:
Which from that former Age so much doth varie,
As all's for what youl give? or nought must bee.
So that this ancient word call'd *Matrimony,*
Is whollie made *A matter now of Mony.*

NULLUM STIMULUM IGNAUIS

Caecus awak't, was tolde the Sunne appeard,
Which had the darknes of the morning cleard:
But *Caecus* sluggish thereto makes replie,
The Sunne hath further farre to goe then I.

IN OBITUM ALIENIUS

Lampus extinct at last in Ashes lyes,
Who when hee liu'd did nought but Gormandize:
On choycest cheere, and Bolles fill'd to the brim,
Which fedde him fatte, for worms that feede on him.

NIL PERDUNT MENDICI

Iack's wondrous sicke, who thinks hee shall goe mad,
And lose his wits (a thing *Iacke* never had:)
Take comfort man, if that be all thou fearest,
A groat will pay thy losse when witts are dearest.

Index